Innovation Systems, Policy and Management

Innovation is a systemic phenomenon in which institutions, such as firms, government entities and public policy incentives, interact in complex ways. Targeting specific sectors of an economy in order to improve the competitiveness and capabilities of domestic firms, interventionist innovation policies can result in the structural transformation of host economies. Numerous examples exist of such policies working successfully in emerging economies and they can be applied to any economic sector, although they are commonly associated with highly innovative industries such as ICT, biotechnology and nanotechnology. *Innovation Systems, Policy and Management* describes how institutions and markets can best be structured in order to promote innovation in key economic sectors. Bringing together some of the leading figures in industrial policy and the economics of innovation and entrepreneurship, this book encourages the reader to think in terms of systems and business dynamics when analysing innovation behaviour, providing an approach useful to policy makers, business leaders and scholars of evolutionary economics.

JORGE NIOSI is Professor Emeritus at the School of Management, University of Quebec at Montreal (UQAM), where he has been a professor since 1970. He was Canada Research Chair on the Management of Technology between 2001 and 2015 and has previously been director of CREDIT (Center for Research on Industrial and Technological Development) and CIRST (Centre for Inter-University Research on Science and Technology). He is the author, co-author, editor or co-editor of sixteen books, most recently *Building National and Regional Innovation Systems* (2010).

Innovation Systems, Policy and Management

Edited by

JORGE NIOSI
University of Quebec, Montreal

CAMBRIDGE
UNIVERSITY PRESS

CAMBRIDGE
UNIVERSITY PRESS

University Printing House, Cambridge CB2 8BS, United Kingdom

One Liberty Plaza, 20th Floor, New York, NY 10006, USA

477 Williamstown Road, Port Melbourne, VIC 3207, Australia

314–321, 3rd Floor, Plot 3, Splendor Forum, Jasola District Centre,
New Delhi – 110025, India

79 Anson Road, #06–04/06, Singapore 079906

Cambridge University Press is part of the University of Cambridge.

It furthers the University's mission by disseminating knowledge in the pursuit of
education, learning, and research at the highest international levels of excellence.

www.cambridge.org
Information on this title: www.cambridge.org/9781108423830
DOI: 10.1017/9781108529525

First published 2018

Printed and bound in Great Britain by Clays Ltd, Elcograf S.p.A.

A catalogue record for this publication is available from the British Library.

ISBN 978-1-108-42383-0 Hardback

Contents

Figures

Tables

Contributors

Fiorenza Belussi is Professor of Management at the Università di Padova, Italy. She completed her PhD in economics at the SPRU, in the United Kingdom, and has published in the *Cambridge Journal of Economics, European Planning Studies, Industry and Innovation, Regional Studies* and *Research Policy* among other journals. Her books include *The Technological Evolution of Industrial Districts* (2003). Her work has received over 1000 citations in SCOPUS and over 3000 in Google Scholar as of December 2016.

Gabriela Dutrénit obtained her PhD at SPRU (UK) and teaches at the Universidad Autónoma Metropolitana in Mexico. Her articles have appeared in *Economics of Innovation and New Technology, Journal of Technology Transfer, Research Policy* and *Science and Public Policy.* She is also the author of several books on the economics of innovation. Her work has received over 2000 citations in Google Scholar and close to 200 in SCOPUS. She has mostly studied innovation in developing countries.

Jan Fagerberg is Professor, both at the University of Oslo, Norway, where he is affiliated with the Centre for Technology, Innovation and Culture (TIK), and at Aalborg University, Denmark, where he is associated with the IKE Research Group (Department of Business and Management). He also has an affiliation with the Centre for Innovation, Research and Competence in the Learning Economy (CIRCLE) at Lund University. Previous affiliations include the Norwegian Ministry of Finance and the Norwegian Institute for Foreign Affairs (NUPI). Fagerberg studied history, political science and economics before he graduated from the University of Bergen in 1980 with a degree in economics. He holds a D. Phil. from the University of Sussex (1989), where he was at the Science Policy Research Unit (SPRU). His research focused on the relationship between technology innovation and diffusion on the one hand and competitiveness, economic growth and development on the other. He has also worked on innovation theory, innovation systems and innovation policy. His books include: *Innovation A Guide to the Literature* (2004), as well as *The Economic Challenge for Europe* (1999, with P. Guerrieri and B. Verspagen). He has published in the *Journal of Economic Geography, Journal of Evolutionary Economic, Research Policy* and *World Development*, among other journals.

Chris Forman is the Brady Family Term Professor at the Scheller College of Business, Georgia Institute of Technology, in the USA. He obtained his PhD at Northwestern University in 2002. His articles have appeared in *Journal of Urban Economics Information Economics and Policy, Information Systems Research, Journal of Urban Economics Management Science* and *MIS Quarterly* and received over 2800 citations in Google Scholar and over 1000 in SCOPUS.

Andrea Ganzaroli is a researcher at the Università degli studi di Milano in the fields of economics and management of the firm. He has published over a dozen articles in refereed journals such as the *European Journal of Innovation Management, Technology Analysis and Strategic Management* and *Technological Forecasting and Social Change.*

Avi Goldfarb is Professor at the Rotman School of Management, University of Toronto, Canada. His articles have appeared in the *American Economic Review, California Management Review, Management Science, Journal of Economics and Management Strategy, Innovation Policy and the Economy* and the *Review of Industrial Organization*. His work received over 1000 citations in SCOPUS and over 4000 in Google Scholar.

Russell Golman is a professor at the Department of Social and Decision Sciences, Carnegie Mellon University, USA. He completed his PhD at the University of Michigan in 2014, and his research interests include game theory, decision theory, behavioural economics, mathematical modeling and complex adaptive systems. He has published articles in *Theory and Decision, RAND Journal of Economics, Journal of Evolutionary Economics, Journal of Economic Behaviour and Organization* and *Public Choice.*

Shane Greenstein is the Martin Marshall Professor of Business Administration at the Harvard Business School, Boston, MA, USA, and co-chair of the HBS Digital Initiative. He teaches in the Technology, Operations and Management Unit. Professor Greenstein is also co-director of the program on the economics of digitization at The National Bureau of Economic Research. He has published nine books and some 64 articles in refereed journals, such as *Industrial and Corporate Change, Journal of Law, Economics, and Organizations, Rand Journal of Economics* and *Review of Economics and Statistics*. He has received over 900 citations in SCOPUS.

Markus Grillitsch received his PhD from the Vienna University of Economics and Business. He teaches and conducts research at the Centre for Innovation at Lund University, Sweden, where he is an associate senior lecturer. He has published in *Annals of Regional Science, Economic Geography, European Planning Studies, Industry and Innovation, The Journal of the Knowledge Economy* and *Regional Studies*. His research areas are economic geography and innovation studies.

Alenka Guzmán completed her PhD in economics at Université Paris 3, France. She is a professor of economics at the Universidad Autónoma Metropolitana, México, Iztapalapa campus, and works in the area of economics of innovation and technological change. She has published several books on intellectual property and the pharmaceutical industry, as well as articles in *Comercio Exterior*, and other Spanish-language journals.

Martin Karlsson is a doctoral student at Linköping University, Sweden.

Steven Klepper was the Arthur Arton Hamerschlag Professor of Economics and Social Science at Carnegie Mellon University (CMU) in Pittsburgh, Pennsylvania. He has published numerous articles on strategy, innovation, entrepreneurship and industry evolution.

Staffan Laestadius is a professor at the KTH (Royal Institute of Technology, Sweden) in the field of industrial organisation.

Keun Lee is Professor at the Department of Economics at Seoul National University. His work has been published in the *Cambridge Journal of Economics, Industrial and Corporate Change, Research*

Policy, Science, Technology Analysis and Strategic Management and *World Development*, and has received over 1200 citations in SCOPUS as of December 2016. Dr Lee is editor of *Research Policy*.

Ignacio Llamas-Huitrón completed his PhD in economics at Stanford University, and became a professor in the Department of Economics at the Universidad Autónoma de México, Iztapalapa campus. He is the author, co-author, editor or co-editor of ten books, and has authored over 40 articles in refereed journals, mostly in Latin America. He works on labour economics and the economics of education.

Edward Lorenz is Professor of Economics at the University of Nice Sophia Antipolis, France. He completed his PhD at the University of Cambridge and has published articles in *Cambridge Journal of Economics, Industrial and Corporate Change, Industrial Relations* and *Politics and Society*, as well as numerous book chapters and working papers. His work has received over 1000 citations in Google Scholar.

Franco Malerba is Full Professor of Applied Economics at the Department of Management and Technology at the Università Luigi Bocconi, Milan, Italy. He obtained his PhD in economics at Yale University. He is president of ICRIOS, Bocconi University, editor of the journal *Industrial and Corporate Change*, advisory editor of *Research Policy* and associate editor of the *Journal of Evolutionary Economics*. He has been president of EARIE (European Association of Research in Industrial Economics) and of the International Schumpeter Society. He has sat on the advisory board of Max Planck Institute of Economics-Jena, SPRU-Sussex University, CRIC-Manchester University, EU High-Level Panels for 'New Innovation Indicators for Europe' and for 'A New European Innovation Policy'. He has been a visiting scholar at the Department of Economics, CEPR and SIEPR, Stanford University; Max Plank Institute-Jena; University of Queensland; University of Stellenbosch and Louis Pasteur University-Strasbourg. He has close to 4000 citations in over 110 articles in SCOPUS. Dr Malerba is among the editors of *Research Policy*.

Ben R. Martin is Professor of Science and Technology Policy Studies at the Science Policy Research Unit (SPRU) University of Sussex. He has carried out research on science policy for some 35 years. His work has appeared in *Research Evaluation, Research Policy, Scientometrics,*

Technological Forecasting and Social Change and *Technology Analysis and Strategic Management*, among other journals. It has received over 10,000 citations in Google Scholar, and over 3400 in SCOPUS as of December 2016. He was Director of SPRU from 1997 to 2004. Since 2004 he has been the editor of *Research Policy*.

Mariana Mazzucato received her PhD in economics at the New School for Social Research in 1999, and is Professor at SPRU, the University of Sussex. She has published in *Industrial and Corporate Change, Industry and Innovation, International Journal of Industrial Organization, The Journal of Evolutionary Economics* and *Small Business Economics*. Her work has received over 260 citations in SCOPUS. Her authored books include *The Entrepreneurial State* (2013) and *Firm Size, Innovation and Market Structure* (2000).

Maureen McKelvey is a professor at the Department of Economy and Society, the University of Gothenburg, Sweden. Professor McKelvey's research addresses innovation and entrepreneurship. Her work has appeared in *Industry and Innovation, the Journal of Evolutionary Economics, R&D Management, Research Policy, Small Business Economics* and *Technovation* and has received close to 4000 citations in Google Scholar and over 700 in SCOPUS as of December 2016.

Pierre Mohnen is a professor of economics of innovation at Maastricht University, The Netherlands. His research deals mainly with the measurement, the determinants, the effects and the interrelationships of R&D, innovation, ICT, competition and productivity. He has published numerous articles in *American Economic Review, Industrial and Corporate Change, Industry and Innovation, Research Policy, Review of Economics and Statistics, Technology Analysis and Strategic Management* and *Technovation*, among other journals.

José Miguel Natera, Universidad Autónoma Metropolitana, Mexico, is a young scholar who completed his PhD in the field of economics and management of innovation, and is a CONACYT Research Fellow in Mexico City. He has published in *CEPAL Review, Research Policy* and *Structural Change and Economic Dynamics*.

Jorge Niosi has been Emeritus Professor at the Department of Management and Technology, Université du Québec à Montréal, Canada, since 2016, where he has taught for some 45 years. He received his doctorate at the Ecole Pratique des Hautes Études in Paris in 1973. He is the author, co-author, editor or co-editor of 15 books, as well as some 60 articles in refereed journals including the *Cambridge Journal of Economics, Industrial and Corporate Change, Journal of Business Research, Journal of Development Studies, Journal of Evolutionary Economics, Journal of Technology Transfer, Research Policy, R&D Management, Small Business Economics, Technovation* and *World Development*. Among his books are *Building National and Regional Innovation Systems* (2010), as well as two books on *Canada's National System of Innovation*, and *Canada's Regional Innovation Systems* (2000 and 2005, respectively). His work had received over 1200 citations in SCOPUS and over 5000 in Google Scholar by December 2016. He has been president of the International Schumpeter Society (2014–16), visiting scholar at the Center for Economic Policy Research Stanford University (1995–96), as well as an invited professor in different universities in Finland, France, Italy and Spain since 1990.

Luigi Orsi, a professor of economics at the Università degli Studi di Milano, Italy, has published in *Research Policy, Technological Forecasting and Social Change, Technology Analysis and Strategic Management* and *Technovation*, among other refereed journals.

Sophie Pommet is Maître de Conférences in Economics at the University of Nice Sophia Antipolis. She specialises in new firms and venture capital. She has published in *Economic Letters*, the *Revue d'économie industrielle, Revue d'économie politique* and other French economic journals.

Martin Puchet Anyul is a professor of economics at Universidad Nacional Autónoma de México (UNAM), Mexico. He has published in *Structural Change and Economic Dynamics* and *Trimestre Económico*, among other SCOPUS journals.

Sanika Sulochani Ramanayake is a doctor in economics from Seoul National University, works at the Indira Ghandi Institute of Development Research in India and is currently a post-doctoral fellow at the Department of Economics, Seoul National University, South Korea. She works with Dr Keun Lee, and has published in the *Journal of the Asia Pacific Economy* and the *Millennial Asia Journal*.

Fernando Santiago is an industrial policy officer at the United Nations Industrial Development Organization in Vienna. He has published on science, technology and innovation policy; the management of human resources for R&D in Mexico; linkages between academia-industry and industrial development. Santiago holds an MSc in Science and Technology Policy from SPRU, University of Sussex and a PhD in economics and Policy Studies of Technical Change from UNU-MERIT/University of Maastricht.

Michaela Trippl is Professor of Economic Geography at the University of Vienna, Austria. She received her PhD from the Vienna University of Economics and Business (Austria) in 2004. She has published in such journals as *Economic Geography, European Planning Studies, Industry and Innovation, Regional Studies, Research Policy* and *Urban Studies*. Her research and teaching have been dedicated to fields in economic geography, innovation studies and regional science with a focus on regional clusters, the geography of innovation, long-term regional structural change, labour mobility and regional development, spatial patterns and institutional foundations of the knowledge economy and regional innovation policies. Her work has received over 1000 citations in Scopus and over 3700 in Google Scholar as of December 2016.

Masaru Yarime received a BEng in Chemical Engineering from the University of Tokyo, an MS in Chemical Engineering from the California Institute of Technology and a PhD in economics and policy studies of technological change from Maastricht University in the Netherlands. Previously he worked as Senior Research Fellow at the National Institute of Science and Technology Policy (NISTEP) of the Japanese Ministry of Education, Culture, Sports, Science and Technology (MEXT). His visiting professorships include Groupe de Recherche en Économie Théorique et Appliquée (GREThA) of the

University of Bordeaux IV in France and the Department of Science and Technology Studies of the University of Malaya in Malaysia. His work has been published in *Science and Public Policy, Sustainability Science, Technological Forecasting and Social Change* and other journals. His publications have received around 1000 citations in Google Scholar.

Preface

In the last quarter century, innovation has consolidated its role as the main factor behind economic growth, and innovation policy as the critical set of incentives that nurtures innovation. Also, the systemic approach, where economic agents have only partial and imperfect knowledge, has gained relevance as opposed to the neoclassical perspective that sees the economy and society as an aggregate of rational individuals maximising their personal welfare. The systemic perspective has flourished on the basis of the work of scholars from different disciplines that analyse the economy as a set of complex adaptive systems. Modelling and simulation replace the approach based on simple equations of known variables. Also in the complex-adaptive systems perspective, small-scale factors have large-scale results (the butterfly effect). Economic systems are adaptive: the system changes its behaviour as a response to the environment. Learning is a form of adaptation to the environment: the system changes its behaviour as a result of its interaction with the environment. The system incorporates some elements from its environment. An analogy would be the plant that climbs and adapts itself to the form of the support it finds.

Developing countries are often slow learners: they modify their response to external changes very gradually. Too often they adopt more efficient organisational patterns and technologies at a leisurely pace. Instantaneous adjustment only occurs in neoclassical models. In the real world, inertia and path dependence as well as slow and tortuous learning processes differ from prompt adjustment and growth.

In addition, following an external shock, systems do not always go back to their previous equilibrium; however, they can attain a new one, several equilibrium states in a row, none or even collapse. The catching up of developing countries – the normal unfolding of human societies according to conventional economics – is far from guaranteed. Instead, catching up is only one possible adaptation of less-developed countries to the changing world economy. Other adaptations may include perpetual backwardness compared to more advanced countries, retrogress or even collapse and disappearance to become regions of larger and more successful nations.

In a nutshell, complexity and the complex adaptive systems (CAS) perspective provide a new and far more fertile, sophisticated and realistic approach to the economic world than conventional neoclassical economics. The economy is not seen in perpetual equilibrium but in continuous change, particularly due to the mutual adaptations of economic agents – individual as well as organisations – with one another. Agents develop strategies, and then change them if they are not successful, or if competition grows. Companies, regions and nations develop new products and new product families, and often neighbours imitate them. Imitation forces the original innovator to change strategies, develop new products or improve them. Often the latecomer becomes the new product – or product-family – leader, forcing the previous leader to innovate or disappear. Thus, perpetual change, but not perpetual stasis, is the substance of macro- and microeconomic analysis. Economic systems are complex adaptive ones, and they must be studied as such.

Acknowledgements

Chris Forman, Avi Goldfarb and Shane Greenstein, 'Agglomeration of invention in the Bay Area: Not just ICT' was originally published in *The American Economic Review Papers and Proceedings* 106 (5): 146–151 (2016).

Russell Golman and Steve Klepper, 'Spinoffs and clusters' was originally published in the *Rand Journal of Economics* 47 (2): 341–365 (2017), under the title 'Spinoffs and clustering'.

The Mariana Mazzucato chapter is a slightly amended version of Mariana Mazzucato, 'From market fixing to market-creating: A new framework for innovation policy', Special Issue of *Industry and Innovation:* 'Innovation policy – can it make a difference?' 23 (2): (2016).

This book could not have been published without the assistance of Andreas Pyka during production. I wish to thank Andreas for offering his assistance when it was most needed.

Abbreviations

AEGIS	Advancing Knowledge-Intensive Entrepreneurship and Innovation for Economic Growth and Social Well-Being in Europe
BFTB	Bang for the buck
BRICS	Brazil, Russia, India, China, South Africa
CIS	Community Innovation Survey
CONACYT	National Council for Science and Technology (Mexico)
DARPA	Defence Advanced Research Projects Agency (USA)
DEA	Data Envelopment Analysis
DMU	Decision-making units
EAEPE	European Association for Evolutionary Political Economy
ECHONET	Energy Conservation and Homecare Network (Japan)
EMA	European Medical Agency
EPO	European Patent Office
EU	European Union
FDA	Food and Drug Administration
FDI	Foreign direct investment
FIT	Feed-in-tariff
GDP	Gross Domestic Product
GEM	Global Entrepreneurship Monitor
GERD	Gross expenditure on R&D
GHG	Greenhouse gas
GNI	Gross national income
HEMS	Home energy management system (Japan)
ICMM	International Council on Mining and Metals
ICT	Information and communication technology
IMIT	Institute for Management of Innovation and Technology
INSERM	National institute for health and medical research, France

ITRI	Industrial technology research institute, Taiwan
JPO	Japan's Patent Office
KIBS	knowledge intensive business services
KIE	knowledge intensive entrepreneurship
KfW	*Kreditanstalt für Wiederaufbau* (Germany)
LDC	Less developed country
MITI	Ministry of Economy, Trade and Industry (Japan)
NEDO	New Energy and Industrial Technology Development Organization (Japan)
NIH	National Institutes of Health, USA
NIS	National innovation systems
NREL	National Renewable Energy Laboratory, USA
NTUA	National Technical University, Greece
OCCTO	Organization for Cross-regional Coordination of Transmission Operators (Japan)
OECD	Organization for Economic Cooperation and Development
ONERA	National Office for Aerospace Study and Research (France)
PEI	Innovation stimulus program, Mexico
PESTI	Public expenditure in STI
PNCyT	National policy for science and technology, Mexico
PPP	Purchasing power parity
REI	Relative Efficiency Index
RIS	Regional innovation system
SBIR	Small Business Innovation Research Act
SIS	Sectoral innovation system
STI	Science, technology and innovation
TEPCO	Tokyo Electric Power Holding Company (Japan)
UNCTAD	United Nations Council on Trade and Development
UCL	University College London
UNU-MERIT	United Nations University – Maastricht Economic and Social Research Institute on Innovation and Technology
USPTO	United States Patent and Trademark Office
WIPO	World Intellectual Property Organization
XIDEA	a software tool for the analysis and evaluation of decision-making units

Introduction
Institution Systems, Policies and Management

JORGE NIOSI

I.1 Introduction

This book is about innovation, its policy, its institutional systems and its management. It is the result of an international conference held in Montreal in July 2016 where 290 speakers presented as many papers on innovation. It collects some of the best presentations on the three related topics of innovation: policy, systems and management.

I.2 On Institutions

Institutions are the canvas on which economic activity is knitted (Nelson 2005). All institutions are different from one country to the next, because they show the 'scars' of history (David 1994). We recognize four types of institutions that have an impact on innovation (Niosi 2010).

(a) Public policies that shape economic activity. They include, of course, R&D and innovation policies, but also education policies, financial policies, immigration policies, and other systemic policies. The market for human capital is built by public policies on education and immigration. Countries that require human capital can either train it at home or attract it with adequate policies; in absence of carefully developed education and immigration policies, the labour market will not offer the skilled people the country requires for innovating and developing. And the adoption of advanced technology requires an educated population.

(b) Organizations: all economic and innovative activity takes place within organizations such as private and government-controlled companies, universities, public research laboratories, venture capital firms and others. Organizations are bundles of routines and

1

capabilities. Firms have different structures in different countries on the basis of human resource availability and strategies required to deal with different environments. Thus, the origins of Japanese and Korean conglomerates are to be found in the small numbers of highly skilled managers in both countries. The routines matter also in public organizations: in some countries (mainly OECD but also some East Asian ones, like Singapore) academic positions are open to all candidates from any nation; in most developing countries, positions are open only to local citizens. Not by chance, research universities in which positions are open to the world are far more productive than those that only recruit local academics (Mohrman et al. 2008). The administration of these organizations has several dimensions, and includes innovation management.

(c) Routines within these organizations: capabilities and routines vary from one organization to the next. All firms are different (Nelson 1994), and also all public organizations are dissimilar. These differences are based on different histories and strategies, and also on the availability of resources in different regional and national contexts. One example will suffice. In most developing countries, government officials are recruited among members of the party in power. In others – mainly OECD and East Asian countries – meritocratic bureaucracies held the key positions in the public administrations. Empirical analysis shows that the quality and stability of public policies depend on the existence of stable and professional meritocratic bureaucracies (Rauch and Evans 2000; Dahlström et al. 2012).

(d) Culture: this is the most 'opaque' but nonetheless determinant, among the four components of the institutional canvas (Inglehart and Baker 2000). Religion, the treatment of women, castes, immigrants and ethnic minorities are among the most important. Religion first: as Weber noticed a century ago, Protestant countries are on average more developed than Catholic, and these more advanced than Islamic countries, but within each nation, values tend to be homogeneous following the cultural majority. Thus German Catholics' cultural and economic behaviour is similar to that of German Protestants. In addition, ethnic and religious fractionalization has a negative effect on economic development because of the probability of civil conflict (Montalvo and Reynal-Querol 2005). Second, culture includes also public attitudes towards women in education and employment: it is clear that countries where women are barred from higher education and job opportunities will experience less innovation and economic development because an important part of the population is excluded from economic activity (Metcalfe 2011). Finally, the treatment of ethnic minorities is also crucial. India is unique in its caste system that affects a quarter of its population, and has not disappeared because of the meritocratic requirements of public office (Subramanian 2015). On the other hand, most OECD countries, including Canada, Finland, Japan, New Zealand, Singapore, South Korea, the United Kingdom and the United States have different affirmative action policies, and several of them welcome educated immigrants. In the Gulf countries, conversely, it is extremely difficult for an immigrant to obtain citizenship, including migrants from other Muslim countries.

I.3 On Innovation Policies

More often than not, neoclassical economics is blind to policy interventions. For many of these economists, at least theoretically if not always in their day-to-day practice, markets are supposed to be efficient enough not to need government inputs: Adam Smith's invisible hand should provide innovation through the benefits of specialization and the division of labour within the market and within the firm (Pavitt 1998). Individuals endowed with rational choice and perfect information do not need advice or incentives from policy makers.

Yet, in Solow's model, innovation is exogenous to the market and thus there is an opportunity for government intervention (mainly through university or public sector research). Another, more recent approach with a more Schumpeterian flavour would argue in favour of endogenous innovation within a neoclassical growth model (Grossman and Helpman 1991). This current would accept policy intervention, but proposes 'one-size-fits-all' horizontal policies such as tax credits for R&D (Mohnen in this volume).

Other economic evolutionary currents exist and they are not Schumpeterian. Rahmeyer (2012) has emphasized that in Marshall, innovation and economic development are a side effect of the normal manufacturing process and the division of labour, an approach that is close to the gradual approach of Adam Smith, where the competitive forces of the environment lead to economic evolution. Also, both the Product life cycle (Vernon 1966) and the Industry life cycle (Klepper 1997) economic approaches are evolutionary but they are not Schumpeterian.

I.3.1 Innovation Policy for Incremental Innovation

Innovation policy has been interpreted in two different senses. The narrow definition is the policies that are meant to affect innovation (i.e. tax credits for R&D). The broad definition includes all policies that have an impact on innovation, such as venture capital policies or higher education policies (Fagerberg 2016).

The differences between incremental and radical innovations have been many times discussed but no generally admitted definition exists. Table I.1 recalls some of the differences between incremental and radical innovation.

Table I.1 *Incremental and radical innovation compared*

Dimension of radicalness	Incremental	Radical	Authors
Impact on the industry	Low	High	Acemoglu & Cao (2015)
Source of subsequent innovation	No	Yes	Ahuja & Lampert (2011)
Older technology remains substitute for new	Yes	No	Arrow (1962)
Cost reductions	Low	High	Green (1995)
Competitive advantage to adopters	Low	High	Kumar et al. (2000)
Benefits brought if successful	Low	High	Kumar et al. (2000)
Adoption risks	Low	High	Kumar et al. (2000)
Technical uncertainty levels	Low	High	O'Connor et al. (2013)
Market uncertainty levels	Low	High	O'Connor et al. (2013)
Resource uncertainty levels	Low	High	O'Connor et al. (2013)
Organizational uncertainty levels	Low	High	O'Connor et al. (2013)

At the basis of an evolutionary economic policy, one must consider several key facts. First, innovative activities are endogenous to the economic system because firms must regularly introduce new products and processes in order to survive in competitive markets. But all firms and sectors are different, thus one-size-fits all innovation policy is not the best type of incentive for innovation. Innovation policies are key components of innovation systems. Second, uncertainty, not just risk, pervades decisions about R&D and innovation; economic agents only know ex-post the results of such investments. Trial and error is part of any technical choice by private firms. Third, therefore, agents do not maximize revenues or profits; within the same industry, firms look for different solutions because they do not know ex-ante the correct answer, and they have different assets and capabilities. Variety is thus another major consequence of bounded rationality. Fourth, asymmetric knowledge is not a hindrance to the performance of the market, but often the source of profits and technological breakthroughs, thus the source of economic growth: some agents know technologies and related opportunities that others do not know, and they create new products or processes that create destruction of competitors (and profits to the innovators) or imitation and radical innovation, or innovation cascades (series of radical innovations). Fifth, externalities do represent market failures,[1] but they are also the sources of economic growth, as knowledge leaks out of the original innovator and creates both consumer and producer benefits. Finally, perfect competition may not be a desirable state of the economic markets: almost all modern inventions have come either from monopolistic and oligopolistic markets, or from universities and government or non-profit laboratories. On the basis of such theoretical premises, Lipsey and Carlaw (1998) arrived to the same policy implications on the basis of the observation of rapid catching-up in South East Asia: there are no ready-made one-size-fits -all policy sets for technological change or human capital. Each catching-up country must devise its own set of innovation policies on the basis of its specific endowment of natural resources, human capital, internal market characteristics and government capabilities. One of the

---

[1] Lipsey and Carlaw propose to keep the market failure concept, but to redefine it. 'Whereas in neoclassical theory the market fails when it does not achieve the unique optimal equilibrium, it fails in the structuralist-evolutionary theory when it does not lead to some desirable and attainable state' (Lipsey and Carlaw 1998).

goals of this book is, however, to try to uncover some important regularities in the implementation of such policies.

Evolutionary economics, comprising uncertainty and risk, believes policy in general and innovation policy in particular is needed to foster economic growth, and proposes to keep open alternatives. Not only do economic agents not have complete knowledge about their choices but also the spectrum of available choices is fairly opaque, and is continuously changing. Take, for instance, today's energy policy. Technical change is very fast in most renewable energy options. The race between solar, hydro, wind, geothermic, biomass and wave solutions is far from showing a clear winner, even if today solar photovoltaic is starting to take the lead. In addition, the combination of these technologies may change from one region to the other according to particular natural conditions. Evolutionary innovation policy would suggest keeping open several of these routes to solve climate change problems and reduce global warming.

The innovation policy choices become more complex and costly when one thinks that innovation institutions form innovation systems: sectoral technologies are complex systems in themselves, and technical solutions evolve. Also, within the same technical choice, several alternative policy instruments may be required, from direct subsidies to private sector innovation and R&D, to mission-oriented policies such as the establishment of government laboratories, incentives to academic research and industry-university consortia, to the development of a venture capital industry or increasingly 'grand-challenge' policies. Table I.2 shows the links between the kind of innovation aimed at and the type of innovation policy.

One short example will suffice. A country adopting solar PV renewable energy will have to decide whether to put efforts into improving solar cells (semiconductors), advanced solar glass, batteries, mechatronics or other components. Also, it has to decide whether to keep doing basic research (i.e. on solar cells and batteries), or aim at applied research on mechatronics, advanced glass or microgrids.

I.3.2 Innovation Policy for Radical and Cascade Innovation: From Path-Following Innovation Policy to Path Creating, Mission-Oriented and Grand Challenge Policies

In addition, neoclassical economics explains government policy on the basis of the need of reducing market failures. Other authors with a less

Table I.2 *Grand challenges, incremental and mission-oriented innovation policies*

Innovation policies	Incremental	Mission-oriented	Grand challenges
Time span	Permanent or long term	Permanent	Short to medium term
Goal	Induce incremental innovation, path following	Continuous support to important sectors, for radical or incremental innovation	Strong effort to solve a STI or a social major problem or create an innovation or a new institutional path
Examples	Tax credits for R&D (i. e. SR&ED, Canada)	Agriculture, climate change, defense, health, green energy, transportation and space policies	Human Genome Project International (1990–2003) US SunShot Initiative (2011/2020)
Initiative of projects	Companies	National Governments	National governments
Institutional forms	An agency runs the program (i.e. IRAP, Canada)	Government laboratory, permanent program	National public/ private partnerships and/ or international coalition
Authors	Bloom et al (2002)	Mowery (2009)	Ulnicane (2016)

neoclassical flavour argue that system failures explain government policy. Such system failures were defined as those related to the 'institutional setting, market structure and governance issues' (Avnimelech and Teubal 2008: 154). Of course, governments are part of the economic system, but only they have the legal authority to modify the institutional setting, the rules of the game, market structures and governance issues. Both types of innovation policy are usually aimed at incremental and path-following technical change. More recently, on the basis of Asian rapid industrialization but also on the experience of OECD countries'

Great Challenges innovation policies (i.e. the EU Framework Programs, the international Human Genome Program or the Human Proteome Program, or the US SunShot Initiative) it has been argued that innovation policy should not concentrate on market or system failures but more on attaining public objectives of great importance, key missions at the national or international levels, and/or market creation. Such goals may also be pursued at the regional level, such as California's stem cell policy or solar policy (Taylor 2008; Foray et al. 2012; Mazzucato 2016). The concept of path creation has also been used to describe regional innovation ruptures from path dependency and local inertia (Dijk and Yarme 2010; Essletzbichler 2012; Lee 2013). Regional path-creating policy strategies are covered by the concept of 'smart specialization strategies' (see Foray in this book). Lee (2013) has analyzed national path-creating catching-up strategies in South Korea. Historical experiences have shown that path dependence and inertia can be broken by an accumulation of resources and political forces in large projects.

Grand challenge policy is more a path-creating than a path-following public intervention (Schienstock 2007; Foray et al. 2012; Sidow et al. 2012). Grand challenge policy is not a short-term type of policy, but a long-term type of public intervention. Some of the most astounding grand challenges were those of the Human Genome and Human Proteome projects that opened entirely new fields of research. But they are far from unique.[2]

This, far from simple, evolutionary innovation policy sees a range of strategy options within innovation systems.

I.4 Innovation Systems

Innovation systems literature represented a major advance in the study of innovation policies. Institutions promoting the production, diffusion

---

[2] In China, the national and provincial governments have been producing grand challenge policies in several areas such as high-speed trains (Sun 2015), satellites (Erikson 2014) and others. Since the early 2000s, more modestly, US DARPA has launched a series of grand challenges. In 2004–5 DARPA launched a grand challenge for a completely automated vehicle. In 2012, the Robotics Grand Challenge aimed at creating a humanoid robot able to execute complex tasks. In June 2014, DARPA launched the Cyber Grand Challenge (CGC), a competition designed to spur innovation in fully automated software vulnerability analysis and repair. Since 2004, the Gates Foundation has launched a series of grand challenges to solve health and development problems.

and adoption of scientific and technical knowledge were shown to be part of a system, a set of organizations, policies, routines and cultures that have a major impact on the economic performance of the national firms of a country (Nelson 1993). Innovation systems literature distinguishes national systems from regional and sectoral systems.

I.4.1 National Systems

Most of the key innovation institutions in any country are national by scope (Nelson 1993). These include the largest public R&D laboratories, the main universities, the inclusive innovation policies such as tax credits for R&D, cluster policies, venture capital incentives, direct subsidies for R&D and the like. Their impact is felt on the entire nation, within national boundaries, depending of course on the absorptive capabilities of each region.

A national system of innovation is the system of interacting private and public firms (either large or small), universities and government agencies aiming at the production of science and technology within national borders. Interaction among these units may be technical, commercial, legal, social, and financial, inasmuch as the goal of the interaction is the development, protection, financing or regulation of new science and technology (Niosi, Saviotti, Bellon and Crow 1993).

The concept was born in the works of Christopher Freeman, Bengt-Ake Lundvall and Richard Nelson, but it has attained widespread global adoption (see Tregua et al. in this volume). Mohnen and Röller (2005) have given empirical and theoretical support to the innovation system concept: they showed that 'the whole is better than the parts', meaning that for companies to adopt innovation practices, a whole package of complementary policies is necessary. Yet, vertically oriented policies tend to increase private firms' innovation efforts.

I.4.2 Regional Innovation Systems

Within any nation, innovative activities are concentrated in particular regions (most often large metropolitan areas) (Feldman and Audretsch 1999).

Regions which possess the full panoply of innovation organizations set in an institutional milieu, where systemic linkage and interactive communication among the innovation actors is normal, approach the designation of regional innovation systems. (Cooke and Morgan 1998: 71)

The regional perspective does not reduce the importance of the national systems approach. It is complementary to it. Provinces, states, *lander*, municipalities and other subnational levels of government may design and implement policies that strengthen their regional innovation capabilities. In federal countries, like Canada, Germany and the United States, subnational governments have their own innovation institutions. Even supranational governments can nurture regional innovation, like the EU Smart Specialization Program (Foray, in this volume). In addition, regional knowledge externalities, based on proximity, are more evident in metropolitan areas than in entire countries, even when the country is small. Regional policies include specialized public research organizations, universities and regional grants.

I.4.3 Sectoral Innovation Systems

From another angle, sectoral innovation systems (innovation institutions centred on a product or group of products) are also components of a national and international system (Malerba, in this volume). Sectoral systems are international by definition. These are sectors like aerospace, biotechnology or nanotechnology. These sectors are often but not only identical to industries defined by a SIC or NAICS code. They include, in addition to industries, the framing institutions such as national laboratories, vertical policies and academic programmes (OECD 2006a). Other key elements of sectoral systems are the appropriability, cumulativeness and opportunity of the technological regime, the number of innovators and their geographical dispersion (Malerba 2004 and 2005). Yet, it has been shown that the number of innovators varies with the industry life cycle and the type of sector (Klepper 1997).

Also, some sectors are born extremely dispersed and then tend to concentrate, such as aircraft and car production, biotechnology and software services, as argued by the PLC-ILC framework. Other sectors are prone to variety, thus to increasing dispersion, such as computers and semi-conductors (Saviotti 1996; Niosi 2000a).

Thus, the Mark I – Mark II classification does not exhaust the different initial conditions and later evolution of sectors and, implicitly, this dychotomic classification suggests that Mark I sectors always remain competitive and Mark II continuously remain concentrated. It is true that some sectors keep dispersed over the decades, such as medical devices and professional equipment: they are the typical Schumpeter Mark I sectors. Medical devices' continuous dispersion is related to the enormous variety of artefacts, and the use of many technologies in each product, including advanced materials, biotechnology, microelectronics and software. Such variety makes the economies of scale required for firm growth and concentration difficult. It was calculated that in 2012 there were over 27,000 medical-device firms worldwide (Industry Canada 2013). Conversely, other sectors are born highly concentrated and keep so for long periods, like commercial space activities, due to the sheer size and cost of the effort (Hansson and McGuire 1999). All in all, some twenty companies dominate the world commercial space sector.

Some sectors contain only one industry. The aerospace sector is one of them. Its key component is the aerospace industry (NAICS 4-digit code 3364, 'Aerospace products and parts manufacturers', with the space and aeronautics industrial segments). But within the sector one finds different markets, different national policies, different products and demand curves. Government support varies from one country to the next. In the United States, direct subsidies and large national laboratories have been preferred to nurture the aerospace sector (Mowery and Rosenberg 1989). Also, even if the United States exports aerospace products to the world, and its components supply chain has been internationalized, most of the innovation activities in the sector are localized in that country. In China, by contrast, the number of national R&D institutes is much larger than in the United States, but the Chinese government has tapped foreign sources of technology, originally from the USSR, and after the China–USSR split, from the United States, the European Union, Brazil and Canada, in order to speed up the country's catching-up process (Niosi and Zhao 2013). More than the US aerospace sectoral system, the Chinese aerospace sector has been truly international since the start.

In terms of policy evaluation, one size does not fit all (Tödtling and Trippl 2005). Assessing innovation systems is more complex than evaluating individual policies. A world of systems requires systems modelling and system evaluation (Arnold 2004; Smits and Kuhlmann 2004). Individual policies should be evaluated in the proper context of the national, regional and sectoral systems in which they are embedded.

And market-creating and path-creating innovation policies require a brand new type of evaluation instruments (Mazzucato, 2016).

I.5 Innovation Management

The quality and quantity of innovation management activities that exist in a country or a region depend on the number and the performance of its policy incentives for business R&D and innovation. The better performing the innovation system is, the larger the number of companies conducting R&D and related innovation activities. It has been shown time and again that the number of R&D-active firms depends on such stimuli (Kim 1997; Niosi 2000b). From 1970 to the present the number of South Korean companies with internal R&D activities has increased from 1 to over 13,000. In Canada, the number of companies with in-house R&D activities has increased from 300 in the 1960s to over 15,000 today. In both cases the innovation system was built in these periods.

These policy incentives lift several of the barriers hampering innovation, such as cost, risk and the provision of highly skilled personnel (D'Este et al. 2012). However, there has been some discussion about how much these policies add to business innovation activity (OECD 2006b). Is there additionality, new innovation activities or just substitution of private funds of the firm with public funds for the same activities? The debates are still raging today.

In most OECD countries, where the sum of system incentives is high, and these incentives are permanently assessed, fine-tuned and renewed, innovation management is a common activity. In most OECD countries, innovation management is taught in universities and there are associations of technology, R&D and innovation managers. Their members are based mostly in North America, Western Europe and a few emerging countries.

Business incubators support the birth and growth of new small firms innovation activities, in many different countries, with different results (Vedovello and Godinho 2003; Grimaldi and Grandi 2005). Incubators are often the result of regional innovation policies aiming at creating new firms and economic activities in a geographical area, but they may also attract external investments of larger firms to the area. If tax credits for R&D are useful incentives for large and medium-sized established companies that have tax responsibilities, business incubators find themselves at the other end of the company lifecycle. The development of the new advanced technologies of biotechnologies, ICTs and nanotechnology, mainly in universities and public research organizations, in the last thirty years has nurtured the birth of incubators. These organizations provide high-level services to new firms, such as contacts with venture capital and angels, skilled personnel, and business model construction and validation, buildings and infrastructure and links to strategic partners. Incubators may often be the first learning experience of technical entrepreneurs in the area of innovation management (Scillitoe and Chakrabarti 2010).

Innovation management includes a vast range of practices internal to organizations, such as R&D management, project management, benchmarking, quality control, information systems management and others. These internal innovation management routines of private firms and government organizations are heavily influenced by public policies. Some authors have identified two modes of learning within firms: one based on science, technology and innovation policy, and the other, more informal, based on Doing, Using and Interacting (DUI). Firms combining the two modes seem to be more innovative that those using just one or the other (Jensen et al. 2007).

One set of innovation policy intervention has direct impacts on innovation management: demand-side policies, such as procurement, regulation, standards and consumer policy (OECD 2011; Vecchiato and Roveda 2014; Edler and Yeow 2016). In many industries, public procurement has triggered the development of both technological innovation and innovation management routines in selected firms. Aerospace, large energy systems, health products and defense are sectors where public procurement has at the same time had an influence on innovation management of those firms, universities and public research institutes participating in the projects.

I.5.1 The Book Contribution

This book moves the debate forward by adding themes and issues that were not entirely analyzed in the past. In his chapter, Malerba studies the evolution of sectoral systems in greater depth. He recalls the well-known fact that technical change produces evolution, and in the process several obstacles can slow down or even block for some time the evolution of the sector. Also, newcomers can use windows of opportunity to challenge incumbents. These windows can be new technologies, new markets and new institutions (policies). In front of these windows, the responses of incumbents can vary and eventually produce changes in leadership. Also, modelling of sectoral systems has been incorporating new actors, such as universities, public laboratories and new public policies supporting the entry of new firms. Thus, sectors evolve and they do it under different patterns and policy frames.

Pierre Mohnen analyzes the effectiveness of direct and indirect support for R&D. He starts by comparing the two main explanations of government support for R&D: market failure and the national system of innovation and mission-oriented public policies. He then concentrates on two of these policies: indirect support via R&D tax incentives (implemented mainly in Australia, Canada, Japan and the Netherlands, and direct aide in the form of grants and subsidies, preferred in Finland, Germany and Sweden). He discusses the effectiveness of tax credits and direct public support for R&D, and concludes that tax credits increase the amount of R&D performed, but there is some level of uncertainty about the effectiveness of the policy. In the analysis of direct funds for R&D, a similar problem exists: many factors can impinge on the results of such policies, such as science, demand, human capital, finance, regulations and entrepreneurship, to name a few.

Mariana Mazzucato recalls that an increasing number of countries are not simply trying to correct market failures but are also creating new markets and technologies through mission-oriented policies. Her chapter puts the accent on four key issues that appear under this new market-creating and technology-creating framework: the direction of change, organizations that can host the discovery process, assessment of both mission-oriented policies and related markets, and the way risks and rewards will be distributed among economic agents under this new policy framework. Her paper highlights the limitations of the market-failure framework; the new policy is more about creating markets and technologies, not about fixing them.

Fiorenza Belussi, Luigi Orsi, G. Ganzarolli and Maria Savarese argue that, considering the importance of alliances for the macro-economy and the firms involved, it is understandable that governments in developed and developing countries support the existence and growth of strategic alliances. Alliances help governments and companies to accelerate the diffusion of knowledge, reduce the amounts of public and private investment and increase the chances that R&D projects will succeed.

I.5.2 Innovation Systems in Developing Countries

Jorge Niosi writes about systems of innovation in developing countries. In the NSI literatures, these systems are often represented as being immature, incomplete, neo-peripheral and/or weak. They are also presented as suffering from inefficiencies and ineffectiveness. The paper discusses these perspectives and adds that empirical studies show that non-meritocratic bureaucracies critically affect developing countries. In such countries, these government bureaucracies fuel economic disparity, stagnation and implement inadequate policies that do not promote economic development. The paper also discusses cultural explanations that constitute barriers to the creation of innovation systems, such as education, religion and the status of women, and argues the need to coordinate innovation systems and policy with industrial policy.

Ed Lorenz and Sophie Pommet analyze the banking systems in developing countries. They start (Section 6.2) with an overview of the links between financial systems, credit restrictions and innovation performance. Then, in a third section, they study the national banking system in thirty-six countries and develop a model that predicts the chances of credit constraints as a result of firm- and country-level variables. In a fourth section, they propose a bivariate probit model to examine the indirect effects of the national banking system on firms' innovation. Then they discuss the policy implications. They give more support to Fagerberg's findings in the sense that there is nothing automatic in the process of catching-up by backward countries. Firms rely on external organizations and banks' support is crucial. Financial constraints are critical as barriers to catching-up.

Gabriela Dutrenit and her colleagues José Miguel Natera, Martin Puchet Anyul, and Fernando Santiago study public expenditure in science, technology and innovation (PESTI) in Mexico, and its relationship with economic growth. They are interested not only on the size but mainly on the causal links between both, using an econometric model. They study the Mexican economy, the second largest in Latin America, one that has moved from an import substitution policy to one with open markets and slow growth. The empirical model is one where GDP is a dependent variable of PESTI, external shocks and fixed capital investments, but also has an effect on them. The period they have studied is 1970–2011. They found that during those four decades,

STI programmes contributed to the instable economic environment. Instead of fostering economic growth, STI investments fluctuate following the economic cycle. Thus STI investment hinders the implementation of long-term strategies, and limits the chances of reducing economic downturns. STI investment – a finding that may probably be extended to other Latin American countries – is both anti-Keynesian and anti-Schumpeterian.

Alenka Guzman and Ignacio Llamas, also from Mexico, study the relative efficiency of national innovation systems in OECD countries. Using Data Envelopment Analysis, they ask some key questions such as the links between NIS investments (mainly R&D) and economic performance. Efficiency is measured by the coefficient between inputs. Do countries with a superior NIS performance display higher economic growth? Using different indicators of efficiency, they found that only the 'utilization' and the 'diffusion' models are significant. This result shows that the diffusion and use of knowledge are related to long-term economic growth, rather than knowledge creation. The general conclusion is that most countries should learn to use existing knowledge, rather than create new knowledge.

Ramanayake and Lee's study explores the possibly differential effects of currency undervaluation or overvaluation in these two different growth paths, that is, manufacturing- versus mineral-exporting economies. Regression results confirm a negative effect of undervaluation on growth in mineral-exporting groups and no significant (positive) effects of undervaluation in manufacturing-exporting groups. This finding is consistent with the fact that if currency is more undervalued in countries that highly depend on natural resource exports, they earn less income in terms of dollars and that natural resource exports are insensitive to exchange rates. This result also underscores a policy dilemma of resource-rich countries aiming to eventually diversify into manufacturing; undervaluation promotes manufacturing exports and, in turn undermines economic growth because of its negative effect on dollar-based earnings from resource exports. Another important contrast between manufacturing versus mineral exporters is that, although depreciation often tends to exert countercyclical effects of recovering exports and growth in economies with a strong manufacturing base (or non-negative effects on average), mineral-exporting economies face the growth-impeding and procyclical effects of undervaluation, which often comes during times of weak performance of the economy with a typical balance-of-payment crisis. This underscores the dilemma of the so-called 'resource-based' development model.

I.5.3 Regional Innovation Systems

Chris Forman, Avi Goldfarb and Shane Greenstein analyze a regional system of innovation: the Bay Area. They recall the abundant literature on co-agglomeration of invention and production. In the United States, the Bay Area represents an increasing fraction of US patents, from under 10 per cent in 1980 to over 30 per cent in 2005. But it is even more noticeable that the Bay Area represents an increasing proportion of US patents in other important areas, such as chemicals, drugs, mechanical and other products. This increase is disproportionate to the rise in population. The authors propose one tentative explanation: the rise in the number of industries that use ICT technologies.

In their chapter about regional innovation policies, Markus Grillitsch and Michaela Trippl argue that low levels of innovation activities can be explained not only by market failures but also by system-level structural deficiencies and capability failures. The authors contend that regional conditions may impede industrial renewal. They propose several types of new developments: path upgrading, modernization, branching, importation and new creation. They also distinguish several types of regional innovation systems, and argue that each of them may suffer from specific failures and barriers to structural change. They also classify different types and mechanisms of path development, such as path extension, path upgrading, path modernisation, path branching, path importation and path creation.

R. Golman and Steve Klepper examine the relationship between clustering and spinoffs. Clusters are the result of new forms locating close to their parents. Spinoffs often discover or produce new submarkets. Firms in clusters share specialized labour, inputs and knowledge. At the origin of clusters there are one or several very successful firms, that other authors have called anchor tenants. Parents' innovation creates the spinoffs and the cluster, in a positive feedback process. The more an industry is innovative, the more it clusters. Larger firms produce more spinoffs and those new entrants outperform spinoffs elsewhere. Cases in point were Olds Motors in Detroit a century ago, Fairchild Semiconductors in Silicon Valley in the early 1960s and Hybritech in the San Diego human biotechnology cluster in the

1970s. While, initially, spinoffs produce similar things to their parents, over time they develop their own line of products. The cluster thus becomes more diversified. Innovation produces both industrial and urban growth.

Masaru Yarime and Martin Karlsson study the transformation of smart cities in Japan. Smart cities are those based on advanced systems of information and energy. These systems improve the efficiency of energy generation and consumption, thus reducing emissions. They include electrification of urban infrastructure, network analysis of the relationships among actors, as well as sophisticated software and hardware. In Japan, METI (the Ministry of Economy, Trade and Industry) is the key actor, through the New Energy and Industrial Technology Development Organization (NEDO), the R&D funding agency. Other major actors are large firms such as Fuji Electric, Hitachi, Mitsubishi, Panasonic, Sharp and Toshiba. Also, the Energy Conservation and Homecare Network, formed in 1997, and the Japan, Smart Community Alliance (2010) are part of NEDO. The network produced social system demonstrations in several cities, using cogeneration, renewable energy, energy storage, electric vehicles and energy management systems (EMSs). The study illustrates an advanced technical innovation system with future applications.

Franco Malerba and Maureen McKelvey are interested in the analysis of knowledge-intensive entrepreneurship (KIE). Advanced knowledge and innovation are the basis of the competitive advantage of these knowledge-intensive firms. Their entry and growth produce economic development through rapid growth and spinoff companies. The purpose of this chapter is to expand the discussion of how to conceptualize the existence and importance of knowledge-intensive entrepreneurship in order to propose directions for future research, through indicators, measurements and related topics. The cases mentioned in the chapter by Golman and Klepper in this book illustrate how KIE produces economic development in specific regions. The Malerba and McKelvey chapter adds figures from a sample of European countries, showing that KIE can also take place in more traditional industries such as machine tools, textiles, food and beverages. Yet, when taken industry by industry, ICT concentrates most of the knowledge-intensive companies in the sample.

I.6 Conclusion

Social sciences evolve towards complexity and dynamic-systems perspectives (Arthur 2007; Sterman 2000). Economics is not an exception to the rule; a complex economics systems approach is slowly progressing within the divided discipline. Economic complexity is evolutionary by nature, due to irreversibility. Increasing information produces increasing complexity (Hidalgo 2015). And the economic world evolves both towards increasing complexity and increasing information (Arthur and Lane 1993).

Innovation is at the centre of long-term economic development. Scattered innovation produces only short-term results. Innovation has an economic impact when it is widely adopted and innovation systems are operating. Innovation systems supersede innovation policies and require system evaluation. The economic system includes both what we understand as macroeconomic processes and also what occurs within smaller systems that we call organizations. Each firm, each innovative organization, is a system in itself.

Armed with system dynamics, evolutionary economics has the potential to unite several heterodox currents under its conceptual roof. These heterodox currents include institutional, post-Keynesian and behavioural economics.

The innovation systems perspective, with its theoretical spin-off known as innovation ecosystems, is the key to the analysis of innovation processes. For innovation systems to develop and prosper, innovation policies need to be assessed and fine-tuned, cultural barriers lifted and organizations redesigned with the addition of appropriate innovation routines.

We have found a plethora of innovation policies with different goals: incremental and radical innovation. Horizontal policies are typically aimed at incremental innovation and path-dependent change, while mission-oriented policies aim at both radical and incremental change, and grand challenge policy is exclusively aimed at radical innovation and path-creating change.

References

Acemoglu, D. and D. Cao. 2015. Innovation by entrants and incumbents. *Journal of Economic Theory* 157: 255–294.

Arnold, E. 2004. Evaluating research and innovation policy: a systems world needs system evaluation. *Research Evaluation* 13(1): 3–17.

Arrow, K. J. 1962. Economic welfare and the allocation of resources for inventions, in R. Nelson (ed.) *The Rate and Direction of Inventive Activity: Economic and Social Factors.* Princeton, NJ: Princeton University Press.

Arthur, W. B. 2007. Complexity and the economy, in H. Hanusch and A. Pyka (eds.) *Elgar Companion to Neo-Schumpeterian Economics.* Cheltenham: Elgar, 1102–1110.

Arthur, W. B. and D. Lane. 1993. Information contagion. *Structural Change and Economic Dynamics* 4(1): 81–104.

Avnimelech, G. and M. Teubal. 2008. Evolutionary targeting. *Journal of Evolutionary Economics* 18: 151–160.

Bloom, N., R. Griffith and J. Van Reenen. 2002. Dotax credits for R&D work? Evidence for a panel of six countries 1979–1997. *Journal of Public Economics* 85(1): 1–31.

Cooke, P. and K. Morgan. 1998. *The Associational Economy: Firms, Regions and Innovation.* Oxford and New York, NY: Oxford University Press.

Dahlström, C., V. Lapuente and J. Teorell. 2012. The merit of meritocratization: politics, bureaucracy and the institutional deterrents of corruption. *Political Research Quarterly* 65(3): 656–668.

David, P. A. 1994. Why are institutions the carriers of history? Path dependence and the evolution of conventions, organizations and institutions. *Structural Change and Economic Dynamics* 5(2): 205–220.

D'Este, P., S. Iammarino, M. Savona and N. von Tunzelmann. 2012. What hampers innovation? Revealed barriers versus deterring barriers. *Research Policy* 41: 482–488.

Dijk, M. and M. Yarme. 2010. The emergence of electric cars: Innovation path creation through co-evolution of supply and demand. *Technological Forecasting and Social Change* 77: 1371–1390.

Edler, J. and J. Yeow. 2016. Connecting demand and supply: The role of intermediation in public procurement of innovation. *Research Policy* 45(2): 414–426.

Erickson, A. 2014. China's pace development history: A comparison of the rocket and satellite sectors. *Acta Astronautica* 103: 142–167.

Essletzbichler, J. 2012. Renewable Energy Technology and Path Creation: A Multi-scalar Approach to Energy Transition in the UK. *European Planning Studies* 20(5): 791–816, DOI: 10.1080/09654313.2012.667926.

Fagerberg, J. 2016. 'Innovation policy and national innovation systems: lessons and challenges', a presentation to the 16th congress of the International Schumpeter Society, Montreal, 5–8 July.

Feldman, M. and D. Audretsch. 1999. Innovation in cities: Science-based diversity, specialization and localized competition. *European Economic Review* 43: 409–429.

Foray, D., D. C. Mowery, and R. R. Nelson. 2012. Public R&D and social challenges: What lessons from mission R&D programs. *Research Policy* 41: 1697–1702.

Grimaldi, R. and A. Grandi. 2005. Business incubation and new venture creation: An assessment of incubating models. *Technovation* 25: 111–121.

Grossman, G. M. and E. Helpman. 1991. *Innovation and Growth in the Global Economy*. Cambridge, MA: Massachusetts Institute of Technology Press.

Hansson, A. and S. McGuire. 1999. Commercial space and international trade rules: An assessment of the WTO's influence on the sector. *Space Policy* 15(4): 199–205.

Industry Canada. 2013. *Medical Devices Industry Profile*. Ottawa. (www.ic.gc .ca/eic/site/lsg-pdsv.nsf/eng/h_hn01736.htm).

Inglehart, R. and W. E. Baker. 2000. Modernization, cultural change and persistence of traditional values. *American Sociological Review* 65(1): 19–51.

Jensen, M. B., B. Johnson, E. Lorenz and B. A. Lundvall. 2007. Forms of knowledge and modes of innovation. *Research Policy* 36: 680–693.

Kim, L. 1997. *Imitation to Innovation, The Dynamics of Korea's Technological Learning*. Boston, MA: Harvard Business School Press.

Klepper, S. 1997. Industry life cycles. *Industrial and Corporate Change* 6(1): 145–181.

Kumar, N., L. Scheer and P. Kotler. 2000. From market driven to market driving. *European Management Journal* 18(2): 129–142.

Lee, K. (2013): *Schumpeterian analysis of Economic catch-up: Knowledge, Path creation and the Middle Income Trap*, Cambridge University Press.

Lipsey, R. and K. Carlaw. 1998. Technology policies in neo-classical and structuralist-evolutionary models. *STI Review* 22: 30–73.

Malerba, F. 2005. Sectoral systems of innovation: A framework for linking innovation to the knowledge base, structure and dynamics of sectors. *Economics of Innovation and New Technology* 14(1): 63–82.

Malerba, F. (ed.) 2004. *Sectoral Systems of Innovation*. Cambridge: Cambridge University Press.

Mazzucato, M. 2016. From market fixing to market creation: A new framework for innovation policy. *Industry and Innovation* 23(2): 140–156.

Metcalfe, B. D. 2011. Women, empowerment and development in Arab Gulf states: A critical appraisal of governance, culture and national human resource development (HRD) framework. *Human Resource Development International* 14(2): 131–148.

Mohnen, P. and L. H. Röller. 2005. Complementarities in innovation policy. *European Economic Review* 49: 1431–1450.

Mohrman, K., W. Ma and D. Baker. 2008. The research university in transition: The emerging global model. *Higher Education Policy* 21(1): 5–27.

Montalvo, J. G. and M. Reynal-Querol. 2005. Ethnic diversity and economic development. *Journal of Development Economics* 76(2): 293–323.

Mowery, D. C. 2009. What does economic theory tell us about 'mission-oriented R&D'? in D. Foray (ed.) *The New Economics of Technology Policy*. Cheltenham: Elgar, 131–147.

Mowery, D. C. and N. Rosenberg. 1989. *Technology and the Pursuit of Economic Growth*. Cambridge: Cambridge University Press.

Nelson, R. R. (ed.) 1993. *National Innovation Systems*. Oxford and New York, NY: Oxford University Press.

Nelson, R. R. 1994. Why do firms differ and how does it matter? in R. P. Rumelt, D. E. Schendel and D. J. Teece (eds.) *Fundamental Issues in Strategy*. Boston, MA: Harvard Business School Press, 247–269.

Nelson, R. R. 2005. *Technology, Institutions and Economic Growth*. Cambridge, MA: Harvard University Press.

Niosi, J. 2000a. Science based industries: A new Schumpeterian taxonomy. *Technology in Society* 22(3): 429–444.

Niosi, J. 2000b. *Canada's National System of Innovation*. Montreal and Kingston: McGill-Queen's University Press.

Niosi, J. 2010. *Building National and Regional Systems of Innovation*. Cheltenham: Elgar.

Niosi, J., P. Saviotti, B. Bellon and M. Crow. 1993. National systems of innovation: In search of a workable concept. *Technology in Society* 15(2): 207–227.

Niosi, J. and J. Zhao. 2013. China's catching up in aerospace. *International Journal of Technology and Globalization* 7(1–2): 80–91.

O'Conner, G. C. and M. P. Rice. 2013. A comprehensive model of uncertainty associated with radical innovation. *Journal of Product Innovation Management* 51: 2–18.

OECD. 2006a. *Innovation in Pharmaceutical Biotechnology. Comparing National Innovation Systems at the Sectoral Level*. Paris.

OECD. 2006b. *Government R&D Funding and Company Behaviour*. Paris.

OECD. 2011. *Demand-side Innovation Policies*. Paris.

Pavitt, K. 1998. Technologies, products and organization in the innovating firm: What Adam Smith tells us and Joseph Schumpeter does not. *Industrial and Corporate Change* 7(3): 433–452.

Rahmeyer F. 2012. Schumpeter, Marshall and Neo-Schumpeterian evolutionary economics. *Jahrbücher für Nationalökonomie und Statistik / Journal of Economics and Statistics* 233(1): 39–63.

Rauch, J. E. and P. B. Evans. 2000. Bureaucratic structure and bureaucratic performance in less developed countries. *Journal of Public Economics* 75: 49–71.

Saviotti, P. P. 1996. *Technological Evolution, Variety and the Economy*. Cheltenham: Elgar.

Schienstock, G. 2007. From path dependency to path creation. *Current Sociology* 55(1): 92–109.

Scillitoe, J. L. and A. K. Chakrabarti. 2010. The role of incubator interactions in assisting new ventures. *Technovation* 30: 155–167.

Sidow, J., A. Windeler, C. Schubert and G. Möllering. 2012. Organizing R&D consortia for path creation and extension: the case of semiconductor manufacturing technologies. *Organization Studies* 33(7): 907–936.

Smits, R. and S. Kuhlmann. 2004. The rise of systemic instruments in innovation policy. *International Journal of Foresight and Innovation Policy* 1(1/2): 4–32.

Sterman, J. 2000. *Business Dynamics, Systems Thinking and Modeling for a Complex World*. Boston, MA: Irwin McGraw-Hill.

Subramanian, A. 2015. Making merit: The Indian Institute of Technology and the social life of caste. *Comparative Studies in Society and History* 57(2): 291–322.

Taylor, M. 2008. Beyond technology-push and demand-pull: Lessons from California's solar policy. *Energy Economics* 30: 2829–2854.

Tödtling, F. and M. Trippl. 2005. One size fits all? Towards a differentiated regional innovation policy. *Research Policy* 34(8): 1203–1219.

Ulnicane, I. 2016. Grand challenges concept: A return of big ideas in science, technology and innovation policy? *International Journal of Foresight and Innovation Policy* 11(1–3): 5–17.

Vecchiato, R. and C. Roveda. 2014. Foresight for public procurement and regional innovation policy: The case of Lombardy. *Research Policy* 43(2): 438–450.

Vedovello, C. and M. M. Godinho. 2003. Business incubators as a technological infrastructure for supporting small innovative firms' activities. *International Journal of Entrepreneurship and Innovation Management* 3(1–2): 4–21.

Vernon, R. 1966. International investment and international trade in the product life cycle. *Quarterly Journal of Economics*, 80: 190–207.

PART I

Innovation Policy and Innovation Systems

1 Moving Forward in Sectoral Systems Research

Taxonomies, Evolution and Modelling

FRANCO MALERBA

1.1 Introduction and Outline of the Chapter

Research on sectoral systems of innovation has progressed significantly in the last decade. Sectoral systems consider sectors as systems and innovation in a sector as the result of the learning, capabilities and strategies of firms and other system components such as non-firm actors and institutions. In a sense, a sectoral system view of innovation puts knowledge, capabilities, systems and institutions at the centre of the analysis.

How much and in which directions has research on sectoral systems progressed? In this chapter I will discuss the major advancements, what we have learned and in which direction research is now evolving. I will be selective in my discussion, with the intention of identifying some core issues and some key challenges.

In Section 1.2 I will examine the early research on sectoral systems and their main findings. Then in Sections 1.3, 1.4 and 1.5 I will move to examine some new challenges and trajectories in research on sectoral systems. I will identify three of them: the creation of taxonomies, the evolution of sectoral systems and modelling. Section 1.5 will present a short reprise and a conclusion.

1.2 Sectoral Systems of Innovation: Early Research and Major Findings

1.2.1 Sectoral Systems

Sectoral systems is a multi-dimensional, integrated and dynamic approach which draws on the work of three areas of research in economics and in innovation studies: the dynamics and transformation of industries, evolutionary theory and the innovation system approach.

According to the sectoral system approach, a sector is seen as a set of activities that are associated with broad product groups and are addressed to an existing or emerging demand; share a common knowledge base; and are affected by a system of actors and institutions (Malerba, 2002). A sectoral systems framework focuses on three main dimensions, which are briefly discussed in the following sections (for a broader discussion see Malerba, 2005 and Malerba and Adams, 2013).

1.2.1.1 Knowledge and Technological Domains

A sector is characterised by a specific knowledge base and technologies. Knowledge plays a central role in the sectoral systems approach. Knowledge is highly idiosyncratic at the firm level, does not diffuse automatically and freely among firms (Nelson and Winter, 1982) and must be absorbed by firms through the capabilities that they have accumulated over time (Cohen and Levinthal, 1990). Knowledge – especially technological knowledge – involves varying degrees of specificity, tacitness, complexity, complementarity and independence (Winter, 1987; Cowan, David and Foray, 2000; Dosi and Nelson, 2011).

1.2.1.2 Actors and Networks

A sector is composed of heterogeneous agents that include firms, non-firm organisations (e.g. universities, financial organisations and industry associations) and individuals (e.g. consumers, entrepreneurs and scientists). These heterogeneous agents are characterised by specific learning processes, competencies, beliefs, objectives and behaviours. They interact through processes of communication, exchange, competition, control and cooperation. Thus, within a sectoral systems framework, innovation is considered to be a process that involves systematic interactions among a wide variety of actors for the generation and exchange of knowledge relevant to innovation and its commercialisation.

1.2.1.3 Institutions

The cognitive frameworks, actions and interactions of agents are influenced by institutions, which include norms, common habits, established practices, rules, laws and standards. Institutions may be more or less binding and more or less formal (i.e. patent laws or specific regulations versus traditions and conventions). Many institutions have national dimensions (i.e. patent laws or regulations concerning the environment), while others are specific to sectors and may cut across national boundaries (such as international conventions or established practices concerning the types of knowledge that are freely exchanged within a sector).

Each of these components of a sectoral system has its own characteristics and its own set of dynamics which are important to understand. But each of these elements is also part of a broader system in which the interaction among the parts drives change and innovation.

1.3 The Early Studies on Sectoral Systems and on Their Differences

1.3.1 Studies of Specific Industries

Early studies regarding sectoral systems have focused on the structure and characteristics of specific sectoral systems in advanced or developing countries. The main features, dimensions and structures of these sectoral systems of innovation from a learning, capability and system perspective have been identified, and major empirical findings and useful appreciative theories have emerged. Mowery and Nelson (1999) have examined innovation and performance of seven industries – semiconductors, computers, software, machine tools, chemicals, pharmaceuticals and diagnostic devices – and have found major differences across industries with respect to several dimensions of sectoral systems which are relevant for innovation, such as demand, suppliers, public policy, universities, financial organizations and institutions. In Malerba (2004) the sectoral systems of pharmaceuticals, chemicals, telecommunications, software, machine tools and services have been examined in various European countries. In Malerba and Mani (2009) the focus was on industries in emerging and developing countries: pharmaceuticals and telecommunication in India, pulp and paper in Brazil, software in Uruguay, aeronautics in Brazil, motorcycles in Vietnam, salmon farming in Chile, capital goods in Korea, ICT in Taiwan and biofuels in Tanzania.

All these studies conclude that major differences exist in the features and structure of sectoral systems of innovation and identify the ways in which these features affect the amount and the direction of innovation in a sector.

1.3.2 Quantitative Analyses of Sectoral Systems

In parallel, another direction of research has conducted quantitative and econometric analyses. These studies have been based on the availability of detailed firm-level data (such as CIS) that is able to capture the effects of knowledge, non-firm actors and institutions on firms' innovation. For example, Castellacci (2007) has used data from CIS, OECD STAN and EUROSTAT to examine sectoral labour productivity growth in twenty-two manufacturing industries between 1996–2001 in nine countries, as affected by key dimensions of sectoral systems such as technological regimes, cooperation in innovation, users, suppliers, science, and market size and openness. Starting from the Pavitt taxonomy and using CIS data, Castellacci (2009) has also analysed cross-sectoral and cross country differences in productivity. He has utilized data on large and small firms' R&D; indicators of process and product innovation; and the role of universities, users and suppliers in firms' innovation. He has found evidence of different types of sectoral systems according to the upstream and the downstream links and the role of universities. He has also found the existence of some cross-country differences in the sectoral system of an industry due to the presence of national innovation systems. Finally, using data for Norwegian firms between 1998 and 2004, Castellacci and Zheng (2010) relate firms' productivity growth to differences in the technological regimes, the knowledge base of sectors and the industry structure.

Similar analyses focusing on the relevance of sectoral systems for innovation and entrepreneurship have been conducted through small surveys (Lenzi et al., 2010) and very large surveys (Caloghirou et al., 2015). They all point to significant differences across industries in the main dimensions of sectoral systems and in their effects on innovation and entrepreneurship.

All these analyses have undoubtedly advanced the measurement and quantitative assessment of the role of specific sectoral system elements in affecting innovation, firm performance and sector development. They have also led to conduct comparisons across sectors in the same country and across countries.

1.3.3 Sectoral Systems and National Systems

The industry studies and the quantitative analyses discussed in the previous section have identified differences across countries in the sectoral system of an industry in terms of the presence and strength of specific actors, linkages and institutions and in the effects that these different features have on innovation and performance in the various countries. This finding has called for a deeper understanding of the relationship between national characteristics and sectoral systems.

Indeed the empirical analyses conducted on various industries indicate that sectoral systems may be affected by national dimensions (i.e. national institutions, national policies and national organizations such as banks or universities), in that national actors and institutional frameworks positively affect those components of a sectoral system that are related or linked to the national ones. For example, the national innovation system that grew up in India was originally based on traditional Indian strengths in university science: India's successes in pharmaceuticals and software reflect this. Over much of its post-war history, Brazil has been strongly pressured to keep the economy open to both trade and foreign direct investment: the Brazilian experience in pharmaceuticals, telecom equipment and automobiles reflects this. Similar considerations may explain why, given their national innovation systems, South Korea has not been able to catch up in software and India has failed to catch up in semiconductors and telecom equipment.

Research on several industries has found, however, that the relationship between national systems and sectoral systems is not one way, going from national to sectoral. It may also go the opposite way. For example, Korean policies of access to foreign knowledge through licences, limited joint ventures and initial protection for the home market proved successful in automobiles and encouraged similar policies for telecommunications and semiconductors, thus becoming more national. Similarly, Indian policies supporting advanced human capital formation and the entry of new firms into software proved successful and were later adopted for pharmaceuticals (Lee, 2013).

Similar reasoning may also explain why attempts by national governments to replicate policies and institutions that have worked well in one sectoral system may not succeed in another. For example, Dodgson et al. (2008) illustrate the case of Taiwan's attempt to replicate its success in ICT clusters by applying similar policies and institutions to biotechnology. But the sectoral innovation system in biotechnology is substantially different from the one in ICT in terms of innovation processes, actors, networks and institutions. It is not surprising, therefore, that policies and institutions successful for ICT were not equally effective in biotechnology. What was required in fact was a set of institutions and policies adapted to the *specific* sectoral innovation system that characterizes biotechnology.

More generally, research on several industries has found that a dynamic interplay between national-system and sectoral-system variables exists: national systems and institutional frameworks positively affect the development and growth of those sectors whose dimensions correspond and fit the national ones. In turn, sectoral actors or institutions that prove effective in a specific sectoral system may be replicated or adopted with success in another sector *if* the two sectoral systems have similar features. However, if the basic features of a successful industry do not fit the characteristics of a targeted industry, any attempt by policy to foster innovation in the targeted industry by replicating the actors or institutions of the successful industry is doomed to failure (Mowery and Nelson, 1999; Malerba and Nelson, 2011; and Gu et al., 2011).

1.3.4 The Role of Public Policy in a Sectoral System Perspective

These early studies on sectoral systems have reached some findings also regarding public policy. The first is that because of the different characteristics of the sectoral system, certain types of policy may be more effective in some sectors than in others in their goal of stimulating innovation. For example, the energy sector may have different innovation policies compared to biotechnology in terms of policy tools. The evidence provided in Mowery and Nelson (1999) and Malerba (2004) for a large number of sectors is quite revealing. As Edquist et al. (2004) point out, a sectoral system approach allows identification of the key variables that need to be targeted if an innovation policy needs to be addressed to specific sectors, such as energy, biotechnology, ICT, environment and so on. Related to this point, the impact of horizontal policies may differ drastically across sectors.

In general, the empirical evidence on sectoral systems indicates that for fostering innovation and diffusion in a sector, technology and innovation policies alone are insufficient. Often a combination of policies addressed to various components of the system is required. Caloghirou et al. (2015) emphasize the need for systems of policies that take into account the interdependencies, links and feedbacks among policies, and the differences that may exist across sectors in the specific combination of these policies. In fact, the most effective combination of policies may vary according to the type of knowledge, actors, networks and institutions of a sector.

One interesting avenue that has been opened recently relates to policy examinations based on quantitative analyses. For example, Bodas Freitas et al. (2016) enquire whether the additionality effects of R&D tax credits vary across sectors and conduct a micro-econometric analysis of three countries – Norway, Italy and France – between 2004 and 2008. They investigate whether the input and output additionality effects of R&D tax credits vary across sectors characterized by different R&D orientation and market structure, key elements of a sectoral system. The results indicate that firms in sectors with a high R&D orientation and a high market concentration are on average more responsive to fiscal incentives to R&D.

In sum, in the last decade major advancements have been obtained in the analyses of specific sectoral systems at the qualitative and quantitative levels; in the examination of the relationship between the national dimensions and the sectoral ones; and in the identification of a system of public policies for sectors. In the next sections I would like to discuss some recent challenges in sectoral system research and the way these challenges have been addressed so far: the development of taxonomies of sectoral systems, the long term evolution of sectoral systems and the formal modelling of sectoral systems.

1.4 Moving Forward: Taxonomies

A first major challenge is to move from studies of the features and structure of single sectoral systems to the identifications of commonalities among several sectoral systems and consequently to the grouping of sectoral systems into distinct typologies along a few key dimensions.

The attempt to create taxonomies of sectoral patterns of innovation goes back decades. The Pavitt taxonomy (1984) is perhaps the best example of sectoral taxonomy. Pavitt started from the consideration that firms' innovative behaviour is constrained by the technological and sectoral context in which they operate. He classified firms into four major groups of industries (science-based, specialized suppliers, supplier-dominated and scale intensive) depending on firms' positioning with respect to sources of technology, type of user, means of appropriation, nature of innovation, firm size and rate of technological diversification. Focusing on other elements of a sector such as the technological regime and the organization of innovative activity within the sector Malerba and Orsenigo (1997) identified two patterns of innovative activities across industrial sectors. In the 'Schumpeter Mark I' (the entrepreneurial regime) pattern, innovation is mainly produced by new and small firms and industrial turbulence is quite high. Instead, in the 'Schumpeter Mark II' (the routinized regime) pattern, innovation originates from the formal R&D activity of larger and already established firms and the stability of innovators is high. Later on, Malerba and Orsenigo (1997) linked these patterns to technological regimes in terms of technological opportunity, innovation cumulativeness and appropriability conditions. Along these lines, Castellacci (2008) identified differences in innovative activities among manufacturing sectors and proposed four sectoral patterns of technological change: 'advanced users-based', 'systemic', 'investment intensive' and 'embodied diffusion'. Finally, Peneder (2010), combining the Schumpeterian distinction between creative and adaptive behaviour with the three characteristics of technological regimes, provided a classification of industries on the basis of their NACE code (both manufacturing and services) along these dimensions.

A recent proposal for a taxonomy of sectoral systems has been advanced by Fontana et al. (2015). This taxonomy is related to innovation and new enterprises and to the factors that affect origin, performance and growth of innovative enterprises. Fontana et al.'s (2015) analysis is based on data coming from the AEGIS survey of 4,004 founders of newly established firms in the period 2001–2007 in ten EU countries. The survey intends to capture firm-level dimensions and contextual factors, such as origin, strategy, demand and institutional setting.

This taxonomy is interesting in the methodology followed and in the results obtained. Using the results from the survey, Fontana et al. (2015) carry out the analysis in four main steps. First, specific questions in the survey which could be used to capture the main characteristics of sectoral systems are selected. Second, on each question a factor analysis is performed in order to pinpoint the main characteristics of the sectoral systems. The factors are extracted using the principal components method. The third step aims at constructing profiles of sectoral systems on the basis of the factors identified in the previous step. Homogeneous groups of sectors are built with the purpose of minimizing the distance in scores of firms within a given cluster and maximizing the distance in scores among companies from different clusters. The outcome of this step is a profile of sectoral systems. The final step is aimed at making sense of the profiles. In order to achieve this aim, Fontana et al. (2015) associate the profiles with the actual sectoral distribution of the firms in our sample based on the NACE (Rev. 1.1) classification. The approach used was 'simple correspondence analysis'.

Starting from the framework of sectoral system, Fontana et al. (2015) isolate several key dimensions: knowledge and its sources, the benefits coming from relationships and networks, the type of participation in formal agreements and the instruments of IP protection. The first characteristic of a sectoral system concerns the *sources of knowledge* considered fundamental by new firms for exploring business opportunities. In this respect, the factor analysis returns three factors. The first factor includes respondents that score highly on items such as *public research institutes, universities* and external commercial labs, R&D firms, technical institutes as well as national and EU-funded programmes as major sources for detecting potential novel sources of knowledge. They score lowly on other items such as clients, suppliers or competitors. These are firms that use 'non–market-based' and 'horizontal' links as sources of knowledge to explore business opportunities and neglect other sources such as clients, suppliers or competitors. The second factor includes respondents that score highly on items such as *clients, suppliers and competitors* as sources of knowledge. These are firms that use 'market-based' and 'vertical' links. The third factor includes instead firms that source *business events* (i.e. trade fairs, conferences and exhibitions) and *publications* (i.e. scientific journals) for knowledge.

The second characteristic analysed relates to the embeddedness of a firm in a *network* as captured by the tendency of the firm to rely upon other actors in order to carry out certain operations. Here the analysis identifies two main factors. The first factor includes firms that score highly on items such as *networking* for assistance in attracting financial resources, for establishing marketing cooperation, for obtaining legal assistance, but also for developing new products and services, managing production, opening new distribution channels and exploring export opportunities. Fontana et al. (2015) have classified these respondents as firms that benefit from networking through access to complementary assets and markets. The second factor includes firms that score highly on items such as *networking for contacting customers and clients and selecting suppliers*. These respondents are classified as firms that use networking for obtaining advantages that are more production-based.

The third characteristic is complementary to the previous one and it refers to the types of new firms' *formal agreements*. Here factor analysis identifies only one factor that has the ability to explain alone the majority of the variance. Two items were poorly represented, namely 'Subcontracting' and 'Marketing/Export promotion', which refer to agreements aimed at establishing production-related and market-based relationships.

The fourth characteristic of the sectoral systems regards the *methods used by new firms to appropriate* the rents from innovation. Here results from factor analysis are straightforward. Three factors are identified. The first factor, labelled 'tacit method of IP protection', scores highly on items like 'confidentiality agreements' and 'secrecy'. The second factor, labelled 'codified and formal methods of IP protection' scores highly on patents, trademarks and copyrights. The third factor, labelled 'informal methods of IP protection', scores highly on 'lead times advantages' and 'complexity of design'.

Using factor scores as a starting base, Fontana et al. (2015) perform a cluster analysis to investigate possible patterns of behaviours which are cross sectional. The statistical analysis identifies more than one profile of sectoral systems in which new firms operate. This result means that the sectoral environment in which entrepreneurs are active can be very diverse, and provides different sources of knowledge, types of networks and means of appropriability of innovation.

In particular, five different profiles of sectoral systems are identified. The first is the '*diffused sectoral system*', in which knowledge diffusion is quite high and the structure of the system is quite atomistic. This system does not present any specificity in terms of the four key dimensions identified. It has been labelled as 'diffused' because new firms in this sectoral system do not exhibit any specific source of knowledge for business opportunity, benefit from specific networking or have a specific type of formal agreement or method of IP protection. Footwear and food are examples of this type of sectoral systems.

The second profile is the '*vertical with production assets sectoral system*'. Here knowledge sources and networks relate mainly to suppliers and customers to deliver products and services within a context characterized by low R&D intensity. The sources of knowledge for business opportunities come from customers and suppliers (as well as from competitors) and identify a vertical relation in the knowledge flows and in the market opportunities. At the same time, the benefits from the involvement in networking with customers and suppliers concern production activities. This profile is very much production related, with vertical flows of knowledge and links. Advertising, publishing, labour recruitment and call centres are examples of this type of sector.

The third profile is *'vertical with complementary assets sectoral system'*. In this case also, knowledge sources and networks relate to suppliers and users, but here networks provide access to complementary assets. As before, the sources of knowledge for business opportunities come from customers and suppliers, but the main benefits from the involvement in ·networking concern the access to distribution channels and networking for activities (such as assistance in obtaining funds, advertising and promotion, developing new products and services, managing production and operations, arranging taxation and exploring export opportunities). In addition, the main methods of IP protection regard patents, trademarks and copyrights and, to a certain extent, informal methods. Therefore, this profile of sectoral system is vertical in terms of knowledge flows but with a variety of both codified and uncodified instruments of IP protection and with benefits from networking that come for the access to complementary assets. Several of the so-called traditional manufacturing sectors as well as machinery are examples of this type of sectoral systems.

The fourth profile is the *'distributed information sectoral system'*, in which problem solving service firms rely on a variety of sources of information as well as on technological alliances, and in which secrecy is a relevant form of protection. The sources of knowledge for business opportunities are related to trade fairs, conferences and external R&D. Networks provide benefits to new firms through their involvement in relationships with customers and suppliers. The types of formal agreements refer to R&D agreements, research contracted out, technical cooperation or licensing agreements. The methods of IP protection concern confidentiality agreements and secrecy. Therefore, this profile is distributed in terms of knowledge and information and the agreements made for technological reasons play a major role in this case. In order to counterbalance the distributed information and knowledge sources, protection of information relies on tacit instruments. Several KIBS sectors such as engineering, computer activities and accounting are examples of this type of sectoral systems.

Finally, the fifth profile is the '*distributed science and technology knowledge sectoral system*', in which a wide variety of knowledge sources are relevant and in which networks complement new firms' internal activities in order to create, integrate and distribute knowledge within a context characterized by medium or high R&D intensity. Here the sources of knowledge for business opportunities are universities, public research organizations and external R&D, and the benefits from networking come from accessing complementary assets related to distribution channels, assistance in obtaining funds, advertising and promotion, developing new products and services, managing production and operations, arranging taxation and exploring export opportunities. Formal agreements are quite common and refer to R&D agreements, research contracted out, technical cooperation and licensing. Relatedly, the methods of IP protection cover a wide range of instruments, from tacit to codified and formal (such as patents, trademarks and copyrights), to informal (such as lead time advantages and complexity of design). Many high technology manufacturing sectors such as telecommunications, computers, medical devices and chemicals are part of this group.

Finally, in order to explain how these profiles are related to all the various industries, Fontana et al. (2015) apply correspondence analysis. They associate the profiles identified in this section (capturing the main features of sectoral systems) and the industries firms belong to as identified by their NACE (Ver. 1.1) classification.

This new taxonomy by Fontana et al. (2015) represents only a first step in identifying consistent groups of sectoral systems. This taxonomy focusses mainly on dimensions such as sources of knowledge, networking, formal agreements and IPR. Future research steps need to enlarge the number and types of dimensions to be taken into account in the analysis and to consider the degree of complementarities among the various dimensions of a sectoral system.

1.5 Moving Forward: The Evolution of Sectoral Systems

A second challenge is understanding the evolution of sectoral systems. We know that one of the major drivers of transformation in sectoral systems is technological change and innovation. Changes in technology may imply a response from the actors (firms and non-firm organizations) of an existing sectoral system that may favour the adoption and diffusion of the new technology and the possibility of incremental changes and adaptations. On the contrary, blocks or misalignments by actors or institutions may impair the adoption of the new technology and the generation of technical change along the new trajectory. For example, the change in the pharmaceutical industry from random screening to molecular biology was associated to a major change in the sectoral innovation system, with an increase in the role of universities, venture capital, star scientists and university start-ups and the emergence of new types of networks that involved a division of labour between big pharma, small biotech firms and universities (McKelvey et al., 2004). Similarly, the change from fixed to mobile phones or from telecommunications before and after the internet was associated with major changes in the sectoral system (Edquist, 2003 and 2004).

In addition to technological change, some other key factors can be related to the evolution of a sectoral system. A recent line of research associates this evolution with openings of windows of opportunities and the changes that they create in the system and in the dynamics of competition and industrial leadership (Lee and Malerba, 2017). The concept of 'windows of opportunity' was first used by Perez and Soete (1988) to refer to the role of the rise of new techno-economic paradigms to generate the leapfrogging of latecomers who take advantage of a new paradigm and surpass the incumbents. Lee and Malerba (2017) expand the notion of windows of opportunity by linking them to several of the building blocks of a sectoral system. They identify three windows – namely technological, demand and institutional – related to three key elements of a sectoral system: the knowledge base and the technological regime; the demand structure and public policy; and regulation and standards. Specifically, a technological window is a radical change in technology; a demand window refers to a new type of demand, a major shake-up in local demand, or a business cycle; and an institutional window opens up through public intervention in the industry or drastic changes in institutional conditions. Lee and Malerba (2017) link these windows to the evolution of specific industries and the changes in international leadership, in particular with reference to emerging countries. For example, a technological window can explain the advances of Korean producers in consumer electronics in the digital era against the incumbent Japanese leaders in the analogue era (Lee et al., 2015). A major increase in demand in China or a new set of consumers (e.g. the demand for low cost cars in India) may create the possibility for the entry of new firms from a latecomer country. A business cycle may create a situation in which incumbents may have difficulty during financial decline, whereas latecomers may have lower entry cost than in normal periods (Mathews, 2005). Finally, public policy windows have been prominent in several catch-up cases, such as in high-tech industries in Korea and Taiwan (Lee and Lim, 2001; Mathews, 2002), telecommunications in China (Lee et al., 2012), and pharmaceuticals in India (Guennif and Ramani, 2012).

Together with the notion of 'windows of opportunity', Lee and Malerba (2017) use the concept of 'responses' by firms and other components of the sectoral system of a latecomer/emerging country to the opening of a window of opportunity in an industry. These responses depend on the learning processes, level of capabilities, types of organization and strategies of the actors of the system, and on the reactions by institutions in terms of public policy, regulations, the educational system and so on. While it is true that all firms in a sectoral system of a latecomer country share the same system conditions, some firms indeed benefit more from the system response and are able to move to a global leadership position. With the opening of a window, the current leaders from a certain country may end up lagging behind because of the lack of effective response attributed to an 'incumbent trap' (Chandy and Tellis, 2000) and of system misalignments or inadequacies in the new sectoral conditions. Firm leaders tend to be complacent and entrenched with the current success and do not pay attention to new technologies, new types of demand or growing markets.

In sum, in the long-term evolution of industries several windows related to a specific component of a sectoral system may open up, prompting different 'responses' by latecomers and incumbents, thus introducing changes in the industrial leadership. Diverse combinations of windows of opportunity and responses from firms and other components of the sectoral system of both the incumbent and latecomer countries determine which pattern of successive catch-ups is most likely to emerge in a sector over a certain time period. This framework has been applied to the long evolution of six sectors, namely, mid-sized aircraft (Daniel Vertesy, 2017), mobile phones (Giachetti and Marchi, 2017), wine (Morrison and Rabellotti, 2017), semiconductor memories

(Shin, 2017), cameras (Kang and Song, 2017), and steel (Lee and Ki, 2017).

This idea of windows and responses in sectoral systems represents a step forward in the analysis of the long-term evolution of industries. Although it has been applied by Lee and Malerba (2017) to industry evolution and changes in industrial leadership that have favoured 'latecomers' or 'emerging countries', the conceptual framework is quite general. In fact, it can be applied to analyses of the long evolution of sectoral systems in advanced countries when some discontinuities emerge and the various components of a sectoral system react to these changes. The next steps of research may involve the analysis of windows which are endogenous and which emerge out of the behaviour and interaction of the actors of the sectoral system.

Another direction of research in the analysis of the long-term evolution of sectoral systems relates to the role of *vertical links among industries*. Since its beginning, research on sectoral systems has pointed to the relevance for innovation of the links that an industry has with its suppliers, users and companies active in related sectors. These links also open up the boundaries of a sectoral system and connect an industry with the knowledge, dynamics and capabilities of other industries. For example, recent work on sectoral systems has paid attention to innovative inputs from upstream industries or to feed backs and innovation form users (Adams et al., 2013). However, no extensive dynamic analysis has been done so far on the relationship between two vertically related industries as an interaction between two sectoral systems. For example, the demand faced by the upstream industry represents industrial demand that emerges from a separate, but related, sectoral system that is affected by the evolution of that system. Analyses in this direction have been at the theoretical and modelling level by Jacobides (2008), Jacobides and Winter (2005, 2008) and Malerba et al. (2016). But no systematic and extensive work has been done at the empirical level.

A first exploration of the joint dynamic effects of these broad types of inter-sectoral links on the long-term evolution of an industry is given by the analysis of the Chinese telecommunication and semiconductor industries in Yu et al. (2016). Yu et al. (2016) examine the evolution of the telecommunications equipment and semiconductor industries in China from 1978 to 2012. By most accounts, the evolution of telecommunications and semiconductors in China is a tale of two very different sectors: the first one is a catch-up story of success, while the second is, as of yet, a story with a much less positive outcome. By the second decade of the new millennium, two of the world's top five telecom equipment manufactures were Chinese, and China had become a leader in mobile telecommunications standards and the largest exporter of telecommunications equipment in Asia. By contrast, China's semiconductor industry remained heavily dependent on foreign technology, and Chinese semiconductor firms competed mainly in low-end product segments. Yu et al. (2016) show that despite these two industries being at similar levels of development in the early 1980s, belonging to the same national innovation system and being inter-related, they have followed quite different trajectories.

The analysis in Yu et al. (2016) points to the key role of the interaction between two vertically related industries as a relationship between two sectoral systems. While demand for semiconductors from telecommunications was large and, for many segments, technologically advanced, domestic telecommunications firms bought only low-end components from the local producers. By contrast, their demand for high-end devices was sourced from international producers. In a sense, user–producer relations were not related to just the size or the type of demand, but also to the features of the sectoral systems of which these producers and users were a component. Demand for high-end devices existed, but the gap between the capabilities of domestic suppliers and the needs of the users hindered an effective interaction between the two vertically related industries. This study therefore indicates that when the demand component of a sectoral system (e.g. semiconductor devices) comes from another industry (e.g. telecommunications equipment), it may be more properly understood as industrial demand coming from a separate downstream sectoral system, which will determine how such demand evolves over time and what requirements are developed with respect to its suppliers.

More generally, the analysis by Yu et al. (2016) indicates the need for further research on the role played by the boundaries of sectoral systems in terms of vertically related industries. Studies that examine other industries connected to a specific sectoral system only as static elements or exogenous factors may miss important dynamics that emerge in the related industry that may greatly affect innovation and growth in the focal industry. Therefore, a relevant future trajectory of research may focus on the relationship between vertically related sectoral systems as a dynamic factor that may foster virtuous or vicious cycles in the development of a sectoral system.

Finally, another interesting and yet relatively unexplored factor that affects the long-term evolution of sectoral systems is *the systemic nature of international linkages*. While the sectoral system framework indeed recognizes the importance of international organizations, cross-national networks and international institutions for innovation and growth, most studies focus on such factors as independent elements acting in one or other of the building blocks of a sectoral system in a separate way. On the contrary, Yu et al. (2016) indicate that international linkages have been major elements in all three components of a sectoral system and that they worked to reinforce each other across the system: in terms of knowledge, international linkages provided access (or lack thereof) to technology and knowledge at the forefront; in terms of actors and networks they opened relations (or lack thereof) with international actors and networks; and in terms of institutions they allowed the participation (or lack thereof) in international agencies and policy-making institutions. The point that Yu et al. (2016) make is that one type of linkage would not have been as effective (or ineffective) without the presence (or absence) of the others.

1.6 Moving Forward: Modelling Sectoral Systems

Most research on sectoral systems has been based on case studies or quantitative analysis. A promising area of research regards the modelling of the structure, the actors and the dynamics of sectoral systems. I see two ways of proceeding. One is through social network analysis and modelling, where the focus is on sectoral systems considered as networks. In this respect, the structure of sectoral systems can be represented and studied in terms of properties and dynamics of networks. The other (which I am more familiar with) is with history-friendly models in which the focus is on the evolution of sectoral systems as composed by different types of actors and institutions. In the next pages I will concentrate on this second modelling style.

History-friendly models (Malerba et al., 2016) are evolutionary models that model the evolution of industries, the dynamics of technologies or industrial change and pay attention to the specificities and histories of an industry. In these models, a fruitful dialogue between empirical analyses of industries, appreciative theorizing derived from these analyses and formal models can be developed. The modelling group has to first identify the empirical evidence on the dynamics to be analysed and the appreciative theories that may explain it, and then develop a model based on that empirical dynamics and on the causal arguments concerning the factors that have shaped it and are expressed in the appreciative theories. The formal model that is created aims to capture the central causal arguments of the appreciative theory in a stylized and simplified form. The building of the model provides a vehicle for checking out the consistency and completeness of the arguments presented in the appreciative theory. Like most evolutionary models, history-friendly models take the form of computer simulations, and are 'agent-based modelling'. History-friendly models can be flexible enough to be able to model different sectors, rich enough to take on board system features and dynamic enough to represent the evolution of an industry. Up to now, history-friendly models have examined the role of some institutions or some non-firm organizations in specific sectoral systems.

The role of a type of knowledge base – science – and of non-firm organizations – universities – has been examined in a history-friendly model of the chemical industry in the nineteenth century (Murman and Brenner, 2003). The paper examines the rise of the German chemical industry with respect to the British one, by modelling the causal impact of the initial number of organic chemists at the start of the industry (1857) and the responsiveness of the German university system on German global market share in the synthetic dye industry in 1913.

The role of another component of a sectoral system – demand – has been explored in terms of users and their effects on innovation and industry evolution in a model of the computer industry (Malerba et al., 2007). In the model, experimental users and niche markets allow the new firms to remain alive long enough so that they can develop a new technology to a point when it then becomes competitive on the main market. Experimental users and niche markets affect, therefore, the ability of the new firms to explore and launch a new technology. Established firms initially have little incentive to adopt the new technology, which initially is inferior to the technology they have mastered. And new firms generally could not survive in head-to-head conflict with established firms on the market that are well served by the latter.

The coupled dynamics of two interdependent industries – discussed in Section 1.5 – have been examined for the semiconductor and computer industries in Malerba et al. (2016). The model illustrates how the structure of the industry in the sectoral system and the vertical integration and specialization in the computer industry change as a function of processes of learning and market selection, both in the upstream and downstream sectors. The level of concentration and the decision to specialize or to integrate depend on the actual capabilities of firms in the industry and how they are transformed – via selection processes – into performance – market shares, growth, etc.

The working of an institution such as IPR in a sectoral system has been examined for the pharmaceutical industry in Garavaglia et al. (2012). Results from this history-friendly model suggest that industrial concentration depends much more on the degree of fragmentation of demand than on the appropriability regime. In fact, in 'homogeneous' markets, concentration tends to be high anyway: stronger patent protection has practically no effect. On the contrary, if the industry is competitive as a result of 'fragmentation' of demand, a stronger appropriability regime may even reduce concentration because through higher profits it makes the discovery of new submarkets easier. What is perhaps more interesting is the simple observation that the consequences of longer patent protection may turn out to be quite different under alternative technological and demand regimes.

Another key element of a sectoral system – the public actor and public policy – has been examined in various papers. In Malerba et al. (2001 and 2008), the role of competition policy in terms of antitrust and entry support in the computer industry has been addressed. The results of simulations show that if strong dynamic increasing returns are operative, both through technological capabilities and through customer tendency to stick with a brand, there is little that competition policy in terms of antitrust and entry policy could do to avert the rise of a dominant firm in mainframes. On the other hand, if the customer lock-in effect had been smaller, either by chance or through policies that discouraged efforts of firms to lock in their customers, the situation might have been different and antitrust and entry-encouraging policies would have been more effective in assuring that concentration would decrease. The leading firm would continue to dominate the market, but its relative power would be reduced. Other types of policies – public procurement, open standards, information diffusion and basic research support – have been analysed for the computer and semiconductor industries (Malerba et al., 2008). Here results show that different policies have quite different effects on key policy targets such as the rate of technical progress in a sector; that there are major inter-industry effects of policies, transmitted vertically and horizontally across markets; and that the unintended consequences of policies may be significant. The degrees of efficacy of policies depend on the specific nature of the dynamic processes driving industry evolution, particularly as it concerns the existence and strength of increasing returns on the supply and demand side and on the nature of the feedback reactions governing the coupled dynamics of vertically and horizontally related industries. The role of public policy on the process of catching up of a latecomer country with respect to an incumbent country has been examined in a history-friendly model inspired by two industries: mobile phones and semiconductors (Landini and Malerba, 2016). In this model, Landini and Malerba (2016) examine the effects of four different types of public policy – strengthening firms' capability building, promoting firms' learning, protectionism and supporting the entry of new domestic firms. This history-friendly model confirms that policies aiming at strengthening firms' capability building and promoting firms' learning are important drivers of catching up in an industry. On the contrary, support for the entry of new domestic firms affects positively the catch-up only if it is combined with a large technological discontinuity. The introduction of protectionism can favour catch-up only in the absence of technological discontinuities. In general, in the presence of a technological discontinuity there is complementarity between capability-related interventions and policy that favours the exploration of technological opportunities, i.e. entry support.

In conclusion, as it is evident from the discussion of these contributions, there are two clear advantages to model sectoral systems and their evolution through history-friendly models. The first advantage is to examine in a rigorous way the direct and indirect effects on innovation and industrial structure of the links of firms – the key elements of a sectoral system – with the other components of the system such as non-firm organizations or institutions. The second advantage of history-friendly models is to look at the dynamic effects of these links in the long run.

The next steps in this direction are to analyse a greater number of different types of actors and institutions, examine their relationship and explore the complementarity or substitutability that may exist among them in affecting innovation and the evolution of industries.

1.7 Conclusions

In conclusion, research on sectoral systems has progressed significantly in the last decade in different directions. The initial case studies and qualitative analyses have enriched our understanding of the structure, working and differences among sectoral systems, while the development of indicators and quantitative analyses have led to an assessment of the strength of the relationships between certain elements of a sectoral system and innovation and productivity growth. From these studies, major differences emerge among sectors in the structure and relevance of some actors and institutions and in the relationships that link these components of a sectoral system. In terms of public policies, these result in horizontal or sector-specific policies that take the differences across sectoral systems directly or indirectly into account.

The progress of research on sectoral systems over the last decade has opened also some major new challenges, which have started to be met by on-going work. The first regards the creation of taxonomies of sectoral systems in order to create groups of sectors that are similar in certain characteristics and structure. This first challenge is greatly helped by the development and availability of detailed and extensive micro-survey data from firms in several sectors and in several countries. The second challenge regards the understanding of the evolution of sectoral systems not just in terms of short-term reactions to changes in some components of the system, but also in terms of the long-run evolution of innovation, industrial structure and all the elements of a sectoral system. This second challenge requires an analysis of the interdependencies and the feedbacks in the system. The third challenge regards the modelling of sectoral systems, their structure and their effects on the innovation and performance of firms. Here the modelling exercise has to start from the wealth of cases, empirical evidence and appreciative theorizing on the sectors that has been accumulated over recent years and build, in a bottom-up way, models that are empirically grounded.

These trajectories of research are exciting and quite promising. At the centre of this future research agenda stands a key topic of paramount importance for all researchers interested in sectoral systems and economic evolution more generally: a full understanding of the co-evolutionary processes among technology, knowledge, industry structure, other non-firm actors, networks and institutions. This calls for a deep and full empirical and theoretical examination of the dynamic and two-way relationship between the various components of a sectoral system along the lines discussed at the general level by Nelson (1994) and Metcalfe (2002) and exemplified at the empirical level for the chemical industry by Murmann (2013).

References

Adams, P., Fontana, R. and Malerba, F. 2013. The magnitude of innovation by demand in a sectoral system: The role of industrial users in semiconductors. *Research Policy* 42(1): 1–14.

Bodas Freitas, I., Castellacci, F., Fontana, R., Malerba, F. and Vezzulli, A. 2016. Sectors and the additionality effects of R&D tax credits: A cross-country microeconometric analysis. *Research Policy* 46(1): 57–72.

Caloghirou Y., Protogerou, A. and Tsakanikas A. 2015. Knowledge Intensive Entrepreneurship: Exploring a taxonomy based on the AEGIS survey, in *Dynamics of Knowledge-Intensive Entrepreneurship: Business Strategy and Public Policy*, ed. F. Malerba, Y. Caloghirou, M. McKelvey and S. Radosevic. New York: Routledge.

Castellacci, F. 2007 Technological regimes and sectoral differences in productivity growth. *Industrial and Corporate Change* 16(6): 1105–1145.

Castellacci, F. 2009 The interactions between national systems and sectoral patterns of innovation. *Journal of Evolutionary Economics* 19(3): 321–347.

Castellacci, F. (2008): Technological paradigms, regimes and trajectories: Manufacturing and service industries in a new taxonomy of sectoral patterns of innovation. *Research Policy* 37: 978–994.

Castellacci, F. and Zheng, J. 2010. Technological regimes, Schumpeterian patterns of innovation and firm-level productivity growth. *Industrial and Corporate Change* 19(6): 1829–1865.

Chandy, R. K. and Tellis, G. J. 2000. The incumbent's curse? Incumbency, size, and radical product innovation. *Journal of Marketing* 64: 1–17.

Cohen W. and Levinthal D. 1990. Absorptive capacity: A new perspective on learning and innovation. *Administrative Science Quarterly* March: 128–152.

Cowan, R., David, P., and Foray, D. 2000. *The Explicit Economics of Knowledge Codification and Tacitness, Industrial and Corporate Change*. Oxford: Oxford University Press, 9(2), 211–253.

Dodgson, M., Mathews, J., Kastelle, T. and Hu. T. 2008. The evolving nature of Taiwan's national innovation system: The case of biotechnology innovation networks. *Research Policy* 37(3): 430–445.

Dosi, G. and Nelson, R. 2010. Technological change and industrial dynamics as evolutionary processes, in *Handbook of the Economics of Innovation*, ed. B. Hall and N. Rosenberg. New York: Elsevier, 51–127.

Edquist, C. 2003. *The Internet and Mobile Telecommunication System of innovation: Development in Equipment, Access and Content*. Cheltenham: Elgar.

Edquist, C. 2004. The fixed internet and mobile telecommunication sectoral system of innovation, in *Sectoral Systems of Innovation*, ed. F. Malerba. Cambridge: Cambridge University Press.

Edquist, C., Malerba, F., Metcalfe, S., Montobbio, F. and Steinmueller, E. 2004. Sectoral systems implications for European innovation policy, in *Sectoral Systems of Innovation*, ed. F. Malerba. Cambridge: University Press Cambridge.

Fontana, R., Malerba, F. and Marinoni A. 2015. Mapping sectoral systems of innovation. An empirical analysis of knowledge, in *Dynamics of Knowledge Intensive Entrepreneurship*, ed. F. Malerba, Y. Caloghirou, M. McKelvey and S. Radosevic. Business Strategy and Public Policy, Albington: Routledge.

Garavaglia, C. Malerba, F. Orsenigo, L. Pezzoni, M. 2012. Technological regimes and demand structure in the evolution of the pharmaceutical industry. *Journal of Evolutionary Economics* 22, 4, 677–709

Giachetti, C. and Marchi, G. 2017. Successive changes in leadership in the worldwide mobile phone industry. *Research Policy* 46(2): 362–364.

Gu, S., Lundvall, B.-Å., Liu, J., Malerba, F., and Schwaag Serger, S. 2009. China's system and vision of innovation: An analysis in relation to the strategic adjustment and the medium- to long-term S&T development plan (2006–20). *Industry & Innovation* 16: 369–388.

Guennif, S. and Ramani, S. V. 2012. Explaining divergence in catching-up in pharma between India and Brazil using the NSI framework. *Research Policy* 41: 430–441.

Jacobides, M. 2008. How capabilities differences, transaction costs and learning curves interact to shape vertical scope. *Organization Science* 19(2): 306–326.

Jacobides, M. and Winter, S. 2005. The co-evolution of capabilities and transaction costs: Explaining the institutional structure of production. *Strategic Management Journal* 26(5): 395–413.

Kang, H. and Song, J. 2017. Innovation and recurring shifts in industrial leadership: Three phases of change and persistence in the camera industry. *Research Policy* 46(2): 376–387.

Landini, F. and Malerba, F. 2016. *Public Policy, Catching Up in Global Industries and Technological Change: A Simulation Model.* Milan: Bocconi University.

Lee, K. 2005. Making a technological catch-up: Barriers and opportunities. *Asian Journal of Technology Innovation* 13(2): 97–131.

Lee, K. 2013. *Schumpeterian Analysis of Economic Catch-Up: Knowledge, Path Creation and the Middle Income Trap.* Cambridge: Cambridge University Press.

Lee, K. and Ki, J., 2017. Rise of latecomers and catch-up cycles in the world steel industry. *Research Policy* 46(2): 365–375.

Lee, K. and Lim, C., 2001. Technological regimes, catching-up and leapfrogging: Findings from the Korean industries. *Research Policy* 30: 459–483.

Lee K. and Malerba F. 2017. Catch-up cycles and changes in industrial leadership: Windows of opportunity and responses of firms and countries in the evolution of sectoral systems. *Research Policy* 46(2): 338–351.

Lee, K., Mani, S. and Mu, Q. 2012. Explaining divergent stories of catch-up in the telecommunication equipment industry in Brazil, China, India, and Korea, in *Economic Development as a Learning Process: Variation across Sectoral Systems,* ed. F. Malerba and R. Nelson. Oxford: Oxford University Press, 21–71.

Lee, K., Lim, C. and Song, W. 2015. Emerging digital technology as a window of opportunity and technological leapfrogging: catch-up in digital TV by the Korean firms. *International Journal of Technology Management* 29(1–2): 40–63.

Lenzi, C., Bishop, K., Breschi, S., Buenstorf, G., Llerena, P., Mancusi, M. L. and McKelvey, M. 2010. New innovators and knowledge intensive entrepreneurship in European sectoral systems: A field analysis, in *Knowledge Intensive Entrepreneurship and Innovation Systems,* ed. F. Malerba. New York: Routledge.

Malerba, F. 2002. Sectoral systems of innovation and production. *Research Policy* 31: 247–264.

Malerba, F. (ed.). 2004. *Sectoral Systems of Innovation: Evidence from Europe.* Cambridge: Cambridge University Press.

Malerba, F. 2005. Sectoral systems, in *Oxford Handbook of Innovation,* ed. J. Fagerberg, D. Mowery and R. Nelson. Oxford: Oxford University Press.

Malerba, F. and Adams P. 2013. Sectoral systems of innovation, in *Oxford Handbook of Innovation Management*, ed. M. Dodgson, D. Gann and N. Phillips. Oxford: Oxford University Press, 183–203.

Malerba, F. and Mani, S. 2009. *Sectoral Systems of Innovation and Production in Developing Countries: Actors, Structure and Evolution*. Cheltenham: Edward Elgar Publishing Incorporated.

Malerba, F. and Nelson, R. R. 2011. Learning and catching up in different sectoral systems: Evidence from six industries. *Industrial and Corporate Change* 20(6): 1645–1675.

Malerba, F. and Nelson, R. R. 2012. *Economic Development as a Learning Process: Variation across Sectoral Systems*. Cheltenham: Edward Elgar Publishing Incorporated.

Malerba F. and Orsenigo L. 1997. Technological regimes and sectoral patterns of innovative activities. *Industrial and Corporate Change* 6(1): 86–118.

Malerba, F., Nelson, R., Orsenigo, L. and Winter, S. 2001. Competition and industrial policies in a 'history friendly' model of the evolution of the computer industry. *International Journal of Industrial Organization* 19(5): 635–664.

Malerba, F., Nelson, R., Orsenigo, L. and Winter, S. 2007. Demand innovation and the dynamics of market structure: The role of experimental users and diverse preferences. *Journal of Evolutionary Economics* 17(4): 371–399.

Malerba, F., Nelson, R., Orsenigo, L. and Winter, S. 2008. Public policies and changing boundaries of firms in a 'history-friendly' model of the coevolution of the computer and semiconductor industry. *Journal of Economic Behaviour and Organization* 67(2): 355–380.

Malerba, F., Nelson, R. R., Orsenigo, L. and Winter, S. 2016. *Innovation and the Evolution of Industries*. Cambridge: Cambridge University Press.

Mathews, J. A. 2002. Competitive advantages of the latecomer firm: A resource-based account of industrial catch-up strategies. *Asia Pacific Journal of Management* 19: 467–488.

Mathews, J. A. 2005. Strategy and the Crystal Cycle. *California Management Review* 47: 6–31.

McKelvey, M., Orsenigo, L. and Pammolli, F. 2004. Pharmaceutical industry analysed through the lens of a sectoral system of innovation, in *Sectoral Systems of Innovation*, ed. F. Malerba. Cambridge: Cambridge University Press.

Metcalfe, J. S. 1995. Technology systems and technology policy in an evolutionary framework. *Cambridge Journal of Economics* 19(1): 25–46.

Metcalfe, J. S. 2002. Introduction to the special issue: Change, transformation and development. *Journal of Evolutionary Economics* 12(1): 1.

Morrison, A. and Rabellotti, R. 2017. Gradual catch up and enduring leadership in the global wine industry. *Research Policy* 46(2): 417–430.

Mowery, D. C. and Nelson, R. R. 1999. *Sources of Industrial Leadership: Studies of Seven Industries*. Cambridge: Cambridge University Press.

Murmann, J. P. 2003. *Knowledge and Competitive Advantage: The Coevolution of Firms, Technology, and National Institutions*. New York: Cambridge University Press.

Murmann, J. P. 2013. The coevolution of industries and important features of their environments. *Organization Science* (1): 58–78.

Murmann, J. P. and Brenner, T. 2003. The use of simulations in developing robust knowledge about causal processes: Methodological considerations and an application to industrial evolution, papers on economics and evolution #0303. Jena: Max-Planck-Institute of Economics.

Nelson, R. and Winter, S. 1982. *An Evolutionary Theory of Economic Change*. Cambridge, MA: Harvard University Press.

Nelson, R. R. 1994. The coevolution of technology, industrial structure and supporting institutions. *Industrial and Corporate Change* 3(1): 47–63.

Pavitt K. 1984. Sectoral patterns of technical change: Towards a taxonomy and a theory. *Research Policy* 13: 343–375.

Peneder, M. 2010. Technological regimes and the variety of innovation behaviour: Creating integrated taxonomies of firms and sectors. *Research Policy* 39(3): 323–334.

Perez, C. and Soete, L. 1988. Catching-up in technology: Entry barriers and windows of opportunity, in *Technical Change and Economic Theory*, ed. G. Dosi, C. Freeman, R. Nelson, G. Silverberg and L. Soete. London: Pinter Publishers, 458–479.

Shin, J.-S. 2017. Dynamic catch-up strategy, capability expansion and changing windows of opportunity in the memory industry. *Research Policy* 46(2): 404–416.

Vertesy, D. 2017. Changing leadership in the regional jet industry. *Research Policy* 46(2): 388–403.

Winter, S. 1987. Knowledge and competence as strategic assets, in *The Competitive Challenge – Strategies for Industrial Innovation and Renewal*, ed. D. Teece. Cambridge, MA: Ballinger (Harper and Row).

Yu, J., Malerba, F., Adams, P. and Zhang, Y. 2016. Diverging Sectoral Systems in China: Telecommunications Equipment and Semiconductors. *Industry and Innovation* Forthcoming.

2 | Effectiveness of Direct and Indirect R&D Support

PIERRE MOHNEN

2.1 Introduction

In the various theories of endogenous or semi-endogenous growth, it is argued that R&D drives productivity growth through increased choice or quality improvements in intermediate inputs or final goods (Grossman and Helpman, 1991; Aghion and Howitt, 1998; Barro and Sala-i-Martin, 2004). Private rates of return to R&D have been estimated to be in the 20 to 30 per cent range (see Hall, Mairesse and Mohnen [2010] for a survey). Ugur, Trushin, Solomon and Guidi (2016), in their meta-analysis of the empirical literature, conclude that the returns are very heterogeneous, maybe lower than the range reported by Hall et al. (2010), but still positive.

Government has a role to play in the funding and the allocation of R&D. There is little disagreement on this. Where scholars disagree is on the way government should intervene and the reason for its intervention. One group argues that government should correct market failures but leave most of the initiatives in the hands of the private sector; the other group places government in charge of a national system of innovation with responsibilities to drive forward science and technology and to take risks that the private sector is unwilling to take.

Defenders of the first argument argue that, for various reasons, the private sector left alone does not spend the amount on R&D that would be optimal for society. The first reason relates to the presence of R&D externalities. The R&D performed by one firm can benefit other firms in the same industry (intra-industry spill overs) and even firms in other industries (inter-industry spill overs). Indeed, knowledge accumulated in one sector can be useful in another sector. Think of the steam engine that was used in the transportation industry after being initially developed for coal extraction (Mowery and Rosenberg, 1998). Besides knowledge transfer there can also be a transfer of rents from the innovator to the downstream sectors. Many empirical studies have shown that R&D yields an above-normal rate of return and that in general R&D generates net positive spill overs (Griliches, 1992; Mohnen, 1996; Parsons and Phillips, 2007; Sveikauskas, 2007). As Bloom, Schankerman and Van Reenen (2013) have shown, there may also be negative externalities of the market-stealing type, but in general the negative spill overs are outweighed by the positive ones. The social benefits thus exceed the private benefits, but firms base their R&D decisions only on the private costs and benefits. The second market failure relates to the financing of R&D and the asymmetry of information. Knowledge is a public good once it is revealed, and therefore firms are cautious not to leak out the knowledge they have obtained by investing in R&D. But fund providers need some information about the new knowledge to evaluate the risk of their lending. Firms, especially small firms and start-ups, may thus be financially constrained and unable to do the desired amount of R&D. Other market failures relate to the indivisibility of certain R&D projects, like space exploration, and hence the impossibility of a single firm financing them alone; the excessive uncertainty of certain projects, like cancer research; and coordination problems, such as the incompatibility of requirements and availability of scientific expertise for particular R&D projects or the adoption of different technological standards (e.g. the VHS and Betamax standards for video recording).

Other scholars argue that government has an even more fundamental role to play than just correcting market deficiencies, namely solving grand societal challenges, like global warming or the elimination of major diseases, and playing a leading role in the advancement of science. As Mazzucato (2013) argues, the State itself is an entrepreneur, and through its innovation programmes like DARPA (Defense Advanced Research Agency), SBIR (Small Business Innovation Research), the Orphan Drug Act and the Nanotechnology Initiative in the United States it has influenced the direction of technological change. Government takes an active and leading role in technological change by funding basic research; conducting its own research in government labs, universities or in collaboration with the private sector; and exploring new technological trajectories. Cantner and Vannuccini (2016) see the role of government as one of defining mission-oriented projects (like the German initiative to steer away from nuclear energy towards green and renewable energy sources). The greatest difference between the two views of innovation policy (the market failures and government initiative-taking camps) lies in the extent to which the direction of technological change should be put in the hands of government or the private sector. Does government lead in the exploration of new technologies and do private firms just follow and finish the job? Or is the private sector the main initiator of change and government only makes sure that the incentives are there for firms to innovate?

There are various ways in which government can participate in the national R&D effort (European Commission, 2014). First, government could do the R&D itself in public laboratories or universities; it would have more means than private firms to finance mammoth projects and it would have societal benefits instead of private profits in mind. Second, government could let the private sector decide on the amount and direction of R&D, but solve the above-mentioned market failures by providing finance through tax incentives, direct grants, research contracts, public procurement, venture capital, soft loans or loan guarantees. It could also via these means decrease the cost of capital so that firms reach the optimal R&D level for society. Additionally, it could make aid for research conditional on the type proposed and thereby steer the research in certain directions that correspond to societal needs. Finally, it could provide inputs into the innovation process by investing in education and creating the necessary human capital that firms need; technology relay centres where firms can get technical assistance; networks where firms can interact and share knowledge (clusters, university–industry collaborations, science parks, etc.); and regulations (e.g. intellectual property rights) that give firms the incentives to invest in R&D and standards that limit the amount of technological uncertainty.

The remainder of this chapter will concentrate on two of these policies: indirect support via R&D tax incentives and direct aid in the form of grants and subsidies.[1] The sum of both support measures amounted in 2007 to a disbursement to private firms at best between 0.35 per cent to 0.40 per cent (see Figure 2.1) of GDP, compared to an amount of

---

[1] For another summary of the literature on the effectiveness of direct and indirect R&D support, see Larédo, Köhler and Rammer (2016) and Cunningham, Gök and Larédo (2016).

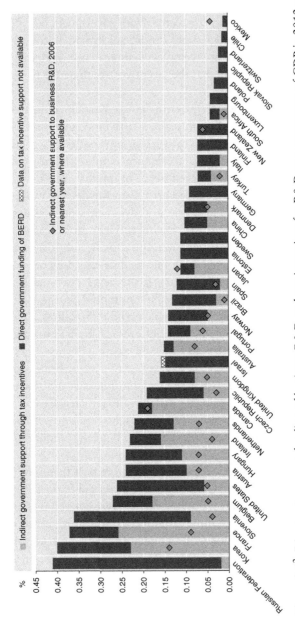

Figure 2.1[2] Direct government funding of business R&D and tax incentives for R&D as a percentage of GDP in 2012 and 2006.

[2] Figures 2.1 and 2.2 are taken from OECD Innovation Strategy, 2015: An Agenda for Policy Action. OECD, Paris.

intramural R&D conducted in government laboratories and universities of around 0.7 per cent of GDP in the OECD countries (see Figure 2.2). A country such as France would spend 0.35 per cent on direct and indirect aid to private firms to encourage them to spend on R&D, but it would spend twice as much on government-performed R&D. There is quite some heterogeneity in the mix of these two innovation support measures. As figures from the OECD STI Scoreboard 2015 show, R&D tax incentives constituted more than 80 per cent of government support for R&D in countries such as Australia, the Netherlands, Canada and Japan in 2013. However, countries such as Germany, Sweden and Finland had no R&D tax incentives in 2014. Since 2010, countries such as Japan, France and the UK have increased their reliance on R&D tax incentives, whereas countries such as Mexico and New Zealand have abolished them, and Canada slightly refocused its support towards more grants and fewer tax incentives. But overall, countries in the OECD zone have increased their use of R&D tax incentives.

To close this introduction, let me assert that few scholars would disagree that innovation policy consists of a whole set of measures and that a holistic approach is necessary. Government needs to manage a national (or regional) system of innovation, including many actors, institutions and linkages. As Fagerberg (2016) clearly puts it, managing a system of innovation means making sure various conditions are satisfied at the same time, namely generating R&D privately or publicly, creating demand for new products, assuring the financing of the innovations, creating the right framework conditions and institutional setup, and providing the right skills to produce the innovations. This complementarity between various aspects of the innovation policy is what is behind the notion of a policy mix. We shall return to this issue at the end of the chapter.

The rest of the chapter is structured as follows. Section 2.2 discusses the various aspects regarding the effectiveness of R&D tax credits and what we know about it. Section 2.3 briefly discusses similar issues regarding direct government support for R&D. Section 2.4 concludes with a discussion on policy recommendations and further issues of research regarding policy effectiveness.

2.2 R&D Tax Incentives

There are many ways in which tax incentives can be used to stimulate private R&D. First, there is the distinction between level-based and

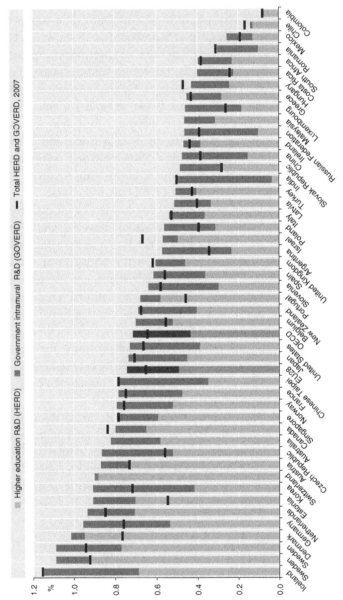

Figure 2.2 Higher education R&D and government intramural R&D as a percentage of GDP in 2012 and 2007.

increment-based tax incentives, i.e. whether the tax credit is proportional to the level of R&D or whether it is proportional to the increment of R&D expenses over a certain base level. As we shall see, this distinction has quite a bearing on the efficiency of this policy. Second, many countries have devised ways to grant the tax credits even in the absence of any taxes to be paid, e.g. by making the tax credits refundable even in the absence of corporate income taxes to be paid, by allowing carry-back or carry-forward provisions or by deducting the tax credits directly from the employer's social security contributions. Third, tax credits are normally supposed to be neutral, but they can also be directed towards certain types of R&D, by giving special or additional tax credits for R&D that is oriented towards health, defence or environmental protection, R&D conducted in collaboration with universities or R&D conducted in small and medium-size enterprises (SMEs). Fourth, a number of countries have introduced a patent-box (or innovation-box) policy that reduces the corporate income taxes to be paid on revenues originating from patents or from innovations ensuing from R&D supported by R&D tax credits. And finally, R&D can be stimulated indirectly by various tax reductions like income taxes on high-skilled immigrants, corporate income taxes from venture capital funding or reductions on capital gains taxes.

Since a huge amount (sometimes in the billions of Euros) of taxpayers' money is devoted to R&D tax incentives and since countries that are devoid of tax incentives debate whether or not they should introduce them, the ex-post evaluation of this policy has attracted a lot of attention. What are the evaluation criteria and what methods have been used to evaluate the effectiveness and the efficiency of these policies along these criteria?

2.2.1 Additionality

The first and foremost criterion to evaluate the effectiveness of R&D tax incentives is that of additionality. Do tax incentives yield additional R&D? If there is crowding-out, firms spend even less on R&D than before receiving indirect government support for it. Possible explanations for the crowding out could be that firms spend too much time on the paperwork related to R&D tax credit applications to the detriment of R&D, or that the involvement of government in private R&D decisions discourages firms from investing in R&D, or that the

additional R&D brought forward from the tax incentives hit the availability of skilled researchers, raising the wages of those researchers so
much that the real amount of R&D plummets. All these reasons are
unlikely to occur. More interesting is, therefore, the following question: do firms spend at least as much additional R&D as the amount of
tax incentives they receive, or do they partially substitute government-
financed R&D for their self-financed R&D?

To address these issues there are two main approaches. One is based
on structural models, modelling the demand for R&D within a firm as
a function of relative input prices, the scale of production, the level of
technology and firm/industry characteristics and estimating these
demands for R&D equations parametrically. R&D tax incentives
then enter either via a dummy variable indicating the presence or not
of R&D tax incentives or via the user cost of R&D, i.e. the price paid
for using a stock of knowledge. In the user cost of R&D, the R&D tax
credits are introduced via a so-called B-index, which represents the
ratio of the net cost of investing one dollar on R&D after deduction
of all quantifiable tax incentives over the net benefit of one dollar of
revenue.[3] The following is a selection of studies that have used the
structural model: Bloom, Griffith and Van Reenen (2002); Dagenais,
Mohnen and Therrien (2004); Caiumi (2011); Lokshin and Mohnen
(2012); Mulkay and Mairesse (2013).

The other approach is based on quasi-natural experiments where
an exogenous feature of the law or an exogenous circumstance allows
the identification of the effect of R&D tax incentives through counterfactuals based on matching methods, difference-in-differences and
regression discontinuity designs. Examples of studies that have used
this approach are Hægeland and Moen (2007); Czarnitzki, Hanel
and Rosa (2011); Duguet (2012); Bronzini and Iachini (2014);
Dechezleprêtre, Einiö, Martin, Nguyen and Van Reenen (2015);
Guceri and Liu (2017).

The major econometric difficulty here is the endogeneity of the use of
R&D tax credits and of the amount of R&D tax credits that can be
claimed. In the absence of refundability of R&D tax credits, firms may
reduce their R&D in periods of economic slowdown at the same time as
government reduces its R&D tax credits. Applying or not for R&D tax

---

[3] The B-index was introduced by McFetridge and Warda (1983). For a critique of
this measure, see Thomson (2013).

credits is an endogenous choice. In some countries, such as Spain, a sizeable proportion of firms that are eligible to claim R&D tax credits make no use of it (Corchuelo and Martínez-Ros, 2008). The determinants of that choice may be correlated with the determinants of the amount invested in R&D. The amount of R&D tax credits may hit a ceiling and fall in a category where the marginal level of support is lower. The dummy variable indicating the reception of tax credits or the user cost related to it should either be instrumented, or exogenous local differences between recipients and non-recipients or different intensities of reception should be exploited to identify the additionality effect.[4]

Many studies have been conducted along one or the other line of investigation over the last thirty years. The results of these studies have been summarized and tabulated in various reviews of the literature: Hall and Van Reenen (2000); Parsons and Phillips (2007); Ientile and Mairesse (2009); European Commission (2014); Becker (2015); Castellacci and Lie (2015).

The price elasticity indicates how much firms respond to R&D tax incentives. If the elasticity is negative and significant we can conclude that firms increase their R&D as the user cost falls in the face of increased tax incentives. Apart from some studies that report non-significant elasticities, there seems to be a consensus that tax incentives increase the amount of R&D. Because of adjustment costs such as those associated with the search for qualified researchers, the setting up of research laboratories and the raising of funds to finance new research projects, the full increase in R&D will take some time to show up. This sluggishness in increasing R&D is confirmed in various studies that estimate dynamic models with lower elasticities in the short run than in the long run (Bloom, Griffith and Van Reenen on data from various countries [2002]; Harris, Li and Trainor [2009] for Northern Ireland; Lokshin and Mohnen [2012] for the Netherlands; Mairesse and Mulkay [2004] and Mulkay and Mairesse [2013] for France; Labeaga, Martínez-Ros and Mohnen [2014] for Spain). Agrawal, Rosell and Simcoe (2014) estimate a higher elasticity of R&D to its user for contract research than for the R&D wage bill, suggesting higher adjustment costs for the latter than for the former.

---

[4] Castellacci and Lie (2015) report lower estimates of the R&D subsidy effects if endogeneity is controlled for.

There may be differences though in responsiveness depending on the size of the firm, the industry, the magnitude of R&D tax credits and the type of R&D tax incentive. Castellacci and Lie (2015) have performed a meta-analysis on results from various studies on the effectiveness of R&D tax credits. They report higher degrees of additionality in low-tech firms, services and SMEs. A higher responsiveness on the part of firms that are liquidity constrained is also reported by Caiumi (2011); Yohei (2011); and Kasahara, Shimotsu and Suzuki (2013). That SMEs react more strongly is also reported in Baghana and Mohnen (2009) for Quebec; Hægeland and Møen (2007) for Norway; Corchuelo and Martínez-Ros (2008) for Spain; and Lokshin and Mohnen (2012) for the Netherlands. Market failure related to financing is probably the reason for this.

2.2.2 The (Direct) Bang for the Buck

There is some confusion in the literature regarding the meaning of additionality. For some experts, there is additionality as soon as firms respond positively to tax incentives by increasing their R&D expenditure. That is the point that we analysed in the previous section. For other analysts, additionality has to do with the absence of a partial crowding out. Do firms spend at least as much additional R&D as the amount of tax reductions that they obtain? If they do, there is additionality; otherwise there is at least partial crowding out. This question is also often referred to as the bang for the buck (BFTB). Per dollar spent by government on fiscal expenses to stimulate private R&D, do firms spend at least one additional dollar of R&D?

Incremental R&D tax credits finance a fraction of firms' additional R&D. This is not the case for level-based R&D tax credits, where the amount of tax credits received is a proportion of the total amount of R&D performed, including the R&D that was done prior to the change in tax incentive. Any change of the R&D tax credit will automatically provide additional support for R&D that would have been done anyway. Supporting existing R&D is a deadweight loss. For the BFTB to be greater than 1, firms need to increase their R&D sufficiently to cover the deadweight loss. More precisely, let R denote R&D expenditure, γ_1 level-based R&D tax credit and γ_2 incremental R&D tax credit, and let superscript $\sim$ denote the new levels of these variables. The BFTB is then given by

$$BFTB = \frac{(\tilde{R}-R)}{[\tilde{\gamma}_1(\tilde{R}-R) + (\tilde{\gamma}_1-\gamma_1)R + \tilde{\gamma}_2(\Delta\tilde{R}-\Delta R) + (\tilde{\gamma}_2-\gamma_2)\Delta R]}.$$

The numerator and the denominator represent, respectively, the difference in R&D and the difference in R&D tax credit disbursements after and before the change in the R&D tax credits. If a firm did no R&D initially, e.g. a start-up firm, the level-based R&D tax credit would be similar to an incremental R&D tax credit. In that case, as in the case of no level-based tax credit and no initial planned increase in R&D, the BFTB would be the inverse of the R&D tax credit. If, however, the firm was doing R&D or was planning to increase its R&D, the second and the fourth term of the denominator, respectively, would represent a deadweight loss, i.e. unnecessary R&D support. The higher the existing R&D expenditure or the higher the planned increase in R&D, the higher the deadweight loss. Large R&D spenders benefit more than small R&D performers from this manna from heaven.

If we take an intertemporal perspective, the BFTB should be calculated as the present value of all additional R&D expenses in the numerator over the present value of all foregone tax incomes in the denominator. As the firm grows and spends more on R&D, given the sunk costs incurred in setting up an R&D laboratory, it becomes more and more likely that some of that R&D would have been done anyway. Therefore, as illustrated in Mohnen and Lokshin (2010), the BFTB tends to decrease over time as more and more periods are taken into account in the intertemporal calculation of the BFTB.

It is therefore not surprising that Mairesse-Mulkay (2004) and Duguet (2012) for France find a BFTB as high as 2.6 and 3.3, respectively, for the period prior to 2003, where France had only incremental R&D tax credits, while Mulkay and Mairesse (2013) report a BFTB of 0.7 under the regime of level-based R&D tax credits that started in 2008. The BFTB found in most other studies where level-based tax credits dominate is below 1 (see Ientile and Mairesse, 2009; Caiumi, 2011; European Commission, 2014). A recent evaluation of the Dutch patent/innovation box also finds a BFTB for that policy that is lower than 1 (Mohnen, Vankan and Verspagen, 2017).

In this sense, an R&D tax incentive policy might be effective in generating additional R&D, but not efficient in terms of the budget multiplier. The most efficient tax policy according to the BFTB criterion of efficiency would be one of incremental R&D tax credit. Recently, however, many governments turned away from incremental R&D tax credits for various reasons: (1) it is more complicated to manage incremental than level-based tax credits both for firms and for the agency that controls them; (2) they entail their own disincentive since any increase in one year raises the bar for getting tax credits in the following years;[5,6] (3) there is a limit to how much firms are willing to accelerate their R&D spending.

2.2.3 Cost-Benefit Analysis

A given tax policy might be effective in raising the R&D level and yet yield a BFTB lower than 1. But a BFTB, as calculated above, lower than 1 is not the end of the story. There may be additional costs and benefits associated with a change in R&D tax credits. A full cost-benefit analysis would take into account price effects, administration and compliance costs, the marginal excess burden of taxation, secondary effects on innovation output or firm performance (productivity or profitability, for example) as well as R&D spill overs.

2.2.3.1 Increases in the Wages of R&D Researchers
Various studies have uncovered price effects of R&D tax credits, which limit the real increase in R&D expenditure. Goolsbee (1998) finds that a 10 per cent increase in US federal R&D expenditure increases the wages of R&D workers by 3 per cent. Marey and Borghans (2000) report an average elasticity of R&D wages with respect to total R&D expenditures of 0.52 in the short run and 0.38 in the long run on Dutch sectoral data. Hægeland and Møen (2007) estimate that for Norway per Euro of R&D tax credit 33 Eurocents go into higher average wages for R&D personnel, especially for SMEs. Lokshin and Mohnen (2013) estimate an elasticity of R&D wages with respect to the fraction of R&D supported by the fiscal incentive

---

[5] It has even been shown (Hollander et al., 1987; Lemaire, 1996) that to get the most out of the incremental tax credit system a spike in R&D spending in one year should be followed by no spending in the following three years (if the base is the average over the last three years), a pattern that may be consistent with concave, but definitely not with convex, adjustment costs in R&D.
[6] Bernstein (1986) calculates that a 1 per cent increase in the rate of incremental R&D tax credit decreases the user cost of R&D by only 0.06 per cent.

scheme in the Netherlands of 0.20 in the short run and 0.24 in the long run.

2.2.3.2 Administration and Compliance Costs
Parsons and Phillips (2007) report the compliance cost in Canada to be of the order of 0.08 and the administration costs to be of the order on 0.02. Similar orders of magnitude are reported by de Jong and Verhoeven (2007) for the Netherlands.

2.2.3.3 Marginal Excess Burden of Taxation
Before being able to spend on R&D tax credits government needs to collect taxes, which may have a social cost because they may lead to distortionary allocations of resources. Parsons and Phillips (2007) use an estimate of the marginal excess burden of taxation of 0.27.

2.2.3.4 R&D Spill Overs
A tax policy that turns out not to be very effective at the micro level may turn out to increase R&D at a higher level of aggregation because the R&D done in one firm leads other firms to also increase their R&D (for reasons of competition, strategic complementarity or complementary between their respective products or services). It may also be, however, that, *ceteris paribus*, firms decrease their own R&D in the face of increased R&D by their competitors, in which case the macro BFTB falls even further below 1. One phenomenon of this sort is tax competition. The R&D done in one state/province/country may also depend on the tax incentives given in neighbouring states/provinces/countries, because firms may move their R&D facilities to locations where the tax system is more generous for R&D (Hines, 1995). Wilson (2005) finds that the R&D price elasticity is close to 1 (in absolute value) if external user costs are excluded from the regression, but that state R&D reacts negatively to more generous tax incentives in neighbouring states, so that the aggregate price elasticity of R&D is close to zero. Sensitivity to foreign R&D tax incentives is also reported in Bloom, Griffith and van Reenen (2002) for nine OECD countries and Corrado, Haskel, Jona-Lasinio and Nasim (2015) for ten European countries.

Parsons and Phillips (2007) take administration and compliance costs, the marginal burden of taxation and R&D spill overs into account and then come up with a net welfare benefit for R&D tax credits in Canada, but they also indicate that small variations in the estimates of these various costs and benefits would yield a welfare loss. Dahlby (2005) finds for Alberta that an additional dollar of R&D tax incentives has to generate close to 2 dollars of additional R&D, with R&D externalities yielding external returns of 30 per cent, for it to be justified if the provincial government's marginal cost of funds for Alberta is of the order of 1.4.

2.2.4 The Returns of Additional R&D

Stimulating R&D is the primary objective of R&D tax credits. But, of course, R&D is not a goal in itself. It would be desirable that the additional R&D yields substantial returns in terms of innovation, patents, productivity or profitability.

2.2.4.1 Output Additionality

Most studies based on the Crépon, Duguet and Mairesse (1998) model find that R&D, especially continuous R&D, has a positive significant effect on innovation (patents, innovation occurrence and share of innovative sales) and that the latter has a positive effect on labour productivity (Mohnen and Hall, 2013). Hence indirectly, tax incentives should raise the productivity level. The studies that have compared beneficiaries and non-beneficiaries of R&D tax incentives do not always reach such positive conclusions, partly because they are not of sufficient duration to let the effects work out. Czarnitzki, Hanel and Rosa (2011) on Canadian data find a positive effect of tax credits on innovation output (introduction of new products, of new-to-the-market products, new product sales intensity), but mixed results regarding firm performance (insignificant effects on profitability and domestic market share, positive effects on international market shares and keeping up with competitors). Cappelen, Raknerud and Rybalka (2012) find a positive effect of the Norwegian SkateFUNN tax incentive system, which mainly targets SMEs, on products new to the firm and on process innovations, but no significant effect on major innovations, i.e. products new to the market or patents.

2.2.4.2 Behavioural Additionality

Receiving R&D tax credits, or for that matter any kind of public support for R&D, can also change the way firms do R&D, such as accelerating their R&D expenditure, changing the allocation of R&D funds to long-term projects, more fundamental research or riskier projects, or changing the balance between research and development activities. Most studies on behavioural additionality have been conducted on R&D support in general. We shall return to it in the next section.

2.2.4.3 Extensive Margin

One aspect of behavioural additionality is the extensive margin. Besides increasing R&D expenses in R&D performing firms, tax incentives can also lower the entrance cost for becoming an R&D performer and hence attract firms to become R&D performers. Corchuelo (2006) reports for Spain that a 1 per cent decrease in the user cost of R&D leads to a 2.6 percentage point increase in the probability of engaging in R&D. Labeaga, Martínez-Ros and Mohnen (2014), also on Spanish data, estimate that a 1 per cent decrease in the user cost of R&D increases the probability of becoming an R&D performer by 4.6 percentage points for large firms and by 19.5 percentage points for SMEs, but no significant effects of the user cost on the probability of stopping R&D. Czarnitzki, Hanel and Rosa (2011) found that almost 30 per cent of Canadian firms that use tax credits would not have done R&D without them.

2.3 R&D Grants and Subsidies

Direct support in the form of grants or subsidies can be channelled to projects with expected high social return, assuming that government can figure out which projects have a high social return, in other words is able to pick winners, or to research areas that are considered as priorities for society (like climate change). In this regard, direct subsidies can be more effective than indirect support in the form of tax credits.

Although early studies treated the subsidies as exogenous, most of the studies since David, Hall and Toole (2000) have evaluated the effectiveness of direct support for R&D using quasi-natural experiments (Czarnitzki and Licht, 2006), instrumental variables (Einiö, 2014), maximum likelihood (González, Jaumandreu and Pazó, 2005) or a control function approach (Hussinger, 2008) to correct for the selection of firms that receive R&D support. Cappelen et al. (2012), Dumont (2013), Guerzoni and Raiteri (2015) and Neicu (2016) find that controlling for unobservables through a control function approach produces fewer positive results than the matching estimators approach based only on observables. A more structural model including decisions to apply for subsidies on the part of the firm, evaluation by experts on the quality of the applications, decisions to grant the subsidies on the part of government and determination by firms of the optimal amount to invest whatever the decision by government has been proposed by Takalo, Tanayama and Toivanen (2013).

2.3.1 Additionality

Surveys of the empirical literature on direct R&D support by David, Hall and Toole (2000), Garcia-Quevedo (2004) and more recently Zuñiga-Vicente et al. (2014) find mixed evidence regarding the crowding out or additionality of direct R&D support, although the latest evidence seems to be tilting towards additionality. Becker (2015) concludes that additionality occurs for small, financially constrained and low-tech firms. In particular, studies based on matching methods find no crowding out but instead crowding in (e.g. Almus and Czarnitzki, 2003; Czarnitzki, Ebersberger and Fier, 2007; Özçelik and Taymaz, 2008). Hottenrott, Lopes-Bento and Veugelers (2006) find more additionality for research grants than for development grants, as the uncertainty is higher for basic research than for development.

2.3.2 Efficiency

The efficiency of the direct support for R&D policy is partly related to the issue of crowding out.

2.3.3 Cost-Benefit Analysis

Takalo, Tanayama and Toivanen (2013) evaluated the expected effects of R&D subsidies in Finland and reached the following conclusions: first, the expected returns are very heterogeneous depending on the quality of the projects, the characteristics of the applicants, the application costs and the externalities; second, the social rate of return of targeted subsidies is of the order of 30–50 per cent and higher than the opportunity costs of public funds; third, the private returns are higher than the externalities (around 60 per cent of the social return is internalized by the firms); and fourth, firms do not apply for subsidies for the most profitable projects.

2.3.4 Output Additionality

Bérubé and Mohnen (2009) find that Canadian firms that receive direct R&D support in addition to R&D tax incentives come up with more world-first innovations than firms that receive only indirect support via R&D tax incentives. Einiö (2014) estimates that in Finland the R&D subsidy programme of TEKES yields in the short run 1.4 additional R&D for firms that are subsidized because of the regional subsidy allocation policy and an even higher effect in the long run. He also uncovers a positive effect on employment and on productivity in the long run.

2.3.5 Behavioural Additionality

Some studies have also shown that R&D subsidies can produce behavioural externalities, i.e. change the way R&D is conducted or the type of innovation that is achieved. Falk (2007) reports that Austrian firms change their R&D behaviour when preparing for funding, in terms of scope, riskiness, scale and timing of their research projects. Neicu, Teirlinck and Klechtermans (2016) for Belgium find that firms that receive R&D subsidies speed up their research projects and do more basic research.

2.3.6 Extensive Margin

Arqué-Castells and Mohnen (2015) found that 21 per cent of the small and 39 percent of the large manufacturing firms in their Spanish sample needed subsidies to start doing R&D but needed no support to continue doing R&D. Because of sunk costs related to creating an R&D laboratory, the entrance costs of R&D are higher than the continuation costs. Evidence for such an extensive margin effect is also reported by González, Jaumandreu and Pazó (2005) for Spain and by Einiö (2014) for Finland.

2.3.7 Multi-Programme Evaluations

Not many studies have evaluated simultaneously R&D subsidies and R&D tax incentive policies in countries where both measures exist.

Lhuillery, Marino and Parrotta (2013) compare the effectiveness of both measures and conclude that in France the marginal impact is higher for R&D tax credits than for R&D subsidies. This conclusion is also reached for Italy by Carboni (2011) and for Belgium by Neicu (2016). Castellacci and Lie (2015) report from their meta-analysis of studies on the effectiveness of R&D tax credits that a lower additionality is obtained if R&D subsidies are controlled for. An interesting question is whether the two measures complement each other or whether the presence of one reduces the effectiveness of the other. Falk (2007) and Neicu (2016) conclude that there is complementarity between the two measures in the sense that their combined presence yields additionality greater than the sum of their individual additionalities. But, as outlined by Falk (2007) and by Busom, Corchuelo and Martínez-Ros (2014), in addition to complementarity at the micro level, there is complementarity at the macro level, in the sense that each measure suits a particular type of firm better: small firms and start-ups with innovations that can be easily imitated, with financial constraints and little taxable income may prefer direct support because it is received ex ante and is not dependent on making profits in the first place, whereas established firms with recurrent profits prefer tax incentives. On the other hand, direct subsidies necessitate more sharing of information and might therefore be less preferred by small firms that do not have a legal service to defend their property rights.

2.4 Conclusion

What can we conclude from this review of the literature on the effectiveness of direct and indirect R&D support?

R&D tax incentives lead firms to increase their R&D spending, but at a cost for society that exceeds the additional R&D outlays. Unless the spill over effects are sufficiently large, from a cost-benefit point of view, it is not an efficient policy, especially if, as is commonly done, the tax incentives are proportional to the level of R&D expenditure. Deadweight losses, R&D duplications, wage effects, tax distortions to raise the money to finance the policy, and administration and compliance costs are the various, to some extent unavoidable, negative side effects of indirect R&D support via tax incentives. This somewhat bleak picture is not much rosier if we consider direct R&D support in the form of grants and subsidies. There is not overwhelming evidence in the literature that direct R&D support leads to additional R&D greater than the cost to support it.

If spill overs are large enough, it may be argued that these costs are worth the effort to steer society to higher levels of R&D. It is encouraging to see that some studies have obtained positive social returns to R&D policies. The returns may also take time to work their way through the system and may not be visible in the relatively short time series we have to perform the evaluations.

The choice between tax incentives and direct support hinges on what is considered to be more important: to have as much neutrality as possible and let the private sector decide which research projects should be pursued, or to proactively discriminate between projects and have the State decide which projects ought to be supported in priority. Does the State have the capacity and the mandate to choose which among many promising projects ought to be supported first?

Given the uncertainty surrounding R&D and innovation, the goal is maybe not to pick the most promising project but to let 'a thousand flowers bloom' (within the budgetary limits) and to set up the right framework conditions to let the best projects find their own path to success. One could also conceive of a solution where through a democratic process research funds are allocated to the resolution of grand societal challenges.

It would make sense if every region or country decided on the best allocation of its funds to the advancement of research and innovation in areas that it considers of prime importance and where it thinks it has the capacities to make progress (the argument of smart specialization). But it would also make sense if, after a while over the many projects that a region or country has invested in, it could recoup part of the costs of that investment to finance future projects. In that sense, incentives to declare the revenues from research projects in the countries that have contributed to the financing of the projects, for example through ex-post patent boxes or innovation boxes, find some justification. But there may be other ways to achieve that sense of equity.

What are some of the future directions of research in this area?

One major concern with the evaluation of R&D policies is the endogeneity issue. Much effort has been expended in the last twenty years to come to grips with this problem by using quasi-natural experiments, by constructing proper counterfactuals or by modelling the decisions of applying for R&D support, of granting the support and of determining the amount that is being granted. More work, though, needs to be done to increase our understanding of what conditions the success of government support.

It would be useful if more data could be used on research projects rather than on firms, sectors or countries to identify the conditions for successful research projects, to control for the ex-ante quality of research projects and to get a better handle of how knowledge disseminates, creates new ideas, builds up and leads to economic rents and aggregate productivity and welfare improvements. Quantitative data allow us to reach conclusions that are not restricted to particular situations, but do not possess the richness that selected qualitative studies can.

Relatively few studies have examined the effectiveness of direct or indirect government support in the presence of the other and the interplay between the two policies. But, as a matter of fact, a whole set of conditions might need to be satisfied for the innovation system to be effective in promoting innovation – science, demand, human capital, finance, regulations and entrepreneurship. It would be interesting to evaluate whole systems or at least to find out to what extent these different conditions need to be present simultaneously. For multinational firms, it would be important to consider their global strategies in matters of research locations, collaborations and marketing of their innovation outputs. This means that data should be collected at the level of multinationals and not just on their operations in particular countries. It also means that the tax incentives and direct support measures of various countries should be brought into play when analysing their RD&I decisions.

References

Aghion, P. and P. Howitt. 1998. *Endogenous Growth Theory*. Cambridge: MIT Press.

Agrawal, A., C. Rosell and T. S. Simcoe. 2014. Do tax credits affect R&D expenditures by small firms? Evidence from Canada, NBER Working Paper 20615.

Almus, M. and D. Czarnitzki. 2003. The effects of public R&D subsidies on firms' innovation activities: The case of Eastern Germany. *Journal of Business and Economic Statistics* 21(2): 226–236.

Arqué-Castells, P. and P. Mohnen. 2015. Sunk costs, extensive R&D subsidies and permanent inducement effects. *Journal of Industrial Economics* 63(3): 458–494.

Baghana, R. and P. Mohnen. 2009. Effectiveness of R&D tax incentives in small and large enterprises in Québec. *Small Business Economics* 33(1): 91–107.

Barro, R. J. and X. Sala-i-Martin. 2004. *Economic Growth* (2nd edition). Cambridge: Massachusetts Institute of Technology Press.

Becker, B. 2015. Public R&D policies and private R&D investment: A survey of the empirical evidence. *Journal of Economic Surveys* 29(5): 917–942.

Bernstein, J. 1986. The effect of direct and indirect tax incentive on Canadian industrial R&D expenditures. *Canadian Public Policy* 12(3): 438–448.

Bérubé, C. and P. Mohnen. 2009. Are firms that receive R&D subsidies more innovative? *Canadian Journal of Economics* 42(1): 206–225.

Bloom, N., R. Griffith and J. Van Reenen 2002. Do R&D credits work? Evidence from a panel of countries 1979–97. *Journal of Public Economics* 85: 1–31.

Bloom, N., M. Schankerman and J. Van Reenen. 2013. Identifying technology spillovers and market rivalry. *Econometrica* 81(4): 1347–1393.

Bronzini, R. and E. Iachini. 2014. Are incentives for R&D effective? Evidence from a regression discontinuity approach. *American Economic Journal: Economic Policy* 6(4): 100–134.

Busom, I., B. Corchuelo and E. Martínez Ros. 2014. Tax incentives or subsidies for business R&D? *Small Business Economics* 43(3): 571–596.

Caiumi, A. 2011. The evaluation of the effectiveness of tax expenditures-A novel approach: An application to the regional tax incentives for business investments in Italy, OECD Taxation Working Papers 5, OECD.

Cantner, U. and S. Vannuccini. 2016. Elements of Schumpeterian catalytic research and innovation policy, presented at the International Schumpeter Society conference in Montreal.

Cappelen, A., A. Raknerud and M. Rybalka. 2012. The effects of R&D tax credits on patenting and innovations. *Research Policy* 41: 334–345.

Carboni, O. A. 2011. R&D subsidies and private R&D expenditures: Evidence from Italian manufacturing data. *International Review of Applied Economics* 25: 419–439.

Castellacci, F. and C. Lie. 2015. Do the effects of R&D tax credits vary across industries? A meta-regression analysis. *Research Policy* 44(4): 819–832.

Corchuelo, M. B. 2006. Incentivos fiscales en I+D y decisiones de innovacíon. *Revista de Economía Aplicada*. XIV(40): 5–34.

Corchuelo Martínez-Azúa, B. and E. Martínez-Ros. 2008. Aplicación de los incentivos fiscales a la inversión I+D en las impresas españolas. *Hacienda Pública Española/ Revista de Economía Pública* 187(4): 9–39.

Corrado, C., J. Haskel, C. Jona-Lasinio and B. Nasim. 2015. Is international R&D tax competition a zero-sum game? Evidence from the EU, paper presented at the NBER/CRIW workshop, Cambridge.

Crépon B., E. Duguet and J. Mairesse. 1998. Research, innovation and productivity: An econometric analysis at the firm level. *Economics of Innovation and New Technology* 7(2): 115–158.

Cunningham, P., A. Gök and P. Larédo. 2016. The impact of direct support to R&D and innovation in firms, in *Handbook of Innovation Policy Impact*, ed. J. Edler, P. Cunningham, A. Gök and P. Shapira. Cheltenham: Edward Elgar.

Czarnitzki, D., B. Ebersberger and A. Fier. 2007. The relationship between R&D collaboration, subsidies and R&D performance: Empirical evidence from Finland and Germany. *Journal of Applied Econometrics* 22: 1347–1366.

Czarnitzki, D., P. Hanel and J. Rosa. 2011. Evaluating the impact of R&D tax credit on innovation: A microeconometric study on Canadian firms. *Research Policy* 40: 217–229.

Czarnitzki, D. and G. Licht. 2006. Additionality of public R&D grants in a transition economy. *Economics of Transition* 14(1): 101–131.

Dagenais, M., P. Mohnen and P. Therrien. 2004. Les firmes canadiennes répondent-elles aux incitations fiscales à la recherche-développement? *Actualité Économique* 80(2/3): 175–206.

Dahlby, B. 2005. A framework for evaluating provincial R&D tax subsidies. *Canadian Public Policy* 31(1): 45–58.

David, P. A., B. H. Hall and A. A. Toole. 2000. Is public R&D a complement for private R&D? A review of the econometric literature. *Research Policy* 29: 497–529.

Dechezleprêtre, A., E. Einiö, R. Martin, K. T. Nguyen and J. Van Reenen. 2015. Do tax incentives for research increase firm innovation? An RDD for R&D, mimeo.

de Jong, J. and Verhoeven, W. 2007. *WBSO evaluation 2001–2005: Impacts, target group reach and implementation, Research Series, Ministry of Economic Affairs*, The Hague. Netherlands.

Duguet, E. 2012. The effect of the incremental R&D tax credit on the private funding of R&D an econometric evaluation on French firm level data. *Revue d'Economie Politique* 122(3): 405–435.

Dumont, M. 2013. The impact of subsidies and fiscal incentives on corporate R&D expenditures in Belgium (2001–2009). *Reflets et Perspectives de la Vie Economique* 1: 69–91.

Einiö, E. 2014. R&D subsidies and company performance: Evidence from geographic variation in government funding based on the ERDF population density rule. *Review of Economics and Statistics* 96(4): 710–728.

European Commission. 2014. A study on R&D tax incentives: Final report, DG TAXUD Taxation Paper 52.

Fagerberg, J. 2016. Innovation policy: Rationales, lessons and challenges. *Journal of Economic Surveys*, forthcoming.

Falk, R. 2007. Measuring the effects of public support schemes on firms' innovation activities: Survey evidence from Austria. *Research Policy* 36(5): 665–679.

Garcia-Quevedo, J. 2004. Do public subsidies complement business R&D? A meta-analysis of the econometric evidence. *Kyklos* 57(1): 87–102.

Gonzáles, X., J. Jaumandreu and C. Pazó. 2005 Barriers to innovation and subsidy effectiveness. *Rand Journal of Economics* 36(4): 930–950.

Goolsbee, A. 1998. Does government R&D policy mainly benefit scientists and engineers? *American Economic Review* 88(2): 298–302.

Griliches, Z. 1992. The search for R&D spillovers. *The Scandinavian Journal of Economics* 94: 29–47.

Grossman, Gene M. and Elhanan Helpman. 1991. *Innovation and Growth in the Global Economy*. Cambridge: MIT Press.

Guceri, I. and L. Liu. 2017. Effectiveness of fiscal incentives for R&D: Quasi-experimental evidence, IMF working paper WP/17/84.

Guerzoni, M. and E. Raiteri. 2015. Demand-side vs. supply-side technology policies: Hidden treatment and new empirical evidence on the policy mix. *Research Policy* 44(3): 726–747.

Hægeland, T. and J. Moen. 2007. Input additionality in the Norwegian R&D tax credit scheme, reports 2007/47, Statistics Norway 2007.

Hall, B. and J. Van Reenen. 2000. How effective are fiscal incentives for R&D? A review of the evidence. *Research Policy* 29: 449–469.

Hall, B., J. Mairesse and P. Mohnen. 2010. Measuring the returns to R&D, in *Handbook of the Economics of Innovation*, ed. B. H. Hall and N. Rosenberg, 1034–1082. Amsterdam: Elsevier.

Harris, R., Q. C. Li and M. Trainor. 2009. Is a higher rate of R&D tax credit a panacea for low levels of R&D in disadvantaged regions. *Research Policy* 38: 192–305.

Hines, James R. Jr. 1995. Taxes, technology transfer, and the R&D activities of multinational firms in *The Effects of Taxation on Multinational Corporations*, 225–252. National Bureau of Economic Research.

Hollander, A., A. Haurie and P. L'Ecuyer. 1987. Ratched effects and the cost of incremental incentive schemes. *Journal of Economic Dynamics and Control* 11: 373–387.

Hottenrott, H., C. Lopes-Bento and R. Veugelers. 2006. Direct and cross scheme effects in a research and development subsidy program, mimeo.

Hussinger, K. 2008. R&D and subsidies at the firm level: An application of parametric and semi-parametric two-step selection models. *Journal of Applied Econometrics* 23: 729–747.

Ientile, Damien and Jacques Mairesse. 2009. A policy to boost the R&D: Does the tax credit work? *European Investment Bank Paper* 14(1): 144–168.

Kasahara, H., K. Shimotsu and M. Suzuki. 2013. Does an R&D tax credit affect R&D expenditure? The Japanese R&D tax credit reform in 2003, CESifo working paper 4451.

Labeaga, J. M., E. Martínez-Ros and P. Mohnen. 2014. The influence of tax incentives, subsidies and other public incentives to stimulate private R&D in Spain, UNU-MERIT working 2014-081.

Larédo, P., C. Köhler and C. Rammer. 2016. The impact and effectiveness of fiscal incentives for R&D, in *Handbook of Innovation Policy Impact*, ed. J. Edler, P. Cunningham, A. Gök and P. Shapira. Cheltenham: Edward Elgar.

Lemaire, I. 1996. Optimal firm response to incremental tax credits, Cahier de recherche du CREST no. 9657.

Lhuillery, S., M. Marino and P. Parrotta. 2013. Evaluation de l'impact des aides directes et indirectes à la R&D en France, Rapport pour le Ministère de l'enseignement supérieur et de la recherche.

Lokshin, B. and P. Mohnen. 2013. Do R&D tax incentives lead to higher wages for R&D workers? Evidence from the Netherlands. *Research Policy* 42(3): 823–830.

Lokshin, B. and P. Mohnen. 2012. How effective are level-based R&D tax credits? Evidence from the Netherlands. *Applied Economics* 44(12): 1527–1538.

Mairesse J. and B. Mulkay. 2004. Une évaluation du crédit d'impôt recherche en France, 1980–1997. *Revue d'Economie Politique* 114(6): 747–778.

Marey, P. and L. Borghans. 2000. *Wage Elasticities of the Supply of R&D Workers in the Netherlands, mimeo, ROA.* University of Maastricht.

Mazzucato, M. 2013. *The Entrepreneurial State.* London: Anthem Press.

McFetridge, D. G. and J. P. Warda. 1983. Canadian R&D incentives: Their adequacy and impact. Canadian Tax Paper No. 70, Canadian Tax Foundation, Toronto.

Mohnen, P. 1996. R&D externalities and productivity growth. *STI Review* OECD 18: 39–66.

Mohnen, P. and B. Lokshin. 2010. What does it take for an R&D tax incentive policy to be effective? in *Reforming Rules and Regulations: Laws, Institutions and Implementation*, ed. V. Ghosal, 33–58. Boston, MA: MIT Press.

Mohnen, P. and B. Hall. 2013. Innovation and productivity: An update. *Eurasian Business Review* 3(1): 47–65.

Mohnen, P., A. Vankan and B. Verspagen. 2017. Evaluating the innovation box tax policy instrument in the Netherlands, 2007–2013. Oxford Review of Economic *Policy* 33(1): 141–156.

Mowery, D. and N. Rosenberg. 1998. *Paths of Innovation. Technological Change in 20th-Century America*. Cambridge: Cambridge University Press.

Mulkay, B. and J. Mairesse. 2013. The R&D tax credit in France: assessment and ex-ante evaluation of the 2008 reform, NBER working paper 19073.

Neicu, D. 2016. Mix and match: Evaluating the additionality of an R&D policy mix, chapter II of PhD dissertation, KU Leuven.

Neicu, D., P. Teirlinck and S. Klechtermans. 2016. Dipping in the policy mix: Do R&D subsidies foster behavioral additionality effects of R&D tax credits? *Economics of Innovation and New Technology* 25(3): 218–239.

Özçelik, E. and E. Taymaz. 2008. R&D support programmes in developing countries: The Turkish experience. *Research Policy* 37: 258–275.

Parsons, Mark and Nicolas Phillips. 2007. An evaluation of the Federal tax credit for scientific research and experimental development, Department of Finance, working paper 2007–08.

Sveikauskas, L. 2007. R&D and Productivity Growth: A Review of the Literature. U.S. Bureau of Labor Statistics, Office of Productivity and Technology, working paper 408.

Takalo, T., T. Tanayama and O. Toivanen. 2013. Estimating the benefits of targeted R&D subsidies. *Review of Economics and Statistics* 95(1): 255–272.

Thomson, R. 2013. Measures of R&D tax incentives for OECD countries. *Review of Economics and Institutions* 4(3): article 4. Also as Melbourne Institute, Working Paper No. 17/12.

Ugur, M., E. Trushin, E. Solomon and F. Guidi. 2016. R&D and productivity in OECD firms and industries: A hierarchical meta-regression analysis. *Research Policy* 45: 269–286.

Wilson, D. 2005. Beggar thy neighbor? The in-state vs. out-of-state impact of state R&D tax credits, Federal Reserve Bank of San Fransisco, working paper 2005–08.

Yohei, K. O. B. A. 2011. Effect of R&D tax credits for small and medium-sized enterprises in Japan: evidence from firm-level data, RIETI Discussion Paper 11-E-066.

Zuñiga-Vicente, J. A., C. Alonso-Borrego, F. J. Forcadell and J. I. Galán. 2014. Assessing the effect of public subsidies on firm R&D investment: A survey. *Journal of Economic Surveys* 28: 36–67.

3 | From Market Fixing to Market Creating

A New Framework for Innovation Policy*

MARIANA MAZZUCATO

3.1 Societal Challenges and Opportunity-Driven Investments

Innovation agencies around the world are increasingly considering socio-economic-technological challenges that can be tackled through innovation policies (*EC Innovation Union; OECD Innovation Strategy*). The idea is that, through such challenges, which can relate to such issues as climate change, cancer, or the demographic-aging crisis, innovation policy should produce solutions for societal problems. The present chapter argues that such challenge-driven innovation policies require the traditional *market failure* justification for policy intervention, and even the *system failure* one, to be complemented with a more active *market creating* framework. To this end, the chapter draws on and advances an analysis of the role of public policy in the economy that can provide a more strategic and *mission-oriented* approach (Mazzucato 2018).

Societal challenges require technological, behavioral, and systemic changes and have much to learn from those *mission-oriented* feats that led to putting humans on the moon and to the emergence of new general-purpose technologies ranging from the Internet to biotechnology and nanotechnology (Foray et al. 2012). It was only possible to achieve those missions when the public and private sectors worked together to create new technologies and sectors (Ruttan 2006; Mowery et al. 2010). Crucially, the public side of such partnerships was not limited to incentivizing, facilitating, or *de-risking* the private

---

*This chapter is a slightly amended version of Mazzucato, M. (2016) From market fixing to market-creating: A new framework for innovation policy. Special Issue of *Industry and Innovation:* Innovation policy – can it make a difference? 23(2).

79

sector. Rather, it required that (public) risks be taken through choosing a particular direction of change (Mazzucato 2013a). Such *directionality* did not occur from the top down, but through a decentralized group of public agencies, what Block and Keller (2011) refer to as a "developmental *network* state." Given the immense risks involved in choosing to develop particular sectors (such as nanotechnology), technologies (such as GPS), and broadly defined areas (such as the green economy), the relevant public institutions had to welcome the underlying uncertainty that such choices entail. Some options win (such as the Internet) while others fail (such as the commercialization of the Concorde airplane). Indeed, the success of innovative public organizations like DARPA in the US Department of Defense, which has been responsible for the financing of Arpanet (the seed of the Internet), has been attributed to the attention it paid to internal organizational dynamics, which nurtured experimentation and learning (Abbate 1999; Block 2008), and "policy as *process*" (Hirschman 1967; Rodrik 2014).

Missions imply setting *directions of change* – that is, tilting (rather than leveling) the playing field to favor certain types of change more than others (Mazzucato and Perez 2015). The IT revolution was picked as was also the biotech and nanotech revolution (Block and Keller 2011). What should be the core of the policy debate is not whether policies require picking and choosing but how to enable such picking to occur in the smartest way possible, nurturing a learning and adaptation process that prevents the system from getting locked into suboptimal circumstances. Missions should be broad enough to catalyze many different sectors (the man on moon mission required a dozen sectors to engage) but concrete enough to translate into specific problems to solve, so that progress toward the mission can be evaluated on a continual basis. Societal challenges, around reducing inequality, improving healthy living and driving sustainability, require missions to be more open, and as equally about social innovation as about technological innovation. They also require a more horizontal interaction with citizens for mission setting (Mazzucato 2018).

Thus, limiting our understanding of the role of the public sector to one that simply "administers," "fixes," "regulates," and at best "facilitates" and "de-risks" the private sector prevents us from thinking creatively about how to allow public sector vision, risk-taking, and investment to lead and structure the necessary transformational changes. A general lack of faith in the power of public institutions, driven by public choice theory (Buchanan 2003), has led to a reduction in the kind of investments that the public sector makes in building its own capabilities and competencies (with a consequent rise in outsourcing, Crouch 2016), which are essential to guide such change. The biased view of the public sector as at best facilitating change, rather than directly creating it, has been symptomatic of not only the market failure approach to policy intervention (discussed further in this chapter), but also of the evolutionary approach that has emphasized the role of public policy in terms of fixing *system failures* (Lundvall 1992). This is because the *systems of innovation* perspective has focused primarily on the need to build horizontal linkages between actors, rather than on direct (vertical) investments, and while this has contributed important insights into the framework conditions required for innovation, it has ignored those more vertical policies required for setting the *direction* of change, and the characteristics of public agencies required to set such a direction. In other words, by viewing public sector action (regulation or investment) as the solution to a problem that arises from different types of failures, whether these be coordination failures or network failures, it has indirectly perpetuated the view of the public sector as a passive force that can only facilitate change, rather than lead it. Consequently, the systems perspective to policy has provided little guidance for the directionality that is required in a world in which different pathways of development can be chosen even within a sector (Stirling 2014), and minimal insights are provided regarding the nature of the actors required. Is a financialized private sector the same as a nonfinancialized one? Are public organizations that aim to create horizontal conditions for innovation organized in the same way as those directed at missions that require picking of specific firms to support, particular technologies to develop, and broadly defined sectors to create?

The key problem is that any framework that focuses on policy only in terms of fixing problems, especially (but not only) market failures, does not embody any explicit justification for the kind of market creation and mission-oriented **directionality** (and "routes" within directions) that was required for innovations such as the Internet and nanotechnology and is required today to address societal challenges (Mazzucato 2015; 2016a/b; 2018). Second, by not considering the state as a lead investor and market creator, such failure-based approaches do not provide insights into the type and structure of public sector **organizations** that are needed in order to provide the depth and breadth of high-risk investments. Third, as long as policy is seen only as an "intervention," rather than a key part of the market creation and shaping process, the type of **evaluation** criteria used to assess mission-oriented investments will inevitably be problematic. Fourth, by not describing the state as a lead risk-taker and investor in this process, the failure-based approaches have avoided a key issue regarding the distribution of **risks and rewards** between the state and the private sector.

The present chapter addresses these four challenges by asking the following questions:

(1) How can public policy be understood in terms of setting the direction and route of change; that is, shaping and creating markets rather than just fixing them (Routes)?

(2) How should public organizations be structured so they accommodate the risk-taking, explorative capacity, and capabilities needed to envision and manage contemporary challenges (Organizations)?

(3) How can this alternative conceptualization be translated into new indicators and evaluation tools for public policies, beyond the micro-economic cost/benefit analysis and macro-economic appraisal of crowding in/crowding out that stem directly from the market failure perspective (Assessment)?

(4) How can public investments along the innovation chain result not only in the socialization of risks, but also of rewards, enabling smart growth to also be inclusive growth (Risks and rewards)?

While the questions may seem broad, it is their potential *connection* that can help build a *market creation* framework. Policies that aim to actively create and shape markets require indicators that assess and measure the performance of a policy along that particular transformational objective. The state's ability and willingness to take risks, embodied in transformational changes, requires an organizational culture (and policy capacity) that welcomes the possibility of failure and experimentation and is rewarded for successes so that failures (which are learning opportunities) can be covered and the next round financed.

This alternative view (policy framework) of policy making builds on the inspirational work of Karl Polanyi (2001 [1944]), an economic historian and sociologist who understood markets as being deeply embedded in social institutions, and policy as not standing on the sidelines, but within the very *market creation* process. In his epic book *The Great Transformation*, Polanyi described the way in which capitalist markets are deeply embedded in social and political institutions, rendering the usual static state vs. market juxtaposition meaningless.

As Polanyi wrote: "[t]he road to the free market was opened and kept open by an enormous increase in continuous, centrally organized and controlled interventionism" (2001 [1944], 144). Polanyi's work has been revolutionary in terms of exposing the myth of the state vs. market distinction: the most capitalist of all markets, the national market, was forcefully pushed into existence by the state. The market is embedded in and shaped by the state (Evans 1995). The present chapter argues, in essence, that the four questions can help govern the dynamics of embeddedness, so that policy choices are rendered more explicit (and hence also more easily debated), and the results of public policies can be measured with metrics that are adequate for a dynamic process.

The remainder of the chapter is structured as follows. Section 3.2 briefly reviews the limits of market failure theory (MFT) in describing transformational change. Section 3.3 considers ways in which recent advances in heterodox economics contain the seeds of an alternative framework to MFT. Section 3.4 considers the four key questions that emerge from considering a market shaping framework. Section 3.5 considers the new research questions that emerge from considering this perspective.

3.2 Market Failure Theory

Market failure theory justifies public intervention in the economy only if it is geared toward fixing situations in which markets fail to efficiently allocate resources (Arrow 1951). The market failure approach suggests that governments intervene to fix markets by investing in areas characterized by positive or negative externalities. For example, positive externalities arising from public goods (which are *nonrivalrous* and *nonexcludable*) will be characterized by underinvestment by the private sector and will therefore require public investment. This is the case for basic research, which has high spillovers that create difficulties in appropriating private returns; consequently, basic research is characterized by too little private investment. Negative externalities, such as those created by pollution, require public measures that cause the private sector to internalize external costs, such as through a carbon tax.

A particular source of market failure comes from negative externalities that arise from the production or use of goods and services such as climate change, traffic congestion, or antibiotic resistance, for which there is *no market*. In this perspective, most societal challenges are seen as negative externalities. Such failures work at the system level; that is, they amount to system failures. The socioeconomic system as a whole results in costly outcomes that are undesirable from a societal point of view. For instance, climate change can be seen as a negative externality from carbon-intensive production methods or the burning of fossil fuels. Indeed, the *Stern Review* (Stern 2006) on the economics of climate change stated that: "Climate change presents a unique challenge for economics: it is the greatest example of market failure we have ever seen" (Stern 2006, 1). Negative externalities are not reflected in the price system: There is no "equilibrium" price because there is no market for negative externalities. Many economists have called for market-based mechanisms (such as carbon pricing or carbon taxes) or neutral technology policies (such as tax breaks) to correct for this type of market failure, both of which leave the market to determine the *direction of change*.

While MFT provides interesting insights, it is at best useful for describing a *steady-state* scenario in which public policy aims to put patches on existing trajectories provided by markets. It is less useful when policy is required to dynamically create and shape new markets; that is, "transformation." This means it is problematic for addressing innovation and societal challenges because it cannot explain the kinds of transformative, catalytic, mission-oriented public investments (Foray et al. 2012) that created new technologies and sectors that did not previously exist. This includes the emergence of the Internet, the nanotechnology sector, the biotechnology sector, and the emerging clean-tech sector (Block and Keller 2011). Such mission-oriented investments coordinated public and private initiatives, built new networks, and drove the entire techno-economic process, which resulted in the creation of new markets (Mazzucato 2015; Mazzucato 2016a/b). This depiction is very different from assuming that the private sector is in a space and simply needs to be incentivized to invest more or less within that space. It is the space itself that has been created by public policy, with the private sector entering only later. The imagination and vision emanated from the policy itself, which actively took risks rather than just *de*-risking.

A key characteristic of market-creating investments is that they are not limited to upstream basic research (the classic public good). Indeed, public investments that led to technological revolutions (IT, biotech, nanotech) and new *general-purpose technologies* (such as the Internet) were distributed *along the entire innovation chain*: basic research through the National Science Foundation (NSF), applied research through DARPA and the National Institutes of Health (NIH), and early-stage financing of companies through agencies like Small Business Innovation Research (SBIR) (Block and Keller 2011). This means that the kinds of innovation instruments (Martin 2016) were spread across a decentralized network of different agencies across the entire innovation chain. While such agencies might not act together in a planned way, the history of agencies like DARPA and NIH teaches us that they were often driven by a *vision* to create new landscapes (in defense or life-sciences) rather than to only fix problems in existing landscapes. In order to understand such mission-oriented policies, and to guide future ones, it is essential to develop a framework that can take into account investments that direct/steer change in particular directions, with the public sector not only de-risking, but also taking risks and uncertainties as lead investor. A *market-creating* framework for policy, to complement the market (and system) *fixing* role, can build on several "heterodox" economics literatures that have emphasized the state's *transformational* capacity. We review these alternative literatures in Section 3.3.

3.3 Insights on Market Shaping/Creating from Alternative Theories

Policies based on building systems of innovation focus on the need for nations to build a "network of institutions in the public and private sectors whose activities and interactions initiate, import, modify and diffuse new technologies" (Freeman 1995). The emphasis here is not on the stock of R&D, but on the circulation of knowledge and its diffusion throughout the economy (Lundvall 1992). Institutional change is not assessed through criteria based on static allocative efficiency, but rather on how such change promotes technological and structural change. This perspective is neither macro nor micro, but more meso, where individual firms are seen as part of a broader network of firms with which they cooperate and compete. The systems of innovation approach has been crucial for highlighting deficiencies in the market failure perspective, as it regards innovation policy (Lundvall 1992; Freeman 1995). It has emphasized the inability of MFT to tackle lock-in effects and to specific types of institutional failures that arise from feedback processes along the entire innovation chain (Verspagen 2006). Key innovation institutions, such as universities, will only allow the innovation system to achieve its potential if they are lined up synergistically with other institutions in the entrepreneurial ecosystem (Brown 2016).

However, while the systems of innovation approach has been key in identifying dynamic system failures, it has not explicitly created an alternative policy framework. This is because it has been too wed to the notion of policy as fixing, rather than wholeheartedly debunking the notion of policy as an "intervention" in the market process. In order to develop an alternative framework, the market itself must be redefined as an *outcome* of the interactions between different agents, including public policy makers (Mazzucato 2013c).

In order to develop a market-creating view of policy, in the spirit of Karl Polanyi's understanding of markets as outcomes embedded in policy processes, the chapter draws on insights from different bodies of thought that have considered the role of the state in achieving *transformation* of the economic landscape. These are: (a) science and technology policy research on *mission-oriented* policies; (b) development economics research on the *developmental state*; (c) evolutionary economics research on shifts in *technological trajectories and the emergence of techno-economic paradigms*; and (d) my own research on the *entrepreneurial state*, which looks explicitly at the risk-taking role of different actors (Mazzucato 2013a). In Section 3.4, I use these insights to consider new questions for economic policy that can help guide a market-creating framework. The fact that these four bodies of thought have not previously been linked, and have not been clearly positioned to critique the key tenets of market failure theory, has prevented them from having the impact they could have on our understanding of how to guide, evaluate, and manage public policy.

3.3.1 Science and Technology Policy Research: Mission-Oriented Innovation Policy

The history of innovation policy, studied especially through the systems of innovation approach (Freeman 1995), provides key insights into the limits of market failure theory with regard to justifying the depth and breadth of investments that have been necessary for the emergence of radical technological change. Innovation policy has historically taken the shape of measures that perform the following four functions: (1) support basic research, (2) aim to develop and diffuse general-purpose technologies, (3) develop certain economic sectors that are crucial for innovation, and (4) promote infrastructural development (Freeman and Soete 1997 [1974]). The *justification* of innovation policies has changed over time. While military motives predominated in the 1950s and 1960s, the aim since the 1970s has been to improve economic and competitive positions. In the 1980s, innovation policy became increasingly justified due to market failure. Innovation policies driven by military motives have been described as mission-oriented because they have aimed to achieve clearly defined technical goals. There have been calls in recent years for a return to such policies to address "grand societal challenges" (Mowery et al. 2010). However, Foray et al. (2012) contrasted missions of the past, such as putting a man on the moon, with such contemporary missions as tackling climate change. While past missions aimed to develop a particular technology (with the achievement of the technological objective signaling that the mission was accomplished), contemporary missions have addressed broader and more persistent challenges, which require long-term commitments to the development of technological solutions. The *Maastricht Memorandum* (Soete and Arundel 1993) provided a detailed analysis of the differences between old and new mission-oriented projects, showing that "older projects developed radically new technologies through government procurement projects that were largely isolated from the rest of the economy, though they frequently affected the structure of related industries and could lead to new spin-off technologies that had wide-spread effects on other sectors. In contrast, [contemporary] mission-oriented environmental [and other] projects will need to combine procurement with many other policies in order to have pervasive effects on the entire structure of production and consumption within an economy" (50).

However, research in this literature has often failed to integrate empirical insights in order to provide a fully-fledged theory that contrasts with MFT. Consequently, these studies have resulted in ad-hoc theoretical understandings and policy advice on how to manage mission-oriented initiatives, without tackling the key justifications for mission-oriented investments in a way that contrasts the justifications that arise from MFT. In particular, the framework has been limited to looking at agencies that focus on science, technology, and innovation policies. Doing so ignores the relationship between types of finance and innovation development. It also overlooks, for example, the rise of public financial institutions like state investment banks (such as KfW in Germany or the China Development Bank) as sources of mission-oriented finance, especially as private finance has increasingly retreated from financing the real economy (Mazzucato 2013b; Mazzucato and Penna 2014). While mission-oriented programs are intrinsically dynamic, with feedback loops between missions and achievements, the tools used to evaluate such public policies have remained static, coming from the MFT toolbox. For these reasons, mission-oriented policy research is currently confined to a small area of policy research and practice and has had minimal impact on how economists understand the role of public policy.

3.3.2 Development Economics: Developmental Network States

Work on the developmental state, a concept from a small group of development economists, has revealed the importance of the "visible hand" of the state in industrialization and technological change (Wade 1990; Amsden 2001). More recently, this literature has also emphasized the importance of a developmental *network* state; that is, a decentralized network of different types of state agencies that can foster innovation and development. While significant attention has been devoted to the role of large agencies or institutions (such as DARPA or the NIH) in historical mission-oriented projects, it is only recently that considerable focus has been placed on the broader network of structures, actors, strategies, and agencies, such as intelligence distributed amongst actors and institutions, flat organizational structures, flexibility, and customization (Perez 2002). Many successful cases of innovation and technology policy strategies have been carried out by networks of decentralized public institutions, which have focused not on creating individual "national champion" firms, but on establishing a constellation of innovative firms (O'Riain 2004). This has been the case in East Asia, Finland, Israel, Taiwan, and even in Silicon Valley in the United States (Block and Keller 2011). Such successful policies have covered a wide range of measures, including R&D support, training, support for marketing and exporting, funding programs (including early-stage venture capital), networking and brokerage services, building of facilities and clusters (so-called science parks), and fostering industrial ties.

From this alternative view, economic development is not the result of natural competitive advantages, but of the endogenous creation of new opportunities that *lead to the establishment* of competitive advantages. This process requires discovery of the cost structure of an economy in order to identify which of the types of goods and services that already exist in world markets can be produced in a domestic economy at low cost (Rodrik 2004). The state plays a central coordinating role in this discovery process and often represents a lead agent in economic development efforts. Because economic development is an endogenous process, the state provides social capital, coordinates initiatives and public-private partnerships, fosters synergies, and promotes the introduction of new combinations that create Schumpeterian rents (Reinert 2007).

3.3.3 Evolutionary Economics: Technological Trajectories and Techno-Economic Paradigm Shifts

Following the Schumpeterian tradition, evolutionary economists aim to "open the black box of technical change" (Rosenberg 1982) with a methodology that is led by empirical regularities and historical analysis in order to understand the process that links technical change (innovation), economic growth, and development. Key concepts developed in evolutionary economics are those of *technological paradigms* and *technological trajectories* (Dosi 1982; Nelson and Winter 1982), which reveal the limitation of market forces in providing direction to economic development. A technological paradigm has a threefold definition: It is an *outlook* of the relevant productive problems confronted by firms (as producers of technologies or innovators); it represents a set of procedures (routines) of how these problems shall be approached; and it defines the relevant problems and associated knowledge necessary for their solution (Dosi 1982, 148).

The evolutionary focus on the coevolution of those processes creating variety between economic agents and the competitive selection process that winnows in on that variety means that an evolutionary perspective on policy must consider adaptation (Witt 2003; Flanagan and Uyarra 2016). Policies should not be viewed as general a priori answers, but as being about learning and emergence. Which policy is best in which environment will emerge from experimentation and trial and error. A technological trajectory, in turn, represents the direction of learning, experimentation, and progress within a technological paradigm. Therefore, technology development is a problem-solving activity, and a technological paradigm "embodies strong prescriptions on the *directions* of technical change" (Dosi 1982, 152). This is why market signals are limited in terms of providing direction to techno-economic development; they only work within the parameters of the paradigm, which means they influence the rate of change more than the direction. When two or more technological paradigms compete, markets may influence which one is selected (the one that minimizes costs). Once established, however, paradigms have a powerful "exclusion effect," whereby some technological possibilities are discarded because they are incompatible with the prevailing paradigm and are therefore "invisible" to agents. Thus, a techno-economic system of innovation may be locked into a self-reinforcing, path-dependent trajectory (Dosi and Nelson 1994). This becomes a problem if the trajectory being followed (or the paradigm itself) is inferior or suboptimal to what could be achieved with technologies that transgress the paradigm (or with a different paradigm).

Perez (2002) expanded the notion of technological paradigm to *techno-economic paradigm* order to account for the nontechnological forces (economic and social institutions) that characterize certain periods of capitalist history and affect both the economic and social systems. Her theory of techno-economic paradigm shifts is a historical perspective on the long-waves of development that accompany technological revolutions. "A techno-economic paradigm is, then, a best-practice model made up of a set of all-pervasive generic technological and organizational principles, which represent the most effective way of applying a particular technological revolution and of using it for modernizing and rejuvenating the whole of the economy" (Perez 2002, 15). When a new technological revolution emerges, the socioeconomic system remains stuck within the bounds of the previous paradigm. This renders market forces incapable of directing the system toward the new paradigm and stifles the modernizing and rejuvenating potential of the new revolution. In other words, there are mismatches between elements of the social and techno-economic systems (for example, social expectations, R&D routines, tax regimes, labor regulations). In order to overcome these mismatches, it is necessary to build new institutions that favor the diffusion of the new paradigm. In all previous technological revolutions, governments have led the process of institution-building that allowed new techno-economic paradigms to replace the old ones. Perez (2002) specifically pointed to the role that public policy plays in allowing the full deployment of technological revolutions, such as the effect of suburbanization on the ability of the mass production revolution to diffuse throughout the economy.

This stream of research on technological and techno-economic paradigms highlights the importance of cognition when establishing the direction of technological change. Paradigms are powerful enabling and constraining institutions that favor certain directions of techno-economic development and obstruct others. In order to redirect techno-economic development on a new, qualitatively different route, a paradigm shift is required that will avoid the constant renewal of prevailing trajectories that occurs if market forces provide directionality to the system. From this perspective, the state has a crucial role to play in terms of creating a new *vision* that will coordinate cognitive efforts of different (public and private) agents and direct their action to areas beyond the existing paradigm. Green innovation can be understood as a redirection of the full deployment of the IT revolution (Mazzucato and Perez 2014). In order to effectively provide the direction of change, a vision must be created and shared. Stirling (2008) correctly focused on the role of bottom-up participatory processes to ensure directionality is taken seriously and shared among actors.

3.3.4 The Entrepreneurial State: The State as Lead Risk-Taker and Investor in the Economy

Alternative approaches to innovation policy, such as those described in this chapter, have questioned particular aspects of the economic dynamics embodied in Neoclassical theory. However, they have not questioned the underlying assumption of business being the only risk taker. The entrepreneurial state agenda has sought to challenge the notion of the entrepreneur being embodied in private business, and policy making being an activity outside of the entrepreneurial process (Mazzucato 2003). This perspective builds on studies in industry dynamics that have documented a weak relationship between entry of new firms into industries and the current levels of profits in those industries (Vivarelli 2013a). Firm entry appears to be driven by expectations about future growth opportunities, even when such expectations are overly optimistic (Dosi and Lovallo 1998). Historically, such technological and market opportunities have been actively shaped by government investment – what Mazzucato (2013a) refers to as the entrepreneurial state; that is, a willingness to invest in, and sometimes imagine from the beginning, new high-risk areas before the private sector does. Business has tended to enter new sectors only *after* the high risk and uncertainty have been absorbed by the public sector, especially in areas of high capital intensity. This has been the case with the IT revolution (Block and Keller 2011), the biotechnology industry (Lazonick and Tulum 2011), nanotechnology (Motoyama et al. 2011), and for the emerging clean tech sector (Mazzucato and Penna 2014). Indeed, Keller and Block (2013) have shown that private venture capital funds have focused on financing firms mid-stage that had previously received early-stage financing by public programs, like the Small Business Innovation Research program (SBIR). The literature has ignored such private piggy-backing on public risk-taking, at best discussing it in terms of "crowding in." What crowding in ignores, however, is the direct risk taking that such (public) activity entails, and hence the occasional failures that will inevitably result.

In the book *The Entrepreneurial State: Debunking Public vs. Private Sector Myths*, Mazzucato (2013a) describes the risk-taking role the state has played in the few countries that have achieved innovation-led growth. Ignoring the high risk and uncertainty that the state has absorbed has caused the fruits of innovation-led growth to be privatized, even though the underlying risk was socialized. It is usually assumed that the returns to the state will occur indirectly through the spillovers that are generated and/or through tax revenue. However, this type of return is based on the assumption that state intervention is limited to upstream areas like basic research (with high spillovers). However, the traditional assumptions break down when the intervention occurs throughout the entire innovation chain, including for applied research for technologies that get appropriated by specific firms, and on early-stage high-risk company financing. This happens because the firms in question often succeed in avoiding tax, and also because there is no reason for the firms to remain in the region/country where the public funding originated. Thus the entrepreneurial state framework implies considering both indirect and direct "reward" mechanisms for the public policies. Such mechanisms can make it easier for public organizations to treat their investments as portfolios, able to make some return on the upside to cover the downside as well as the next round of investments. More evidence is needed from around the world regarding the challenges and opportunities related to different types of return-generating mechanisms for public investments, such as those in Israel (through Yozma), the United States (through In-Q-tel), and Finland (through SITRA). This will help generate insights into the role of the state as a spender, facilitator, and regulator, but also as an investor and venture capitalist (Mazzucato 2013a; Rodrik 2015). How to do this, while retaining a mission-oriented perspective (not limited by cost–benefit analysis), is a key challenge.

3.4 Beyond Market Failure: Routes, Organization, Assessment, and Rewards

New economic thinking is required in order to build a policy framework that can be oriented toward market creating, rather than just market fixing, and can be focused on *transforming* the economic landscape rather than just facilitating it. This section brings together key concepts from the four heterodox frameworks reviewed in the previous section, drawing especially on the empirical research conducted within these perspectives, in order to provide a new theoretical conceptualization for guiding state action to tackle transformational change. The section considers four new policy questions, which can help build a market-creating policy agenda (Mazzucato 2016a), which can be conveniently labelled as ROAR, rethinking innovation in terms of Routes, Organizations, Assessment, and Rewards.

Routes: Understanding the role of policy as setting the direction of change. Policies that aim to correct markets assume that once the sources of the failure have been addressed, market forces will efficiently direct the economy to a path of growth and development. However, markets are "blind" (Dosi 1982) and the direction of change provided by markets often represents suboptimal outcomes from a societal point of view. This is why, in addressing *societal challenges*, states have led the process and provided the direction toward new techno-economic paradigms that did not emerge spontaneously out of market forces. Governments made direct investments in the technologies that enabled the mass production and IT revolutions to emerge, and formulated bold policies that allowed these phenomena to be fully deployed throughout the economy (Ruttan 2006; Block and Keller 2011). This fact seems to point to different analytical problems facing policy makers: namely, choosing whether the correct course of action is to direct or stand back; understanding *how* particular directions and routes can be picked; and determining how to mobilize and manage activities that can lead to the achievement of dynamic social and technological challenges.

The problem is not whether to pick a direction, but how to learn from the successful picking of the past, and to enable the directions picked to be broad enough to allow bottom-up exploration, discovery, and learning. This is sometimes referred to as "smart specialization" (Foray, David, and Hall 2009) and is explicitly a results- and outcome-oriented agenda, not an input- or outputs-oriented one (Rodrik 2004). However, the fact that it has hitherto been based on a market failure framework means that smart specialization is, at best, considered a "discovery" process with which stakeholders and policy-designers can jointly identify bottlenecks, market failures, and missing links. Smart specialization has not addressed the way in which innovation-led growth in places like Silicon Valley *actually happened*. Doing so requires not only the identification of missing links, but the formation of concrete strategies toward producing market landscapes that simply did not exist in the past. It also requires that the playing field be *tilted* in the direction pursued, rather than *leveled* (Mazzucato and Perez 2015). It also requires new thinking about how 'mission setting' can be applied to societal challenges that embody social innovation as much as technological, and a more participatory process in selecting missions (Mazzucato 2018).

Organization: Transforming public organizations into ones that welcome learning, experimentation, and self-discovery. If brought to its extreme, as advocated by critics from public choice theory, MFT calls for the state to intervene as little as possible in the economy, in a way that minimizes the risk of government failure, from crowding out to cronyism and corruption. This view requires a structure that *insulates* the public sector from the private sector (to avoid issues such as agency capture) and has resulted in a trend of outsourcing that often rids government of the knowledge capacities and capabilities (in relation to IT, for example) that are necessary for managing change (Kakabadse and Kakabadse 2002). Studies have examined the influence of outsourcing on the ability of public institutions to attract top-level talent with the relevant knowledge and skills to manage transformative mission-oriented policies. Without such talent and expertise it is nearly impossible for the state to fulfill its role of coordinating and providing direction to private actors when formulating and implementing policies that address societal challenges. In order to promote transformation of the economy, by shaping and creating technologies, sectors, and markets, the state must organize itself so that it has the intelligence (policy capacity) to think big and formulate bold policies. If the state is essential to the process of transformative technological and socioeconomic change, it is also essential to understand the appropriate structure of public organizations. Innovation is subject to extreme uncertainty, which creates the need for both patience ("patient long-term capital," Mazzucato 2013b) and the ability to experiment and explore the underlying landscape (Rodrik 2004). Therefore, a crucial element in organizing the state for its market-creating role is building its *absorptive capacity* (Cohen and Levinthal 1990), a concept that has hitherto been restricted to private organizations. This absorptive capacity will enable public agencies to learn in a process of investment, discovery, and experimentation, and see policy as process (Hirschman 1967).

A key concern should be to establish skills/resources, capabilities, and structures that can increase the chances that a public organization will be effective, both at *learning* and at *establishing symbiotic partnerships with the private sector*, and ultimately succeed in implementing mission-oriented and transformative policies. Public and private organizations must re-rethink their roles when working together. Public–private partnerships have often limited the public part in de-risking the private part. This ignores the capabilities and challenges involved in public sector risk taking. De-risking assumes a conservative strategy that minimizes the risks of picking losing projects, but does not necessarily maximize the probability of picking winners, which requires the adoption of a portfolio approach for public investments (Rodrik 2013). In such an approach, the success of a few projects can cover the losses from many projects, and the public organization in question also learns from its loss-making investments (Mazzucato 2013a). Here, the matching between failures and fixes is less important than having an institutional structure that ensures that winning policies provide enough rewards to cover the losses, and that losses are used as lessons to improve and renew future policies. Research on the *developmental state* (Block and Keller 2011) suggests that these goals are best achieved not through top-down policies, but through a decentralized structure in which the organization-(s) involved remain nimble, innovative, and dynamic from within. This strand of thinking can benefit from looking at the ways in which public–private partnerships were created when seeking the joint creation of new products and services, including vaccines (Chataway et al. 2007) and also new forms of partnerships between not only public and private actors but also third sector actors and civil society, so to increase the bottom-up processes necessary for exploration of new opportunities and landscapes, and new "voices" that can help welcome the serendipity of change (Hirschman 1967).

Assessment: Transforming static metrics into dynamic ones. The market failure framework has developed concrete indicators and methods to evaluate government investments, which stem directly from the framework itself, usually through a cost–benefit analysis that estimates whether the benefits of public intervention compensate for the costs associated with the market failure and with the implementation of the policy (including governmental failures). The problem is that there is a mismatch between the intrinsically dynamic character of economic development and the static tools used to evaluate the role of public policy in the process.

Failure to allow for the possibility that government can transform and create new landscapes that did not previously exist will affect the ability to measure such impact. This is evident in innovation and also for public services (Crouch 2016). This situation then leads to accusations of government crowding out business, which implies that the areas that government moves into could have been areas for business investment. Such claims are best defended through a *crowding in* argument, which relies on showing how government investments create a larger national output pie (hence higher savings for private investment to dip into). Indeed, as shown by Engel, Rothgang, and Eckl (2016), public investments in R&D often crowd in further R&D investments by business.

However, this defense does not account for the fact that businesses are risk-averse and unwilling or unable to transform existing and create new landscapes, which is about creating *new pies*, not increasing existing ones. Without *indicators* for such transformative action, the static toolbox affects the government's ability to determine whether it is simply operating in existing spaces or making new things happen that would not have happened anyway (its "additionality"). This often leads to investments that are overly narrow or directed within the confines of the boundaries set by the business practices of the prevailing techno-economic paradigm (Abraham 2010).

Therefore, it is crucial to develop a new toolbox and indicators for evaluating and measuring the degree to which state investments open up and transform sectoral and technological landscapes, rather than tinkering with existing ones. The indicators must take into account the underlying risk and uncertainty absorbed in transforming such landscapes.

Risks and Rewards: building symbiotic private–public partnerships. MFT says little about cases in which the state is the *lead investor and risk taker* in capitalist economies. Having a vision about the direction in which to drive an economy requires direct and indirect investment in particular areas, not just creating the (framework) conditions for change. Crucial choices must be made, the fruits of which will create some winners, but also many losers. For example, the US Department of Energy recently provided guaranteed loans to two green-tech companies: Solyndra ($500 million) and Tesla Motors ($465 million). While the latter is often glorified as a success story, the former failed miserably and became the latest example in the media of government being inefficient and unable to *pick winners* (Wood 2012). However, any venture capitalist will admit that for every winning investment (such as Tesla) there are many losses (such as Solyndra). In making its downstream investments, therefore, governments can learn from portfolio strategies of venture capitalists, structuring investments across a risk space so that lower risk investments can help to cover the higher risk ones. In other words, if the public sector is expected to compensate for the lack of private venture capital (VC) money going to early-stage innovation, it should at least be able to benefit from the wins, as private VC does. Otherwise, the funding for such investments cannot be secured. As argued in Mazzucato and Wray (2015), even if money could be secured for public investments endogenously (through money creation), it is desirable to allow the state to reap some of the rewards from its investments for a number of other reasons. Matching this type of spending with the corresponding return would provide a measure of efficiency, holding policymakers accountable; government net spending has limits dictated by the real resource capacity of the economy; and voters will be more willing to accept the (inevitable) failures if they see that those are compensated by important successes.

The public sector can use a number of return-generating mechanisms for its investments, including retaining equity or royalties, retaining a golden share of the IPR, using income-contingent loans, or capping the prices (which the tax payer pays) of those products that emanate, as drugs do, from public funds (Mazzucato 2013a). Before exploring the details of each mechanism, however, it is crucial for the policy framework to even allow the question to be asked. In a market-shaping framework, does government have the right to retain equity more than in a market failure framework? Are taxes currently bringing back enough return to government budgets to fund high-risk investments that will probably fail?

3.5 Conclusion

This chapter has considered the limitations of the market failure framework that continues to guide innovation policy. It has argued that putting innovation at the center of growth policy requires an emphasis on shaping and creating markets rather than just fixing them and that an alternative framework must also go beyond fixing system failures. To guide a market-creating view, the chapter has considered insights from alternative (heterodox) literatures on the role of the state in producing structural change and transformation. Four critical issues must be considered when building such a framework: (1) the *direction* of change promoted by policy; (2) the nature of (public and private) *organizations* that can welcome the underlying uncertainty and discovery process; (3) the *evaluation* of mission-oriented and market-creation policies; and (4) the ways in which both *risks and rewards* can be shared so that smart growth can also result in inclusive growth.

Considering the need for government policy to transform, be catalytic, and create and shape markets rather than just fix them helps reframe the key questions of economic policy from static ones that deal with crowding out and picking winners to more dynamic ones that help form the types of public–private interactions that can create new innovation and industrial landscapes. The point is not to prescribe specific technologies, but to provide directions of change around which bottom-up solutions can then experiment. As Stirling (2014, 2) put it: "The more demanding the innovation challenges like poverty, ill health or environmental damage, the greater becomes the importance of effective policy. This is not a question of 'picking winners' – an uncertainty-shrouded dilemma which is anyhow equally shared between public, private and third sectors. Instead, it is about engaging widely across society, in order to build the most fruitful conditions for deciding what 'winning' even means." While identifying key societal challenges is straightforward – climate change, ageing, resource security, housing, urbanization, etc. – translating challenges into concrete missions will require the involvement of an array of stakeholders concerned with sectors and sociotechnical fields affected by the challenge itself. Therefore, defining the direction of investments should be based on sound diagnosis of each challenge by the state *together* with other stakeholders.

Acknowledgments

This chapter has received funding from the European Union's Horizon 2020 Framework for Research and Innovation under grant agreement No. 649186 – Project ISIGrowth. Comments from Caetano Penna and an anonymous referee from the SPRU working paper series are greatly appreciated. All errors remain the author's.

References

Abbate, J. 1999. *Inventing the Internet.* Cambridge, MA: MIT Press.

Abraham, J. 2010. Pharmaceuticalization of society in context: Theoretical, empirical and health dimensions. *Sociology* 44(4): 603–622.

Amsden, A. H. 2001. *The Rise of "the Rest": Challenges to the West from Late-Industrializing Economies.* Oxford: Oxford University Press.

Angell, M. 2005. *The truth about the drug companies: How they deceive us and what to do about it.* New York: Random House.

Arrow, K. 1951. *An Extension of the Basic Theorems of Classical Welfare Economics.* Chapter presented at the Second Berkeley Symposium on Mathematical Statistics and Probability, Berkeley, CA.

Block, F. L. 2008. Swimming against the current: The rise of a hidden developmental state in the United States. *Politics and Society* 36(2, June): 169–206.

Block, F. L. and M. R. Keller. 2011. *State of Innovation: The U.S. Government's Role in Technology Development*. Boulder, CO: Paradigm Publishers.

Brown, R. 2016. "Mission impossible? Entrepreneurial universities in peripheral regional innovative systems." *Industry and Innovation* 23(2).

Buchanan, J. M. 2003. Public choice: The origins and development of a research program. *Champions of Freedom* 31: 13–32.

Chataway, J., S. Brusoni, E. Cacciatori, R. Hanlin, and L. Orsenigo. 2007. The international AIDS vaccine initiative (IAVI) in a changing landscape of vaccine development: A public/private partnership as knowledge broker and integrator. *The European Journal of Development Research* 19(1): 100–117.

Cohen, W. M. and D. A. Levinthal. 1990. Absorptive capacity: A new perspective on learning and innovation. *Administrative Science Quarterly* 35(1): 128–152.

Crouch, C. 2016. The paradoxes of privatization and public-service outsourcing, in *Rethinking Capitalism*, ed. M. Jacobs and M. Mazzucato. Wiley Press.

Dosi, G. 1982. Technological paradigms and technological trajectories: A suggested interpretation of the determinants and directions of technical change. *Research Policy* 11(3): 147–162.

Dosi, G. and D. Lovallo 1998. Rational entrepreneurs or optimistic martyrs? Some considerations on technological regimes, corporate entries, and the evolutionary role of decision biases, in *Foresights and Oversights in Technological Change*, ed. R. Garud, P. Nayyar, and Z. Shapiro, 41–68. Cambridge: Cambridge University Press.

Dosi, G. and R. R. Nelson. 1994. An introduction to evolutionary theories in economics. *Journal of Evolutionary Economics* 4(3): 153–172.

Engel, D., M. Rothgang, and V. Eckl. 2016. Systemic aspects of R&D policy subsidies for R&D collaborations and their effects on private R&D. *Industry and Innovation* 23(2).

Evans, P. 1995. *Embedded Autonomy: States and Industrial Transformation* (First edition). Princeton, N.J.: Princeton University Press.

Flanagan, K. and E. Uyarra. 2016. Four dangers in innovation policy studies – and how to avoid them. *Industry and Innovation* 23(2).

Foray, D., P. A. David, and B. Hall. 2009. Smart specialization: The concept, in *Knowledge for Growth. Prospects for Science, Technology and Innovation*. Selected chapters from Research Commissioner Janez Potočnik's Expert Group, 20.

Foray, D., D. Mowery, and R. R. Nelson. 2012. Public R&D and social challenges: What lessons from mission R&D programs? *Research Policy* 41(10): 1697–1902.

Freeman, C. 1995. The "National System of Innovation" in historical perspective. *Cambridge Journal of Economics* 19(1): 5–24.

Freeman, C. and L. Soete. 1997 [1974]. *The Economics of Industrial Innovation* (3rd edn.). Cambridge, MA: MIT Press.

Hirschman, A. O. 1967. *Development Projects Observed.* Washington, DC: Brookings Institution Press.

Kakabadse, A. and N. Kakabadse. 2002. Trends in outsourcing: Contrasting USA and Europe. *European Management Journal* 20(2): 189–198.

Keller, M. R. and F. Block. 2013. Explaining the transformation in the US innovation system: the impact of a small government program. *Socio-Economic Review* 11(4): 629–656.

Lazonick, W. and O. Tulum. 2011. US biopharmaceutical finance and the sustainability of the biotech business model. *Research Policy* 40(9): 1170–1187.

Lundvall, B. A. 1992. *National Innovation System: Towards a Theory of Innovation and Interactive Learning.* Pinter: London.

Martin, B. R. 2016. R&D policy instruments – a critical review of what we do and don't know. *Industry and Innovation* 23(2).

Mazzucato, M. 2013a. *The Entrepreneurial State: Debunking the Public vs. Private Myth in Risk and Innovation.* London: Anthem Press.

Mazzucato, M. 2013b. Financing innovation: Creative destruction vs. destructive creation. *Industrial and Corporate Change* 22(4): 851–867.

Mazzucato, M. 2013c. Debunking the market mechanism: a response to John Kay. *Political Quarterly* 84(4): 444–447.

Mazzucato, M. and Perez, C. 2015a. "Innovation as growth policy," in *The Triple Challenge: Europe in a New Age.* J. Fagerberg, S. Laestadius, and B. Martin (eds.), Oxford: Oxford University Press.

Mazzucato, M. 2015b. Innovation systems: From fixing market failures to creating markets. *Intereconomics* 50(3): 120–125.

Mazzucato M. 2016a. From market fixing to market-creating: A new framework for innovation policy. Special Issue of *Industry and Innovation*: "Innovation policy – can it make a difference?" 23(2).

Mazzucato, M. 2016b. Innovation, the state and patient capital, in *Rethinking Capitalism Economics and Policy for Sustainable and Inclusive Growth*, chapter 6, ed. M. Jacobs and M. Mazzucato. London: Wiley-Blackwell.

Mazzucato, M. and C. C. R. Penna. 2014. Beyond market failures: State investment banks and the "mission-oriented" finance for innovation. *SPRU Working paper Series* 21.

Mazzucato, M. and C. Perez. 2014. Innovation as growth policy. *SPRU Working Paper Series* 13.

Mazzucato, M. and R. Wray. 2015. Financing the capital development of the economy: A Keynes-Schumpeter-Minsky synthesis." *Levy Institute Working Paper* No. 837.

Mazzucato, M. 2018. Mission oriented research and innovation in the EU: A problem solving approach to fuel innovation-led growth, ISBN 978-92-79-79918-1 https://publications.europa.eu/en/publication-detail/-/publication/5b2811d1-16be-11e8-9253-01aa75ed71a1/language-en (accessed 1/4/2018)

Motoyama, Y., R. Appelbaum, and R. Parker. 2011. The national nanotechnology initiative: Federal support for science and technology, or hidden industrial policy? *Technology in Society* 33(1–2): 109–118.

Mowery, D. C., R. R. Nelson, and B. R. Martin. 2010. Technology policy and global warming: Why new policy models are needed (or why putting new wine in old bottles won't work). *Research Policy* 39(8): 1011–1023.

Nelson, R. R. and S. G. Winter. 1982. *An Evolutionary Theory of Economic Change.* Cambridge, MA: Belknap Press.

O'Riain, S. 2004. *The Politics of High Tech Growth: Developmental Network States in the Global Economy.* Boston, MA: Cambridge University Press.

Perez, C. 2002. *Technological Revolutions and Financial Capital: The Dynamics of Bubbles and Golden Ages.* Cheltenham: Edward Elgar.

Polanyi, K. 2001 [1944]. *The Great Transformation: The Political and Economic Origins of Our Time* (2nd Beacon Chapterback edn.). Boston, MA: Beacon Press.

Reinert, E. S. 2007. *How Rich Countries Got Rich and Why Poor Countries Stay Poor.* London: Constable.

Rodrik, D. 2004. Industrial policy for the twenty-first century. *John F. Kennedy School of Government Working Paper Series* rwp04–047.

Rodrik, D. 2013. Green industrial policy. *Princeton University Working Paper.*

Rodrik, D. 2015. From welfare state to innovation state, *Project Syndicate* www.project-syndicate.org/commentary/labor-saving-technology-by-dani-rodrik-2015–01 (accessed March 3, 2015).

Rosenberg, N. 1982. *Inside the Black Box: Technology and Economics.* Boston, MA: Cambridge University Press.

Ruttan, V. W. 2006. *Is War Necessary for Economic Growth? Military Procurement and Technology Development.* University of Minnesota: Department of Applied Economics.

Soete, L. and A. Arundel. 1993. *An Integrated Approach to European Innovation and Technology Diffusion Policy: A Maastricht Memorandum.* Luxembourg: Commission of the European Communities, SPRINT Programme.

Stern, N. H. 2006. *The Economics of Climate Change (Stern Review).* HM Treasury.

Stirling, A. 2008. "Opening up" and "closing down" power, participation, and pluralism in the social appraisal of technology. *Science, Technology & Human Values* 33(2): 262–294.

Stirling, A. 2014. Making choices in the face of uncertainty. *Themed Annual Report of the Government Chief Scientific Adviser*, Chapter 2 (June). Draft mimeo.

Verspagen, B. 2006. Innovation and economic growth, in *The Oxford Handbook of Innovation*, ed. J. Fagerberg, D. C. Mowery, and R. R. Nelson, 487–513. New York, NY: Oxford University Press.

Vivarelli, M. 2013a. Is entrepreneurship necessarily good? Microeconomic evidence from developing and developed countries. *Industrial and Corporate Change* 22(6): 1453–1495.

Wade, R. 1990. *Governing the Market: Economic Theory and the Role of Government in East Asian Industrialization.* Princeton, NJ: Princeton University Press.

Witt, U. 2003. Economic policy making in evolutionary perspective. *Journal of Evolutionary Economics* 13(2): 77–94.

Wood, R. 2012. Fallen Solyndra won bankruptcy battle but faces tax war. *Forbes*, June 11. (www.forbes.com/sites/robertwood/2012/11/06/fallen-solyndra-won-bankruptcy-battle-but-faces-tax-war/) (accessed June 29, 2014).

4 | Strategic Alliances
Identifying Recent Emerging Sub-Fields of Research

FIORENZA BELUSSI, LUIGI ORSI,
AND ANDREA GANZAROLI

4.1 Introduction

Research in both journals and books on strategic alliances has increased rapidly since the 1990s. Numerous related topics have been explored, such as globalisation, governance structure, learning capability, and alliance stability. The founding fathers of this literature were analysed by Ling and Chen (2012) in their bibliometric survey, which covered more than 1500 publications and 82,614 citations. Dyer and Singh (1998), Gulati (1995; 1998), Hamel (1991), Kogut (1988), Dyer (1997), Doz and Hamel (1998), and Hamel, Doz, and Prahalad (1989) emerged as the most cited authors. By using the bibliometric technique, it is possible to create a map of science in a specific field or discipline. In the scientific literature, mapping of science can facilitate an understanding of the contemporaneous state of knowledge as the first requirement for a good history of science, facilitating the understanding of conceptual relations. While the analyses of citations and co-citations refer to influential articles of the past, they do not represent the core subfield of contemporary research that is, indeed, the main aim of the bibliographic coupling analysis used in this chapter.

4.2 The Theoretical Frame

The rate of alliance formation has increased significantly during recent decades. A strategic alliance is a short- or long-term voluntary agreement among independent organisations aimed at sharing access and exchanging resources and knowledge, and engaging in a new market entry. The types of alliance can be categorised as equity agreements (such as joint ventures, minority equity, and equity swaps), or non-equity agreements (such as joint R&D, long-term sourcing agreements, reciprocal distribution, and franchising and licensing). Alliances represent a useful tool to source new knowledge and competences, to increase firms' scale economies, to increase the speed of launching new products into markets, and to reduce risks and costs (Gulati and Singh 1998; Hagerdorn 2002; Dacin et al. 2007).

An important stream of literature has applied a knowledge perspective (Eisenhardt and Schoonhoven 1996; Mowery et al. 1996; Powell et al. 1996) to address the benefits and risks of alliances between firms. In particular, it studies the technological dynamics enabled by alliances to firms belonging to high-tech sectors (and, above all, to the bio-pharma industry, Baum et al. 2000) and the asymmetries stemming from the heterogeneity of partner selection (Inkpen and Beamish 1997). R&D alliance formation is considered a contractual agreement alternative to a more concentrated and verticalised mode of governance, where R&D activities are internalised in large laboratories owned by the largest firms (Dyer and Singh 1998). For many firms, alliances are a necessary step in order to boost innovative performances (Shan et al. 1994), the development of new products (Deeds and Hill 1996; Rothaermel and Deeds 2004), and, more generally, performance (Baum et al. 2000). Contributions based on the resource-based view of firms (Barney 1991; Wernerfelt 1995) and on the knowledge-based view of firms (Levitt and March 1988; Nelson 1991; Nonaka 1991; Conner and Prahalad 1996; Grant 1996; Cloodt et al. 2006) provide useful insights to understand this phenomenon. In order to generate and support a competitive advantage compared to other companies, firms rely heavily on unique and innovative capabilities, i.e. specific expertise and competences related to the development and introduction of new processes and products (Rumelt 1974; Hagedoorn and Duysters 2002a). Such capabilities can be either endogenous or exogenous. Moreover, knowledge is often tacit, especially in technological- and knowledge-intensive contexts, and thus difficult to transfer from one firm to another (Larsson et al. 1998). Moreover, markets are imperfect mechanisms: thus, alliances or acquisitions may be better options. Despite the evidence that alliance portfolios are beneficial for firms, the question of *who allies with whom* within entrepreneurial technology ventures remains largely unexplored (Gans and Stern 2003). These partnerships, which often involve co-development contracts, challenge the traditional business models centred on the idea of developing an in-house product. Moreover, they create business model options that can significantly reduce R&D expenses, increase innovation output, and open new markets: the so-called markets for technology (Arora et al. 2001). This theoretical approach is in line with the open innovation study tradition (Hagedoorn and Duysters 2002b; Chesbrough 2003) through the acknowledgement of the complexity inherent in the innovation process itself, where several sources (internal and external to the firm) are used to recombine different pieces of knowledge into a new piece of knowledge.

Through alliances, firms gain access to external sources of innovation (Arora and Gambardella 1994; Hitt et al. 1996; Graebner and Eisenhardt 2004), develop and extend their resources and capabilities (Vermeulen and Barkema 2001; Uhlenbruck et al. 2006), and overcome local searching boundaries (Rosenkopf and Nerkar 2001; Rosenkopf and Almeida 2003). From the extensive literature analysed, it is possible to argue that exploration is better developed within alliances, but acquisition processes drive a more exhaustive exploitation of resources (Belussi and Orsi 2016). Through acquisition, firms can reduce the risk of erroneous selection and subsequent difficulties in knowledge integration (Hennart 1988).

4.3 Data Collection and Method

The Bibliometric approach represents the collection and management of bibliographic data derived from scientific works, and the use of robust quantitative methods to improve the findings of more subjective literature reviews. It is a useful tool to achieve an overview of the intellectual structure of the field, and recognise core publications and epistemological orientations (De Bakker et al. 2005). Moreover, it allows evaluation of citation patterns by exploiting various techniques, such as authors' citation analysis, citation networks mapping, co-citation, and bibliographic coupling analysis (Schildt et al. 2006).

Certain elements decrease the reliability of bibliometric research evaluation (MacRoberts and MacRoberts 2007). Criticisms concerning research databases are: the limited coverage, the exclusion of certain types of documents, the classification of journals by discipline, changes in journal titles, names spelled in a different way, or the number of authors (Beall and Kafadar 2007). Other critical aspects regard excessive, selective, secondary, erroneous, negative, or criticism-oriented citations, self-citation, and personal strategies (Baumgartner and Pieters 2003). A further criticality concerns the lower likelihood of recent studies being cited over those published around the beginning of the decade. Since citations tend to grow exponentially over time, even measuring the average number of citations by year, the more recent studies are inclined to remain on the sidelines of the citations network. Finally, all mentioned criticalities suggest that the dataset of publications selected represents only the core of the discipline or of the topic under investigation (White and McCain 1998).

In order to build the dataset for this study, the authors relied on the ISI-Thomson Web of Science platform to ensure the quality of the sample of the publications.

The analysis is based on the Thomson Reuter's ISI Web of Science database (WOS). The Web of Science provides access to current and retrospective multidisciplinary information from more than 10,400 of the most prestigious, high-impact research journals worldwide in sciences, social sciences, and arts and humanities, with coverage that goes back to 1900 for sciences, 1956 for social sciences, and 1975 for arts and humanities. For the purpose of this chapter, articles were downloaded from the 'Core Collection'; the time span covered: all years until the end of 2015; and the WOS indexes covered: SCI-EXPANDED, SSCI, A&HCI, CPCI-S, CPCI-SSH, and ESCI. The keyword used was 'strategic allianc*' in topic 'or' title. Since the term 'strategic allianc*' is used by a variety of disciplines, the research was limited to the fields of management, business, and operations research management science. A sample of 2939 articles and books was obtained, classified as follows: (1) 2283 in the management field, (2) 1680 in the business field, and (3) 492 in the operations research management science field. There may be overlays among the different fields, thus the sum of the three categories is not equal to 2939. Even if WOS has been criticised for a number of limitations, and other databases such as Scopus and Google Scholar have recently increased in popularity, WOS includes the most influential, relevant, and credible journals by examining, according to a 'publisher-neutral' approach, basic publishing standards, timeliness, and editorial scope and objectives. Thus, it is the most used source for bibliometric analysis (e.g. Casey and McMillan 2008; Tsai and Yang 2010).

The whole sample was analysed using two types of software: BibExcel (Persson et al. 2009) and VOSviewer. BibExcel is used to organise the dataset, the main descriptive statistics on the sample, and the bibliographic coupling matrix (Appio et al. 2014). VOSviewer is used to analyse bibliometric networks (in our case the bibliographic coupling network) through the mapping and clustering technique. It uses proximity to show relationships between nodes. The closer the nodes, the stronger the relationship; and the farther, the weaker. This corpus of scientific knowledge was analysed by using bibliometric tools, in particular the bibliographic coupling method. Bibliometric techniques introduce objective evaluation measures of scientific publications that contrast the potential bias embedded in a subjective evaluation, and thus represent an important complement to researchers' analytical ability (Appio et al. 2014). By using the bibliometric technique, it is possible to create a map of science in a specific field or discipline. In the scientific literature, the map of science can facilitate the understanding of the contemporaneous state of knowledge, considered by Holton (2000) as the first requirement of a good history of science, allowing the understanding of conceptual relations (Small 1999). The bibliographic method has its roots in the social network analysis that, since the 1930s, has been used by researchers and theorists, especially in sociological studies, to understand the characteristics and relationships of social structures. Social network analysis represents an application of the 'graph theory,' a branch of mathematics, where graphs are used to model pairwise relations among individual entities. This corpus of scientific knowledge was analysed by using the bibliographic coupling method. For this analysis, a node represents a single paper/document and the edges represent the number of couplings between papers.

Bibliographic coupling, like co-citation, is a similarity measure that uses citations to determine a similarity linkage between papers/documents. Bibliographic coupling occurs when two scientific documents have a common source in their references. This can be used as a proxy when two scientific documents handle related subject matter, and the 'coupling strength' of two given documents is higher the more they share citations with other documents. Moreover, in our analysis, the influence of publications with many citations or many references can be reduced using a fractional counting approach. The common procedure for bibliographic coupling is: (1) to select a set of papers; (2) to estimate similarities between pairs of papers/documents using bibliographic coupling counts; and (3) to allocate citing papers to clusters using similarity measures (Boyack and Klavan 2010). Co-citation analysis has been adopted as standard since the 1970s, but recently there has been a rebirth in the use of bibliographic coupling that is challenging the historical preference for co-citation analysis (Boyack 2009; Boyack and Klavan 2010; Jarneving 2005, 2007a,b; Sandström 2009).

4.4 A Descriptive Analysis of the Data Source Used

Analysis of the ISI Web of Science database (WOS) allows understanding of the publication trend in the topic of strategic alliance. The issue of strategic alliances started in the mid-1990s with a steady growth that reached maturity at the end of the second millennium, when more than

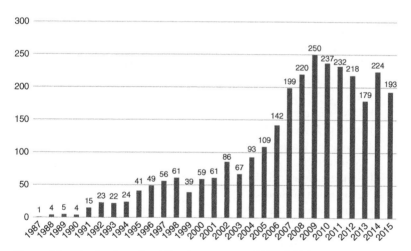

Figure 4.1 Distribution of publications per year 1987–2015. (*Sources:* Our elaboration from ISI web of Science)

Table 4.1 *Top 25 scientific journals by number of articles (on the left) and the top 25 most prolific authors in the field of strategic alliances (on the right)*

	Top 25 journals by number of articles	Freq.	Top 25 most prolific authors	Freq.
1	Strategic Management Journal	157	Reuer JJ	30
2	International Journal of Technology Management	80	Duysters G	28
3	Organization Science	79	Das TK	18
4	Industrial Marketing Management	73	Hagedoorn J	18
5	Journal of Business Research	73	Luo YD	18
6	Journal of International Business Studies	73	Gulati R	15
7	Journal of Management Studies	68	Hitt MA	15
8	Technovation	67	Li Y	15
9	Research Policy	61	Vanhaverbeke W	15
10	Long Range Planning	57	Singh H	14
11	Academy of Management Journal	49	Arino A	13
12	International Business Review	48	Beamish Pw	13
13	Journal of Product Innovation Management	46	Lavie D	12
14	Management Decision	44	Teng BS	12
15	Journal of Business Venturing	39	Inkpen AC	11
16	Journal of World Business	39	Liu Y	11
17	R D Management	39	Rothaermel FT	11
18	Journal of Management	38	Baum JAC	10
19	Technology Analysis Strategic Management	38	Cavusgil ST	10
20	International Journal of Production Economics	28	Faems D	10
21	Organization Studies	25	Lichtenthaler U	10
22	Journal of Engineering and Technology Management	24	Parkhe A	10
23	Technological Forecasting and Social Change	23	Santoro MD	10

Table 4.1 (*cont.*)

Top 25 journals by number of articles	Freq.	Top 25 most prolific authors	Freq.
24 Academy of Management Review	22	Shenkar O	10
25 Journal of Operations Management	21	Tyler BB	10

(*Sources:* Our elaboration from ISI web of Science)

200 documents were annually published for a total of 2939 publications (Figure 4.1).[1]

Table 4.1 shows the top twenty-five scientific journals on the basis of the number of articles published in the field of strategic alliances, and the most prolific author per number of articles in the same topic. The most important journals are those in the field of management studies (*Strategic Management, Organization Science, Industrial Marketing Management, Journal of Business Research,* and *Journal of Management Studies*) and international business literature (the *Journal of International Business Studies*). In addition, there are also journals whose focus is mainly devoted to the analysis of innovation and technological change, such as *Technovation, Research Policy,* and the *Journal of Product Innovation Management.*

Table 4.1, in the right-hand column, provides a list of authors with the highest number of publications in the field of strategic alliances. Professor Reuer is the most prolific author in this field, with thirty publications updated at the beginning of 2016. Reuer is mostly active in entrepreneurship and strategy. Reuer's research uses organisational economics to investigate firms' external corporate development activities and growth options (e.g. strategic alliances, international joint ventures, acquisitions, and initial public offerings). Recent works concern the governance and design of alliances, collaborative strategies, and applications of information economics to various problems in strategy, international business, and entrepreneurship.

---

[1] We excluded from the chart twenty-six publications for year 2016, because we do not have complete data for the whole year.

Professor Duysters' studies focus mainly on international business strategies, innovation strategies, mergers and acquisitions, technology catch-up strategies of developing countries, network analytical methods, and strategic alliances.

Professor Hagedoorn, with eighteen articles in this field, deals with organisation and strategy, especially within the field of economics of knowledge and innovation.

Professor Das' research (eighteen papers) concerns strategic management, with a clear focus on trust, control, and risk in strategic alliances.

Professor Luo's research (eighteen articles) concerns global strategy, international management, and emerging market business. An important aspect studied is the topic of partners' selection strategies. Other active scholars in the field of strategic alliances are the following: Gulati (fifteen articles), Hitt (fifteen), Li (fifteen), and Vanhaverbeke (fifteen).

The literature focused on alliances sees the dominant position of Anglo-Saxon contributors, where the United States, the United Kingdom, Canada, and Australia cover more than 50 per cent of all the articles published (see Table 4.2). Interestingly, China ranks second with 448 publications and Taiwan ranks sixth with 173 articles. In particular, two Chinese authors (Luo and Li) are in the top list of the twenty-five most prolific authors (see Table 4.1). Many authors are also European; especially, from the Netherlands (201 documents, ranking 4th), Spain (159 docs, ranking 7th), France (114 docs, ranking 8th), Germany (113 docs, ranking 9th), and Italy (85 docs, ranking 12th). Regarding the most prolific institutions (Table 4.2), we can also in this case note the leadership of US universities (Pennsylvania, Indiana, North Carolina, and Illinois rank among the first five institutions), and UK and Dutch schools.

Table 4.3 reports the most cited publications and authors extracted by this study's sample of 2939 documents. The top positions are held by three fundamental works in the field of management and strategy. The first article, written by Powell, Koput, and Smithdoerr in *Administrative Science Quarterly* (2411 citations updated at the beginning of 2016), argues that when the knowledge base of an industry is complex and the competences are dispersed, the locus of innovation is in networks rather than in individual firms. Using the biotech industry, the authors developed a network approach that links research and development activities and alliances, and discusses

Table 4.2 *Top 25 authors' provenance countries (on the left) and the top 25 most prolific institutions in the field of strategic alliances (on the right).*

	Authors' provenance (top 25 countries)	Freq.	Top 25 institutions	Freq.
1	USA	1107	Pennsylvania Commonwealth System of Higher Education PCSHE	60
2	Peoples R China	448	Indiana University System	46
3	England	258	Tilburg University	45
4	Netherlands	201	University of North Carolina	45
5	Canada	176	University of Illinois System	43
6	Taiwan	173	University of London	43
7	Spain	159	University System of Georgia	43
8	France	114	Erasmus University Rotterdam	42
9	Germany	113	Xi An Jiaotong University	42
10	South Korea	98	Wuhan University of Technology	38
11	Australia	94	Maastricht University	37
12	Italy	85	Florida State University System	36
13	Finland	58	University of Manchester	36
14	Singapore	53	Eindhoven University of Technology	34
15	Sweden	51	Indiana University Bloomington	33
16	Belgium	49	University of Pennsylvania	32
17	Denmark	47	Michigan State University	31
18	Switzerland	46	Baruch College Cuny	30
19	Turkey	38	City University of New York Cuny System	30
20	Norway	31	Copenhagen Business School	30
21	Japan	30	Insead Business School	29
22	Israel	26	National University of Singapore	29
23	Austria	24	Ohio State University	29
24	Scotland	24	University of Illinois Urbana Champaign	29
25	Portugal	18	Vu University Amsterdam	29

(*Sources:* Our elaboration from ISI web of Science)

Table 4.3 *Ranking of the top 25 most cited articles and authors*

	Publication title	Authors	Publication year	Total citations	Average per year
1	Interorganisational collaboration and the locus of innovation: Networks of learning in biotechnology	Powell, WW; Kogut, KW; Smithdoerr, L	1996	2411	114,81
2	Absorptive capacity: A review, reconceptualisation, and extension	Zahra, Sa; George, G	2002	1764	117,6
3	Competition for competence and inter-partner learning within international strategic alliances	Hamel, G	1991	1411	54,27
4	Alliances and networks	Gulati, R	1998	1223	64,37
5	The art of continuous change: Linking complexity theory and time-paced evolution in relentlessly shifting organisations	Brown, Sl; Eisenhardt, Km	1997	1033	51,65
6	Strategic alliances and interfirm knowledge transfer	Mowery, Dc; Oxley, Je; Silverman, Bs	1996	949	45,19
7	Between trust and control: Developing confidence in partner cooperation in alliances	Das, Tk; Teng, Bs	1998	868	45,68
8	Characteristics of partnership success – partnership attributes, communication behaviour, and conflict-resolution techniques	Mohr, J; Spekman, R	1994	861	37,43
9	Strategic alliance structuring – a game-theoretic and transaction cost examination of interfirm cooperation	Parkhe, A	1993	848	35,33

	Title	Authors	Year		
10	Learning and protection of proprietary assets in strategic alliances: Building relational capital	Kale, P; Singh, H; Perlmutter, H	2000	821	48,29
11	Social structure and alliance formation patterns: A longitudinal analysis	Gulati, R	1995	777	35,32
12	The evolution of cooperation in strategic alliances: Initial conditions or learning processes?	Doz, YL	1996	730	34,76
13	Network location and learning: The influence of network resources and firm capabilities on alliance formation	Gulati, R	1999	729	40,5
14	Social capital, networks, and knowledge transfer	Inkpen, Ac; Tsang, Ewk	2005	724	60,33
15	Interorganisational endorsements and the performance of entrepreneurial ventures	Stuart, Te; Hoang, H; Hybels, Rc	1999	723	40,17
16	Understanding the rationale of strategic technology partnering – interorganisational modes of cooperation and sectoral differences	Hagedoorn, J	1993	715	29,79
17	Resource-based view of strategic alliance formation: Strategic and social effects in entrepreneurial firms	Eisenhardt, Km; Schoonhoven, Cb	1996	713	33,95
18	Don't go it alone: Alliance network composition and startups' performance in Canadian biotechnology	Baum, Jac; Calabrese, T; Silverman, Bs	2000	706	41,53
19	The architecture of cooperation: Managing coordination costs and appropriation concerns in strategic alliances	Gulati, R; Singh, H	1998	682	35,89

Table 4.3 (*cont.*)

	Publication title	Authors	Publication year	Total citations	Average per year
20	The network paradigm in organisational research: A review and typology	Borgatti, Sp; Foster, Pc	2003	619	44,21
21	The changing-role of marketing in the corporation	Webster, Fe	1992	613	24,52
22	Redundant governance structures: An analysis of structural and relational embeddedness in the steel and semiconductor industries	Rowley, T; Behrens, D; Krackhardt, D	2000	604	35,53
23	A resource-based theory of strategic alliances	Das, Tk; Teng, Bs	2000	600	35,29
24	Ambiguity and the process of knowledge transfer in strategic alliances	Simonin, BL	1999	595	33,06
25	Interorganisational alliances and the performance of firms: A study of growth and innovation rates in a high-technology industry	Stuart, TE	2000	541	31,82

(*Sources:* Our elaboration from ISI web of Science)

the role of experience in managing inter-firm relationships, analysing firms' network position, rate of growth, and portfolios of collaborative activities. The second most cited article (1764 citations) is a review on the topic of firms' absorptive capacity, written by Zahra and George in the *Academy of Management Review*. In this article, the authors distinguish between firms' potential and realised capacity, highlighting the conditions under which firms' potential and realised capacities can influence the creation and maintenance of a competitive advantage. This second article has an ample focus for different areas of management, strategy, and organisation studies. The third article (1411 citations) is 'Competition for competence and inter-partner learning within international strategic alliances' written by Hamel and published in the *Strategic Management Journal*. It focuses on global competition and specifically on how collaborations may provide an opportunity for one partner to internalise the skills of the others, thus improving its position by means of alliances. This study suggests that not all partners are equally able to learn. Asymmetries in learning may also subsequently alter the relative bargaining power of partners. In the fourth most cited document (1223 citations), 'Alliances and networks,' published in the *Strategic Management Journal*, Gulati introduces a social network perspective to the study of strategic alliances. The author identifies five key issues for the study of alliances: (1) alliance formation, (2) the choice of governance structure, (3) alliance dynamic evolution, (4) the performance of alliances, and (5) future consequences over performance experimented by firms entering alliances. Brown and Eisenhardt rank fifth with an article published in the *Administrative Science Quarterly* journal titled 'The art of continuous change: Linking complexity theory and time-paced evolution in relentlessly shifting organizations' (1033 citations). In this article the authors examine how organisations engage in continuous change in the computer industry. Successful firms rely on a wide variety of multi-product strategies. Other important studies for this field of research are: 'Strategic alliances and interfirm knowledge transfer,' written by Mowery et al. (949 citations); 'Between trust and control: Developing confidence in partner cooperation in alliances,' written by Das and Teng (868 citations); 'Characteristics of partnership success – partnership attributes, communication behavior, and conflict-resolution techniques,' written by Mohr and Spekman (861 citations); 'Strategic alliance structuring – a game-theoretic and transaction cost examination of interfirm cooperation,' written by Parkhe (848 citations); and lastly, 'Learning and protection of proprietary assets in strategic alliances: Building relational capital,' written by Kale et al. (821 citations), closes the top 10 of the most cited articles related to strategic alliances.

4.5 Bibliographic Coupling Results

The bibliographic coupling analysis looks at emergent trends in the literature. The mentioned analysis does not look at the past; rather, it explores the future direction of the literature. In the authors' analysis eighteen clusters were found, but only the most important seven were considered. The others were excluded because of their low degree of centrality (a measure linked to the number of citations). For each cluster considered, only the most relevant papers were selected in terms of degree of centrality. Results are shown in Figure 4.2 and Table 4.4. In Figure 4.2, the main six clusters are reported. Other minor clusters are represented in grey.

Cluster 1 is defined as 'alliances in an international context.' It considers numerous articles focused on the issue of international management research. When a company decides to internationalise its activities, international management becomes relevant, and hence needs to be carefully analysed (Werner 2002) from different viewpoints. In particular, several aspects are analysed, such as the descriptions and measurement of internationalisation (including levels and speed), the antecedents and consequences of internationalisation, the entry mode choice and the predictors of the entry mode choice, partners' selection and relations, and the process of knowledge transfer (transfer of experts, geographical knowledge flows, access to knowledge networks, patent sharing or licensing, the role of subsidiary and multinational team management, and expatriate management). Reid et al. (2001) discuss the process of alliance formation through interfirm collaborations among knowledge-intensive firms. Particular attention is paid to the stage of critical alliance formation. Firms' performance in knowledge creation is evaluated considering a number of factors, including: (a) the motivation for an alliance, (b) partner firm characteristics (the ability to develop and support valuable resources),

Table 4.4 Clusters of articles from bibliographic coupling

Author and source	Degree	Cluster	
Werner (2002) *Journal of Management*	2000.005	1	
Reid et al. (2001) *International Journal of Management Reviews*	1240.001	1	
Sanchez-Peinado and Menguzzato-Boulard (2009) *Industrial Marketing Management*	1160.001	1	
Lavie and Miller (2008) *Organization Science*	1140.001	1	
Beamish and Lupton (2009) *Academy of Management Perspectives*	1090.001	1	Alliances in an
Nielsen (2007) *International Business Review*	1050.001	1	international
Schuler (2001) *International Journal of Human Resource Management*	1040.005	1	context
Franco (2011) *European Journal of International Management*	1030.005	1	
Kauser and Shaw (2004) *International Marketing Review*	1020.003	1	
Lei (2000) *International Journal of Technology Management*	1000.001	1	
Gimeno and Woo (1996) *Advances In Strategic Management*	1000.001	1	
Veiga and Franco (2015) *Management Research Review*	990.004	1	
Schilke and Cook (2015) *Strategic Management Journal*	1190.005	2	
Silva et al. (2012) *International Business Review*	1130.005	2	
Graebner (2009) *Academy of Management Journal*	1100.005	2	
Mccarter et al. (2011) *Academy of Management Review*	1020.004	2	Trust &
Bensaou and Anderson (1999) *Organization Science*	1000.001	2	cooperation
Lakhal and H'mida (2009) *International Journal of Technology Management*	970.005	2	
Deitz et al. (2010) *Industrial Marketing Management*	920.005	2	
Francis et al. (2009) *International Business Review*	920.004	2	
Jiang et al. (2013) *Industrial Marketing Management*	910.004	2	
Wei et al. (2012) *International Journal of Production Economics*	900.001	2	

Table 4.4 (*cont.*)

Author and source	Degree	Cluster	
Ahuja et al. (2008) *Academy of Management Annals*	3280.005	3	
Phelps (2010) *Academy of Management Journal*	1370.003	3	
Vanhaverbeke et al. (2015) *Journal of Product Innovation Management*	1270.035	3	
Lichtenthaler Muethel (2012) *Journal of Engineering and Technology Management*	1080.034	3	Impact of alliance on innovation performance
Bogers and Lhuillery (2011) *Industry and Innovation*	1020.034	3	
Lavie and Drori (2012) *Organization Science*	1000.003	3	
Haeussler et al. (2012) *Journal of Business Venturing*	970.004	3	
Beck et al. (2014) *European Journal of International Management*	940.034	3	
Hung and Chou (2013) *Technovation*	940.034	3	
Xia and Roper (2008) *Technovation*	920.034	3	
Foss et al. (2010) *Journal of Management Studies*	1430.003	4	
Liu et al. (2010) *Journal of World Business*	1330.005	4	
Heimeriks et al. (2007) *Strategic Organization*	1330.001	4	Knowledge sharing, absorption, transfer, and exchange, within firms' alliance
Heimeriks and Duysters (2007) *Journal of Management Studies*	1240.001	4	
Maurer et al. (2011) *Organization Studies*	1130.003	4	
Van Wijk et al. (2008) *Journal of Management Studies*	1150.003	4	
Yang et al. (2014) *Industrial Marketing Management*	1140.003	4	
Najafi-Tavani et al. (2012) *Management International Review*	1030.003	4	
Badir and O'Connor (2015) *Journal of Product Innovation Management*	930.003	4	
Tzabbar et al. (2008) *Strategic Organization*	921.667	4	
Brass et al. (2004) *Academy of Management Journal*	1970.001	5	

Reference	Value	Group	Description
Phelps et al. (2012) Journal of Management	1810.003	5	
Huggins (2010) International Journal of Management Reviews	1470.003	5	
Gonzalez-Campo (2010) Innovar-Revista De Ciencias Administrativas Y Sociales	1470.001	5	Network dimension of strategic alliances
Huggins and Johnston (2010) Entrepreneurship and Regional Development	1440.001	5	
Castro and Roldan (2013) International Business Review	1400.001	5	
Sytch et al. (2012) Organization Science	1300.003	5	
Goerzen (2007) Strategic Management Journal	1220.001	5	
Alguezaui and Filieri (2010) Journal of Knowledge Management	1180.003	5	
Lavie (2007) Strategic Management Journal	1150.005	5	
Rice et al. (2012) Journal of Management & Organization	750.004	6	
Hardy et al. (2003) Journal of Management Studies	670.001	6	
Rivera-Santos and Rufin (2010) Journal of Business Ethics	660.833	6	
Tian et al. (2013) Systems Research and Behavioral Science	630.034	6	Governance mechanism in strategic alliance
Park et al. (2014) Industrial Marketing Management	600.004	6	
Czernek and Czakon (2016) Tourism Management	560.004	6	
Talke and Hultink (2010) Journal of Product Innovation Management	560.004	6	
Ritala and Hurmelinna-Laukkanen (2009) Technovation	560.004	6	
Arya and Salk (2006) Business Ethics Quarterly	530.833	6	
Ritala and Sainio (2014) Technology Analysis & Strategic Management	520.004	6	

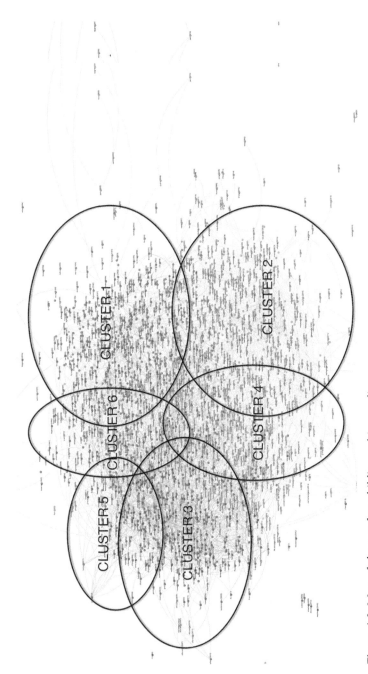

Figure 4.2 Map of clusters from bibliographic coupling
Source: Elaboration of the authors with VOSviewer.

(c) absorptive capacity, (d) combinative capability, (e) experience with alliances, and (f) appropriate design for knowledge exchange.

Sanchez-Peinado and Menguzzato-Boulard (2009) provide empirical evidence on the use of international strategic alliances to support diversification strategies. They find that international strategic alliances play an important role in overcoming market barriers and learning how and where to diversify. Firms seem to use these strategic options as learning instruments to acquire the know-how and capabilities necessary to grow into new businesses. Strategic alliances appear an efficient option in addition to internal development or acquisition, especially when the degrees of the desired diversification are significant, but not very high (in the latter case full integration appears to be a better choice). Lavie and Miller (2008) introduce the notion of alliance portfolio internationalisation (API), which refers to the degree of partners' foreignness in a firm's collection of several alliance relationships. They develop a framework to explain alliances' impact on firms' performance. The former is expected to initially decline, then improve, and finally decline again. This sigmoid relationship is ascribed to evolving learning effects that shape the net benefits of alliances. When firms' alliance portfolio, on average, consists of proximate foreign partners, firms may fail to recognise latent national differences. However, at moderate levels, the absorptive capacity and specialised collaborative routines support the exchange of valuable network resources. Nevertheless, high levels of alliances undermine firms' performance because of the failure of collaborative routines and mounting liabilities of cross-national differences. The study of Nielsen (2007) contributes to the understanding of the role of both structure (prior experience, partner reputation, and country risk) and the alliance process (collaborative know-how, trust, protectiveness, complementarities, and cultural distance) in determining alliance performance. While some argue that process matters more than structure (e.g. Kauser and Shaw 2004), it seems that structure and process are complements in determining alliance performance. Schuler (2001) focuses on the critical aspects of the various international alliance stages, considering many alliance failures, in conjunction with the reasons for their establishment, development, implementation, and advancement. A focal point is the indication that the quality of human resource management is critical to alliance success. Moreover, international strategic alliances can significantly facilitate new product development (Lei 2000), although it is necessary to consider the impact of both behavioural and organisational characteristics for the success of international strategic alliances. In the theoretical framework developed by the various authors, the component of firms' growth remains at the periphery, while in several contributions alliances appeared as the major determinant of growth, together with patent propensity, innovation, and firms' specialisation (Niosi 2003).

A gap in this literature is the lack of more extensive empirical testing: each article focuses only on a specific aspect, using a specific country sample. Thus, no general verification of the various hypotheses has been carried out, and a weak link is established with the literature of international business, where multiple county studies are frequently developed.

Cluster 2 is defined by inserting the approach of trust and cooperation within the analysis of alliances. The article with the highest degree of similarities is that of Schilke and Cook (2015), which reflects on the relative importance of the calculative and relational perspective, providing an integrative model. The main assumption tested is that the calculative perspective (represented by the various contractual safeguards) has higher predictive power when the partner lacks a favourable reputation. In contrast, the relational perspective (represented by organisational culture) predicts trustworthiness more strongly when familiarity with the partner organisation is high. Silva et al. (2012) reflect on the positive relationship between trust and performance. Trust, measured in its various dimensions – such as confidence, goodwill trust, competence trust, and contractual trust – works as a catalyser for doing what is right and avoiding what may hurt the partner's interests, therefore increasing satisfaction within the alliance. The reciprocity of attitudes is likely to feed this process. The results reported by the article suggest that when controlled for the experience and size of a firm, trust has a strong and positive effect on performance. In contrast, Graebner (2009) examines the acquisition process and decision making from the viewpoints of both buyers and sellers. She highlights that, unlike the common view that members of a dyadic relation share symmetric trusting beliefs, often asymmetries between buyers and sellers emerge, caused by errors and wrong perceptions. These imbalances may cause seller vulnerability and buyer deceit. Prior literature on international alliances had primarily focused on the process of setting the deal. Many articles are now reflecting on the different alliance stages – such as initiation, reconfiguration, or termination – discussing the impact that changes have on the stability of the alliance itself and on knowledge leakages (Jiang et al. 2013). Jiang et al. found that only moderate levels of trust in partners' goodwill constrain knowledge leakage, while either low or high levels trigger it. In other words, too little or too much trust in partners' goodwill induces opportunism in knowledge transfer between alliance firms. In contrast to the effect of trust in goodwill, trust in competence effectively avoids knowledge leakage because the focal firm's belief in a partner's competence triggers intense monitoring efforts in knowledge sharing. By combining those findings, this research provides a more refined view of the relationships between trust in alliances and knowledge leakage. For Deitz et al. (2010), the effect of trust in alliances must be separated from the issue of complementarity. Their results illustrate the distinct effects of resource complementarity and trust upon JV stability and cooperation: trust is most influential in newer JVs, while the presence of resource complementarity is more critical in older ventures. The effect of both personal relationships and trust is studied by Francis et al. (2009), analysing the link between trust, inter-firm adaptation, and performance. Trust is a key variable that initially links two firms, as trust is the basis for establishing meaningful communication. After trust and communication are established, the creation of valuable resources significantly impacts firms' adaptation, and, therefore, firms' performance. A different aspect is studied by Wei et al. (2012): logistic information integration in relation to inter-organisational trust in the case of the buyer–supplier chain. Transactional and relational mechanisms, once supported by trust and by logistic integration, are helpful for improving performance.

Trust and cooperation are studied particularly in two contexts: (a) within buyer and supplier inter-organisational relationships, and (b) within R&D networks.

This stream of literature on alliances, trust, and cooperation is quite creative, but it has not yet developed unified methodologies to measure and evaluate this phenomenon. Different levels and forms of trust escape from the analysis and many different proxies have been implemented with unsatisfactory results.

Cluster 3 is primarily focused on the impact of alliances on innovation performance. Strategic alliances are a means to gain access to knowledge, resources, and capabilities. The approach developed by this stream of literature is in line with a post-Schumpeterian view, overcoming the idea that only large monopolistic firms can be considered the key sources of innovation in modern economies, and a broader set of innovation determinants are investigated. The work of Ahuja et al. (2008) is the article that is most representative of this cluster, and puts forward an interesting theoretical framework making a distinction between the determinants of innovative efforts (more related to specific incentives/possibilities to R&D investment) and innovative outputs (where innovation is less programmable, being more related to specific research paths, technological opportunities, creativity, and serendipity). Thus, the determinants of the former are not the same as of the latter. The article explicitly focuses on the management literature in this area, recognising four broad issues: the industry's structure, firm characteristics, intra-organisational attributes, and institutional influences (the supply of science, the nature and degree of science–industry relationships, and the appropriability regime). The market's structure reflects the influence of competition and collaboration, as well as the roles of buyers and suppliers in influencing innovation performance, like the many observable attributes of a firm, such as size, scope, and access to external sources of knowledge through alliances. In addition to that, the market structure depends on the number of independent research efforts promoted and on the presence of a substructure of inter-firm linkages which may act as an information channel providing speedy access to knowledge spill-overs. Industries with poorly connected substructures may convey information less efficiently than industries marked by more efficiently connected substructures, leading to differences in the rates of technical advance.

In general, the literature shows that external technology acquisition through alliances positively affects firms' performance, testing the influence of the structure and composition of firms' alliance networks (examining different characteristics, such as: diversity, density, type of collaboration being upstream, horizontal or vertical, repeated ties, and alliance duration) and firms' exploratory innovation (knowledge which is new, compared to the firm's extant knowledge). According to the findings of Phelps (2010), alliances can spur exploratory innovation when they provide access to technologically diverse partners that are densely connected to each other (network closure: wherein a firm's partners are also partners).

Interestingly, many authors (Bogers and Lhuillery 2011; Haeussler et al. 2012; Beck and Schenker-Wicki 2014) have found that the availability of internal resources, like intensity or continuity of R&D, can either complement or substitute for collaboration, depending on its optimal level, where the degree of specialisation of technological capabilities may play a moderating role. This is an intellectual statement that deserves future studies. As expected, academic collaborations with fellow university scientists drive knowledge creation, whereas collaboration with industrial partners drives knowledge application (Lavie and Drori 2012).

More specifically, cluster 4 deals with the issue of knowledge sharing, knowledge absorption, knowledge transfer, and knowledge exchange within firms' alliances: thus with the complex phenomenon of vicarious and voluntary learning. Knowledge governance – choosing structures and mechanisms that can influence the processes of sharing and creating knowledge – has become a distinct issue in several articles using both a theoretical (Foss et al. 2010) and an empirical (Liu et al. 2010; Heimeriks et al. 2007) perspective. Although alliance structures and similarities among alliance partners may facilitate knowledge acquisition, the main results of the research presented suggest that learning opportunities are not limited by the mode or symmetry of the partnerships, but many other factors seem to intervene, such as the presence of a high level of knowledge stocks (proxied by accumulated R&D, patents and star scientists), and high level of quality patents (proxied by forwards citations). Clearly, high levels of trust also facilitate knowledge learning and positive outcomes of alliances (Liu et al. 2010). Another interesting theme developed is the so called ambidexterity dimension (Yang et al. 2014), in which firms are involved both in knowledge exchange and knowledge protection. Moreover, they have to find the right balance, maximising the benefits of alliances while reducing the risk of partner opportunism and knowledge leakages.

Articles in cluster 5 look at strategic alliances as inter-organisation constructs embedded in social and inter-unit networks offering both opportunities for and constraints on behaviour. Networks are seen as a multidimensional structures ranging from interpersonal to inter-organisational. The two most central articles in this cluster are both literature reviews. This explains why said articles occupy a central position in the cluster, and highlights the existence of an extensive literature on this matter. The article of Brass et al. (2004) reviews the literature on antecedents and the consequences of network at different levels of analysis. It looks at the main drivers explaining the forming of inter-organisational networks and the role of the networking experience in explaining firms' different learning capabilities. Great attention is paid to the issue of trust, and how the interplay between different forms of trust affects the development of strategic networks in the different phases of their life cycle. Other antecedents that significantly affect the forming of strategic networks are the existence of shared norms, the role of monitoring capacity, the issue of equity, and the role of the historical and institutional context. With respect to the consequences, inter-organisational networks stimulate the socialisation of information, mutual imitation, learning, and innovation, enhancing the chances of firms' survival and improving their performances. Phelps et al. (2012) look at the relation between network and knowledge outcomes. Their review confirms that structural, relational, nodal, and knowledge properties of strategic networks affect the capability of firms to create, learn, and absorb knowledge. However, it also points to a number of deficiencies requiring additional research, such as the excessive emphasis on the structural and relational properties of networks and the need to look more to the institutional context in which those networks are embedded; second, the tendency to consider casual mechanisms linking elements of the network to knowledge outcomes as isomorphic across levels; third, the structure of the network is often assumed exogenous rather than endogenous to knowledge-related dependent variables and to unobserved characteristics of nodes. The latter point is common to Brass et al. (2004), who claim the need to focus on the dynamic explanation of the evolution of networks across time. In a similar vein, Huggins (2001) looks at knowledge networks and more specifically at networks as strategic resources to access knowledge. His contribution is mainly theoretical. He points out the need to distinguish between social capital and network capital. The second is defined as an investment in calculative relations through which firms gain access to knowledge to enhance expected economic returns. Differently from social capital, network capital can be strategically managed to influence knowledge flows across companies. This distinction is operationalised by Huggins and Johnston (2010), who show that social capital is more significant among firms belonging to the same region. In contrast, the calculative and strategic nature of network capital plays a more significant role among firms belonging to different institutional settings. Castro and Roldán (2013) also study the role of social capital. However, they look at its mediating role with respect to international performances of multinational companies. Their findings suggest that two dimensions of social capital (relational and resource-based) mediate the effect of structural variables on international market share. The issue of social capital is also investigated in Alguezaui and Filieri (2010), highlighting the different effects of two alternative configurations: sparse versus cohesive networks. The remaining articles look at strategic alliances in networks from different perspectives. Gulati et al. (2012) focus on strategic alliances as bridging ties. They point out how firms entering this kind of relationship are motivated by incentives and opportunities embedded in their existing network structure in terms of value-creation and value-distribution. Goerzen (2007) highlights the negative effect of repeated strategic partnering. Finally, Lavie (2007) looks at the portfolio of strategic alliances, highlighting both the effect of resource availability and the competitive position of the parties involved.

To conclude, the articles in cluster 5 focus more on the network effects and the properties of networks in which strategic alliances are embedded. They devote their analysis to network properties, which in turn are influenced by network structure (density, centrality, and cohesion), and to the characteristics of each node (i.e. network position, ego network, relative bargaining power of actors, and type of relations). It may be that decentralised networks are superior when they are organised according to 'small world' principles (Brass et al. 2004). Moreover, network cohesion among venture alliances may increase the likelihood that these alliances will promote market sales. In the evolution of networks, nodes with more proximate ties, bridging across many network communities, are creating more bridging ties in subsequent periods. As a consequence, they activate an unbalanced path of growth (Gulati et al. 2012).

In this perspective, these articles highlight the multidimensional character of these networks, and the distinction between structural and relational properties of these networks and resource accessibility and availability. The focus is either on knowledge or internationalisation outcomes. Great attention has been paid to the concept of social capital and the difference compared to network capital as a more calculative and strategic form of social capital. Many authors suggest the need to look at the evolution of strategic networks over time, and in relation to strategic alliances as micro foundations of the networking process. There are others that suggest the need to decompose social capital in its dimensions in order to understand how they are related with each other and affect knowledge and internationalisation outcomes.

Articles in cluster 6 focus on the effect of different governance mechanisms on the performance of strategic alliances. By using a sample from Australian small-and-medium-sized manufacturing enterprises, Rice et al. (2012) analyse the importance of alliances as vehicles allowing firms to access or acquire external resources, hence shoring up capability gaps and building new capabilities. In contrast, Hardy et al. (2003) focus on how knowledge outcomes of strategic alliances relate to the nature of collaboration. Their findings suggest both embeddedness and involvement as critical factors in influencing partners' capability to achieve expected knowledge outcomes in strategic alliances. Moreover, not only does the acquisition of new resources play a leading role in alliance governance and success but also the partners' sector, because it makes alternative mechanisms available to partners (Rivera-Santos and Rufín 2010). In particular, the latter article looks at strategic alliances between business and non-governmental organisations and finds that this peculiar form of strategic alliance relies more on trust-based mechanism even if those mechanisms are harder to build than in business-to-business alliances. In contrast, Tian et al. (2013) focus on managerial incentives and find that wealth-oriented incentives, unlike career incentives, have an inverted U-shaped effect on knowledge acquisition through strategic alliances. Articles in this cluster pay great attention to the issue of coopetition, which is collaboration between competing firms. Park et al. (2014) look at the interplay between competition and cooperation in strategic alliances among firms in the semiconductor industry. Their findings suggest that firms need to balance cooperation and competition. Every time one of these dimensions becomes dominant in the strategic alliance, firms' performances tend to deteriorate. Czerneka and Czakon (2016) focus on the role of trust in sustaining coopetition among strategic partners in the tourist sector. Their findings, consistently with the articles in cluster 2, suggest that different trust mechanisms affect the outcomes of strategic alliances in various ways. Ritala and Hurmelinna-Laukkanen (2009) focus on the factors that distinguish coopetition from collaboration. They find that the ability of a firm to reap benefits in innovation-related coopetition is contingent on factors that enable the creation of a collective value, and on those that facilitate the individual appropriability of innovation and related profits involved. The effectiveness of these factors depends on the novelty of the innovation with respect to current markets and technology. Ritala and Sainio (2014) extend those findings, showing that coopetition is negatively related to technological radicality but positively related to new radical business models. Finally, Talke and Hultink (2010) highlight the need to extend the gaze to stakeholders' barriers rather than only to those of customers, in order to enhance the likelihood of success in launching new products. The review of the literature developed around this cluster suggests that there is still a lot of work to be done in order to develop a clear conceptualisation of the meaning of governance in strategic alliances. Moreover, a lot of work is likewise necessary to build a systematic framework of verified and tested hypotheses, going beyond the effort to find positive and/or negative relationships to strategic performances of alliances. Authors in this cluster could benefit extensively from confronting themselves with cluster 2, integrating the issue of trust and cooperation.

4.6 Discussion and Conclusions

Alliances have become an important and dominant field in international business and management studies. Studies on strategic alliances have also highlighted that alliances are drivers of superior performance (Hagedooorn and Schakenraad 1994; Lavie and Drori 2012). The increasing relevance of this new organisational form is rooted in the changes of global economies, where economic fragmentation is linked to new global supply chains and new conditions of trades, and where the globalisation of knowledge production implies a new network-based cooperative model of research activity. In his book on alliances, Niosi (1995) proposed the evolutionary explanation that alliances are a new routine that responds to three new major environmental changes, that is: (a) increasing international competition, with the entry of Asian and other emerging countries, (b) the triple technological revolution of biotech, ITC and nanotech, and (c) an explosion in the number of innovation agents (more R&D firms, research universities, and public R&D labs). Alliances allow firms to increase their competitive scale also at global level, to use complementary and similar knowledge to better perform research activities, and to use public knowledge to accelerate the rate of invention and the process of science commercialisation.

No dominant theorisation is emerging in the current managerial and business literature, and the transaction cost theory represents a weak analytical support for the explanation of why alliances exist. It underestimates the role of cooperative research in making hierarchies a more efficient choice to deal with the creation of knowledge and new technology. However, in a post–Schumpeterian-evolutionary view, hierarchies and large organisations are not the only efficient alternatives within the economic system. Mobile enterprise boundaries are allowed by alliances outside the paradigm of market-hierarchies. Alliances allow the use of external capabilities and knowledge. It is important to specify that we do not allude simply to an open model where knowledge sources are external (Chesbrough 2006), but to a specific new model: a new learning process where actors are in part external to the focal firms, as originally discussed by Powel et al. (1996). Once we implement a firm-specific strategy, we focus on different characteristics influencing the performance of the economic agent linked by a close relationship (Niosi 1995): reduction of uncertainty, reduction of costs, sharing of resources, sharing of knowledge and R&D costs, copying with short life cycles of products, searching of standards and technical compatibility, improvement in reaching the market, acceleration of innovation, better use of knowledge possessed by users, and access to localised externalities.

An important element that has emerged in the current literature is the existence of non-linearity of the phenomena under observation.

Curvilinear modes have emerged in analysing the relationships among innovation, alliance type, knowledge similarity/complementarity, trust and performance, network dimension, and models of governance. Thus, we entered into a dynamic non-neoclassical world of multiple equilibria, equifinality (similar performances are reached by different structures), and localised ecologies (multiple actors, private and public, are co-evolving towards different patterns of growth). The literature covered in this work has left unexplored the intellectual issue of providing more sound empirical evidence for the analysed phenomena.

In fact, *ad-hoc* hypotheses are tested in *ad-hoc* contexts, but their generalisation (possible only with replicated tests/results) is still not a prevailing research path. We need more research pieces based on multi-country/multi-sector/multi-firm studies. No dominant journals have played the role of unifying the dispersed analytical efforts, and the fields of management and international business appear very poorly integrated.

Several future important open issues remain unanswered such as, for instance, a clearer analysis regarding partners' selection (Who allies with whom); the role played by knowledge similarity vs. knowledge complementarity in determining alliances' success (Rothaermel and Deeds 2006); the specific role played by alliances vs. acquisitions in knowledge exploration or exploitation, and the role played by the geography of connectedness in close clusters and districts versus larger networks, based on regional or global scale (Hagedoorn and Wang 2012); the way in which alliances foster knowledge access, and/or knowledge integration, and/or knowledge acquisition; and the importance of prior alliances post-acquisition (Hakanson 1995; Bresman et al. 2010). In between these research perspectives, researchers are focusing more and more on the structures of networks as a driver of both knowledge flows and governance structuring. However, networks are the results of partners' selection, and dependent and independent variables are often treated alternatively as endogenous or exogenous: thus endogeneity is not avoided.

In this chapter, a bibliographic coupling analysis was implemented to identify the emerging clusters in the field of strategic alliances among authors sharing the same bibliography, and thus, working on a similar path research. Unlike co-citation analysis, which is backward looking and where clusters are formed according to the frequency with which authors are cited together (in a database of papers), bibliographic coupling is forward looking, because it clusters papers that share a common bibliography. Our analysis confirms that strategic alliances are a complex and articulated field of study.

Six potential clusters were identified with the highest degree of centrality. The in-depth analysis of these six clusters highlighted the persistence of several issues in this field of study: (1) strategic alliance internationalisation, (2) trust and cooperation, (3) impact of alliances on firms' innovative performance, (4) impact on knowledge creation and appropriation, (5) analysis of the bi-univocal relationship between network structure and alliance performance, and (6) impact of the different types of governance on alliances' evolution and innovative performance.

After acknowledging the positive role played by alliances in the economy, we have to ask ourselves about the policy implications of our work. Should governments be more effective in promoting alliances? Is the ever-growing interest in the intensification of incentives on alliances-related innovation policy justified? The increasing public support for technical cooperation in all advanced and emerging countries appears to be a beneficial trend. Many government programmes (US- and EU-based) have supported several programmes, in high-tech sectors (Niosi 1995), in health promotion (Gillies 1998), in cluster policy initiatives (Borras and Tsagdis 2008), and considering environmental policies (del Brío et al. 2003), accelerating the introduction of technical change and avoiding R&D duplication efforts. However, the government should enforce the overall reduction of management costs associated to large alliances or consortia. Industry–university alliances were found to be more exploration-oriented while inter-firm alliances were generally more exploitative. However, Ganzaroli et al. (2016) highlighted that the effective assimilation and utilisation of acquired knowledge is also related to the technological distance of firms. Technological distance enhances technological performance, influencing above all explorative performances in terms of innovation.

Governments should regularly evaluate their programmes, thus improving their ability to take corrective actions. Value creation and value appropriation in alliances is another key issue, extensively discussed in the papers examined. Experience is positively associated with good alliance performances, but there is a mechanism of decreasing returns at work with the increasing number of alliances that a firm is able to organise. Managers should adopt alliance activity, balancing advantages and disadvantages. The latter are often underestimated: the loss of proprietary information, the complexity of management, financial and organisational risks, the risk of becoming dependent (where the partner exhibits opportunistic behaviour), the loss of decision autonomy, the loss of flexibility, and long-term viability (Tjemkes et al. 2013). In addition, internal and/or external contingencies constitute a threat to long-term stability (Das and Teng 2000). Paradoxically, although firms have increased the use of alliances, the failure rate seems to keep climbing (Dacin et al. 1997; De Man 2005; Hoang and Rothaermel 2005). Managers should carefully evaluate their decisions along the entire development stage of an alliance: formulation, partner selection, negotiation, design, management, evaluation, and termination (Das 2010).

Clearly, this work suffers from several limitations. In this paper, bibliographic coupling is applied in a static way. This served to identify the main clusters of common research. A further development could be to investigate the evolution of this field of study implementing bibliographic coupling to the shortest time-defined segments of the literature. This would allow an understanding of how the process of specialisation is progressing over time, and the contents of the new research paths.

References

Ahuja, G., Lampert, C. M., and Tandon, V. 2008. Moving beyond Schumpeter: Management research on the determinants of technological innovation. *The Academy of Management Annals* 2(1): 1–98.

Alguezaui, S. and Filieri, R. 2010. Investigating the role of social capital in innovation: Sparse versus dense network. *Journal of Knowledge Management* 14(6): 891–909.

Appio, F. P., Cesaroni, F., and Di Minin, A. 2014. Visualizing the structure and bridges of the intellectual property management and strategy literature: A document co-citation analysis. *Scientometrics* 101(1): 623–661.

Arora, A., Fosfuri, A., and Gambardella, A. 2001. *Markets for Technology: Economics of Innovation and Corporate Strategy*. Cambridge, MA: The MIT Press.

Arora, A. and Gambardella, A. 1994. Evaluating technological information and utilizing it: scientific knowledge, technological capability, and external linkages in biotechnology. *Journal of Economic Behavior & Organization* 24(1): 91–114.

Barney, J. 1991. Firm resources and sustained competitive advantage. *Journal of Management* 17(1): 99–120.

Baum, J., Calabrese, T., and Silverman, B. 2000. Don't go alone: alliance network composition and startups' performance in Canadian biotechnology. *Strategic Management Journal* 21: 267–294.

Baumgartner, H. and Pieters, R. 2003 The structural influence of marketing journals: a citation analysis of the discipline and its subareas over time. *Journal of Marketing* 17(2): 123–139.

Beall, J. and Kafadar, K. 2007 Measuring typographical errors' impact on retrieval in bibliographic databases. *Cataloging & Classification Quarterly* 44(3–4): 197–211.

Beck, M. and Schenker-Wicki, A. 2014. Cooperating with external partners: the importance of diversity for innovation performance. *European Journal of International Management* 8(5): 548–569.

Belussi, F. and Orsi, L. 2016. (eds.) *Innovation, Alliances, and Networks in High-Tech Environments*. Abingdon: Routledge.

Bogers, M. and Lhuillery, S. 2011. A functional perspective on learning and innovation: Investigating the organization of absorptive capacity. *Industry and Innovation* 18(6): 581–610.

Borrás, S. and Tsagdis, D. 2008. *Cluster Policies in Europe*. Cheltenham, UK: Edward Elgar Publishing.

Boyack, K. W. 2009. Using detailed maps of science to identify potential collaborations. *Scientometrics* 79(1): 27–44.

Boyack, K. W. and Klavans, R. 2010. Co-citation analysis, bibliographic coupling, and direct citation: Which citation approach represents the research front most accurately? *Journal of the American Society for Information Science and Technology* 61(12), 2389–2404.

Brass, D. J., Galaskiewicz, J., Greve, H. R., and Tsai, W. 2004. Taking stock of networks and organizations: A multilevel perspective. *Academy of Management Journal* 47(6): 795–817.

Bresman, H., Birkinshaw, J., and Nobel, R. 2010. Knowledge transfer in international acquisitions. *Journal of International Business Studies* 41(1): 5–20.

Brown, S. L. and Eisenhardt, K. M. 1997. The art of continuous change: Linking complexity theory and time-paced evolution in relentlessly shifting organizations. *Administrative Science Quarterly* 42(1): 1–34.

Casey, D. L. and McMillan, G. S. 2008. Identifying the 'invisible colleges' of the 'industrial & labor relations review': A bibliometric approach. *Industrial and Labor Relations Review* 62(1): 126–132.

Castro, I. and Roldán, J. L. 2013. A mediation model between dimensions of social capital. *International Business Review* 22(6): 1034–1050.

Chesbrough, H. 2003. The era of open innovation. *The Mit Sloan Management Review* Spring: 35–41.

Chesbrough, H. W. 2006, *Open Business Models. How to Thrive in the New Innovation Landscape*. Boston, MA: Harvard Business School Press.

Cloodt, M., Hagedoorn, J., and Van Kranenburg, H. 2006. Mergers and acquisitions: Their effect on the innovative performance of companies in high-tech industries. *Research Policy* 35(5): 642–654.

Conner, K. R. and Prahalad, C. K. 1996. A resource-based theory of the firm: Knowledge versus opportunism. *Organization Science* 7(5): 477–501.

Czernek, K. and Czakon, W. 2016. Trust-building processes in tourist coopetition: The case of a Polish region. *Tourism Management* 52: 380–394.

Dacin, M. T., Hitt, M. A., and Levitas, E. 1997. Selecting partners for successful international alliances: Examination of US and Korean firms, *Journal of World Business*, 32(1): 3–16.

Dacin, M. T., Oliver, C., and Roy, J. P. (2007). The legitimacy of strategic alliances: An institutional perspective. *Strategic Management Journal* 28(2): 169–187.

Das, T. K. 2010. *Researching strategic alliances: emerging perspectives.* Charlotte, NC: IAP.

Das, T. K. and Teng, B. S. 1998. Between trust and control: Developing confidence in partner cooperation in alliances. *Academy of Management Review* 23(3): 491–512.

Das, T. K. and Teng, B. S. 2000. Instabilities of strategic alliances: An internal tensions perspective. *Organization Science* 11(1): 77–101.

De Bakker, F. G. A., Groenewegen, P., and Den Hond, F. 2005. A bibliometric analysis of 30 years of research and theory on corporate social responsibility and corporate social performance. *Business & Society* 44(3): 283–317.

Deeds, D. L. and Hill, C. W. 1996. Strategic alliances and the rate of new product development: An empirical study of entrepreneurial biotechnology firms. *Journal of Business Venturing* 11(1): 41–55.

del Brío, J. Á. and Junquera, B. 2003. A review of the literature on environmental innovation management in SMEs: Implications for public policies. *Technovation* 23(12): 939–948.

De Man, A. P. 2005. Alliance capability: A comparison of the alliance strength of European and American companies. *European Management Journal* 23(3): 315–323.

Deitz, G. D., Tokman, M., Richey, R. G., and Morgan, R. M. 2010. Joint venture stability and cooperation: Direct, indirect and contingent effects of resource complementarity and trust. *Industrial Marketing Management* 39(5): 862–873.

Doz, Y. and Hamel, G. 1998. *Alliances Advantage. The Art of Creating Value through Partnering*. Boston, MA: Harvard Business School Press.

Dyer, J. H. 1997. Effective interfirm collaboration: How firms minimize transaction costs and maximise transaction value. *Strategic Management Journal* 17: 271–291.

Dyer, J. H. and Singh, H. 1998. The relational view: Cooperative strategy and sources of interorganizational competitive advantage. *Academy of Management Review* 23(4): 660–679.

Eisenhardt, K. M. and Schoonhoven, C. B. 1996. Resource-based view of strategic alliance formation: Strategic and social effects in entrepreneurial firms. *Organization Science* 7(2): 136–150.

Foss, N. J., Husted, K., and Michailova, S. 2010. Governing knowledge sharing in organizations: Levels of analysis, governance mechanisms, and research directions. *Journal of Management studies* 47(3): 455–482.

Francis, J., Mukherji, A., and Mukherji, J. 2009. Examining relational and resource influences on the performance of border region SMEs. *International Business Review* 18(4): 331–343.

Gans, J. and Stern, S. 2003. The product market and the market for ideas: Commercialization strategies for technology entrepreneurs. *Research Policy* 32(2): 333–350.

Ganzaroli, A., De Noni, I., Orsi, L., and Belussi, F. 2016. The combined effect of technological relatedness and knowledge utilization on explorative and exploitative invention performance post-M and A. *European Journal of Innovation Management* 19(2): 167–188.

Gillies, P. 1998. Effectiveness of alliances and partnerships for health promotion. *Health Promotion International* 13(2): 99–120.

Goerzen, A. 2007. Alliance networks and firm performance: The impact of repeated partnerships. *Strategic Management Journal* 28(5): 487–509.

Graebner, M. E. 2009. Caveat venditor: Trust asymmetries in acquisitions of entrepreneurial firms. *Academy of management Journal* 52(3): 435–472.

Graebner, M.E. and Eisenhardt, K.M., 2004. The seller's side of the story: Acquisition as courtship and governance as syndicate in entrepreneurial firms. *Administrative Science Quarterly* 49(3): 366–403.

Grant, R. M. 1996. Prospering in dynamically-competitive environments: Organizational capability as knowledge integration. *Organization Science* 7(4): 375–387.

Gulati, R. 1995. Does familiarity breed trust? The implications of repeated ties for contractual choice in alliances. *Academy of Management Journal* 38(1): 85–112.

Gulati, R. 1998. Alliances and networks. *Strategic Management Journal* 19: 293–317.

Gulati, R. and Singh, H. 1998. The architecture of cooperation: Managing coordination costs and appropriation concerns in strategic alliances. *Administrative Science Quarterly* 43: 781–814.

Gulati, R., Sytch, M., and Tatarynowicz, A. 2012. The rise and fall of small worlds: Exploring the dynamics of social structure. *Organization Science* 23(2): 449–471.

Haeussler, C., Patzelt, H., and Zahra, S. A. 2012. Strategic alliances and product development in high technology new firms: The moderating effect of technological capabilities. *Journal of Business Venturing* 27(2): 217–233.

Hagedoorn, J. 2002, Inter-firm R&D partnerships: An overview of major trends and patterns since 1960. *Research Policy* 31(4): 477–492.

Hagedoorn, J. and Schakenraad, J. 1994. The effect of strategic technology alliances on company performance. *Strategic Management Journal* 15(4): 291–309.

Hagedoorn, J. and Duysters, G. 2002a. External sources of innovative capabilities: The preferences for strategic alliances or mergers and acquisitions. *Journal of Management Studies* 39(2): 167–188.

Hagedoorn, J. and Duysters, G. 2002b. The effect of mergers and acquisitions on the technological performance of companies in a high-tech environment. *Technology Analysis & Strategic Management* 14(1): 67–85.

Hagedoorn, J. and Wang, N. 2012. Is there complementarity or substitutability between internal and external R&D strategies? *Research Policy* 41(6): 1072–1083.

Hakanson, L. 1995. Learning through acquisitions: Management and integration of foreign R&D laboratories. *International Studies of Management and Organization* 25(1–2): 121–157.

Hamel, G. 1991. Competition for competence and interpartner learning within international strategic alliances. *Strategic Management Journal* 12(1): 83–103.

Hamel, G., Doz, Y. L., and Prahalad, C. K. 1989. Collaborate with your competitors and win. *Harvard Business Review* 67(1): 133–139.

Hardy, C., Phillips, N., and Lawrence, T. B. 2003. Resources, knowledge and influence: The organizational effects of interorganizational collaboration. *Journal of Management Studies* 40(2): 321–347.

Heimeriks, K. H., Duysters, G., and Vanhaverbeke, W. 2007. Learning mechanisms and differential performance in alliance portfolios. *Strategic Organization* 5(4): 373–408.

Hennart, J. F. 1988. A transaction costs theory of equity joint ventures. *Strategic Management Journal* 9(4): 361–374.

Hitt, M. A., Hoskisson, R. E., Johnson, R. A., and Moesel, D. D. 1996. The market for corporate control and firm innovation. *Academy of Management Journal* 39(5): 1084–1119.

Hoang, H. and Rothaermel, F. T. 2005. The effect of general and partner-specific alliance experience on joint R&D project performance. *Academy of Management Journal* 48(2): 332–345.

Holton, G. J. 2000. *Einstein, History, and Other Passions: The Rebellion against Science at the End of the Twentieth Century.* Cambridge, MA: Harvard University Press.

Huggins, R. 2001. Inter-firm network policies and firm performance: evaluating the impact of initiatives in the United Kingdom. *Research Policy* 30(3): 443–458.

Huggins, R. and Johnston, A. 2010. Knowledge flow and inter-firm networks: The influence of network resources, spatial proximity and firm size. *Entrepreneurship & Regional Development* 22(5): 457–484.

Inkpen, A. and Beamish, P. W. 1997. Knowledge, bargaining power, and the instability of international joint ventures. *Academy of Management Review* 22(1): 177–202.

Jarneving, B. 2005. A comparison of two bibliometric methods for mapping of the research front. *Scientometrics* 65(2): 245–263.

Jarneving, B. 2007a. Bibliographic coupling and its application to research-front and other core documents. *Journal of Informetrics* 1(4): 287–307.

Jarneving, B. 2007b. Complete graphs and bibliographic coupling: A test of the applicability of bibliographic coupling for the identification of cognitive cores on the field level. *Journal of Informetrics* 1(4): 338–356.

Jiang, X., Li, M., Gao, S., Bao, Y., and Jiang, F. 2013. Managing knowledge leakage in strategic alliances: The effects of trust and formal contracts. *Industrial Marketing Management* 42(6): 983–991.

Kale, P., Singh, H., and Perlmutter, H. 2000. Learning and protection of proprietary assets in strategic alliances: Building relational capital. *Strategic Management Journal* 21(3): 217–237.

Kauser, S. and Shaw, V. 2004. The influence of behavioral and organizational characteristics on the success of international strategic alliances. *International Marketing Review* 21(1): 17–51.

Kogut, B. 1988. Joint ventures: Theoretical and empirical perspectives. *Strategic Management Journal* 9(4): 319–332.

Larsson, R., Bengtsson, L., Henriksson, K., and Sparks, J. 1998. The interorganizational learning dilemma: Collective knowledge development in strategic alliances. *Organization Science* 9(3): 285–305.

Lavie, D. 2007. Alliance portfolios and firm performance: A study of value creation and appropriation in the US software industry. *Strategic Management Journal* 28(12): 1187–1212.

Lavie, D. and Drori, I. 2012. Collaborating for knowledge creation and application: The case of nanotechnology research programs. *Organization Science* 23(3): 704–724.

Lavie, D. and Miller, S. R. 2008. Alliance portfolio internationalization and firm performance. *Organization Science* 19(4): 623–646.

Lei, D. T. 2000. Industry evolution and competence development: The imperatives of technological convergence. *International Journal of Technology Management* 19 (7–8): 699–738.

Levitt, B. and March, J. G. 1988. Organizational learning. *Annual Review of Sociology* 14: 19–340.

Ling, T. J. and Chen, Y. Y. 2012. Changes in the intellectual structure of Strategic Alliances Research 1980–2010. *Management Review* 31, October: 131–141.

Liu, C. L. E., Ghauri, P. N., and Sinkovics, R. R. 2010. Understanding the impact of relational capital and organizational learning on alliance outcomes. *Journal of World Business* 45(3): 237–249.

MacRoberts, M. H. and MacRoberts, B. R. 2007. Problems of citation analysis: a critical review. *Journal of the American Society for Information Science* 40(5): 342–349.

Mohr, J. and Spekman, R. 1994. Characteristics of partnership success: Partnership attributes, communication behavior, and conflict resolution techniques. *Strategic Management Journal* 15(2): 135–152.

Mowery, D., Oxley, J. and Silverman, B. 1996. Strategic alliances and interfirm knowledge transfer. *Strategic Management Journal* 17 (Suppl. Winter): 77–91.

Nelson, R. 1991. Why do firms differ, and how does it matter? *Strategic Management Journal* 12: 61–74.

Nielsen, B. B. 2007. Determining international strategic alliance performance: A multidimensional approach. *International Business Review* 16(3): 337–361.

Niosi, J. 1995. *Flexible Innovation: Technological Alliances in Canadian Industry.* Montreal: McGill-Queen's Press-MQUP.

Niosi J. 2003. Alliances are not enough explaining rapid growth in biotech firms. *Research Policy* 32(5): 737–750.

Nonaka, I. 1991. The knowledge-creating company. *Harvard Business Review* 69(6): 96–104.

Park, B. J. R., Srivastava, M. K., and Gnyawali, D. R. 2014. Walking the tight rope of coopetition: Impact of competition and cooperation intensities and balance on firm innovation performance. *Industrial Marketing Management* 43(2): 210–221.

Parkhe, A. 1993 Strategic alliance structuring: A game theoretic and transaction cost examination of interfirm cooperation. *Academy of Management Journal* 36(4): 794–829.

Persson, O., Danell, R., and Schneider, J. W. 2009. How to use Bibexcel for various types of bibliometric analysis. Celebrating scholarly communication studies: A Festschrift for Olle Persson at his 60th Birthday, 9–24.

Phelps, C. C. 2010. A longitudinal study of the influence of alliance network structure and composition on firm exploratory innovation. *Academy of Management Journal* 53(4): 890–913.

Phelps, C., Heidl, R., and Wadhwa, A. 2012. Knowledge, networks, and knowledge networks a review and research agenda. *Journal of Management* 38(4): 1115–1166.

Powell, W. W., Koput, K. W., and Smith-Doerr, L. 1996. Interorganizational collaboration and the locus of innovation: Networks of learning in biotechnology. *Administrative Science Quarterly* 41(1): 116–145.

Reid, D., Bussiere D., and Greenaway K. 2001. Alliance formation issues for knowledge-based enterprises. *International Journal of Management Reviews* 3(1): 79–100.

Rice, J., Liao, T. S., Martin, N., and Galvin, P. 2012. The role of strategic alliances in complementing firm capabilities. *Journal of Management & Organization* 18(6): 858–869.

Ritala, P. and Hurmelinna-Laukkanen, P. 2009. What's in it for me? Creating and appropriating value in innovation-related coopetition. *Technovation* 29(12): 819–828.

Ritala, P. and Sainio, L. M. 2014. Coopetition for radical innovation: technology, market and business-model perspectives. *Technology Analysis & Strategic Management* 26(2): 155–169.

Rivera-Santos, M. and Rufín, C. 2010. Odd couples: Understanding the governance of firm–NGO alliances. *Journal of Business Ethics* 94(1): 55–70.

Rosenkopf, L. and Almeida, P. 2003. Overcoming local search through alliances and mobility. *Management Science* 49(6): 751–766.

Rosenkopf, L. and Nerkar, A. 2001. Beyond local search: Boundary-spanning, exploration, and impact in the optical disk industry. *Strategic Management Journal* 22(4): 287–306.

Rothaermel, F. T. and Deeds, D. L. 2004. Exploration and exploitation alliances in biotechnology: A system of new product development. *Strategic Management Journal* 25(3): 201–221.

Rothaermel, F. T. and Deeds, D. L. 2006. Alliance type, alliance experience and alliance management capability in high-technology ventures. *Journal of Business Venturing* 21(4): 429–460.

Rumelt, R. P. 1974. *Strategy, Structure, and Economic Performance.* Boston, MA: Division of Research, Graduate School of Business Administration, Harvard University.

Sánchez-Peinado, L. and Menguzzato-Boulard, M. 2009. Antecedents of entry mode choice when diversifying. *Industrial Marketing Management* 38(8): 971–983.

Sandström, U. 2009. *Bibliometric Evaluation of Research Programs: A Study of Scientific Quality.* Report 6321: Swedish Environmental Protection Agency.

Schildt, H. A., Zahra, S. A., and Sillanpää, A. 2006. Scholarly communities in entrepreneurship research: A co-citation analysis. *Entrepreneurship Theory and Practice* 30(3): 399–415.

Schilke, O. and Cook, K. S. 2015. Sources of alliance partner trustworthiness: Integrating calculative and relational perspectives. *Strategic Management Journal* 36(2): 276–297.

Schuler, R. S. 2001. Human resource issues and activities in international joint ventures. *International Journal of Human Resource Management* 12(1): 1–52.

Shan, W., Walker, G., and Kogut, B. 1994. Interfirm cooperation and startup innovation in the biotechnology industry. *Strategic management journal* 15(5): 387–394.

Silva, S. C., Bradley, F., and Sousa, C. M. 2012. Empirical test of the trust–performance link in an international alliances context. *International Business Review* 21(2): 293–306.

Small, H. 1999. Visualizing science by citation mapping. *Journal of the American Society for Information Science* 50(9): 799–813.

Talke, K. and Hultink, E. J. 2010. Managing diffusion barriers when launching new products. *Journal of Product Innovation Management* 27(4): 537–553.

Tian, Y., Li, Y., and Wei, Z. 2013. Managerial incentive and external knowledge acquisition under technological uncertainty: A nested system perspective. *Systems Research and Behavioral Science* 30(3): 214–228.

Tjemkes, B., Vos, P., and Burgers, K. 2013. *Strategic Alliance Management.* London: Routledge.

Tsai, H. H. and Yang, J. M. 2010. Analysis of knowledge management trend by bibliometric approach. *Proceeding (s) of the WASET on Knowledge Management* 62(1): 174–178.

Uhlenbruck, K., Hitt, M.A., and Semadeni, M. 2006. Market value effects of acquisitions involving Internet firms: A resource-based analysis. *Strategic Management Journal* 27(10): 899–913.

Vermeulen, F. and Barkema, H. 2001. Learning through acquisitions. *Academy of Management Journal* 44(3): 457–476.

Wei, H. L., Wong, C. W., and Lai, K. H. 2012. Linking inter-organizational trust with logistics information integration and partner cooperation under environmental uncertainty. *International Journal of Production Economics* 139(2): 642–653.

Werner, S. 2002. Recent developments in international management research: A review of 20 top management journals. *Journal of Management* 28(3): 277–305.

Wernerfelt, B. 1995. The resource-based view of the firm: Ten years after. *Strategic Management Journal* 16(3): 171–174.

White, H. D. and McCain, K. W. 1998 Visualizing a discipline: An author co-citation analysis of information science, 1972–1995. *Journal of the American Society for Information Science* 49(4): 327–355.

Yang, S. M., Fang, S. C., Fang, S. R., and Chou, C. H. 2014. Knowledge exchange and knowledge protection in interorganizational learning: The ambidexterity perspective. *Industrial Marketing Management* 43(2): 346–358.

Zahra, S. A. and George, G. 2002. Absorptive capacity: A review, reconceptualization, and extension. *Academy of Management Review* 27(2): 185–203.

PART II

Innovation in Developing and Emerging Countries

5 National Systems of Innovation in Developing Countries

JORGE NIOSI

5.1 Introduction

Innovation is the main determinant of long-term economic development. In order to have a long-lasting effect, innovation must be produced and diffused regularly by innovation systems.

5.2 National Systems of Innovation (NIS) Defined

Chris Freeman, Bengt-Ake Lundvall and Richard Nelson, put in the public scientific domain the concept of national innovation systems. Many other publications, including those of Nelson, followed (Nelson and Sampat 2001; Nelson 2006). The literature has grown exponentially since the late 1980s.

"The network of institutions in the public and private sectors whose activities and interactions initiate, import, modify and diffuse new technologies." (Freeman 1987)

"The set of institutions whose interaction determines the innovative performance of national firms" (Nelson and Rosenberg 1993).

"A national system of innovation is the system of interacting private and public firms (either large or small), universities and government agencies aiming at the production of science and technology within national borders. Interaction among these units may be technical, commercial, legal, social, and financial, inasmuch as the goal of the interaction is the development, protection, financing or regulation of new science and technology" (Niosi, Bellon, Saviotti, and Crow 1993).

"The national institutions, their incentive structures and their competencies that determine the rate and direction of technological learning (or the volume and composition of change generating activities) in a country" (Patel and Pavitt 1994).

NIS are composed of several regional and several sectoral systems. The innovative regions are most often large metropolitan areas such as Chicago, Los Angeles, New York/New Jersey, Silicon Valley, and Washington metropolitan areas in the United States (Feldman and Audretsch 1999). In countries like the United States, Canada, or Australia, regional systems correspond roughly with metropolitan areas; in smaller and highly populated nations such as Japan, they may correspond to prefectures.

The main sectoral systems are those actively involved in innovation and R&D. Sectoral systems are defined by their knowledge base, their technologies, and their network of actors. In each OECD country, a small number of such sectors represent the majority of the innovative effort of the country. In older industrial countries, the initial distribution of the main sectors was a matter of historical evolution and market opportunities, rather than governmental choice. Over time, however, and particularly after WWII, governments started accompanying private sector efforts. Thus, for instance, in the United States the most innovative manufacturing sectors were the aerospace, chemical (including pharmaceuticals), and computer/electronic products industries. In the service sector, software publishers are the main innovators (NSF 2010). If measured by R&D expenditure, the same sectors (R&D is highly correlated with innovation activities) appear at the top of the list.

In most countries, traditional sectors such as agriculture, food, garment, leather products, and textiles involve little public support, other than basic regulations regarding food security. The sectors that involve the highest ratio of R&D to sales, thus comprising more risky activities, are those that entail more government support. This is also true for sectors that are part of "national missions" such as defense, health, and the environment. The institutions that support those sectoral systems vary. In biotechnology, universities and government laboratories are at the origins of some of the main regional and sectoral systems (Chen and Lin 2015). Government demand for aircraft before and during the wars has given a major boost to the aerospace industry. Pharmaceuticals and biotechnology have enormously benefitted from government support to public health, often through public research organizations such as the National Institutes of Health in the United States. Also, environmental missions have helped develop such institutes as the National Renewable Energy Laboratory in the United States, Japan's New Energy and Industrial

Technology Development Organization (NEDO), or the French government's *Laboratoire des sciences du climat et de l'environnement.*

5.3 Regional Innovation Systems Defined

"Regions which possess the full panoply of innovation organizations set in an institutional milieu, where systemic linkage and interactive communication among the innovation actors is normal, approach the designation of regional innovation systems" (Cooke and Morgan 1998: 71).

"Regional systems of innovation are sets of institutions (innovating firms, research universities, research funding agencies, venture capital firms and government laboratories, and other appropriate public bodies) and the flows of knowledge, personnel, research monies, regulation and embodied technology that occur within a region (metropolitan area, sub-national unit or other)" (Niosi 2005: 16).

5.4 Sectoral Innovation Systems Defined

"More accurately, a Sectoral Innovation System (SIS) can be defined as that system (group) of firms active in developing and making a sector's products and in generating and utilizing sector technologies: such a system of firms is related in two ways: through processes of interaction and cooperation in artifact technology development and through processes of competition and selection in innovation and market activities" (Breschi and Malerba 1997: 131).

5.5 Systems of Innovation in Developing Countries: The Literature

This new literature on developing countries stands on the shoulders of other authors, as Lundvall (2007) has already underlined. These include, of course, Albert Hirschman (1958), Gunnar Myrdal (1970), Raul Prebisch (1963), and Francis Stewart (1977). The new approach was launched by authors from both developed and developing countries, but in reduced numbers, compared to the OECD literature on innovation systems. In a sense, the works appear more often to be expressions of grief than thorough analyses of the causes, consequences, and potential ways out of such a situation. A short review of this literature follows.

5.5.1 Immature Systems

Albuquerque (2003) argued that Latin American innovation systems are "immature": too young. This explanation is unconvincing. In fact, compared with their much younger East Asian systems (i.e. Singapore or Taiwan), and after 200 years of independence, Latin American systems seem instead to have experienced an unexplained lag. Albuquerque made an effort to define "immature systems" through quantitative thresholds but without making clear the processes through which NIS may mature; other authors used the term without defining it and without drawing any policy implications (Carlsson et al. 2002). Thus, we don't know whether immature systems may one day become "mature" systems, and how. The biological metaphor is not extremely helpful in this context. We do not know why some of these systems do not mature.

5.5.2 Incomplete Systems

According to other authors, innovation systems in developing countries are incomplete, particularly at the level of their connections (Ernst 2002; Metcalfe and Ramlogan 2008). In developing countries, innovation systems usually lack research universities, public R&D laboratories, venture capital firms, and innovative firms. With few research universities and R&D laboratories, as well as R&D-active firms, it comes as no surprise that they lack connections: There are few incentives for businesses to collaborate with universities. Also, teaching-only universities will have few links with business organizations. University–industry connections, when they exist, will be rudimentary and limited.

5.5.3 Weak Systems

According to other authors, innovation systems in less-developed countries are weak and fragmented, with institutional and infrastructural problems (Intarakumnerd and Chaminade 2011; Chaminade et al. 2012). The weaknesses come from low and inappropriate government expenditure: unstable R&D investments in higher education and government R&D, as well as shaky support for innovation in industrial firms. As in the previous case, lack of backing for R&D and innovation yields a lack of connections among the elements of the system. These approaches usually lack the policy implications relating to where these countries need to go in order to reinforce those systems.

5.5.4 Neo-Peripheral Systems

In this approach, MNC are the active elements in the system (Arocena and Sutz 2002). The problem with this approach is that it does not explain why local agents, and particularly the state in developing countries, are so passive. Yet, some Eastern Asian countries such as China, Singapore, South Korea, and Taiwan (province of China) are actively promoting investment of MNC, and at the same time furthering learning in local organizations. This "neo-peripheral" perspective seems less useful, as it does not explain the passiveness of local organizations in most developing countries.

5.5.5 Inefficiency and Ineffectiveness

Inefficiency and ineffectiveness also affect innovation systems (Niosi 2002; Kravtsova and Radosevic 2012). These characteristics are determined by path dependency, organizational inertia, badly designed contracts, inadequate system rules, weak coordination among institutions, and small budgets for key activities including student grants and grant loans, university–industry research centers, or university patenting.

Most, if not all, of the above perspectives present innovation systems divorced from both industrial policy and the quality of the bureaucracy that designs, implements, and assesses innovation system policies. Thus, the IS current has often paid little or no attention to the parallel literature on the impact of the quality of public bureaucracy and industrial policy on development.[1] Almost all of the above-mentioned IS approaches underlie the idea that all government bureaucracies are equally effective and efficient, and that industrial policy is a different chapter in the study of economic development, without close links to innovation systems. This is remarkable when one considers that

---

[1] In a book about innovation systems in developing countries, there is barely mention of either industrial policies, culture, or the quality of public bureaucracies (Lundvall et al. 2011).

innovation systems literature originated in Friedrich List's original work on national industrial policy (List 1841).

A further problem is that these literatures forgot another key element of the required institutions: culture. The cultural explanation comes in different variants. All of them nevertheless put the accent on ancient ways of thinking, be they religious (Catholicism, Islam) or the order of preferences of states. In countries having inherited Catholic institutions from Italy, Portugal, or Spain, such as those in Latin America, science, rational thinking, and technology have lagged, for centuries, behind religious priorities (Eisenstein 2015). Education is underfunded, and traditional thought is common. David Landes (1998) has been the main flag bearer of this "cultural" current.

5.6 Meritocratic Bureaucracies and Their Advantages

Countries with meritocratic bureaucracies are usually those with strong innovation systems. But how did the idea and the practice of the meritocratic bureaucracy take hold?

"Replacing patronage systems for state officials by a professional bureaucracy is a necessary (though not sufficient) condition for a state to be developmental" (Rauch and Evans 2000: 50).

5.6.1 Historical Origins in China and Britain: Conceptual Origins in Max Weber

The idea of embedding meritocracy into public service is as old as the Chinese empire. Mandarins had to pass examinations in order to be employed in the imperial service. The British rulers in India imitated Chinese bureaucracies and introduced tests for public offices in their Indian possessions. In Europe, several countries adopted and gave more modern and precise dimensions to the policy. Under Napoleon, France made an effort to abolish inherited privilege in the public service and created a powerful government bureaucracy. In the United Kingdom, the Northcote-Trevelyan Report (1854) recommended radical changes in the British public bureaucracy, replacing patronage with examination in order to recruit skilled personnel for the British Civil Service, as well as substituting seniority by merit as the basis for promotion (Edwards 2011). In the United States, the Pendleton Civil Service Reform Act, created in 1883, and inspired by the British recruitment system, stipulated that jobs in the public sector would be based on merit (exams). The United States law also created the US Civil Service Commission, recently changed to the Office of Personnel Management and the Merit System Protection Board. By 1983, some 55 percent of all US civil employees had some higher education training; they included 22,000 Ph.D.s, and 150,000 who had a Master's degree (Cigler 1990). The organizational change increased public-sector efficiency, and was soon adopted by other European and English-speaking countries.

In the area of the academic explanation, Max Weber is unanimously considered the first to show the advantages of permanent government bureaucracy. He suggested that rational government behavior could only be imposed on society by means of a highly skilled professional public civil service. For Max Weber, Germany was the quintessential case of such a bureaucracy.

5.6.2 *The Advantages of Meritocracy*

A more recent strand of literature, in agreement with Weber's ideas, shows that economic development requires "quality of government": a meritocratic, skilled, and professional bureaucracy, able to collect taxes, design public policy programs, and create incentives for education and industrial innovation. Democracy and a high level of development are not preconditions – but rather the results – of such public service (Cho et al. 2013). Neither the level of salaries nor civil servants' tenure made a difference: only meritocracy did. Such a civil service is most often absent in developing countries, where corrupt, clientelistic, and politically appointed bureaucracies are often the norm (Charron et al. 2011; Dahlström et al. 2012; You 2015). Corrupt bureaucracies chosen by political appointees are neither able nor interested in designing, implementing, and monitoring policies conducive to economic development.

Stiglitz (1996) has suggested that governments complement markets; they do not substitute them. In particular, he stressed that in East Asia, several governments implemented:

- "Policies that actively sought to ensure macroeconomic stability.
- Making markets work more effectively by, for instance, regulating financial markets.
- Creating markets where that did not exist;
- Helping to direct investment to ensure that resources were deployed in ways that would enhance economic growth and stability;

- Creating an atmosphere conducive to private investment and ensured political stability." (Stiglitz 1996: 156)

Comparing several Asian countries, You (2015) found that economic inequality in the Philippines fostered a patronage-prone bureaucracy, one that in turn fueled stagnation and economic disparity in a sort of "vicious circle," or feedback loop. More equal societies, such as those of South Korea and Taiwan, on the other side, fostered a meritocratic public service, which in turn promoted economic development.

The advantages of meritocratic civil services in economic development are many; the capacity to provide a reasonable selection of industrial sectors to nurture, and the design, implementation, and monitoring of industrial policy require a sophisticated government bureaucracy, one that understands the costs and benefits of different education, science, technology, and innovation incentives and their eventual pitfalls. Thus, a permanent, professional, and meritocratic public bureaucracy is a necessary condition of industrial growth. Among modern authors, comparing Asian and Latin American countries, Evans was one of the first to argue "the efficacy of the developmental state depends on a meritocratic bureaucracy ... " (Evans 1989: 561). Later on, Rauch and Evans showed that a meritocratic bureaucracy is a necessary condition for economic growth (Evans and Rauch 1999).

5.6.3 *The Opposition to Meritocratic Bureaucracies*

Opponents of the Weberian civil service abound. In neoclassical economics, markets are supposed to be more flexible and efficient than governments. Opposition to public bureaucracy, rational or otherwise, became vocal in the Public Choice school of thought (J. Buchanan and G. Tullock) during the 1960s; bureaucracy was identified with rent seeking. Markets were considered efficient by their own nature, and citizens did not need a bureaucracy. This was the idea behind Ronald Reagan's and Margaret Thatcher's reduction of the size of the state, respectively in the United States and the United Kingdom, in the 1970s, as well as the similar process in Canada under the Conservative governments of Brian Mulroney and Stephen Harper. It was based on the application of neoclassical economics in its public choice variety.

More recently, a new attack on the meritocratic form of government has come from law: those meritocratic states are usually composed of nonelected civil servants, who share governmental responsibilities with elected officials. These elected personnel should, in a purely democratic state, be the only ones allowed to impose laws and regulations (Hamburger 2014). The civil service should be composed, as much as possible, of elected officials. People should elect judges, food and health administrators, and science officials.

Hamburger's approach is a radical form of libertarianism. For him, central bank officials establishing interest rates and quantitative easing should be replaced by elected officials, together with health authorities deciding which drugs can be accepted, or security forces. Hamburger proposes a sort of radical weakening of the state.[2] His proposal is based on the perfect rationality of agents in neoclassical economics. All economic agents have complete information about the past and rational expectations about the future. In a sense, Hamburger ignores history, namely what France discovered under Napoleon, Britain in the 1850s, and the United States in the 1890s: The necessity to curb clientelism and nepotism, and to increase performance in the public sector, abolishing the old ways of doing that, has existed for millennia; "to the victor the spoils."

At the very opposite of "neoclassical law," we find those authors that link underdevelopment to inefficient states (Acemoglu et al. 2006). Not far from them are those authors that link underdevelopment to weak and/or inefficient science, technology, and innovation institutions (Arocena and Sutz 2000; Niosi 2002, 2010a).

5.6.4 The Difficulties of Implementing Meritocratic Bureaucracies in LDCs

A few authors have analyzed the difficulties of developing meritocratic structures in Latin American public services (Perlman 1989; Palma 2010; Roll 2014). Perlman (1989) found that the public sector in Latin America was vastly inefficient and resisted modernization. Shepherd and Valencia (1996: 1) suggested that "The public administrations of many Latin American countries are typically dysfunctional – are over-dimensioned, inefficient, unable to deliver services to the most needy, and bastions of opportunistic behavior."

---

[2] Many of them went back to ISI policies, including Argentina and Brazil. In the 2010s they became the two most protectionist countries in the world.

In Latin America, for instance, governments undermined financial stability by the creation of excessive government debt. As a consequence, the region has often been in default (Reinhart and Rogoff 2009). In order to wipe out the debt, governments have promoted high inflation by printing too much money. Social unrest followed, and political stability was undermined. The low-quality bureaucracy was unable to react. The vicious circle continued to unfold.

5.7 Cultural Explanations

Cultural explanations also have a clear Weberian flavor. Max Weber had argued that Protestant countries had a clear proclivity to save and invest. The Protestant ethic would explain such spirit of capitalism. Conversely, Weber saw the Muslim religion as one of a warrior group, tending to patrimonial states.

Several experts in economic history have put these explanations forward. They argue that in Muslim countries, representing 1.6 billion people, religion has erected a number of barriers against economic development (Kuran 2004a, 2004b). These include the Islamic law of inheritance, the lack of a concept of the corporation, and the waqf, a form of trust that locked large economic resources into pious public institutions such as the madrassas (Kuran 2004b). Also, another barrier is the Zakat, the Islamic tax on wealth and income, which is compulsory in Malaysia, Pakistan, Saudi Arabia, and Sudan, and common among other Muslim countries. Interest-free banking also discourages savings. Polygamy, with scarce household resources divided among numerous children, following the Prophet's example, does not help education either. Neither does the general perception that modern economic and political problems have a solution in ancient formulas provided by the Book, and their more or less imaginary past successes. Also, Barro (1991) noted the strong negative correlation between population growth and investment in human capital. Most Muslim countries are affected by rapid and uncontrolled population growth. In addition, Islamic law is not derived from a rational code, but from revelation, and the judges (*qadi*) can interpret it at will, thus lacking generality and stability in human relations (Turner 1974).

In Islamic countries, women are at a disadvantage in both education and working opportunities. Comparing gender statistics in six Arabic Gulf countries with the UK and the United States, Metcalfe (2011) found that few women in Arab countries have seats in parliament, that their labor force participation is low, and that public law is always interpreted using Sharia law, custom, and cultural practices. Also, the World Economic Forum publishes a yearly Global Gender Gap Report. The gender gap is smaller in Nordic countries. The twenty-four lowest-ranked (more gender unequal) countries were Islamic.[3]

Cultural obstacles have not only affected Islamic countries. Several authors (Eisenstein 2015) have argued that economic development in Southern Europe (mostly Catholic) may have been retarded by the centuries-old fight of the church against the printing press, and against science in general, the Index being the Church's main weapon. Out of 142 countries, the average Latin American position was number 58. The average Catholic South European country was in 38th.

5.8 Innovation Systems and Industrial Policy: Why They Need to Be Coordinated

The necessity of coordinating and integrating innovation policy and industrial policy has been put forward several times (Oughton et al. 2002; Cimoli et al. 2009). The concept of innovation systems was not part of this argument.

With the exception of the Far East, many developing countries adopted the view that industrial policy resulted in inefficiency and poor economic growth. Ample historical evidence shows that industrial policy does work, when the right technologies and industries are supported and when appropriate combinations of policy measures are implemented. (Cimoli et al. 2009)

However, some authors have made an effort to link industrial policy with other areas of public policy (Aiginger 2007, 2012). Yet others differentiate and separate innovation policy and industrial policy due to the "suspicious" connotation of the latter (Edquist and Hommen 1999; Warwick 2013). Soete (2007) sees the evolution of industrial policy into innovation policy in a favorable light.

In this chapter, we argue that industrial policy is required for the success of innovation policy for several reasons.

---

[3] http://reports.weforum.org/global-gender-gap-report-2014/rankings/.

(a) First of all, innovation needs to be protected not only by patents, industrial design, copyright, and trademark legislation. All these are weak barriers against imitation: Patents can be "worked around"; designs can be copied; and copyrights and trademarks are even easier barriers to overcome. Being first to the market, obtaining economies of scale and scope, and searching market leadership (all linked to industrial policy) are far better ways to protect innovation.

(b) Second, no country can excel in all industries. Even the largest economies, such as those of China and the United States, have competitive advantages in a few sectors and are uncompetitive in others. Both industrial and innovation policy should promote the same industries, in a coordinated way.

(c) Finally, even if one agrees that governments have, since the industrial revolution, supported different industries, no state can provide specialized human capital and support for all industries. Public resources are limited. Thus sectors must be chosen.

In this chapter we adopt the view that innovation policy is only effective when coordinated with industrial policy, as successful cases of catching-up in Eastern Asia clearly show. Investments in innovation, particularly when they are not directed at a specific sector, run the risk of being dispersed into too many industries and firms.

In the next section, two opposite sets of countries are analyzed.

5.8.1 Disconnecting Industrial and Innovation Policies: ISI in Brazil and Argentina

Import Substitution Industrialization (ISI), developed in Latin America in the 1940s and 1950s, is the paradigmatic case of industrial policy not linked to any kind of innovation policy. Governments protected all sorts of industries without selection or emphasis on innovation, and did not provide any incentive for these industries to improve products, processes, or organizations. In Latin America, Argentina and Brazil are the classic cases of the inefficient results of badly designed ISI industrial policy after WWII; India, Indonesia, and Turkey are their Asian counterparts.

Inefficient bureaucracies, corruption, and low capacity to design, implement, and monitor or assess public policies have, for decades, characterized countries implementing ISI policies. The generally permanent tariff protection for most if not all industries resulted in high prices for low quality goods. Also, in these countries, governments have renamed ISI a "neo-structuralist" policy (Bielschowsky 2009) similar to ISI's original structuralist approach, i.e. an ISI set of policies under another name. This set of policies encouraged capital-goods imports, strong investment in industry, and some level of planning.

Massive protectionism – mostly through tariffs – discouraged learning, as local producers and consumers were unable to compare domestic products' qualities and prices with those of foreign-made goods and services (Bruton 1998). Thus ISI products became increasingly obsolete, without this process being noticed by local authorities, producers, and consumers.

5.8.2 Linking Industrial and Innovation Policies: Taiwan, Korea, Singapore, and China

In the EU, the return of industrial policy after 2000 is associated to the very successful industrial catching up of East Asian countries after Japan: South Korea, Taiwan, Singapore, and then the P.R. of China (Amsden 1992, 2001; Lim 1997; Amsden and Chu 2003; Fu 2015). Their catching up was based on a careful selection of industries, and an equally cautious selection of industrial policy incentives. Also, Lee (2014) has shown that catching up occurs industry-by-industry, or sector-by-sector, as Malerba would say. In Abramovitz (1986), macroeconomic catching up could be studied by itself, without mentioning the engine industries. Today, macroeconomic catching up is seen as the result of industrial catching up in particular sectors.

It was argued that the "flying geese" policy of several countries in East Asia explains their success (Ozawa 2003). Others replied that the "flying geese" policy is a useful model but fails to capture the diversity of development paths in the region. The above-mentioned NICs are by themselves important and distinct sources of East Asian technological progress, competitiveness, and regional investment, in addition to the general flying geese model. "The flying geese model would also underplay the significance of the US economy, both as a market and as a source of technology and investment" (Hobday 1995).

Furthermore, Cline (1982) maintained that the East Asian model of export-led development in Hong Kong, Singapore, South Korea, and

Taiwan could not be generalized without triggering a protectionist response in industrial countries. Still, China has multiplied the East Asian model by a factor of ten without launching, at least yet, a massive protectionist response in rich countries where deindustrialization is evident.

It may be argued that East Asian countries started with a general imitation of the Japanese model of development, attaining technology and organization in the most advanced countries, while each East Asian country implemented its own set of specific policies. But these nations did more than simply "innovate" in products, processes, and organization; they successfully launched new forms of incentives, new and improved products in the global market, with a view to capturing a substantial portion of it. Singapore has attracted foreign direct investment to nurture new industries. South Korea has relied on their own *chaebols* to catch up in key industries. Taiwan has been more creative in its combined innovation and industrial policy, putting a nonprofit government lab (ITRI) at the center of its development efforts. Whatever the specific innovation and set of industrial policies, these countries protected innovation through successful entries in world markets.

Also, the highest-growing Asian countries have relied on active industrial policy (Amsden 1989, 2001; Stiglitz 1996; Liu and White 2001; Fu 2015), supported by the state through soft lending by different public organizations, such as the China Development Bank and the China Export-Import Bank; cluster creation such as Biopolis and Futuropolis in Singapore; and government R&D laboratories and other public agencies in South Korea and Taiwan.

What kind of industrial policies matter? Those that succeed favor the absorption of external knowledge and global externalities, particularly organizational and technological upgrading. As Giuliani et al. (2005) have underlined, the literature on clusters has emphasized local sources of knowledge. The East Asian countries, conversely, have put the accent on external sources of knowledge, which have been more useful for catching up. They imitate technologies, organizational forms, and policies from more advanced countries. The ISI industrial policy model does not select sectors. Yet, different types of industries require specific innovation incentives. Two sets of policies have been put forward to address this problem: the decades-old flying geese and the most recent smart specialization policy approach. They are compared with the ISI model in Table 5.1.

Table 5.1 *Some industrial policies compared*

	Flying Geese	Import substitution	Smart specialization	Developmental state
Context of emergence	Japanese catching up in the 1930s	1940s–1970s LA and Asian catching up,	EU productivity gap with USA (2000–)	East Asia catching up after 1960s
Policies related	Industrial policy evolution	Infant industry	Regional policies	Infant industry
Sector strategy	New sector creation	None	Discover and enhance sectors with EU advantage	New sector and new activity creation
Roles of the state	Export incentives and price discrimination	Tariff and non-tariff protection	Increase EU integration	Picking activities, funding and coordination
	Investment subsidies	Investment subsidies	Purveyor of funds	Purveyor of funds & strategic advice
Critiques & problems	Confusion created by numerous versions of the model	Informational barriers to entry; trade deficits; old technology out-competes new one	Innovation comes from variety and recombination rather than specialization; composite regional innovation systems more productive	Successes (Korea car & ICT industry) but some failures (i.e. Korea aircraft industry; car industry in Taiwan)
To read more	T. Ozawa	R. Prebisch, B. Balassa R. E. Baldwin	D. Foray (2015)	A. Amsden, R. Wade

Smart specialization is the latest response of European countries to industrial decline following East Asian – and particularly Chinese – competition. It has some similarities with Michael Porter's policy arguments aiming at reinforcing industrial clusters and innovative regions (Niosi 2010). While some countries like Canada and Finland have tried to develop new innovative regions from scratch, Porter's recommendations aimed at reinforcing some capabilities already existing in the cluster or innovative region, while at the same time building up value chains and skilled activities. Such a perspective has the advantage of building on some knowledge already present in the region. The concept has undeniable merits. The European Union has built a Smart Specialization Platform, helping regions to discover and enhance their strengths and potential. Thus this variety of industrial strategy is based on regions, more than countries. Thus for instance, Andalusia in Spain found a potential for dual use technologies in the area of sustainable construction, and logistics. An Action Plan was devised and a budget of 529 million euros was voted. From 2014 on, these smart strategies were put forward in the European Union. The results will be evaluated in the years to come.

Before leaving this section it is important to underline that those countries that claim not to apply industrial strategies have in fact put forward several ad hoc ones. During the 2008–10 crisis, the United States has supported their assurance, automobile, banking, and other industries with billions of dollars of credits.

ISI has been criticized for decades: It brought informational deficits through which developing countries nurtured inefficient industries with high prices and old technologies. Today, except in a few countries such as Argentina, Brazil, and Indonesia, it has been abandoned everywhere.

Both Flying Geese (FG) and Smart Specialization (SS) concepts run against received ideas, according to which governments should pick neither winning firms nor sectors. In conventional economics, governments should let markets alone decide in which firms and sectors investors should put their capital. However, as Ozawa has argued: "In essence, the market is merely a resource-allocation mechanism, not a goal-oriented and – filling entity. Directions need to be given by states that represent collective desires at the national level. Effective masters are in great demand" (Ozawa 2010: 23). Both concepts are similar on some dimensions and complementary on other ones. They are similar in the sense that both assume that industrial policy is needed to catch up with more advanced nations. But they differ in some key elements. The FGP aims at launching new sectors, while the SSA proposes revamping existing sectors, mainly by adding General Purpose Technologies (GPT), of which ICT is the most relevant.

The concept of a "developmental state" arrived later, first with Johnson (1962) and the "governing the market" concept, with Wade (1990). In both cases industrial policy was put forward. However, neither the FGP nor the developmental state have avoided Japan's decades-long stagnation that started in the early 1990s and continues to this day. The second generation of geese (Taiwan, South Korea, and Singapore) are doing exceedingly well, and, among the third generation, China is now the second industrial power in the world.

Among the explanations for the success of East Asian developmental states, several appear outstanding. Evans and Rauch (1999) have insisted on the role of meritocratic bureaucracies in Asia in the planning, design, implementation, and upgrading of public policies. Lee (1997) has underlined that local governments strongly pressed new Asian industries to export from the start, thus avoiding the huge trade deficits that characterized Latin American and other ISI-addicted countries. Also, Korean companies were immersed in a situation of strong market competition within the local market, even if price discrimination was allowed. In addition, like in Japan, the government preannounced well in advance the end of quotas, trade protection, and other perks. Local industrialists knew from the start that the bonanza of infant industry protection was short term. Also, in all Eastern Asian countries, government R&D laboratories reduced the informational barriers to entry by bringing technology from abroad, producing prototypes, and transferring technology to the private sector.

In East Asia, infant industry protection existed, but it was a short-term policy, and often took the form of quotas, thus allowing learning from foreign goods in the local market and avoiding situations of total informational disadvantage from consumers and producers (Militz 2005).

The following table gives an idea of the sectors and their incentives.

Acronyms: EMA: European Medical Agency; FDA: Food and Drug Administration; NREL: New Renewable Energy Laboratory; SBIR: Small Business Innovation Research program; NRC: National Research Council; INSERM: Institut national de la santé et de la recherche médicale; NEDO: New Energy and Industrial Technology; NIH: National Institutes of Health.

Table 5.2 *Industrial sectors and frequent innovation incentives*

Sector	Type of innovation projects	Type of support	Countries, regions and examples
Mining industry	Long and costly capital-intensive R&D projects	Government laboratories for exploration, extraction, fabrication and composite materials	USA (Geological Survey; Advanced Program on Composite Materials) Canada (Geological Survey)
Pharmaceuticals	Long and human-capital intensive R&D projects	Government R&D subsidies to academia and industry, tax credits, public R&D laboratories	USA (FDA, NIH) European Union (EMA, government subsidies through Frameworks Programs)
Aerospace	Large projects for aircraft designs, new engines and subsystems	Large projects for aircraft designs, new engines and subsystems	USA (Aerospace Corporation, Jet Propulsion Labs), France (ONERA), Canada (NRC Aerospace labs)
Software	Shorter and less expensive R&D projects	University grants for computer software, public R&D contracts with private firms	USA, Canada, European Union, Japan public subsidies and procurement
Biotechnology	Long, costly, and human-capital intensive R&D projects	University and public grants for R&D in academia and dedicated biotech firms, large public R&D laboratories	USA (NIH laboratories), Canada (NRC biotechnology federal laboratories), France (INSERM)
Nanotechnology	Long and human-capital intensive R&D projects	University grants for nanotech R&D; public grants for dedicated biotech firms, public R&D	USA (National Nanotechnology Initiative); Canada (NRC Institute for Nanotechnology)
Renewable energy	Long and human-capital intensive R&D projects	Public grants for R&D in academia and dedicated energy firms, public R&D labs	USA (NREL, SBIR DOE grants), Japan (NEDO), Canada (CANMET-Energy)

Table 5.3 *Types of policy preferred for different types of innovation*

Goal	Type of policy preferred	Examples
Incremental innovation and path following policies	R&D tax credits Subsidies for SME innovation	Canada or US tax credits for R&D
Radical innovation and path creation	Mission-oriented laboratories	US NIH, Jet Propulsion Lab
Innovation cascades and path creation	Grand challenge policy	SunShot Initiative, Human Genome Project

5.9 Policy Implications

The different policies that need to be implemented in LDCs in order to replicate Asian success require correct progression, strategy, and application. A classification of innovation policies is presented.

The first phase of institutional building includes designing and presenting industrial, innovation, and cultural policies, which require a meritocratic and professional bureaucracy. Eventually, foreign personnel may need to be recruited for that purpose. Several examples come to mind. The revolution in Turkish education came along with President Kemal Ataturk in the mid-1920s. It was promoted by the visit made by the great US educator John Dewey (1859–1952) at that time, and his report and proposals to the Turkish government about the necessary reforms in the educational system of the new republic. Dewey made recommendations about the organization of the Ministry of Education, the training and treatment of teachers, the education curriculum, and other topics (Ata 2000).

Similarly, the hiring of US MIT Professor of aerospace engineering Richard Smith as the first rector of the Brazilian Aeronautics Institute of Technology in the late 1940s accelerated the successful development of the Brazilian aeronautical industry. Soon, the school would boast the hiring of distinguished professors from twenty different countries.

How long did these meritocratic civil services take before they were fully operational? A ten-year period seems a reasonable minimum deadline. Several factors explain the delay. First, people need to be recruited from the domestic or international labor markets. This is not always easy or evident. Second, new institutions have to be built or revamped: government departments, public management schools, and university programs. Finally, the new managers have to become acquainted with their responsibilities, and receive public support. Only such a meritocratic bureaucracy can bring the necessary cultural, industrial, and innovation policy reforms. How long do these reforms need in order to succeed? Few cases of such reforms come to mind. In five to ten years, the Republic of Turkey abolished the caliphate, changed the alphabet from Arabic to Western (the Revolution of the Signs), gave voting rights to women, created a laic education system, adopted European law systems, changed the Muslim calendar for the Western one, and abolished polygamy. The adoption of a family name followed in 1934.

In China, the revolution in culture extended itself over a century, starting with the creation of the Republic of China by Sun Yat-sen in late 1911, and up to this day. India's cultural revolution started with Gandhi, decades before the declaration of independence in 1947. In India, almost seventy years after independence and the fight against caste discrimination, difference based on caste still persists in educational attainment and marriage preference (Azam and Bhatt 2015; Emran and Shilpi 2015). Dozens of other major cultural changes have been launched in many countries, with different levels of success. Most often than not they have either failed or were prolonged over decades. The case of South Africa's fight against apartheid has been documented time and again, as well as its drawbacks and resistance (Suransky and van der Merwe 2016).

Finally, institutions able to design, implement, assess, and improve industrial and innovation policy need to be built. Chang identified three types of institutions that were crucial in Asian countries' rapid economic catching up: "institutions for coordination and administration, institutions for learning and innovation, and institutions for income redistribution and social cohesion" (Chang 1998: 64). In Japan, the case of MITI was underlined many times (Johnson 1982). In Taiwan, ITRI had a major role as the purveyor and local window on foreign technologies.

The innovation system perspective, and China's experience, suggests that in less-developed countries, the exclusive adoption of "incremental innovation policies" such as tax credits for R&D and subsidies for SME innovation, though useful, are not what is required to pull them out of quasi-stagnation. Mission-oriented and grand challenge policies may be far more useful to build innovation systems in the global south.

5.10 Conclusion and Theoretical Implications

Innovation systems in developing countries are often incomplete, and fairly ineffective, inefficient, and thus weak. They often lack some key institutions (appropriate public policy incentives for industrial R&D, research universities, and public R&D laboratories) as well as connections among the components of the system. The existing literature has appropriately described some of the characteristics of IS in less-developed nations.

But the literature has forgotten how to explain why this state of affairs occurs. In its first conclusion, this chapter suggests that as the basis of this ineffectual set of structures one must find *the lack of a meritocratic public bureaucracy*, one that is able to design, implement, monitor, and continuously improve public policy, including the set of innovation policies that compose IS. Also, the literature shows how these meritocratic bureaucracies were built in countries such as Germany, the United Kingdom, and the United States. These processes took decades before the effects of the changes in the civil service were felt.

A second conclusion is that, in order to develop, these less-developed countries also *lack a set of effective industrial policies*, such as the selection of industrial sectors, either in a flying geese approach or a "smart specialization" strategy, that allow progressive upgrading (or abandoning) of their low-tech industries and incorporation of medium- and high-tech industries, particularly those that bring the largest knowledge externalities. The original sectors that these countries have to promote depend on their endowment of human and natural resources, as well as on the possibility of investing in human capital and using foreign natural resources. It is clear that no country, except maybe China or India, can expect to be internationally competitive in a large set of industries.

ISI policies have been applied for decades, and on the whole they have been criticized and, except in a few cases, abandoned. The debate about flying geese/developmental state policies in East Asia has been fairly abundant. The impression of this author (following the points of view of Amsden 1989, 2001; Lee 1997; Evans and Rauch 1999; and

Wade 1990) is that they have been enormously successful. It is too easy to judge the value of smart specialization policies.

A third conclusion is that *cultural barriers* and heritages are highly important and that they are as difficult to overcome as the two others. In spite of their large endowment of natural resources, most African, Asian, Latin American, and Middle Eastern countries seem unable to expand their economies. Religious and other cultural obstacles may be part of the explanation of their secular stagnation.

In order to develop, design, implement, and monitor such sector selection and adequate innovation and industrial policy incentives, they need to build an effective meritocratic public bureaucracy, one that exists in not more than fifty countries in the world. Building such a bureaucracy is not an easy task: They will have to progressively replace hundreds of thousands of public employees recruited on the basis of clientele principles with a smaller number of meritocratic and highly efficient ones.

A further theoretical conclusion is due. It is time to expand the concepts behind Myrdal's vicious circle of poverty.[4] Underdevelopment is not only the result of a short set of related variables such as poverty, lack of health, and lack of education mutually reinforcing each other. One must add to the circle the effects of corruption, inefficient and weak government, including STI institutions, and erroneous economic (industrial and financial) policy.

So, what are the policy implications; where do we go from here? How do we build a meritocratic bureaucracy? In terms of how to change, I suggest building the meritocratic institutions through a fast but evolutionary process, one that includes policy transfer, benchmarking, and selective hiring. Instead of recruiting hordes of badly paid loyal supporters, governments in developing countries should hire highly educated bureaucrats in short numbers, and recruit them through examinations and curricula. Such an institution-building process should start with STI institutions as well as public financial organizations. Universities,

---

[4] "He again used the concept of cumulative causation, this time to explain the vicious circle of poverty, poor health, lack of education and underutilisation of the labour force in less developed countries in South Asia. To break the vicious circle of poverty and start a virtuous circle of development through the process of cumulative causation, he advocated government development planning involving a number of measures including institutional reform." http://prizei neconomics.blogspot.ca/2008/03/gunnar-myrdal-18981987.html.

government laboratories, the central bank, and the national development bank should be the priorities. At the same time, a transparency law should be passed: All tax-paying individuals and organizations must have the right to request information about the use of public monies, public assets, and government loans. Transparency is the best antidote against corruption. Institutional reform is required. Governments should concentrate on subsidizing education through scholarships, high salaries for teachers, recruiting foreign talent, excellent education facilities, and the like.

The East Asian miracle was built on education. Publication and patent figures in these countries may shame Latin American countries. (Singapore produces many more patents than Latin America every year.) STI policies will be based on education. However, financial institutions should not be let astray. So many developing countries have lost their course due to excessive debt and subsequent runaway inflation triggered in order to liquidate the debt, Argentina being probably the most outstanding example, that attention needs also to be put on public financial organizations (Reinhart and Rogoff 2009).

Another key component was industrial policy. Smart specialization may succeed, based on a careful selection of industries by the planning bureaucracy. Successful Asian countries use smart specialization; Latin America is, with Africa, the last remaining region to believe in the power of markets.

A final section will be on timeframes. How long does it take to build an NIS? Take the miracle countries of the first half of the twentieth century. Up to 1940, Argentina, Australia, and Canada displayed many similarities. Between 1940 and 1970 Canada built a system of advanced universities, public research organizations, and created powerful incentives for private firms to innovate (Niosi 2000). Similar periods of time appear in the books authored by Kim (1997) on Korea, and Amsden and Chu (2003) on Taiwan, and in Lemola's article on Finland (2012), to name a few. The construction of a national innovation system may require thirty to fifty years. Starting in 1978, China's completion of its NIS will take, in all, thirty to fifty years (Fu 2015).

Bibliography

Abramovitz, M. 1986. Catching up, forging ahead, and falling behind. *The Journal of Economic History* 46(2): 385–406.

Acemoglu, D., D. Ticchi, and A. Vindigni. 2006. *Emergence and Persistence of Inefficient States*. Cambridge, MA: NBER Working Paper 1278.

Aiginger, K. 2007. Industrial policy: A dying breed or a re-emerging phoenix. *Journal of Industry, Competition and Trade* 7 (3–4): 297–323.

Aiginger, K. 2012. *A Systemic Industrial Policy to Pave a New Growth Path for Europe*, WIFO WP. 421.

Albuquerque, E. 2003. *Immature Systems of Innovation*. Belo Horizonte: UNMG, CEDEPLAR, Working Paper.

Amsden, A. 2001. *The Rise of the Rest*. Oxford: Oxford University Press.

Amsden, A. and W. Chu. 2003. *Beyond Late Development: Taiwan's Upgrading Policies*. Boston, MA: Massachusetts Institute of Technology Press.

Arocena, R. and J. Sutz. 2000. Looking at national systems of innovation from the South. *Industry and Innovation* 7(1): 55–75.

Arocena, R. and J. Sutz. 2002. *Innovation Systems and Developing Countries*. Aalborg: Aalborg University, Druid WP.

Ata, B. 2000. The influence of an American educator on the Turkish educational system, in *Turkish Yearbook of International Relations*, Volume XXXI, Ankara: University of Ankara.

Azam, M. and V. Bhatt. 2015. Like father, like son, Intergenerational educational mobility in India. *Demography* 52(1): 1929–1959.

Barro, R. 1991. A cross-country study of growth, saving, and government, in B. D. Bernheim and J. B. Sholen (eds.), *National Savings and Economic Performance*. Chicago: University of Chicago Press, 271–304.

Bielschowsky, R. 2009. Sixty years of ECLAC: structuralism and neo-structuralism. *CEPAL Review* 97: 171–192.

Breschi, S. and Malerba, F. 1997. Sectoral innovation systems: Technological regimes, Schumpeterian dynamics, and spatial boundaries, in C Edquist (ed.), *Systems Of Innovation: Technologies, Institutions, and Organizations*. London: Pinter Publishers.

Bruton, H. J. 1998. A reconsideration of import substitution. *Journal of Economic Literature* 32(6): 902–936.

Carlsson, B., Jacobsson S., Holmen M. and Rickne A. 2002. Innovation systems: analytical and methodological issues. *Research Policy* 31(2): 233–245.

Chang, H. 1998. The role of institutions in Asian development. *Asian Development Review* 16(2): 64–95.

Charron, N. L., Apuente V. and Rothstein B. 2011. Measuring Quality of Government and Sub-National Variation. Report for the European Commission of Regional Development. European Commission Directorate-General Regional Policy Directorate Policy Development, Brussels.

Chen, S.-H. and W. T. Lin. 2015. The dynamic role of universities in developing an emerging sector: a case study of the biotechnology sector, *Technological Forecasting and Social Change*, (article in press).

Cho, W., T. Im, G. A. Porumbescu, H. Lee and J. Park. 2013. A cross-country study of the relationship between Weberian bureaucracy and government performance. *International Review of Public Administration* 18(3): 115–137.

Cigler, B. A. 1990. Public administration and the paradox of professionalization. *Public Administration Review* 50(6): 637–653.

Cimoli, M., G. Dosi and J. E. Stiglitz (eds.). 2009. *Industrial Policy and Development*. Cambridge: Cambridge University Press.

Cline, W. 1982. Can the East Asian model of development be generalized? *World Development* 10(2): 81–90.

Cooke, P. and Morgan, K. 1998. *The Associational Economy: Firms, Regions, and Innovation*. Oxford, UK: Oxford University Press.

Dahlström, C., V. Lapuente, and J. Teorell. 2012. The merit of meritocratization. *Political Research Quarterly* 65(3): 656–68.

Edquist, C. 1997. Systems of innovation approaches – their emergence and characteristics, in C. Edquist (ed.), *Systems of Innovation*. London: Pinter, 1–35.

Edquist, C. 2005. Systems of innovation, in J. Fagerberg, D. C. Mowery, and R. R. Nelson (eds.), *The Oxford Handbook of Innovation*. Oxford: Oxford University Press, 181–208.

Edquist, C., and Hommen L. 1999. Systems of innovation: Theory and policy for the demand side. *Technology in Society* 21: 63–79.

Edwards, J. R. 2011. Professionalizing the British central bureaucracy: The accounting dimension. *J. Account. Public Policy* 30: 217–235.

Einsenstein, E. 2015. *The Printing Revolution in Early Modern Europe*. Cambridge: Cambridge University Press (3rd edition).

Emran, M. S. and F. Shilpi. 2015. Gender, geography and generations: Intergenerational educational mobility in India. *World Development* 72(1): 362–380.

Ernst 2002. Global production networks and the changing geography of innovation systems. Implications for developing countries. *Economics of Innovation and New Technology* 11(6): 497–523, DOI: 10.1080/10438590214341.

Evans, P. 1989. Predatory, developmental and other apparatuses: A comparative political economy perspective on the Third World state. *Sociological Forum* 4(4): 561–587.

Evans, P. and J. E. Rauch. 1999. Bureaucracy and growth; a cross-national analysis of the effects of "Weberian" state structures on economic growth. *American Sociological Review* 64: 748–765.

Feldman, M. and D. Audretsch. 1999. Innovation in cities: Science-based diversity, specialization and localized competition. *European Economic Review* 43: 409–429.

Foray, D. 2015. *Smart Specialization. Opportunities and Challenges for Regional Innovation Policy*. London: Routledge.

Freeman, C. 1987. *Technology Policy and Economic Performance*. London: Pinter.

Fu, X. 2015. *China's Path to Innovation*. Cambridge: Cambridge University Press.

Giuliani, E., C. Petrobelli and R. Rabellotti. 2005. Upgrading in global value chains: Lessons from Latin American clusters. *World Development* 33(4): 549–573.

Hamburger, P. 2014. *Is Administrative Lw Unlawful?* Chicago: University of Chicago Press.

Hirschman, A. 1958. *The Strategy of Economic Development*. New Haven, CT: Yale University Press.

Hobday, M. 1995. Innovation in East Asia: diversity and development. *Technovation* 15(2): 55–63.

Intarakumnerd, P. and C. Chaminade. 2011. Innovation policies in Thailand: Towards a system of innovation approach? *Asia Pacific Business Review* 17(2): 241–256.

Johnson, C. 1982. *MITI and the Japanese Miracle: The Growth of Industrial Policy, 1925–1975*. Stanford, CA: Stanford University Press.

Kim, L. 1997. *Imitation to Innovation*. Boston, MA: Harvard Business School Press.

Kravtsova, V. and S. Radosevic. 2012. Are systems of innovation in Eastern Europe efficient? *Economic Systems* 36: 109–126.

Kuran, T. 2004a. *Islam and Mammon: The Economic Predicaments of Islamism*. Princeton, NJ: Princeton University Press.

Kuran, T. 2004b. Why the Middle East is economically underdeveloped: Historical mechanisms of institutional stagnation. *Journal of Economic Perspectives* 18(3): 71–90.

Landes, D. S. 1998. *The Wealth and Poverty of Nations*. New York, NY: Norton.

Lee, J. 1997. The maturation and growth of infant industries: The case of Korea. *World Development* 25(8): 1271–1281.

Lee, K. and C. Lim. 2001. Technological regimes, catch-up and leapfrogging: Findings from the Korean industries, *Research Policy*, 30: 459–476.

Lee, K. (2014): *Schumpeterian Analysis of Technological Catch-up*, Cambridge U. Press.

Lemola, T. 2012. Convergence of national science and technology policies: The case of Finland. *Research Policy* 31: 1481–1490.

List, F. 1841. *Das nationale System der politischen Ökonomie*. Stuttgart/ Tübingen: Cotta Verlag.

Liu, X. and S. White. 2001. Comparing innovation systems: A framework and application to China's transitional context. *Research Policy* 30: 1091–1114.

Lundvall, B. A. 2007. National innovation systems—analytical concept and development tool. *Industry and Innovation* 14: 95–119.

Lundvall, B. A., K. J. Joseph, C. Chaminade, and J. Vang. 2011. *Handbook of Innovation Systems in Developing Countries*. Cheltenham: Elgar.

Metcalfe, B. D. 2011. Women empowerment and development in Arab Gulf states: A critical appraisal of governance, culture and national human resource development (HRD) frameworks. *Human Resource Development International* 14(2): 131–148.

Metcalfe, S. and Ramlogan, R. 2002. Innovation systems and the competitive process in developing economies. *Quarterly Review of Economics and Finance* 48(2): 433–446.

Millitz, M. J. 2005. When and how should infant industries be protected? *Journal of International Economics* 66: 177–196.

National Science Foundation. 2010. NSF releases new statistics on business innovation (www.nsf.gov/statistics/).

Nelson, R. R. and Rosenberg, N. 1993. American universities and technical advances in industry. *Research Policy* 23: 323–348.

Niosi, J. 2000. *Canada's National System of Innovation*. Montreal and Kingston: McGill- Queen's University Press.

Niosi, J. 2002. National systems of innovation are x-efficient (and x-effective): why some are slow learners. *Research Policy* 31: 291–302.

Niosi, J. 2005. *Canada's Regional Innovation System: The Science-Based Industries*. Montreal, Canada: McGill Press.

Niosi, J. 2010. Rethinking science, technology and innovation (STI) institutions in developing countries. *Innovation: Organization and Management* 12: 250–268.

Niosi, J. 2010a. *Building National and Regional Systems of Innovation*. Cheltenham: Elgar.

Niosi, J. 2010b. Rethinking science, technology and innovation (STI) institutions in developing countries. *Innovation Management, Policy and Practice* 12(3): 250–268.

Niosi, J., Bellon, B., Saviotti, P. P. and Crow, M. 1993. National systems of innovation: in search of a workable concept. *Technology in Society* 15: 207–227.

Oughton, C., M. Landabasso and K. Morgan. 2002. The regional innovation paradox: Innovation policy and industrial policy. *The Journal of Technology Transfer* 27: 97–110.

Ozawa, T. 2003. Pax Americana-led macro-clustering and flying-geese-style catch-up in East Asia: mechanisms of regionalized endogenous growth. *Journal of Asian Economics* 13: 699–713.

Palma, J. G. 2010. Flying geese and waddling ducks: The different capabilities of East Asia and Latin America to "demand-adapt" and "supply-upgrade" their export productive capacity, in M. Cimoli et al. (eds.), *Industrial Policy and Development*. Oxford: Oxford University Press.

Patel, P. and Pavitt, K. 1994. National innovation systems: Why they are important, and how they might be measured and compared. *Economics of Innovation and New Technology* 3(1): 77–95.

Perlman, B. J. 1989. Modernizing the public service in Latin America: Paradoxes of Latin American public administration. *International Journal of Public Administration* 12(4): 671–704.

Prebisch, R. 1963. *Hacia una dinámica del desarrollo latinoamericano*. México: FCE.

Rauch, J. E. and P. B. Evans. 2000. Bureaucratic structure and bureaucratic performance in less developed countries. *Journal of Public Economics* 75: 49–71.

Reinhart, C. and K. Rogoff. 2009. *This Time Is Different*. Princeton, NJ: Princeton University Press.

Roll, M. 2014. The state that works: A pocket of effectivness perspective in Nigeria and beyond, in: Bierschank, t., de Sardan, J.P.(eds.), *States at Work, Dynamics of African Bureaucracies*, Leiden, 365–397.

Shepherd, G. and S. Valencia. 1996. Modernizing the public administration in Latin America: Common problems, no easy solutions, *Conference Reforma del Estado en América Latina y el Caribe*. Madrid, October 14–17, 1996.

Soete, L. 2007. From industrial to innovation policy. *Journal of Industrial Competition and Trade* 7: 273–284.

Stewart, F. 1977. *Technology and Underdevelopment*. London: Macmillan.

Stiglitz, J. 1996. Some lessons from the East Asian Miracle. *The World Bank Research Observer* 11(2): 151–177.

Suransky, C. and J. van der Merwe. 2016. Transcending apartheid in higher education: Transforming an institutional culture. *Race, Ethnicity and Education* 19(3): 577–597.

Turner, B. 1974. Islam, capitalism and the Weber theses. *British Journal of Sociology* 25(2): 230–243.

Wade, R. 1990. *Governing the Market*. Princeton, NJ: Princeton University Press.

Warwick, K. 2013. Beyond industrial policy: Emerging issues and new trends, *OECD Science, Technology and Industry Policy Papers*, No. 2. OECD Publishing.

You, J. S. 2015. *Democracy, Inequality and Corruption: Korea, Taiwan and the Philippines Compared*. Cambridge: Cambridge University Press.

6 | Innovation, Credit Constraints, and National Banking Systems

A Comparison of Developing Nations *

EDWARD LORENZ AND SOPHIE POMMET

6.1 Introduction

The importance of innovation and technical change for economic development has been investigated in a large range of literature, both theoretical and empirical. One key finding of this research is that it is important to distinguish between innovations in the sense of cutting edge developments at the technological frontier and the incremental processes associated with the adoption and diffusion of existing technologies. Kim (1997), in his now classic study on the role of technological catch-up in Korea's rapid economic growth from the 1960s, refers to "innovation through imitation," and Lee (2005), in his analysis of the opportunities and barriers to technological catch-up, also emphasizes the importance of imitation in the early so-called OEM (own equipment manufacturing) stage of the process. In a similar vein, Fagerberg et al. (2010), in a recent review of the empirical research on innovation and development, observe that cutting edge technological development tends to be located in the "developed" world, while innovation in the sense of imitation and diffusion tends to characterize the "developing" world. The largely imitative nature of innovation activity in developing nations, however, doesn't make it any less significant economically.

A closely related finding based on the results of innovation surveys is that innovation, in the sense of imitation and diffusion, far from being exceptional is a quite frequent and even common phenomenon in developing countries (Crespi and Peirano 2007; Fagerberg et al. 2010; Goedhuys 2007; Srholec 2011). It may be

* Preliminary versions of this paper were presented at the internal seminar of the IKE Group, Aalborg University, Denmark and at the sixteenth Annual Schumpeter Society Conference, Montreal, Canada. We would like to thank the participants for their useful comments on the earlier versions.

the necessary condition for firms to sustain a competitive position in their local or national markets. Moreover, the opportunities for innovating in the sense of introducing products or technologies that are new to the firm but not necessarily new on world markets may well be greater in nations that are behind technologically, simply because the amount of mature technology available on international markets for enterprises in these nations to "absorb" is greater. This issue is addressed in the literature on technological gaps and convergence between low income and high income nations (Fagerberg 1987; Verspagen 1991).

An important conclusion coming out of these related strands of research is that there is nothing "automatic" about the process whereby firms in less-developed countries acquire the technological and organizational capabilities necessary to assimilate and possibly modify technologies and products first developed elsewhere (Fagerberg 1994: 155–162 for an overview). While these capabilities are internal to the enterprise, their development depends in part on the characteristics of the national and local institutions and support structures the enterprise is embedded in. This reflects the fact that firms rely on their relations with different external organizations and institutions for the development of their core competences. Firms depend on relations with education institutions and training providers for securing supplies of labor with the required basic and domain-specific skills, and on relations with universities and public and private research institutions for the development of their research and innovation capabilities. To varying degrees they depend on their relations with banks and other financial institutions for access to credit in order to develop, produce, and commercialize new products and technologies. The importance of the nationally specific institutional setting is investigated in a large range of literature on national and regional innovation systems in both developed and developing nations (Lundvall 1992; Niosi et al. 1993; Dahlman and Nelson 1995; Freeman 1995; Arocena and Sutz 2000).

In this chapter we focus on one dimension of the national institutional setting that is recognized as being central to the ability of developing-country firms to acquire the resources and develop the capabilities needed for innovation: the national financial system. We investigate the links between innovation and financial system characteristics for a sample of thirty-six developing nations spread across five regions of the world: Sub-Saharan Africa, the Middle East and North Africa, East Asia and Pacific, South Asia, and Central Asia. We seek to extend existing micro-level studies on the financing decisions of enterprises in developing countries by explicitly connecting these decisions to firms' innovation outcomes and to the wider institutional framework formed by the national banking system. Our results show that credit constraints have a significant negative impact on innovation and that the characteristics of the national banking system indirectly affect innovation through their impact on the likelihood that firms face these financing constraints.

The chapter is structured in the following way. Section 6.2 presents a brief overview of research examining the links between financial system development, credit constraints, and innovation performance. Section 6.3 contrasts the national banking systems of the thirty-six developing nations investigated in this chapter and it develops a probit model predicting the likelihood of credit constraints as a function of both firm-level characteristics and country-level variables, measuring the national banking systems. The sources of firm-level and country-level data are described. Section 6.4 extends the analysis by developing a recursive bivariate probit model in order to examine the indirect effects of national banking system characteristics on firms' innovation outcomes. Section 6.5 concludes with a discussion of the policy implications.

6.2 Financial Systems, Credit Constraints, and Innovation

Macroeconomic research has identified a positive relation between economic development and the development of the financial system. Contemporary cross-country econometric research starts with papers by King and Levine (1993) building on earlier work by Goldsmith (1969). Rajan and Zingales (1998), in an influential paper using industry and firm data, find that financial development has a substantial impact on industrial growth in part though the availability of credit for new firm formation. These papers provide evidence for a "first-order" positive relationship between financial development and economic growth (Levine 2005 for an overview).

At a more micro level, a number of studies focusing on both developed and developing nations have shown that firms face more or less important financing obstacles or constraints linked to the level of development of their national financial systems. Beck et al. (2006)

explore the relationship between the characteristics of the financial system and the financing obstacles firms face for a sample of eighty countries using micro data from the World Bank's Enterprise Surveys (WBES). They show that firms in countries with higher levels of financial intermediary and stock market development, legal system efficiency, and higher GDP per capita report, on average, lower financing obstacles. Presbitero and Rabellotti (2013) focus on the Latin America region and show that the financing constraints of firms depend in part on the degree of bank penetration (as measured by the number of bank branches) and bank competition. This literature also shows that the size of firms is an important determinant of access to external finance. There is substantial evidence that small and medium enterprises (SMEs) are financially more constrained than large firms and have less access to formal sources of external finance (Shiffer and Weder 2001; Beck and Demirgüç-Kunt 2006).

There are a number of micro-level studies examining the relation between the obstacles firms face in gaining access to credit and their R&D expenditure and innovation performance. Fazzari et al. (1988), in a path-setting study, focused on the relation between investment and R&D expenditure and cash flows. They argued that higher investment-cash flow sensitivities provide a useful measure of financing or credit constraints. This gave rise to a literature focusing on advanced industrialized nations, giving particular attention to the financing decisions of small firms in high-tech or R&D intensive industries (Hall and Lerner 2010 for a survey). Mulkay et al. (2001), for example, compared a panel of US and French firms and showed that investment-cash flow sensitivities are higher in the United States, and Bond et al. (1999) compared firms in the UK and Germany, finding that UK firms were more sensitive to financing constraints. The broad conclusions of this literature, however, were that the investments of firms that had exhausted all of their relatively low-cost internal funds would be more sensitive to fluctuations in their cash flow than firms with higher liquidity.

More recent literature addresses these issues using direct measures of both firms' financing constraints and their innovation performance. Savignac (2006), for example, uses data from the French Financing of Technological Innovation (FIT) survey carried out in 2000, focusing on the financial resources used for funding innovative projects. The survey provides direct measures of innovation based on the Oslo Manual definitions and direct measures of financial constraint based on asking respondent firms whether a lack of financing sources or too high interest rates have been obstacles preventing them from undertaking innovation projects. The analysis of Gorodnichenko and Schnitzer (2013) similarly uses direct measures of innovation and credit constraints derived from the World Bank's Business Environment and Enterprise Performance Surveys (BEEPS), which cover Eastern Europe and Commonwealth Independent States (CIS). This approach based on direct measures not only avoids potential problems with using investment-cash flow sensitivities as a proxy for financing constraints but also overcomes the well-known weaknesses associated with using R&D expenditures as proxy for innovation.[1] Not only is R&D only one among several important inputs to innovation, but as research based on the Community Innovation Surveys or surveys adopting the Oslo Manual definitions of innovation have shown, many firms innovate without having undertaken any formal R&D (Arundel et al. 2008; Rammer et al. 2009; Leitner and Stehrer 2013).

In summary, one body of literature has shown that the level of development of the national financial system has an important impact on the ability of firms to gain access to credit and another has made the case for the importance of credit constraints for firms' investments in innovation activities. A main objective in this chapter is to link these different insights and findings in a model investigating for a sample of developing countries the channels through which the banking system impacts indirectly on enterprise innovation performance through its effect on firms' financing constraints.

In order to do this, we make use of recently available harmonized enterprise-level data from the World Bank Enterprise Survey (WBES), in combination with aggregate measures of national banking systems available from the World Bank's Global Financial Development database. Different units within the World Bank have conducted firm-level surveys providing information on the financing decisions of enterprises since the 1990s. Since 2005–2006, data collection has been centralized in the Enterprise Analysis Unit using a harmonized methodology,[2] and beginning with the 2010 survey wave questions on innovation outcomes conforming to the Oslo Manual definitions have been

---

[1] See notably Kaplan and Zingales (1997), who present evidence showing a non-monotonic relation between investment-cash flow sensitivities and the extent of financing constraints.

[2] See Annex 1 for a description of the sample frame and survey methodology.

included in the separate manufacturing and services questionnaires in selected nations.[3] In this chapter, we analyze the subset of developing nations surveyed by the World Bank during the period 2010–2014 for which innovation indicators are available for both manufacturing and service sector enterprises and for which aggregate indicators characterizing the national banking system are obtainable from the World Bank's Global Financial Development database.[4] Table 6A.1 in the Annex lists the thirty-six countries analyzed and shows both their GDP and their GNI per capita in 2012 US dollars. Gross national income per capita for the sample of nations in 2012 ranges from a low of 320 US dollars in Malawi to a high of 9780 US dollars in Kazakhstan. The majority of nations that are classified as low income by the World Bank (less than 1025 US dollars in 2012) are located in Sub-Saharan Africa and in South Asia.

6.3 National Banking Systems in Comparative Perspective

As securities markets play a minor or insignificant role in the provision of external finance in the majority of the countries analyzed in this chapter, we focus on the characteristics of the national banking system. This applies to a considerable extent even to fast-growing Asian countries like China and India that experienced large increases in equity market capitalization during the 2000s. According to Didier and Schmukler (2014), the use of equity financing remains quite limited across East Asian nations and tends to be concentrated in a few firms. For example, the national shares raised by the top five issuers in China and India in the 2000s were 45 percent and 55 percent, respectively, and trading is similarly concentrated with the top five capturing about 40 percent. Only a few firms in China and India use equity and bond markets on a recurrent basis and even fewer capture the bulk of capital market financing.

In comparing national systems we focus on measures of banking system depth, breadth, market concentration, and the cost of financial

---

[3] Earlier waves of the WBES conducted between 2003 and 2006 also included questions on innovation in selected countries. However, the survey methodology was not uniform in terms of the sample frames, stratification, and the use of post-stratification weights.

[4] We have excluded the Latin American and Caribbean nations surveyed in the 2010 wave of the WBES, as innovation data were only collected for the manufacturing sector.

184   *Edward Lorenz and Sophie Pommet*

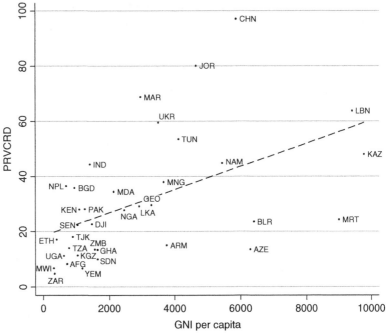

Figure 6.1 Scatter plot for PRVCRD and GNI per capita
Source: World Bank Global Financial Development Database

mediation as reflected in net interest margins. A standard measure of
the level of development or the "depth" of the banking system is private
bank credit as a percentage of GDP (PRVCRD). A number of cross
national studies have identified a positive relation between this measure
and the share of private sector firms having access to a line of credit
from a financial institution (Fisman and Love 2003; Beck et al. 2006).
The unweighted population average for PRVCRD in 2008 is 30.7
percent of GDP, with values ranging from a low of 4.8 percent of
GDP in the Democratic Republic of Congo to a high of 97 percent in
China.[5] Figure 6.1 identifies a positive relationship between private
bank credit as a percentage of GDP and the level of economic

---

[5] 2008 is the most recent year for which values of PRVCRD for all thirty-six
nations are available on the World Bank's Global Financial Development
database.

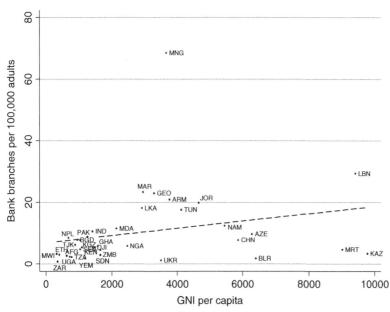

Figure 6.2 Scatter plot for BRNCH and GNI per capita
Source: World Bank Global Financial Development Database

development as measured by GNI per capita. As previous comparative work has observed, the banking systems of Sub-Saharan African nations stand out in comparison to those of other regions of the world for their lack of depth (Beck et al. 2011). The only Sub-Saharan African nation included in the analysis with a value of private bank credit as a percentage of GDP over the population average is Namibia.

Figure 6.2 shows the correlation between GNI per capita and the number of bank branches per 100,000 adults (BRNCH), a standard measure of banking system breadth or outreach. The figure identifies a weak positive correlation. Banking system outreach may be especially important for SMEs that tend to rely more than larger firms on relationship banking depending on geographical proximity and face-to-face contacts (Berger and Udell 1998). The nations of Sub-Saharan Africa are also notable for their lack of banking system outreach, with Namibia at 12.4 branches being the only country with a value over the population average of 10.3 branches per 100,000 adults. Especially

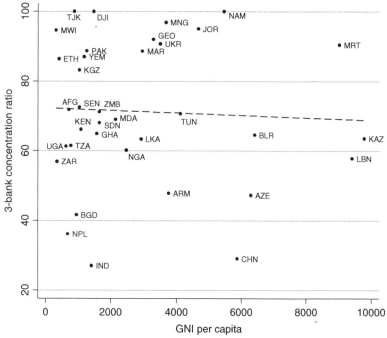

Figure 6.3 Scatter plot for bank concentration and GNI per capita
Source: World Bank Global Financial Development Database

low values are reported in a number of Central Asian nations, including Ukraine, Belarus, and Kazakhstan. Mongolia stands out as an outlier with over sixty bank branches per 100,000 adults.

Figure 6.3 presents the correlation between GNI per capita and the 3-bank concentration ratio (CONCTR). Concentration ratios range from a low of 27 percent in India to a high of 100 percent in Namibia, Djibouti, and Tajikistan. The impact of concentration on access to credit and firm growth has been debated in the literature, especially as regards its impact on SMEs. Comparing states across the United States, Black and Strahan (2002) find that higher levels of concentration result in lower rates of new firm formation. However, Petersen and Rjan (1995), using data from the US National Survey of Small Business Firms, find that credit-constrained firms are more likely to gain access to credit in concentrated credit markets because the lenders are more easily able to internalize the benefits of assisting them. From the cross-national perspective, Beck et al. (2004), in a seminal study using World Bank data for seventy-four developed and developing countries, found that concentration had a negative impact on access to credit and that the negative impact is stronger for SMEs. This result is qualified, however, by the finding that the negative impact is dampened or rendered insignificant by higher levels of institutional development, in the sense of more respect for rule of law and lower levels of corruption, and by the importance of foreign banks as a share of all banks.

Interest rate spreads and net interest margins are often used as proxies for financial intermediation efficiency. Costly finance, as reflected in high net interest margins, may result in credit rationing, with some borrowers unable to borrow all they want or even impeded from having any access to bank finance. Beck et al. (2011: ch. 2), focusing on finance in Sub-Saharan Africa, argue that the generally high interest rate spreads and margins in this region may be the counterpart of the small size and inefficiency of the national financial systems. Figure 6.4 shows a negative relation for the thirty-six nations

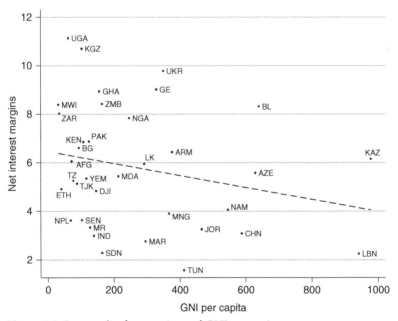

Figure 6.4 Scatter plot for margins and GNI per capita
Source: World Bank Global Financial Development Database

between the size of net interest margins and the level of economic development as measured by GNI per capita. Values range from a high of 11.1 percent in Uganda to a low of 1.6 percent in Tunisia.

6.3.1 The Relation between National Banking Systems and Credit Constraints

In order to measure whether or not firms are credit constrained, we use the approach developed by Kuntchev et al. (2012), which draws on the rich information collected in the WBES on the financing decisions of establishments during the year prior to survey. Credit constrained establishments (FC) are defined as establishments that either applied for a loan or a line of credit and had their application rejected, or did not apply for a loan or a line of credit for reasons other than having enough capital for their needs. The possible reasons include the following terms and conditions implying that these firms, at least to some extent, were rationed out of the market: interest rates were not favorable, collateral requirements were too high, the size of the loan and maturity were insufficient, they did not think the application would be approved, or the application procedures were too complex. In short, credit-constrained firms are defined as firms that would like additional credit to meet their investment needs but have been unable to gain access to it.[6]

The national share of firms that are credit constrained varies from a high of about 58 percent in Tanzania and Ghana to a low of about 11 percent in Mongolia. Figure 6.5 points to a negative relationship between the share of establishments in each nation that are credit constrained and GNI per capita. Nations in the Sub-Saharan African region stand out for the high shares of their establishments that are credit constrained, with Namibia and Kenya being the only nations with a share below the sample average of 34 percent.

In order to explore the impact of the characteristics of national banking systems on the probability that a firm is credit constrained, we use a probit model that takes the following form:

---

[6] Our category of credit constrained firms combines the categories of "fully" and "partially" credit constrained firms in the terminology of Kuntchev et al. (2012: 10). They define partially credit constrained firms as firms that while meeting the conditions in the definition above did make some use of external finance during the previous fiscal year and/or had an outstanding loan at the time of the survey.

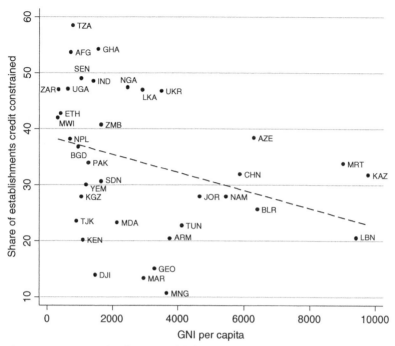

Figure 6.5 Scatter plot for % establishments credit constrained and GNI per capita
Sources: World Bank Global Financial Development Database, World Bank Enterprise Survey and authors' calculations

$$W^* = X'_1\beta_1 + \varepsilon_1 \quad W = 1 \text{ if } W^* > 0, 0 \text{ otherwise where } \varepsilon_1 \sim N(0, 1)$$
$$(6.1)$$

Where W^* is a latent variable that can be interpreted as the unobservable severity of financing constraints.

Equation 6.2 presents the baseline probit model without country-level covariates. At the enterprise level we control for a set of firm characteristics that are likely to impact on the probability of being credit constrained. *LogEmp* refers to size of the firm as measured by the natural logarithm of the number of full-time employees, and *Foreign* measures whether or not the firm's ownership is over 20 percent foreign. We expect that larger establishments with a greater sales volume will be less likely to be credit constrained and that firms with foreign ownership will have better access to sources of external credit. *Young* is a binary equal to 1 if the firm was established within the last three years. It is assumed that other things being equal, younger firms without established reputations will be more likely to be credit constrained. *Export* is a variable equal to 1 if the firm exports any of its output, either directly or indirectly. It is assumed that exporters will have better access to credit and will be less constrained than non-exporters. The regressions control for whether the sector of activity is manufacturing, mining and utilities, or service (*Sector*). The data is weighted and, as with Beck et al. (2006a) and Presbitero and Rabellotti (2013), we use cluster-controlled standard errors in order to correct for within-country error correlation. Table 6A.2 in the Annex gives the definitions and descriptive statistics for the enterprise-level variables.

$$Prob(FC = 1) = f(LogEmp, Foreign, Young, Export, Sector) \quad (6.2)$$

Table 6.1 presents the results for the probit regressions. Column 1 shows the results for a model without country-level variables and column 2 includes the four aggregate indicators for banking system depth, breadth, concentration, and net interest margins.[7] In column 3 we add an interaction term (*PRVCRD * BRNCH*) in order to assess whether the level of banking system depth moderates the impact of banking system breadth. Our expectation is that if an increase in the number of bank branches is accompanied by a simultaneous increase in the total value of private bank credit available for lending, the negative effect on the financing constraints of firms will be enhanced.

The column 1 results show that there is a negative and statistically significant impact of the variables *LogEmp*, *Foreign*, and *Export* on the probability of the firm being credit constrained. Larger firms, firms with foreign ownership, and firms that export are less likely to be credit constrained than their counterparts. These results are consistent with those in the literature discussed earlier in the chapter. The results also show that the firms belonging to the manufacturing sector have a higher probability of being financially constrained than those belonging to the services sector. The variable *Young* has a negative but not statistically significant impact.

---

[7] See Table 6A.2 in the Annex for descriptive statistics for the four aggregate indicators.

Table 6.1 *Probit model estimating credit constraints*

Variables	(1) FC	(2) FC	(3) FC
Foreign	−0.135**	−0.116***	−0.115***
	(0.0538)	(0.0322)	(0.0314)
LogEmp	−0.164***	−0.163***	−0.164***
	(0.0536)	(0.0536)	(0.0536)
Young	−0.119	−0.190***	−0.189***
	(0.0799)	(0.0699)	(0.0697)
Sector	0.144***	0.337***	0.334***
	(0.0456)	(0.0279)	(0.0283)
Export	−0.276***	−0.258***	−0.258***
	(0.00519)	(0.0190)	(0.0193)
CONCTR		−0.00445***	−0.00184
		(0.00124)	(0.00154)
BRNCH		−0.0237***	0.00367
		(0.00675)	(0.0144)
PRVCRD		−0.00600***	−0.00125
		(0.000593)	(0.00224)
MARGIN		−0.00159	−0.0253
		(0.0225)	(0.0188)
BRNCH*PRVCRD			−0.000628**
			(0.000280)
Constant	0.171	0.850***	0.648***
	(0.147)	(0.206)	(0.220)
Pseudo R²	0.0309	0.0347	0.0348
Prob>Chi2	0.0000	0.0000	0.0000
Observations	25,485	25,485	25,485

Robust standard errors in parentheses.*** p<0.01, ** p<0.05, * p<0.1***, **, * denote significance at the 0.01, 0.05, 0.10 levels, respectively. The data are weighted and the regressions control for clustering of errors within countries.

The column 2 results show that the aggregate banking system indicators measuring breadth, depth, and concentration have a negative and statistically significant impact on the probability of a firm being credit constrained, with the effect being relatively strong in the case of BRNCH. The coefficient on MARGIN is negative but not statistically significant. Contrary to expectations, the results show that higher levels of banking concentration reduce the probability of a firm being credit constrained after controlling for the other characteristics of the national banking system.

The column 3 results show that the interaction term between the system depth and breadth is negative and statistically significant, supporting the hypothesis that the negative impact of increasing the number of bank branches on financing constraints will be larger as private bank credit as a percent of GDP increases. This implies that policies designed to reduce financing constraints by increasing banking system outreach will have a greater impact when combined with measures to increase the amount of private bank credit in the economy.

6.4 The Relation between Innovation, Credit Constraints, and National Banking Systems

In this section we focus on how the characteristics of national banking systems indirectly affect enterprise innovation performance through their impact on the probability that the enterprise is credit constrained. In keeping with the basic Oslo Manual definition, innovation is measured as the introduction onto the market during the three years prior to the survey of a product or service that is new-to-the firm (NewFrm). This measure captures processes of imitation and technology diffusion that tend to characterize innovation in developing countries, as it includes the introduction of product and services that although new to the firm are already available elsewhere, either on the national or international market. Column 4 in Table 6A.1 in the Annex shows the share of firms in each country that have introduced a new product or service. Values range from a high of about 68 percent in Kenya to a very low value of about 2 percent in Azerbaijan.

As a number of authors has observed, the cross-sectional nature of the data used in estimating the probability of innovation creates a potential problem of endogeneity resulting in biased estimates of the impact of financial constraints on innovation performance (Savignac 2006; Gorodnichenko and Schnitzer 2013). The simplest way to understand this is to observe that for reasons of asymmetric information associated with the intangible nature of the human and knowledge assets used in the early stages of an innovation project involving search and possibly prototype development, firms wishing to innovate generally rely on internal financing. To the extent that their internal funds are exhausted during the early stages of innovation activities, firms wishing to innovate will be forced to turn to relatively costly external financing in the form of bank loans or equity financing for the latter stages, including the production and marketing of the new products or services. For these reasons, firms trying to innovate are more likely to face credit constraints, in the form of having their applications to banks for a loan or a line of credit rejected or of being rationed out of the market by terms and conditions, than firms that did not even try to innovate, since these non-innovators will be less likely to have exhausted their internal funds (Gorodnichenko and Snitzer 2013). This endogeneity means that the coefficients in a regression model estimating the impact of financial constraints on innovation outcomes will tend to be biased upward, and they may even show a positive relation between financial constraints and innovation, whereas the direction of the impact is actually negative.

One approach to addressing the endogeneity problem is through the use of instrumental variables. However, finding variables that meet the criteria for good instruments often poses a problem since many of the variables that have a direct effect on the endogenous variable will also have an effect on the dependent variable. To circumvent the difficulty in identifying valid instruments, we adopt the approach used by Savignac (2006) and use a bivariate probit model with correlated disturbances and an endogenous binary variable. This is a recursive simultaneous equation model where the binary dependent variable in the first equation appears as an endogenous variable on the right-hand side of the second structural equation (Greene 2012 for a presentation). As Wilde (2000) has shown, under the standard assumption that the correlated disturbance terms between the two equations are bivariate normally distributed, the endogenous nature of one of the variables on the right-hand side of the structural equation can be ignored in formulating the log-likelihood. The only restriction on the parameters that needs to be imposed in order for complete identification is that the two equations in the simultaneous model contain a varying exogenous regressor.[8]

6.4.1 The Baseline Bivariate Probit Model

The bivariate probit model with an endogenous binary variable takes the following form:

$$W^* = x'_1\beta_1 + \varepsilon_1 \quad W = 1 \text{ if } W^* > 0, 0 \text{ otherwise,}$$
$$y^* = x'_2\beta_2 + \gamma W + \varepsilon_2 \quad y = 1 \text{ if } y^* > 0, 0 \text{ otherwise,}$$
$$\varepsilon_1, \varepsilon_2 \sim N(0, 1) \text{ et } Cov(\varepsilon_1, \varepsilon_2) = \rho \qquad (6.3)$$

where W^* and y^* are unobserved latent variables. The latent variable y^* can be interpreted as the expected returns from innovating and W^* is the unobservable severity of financing constraints. The assumption is that the error terms of the two equations are bivariate normally distributed and correlated with the covariance equal to ρ.

Equation (6.4) presents the baseline bivariate probit model estimated to determine the impact of credit constraints on the probability of innovating. The first equation modelling the probability of being credit constrained takes the same basic form as Equation (6.1) in the ordinary probit model developed in Section 6.3.

$$Prob(FC = 1) = f(LogEmp, Foreign, Young, Export, Sector)$$
$$Prob(NewFrm = 1) = f(FC, R\&D, Train, Export, LogEmp,$$
$$LogEmp^2, Sector) \qquad (6.4)$$

In the second structural equation explaining innovation outcomes, the enterprise level covariates include FC, the endogenous binary variable measuring credit constraints, RD, a binary variable equal to 1 if the establishment undertakes R&D expenditures, *Train*, a binary variable equal to 1 if the establishment offers formal training to its permanent employees, and the control variables appearing in the first equation. The variable *Export* in the second equation is designed to capture

---

[8] As Savignac (p. 17) observes, there is some confusion on this point due to the claim by Maddala (1983: 222) that further exclusion restrictions on the exogenous variables comparable to the linear case are required for identification in the bivariate probit model. Wilde (2000) shows that this is only true in the special case treated by Maddala of the simple intercept model, where the exogenous variable in each equation is a constant. Wilde provides an example where a varying dichotomous variable enters the right-hand side of both equations.

horizontal linkages, and it reflects the hypothesis that exporters will be more innovative through their contacts with more knowledgeable foreign customers or due to the increased pressure of international competition. We also assume that larger establishments are more likely to innovate as they have more resources than smaller establishments. Returns to scale are hypothesized to be decreasing due to problems of managerial inefficiency and organizational inertia in larger establishments, and this is captured by including the square of the natural logarithm of employment (*LogEmp2*). As for the first equation we control for sector of activity. The data are weighted as in the ordinary probit regressions in Section 6.3 and we use cluster-controlled standard errors throughout to correct for within-country error correlation. Table 6A.2 in the Annex presents descriptive statistics for the enterprise-level covariates.

6.4.2 Results for the Baseline Bivariate Probit Model

Table 6.2 presents the results for both the univariate probit model estimating the probability of innovating (column 1) and for the baseline bivariate probit model taking into account the endogeneity of firm-level credit constraints (column 2). The value for *rho* in the bivariate model is 0.799 and highly statistically significant, showing that the disturbances of two univariate probit models are highly correlated. This result supports the hypothesis that credit constraints are endogenous to the decision to innovate and that firms that engage in innovation development projects are more likely to face financial constraints than firms that don't even try to innovate.[9] The importance of the bias introduced by the endogeneity can be appreciated by comparing the results for the univariate probit model shown in column 1 with those for the bivariate probit model in column 2. In the univariate model the coefficient on the financial constraint variable (*FC*) is weakly negative and non-statistically significant, while in the structural equation predicting innovation outcomes in the bivariate probit model the negative coefficient on *FC* is both considerably larger in absolute size and highly statistically significant.

---

[9] See Knapp and Seaks (1998) for a demonstration that a likelihood ratio (LR) test of the hypothesis that rho = 0 is equivalent to a Hausman test for endogeneity.

Table 6.2 *Baseline Bivariate Probit Model*

	(1) Univariate probit	(2) Bivariate probit model
Innovation equation	Dependent variable : NewFrm	
FC	−0.128	−1.373***
	(0.0894)	(0.153)
R&D	1.253***	0.980***
	(0.0154)	(0.0181)
Train	0.0405*	0.0132
	(0.0238)	(0.0121)
LogEmp	0.210***	0.0599***
	(0.0490)	(0.0119)
LogEmp²	−0.0221***	−0.0135***
	(0.00734)	(0.00395)
Export	0.515***	0.274***
	(0.0645)	(0.0348)
Sector	−0.312***	−0.159***
	(0.0570)	(0.0432)
Constant	−1.034***	−0.0571
	(0.0764)	(0.113)
Credit constraint equation	Dependent variable : FC	
LogEmp		−0.167***
		(0.0542)
Foreign		−0.244***
		(0.0466)
Young		−0.00925
		(0.0201)
Export		−0.279***
		(0.00870)

Table 6.2 (*cont.*)

	(1) Univariate probit	(2) Bivariate probit model
Credit constraint equation		Dependent variable : *FC*
Sector		0.146***
		(0.0484)
Constant		0.186
		(0.145)
Rho		0.799
(Wald test of rho=0) Prob>Chi2		0.000
Observations	25,485	25,485

Robust standard errors in parentheses. *** p<0.01, ** p<0.05, * p<0.1***, **, * denote significance at the 0.01, 0.05, 0.10 levels, respectively. The data are weighted and the regressions correct for clustering of errors within countries.

Both the univariate probit and the bivariate probit models show that there is a positive and statistically significant impact of R&D expenditures on the probability of innovating. The variable measuring the provision of formal training for the firm's full-time employees is positive in the univariate model, although it is of borderline statistical significance. It is no longer statistically significant in the bivariate probit model. The results also show that being an exporter has a statistically significant impact on the probability of innovating and that firms in the manufacturing, mining, or utilities sectors have a lower probability of innovating compared to service sector enterprises. The results for the impact of *LogEmp* on innovation activity do not differ between the univariate and bivariate probit models, showing that larger firms have a higher probability of innovating. There is evidence to support the presence of decreasing returns to scale in the effect of establishment size on innovation, with the squared employment term being negative and significant in both models.

Table 6.3 presents the results for the bivariate models including the national banking system indicators in the equation predicting the

Table 6.3 *Bivariate Probit Model with country-level covariates*

	(1) Bivariate probit model	(2) Bivariate probit model
Innovation equation	Dependent variable: *NewFrm*	
FC	–1.277***	–1.284***
	(0.302)	(0.285)
R&D	1.040***	1.037***
	(0.0955)	(0.0884)
Train	0.0769	0.0760
	(0.0535)	(0.0523)
LogEmp	0.0707***	0.0699***
	(0.0201)	(0.0180)
LogEmp^2	–0.0144***	–0.0143***
	(0.00368)	(0.00377)
Export	0.337***	0.335***
	(0.0455)	(0.0410)
Sector2	0.143**	0.144**
	(0.0612)	(0.0592)
LnGNICAP	–0.285***	–0.284***
	(0.0259)	(0.0252)
Constant	1.918***	1.915***
	(0.179)	(0.166)
Credit constraint equation	Dependent variable: *FC*	
Foreign	–0.236***	–0.234***
	(0.0320)	(0.0320)
LogEmp	–0.167***	–0.167***
	(0.0549)	(0.0548)
Young	–0.0484	–0.0451
	(0.0461)	(0.0441)
Export	–0.264***	–0.263***
	(0.0270)	(0.0274)

Table 6.3 (*cont.*)

	(1) Bivariate probit model	(2) Bivariate probit model
Credit constraint equation	Dependent variable: *FC*	
Sector2	0.345***	0.341***
	(0.0389)	(0.0383)
CONCTR	−0.00239	0.000887
	(0.00169)	(0.00199)
PRVCRD	−0.00533***	0.000749
	(0.000888)	(0.00252)
BRNCH	−0.0144*	0.0204
	(0.00805)	(0.0139)
MARGIN	−0.0115	−0.0410
	(0.0299)	(0.0255)
PRVCRD*BRNCH		−0.000801***
		(0.000301)
Constant	0.693***	0.434**
	(0.168)	(0.182)
Rho	0.7269	0.7317
(Wald test of rho=0) Prob>Chi2	0.0061	0.0032
Observations	25,485	25,485

Robust standard errors in parentheses. *** p<0.01, ** p<0.05, * p<0.1***, **, * denote significance at the 0.01, 0.05, 0.10 levels, respectively. The data are weighted and the regressions correct for clustering of errors within countries.

probability of being credit constrained. The column 2 results are for the model including an interaction term between banking system breadth and depth. In the innovation equation we control for the level of economic development by including the natural logarithm of GNI per capita (*LnGNICAP*).

The column 1 results show that the coefficients on the measures of banking system depth (*PRVCRD*) and breadth (*BRNCH*) are negative and statistically significant, as in the univariate probit model presented in Section 6.3. In the innovation equation the coefficient on *LnGNICAP* measuring the level of economic development is negative and statistically significant. To the extent that the size of technological gap is larger in less economically developed nations, this result supports the hypothesis that firms in nations that are more distant from the technological frontier will have a higher probability of innovating due to the greater amount of mature technology available on national and international markets for diffusion and adoption. The statistically significant negative coefficient on the interaction term between banking system depth and breadth in column 2 points to complementarities with the negative impact of banking system breadth on the probability of being credit constrained being greater when the level of private bank credit as a percentage of GDP is greater.

6.4.3 The Indirect Impact of the National Banking System on Innovation

In order to estimate the indirect effects of the level of development of the national banking system on innovation performance through its impact on firm-level financing constraints, we calculate the marginal effects of the enterprise and country-level covariates in the bivariate probit model on the probability of innovating being conditional on the firm being credit constrained. Table 6.4 reports both the indirect and direct average marginal effects for the covariates in the column 2 model in Table 6.3. The table distinguishes between those variables having a direct effect, those having an indirect effect, and those having both direct and indirect effects on the probability of innovating. The marginal effects reported for the four macro financial systems variables are indirect and reflect the way they affect innovation through their impact on the endogenous dependent variable FC, measuring whether or not the firm is credit constrained. For the binary variables, the marginal effects measure discrete changes and show how the probability of innovating changes as a binary variable changes from 0 to 1.

The results show on average that being credit constrained reduces the probability of innovating by about 38 percent. Undertaking R&D expenditure increases the probability of innovating by about 30 percent and exporting increases the probability of innovating by about 14 percent. Foreign ownership, through its negative impact on

Table 6.4 *Conditional direct and indirect marginal effects on the probability of innovating*

Variables	Marginal effects	p-value
Direct effects		
FC	–0.3761	0.000
R&D	0.3037	0.000
Train	0.0223	0.209
LnGNICAP	–0.0832	0.000
Indirect effects		
Foreign	0.0362	0.000
Young	0.0070	0.254
CONCTR	–0.0001	0.660
PRVCRD	0.0009	0.000
BRNCH	0.0075	0.001
MARGIN	0.0063	0.121
Direct and indirect effects		
LogEmp	0.0463	0.000
Export	0.1389	0.000
Sector	–0.0107	0.366

The data are weighted and the regression corrects for clustering of errors within countries.

the probability of being credit constrained, indirectly increases the probability of innovating by about 4 percent. The effect of undertaking training and the effect of the firm being established within the previous three years are not statistically significant.

With respect to the aggregate banking system variables, the results show that on average the indirect effects of *BRNCH* and *PRVCRD* on the probability of innovating are positive and statistically significant. The estimated indirect effect of *PRVCRD* is quite small and it implies that a 10 percent increase in the value of bank credit as a share of GDP would lead to an approximate 1 percent increase in the probability of

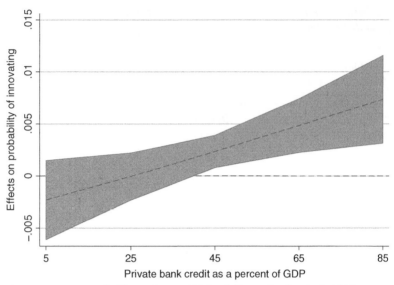

Figure 6.6 Marginal effects of BRNCH for different levels of PRVCRD

innovating. In the case of *BRNCH*, the marginal effect is considerably larger with an increase in the number of bank branches per 100,000 adults by 10, increasing the probability of innovating by about 7.6 percent. For countries like Yemen, Uganda, and the Democratic Republic of Congo this could account for an approximate 20 percent shortfall in the probability of innovating when compared with countries with relatively well-developed banking systems like Tunisia, Morocco, and Jordan.

The negative coefficient on the interaction term between *BRNCH* and *PRVCRD* shown in Table 6.3 implies that the marginal effects on innovation of an increase in banking system breadth will be larger for higher levels of banking system depth. To explore this relation in more detail, Figure 6.6 shows the average marginal effects with 95 percent confidence intervals of an increase in *BRNCH* conditional on the level of private bank credit as a percent of GDP. The results show that the average marginal effects on the probability of innovating of an increase in *BRNCH* increase in size as *PRVCRD* increases, and that they are positive for values of *PRVCRD* above 30 percent. The positive effect is only statistically significant for values of *PRVCRD* over 40 percent.

The first quartile of the sample of thirty-six nations investigated here have values of *PRVCRD* under 23 percent of GDP and half of the nations have values under 40 percent. The results presented in Figure 6.4 imply that for the majority of nations an increase in banking system outreach or breadth will have only a limited or no positive impact on enterprise innovation performance. The results point to a threshold value of *PRVCRD*, over 30 percent of GDP, which needs to be attained in order for innovation performance to possibly benefit from increases in banking system breadth. These results support the view that institutions matter and moreover provide insight into the factors that may slow or inhibit innovation and technological catch-up in low income nations with a very low level of financial institutional development.

6.4.4 The Indirect Effect of Firm Size on Innovation Performance

There is considerable evidence to show that smaller firms are more likely to be credit constrained than larger ones. At the same time, increases in the breadth or outreach of the banking system (in the sense of the number of branches and their geographic spread) will arguably improve the relative position of smaller firms that tend to rely more on relational banking than larger ones. To provide evidence relevant to this, we present in Table 6.5 the results of regressions including firm size categories, and we estimate their interactions with the measures of banking system breadth and depth. We use a three-level categorical variable to measure size, with small firms employing less than 20 employees, medium firms employing 20 to 99 employees, and large firms employing over 99 employees. Large firms are the reference category in the regressions. We remove the continuous variable used in the previous regressions that measured firm size as the natural logarithm of the number of employees.

The results in column 1 show that relative to large firms, small and medium-sized firms are more likely to be credit constrained, with the effect being greater in the case of small firms. Expressed in terms of marginal effects, the indirect negative effects on the probability of innovating for small and medium-sized firms, respectively, compared to large firms come to about 6 and 2 percent.

In column 2, the model includes interaction effects. There is a clear difference between how firm size interacts with the level of *BRNCH*

Table 6.5 *Bivariate Probit Model with interaction effects on firm size*

	(1) Bivariate probit model	(2) Bivariate probit model
Innovation equation	Dependent variable: *NewFrm*	
FC	−1.008***	−0.776**
	(0.175)	(0.303)
R&D	1.145***	1.204***
	(0.0589)	(0.0396)
Train	0.0883*	0.106*
	(0.0475)	(0.0605)
Export	0.385***	0.444***
	(0.0570)	(0.0353)
Sector	0.108***	0.0856*
	(0.0303)	(0.0476)
LnGNICAP	−0.290***	−0.292***
	(0.0195)	(0.0166)
Constant	1.857***	1.745***
	(0.1332)	(0.1808)
Credit constraint equation	Dependent variable: *FC*	
Foreign	−0.182***	−0.145***
	(0.0565)	(0.0213)
Young	−0.0705**	−0.0515**
	(0.0337)	(0.0239)
Size (small)	0.468***	−0.0438
	(0.139)	(0.315)
Size (medium)	0.183***	0.256*
	(0.0359)	(0.145)
Export	−0.280***	−0.258***
	(0.0279)	(0.0489)
Sector	0.308***	0.260***
	(0.0301)	(0.0241)

Table 6.5 (*cont.*)

	(1) Bivariate probit model	(2) Bivariate probit model
Credit constraint equation	Dependent variable: *FC*	
CONCTR	−0.00327**	−0.00285*
	(0.00156)	(0.00159)
PRVCRD	−0.00606***	−0.0111***
	(0.000629)	(0.00203)
BRNCH	−0.0169**	0.0118
	(0.00770)	(0.0181)
MARGIN	−0.00725	0.00397
	(0.0279)	(0.0261)
Size (small)*PRVCRD		0.00995***
		(0.00256)
Size (medium)*PRVCRD		0.00208**
		(0.00102)
Size (small)*BRNCH		−0.0410*
		(0.0215)
Size (medium)*BRNCH		−0.0317***
		(0.00884)
Constant	−0.0330	0.159
	(0.164)	(0.284)
Rho	0.550	0.401
(Wald test of rho=0) Prob>Chi2	0.0004	0.0174
Observations	25,482	25,482

Robust standard errors in parentheses. ***, **, * denote significance at the 0.01, 0.05, 0.10 levels, respectively. The data are weighted and the regressions control for clustering of errors within countries. Here, we have a sample of 25,482 observations because three firms were not classified in one of the three groups in the data.

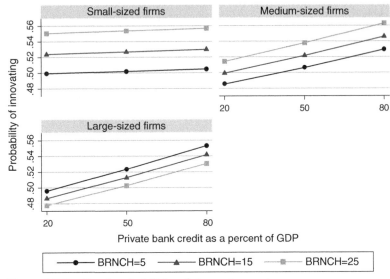

Figure 6.7 Predicted probabilities of size on innovation

and *PRVCRD*. In the case of *BRNCH*, the coefficients on the interaction terms are negative and statistically significant, implying that the probability of being credit constrained for small and medium-sized firms decreases relative to larger ones when the number of bank branches per 100,000 adults increases. The effect is stronger for the small firm category. In the case of *PRVCRD*, while the interaction effects are much weaker, they work in the opposite direction, implying that the relative positon of larger firms improves as the amount of private bank credit in the economy increases. Again the size of the effect is larger for small firms than for medium-sized ones.

In Figure 6.7 we take a closer look at how the innovative performance of small and medium-sized firms is affected by banking system breadth and depth. The figure shows the predictive margins or probabilities of innovating for each size category of firm for different levels of banking system depth and breadth. The results show that for all levels of private bank credit as a percent of GDP, the innovative performance of small firms and, to a lesser extent, medium-sized firms benefits from increases in the number of bank branches. This supports the hypothesis that increases in banking system outreach are relatively advantageous for smaller establishments. The innovative performance of both medium- and large-sized firms improves from increases in the amount private bank credit in the system regardless of the level of banking system breadth or outreach. For medium-sized firms, this improvement means that their probability of innovating is slightly greater than that for smaller firms at very high levels of private bank credit as a share of GDP. In the case of large firms, at very high levels of private bank credit their probability of innovating is equal to or outstrips that of small firms, except in the case where the number of bank branches per 100,000 adults is well above the sample average.

6.5 Conclusions

There is considerable evidence at the country level that financial system development is positively correlated with economic development. At the same time, micro-level studies drawing on firm-level data have identified a significant negative relation between financing constraints and firms' investments in their R&D and innovation activities. These combined results are suggestive of a channel through which financial development may influence innovation and technological change, and hence promote economic development. A main objective in this chapter is to contribute to the modelling of this channel by showing how the level of development of the national banking system indirectly influences enterprise innovation activity through its effects on firms' financing constraints. Our results show that low levels of financial system development may hinder or slow processes of innovation and technical change.

When estimating the impact on innovation of measures of country-level banking system depth and breadth, we obtain a number of important results. At the margin, the indirect effects of increases in the depth and breadth of national banking systems on the probability of innovating are important, and we show that the impact of an increase in banking system breadth or outreach only becomes positive above a threshold level of private bank credit as a percentage of GDP. This result illuminates a possible obstacle to technological catch-up in lower income nations with relatively shallow financial systems, and it may, as Levine (1997) has suggested, be a contributing factor to the creation of a "poverty trap."

Our results are relevant to understanding the position of small enterprises, which account for the majority of businesses in developing nations and for about 56 percent of our sample. Consistent with other research we find that small firms are more likely to be credit constrained than medium and large-sized firms, and we show that this disadvantages the innovation performance of small firms relative to larger firms. We also identify important differences in the effects of increases in banking system depth and breadth on innovation performance according to firm size. Large firms tends to benefit disproportionately from increases in banking system depth, while small firms and, to a lesser extent, medium-sized firms reap relative innovation benefits from increases in banking system breadth. Our results show that the majority of enterprises will garner limited benefits from policies focusing narrowly on increasing the amount of available credit in the banking system without concomitant increases in the number of bank branches.

Our research could be usefully extended in a number of directions. The measure of innovation we use is the basic one proposed by the Oslo Manual, defined as the introduction of a product or service that is new-to-the firm. While this measure allows us to capture processes of imitation and diffusion of technologies and products, it fails to characterize differences in the importance of the firm's in-house contribution to the innovation activity. While in some cases firms will be creatively adapting or modifying products or services developed by other organizations, in other cases they may be simply adopting and selling on new products or services developed by other organizations without any significant contribution. While the adoption of existing technologies and products without modifications requires in-house learning activity and may require investments in workforce training, we would expect financing constraints to be more binding in the case of the more substantial investments needed for the creative forms of adaptation and modification. The WBES group is currently undertaking follow-up surveys in selected nations, providing a rich characterization of the innovation process, including marketing and organizational innovations. As this survey work continues and provides coverage for a large number of nations worldwide, it will become possible to extend the analysis we have undertaken here to take into account differences in the firm's in-house creative contribution to innovation.

Another useful extension would be to explore more explicitly the links between the level of development of the financial system, the existence of a technology gap, and processes of catch-up. Our results are suggestive in this respect. On the one hand we find that the probability of innovating tends to be greater in nations at lower levels of economic development, as measured by GNI per capita, which is suggestive of positive catch-up through technology diffusion. At the same time, we have shown that having a relatively shallow financial system decreases the probability of firms innovating. These results could be strengthened by determining whether there are threshold levels of economic development below which processes of catch-up tend to slow. By relating these thresholds to the level of institutional development, such an analysis could contribute to a better understanding of the factors that hinder or even block economic development in the world's weakest nations.

ANNEX

World Bank Enterprise Survey Methodology

The World Bank Enterprise Surveys (ES) are conducted by private contractors on behalf of the World Bank (WB). According to the World Bank, an ES is a firm-level survey of a representative sample of an economy's private sector. The survey topics include firm characteristics, gender participation, access to finance, annual sales, costs of inputs/labor, workforce composition, bribery, licensing, infrastructure, trade, crime, competition, capacity utilization, land and permits, taxation, informality, business-government relations, innovation and technology, and performance measures. Over 90 percent of the questions objectively ascertain characteristics of a country's business environment. The remaining questions assess the survey respondents' opinions on what are the obstacles to firm growth and performance. The mode of data collection is face-to-face interviews.

The manufacturing and services sectors are the primary business sectors of interest and the firms targeted for interview are formal (registered) companies with five or more employees. Firm-level surveys have been conducted since the 1990s. Since 2005, the WB has used a standardized methodology of implementation, sampling, and quality control in most countries, which allows for better international comparisons. ES are composed of representative random samples of firms and all samples are constructed following a stratified random selection. The survey questionnaire is answered by business owners and top managers. Sometimes the survey respondent calls company accountants and human resource managers into the interview to answer questions in the sales and labor sections of the survey. Typically 1200–1800 interviews are conducted in larger economies, 360 interviews are conducted in medium-sized economies, and for smaller economies, 150 interviews take place. The strata for ES are firm size, business sector, and geographic region within a country. Firm-size levels are: small (5–19 employees), medium (20–99 employees), and large (100 and more employees). Sector breakdown is usually: manufacturing, retail, and other services, and geographic regions are selected based on which cities/regions collectively contain the majority of economic activity. For more details on the sample frame and survey methodology, see the following link: (www.enterprisesurveys.org/methodology).

Table 6A.1 *Country descriptive statistics*

Region	Country	GDP (billion $)	GNI per capita	NEWFRM	CONSTR
East Asia & Pacific	Mongolia (MNG)	12.293	3670	26.18	10.74
	China (CHN)	8461.623	5870	46.81	31.96
	Tajikistan (TJK)	7.633	890	16.43	23.58
	Kyrgyz Republic (KGZ)	6.605	1040	38.43	27.89
	Moldova (MDA)	7.285	2140	29.81	23.3
Central Asia	Georgia (GEO)	15.846	3290	10	15.1
	Ukraine (UKR)	175.781	3500	20.04	46.77
	Armenia (ARM)	10.619	3760	15.83	20.51
	Azerbaijan (AZE)	68.731	6290	2.05	38.46
	Belarus (BLR)	63.615	6400	31.01	25.67

Table 6A.1 (*cont.*)

Region	Country	GDP (billion $)	GNI per capita	NEWFRM	CONSTR
	Kazakhstan (KAZ)	203.517	9780	19.33	31.81
	Nepal (NPL)	18.852	690	44.4	38.23
	Afghanistan (AFG)	20.537	720	45.07	53.69
	Bangladesh (BGD)	133.356	950	34.1	36.84
South Asia	Pakistan (PAK)	224.646	1260	29.79	33.97
	India (IND)	1831.781	1410	44.91	48.53
	Sri Lanka (LKA)	68.434	2920	31.03	47.02
	Yemen. Rep. (YEM)	32.075	1180	40.79	30.03
	Djibouti (DJI)	1.354	1471	35.14	13.99
Middle East & North Africa	Morocco (MAR)	98.266	2960	31.34	13.37
	Tunisia (TUN)	45.131	4120	27.2	22.83
	Jordan (JOR)	30.937	4660	23.89	27.98
	Lebanon (LBN)	43.205	9410	43.85	20.62
	Malawi (MWI)	4.24	320	53.86	41.97
Sub-Saharan Africa	Congo. Dem. Rep. (ZAR)	27.463	350	41.59	47.09
	Ethiopia (ETH)	43.311	410	42.55	42.73
	Uganda (UGA)	23.237	630	64.3	47.16

Table 6A.1 (*cont.*)

Region	Country	GDP (billion $)	GNI per capita	NEWFRM	CONSTR
	Tanzania (TZA)	39.088	780	51.66	58.52
	Senegal (SEN)	14.046	1040	47.57	49.03
	Kenya (KEN)	50.41	1090	67.87	20.21
	Mauritania (MRT)	4.845	1290	55.33	33.85
	Ghana (GHA)	41.94	1570	51.25	54.24
	Zambia (ZMB)	24.939	1650	55.44	40.76
	Sudan (SDN)	62.689	1650	53.06	30.68
	Nigeria (NGA)	460.954	2470	49.85	47.43
	Namibia (NAM)	13.016	5450	63.87	27.95

Source: World Bank Development Indicators

Table 6A.2 *Descriptive statistics*

Variable	Mean	St. dev.
NewFrm (= 1 if firm has introduced onto the market a product or service that is new-to-the firm, 0 otherwise)	0.411	0.492
Constr (= 1 if the firm is credit constrained, 0 otherwise)	0.398	0.489
R&D (= 1 if the firms has spent on R&D over the last year, 0 otherwise)	0.238	0.426
Train (= 1 if firm offers formal training to its permanent employees, 0 otherwise)	0.346	0.476
Export (= 1 if the firm has positive direct of indirect exports, 0 otherwise)	0.191	0.393

Table 6A.2 (*cont.*)

Variable	Mean	St. dev.
LnGNICAP (= natural logarithm of GNI per capita)	7.492	0.766
LogEmp (= natural logarithm of number of permanent employees)	3.259	1.364
LogEmp^2 (= square of LogEmp)	12.484	10.780
Foreign (=1 if over 20 percent foreign ownership, 0 otherwise)	0.056	0.229
Young (= 1 if the firm was established within the last 3 years	0.048	0.215
Sector (= 1 if manufacturing, mining or utilities, 0 = services)	0.606	0.489
Size (small) (= to 1 if < 20 employees)	0.460	0.498
Size (medium) (= to 1 if 20–99 employees)	0.357	0.479
Size (large) (= to 1 > = 100 employees)	0.183	0.386
BRNCH (= number of bank branches per 100,000 adults)	9.237	7.383
CONCTR (= 3-bank concentration ratio as expressed in %)	55.479	24.652
PRVCRD (= private bank credit as a percentage of GDP)	38.079	22.139
MARGIN (=bank net interest margin as expressed in %)	5.153	2.496

References

Arocena, R. and Sutz, J. 2000. Looking at national systems of innovation from the South. *Industry and Innovation* 7(1): 55–75.

Arundel, A., Bordoy, C., and Kanerva, M. 2008. Neglected innovators: How do innovative firms that do not perform R&D innovate? Results of an analysis of the Innobarometer 2007 survey No. 215 INNO-Metrics Thematic Paper, MERIT.

Beck, T., Demirguc-Kunt, A., and Maksimovic, V. 2004. Bank competition and access to finance: International evidence. *Journal of Money, Credit, and Banking* 36(3): 627–648.

Beck, T. and Demirgüç-Kunt, A. 2006. Small and medium-size enterprises: Access to finance as a growth constraint. *Journal of Banking & Finance* 30: 2931–2943.

Beck, T., Demirgüç-Kunt, A., Laeven, L. and Maksimovic, V. 2006a. The determinants of financing obstacles. *Journal of International Money and Finance* 25: 932–952.

Beck, T. and Demirgüç-Kunt, A. 2008. Access to finance: An unfinished agenda. *World Bank Economic Review* 22(3): 383–396.

Beck, T., Maimbo, S. M., Faye, I., and Triki, T. 2011 *Financing Africa: Through the Crisis and Beyond.* Washington, DC: World Bank.

Berger, A. N. and Udell, G. F. 1998. The economics of small business finance: The roles of private equity and debt markets in the financial growth cycle. *Journal of Banking & Finance* 22(6): 613–673.

Black, S. E. and Strahan, P. E. 2002. Entrepreneurship and bank credit availability. *The Journal of Finance* 57(6): 2807–2833.

Bond, S., Harhoff, D., and Van Reenen, J. 1999. Investment, R&D, and Financial Constraints in Britain and in Germany, IFS working paper, n° 99/5.

Crespi, G. and Peirano, F. 2007. Measuring innovation in Latin America: What we did, where we are and what we want to do, WP Paper prepared for the MEIDE conference, Maastricht.

Dahlman, C. and Nelson, R. 1995. Social absorption capability, national innovation systems and economic development, in Koo, B. and Perkins, D. (eds.), *Social Capability and Long-Term Economic Growth*. London: Macmillan.

Didier, T. and Schmukler, S. L. 2014. Financial development in Asia: Beyond aggregate indicators, World Bank Policy Research Working Paper No. 6761.

Fagerberg, J. 1987. A technology gap approach to why growth rates. *Research Policy* 16: 87–99.

Fagerberg, J. 1994. Technology and international differences in growth rates. *Journal of Economic Literature* 32(3): 1147–1175.

Fagerberg, J., Srholec, M., and Verspagen, B. 2010. The role of innovation in development. *Review of Economics and Institutions* 1(2): 1–29.

Fazzari, S., Hubbard, R. G., and Petersen, B. C. 1988. Financing constraints and corporate investment. *Brookings Papers on Economic Activity* 1988 (1): 131–195.

Fisman, R. and Love, I. 2003. Trade credit, financial intermediary development, and industry growth. *The Journal of Finance* 58(1): 353–374.

Freeman, C. 1995. The "National System of Innovation" in historical perspective. *Cambridge Journal of Economics* 19(1): 5–24.

Goedhuys, M. 2007. Learning, product innovation, and firm heterogeneity in developing countries; Evidence from Tanzania. *Industrial and Corporate Change* 16(2): 269–292.

Goldsmith, R. W. 1969. *Financial Structure and Development.* New Haven, CT: *Yale University Press.*

Gorodnichenko, Y. and Schnitzer, M. 2013. Financial constraints and innovation: Why poor countries don't catch up. *Journal of the European Economic Association* 11(5): 1115–1152.

Greene, W. H. 2012. *Econometric Analysis,* 7th Edition. New York: Prentice Hall.

Hall, B. and Lerner, J. 2010. The financing of R&D and innovation, in Hall, B. and Rosenberg, N. (eds.), *The Handbook of Innovation.* North Holland: Elsevier.

Kaplan, S. N. and Zingales, L. 1997. Do investment-cash flow sensitivities provide useful measures of financing constraints? *Quarterly Journal of Economics* 112(1): 169–215.

Kim, L. 1997. *Imitation to Innovation: The Dynamics of Korea's Technological Learning.* Boston: Harvard Business School Press.

King, R. G. and Levine, R. 1993. Finance, entrepreneurship and growth. *Journal of Monetary economics* 32(3): 513–542.

Knapp, L. G. and Seaks, T. G. 1998. A Hausman test for a dummy variable in probit. *Applied Economics Letters* 5(5): 321–323.

Kuntchev, V., Ramalho, R., Rodríguez-Meza, J., and Yang, J. S. 2012. What have we learned from the Enterprise Surveys regarding access to finance by SMEs? Enterprise Analysis Unit of the World Bank. Research report.

Lee, K. 2005. Making a technological catch-up: Barriers and opportunities. *Asian Journal of Technology Innovation* 13(2): 97–113.

Leitner, S. M. and Stehrer, R. 2013. R&D and non-R&D innovators in the financial crisis: The role of binding credit constraints. Wiener Inst. für Internat. Wirtschaftsvergleiche (WIIW).

Levine, R. 1997. Financial development and economic growth: Views and agenda. *Journal of Economic Literature* XXXV: 688–726.

Levine, R. 2005. Finance and growth: Theory and evidence, in *Handbook of Economic Growth,* Vol. 1, 865–934.

Lundvall, B. A. 1992. *National Systems of Innovation: Toward a Theory of Innovation and Interactive Learning.* London: Pinter Publishers.

Maddala, G. S. 1983. *Limited-Dependent and Qualitative Variables in Econometrics.* Cambridge: Cambridge University Press.

Mulkay, B., Hall, B., and Mairesse, J. 2001. Firm level investment and R&D in France and the United States: A comparison, in *Investing Today for the World of Tomorrow Studies on the Investment Process in Europe.* Berlin: Springer Verlag, 229–273.

Niosi, J., Saviotti, P., Bellon, B., and Crow, M. 1993. National systems of innovation: In search of a workable concept. *Technology in Society* 15(2): 207–227.

Petersen, M. A. and Rajan, R. G. 1995. The effect of credit market competition on lending relationships. *The Quarterly Journal of Economics*: 407–443.

Presbitero, A. F. and Rabellotti, R. 2013. Is access to credit a constraint for Latin American enterprises? An empirical analysis with firm-level data, Working Paper 101: Money and Finance Research group (Mo.Fi.R).

Rajan, R. G. and Zingales, L. 1998. Financial dependence and growth. *The American Economic Review* 88(3): 559–586.

Rammer, C., Czarnitzki, D. and Spielkamp, A. 2009. Innovation success of non-R&D-performers: Substituting technology by management in SMEs. *Small Business Economics* 33(1): 35–58.

Savignac, F. 2006. The impact of financial constraints on innovation: Evidence from French manufacturing firms, Working Paper, Centre d'Economie de la Sorbonne, Paris.

Schiffer, M. and Weder, B. 2001. *Firm Size and the Business Environment: Worldwide Survey Results*, International Finance Corporation discussion paper; no. IFD 43*IFC working paper series. Washington, DC: The World Bank.

Srholec, M. 2011. A multilevel analysis of innovation in developing countries. *Industrial and Corporate Change* 20(6): 1539–1569.

Verspagen, B. 1991. A new empirical approach to catching up or falling behind. *Structural Change and Economic Dynamics* 2(2): 359–380.

Wilde, J. 2000. Identification of multiple equation probit models with endogenous dummy regressors. *Economics letters* 69(3): 309–312.

7 | Pro-Cyclical Dynamics of STI Investment in Mexico

The Inversion of the Schumpeterian Reasoning*

GABRIELA DUTRÉNIT, JOSÉ MIGUEL NATERA,
MARTÍN PUCHET ANYUL AND FERNANDO
SANTIAGO

7.1 Introduction

Determining the causal relationship between innovation and growth is a classic quest of the economics of innovation studies. However, empirical research that goes beyond verifying the existence of causality, to investigate the direction, intensity, and mechanisms that explain those causal links is still a green field (Foster and Pyka 2014). Investment in the public goods associated with science, technology, and innovation (STI) activities depends on a country's available public resources, which opens up a causal loop that may be associated with either growth and welfare or poverty traps. This interaction between investment in STI and growth remains at the core of many theoretical discussions, especially in developing countries, where this investment is expected to drive economic growth, sustain catching up processes, and assist in poverty alleviation. From an evolutionary perspective, in this chapter we argue that to better understand how STI can foster economic growth, as well as differences in development trajectories between countries, consideration of the "time" dimension is a fundamental drawback in the analysis.

The "time" dimension helps to track the development path followed by a given society. In the literature, two approaches have been adopted.

* An earlier version of this chapter was presented at the 16th Congress of the International Joseph A. Schumpeter Society, Montréal, Canada, July 6–8, 2016. Comments from participants are appreciated.

One is closely linked to historical analysis where the description of the crucial events that have shaped the evolution of an economic system is combined with evidence based on appreciative theorizing, including a policy perspective (Lundvall 1992; Nelson 1993; Hobday 1995; Kim 1997; Lundvall et al. 2009). The other approach has a quantitative base; it uses data to describe the nature and the causal relationships of changes observed over time. By studying autoregressive vectors, the approach seeks to determine the existence and direction of the causal links between different dimensions of the innovation process and economic growth (Castellacci and Natera 2016). The two approaches are powerful tools to explain the development paths that countries follow. However, they are seldom combined to disentangle the complexity of the causal relation between investment in STI and the dynamics of an economy.

Building on data about Mexico, this chapter explores the relation that exists between public expenditure in STI (PESTI) and the dynamics of the Mexican economy, measured in terms of the gross domestic product (GDP). The analysis looks into the causal links between the two variables, and the direction and intensity of the causal effects. The paper characterizes the evolution of STI policy in Mexico, giving due consideration to the most relevant changes in both STI and economic system over a period of more than forty years. Against this background, and using data on GDP, PESTI for the period 1970–2012, we applied a Johansen System Co-integration approach (Hoover, Johansen, and Juselius 2008) to propose a model that links economic growth to public efforts in STI and total investment.

To achieve this, it is important to understand the effect not only of the size but also the manner in which this effort is undertaken. STI activities are highly dependent on their history and how they have evolved over time. Hence, we analyze the causal relationship between STI efforts and economic growth in Mexico by combining qualitative and quantitative approaches.

After this introduction, Section 7.2 reviews the literature on the links between efforts in STI and economic growth; the discussion includes both theoretical research designs and approaches to deal with empirical evidence. Section 7.3 describes our research design. Section 7.4 presents a historical account of the evolution of STI policy, as well as the context around investment and economic dynamics in Mexico. Section 7.5 introduces the methodology underpinning the quantitative model used to analyze the causal links between the variables of interest. The section includes a discussion around the evidence used in this paper. Section 7.6 discusses the results from our econometric models. Finally, Section 7.7 concludes.

7.2 Efforts in STI and Economic Growth

7.2.1 Theoretical Approaches and Research Designs

Assessing the relationship between innovation, economic growth, and development has been a constant in evolutionary economics research. In fact, some relevant concerns, related to learning processes and the integration of innovation into productive systems, date back to Adam Smith's discussions around labor division in 1776, and Friedrich List's work on national systems of production and learning in 1841 (Lundvall et al. 2002).

A pending issue in the innovation studies tradition is that if historical perspectives are fundamental to explain development, then path dependence and nonreversibility cannot be left out of the analysis (Cowan and Foray 2002). Case studies are the preferred methodological approach to accomplish this task. A great amount of empirical evidence has been collected from qualitative and historical research. Freeman's (1987, 1991) study of agents' interactions and the importance of the state for a country's innovation performance set an important reference for the field; Nelson's (1993) comparative analyses of national innovation systems pointed out the heterogeneity of the historical processes that underpin the building of innovation systems. Lundvall et al. (2009) and Edquist and Hommen (2008) have provided insights on the different policy and institutional settings that split developing and developed countries.

An alternative stream of research, more centered on sectorial perspectives, builds history-friendly models (Malerba et al. 1999, 2016; Malerba 2002). Researchers in this field have focused on tracking the evolution of specific technological niches, identifying key structural changes that have impacted on the structure and functioning of productive systems. These distinct approaches to research seldom combine, at least to a desirable level, econometric evidence with historical insights around the process under study.

Econometric approaches to study growth and innovation have explored the relationship between these variables using cross-country comparative analyses. A review by Fagerberg (1994) included more than twenty empirical papers that had assessed – back then – the relationship between economic growth and technology, on the one hand, and productivity measures such as GDP per capita on the other. These early contributions to the literature controlled for variables such as the share of the public sector in the economy, population growth, and economic openness, while typical innovation indicators included education variables, investment in research and development (R&D), and patents. Recent contributions to this body of literature have increased the number of countries considered in the analysis, including less developed countries when data were available (Fagerberg and Verspagen 2002; Fagerberg, Srholec, and Knell 2007; Castellacci and Archibugi 2008; Castellacci 2008; Lee and Kim 2009). Castellacci and Natera (2013, 2016) have proposed alternatives to these empirical exercises; the authors have fully integrated the time dimension into the analysis of a systemic approach to innovation and development. However, because of their focus on a broad set of countries, it is difficult to undertake a more in-depth historical analysis of how innovation capabilities have evolved over time across countries.

The empirical evidence indicates that most catching up processes have been driven by a notable accumulation of innovation capabilities. Although investments in science, or in research and development (R&D), have been important for this accumulation (Lee 2013; Wong 2016), learning from experience has had at least the same importance (Hobday 1995; Kim 1997; Bell and Figueiredo 2012; Dutrénit et al. 2013). However, while in recent years it is possible to observe some changing conditions for catching up and development, the Schumpeterian literature on coevolution is yet to develop a basic analytical framework suitable to accommodate those new processes. In effect, we need better frameworks to connect recent catching up processes with broader discussions around development as an evolutionary process; likewise renewed approaches that link innovation with economic development are missing. Some solid efforts to address some of these questions can be found in Fagerberg, Guerrieri, and Verspagen (1999), Fagerberg and Verspagen (2007), Sotarauta and Srinivas (2006), and Saviotti, Cassiolato, and Pessoa de Matos (2014).

7.2.2 Empirical Evidence

There is consensus on the centrality of scientific and technological advances as drivers of economic growth (Schumpeter 1942; Solow 1956; Abramovitz 1956, 1986). Based on the experience of the United Kingdom, the work by Haskel, Hughes, and Bascavusoglu-Moreau (2014) is one of the most recent contributions to this line of research. Castellacci and Natera (2013) present evidence on the significant contribution that investment in STI has had on the growth dynamics of eighty-seven countries; the authors used time series data for the period 1980 through 2008.

The evidence suggests that the dynamics of investment in STI should consider the characteristic of a given economy. Such characteristics determine the impacts that can reasonably be associated with an amount of this investment. At the same time, it is possible to study why the benefits from investment in STI can differ between countries.

Two recent studies by Capdevielle et al. (2013) and Santiago and Natera (2014) have proposed different scenarios that help to explain the joint long-term dynamics of STI investment, GDP growth, and labor productivity in Mexico. In particular, the authors documented trends that define the historical performance of STI-related indicators, such as Gross Expenditure in Experimental Development (GIDE for its Spanish acronym), and the federal government's expenditure in STI (PESTI). Essentially, these studies have proposed a set of scenarios for the dynamics of STI expenditures, GDP growth, and other macroeconomic variables consistent with a level of investment in STI equivalent to 1 percent of Mexico's GDP. In both cases, a critical assumption is that the patterns of investment in STI observed since 1970 remain unchanged over a time horizon of 10–25 years.[1]

---

[1] Capdevielle et al. (2013) and Santiago and Natera (2014) coincided in setting 1970 as the base year for the analysis. This date marks the creation of the Council for Science and Technology (CONACYT), which is considered one of the most significant developments around the formalization of STI policy in Mexico (Corona et al. 2014). It is in this period that Mexican STI authorities began to more systematically collect statistical data on the country's performance in STI.

From a methodological perspective, Capdevielle et al. (2013) introduced vector autoregressive models (VAR) to analyze, in Mexico, the magnitude of the impact on labor productivity and GDP per capita that can be associated with changes in STI investment. The study showed that a positive relationship exists between investment in STI, aggregate investment, and GDP growth. The authors illustrated the recursive effects between STI efforts and macroeconomic performance; in effect, they documented the mutually reinforcing effects between STI policy interventions and economic policies. These findings have significant implications on the levels of public investment in STI, measured in terms of the PESTI that would be required to achieve a desired effect on both GERD and GDP. Ceteris paribus, in order to reach a level of investment in STI equivalent to 1 percent of Mexico's GDP by 2018, the PESTI would have needed to increase at a sustained pace of about 11.6 percent per annum between 2011 and 2018. The associated effect on the dynamics of the Mexican economy would have been a long-term rate of expansion of around 3.4 percent in GDP per capita, and about 1.72 percent in labor productivity (Capdevielle et al. 2013).

Santiago and Natera (2014) expanded the analysis in Capdevielle et al. (2013) to include a time dimension into the dynamic relationship between changes in STI investment, GDP per capita, and labor productivity. The authors distinguished two stages in the expansion of GDP per capita and labor productivity associated with an initial increase in PESTI. The first stage, which the authors name "growth stage," takes place during the five-year period immediately following the initial expansion in PESTI. In this period, both GDP per capita and labor productivity record rapid growth rates. In the second phase, the economy steadily returns to stability, with a steady rate of GDP expansion. This second phase spans about a decade after the initial increment in STI investment. The expected results are consistent with those of Capdevielle et al. (2013); an annual increment of 1 percent in PESTI led to an expansion of about 0.1 percent in both GDP per capita and labor productivity.

The information on the magnitude of the effect that can be associated with changes in STI investment is useful to identify the potential benefits and social returns associated with public investment in STI. These findings are particularly relevant for emerging economies such as Mexico, where careful priority-setting and planning are required to maximize the use of scarce resources available to support STI activities.

In this chapter we take the analysis a further step forward; having established the existence of causal links between STI investment and GDP growth, we explore the direction and intensity of such causality.

7.3 Research Design

To analyze the causal relationship between STI efforts and economic growth in Mexico this chapter combines qualitative and quantitative approaches. The qualitative approach consists of a historical analysis of the evolution of STI policy since the creation of CONACYT in 1970. The discussion establishes the links between the scope of STI policy interventions and some of the observed performance of Mexico's STI system over time; in particular, we show how specific objectives of research capacity building and research productivity have dominated the scene, while efforts to promote innovation are relatively more recent. The quantitative approach consists of a Johansen System Co-integration approach to propose a model that links economic growth to public efforts in STI and aggregate investment. The model was built starting with an analytical revisit of the document of Capdevielle et al. (2013). Following this road, we include a more explicit consideration of the temporal dynamics that characterizes the relationship between those variables.

Our historical analysis builds on a timeline that characterizes the main tenets of STI policy in Mexico, which, according to Crespi and Dutrénit (2014), can be considered structured developmental stages. The evolution of science policy and science itself is related to the economic context. The narrative is based on secondary information obtained from national S&T and STI strategies, reports, and evaluations of the main institutions with a stake in STI in Mexico, documents that reconstruct the history of institutions, and documents containing interviews with key actors in the sector.

During the last two decades, the number of econometric analyses that investigate evolutionary matters has grown. One reason is data availability on key indicators such as expenditure on R&D activities, opening the door for time series and panel econometrics. Also, new methods have been developed to include the effect of past events as determinants of the structures and patterns that define economic systems. One of those advanced methods is the vector autoregressive model, which allows for full endogeneity and cross effects of the variables in the system, incorporating information from the past to explain current states (Greene and Zhang 1997). A specific case of this method that suits the purpose of our analysis is co-integration methodology, mainly developed by Johansen (1991, 1995). This methodology helps to disentangle relationships among variables that co-evolve, growing over time as a system. If co-integration is confirmed, it is possible to distinguish different relationships. On the one hand, long-run relations at the core of the system, and on the other hand, the short-run structure, that represents how the system reacts to changes (Hendry and Juselius 2000; Juselius 2006).

The characterization of the short-run structure of the system helps to analyze causality among the variables and establish the dynamics of the system. The way the variables adapt to changes in the long-run structure of the system and how they transitorily adjust to the new conditions is a rich source of information (Juselius 2006). The co-integration methodology provides evidence of the forces driving the economic system, of the relationships that the time structure reveals, of agents' aggregate interactions. Furthermore, this methodology obviates the need to impose strong restrictions onto the system; it is orientated to draw from the information contained in the data to shed light on systemic relationships. As such, the methodology is an alternative to rigid models that test approaches in which theories are confirmed or rejected; it aims at documenting empirical facts that can inform improved theorizing efforts (Frydman and Goldberg 2008; Hoover et al. 2008; Colander et al. 2009).

The econometric analysis investigates the time series properties of the relationship between investment in STI and economic growth in Mexico over the period 1970–2011.

7.4 Historical Analysis

The formalization of STI policy in Mexico dates back to 1970, a year that marks the creation of the National Council for Science and Technology (CONACYT for its Spanish acronym) as the national agency responsible for planning, coordinating, and executing STI policy in the country (Casas et al. 2013).[2] The creation of CONACYT

---

[2] Historically, policy formulation focused on science and technology; in the 1990s explicitly it recognized that fostering innovation is an activity with its own

built on a series of scoping and diagnostic studies and consultations with diverse organizations and communities with a stake in STI in Mexico. The studies documented the fragmented nature of the STI system in Mexico; STI activities built on individual efforts, with extremely low levels of investment and little or no connection to national development strategies (PNPCyT 1970).

The creation of CONACYT is interpreted as a symbol of the formal recognition of the Mexican government of the potential contribution that STI activities can have for the successful implementation of long-term development strategies. Specific measures were introduced to overcome shortcomings in the functioning of the STI system. In particular, the strengthening of the financial commitments around STI, and initiatives to mobilize and capture the benefits associated with a growing, yet small, base of highly qualified human resources in the country. CONACYT was expected to assume a leading role in the governance and institutional strengthening of Mexico's STI system; the agency became responsible for designing, implementing, monitoring, and evaluating STI policies in the country (Casas et al. 2013).

The ambitious changes introduced into the incipient STI system took place amid a dramatic transformation and strategic reorientation of the Mexican economy. Over the course of the last forty years or so, the Mexican economy moved away from an import substitution model orientated to the development of domestic markets for products and services, to an alternative model guided by principles of free, open, and deregulated markets. The Mexican economy became increasingly linked to global markets. Moreover, Mexico moved away from a situation of recurrent financial and economic crises, to a situation of relative macroeconomic stability yet low economic growth. Notwithstanding the initial impulse granted to STI activities as an engine of growth, the true is that in both the import substitution model and the current stage of an outward looking economy, one of the greatest bottlenecks faced by the Mexican economy has been, and still is, the limited investment in STI.

The evolution of STI policy in Mexico can be organized into three broad periods, described in the following paragraphs.

identity and is subject to specific support. Since then a policy of STI has been designed. However, for the purposes of this chapter we use the concept of "STI policy" for the entire period.

7.4.1 A Supply Push Approach (1930s through Early 1980s)

During the long period starting in the 1930s and up to the early 1970s, the demand for technology and associated services and human resources in Mexico was influenced by the dynamism of an industrialization process orientated, first, toward export markets, and then, by a rapid reorientation toward an import substitution model. In such a context, the approach to STI was characterized by a supply driven, linear model dominated by public education and research organizations. This was a period of accumulation of basic STI capacities in the country.

Starting in 1970, the official STI strategy became increasingly formalized based on the adoption of a series of plans and programs to support STI activities. The actual lifespan and scope of those programs have varied significantly, although it is possible to establish a direct link with the term of the president in office at the time (Table 7.1). In 1970, and for the first time in the recent history of STI activities in Mexico, the adoption of a National Policy and Programs for Science and Technology (*Política Nacional y Programas en Ciencia y Tecnología*, PNPCyT for its Spanish acronym) included STI policies informed by a series of diagnostic studies on the state of STI in the country (Casas et al. 2013).

During this period, the federal government's financial commitments to STI recorded significant transformations (Table 7.1). In real terms, between 1970 and 1981, the PESTI observed a rapid expansion, with annual average growth rates (18.7 percent) greater than that corresponding to GDP growth (6.0 percent). This dynamic was sustained during the term of President López Portillo, with annual average growth rates of 11.9 percent and 6.7 percent, for PESTI and GDP, respectively. As a result, the ratio of PESTI to GDP increased from 0.15 percent in 1970, to about 0.40 percent in 1982.

The enhanced PESTI was directed to support public higher education institutions and public research centers. In addition, CONACYT's operational budget received a substantial increase (Corona et al. 2014).

The initial boost to PESTI lost momentum between 1970 and 1982, although the breaking point took place during the 1980s. Early in the decade, and to a large extent due to the fall in oil prices, the Mexican economy entered into what was to become one of the first major economic crises that have affected it since the 1980s. The crisis made

Table 7.1 *STI policies and plans aligned with different government administrations in Mexico*

National plan/Program	Validity	Federal government	Average annual growth rate*		PESTI/GDP
			GDP	GFCT	
Política Nacional y Programas en Ciencia y Tecnología (PNPCyT).	1970	Luis Echeverría Álvarez	6.0	18.7	0.15
Programa Nacional de Ciencia y Tecnología (PNCyT).	1978–1982	José López Portillo	6.7	11.9	0.40
Programa Nacional de Desarrollo Tecnológico y Científico (PNDTyC).	1984–1988	Miguel de la Madrid	0.5	-8.6	0.32
Programa Nacional de Ciencia y Modernización Tecnológica (PNDyMT).	1990–1994	Carlos Salinas de Gortari	3.6	14.0	0.34
Programa de Ciencia y Tecnología (PCyT).	1995–2000	Ernesto Zedillo	5.5	9.1	0.40
Programa Especial de Ciencia y Tecnología (PECyT).	2001–2006	Vicente Fox	2.9	-2.2	0.36
Programa Especial de Ciencia, Tecnología e Innovación (PECITI-I).	2008–2012	Felipe Calderón	0.9	-0.9	0.36
Programa Especial de Ciencia, Tecnología e Innovación (PECITI-II)	2014–2018**	Enrique Peña Nieto	2.5	7.8	0.44

Notes: The programs adopted in 1970 and 1976 did not specify their period of validity. In these cases, growth rates were calculated based on their actual validity, 1970–1976 and 1976–1978. *The current administration began in 2012. **Data correspond to the period 2012–2014, the first years of this administration.

Source: Authors based on data from INEGI, Capdevielle et al. (2013), and CONACYT.

evident the structural challenges of the economy, including the significant technological backwardness that resulted from the import substitution model. Low STI capacities limited the opportunities for the Mexican economy to integrate solid value chains in the domestic market, particularly around areas of strategic importance for the economic development of the country. These included natural resource-based industries, capital goods, or industries with high technological content. It is in this period that manufacturing assumed leadership as the main driver of the Mexican economy, although competitiveness and integration of the sector with the global economy were really poor.

Mexico initiated a comprehensive economic and structural adjustment program intended to lay the foundations for a new economic development strategy. This period was characterized by an abrupt fall in the economic activity, and a subsequent period of economic stagnation; GDP growth recorded annual rates in the order of 0.5 percent between 1984 and 1988. Investment in STI took a direct hit; PESTI fell at an average rate of 8.6 percent per annum over the same period.

It is in this period that we observe the creation of some programs, in place to date, intended to contain the negative effects of the economic crisis on the scientific community in Mexico. In a way, the intention was to minimize the loss of STI capacities accumulated until then. This is the case of, for example, the System of National Researchers (SNI for its Spanish acronym). This system, created in 1984 with the intention to retain the existing base of researchers in Mexico during the crisis, grants a series of incentives linked to researchers' individual productivity. Over time, the System of National Researchers has greatly enhanced its scope and mandate; it is now the main instrument at the disposal of the Mexican government to recognize research productivity and promote careers in STI; moreover, it serves as the leading mechanism to assess the quality of S&T production in Mexico (FCCT-AMC 2005; Santiago 2006; Vega y León 2012).

7.4.2 Demand Pull (Late 1980s – 2000s)

This period started with the painful transition from the import substitution model through the structural adjustment process inspired by policies modeled according to the principles of the Washington consensus. Structural reforms included the steady withdrawal of the Mexican government from direct intervention in economic activity, a substantive deregulation program, economic and financial liberal-ization, the privatization of public assets, and the intention to promote the development of a strong private sector. A segment of export-oriented firms was expected to lead recovery and, subsequently, the expansion of the Mexican economy.

This emerging context of economic deregulation and enhanced rul-ing of the market failed to reverse the bottlenecks observed in the area of STI. The limited STI capacities led to a productive specialization centered on activities with low technological content and limited inte-gration with domestic and global value chains. The increased presence of Mexican manufacturing products in export markets was led by traditional industries specialized in the processing of natural resources, while competitiveness was underpinned by lowering labor costs. The pace of economic growth was considerably below the one observed during the best years of the import substitution model, and subject to greater volatility, notwithstanding some improved macroeconomic stability.

In regards to STI policy, the change in the economic strategy had two main effects. From the perspective of supply, the political weight of the organisms responsible for the promotion of STI weakened relative to other instances of the Mexican government. At the same time, the financial restrictions characteristic of the 1980s led to severe reductions in public funding for STI organizations and actual STI activities. Significant changes were introduced to the processes governing the allocation of public support to STI, particularly R&D. It is in this period that novel mechanisms based on competitive funds and open calls for projects were adopted as the preferred approach to support STI in Mexico.

The early 1990s observed a steady recovery of the Mexican econ-omy. This is the time of the mandate of President Salinas de Gortari. This period was characterized by an average expansion in GDP of around 3.4 percent and the consolidation of the structural adjustment program. Likewise observed was a substantial recovery in PESTI, at a pace of 14 percent between 1990 and 1994. However, the economic crisis initiated in 1994 eventually resulted in a new hit on the resources available for the STI system. A new wave of economic reforms and recovery programs was adopted between 1995 and 2000, while real GDP growth rates rose to 5.5 percent on average per annum. The STI system managed to capture some benefits from the economic recovery;

PESTI grew by an average of 9.9 percent, while the ratio of PESTI/GDP returned to a level of around 0.40 percent.

In terms of the demand for technology, economic liberalization facilitated the import of capital goods and induced a substitution process from locally produced capital goods in favor of imported machinery and equipment. Although the effect was positive on the technological modernization of the local economy, the parallel effect was a significant loss of local capacities to produce capital goods. While there was a clear goal of attracting multinational enterprises to promote competition and technology transfer, productive specialization, and the insertion in global value chains, the result was the fragmentation of local production capacities and a crowding out of locally owned small and medium-size firms. Attempts to promote private investment in R&D were really timid and poorly resourced. In the late 1990s a decision was made to introduce a tax credit program to promote R&D.

7.4.3 Toward a Systemic Approach (2000s Onwards)

With the start of the new millennium, a growing consensus could be observed that the promotion of competitiveness based on individual enterprises was insufficient to sustain faster rates of economic growth. Economic transformation required a more systemic approach. A renewed interest in supply-driven economic policies was evident, this time as a mechanism contributing to attract private investments. At the same time, there was the intention to improve articulation and coordination between knowledge supply and knowledge demand. The start of this period also marked the beginning of a stage in which, for the first time, greater emphasis in learning and experimentation provides the basis for the design and implementation of STI policy.

In regards to the reform of the STI system, in 2002 a new Science and Technology (S&T) Bill was approved by the Mexican Legislative, together with other regulations and by-laws; a new mix of policy instruments was also introduced as part of the new approach to STI support. Some major features of the new S&T Bill were, (1) the adoption of a new legal framework to govern the STI system, under the leadership of CONACYT; (2) the introduction of a new systemic approach to STI, with renewed emphasis on the regionalization of STI capacities; (3) the articulation of federal and regional and local STI policies, and the democratization of decision-making around STI, with an increased presence of the research communities, and stronger leadership of the Mexican Presidency.[3] Although the scope of the new 2002 S&T Bill centered on the functioning of the STI system, in 2011 a reform to the bill introduced some important changes to make more explicit the notion of innovation. The official discourse recognized innovation as a third pillar for public policy intervention, next or in principle, at a level of importance similar to science and technology. Likewise recognized was the need to build a National System of STI. A new S&T Special Program 2002–2006 was published in 2002 (PECYT for its Spanish acronym).[4]

This renewed view of the contribution of STI to economic dynamics took place in the context of sluggish economic activity. Indeed, beginning in 2001 the Mexican economy experienced a new slowdown, eventually exacerbated by the effects of the global economic crisis of 2008 and 2009. During the administration of President Felipe Calderón (2008–2012), Mexico recorded its second poorest economic performance of the last forty years; GDP growth stalled to about 0.9 percent on average per annum. In regards to public expenditure in STI, PESTI systematically recorded negative growth rates, a situation that contrasted significantly with the federal government's ambitious plans to reform the STI system (PECITI 2008–2012).

Beginning with the PECYT 2002–2006, the subsequent PECITI I (2008–2012), and PECITI II (2014–2018), new policy instruments have been added to the suite available for STI authorities: new thematic competitive funds – sectorial funds and regional funds – programs to support scientific research orientated to address specific development problems, programs specifically designed to promote research collaboration particularly between academia and the productive sector, and programs to incentivize innovation by the private sector. The latter included an R&D tax credits program (2003–2009) and the current Innovation Stimulus Program (*Programa de Estímulos a la Innovación*, PEI).

A persistent structural weakness of Mexico's STI system is the low level of investment in STI, both public and private. Moreover, erratic dynamics characteristic of PESTI has hindered the capacity to induce

---

[3] The Mexican president assumed leadership of the General Council for Scientific Research, Technology Development and Innovation, which is the highest governing body of the STI system in Mexico.

[4] For a more complete discussion of the reforms to the STI system implemented since 2002, please refer to FCCyT (2006) and Dutrénit et al. (2010).

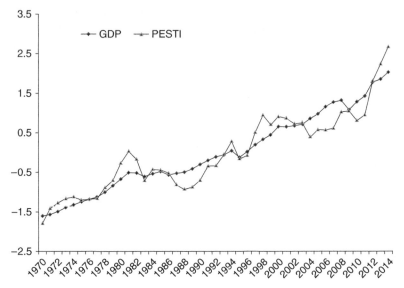

Figure 7.1 Evolution of GDP and PESTI, 2007–2014 (standardised values)
Source: INEGI, Capdevielle et al. (2013) and CONACYT.

meaningful quantitative changes in STI expenditures relative to GDP. Both PESTI and GERD have consistently been below 0.5 percent relative to GDP. By 2015 CONACYT reported that the ratio was approaching 0.6 percent but it is still too early to see if this effort can be sustained and augmented, even.

The observed trend in the PESTI to GDP ratio can be put in context if one considers that in the early 1970s, UNESCO's recommendation was for a level of investment in STI equivalent to 0.5 percent of GDP. In México, such ratio was just 0.15 percent of GDP (Dutrénit et al. 2010). By 2014, while the recommended level of investment was a minimum 1 percent of GDP, the actual level recorded in Mexico was about 0.40 percent for PESTI and 0.54 percent in the case of GERD[5] (Figure 7.1).

In terms of governance of the STI system in Mexico, CONACYT faces significant challenges (Corona et al. 2014). It has difficulties in designing and implementing STI policies with a long-term perspective.

---

[5] http://stats.oecd.org/Index.aspx?DataSetCode=MSTI_PUB, visited June 18, 2016.

One reason is the limited budgetary appropriations received from the federal government. As already noted, sitting at less than 0.6 percent, the GERD/GDP ratio is far from the 1 percent target established by the 2012 S&T Bill. Moreover, CONACYT has control of approximately half of PESTI, while the other half is distributed between myriad federal government organizations.

Imbalances in budgetary appropriations accompany differences in decision-making capacities around STI policy; CONACYT falls somewhat behind other federal government organizations with a stake in STI. Moreover, CONACYT has limited capacity to implement the directives received from the different organizations with a stake in STI, including the Mexican presidency.

This overview of the functioning of STI policy in Mexico suggests that more than a systematic progression in STI policy capacities, in practice, it is possible to identify public policy interventions that target short-term objectives. This narrow horizon for STI policy implementation is seldom articulated with a long-term development strategy that builds on an intensive use of STI activities. STI policy interventions lack continuity and consistency, with limited capacity to sustain the steady accumulation and consolidation of STI capacities in the country. Likewise missing are monitoring and evaluation approaches that make it possible to define and articulate short, medium, and long-term development outcomes with specific STI policy interventions. Moreover, there is a strong disconnection between policy objectives and actual commitment of resources over a long-term perspective.

7.5 Causal Analysis: The Quantitative Model

The econometric analysis presented in this chapter investigates the time series properties of the relationship between investment in STI and economic growth in Mexico. The data used cover the period 1970–2011. We make use of time series co-integration analysis, building on the system approach developed by Johansen.

The co-integration approach analyses the relationships between nonstationary time series by looking at their long-run equilibrium relationship as well as the process of short-run adjustment (Engle and Granger 1987). More precisely, if two or more variables are integrated of the same order (e.g. they are both I (1) series), there might exist a linear combination of them whose residuals are stationary – in other words, the two series are not stationary but one (or more) linear combination of them is.[6] If this is the case, the variables are said to be co-integrated. The Johansen co-integration method has one major characteristic that makes it suitable to analyze the time series properties of a model. Based on a Vector Error Correction (VEC) econometric specification, the approach helps to distinguish between long- and short-run structures; hence it is possible to identify the long-run causal effect of each explanatory variable on a country's growth rate along its development path. This is the crucial task that our analysis undertakes.

The method proceeds in three steps. First, it investigates the presence of unit roots in the variables. This can be done through two different tests, namely the Augmented Dickey Fuller (ADF) test and the Phillips and Perron (PP) test. Second, it studies the existence of co-integration relationships among the variables of interest. In order to do so, we specified a VEC model comprising K variables:

$$\Delta Y_t = \Pi Y_{t-1} + \sum\nolimits_{p-1}^{i=1} \Gamma_i \Delta Y_{t-i} + \nu + \eta t + \varepsilon_t \qquad (7.1)$$

where Y_t is the vector that contains the K variables of the model, Π is the matrix that contains the Error Correction Term (ECT), Γ_i are the matrices related to the transitory effects (part of the short-term structure), p is the lag order, ν and ηt are the deterministic components, and ε_t are independently and identically distributed (i.i.d.) errors with mean zero and a finite variance σ^2. Engle and Granger (1987) show that if variables are co-integrated, the Π matrix in Equation 7.1 should have a reduced rank r, such that $K > r > 0$. The Johansen (1991, 1995) co-integration rank test seeks to determine those r co-integrating relationships by adopting Trace Test and Maximum Likelihood specifications. Under the null of finding an additional co-integrating relation, it uses a recursive test starting with $r = 0$ until the first rejection is encountered.

The third and crucial step is estimation and identification of the model. The ECT term comprises all the information about the long run structure of the system. The Π matrix can be expressed as:

---

[6] It is also possible to find co-integration between I(1) and I(0) series. Some authors argue that the restriction of having only I(1) variables within the estimation is unnecessary; as long as there exists a stable combination of the variables, co-integration techniques can be used – see Juselius (2006) and Loayza and Ranciere (2005).

$$\Pi = \alpha\beta' \qquad\qquad (7.2)$$

where β is a matrix with the co-integrating relations – representing the long-run equilibrium relationships – whereas α represents the set of long-run Granger causality effects, measuring how variables react to deviations from the long-run equilibrium path (Granger 1969). Specifically, the Johansen approach allows us to determine two distinct types of causality. On the one hand, we can analyze *short-run causality* by using the Γ_i matrices to investigate how variables react to short-term external shocks (i.e. the effect of one variable change on another variable change). On the other hand, for our study it is more interesting to investigate *long-run causality* patterns, namely how variables react to deviations from the long-run equilibrium β. Hence, we will focus on the estimation results for the α matrix, which represents the way variables react when an exogenous shock (i.e. changes on STI investment) tends to move the system out of its long-run equilibrium path.

More precisely, a *positive* value for an estimated α coefficient would indicate that a change in the variables investment has a driving force effect on the rate of growth of another variable (i.e. GDP per capita) over this four-decade period of its transitional dynamics. By contrast, a *negative* value of α coefficient would imply that changes in the variables have had an equilibrium-correcting effect on the growth rate of the economy along its transition path: A negative sign provides evidence of a pro-cyclical relationship, since it captures the inertia behavior of the system to remain unaltered.

Econometric time series analyses describe the dynamics of processes that change over time. In particular, if these processes are closely related and show signs of coevolution, it is possible to demonstrate that such link exists in a period. Evidence suggests that socioeconomic variables, such as GDP, are related with scientific and technological variables such as investment in STI over time. Johansen's co-integration system approach allows verification of the existence of these relationships. As discussed in Section 7.3, the causality analysis here outlined is based on this approach: We aim to find evidence on the existence but also on the characteristics of the long-run causality between economic activity and STI investment. It is important to note that STI investment is only a fraction of total aggregate investment in the country; because of this it is necessary to consider the impact of Fixed Capital formation on the economy.

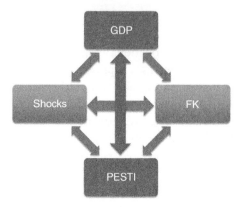

Figure 7.2 Schematic representation of the empirical model

We present a stylized model that considers a system composed of three elements (all measured in per capita terms): GDP, Fixed Capital Investment (FK), and STI expenditure (PESTI). We have also added dummy variables to better characterize the external shocks that have occurred in the economy, as described in the historical analysis. Nevertheless, even when the configured model considers all these features, we will still focus on the relationship between GDP and STI investment. Figure 7.2 is a schematic representation of the model.

As shown in Figure 7.2, the outline model has a systemic design, in which each element is considered in terms of its relation with the other. This allows us to analyze causality in a more complex way, by including the effects from other dimensions on the existence and direction of causal link between GDP and STI investment.

7.5.1 Data

We collected data to proxy the variables of the conceptual model for the period 1970–2011. We are considering data in per capita terms since it is more appropriate to measure welfare levels.[7] Data have been homogenized according to the country's methodological measurement changes during the period and it is presented in real terms (year 2003). Dimensions have been proxied as follows:

---

[7] We also have data on labor. We are not including those as part of the empirical exercise since we believe it is more suitable for a productivity analysis rather than

- **GDP**: GDP per capita in purchase power parity, derived from growth rates of overall consumption, government consumption, and investment. This is the proxy for economic welfare in our estimations.
- **STI public expenditure (PESTI)**: we are using Government Expenditure on STI (PESTI) activities in per capita terms. We acknowledge that we are missing private investment on STI; nevertheless, in Mexico the public sector is the main force of the innovation system and has a strong traction force on private investment. In fact, the indicator commonly used to measure the national effort on STI is the gross expenditure on R&D (GERD). In the case of Mexico, it has time series of government-financed GERD since 1970. In contrast, data on the total GERD is collected since 1993, when information about the business enterprise expenditure on R&D (BERD) began to be systematically collected from the R&D surveys. Therefore, for an analysis of time, you can only use public investment in STI. Mexico is a federation as this indicator is called "Federal Spending on STI." Data from 1993 show that private spending is reduced, and is less than federal government spending; BERD has not exceeded 35 percent of GERD. In fact, evidence suggests that over time private spending has been associated with public effort (Capdevielle et al. 2013). Therefore, federal government-financed GERD is a good indicator of the national effort in STI.
- **Fixed Capital investment (FK)**: total investment in the country, in per capita terms.
- **Shocks (DS)**: During the last forty years, as has been shown in the historical analysis, Mexico has undergone important economic and political transformations, and many of them have sometimes experienced episodes of crises and stability. These structural breaks have important effects on the aggregate time series dynamics, and must therefore be considered in the econometric analysis. The inclusion of *permanent* time dummies, for long-lasting external shocks, allows us to control for the presence of these exogenous events in the empirical exercise. We have added three dummy variables to mark important shocks in Mexican economic history, namely in 1982, 1988, and 1994. All these shocks are discussed in detail in the historical analysis (Section 7.4).

an economic growth discussion. Nevertheless, because of their close relationship, we have also applied the conceptual model using data in labor terms; results are included in Table 7A.1 and support the empirical findings of this document.

7.5.2 Model Results

We have applied the Johansen System Co-integration approach in order to estimate our model. In Table 7A.2, we present the preliminary tests required to build the empirical exercise: variables' unit root analysis, co-integration tests, and lag structure. Based on those tests, we found evidence of co-integration with rank $r = 2$, defining two co-integrating equations.[8] We have identified the model in such a way that the long-run causality between GDP and STI could be directly evaluated. The corresponding mathematical representation of our system is as follows[9]:

$$\Delta\,GDP_t = \alpha_{11}(GDP_{t-1} - \beta_1\,PESTI_{t-1} + \varphi_1 DS1982_{t-1} + \delta_1$$

$$DS1988_{t-1} + \lambda_1 DS1994_{t-1} + \eta_1 t + c_1)$$

$$+\alpha_{12}(GDP_{t-1} - \beta_2\,FK_{t-1} + \varphi_2 DS1982_{t-1} + \delta_2 DS1988_{t-1}$$

$$+\lambda_2 DS1994_{t-1}\eta_2 t + c_2) + \sum\nolimits_j (T_{1j}\Delta GDP_{t-j})$$

$$+\sum\nolimits_j (S_{1j}\Delta FK_{t-j}) + \sum\nolimits_j (R_{1j}\Delta STI_{t-j})$$

$$+\sum\nolimits_j (X_{1j}\Delta DS1982_{t-j}) + \sum\nolimits_j (Y_{1j}\Delta DS1988_{t-j})$$

$$+\sum\nolimits_j (Z_{1j}\Delta DS1994_{t-j}) + 1 + \varepsilon_{1t} \qquad\qquad (7.3)$$

$$\Delta\,PESTI_t = \alpha_{21}(GDP_{t-1} - \beta_1 PESTI_{t-1} + \varphi_1 DS1982_{t-1}$$

$$+\delta_1 DS1988_{t-1} + \lambda_1 DS1994_{t-1} + \eta_1 t + c_1)$$

$$+\alpha_{22}(GDP_{t-1} - \beta_2 FK_{t-1} + \varphi_2 DS1982_{t-1} + \delta_2 DS1988_{t-1}$$

$$+\lambda_2 DS1994_{t-1}\eta_2 t + c_2) + \sum\nolimits_j (T_{2j}\Delta GDP_{t-j})$$

---

[8] We have run all the tests needed to verify cointegration: (i) unit root tests (Augmented Dickey-Fuller Test and Phillips-Perron Test); (ii) Unrestricted Cointegration Rank Trace Test, finding r=2; and (iii) Inverse Roots of AR Characteristic Polynomial, to check the lag structure. We found results that support our cointegration analysis.

[9] We also hold the results for the equation where FK is the dependent variable. Since our focus is not on this dimension, we are not including it in the empirical results. It is sufficient to say that results on FK shows a driving force from GDP (meaning that GDP growth foster capital investment in the country) and an equilibrium correcting behavior from STI (STI follows a procyclical behavior to FK). These results are included in the Appendix, Table 7A.1 and Table 7A.2.

$$+\sum_{j}(S_{2j}\Delta FK_{t-j}) + \sum_{j}(R_{2j}\Delta STI_{t-j})$$

$$+\sum_{j}(X_{2j}\Delta DS1982_{t-j}) + \sum_{j}(Y_{2j}\Delta DS1988_{t-j})$$

$$+\sum_{j}(Z_{2j}\Delta DS1994_{t-j}) + 2 + \varepsilon_{2t} \qquad (7.4)$$

where the vector $[(\beta_1; \varphi_1; \delta_1; \lambda_1; \eta_1; c_1)\ (\beta_2; \varphi_2; \delta_2; \lambda_2; \eta_2; c_2)]$ represents the long-run co-integration (equilibrium) relationships, and the vector $[(\alpha_{11}; \alpha_{12})\ [(\alpha_{21}; \alpha_{22})]$ provides a measure of the extent to which the growth rate of the economy responds to a (level) change in STI expenditure (e.g. due to a policy change). The first co-integrating equation (the one that contains the parameters $\beta_1; \varphi_1; \delta_1; \lambda_1; \eta_1; c_1$) shows the long run relationship between GDP and STI expenditure. The second co-integrating equation (the parameters $\beta_2; \varphi_2; \delta_2; \lambda_2; \eta_2; c_2$) expresses the long run relationship between GDP and FK. In Table 7.2, we show the result from the long-run co-integration relationships:

Arranging the model in this fashion allows us to test the direct effect of STI expenditure on GDP. As explained in Section 7.3, by looking at the sign and significance of the α coefficients, we are able to identify the kind of long-run causality that is evidenced between those variables:

- Causality from PESTI to GDP: applying a Wald test on the α_{11} coefficient, we can explore whether there is evidence of a causal relationship between STI and GDP. Furthermore, if the coefficient is statically significant, a positive sign would mean that PESTI is a driving force for GDP growth; while a negative sign would imply that PESTI has a procyclical behavior.
- Causality from GDP to PESTI: since GDP takes part in both co-integrating equations, in order to check for the existence of this causal link, we should apply a joint Wald test on the coefficients α_{21} and α_{22}. In this case, the analysis of the type of causality is more complex: provided that the joint Wald test is statically significant, a positive sign in α_{21} implies reinforcing relation between PESTI and GDP, while a negative one would imply an inertial behavior; a positive sign on α_{22} provides evidence that economic growth and capital investment are the ones that could foster STI expenditure; to the contrary, a negative sign would be evidence of an

Table 7.2 *Long run co-integration equations (the β vector)*

		Cointegration equation 1	Cointegration equation 2
GDP	Coefficient	1	1
	Standard error	-	-
	T-Statistic	-	-
FK	Coefficient	-	[-0.335631]
	Standard error	-	(0.02444)
	T-Statistic	-	-13.7335***
PESTI	Coefficient	[-0.168137]	-
	Standard error	(0.01853)	-
	T-Statistic	-9.07359***	-

Significance level: *** 1% sig. level; ** 5% sig. level; * 10% sig. level.
Coefficients in brackets [ ]
Standard errors in parenthesis ( )

inertial behavior. The final effect of GDP on PESTI would depend on the combined effect of both parts of the equation.

The causality results are presented in Table 7.3.

The causality analysis provides evidence of the procyclical behavior of STI expenditure in the last four decades in Mexico. The a_{11} coefficient is negative and significant: STI expenditure has an equilibrium correcting behavior on GDP per capita, it has not been a driving force of the country's economic growth. The joint Wald test on the coefficients a_{21} and a_{22} is significant, but they have opposite signs: a_{21} is negative; it indicates that PESTI and GDP follow the same inertial path; on the other hand, a_{22} is positive and greater than a_{21}, meaning that it is the combination of FK and GDP that are the driving forces for PESTI. In a nutshell, STI expenditure has depended on the availability of economic resources. Evidence suggests that STI expenditure has not been seen as a tool to foster economic growth but as a generic expenditure that is assumed only when an economic surplus is available.

7.6 Discussion

Quantitative results show evidence of co-integration and bidirectional causality between expenditure in STI and macroeconomic aggregates.

Table 7.3 *Causality analysis*

From	To	Chi-Squared statistic	Cointegration equation 1 (α_{k1})	Cointegration equation 2 (α_{k2})
PESTI	GDP	24.28975***	[−1.2331] (0.2502)	-
GDP	PESTI	6.561536**	[−0.651253] (1.06466)	[2.844135] (1.170513)

Significance level: *** 1% sig. level; ** 5% sig. level; * 10% sig. level.
Coefficients in brackets []
Standard errors in parenthesis ()

However, not all of the causal links work in the same fashion: STI investment has had an "equilibrium correcting" behavior on economic growth; it has sustained the economic growth cycle. However, it has been unable to change the direction of the long-term economic trend. At the same time, economic growth has had an "equilibrium divergent" behavior on public efforts in STI. In other words, long-term trends in STI efforts are dependent on the availability of economic resources.

The qualitative analysis shows that STI policies have changed from one political cycle to the other. In fact, during the last four decades, nine different STI policy programs have been implemented in Mexico, generating an unstable environment, discontinuity, and poor coordination of STI efforts over time. In this chapter we document some of the impacts that this environment has had on STI investment in Mexico.

The combination of quantitative and qualitative methodological tools that we propose for analyzing the relationship between STI and economic growth in Mexico's recent history sheds light on a series of unfortunate events (Corona et al. 2014). Contrary to the ambition that STI activities would foster economic growth and the country's development path, our findings suggest that a procyclical behavior exists: Investment in STI fluctuates following economic growth trends, and at the same time, economic ups and downs may completely change STI investment trends. The impact of this evidence is multidimensional: (i) it is clear that STI activities have not been incorporated in governments' agendas as a priority: Mexico has not followed a knowledge-driven economic development strategy; (ii) the capability building process that the STI system requires is unlikely to be developed, as uncertainty on the governmental financial efforts in STI hinders the implementation of long-term strategies; and (iii) the country is limiting its possibilities to react to economic turndowns, since the capabilities already existing in the country lack institutional support to deliver expected benefits, generating a poverty trap. In a nutshell, contrary to what we found in the literature, STI activities in Mexico do not steer the wheel of economic growth, on the contrary, they go with the wind of the economic cycle.

Schumpeter (1939), almost eight decades ago, already proposed that innovation efforts should be contra-cyclical to economic growth. When in the low valley of business cycles, countries should make an effort to foster innovative activities in order to generate new sources of economic growth. In Mexico, the causality analysis has shown the opposite behavior: STI activities are pushed by economic growth. When food is scarce, we fail to feed the goose that laid the golden eggs.

7.7 Conclusions

The contribution of this chapter to the literature is twofold. First, we offer an alternative way to analyze causality, since we incorporate the time dimension using a mix method approach: historical policy analysis and Johansen's co-integration system. Second, we challenge the literature by characterizing the causal links between STI activities and economic growth: It is not sufficient to find evidence of the existence of causality; the direction and intensity of the causal link have major implications on the behavior of the system.

Our causality analysis results show (i) an equilibrium correcting force from STI investment to economic growth and (ii) a driving force from economic growth and total investment on STI activities. These results are contradictory to usage of innovation capabilities as a tool to foster economic growth as it has been evidenced in most of the empirical analysis that investigate the relationship between innovation and growth (Hobday 1995; Kim 1997; Fagerberg et al. 1999, Sotarauta and Srinivas 2006; Fagerberg and Verspagen 2007; Castellacci and Natera 2013, 2016). The evidence suggests a tragic scenario for the future of Mexico.

As expected, a study of this type faces some limitations. As mentioned earlier, because the models used in this document utilize information on only three variables, there is the possibility that the results concerning the level of impact on GDP associated with changes/increases in PESTI could be overestimated. Any inference or policy recommendation should address this limitation.

Finally, an active policy of STI also requires understanding the behavior of the different policy tools available, whose evolution over time can alter the dynamic trend of the aggregate product. Unfortunately, in the current context of limited continuity of the instruments of STI in Mexico, particularly in terms of plans, programs, and instruments of direct support for innovation, an exercise in long-term analysis is problematic because it does not have sufficient data. Similar limitations prevent the realization of sectoral and detailed studies on the contributions differentiated by type of industry. Such further studies are proposed for an agenda for future research.

Appendix

Table 7A.1 *Long run co-integration equations (the β vector)*

		Cointegration equation 1	Cointegration equation 2
Productivity	Coefficient	1	1
	Standard error	-	-
	T-Statistic	-	-
FK	Coefficient	-	[−0.6287]
	Standard error	-	(0.0371)
	T-Statistic	-	−16.9372***
PESTI	Coefficient	[−0.1521]	-
	Standard error	(0.0467)	-
	T-Statistic	−3.25765**	-

Significance level: *** 1% sig. level; ** 5% sig. level; * 10% sig. level.
Coefficients in brackets [ ]
Standard errors in parenthesis ( )

Table 7A.2 *Causality analysis*

From	To	Chi-squared statistic	Cointegration equation 1 (a_{k1})	Cointegration equation 2 (a_{k2})
PESTI	Productivity	5.945366**	[−0.342675] (0.140538)	-
Productivity	PESTI	17.69427***	[0.703682] (0.474726)	[1.47234] (0.351955)

Significance level: *** 1% sig. level; ** 5% sig. level; * 10% sig. level.
Coefficients in brackets [ ]
Standard errors in parenthesis ( )

References

Abramovitz, M. 1956. Resource and output trends in the United States since 1870, in *Resource and output trends in the United States since 1870* (1–23). Cambridge, MA: NBER.

Abramovitz, M. 1986. Catching up, forging ahead, and falling behind. *The Journal of Economic History* 46(2): 385–406. doi:10.1017/S0022050700046209.

Bell, M. and Figueiredo, P. N. 2012. Innovation capability building and learning mechanisms in latecomer firms: Recent empirical contributions and implications for research. *Canadian Journal of Development Studies/Revue Canadienne D'études Du Développement* 33(1): 14–40. doi:10.1080/02255189.2012.677168.

Capdevielle, M., Enríquez, L., Farías, A., Puchet, M., Sánchez, A., Solano, M. E., and Zaragoza, M. M. L. 2013. Efectos económicos y sociales de la inversión en ciencia, tecnología e innovación, in *Propuestas para contribuir al diseño del PECiTI 2012–2037* (p. 1). Working paper. Mexico: Foro Consultivo Científico y Tecnológico.

Casas, R., Corona, J. M., Jaso, M. and Vera-Cruz, A. O. 2013. *Construyendo el Diálogo entre los Actores del Sistema de Ciencia, Tecnología e Innovación*. Mexico: Foro Consultivo Científico y Tecnológico.

Castellacci, F. 2008. Technology clubs, technology gaps and growth trajectories. *Structural Change and Economic Dynamics* 19(4): 301–314. doi:10.1016/j.strueco.2008.07.002.

Castellacci, F., and Archibugi, D. 2008. The technology clubs: The distribution of knowledge across nations. *Research Policy* 37(10): 1659–1673. doi:10.1016/j.respol.2008.08.006.

Castellacci, F. and Natera, J. M. 2013. The dynamics of national innovation systems: A panel cointegration analysis of the coevolution between innovative capability and absorptive capacity. *Research Policy* 42(3): 579–594. doi:10.1016/j.respol.2012.10.006.

Castellacci, F. and Natera, J. M. 2016. Innovation, absorptive capacity and growth heterogeneity: Development paths in Latin America 1970–2010. *Structural Change and Economic Dynamics* 37: 27–42. doi:10.1016/j.strueco.2015.11.002.

Colander, D., Goldberg, M., Haas, A., Juselius, K., Kirman, A., Lux, T., and Sloth, B. 2009. The financial crisis and the systemic failure of the economics profession. *Critical Review* 21(2–3): 249–267. doi:10.1080/08913810902934109.

Corona, J. M., Dutrénit, G., Puchet, M., and Santiago, F. 2014. The changing role of science, technology and innovation policy in building systems of innovation: The case of Mexico, in G. Crespi and G. Dutrénit (eds.), *Science, Technology and Innovation Policies for Development: The Latin American Experience* (15–43). Cham: Springer International Publishing.

Cowan, R. and Foray, D. 2002. Evolutionary economics and the counterfactual threat: on the nature and role of counterfactual history as an empirical tool in economics. *Journal of Evolutionary Economics* 12(5): 539–562. doi:10.1007/s00191-002-0134-8.

Crespi, G. and Dutrénit, G. 2014. Introduction to science, technology and innovation policies for development: The Latin American experience, in G. Crespi and G. Dutrénit (eds.), *Science, Technology and Innovation Policies for Development: The Latin American Experience* (1–14). Cham: Springer International Publishing. doi:10.1007/978–3-319-04108-7_1.

Dutrénit, G., Capdevielle, M., Corona, J. M., Puchet, M., Santiago, F., and Vera-Cruz, A. O. 2010. *El sistema nacional de innovación mexicano: estructuras, políticas, desempeño y desafíos*. CDMX: UAM/Textual S.A.

Dutrénit, G., Lee, K., Nelson, R., Soete, L., and Vera-Cruz, A. 2013. *Learning, Capability Building and Innovation for Development*. London: Palgrave Macmillan. doi:10.1057/9781137306937.

Edquist, C. and Hommen, L. 2008. *Small Country Innovation Systems: Globalization, Change and Policy in Asia and Europe*. Cheltenham: Edward Elgar Publishing. Retrieved from http://books.google.es/books?id=s9giP7KhtJ0C.

Engle, R. F. and Granger, C. W. J. 1987. Co-integration and error correction: Representation, estimation, and testing. *Econometrica* 55(2): 251–276. doi:10.2307/1913236.

Fagerberg, J. 1994. Technology and international differences in growth rates. *Journal of Economic Literature* 32(3): 1147–1175.

Fagerberg, J., Guerrieri, P., and Verspagen, B. 1999. *The Economic Challenge for Europe: Adapting to Innovation Based Growth*. Cheltenham: Edward Elgar.

Fagerberg, J., Srholec, M., and Knell, M. 2007. The competitiveness of nations: Why some countries prosper while others fall behind. *World Development* 35(10): 1595–1620. doi:10.1016/j.worlddev.2007.01.004.

Fagerberg, J. and Verspagen, B. 2002. Technology-gaps, innovation-diffusion and transformation: An evolutionary interpretation. *Research Policy* 31(8–9): 1291–1304. doi:10.1016/S0048-7333(02)00064-1.

Fagerberg, J. and Verspagen, B. 2007. Innovation, growth and economic development: Have the conditions for catch-up changed? *International*

Journal of Technological Learning, Innovation and Development 1(1): 13–33.

FCCT. 2006. *Diagnóstico de la Política Científica, Tecnológica y de Fomento a la Innovación en México (2000–2006)*. Mexico: Foro Consultivo Científico y Tecnológico.

FCCT-AMC. 2005 [Foro Consultivo Científico y Tecnológico-Academia Mexicana de Ciencias] *Una Reflexión Sobre el Sistema Nacional de Investigadores a 20 Años de su Creación*. Mexico: Foro Consultivo Científico y Tecnológico, 146; www.foroconsultivo.org.mx/libros_edita dos/20_sni.pdf.

Foster, J. and Pyka, A. 2014. Introduction: Co-evolution and complex adaptive systems in evolutionary economics. *Journal of Evolutionary Economics* 24(2): 205–207.

Freeman, C. 1987. *Technology, Policy, and Economic Performance: Lessons from Japan*. London: Pinter Publishers.

Freeman, C. 1991. Networks of innovators: A synthesis of research issues. *Research Policy* 20(5): 499–514. doi:10.1016/0048-7333(91)90072-X.

Frydman, R. and Goldberg, M. D. 2008. Macroeconomic theory for a world of imperfect knowledge. *Capitalism and Society* 3(3). doi:10.2202/1932-0213.1046.

Greene, W. H. and Zhang, C. 1997. *Econometric Analysis* (Vol. 3). Upper Saddle River, NJ: Prentice Hall. Retrieved from http://cs5538.userapi.com /u11728334/docs/2ff8c8aa9672/William_H_Greene_Econometric_analy sis_283011.pdf.

Granger, C. J. 1969. Investigating causal relations by econometric models and cross-spectral methods. *Econometrica* 37(3): 424-438.

Haskel, J., Hughes, A., and Bascavusoglu-Moreau, E. 2014. The economic significance of the UK science base. Report. London: Campaign for Science and Engineering. Retrieved from file:///Users/GabMacAir/ Downloads/economicsignificanceofuksciencebase2014.pdf

Hendry, D. F. Juselius, K. 2000. Explaining cointegration analysis: Part 1. *Energy Journal* 21(1): 1. Retrieved from http://content.ebscohost.com/C ontentServer.asp?T=P&P=AN&K=2692256&S=R&D=aph&EbscoCon tent=dGJyMNLr40SeqLQ4y9fwOLCmr0uep69Sr6a4S6+WxWXS&Co ntentCustomer=dGJyMPGusU+wrLRQuePfgeyx44Dt6fIA.

Hobday, M. 1995. Innovation in East Asia: Diversity and development. *Technovation* 15(2): 55–63. doi:10.1016/0166-4972(95)96610–6.

Hoover, K. D., Johansen, S., and Juselius, K. 2008. Allowing the data to speak freely: The macroeconometrics of the cointegrated vector autoregression. *The American Economic Review* 98(2): 251–255. doi:10.2307/29730029.

Johansen, S. 1991. Estimation and hypothesis testing of cointegration vectors in gaussian vector autoregressive models. *Econometrica* 59(6): 1551–1580. doi:10.2307/2938278.

Johansen, S. 1995. Identifying restrictions of linear equations with applications to simultaneous equations and cointegration. *Journal of Econometrics*. 69(1): 111–132. doi:10.1016/0304-4076(94)01664-L.

Juselius, K. 2006. *The Cointegrated VAR Model: Methodology and Applications*. Oxford: Oxford University Press. Retrieved from http://bo oks.google.es/books?id=N6LmgE8vl1EC.

Kim, L. 1997. *Imitation to Innovation: The Dynamics of Korea's Technological Learning*. Cambridge, MA: Harvard Business Press.

Lee, K. 2013. *Schumpeterian Analysis of Economic Catch-Up: Knowledge, Path-Creation, and the Middle-Income Trap*. Cambridge: Cambridge University Press.

Lee, K. and Kim, B.-Y. 2009. Both institutions and policies matter but differently for different income groups of countries: Determinants of long-run economic growth revisited. *World Development* 37(3): 533–549. doi:10.1016/j.worlddev.2008.07.004.

Loayza, N. and Ranciere, R. 2005. Financial development, financial fragility, and growth. *Financial Fragility, and Growth (September 2004)*. Retrieved from http://papers.ssrn.com/sol3/papers.cfm?abstract_id=859565.

Lundvall, B.-A. (ed.). 1992. *National Innovation System: Toward a Theory of Innovation and Interactive Learning*. London: Pinter publishers.

Lundvall, B.-Å., Johnson, B., Andersen, E. S., and Dalum, B. 2002. National systems of production, innovation and competence building. *Research Policy* 31(2): 213–231. doi:10.1016/S0048-7333(01)00137-8.

Lundvall, B.-Å., Joseph, K. J., Chaminade, C., and Vang, J. 2009. *Handbook of Innovation Systems and Developing Countries: Building Domestic Capabilities in a Global Setting*. Cheltenham: Edward Elgar Publishing.

Malerba, F. 2002. Sectoral systems of innovation and production. *Research Policy* 31(2): 247–264. doi:10.1016/S0048-7333(01)00139-1.

Malerba, F., Nelson, R., Orsenigo, L., and Winter, S. 1999. "History-friendly" models of industry evolution: The computer industry. *Industrial and Corporate Change* 8(1): 3–40. doi:10.1093/icc/8.1.3.

Malerba, F., Nelson, R., Orsenigo, L., and Winter, S. 2016. *Innovation and the Evolution of Industries: History Friendly Models*. Cambridge, UK: Cambridge University Press.

Nelson, R. R. 1993. *National Innovation Systems: A Comparative Analysis*. Oxford: Oxford University Press.

PNPCyT [Política Nacional y Programas en Ciencia y Tecnología]. 1970. Mexico: CONACYT. Retrieved from www.siicyt.gob.mx/siicyt/cms/pagi nas/PolNacProgCyT70.jsp.

Santiago, F. and Natera, J. M. 2014. *Tiempos de respuesta de la dinámica económica asociados a la inversión en ciencia, tecnología e innovación en México.* Working Paper. Mexico: Foro Consultivo Científico y Tecnológico. Retrieved from www.foroconsultivo.org.mx/libros_edita dos/tiempos_respuesta_fernando_santiago.pdf.

Santiago, F. 2006. Valoración del Sistema Nacional de Investigadores in FCCT (2006), *Diagnóstico de la Política Científica, Tecnológica y de Fomento a la Innovación en México (2000–2006),* (Estudio 2; 158–174). Mexico: Foro Consultivo Científico y Tecnológico.

Saviotti, P. P., Cassiolato, J. E., and Pessoa de Matos, M. 2014. The role of the National Innovation System in the growth of Latin American countries. Paper presented at the 12th Globelics International Conference, Addis Ababa, Ethiopia, 28–31 October. www.researchgate.net/publication/27 1828038_The_role_of_the_National_Innovation_System_in_the_growt h_of_Latin_American_countries.

Schumpeter, J. 1939. Business cycles: A theoretical, historical and statistical analysis of the capitalist process. *NBER Books,* 1950(1939): 461. doi:10.1016/j.socscimed.2006.11.007.

Schumpeter, J. A. 1942. *Socialism, Capitalism and Democracy.* London: Harper and Brothers.

Solow, R. M. 1956. A contribution to the theory of economic growth. *The Quarterly Journal of Economics* 70(1): 65–94. doi:10.2307/1884513.

Sotarauta, M. and Srinivas, S. 2006. Co-evolutionary policy processes: Understanding innovative economies and future resilience. *Futures* 38(3): 312–336. doi:10.1016/j.futures.2005.07.008.

Vega y León, S. (coord.) 2012. *Sistema Nacional de investigadores. Retos y perspectivas de la ciencia en México.* Mexico: Universidad Autónoma Metropolitana-Xochimilco.

Wong, C.-Y. 2016. Evolutionary targeting for inclusive development. *Journal of Evolutionary Economics* 26(2): 291–316. doi:10.1007/s00191-015-0441-5.

8 Gaps in the Relative Efficiency of National Innovation Systems and Growth Performance across OECD and BRICS Countries[*]

ALENKA GUZMÁN AND IGNACIO
LLAMAS-HUITRÓN

8.1 Introduction

The aim of this chapter is to analyze how the relative performance of National Innovation Systems (NIS) in the Organization for Economic Cooperation and Development (OECD) and the BRICS countries of Brazil, the Russian Federation, India, China, and South Africa could impact countries' long-run economic growth rates. To that end, we first estimated the relative efficiency of national innovation systems and their main objectives in those countries, creation, diffusion, and utilization, using Data Envelopment Analysis (DEA) software. Then we analyzed how relative NIS performance (efficiency) could impact each country's economic growth.

This research has two main influences. The first is from authors who recognize that technological progress is a fundamental factor in explaining economic growth (Schumpeter 1942 and Solow 1957, in neoclassical theory, and Romer 1990, in the new endogenous growth theory). The second comes from authors whose research has focused on NIS (Freeman 1987, 1995; Lundvall 1992; Nelson 1993; Metcalfe 1995; and Niosi 2002, among others).

Despite their theoretical differences, Schumpeter, Solow, and Romer recognize the key role of innovation or technological progress in economic growth. Sources of innovation include human capital and R&D (Research and Development). According to Romer (1990), dissimilar R&D levels (population involved in R&D activities) and uneven

[*] We are grateful for the collaboration of master's degree student Juan Carlos Vilchis in researching statistical information and estimates of DEA models.

249

productivity performance in the research sector explain per capita income differentials across countries. Although Romer considers patents a key factor in his research sector analysis, he does not include various institutional factors that can influence decisions to increase countries' R&D efforts. Nelson (1993) points out how the new endogenous growth theory does not include in its models certain institutional variables that a growing number of authors have already accepted as essential to analyze economic growth. In this sense, the second theoretical group has pointed out that the systemic approach provides relevant and additional elements to assess success in generating new ideas (innovation) through the combined efforts of various institutions and agents, whose activities and interactions create, modify, and disseminate new technologies (Freeman 1987), and also includes the utilization of new, economically useful knowledge (Lundvall 1992).

This study estimates the national innovation system's relative efficiency index (NIS-REI) in OECD and BRICS countries, using DEA methodology (Charnes, Cooper and Rhodes 1978; Ramanathan 2009).[1] A subsequent estimate is made of the effect of this performance on countries' long-term economic growth. Most studies on this topic have focused on estimating whether a system is efficient as a whole. Unlike previous studies (Nasierowski and Arcelus 2003; Lee and Park 2005; Hollanders and Celikel 2007; Pan 2007; Pan, Hung and Lu 2010; Cai 2011; Cai and Hanley 2012), our goal is to contribute to measuring NIS-REI by objectives, in addition to assessing its global efficiency. We considered it appropriate for the NIS-REI measurement to be based on the achievement of each central NIS objective: creating, disseminating, and using new knowledge (Whitley 2001).

The OECD has contributed to the performance analysis of individual and comparative NIS of its member states and of other emerging

---

[1] DEA was created as a mathematical technique based on linear programming models to measure the relative performance of a set of similar units. However, today the scope of its scientific use is larger, as developed by different authors, evolving to encompass many more extensions and finding a number of practical applications. In the 1980s and 1990s, Charnes and Cooper et al. made interesting contributions in the DEA applications, such as DEA to measure the efficiency of maintenance units in the US Air Force and large commercial banks. An interesting article in the field of microeconomics is Charnes, A., Cooper, W. W., Golany, B., Seiford, L., and Stutz, J. (1985b). Foundations of data envelopment analysis for Pareto-Koopmans efficient empirical production functions, *Journal of Econometrics* 30(1/2): 91–107 (Cited by Ramanathan 2009).

nations – such as the BRICS. As our contribution to such NIS analyses, we have estimated the NIS-REI of thirty-nine OECD (thirty-five) and BRIC (four) countries. We sought to measure relative NIS efficiency across OECD and non-OECD emerging countries, such as Brazil, China, India, the Russian Federation, and South Africa. We also sought to explain how the systemic performance of innovation might impact each country's long-term economic growth. We asked whether countries with a weak R&D sector and disjointed NIS could have positive relative efficiency compared with countries that have built strong technological capabilities and appear to have institutional and social agents interacting to foster innovative efforts, and how their innovation performance impacts their economic growth rate. In other words, we asked whether it is possible for countries lacking a strong research sector and which are dependent on technology transfer or importing capital goods to produce new ideas. We also asked if such countries could create, disseminate, and use new technological knowledge efficiently, compared with countries that possess a research sector and entrepreneurs linked to the innovation frontier. Finally, we asked whether those countries could link new ideas and technological knowledge to their growth performance.

The key questions in this research are: do countries, which invest the most in each of the three NIS objectives, achieve higher relative efficiency? Even if some NIS are efficient in achieving one or two of their objectives, might they be inefficient in achieving the others? How does this relative NIS performance affect long-term economic growth? As a hypothesis, we propose that OECD and BRICS countries with the greatest GDP results derived from investing most heavily in the three core NIS objectives should achieve greater NIS-REI levels than those countries channeling fewer resources into that area. We also expected that some NIS are relatively efficient in relation to some objectives but inefficient in relation to others. Finally, we expected that those countries with better relative NIS performance would report higher sustained economic growth.

In the second of the five parts comprising this chapter, we analyzed the relevance of NIS and their comparative evaluation. In the third, we briefly described the Data Envelopment Analysis (DEA) methodology and outlined some findings in measuring NIS with DEA. In the fourth part, we estimated the efficiency indices of each of the following objectives: creation, diffusion, and utilization, using XLDEA software. Part five is a study of the impact of relative NIS efficiency on economic growth across countries by means of an econometric model. In conclusion, we summarize our main findings.

8.2 Why Are National Innovation Systems Important and How Can We Measure Their Relative Efficiency?

The National Innovation Systems approach provides the theoretical tools to analyze all the components that combine to make innovation possible. This holistic[2] approach assumes that firms join efforts with other organizations in an institutional framework in order to create, disseminate, and use technological knowledge (Edquist 1997; Soete, Verspagen, and Weel 2010).[3] Institutions and organizations as a whole are key in arriving at innovation events (Balzat 2002; Balzat and Hanusch 2004). Their importance differs depending on whether countries have developed an institutional framework, cultural heritage, and policies to foster innovation.[4]

Although this approach emphasizes the national dimension within a nation-state's geographic boundaries (OECD 1997; Lundvall 1992; Niosi 2002), today, international institutions and organizations interact with national agents, increasing their influence on national science, technology, and innovation policy.[5] In the context of globalization processes, international trade agreements (or other kinds of arrangements) or the enactment of international legislation, such as the TRIPS, seem to affect some countries' NIS performance, either in whole systems or in parts of systems. However, it is relevant to

---

[2] Holistic means that every system's property depends on each part of the whole system. It outlines the multidisciplinary innovation study by taking into account social, political, organizational, and developmental elements.

[3] Development, absorption, and diffusion have been identified as the core that organizations and institutions could influence in a national innovation system framework (Lundvall 1992), Lundvall and Tomlinson 2001; and Nooteboom 2000). Specifically, Edquist (1997) considers that an innovation system is made up of "all important economic, social, political, organizational, and other factors that influence the development, diffusion, and use of innovations" (Edquist 1997: 14).

[4] The OECD (1997) considers that the main NIS agents' interactions include competitions, transactions or agreements, and network creation.

[5] In the specific case of OECD countries, constant observation has been implemented to suggest policies orientation regarding what can and should be done for a catching up process.

analyze those national factors, and also international factors affecting endogenous systemic elements, their properties, and their ties to key NIS objectives (such as foreign direct investment (FDI), technology transfer (TT), and information and communications technology (ICT) imports).

There are various approaches to analyze innovative performance and national innovative capacity (Furman et al. 2002; Porter and Stern 2001). For this study, we chose to analyze NIS efficiency based on three main objectives: (i) creation, (ii) diffusion, and (iii) utilization (Whitley 2001).

8.3 Measuring Relative NIS Efficiency with the DEA Model

Data Envelopment Analysis (DEA) is a useful tool for evaluating the relative efficiency of a set of decision-making units (DMUs). The DEA uses a variety of inputs (means) to achieve the production of goods and services (ends). The tool takes as reference the most efficient DMUs, to which it assigns an efficiency index of one, and evaluates the relative performance of the least efficient DMU, which it values between zero and one (Niosi 2002) (see Annex).

We evaluated relative NIS efficiency by means of DEA, using Science & Technology (S&T) indicators, which can be quantitative or qualitative, and may be used as input or output. According to Grupp and Schubert (2010), the methodology for choosing indicators is a multidisciplinary decision based on two main ideas. The first is that innovation is a process that, when successful, may generate monopolistic profits. The second is that statistics validate the performance of each step of the innovation process. The individual indicators could be partial, not measuring innovation as a whole, and often are indirect because innovation is sometimes intangible. But there are also indicators intended to generate statistics on innovation, such as R&D expenditure and patents, among others.[6]

Different studies on the relative efficiency of NIS through DEA models use R&D expenditure as input (Nasierowski and Arcelus

---

[6] There is a great variety of DEA programs to calculate efficiency (see Barr 2004).

2003; Lee and Park 2005; Hollanders and Celikel 2007; Pan 2007; Pan, Hung, and Lu 2010; Cai 2011; Cai and Hanley 2012); differentiate between public R&D (Matei and Aldea 2012) and private R&D (Zhang 2013), or R&D capital stocks (Guan and Chen 2012; Zhang 2013; Hu, Yang, and Chen 2014). All those authors take human capital into account as input under different specific variables. As output variables, it is common that the authors use patents granted by different offices (WIPO, USPTO, EPO, JPO) and scientific and technical journal articles. The authors use different output variables, such as royalty and licensing fees (Nasierowski and Arcelus 2003; Hu, Yang, and Chen 2014); high-technology export and national productivity (Zhang 2013), especially ICT products (Cai-Yuezhou 2011) or medium and high-tech product exports as % total product exports (Matei and Aldea 2012); employment in knowledge-intensive activities (manufacturing services) as % of total employment; knowledge-intensive services exports as % total service exports (Matei and Aldea 2012), and computers per capita (Afzala 2014) (see Table 8.1).

8.4 Relative NIS Efficiency across OECD and BRICS Countries by Data Envelopment Analysis

Studies of NIS relative efficiency using DEA models usually include different numbers of countries, most of them developed and emerging countries (see Table 8.1). Kotsemir (2013) points out that it is suitable to use a sample of more than forty nations, including developed, developing, and transition countries. From the literature we reviewed, only Nasierowski and Arcelus (2003) and Pan (2007) satisfy this recommendation; these authors studied forty-five and forty countries, respectively. Hollanders and Celikel (2007) studied thirty-seven countries, approaching that recommendation. Our study is close to that recommendation as well. We studied the National Innovation Systems of thirty-nine OECD and BRICS countries, estimating relative efficiency indices, one for each of the NIS objectives: creation, diffusion, and utilization, and one for the general system.

We estimated the relative efficiency indices of each of the following objectives of NIS for OECD and BRICS countries: creation, diffusion, and utilization. In DEA, the most efficient NIS received an efficiency index of one, and we evaluated the relative performance of the less

Table 8.1 *National Innovation Systems relative efficiency studies*

Author (s)	Number of countries studied	Inputs	Outputs	Main findings
Hu, Yang, and Chen (2014)	24 countries, 1998–2005 periods	1) Total R&D manpower; 2) R&D capital stocks	1) Patents; 2) Royalty and licensing fees; 3) Scientific journal articles	The authors aim for comparing R&D efficiency and its determinants across countries, and the role of NIS. They find an average R&D efficiency of 0.8286 in 1998 with an improvement of 18.138 in 2015. Germany, Ireland, Netherlands, Israel, Canada, and Unites States had the higher R&D efficiency scores (more than 0.9). Romania had the lowest efficiency score of 0.2688 in 2015. The higher intellectual property rights protection, higher education investment intensity, the technological cooperation within business sector, knowledge flows(transfer) between business sector, and universities, agglomeration of R&D facilities contribute to improve national R&D.
Afzala (2014)	20 emerging and developed countries	i) Openness as % of GDP; 2) Legal & regulatory framework; 3) R&D/GDP; 4)	1) Real GDP growth; 2) Scientific and technical journals; 3) Computers per capita; 4) High	The efficiency scores obtained allow identification of which countries were innovation leaders. Based on the Tobit regression model and DEA, with constant returns to scale, technical efficiency scores, the study concluded that inefficient countries could improve their

Table 8.1 (*cont.*)

Author (s)	Number of countries studied	Inputs	Outputs	Main findings
		Transparency; 5) FDI/GDP; 6) Total education expenditure/GDP; 7) Secondary school enrolment; 8) Knowledge transfer	technology exports; 5) Inflation	innovation capabilities through increases in three main variables: the secondary school enrolment ratio; the labor force (ages 15–65), as a percentage of the total population; and domestic credit expansion by the business sector, as a percentage of GDP.
Kotsemir (2013)	Review of 11 empirical studies on cross-country analysis of NIS efficiency			The author detects general trends and differences in the sets of variables and the content of country samples. It seems suitable for estimating the NIS' relative efficiency through DEA model, using a sample of more than 40 countries. He recommended including highly developed countries, developing countries, and countries in transition (as Eastern European countries). There is a discussion of the set of input and output variables and also how to weigh the output variables.
Zhang (2013)	China comparing	1) Firm expenditure on R&D; 2) Higher	Indicators of output are divided into: a)	Chinese innovation system has achieved significant improvement in the last ten years, and narrowed the

Study	Sample	Indicators	Findings
	with 11 countries (US, Germany, Japan, UK, Italy, France, Canada, Republic of Korea, Singapore, Brazil, Russia)	education expenditure on R&D; 3) Government expenditure on R&D; 4) Firm R&D personnel ; and 5) Government R&D personnel. Technological output (Triadic patent; Scientific articles) and b) Economic output (market share of high-technology export and national productivity).	overall gap with developed countries. The economic efficiency is not a satisfactory one; it has been the bottleneck of the Chinese innovation system.
Matei and Aldea (2012)	EU 27 countries, 2011	1) New doctorate graduates per 1000 population aged 25–34; 2) International scientific co-publication per million; 3) Public R&D expenditure as % of GDP; 4) Business R&D expenditure as % of GDP; 5) Public-private co-. 1) Employment in knowledge-intensive activities (manufacturing services) as % of total employment; 2) Medium and high-tech product exports as % of total product exports; 3) Knowledge-intensive service exports as % total service exports	The authors identify five performance groups: i) Innovation leaders, countries above the EU27 average: Denmark, Finland, Germany, and Sweden; do not always have the most efficient innovation system; ii) *Innovation followers* countries with a performance next to the EU27 average (Austria, Belgium, Cyprus, Estonia, France, Ireland, Luxembourg, Netherlands, Slovenia, and UK; iii) *Moderate innovators* countries with a performance below that of EU27 average (Czech Republic, Greece, Hungary, Italy, Malta, Poland, Slovakia, and Spain, and iv) *Modest innovators* countries with a performance considerably below the EU27 average. The DEA estimations of relative

Table 8.1 (*cont.*)

Author (s)	Number of countries studied	Inputs	Outputs	Main findings
		publications per million population; 6) PCT patent applications per billion GDP; 7) Community trademarks per billion GDP		efficiency corrected show three countries with the highest NIS efficiency: Malta, Ireland, and UK. Although, Romania and Turkey had an efficiency score equal to one, they were in 4th and 6th place. The inefficient countries were Greece, Portugal, and Lithuania. Taking into account the first classification and the DEA efficiency scores, the authors conclude that Ireland, UK, and Germany may be considered best practices in terms of innovation policies, even if they are not necessarily efficient.
Guan and Chen (2012)	OECD 22 countries	1) Number of full-time equivalent scientists and engineers; 2) Incremental R&D expenditure funding innovation activities; 3) Prior accumulated knowledge stock	1) Number of USPTO patents; 2) International scientific papers; 3) Added value of industries; 4) Export of new products in high-tech industries.	Various factors were chosen to represent the embedded policy-based institutional environment (IPR, Legal environment for technological development and application; openness for international trade; Private R&D funding; University R&D performance; Venture capital; University industry collaboration; Technological cooperation between enterprises). These factors had a significant influence on the efficiency

Study	Sample		Inputs	Outputs	Description
Cai-Yuezhou (2011)	22 countries (Including BRICS and G7 countries), 2000–2008	breeding upstream knowledge production; 4) Prior accumulated knowledge stock participating in downstream knowledge commercialization; 5) Consumed full-time equivalent labor for non R&D.	1) R&D expenditure; 2) Total R&D personnel	1) WIPO Patents granted; 2) Scientific and technical journal articles; 3) high-technology and ICT exports	performance of the two individual component processes (an upstream knowledge production process (KPP) and a downstream knowledge commercialization process (KCP) confirming the impact of public policy interventions undertaken by the government on the innovation performance of NIS.
Hollanders and Celikel (2007)	37		Fifteen indicators in three dimensions: 1) Innovation drivers; 2) knowledge	Ten indicators in two dimensions: 1) Applications measures the	BRICS have a very different relative efficiency of NIS. On one hand, Russia, India, and China have relatively high efficiency scores and, on the other hand, Brazil and South Africa have not. Some factors affecting the NIS performance are ICT infrastructure, enterprise R&D activities, economic scale, economic openness, financial structure, market circumstance, governance, education system, and natural endowments. Classification of NIS relative efficiency according to the average efficiency performance using different input combinations on two outputs dimensions: *innovation leadership* (with the highest values); *innovation*

Table 8.1 (*cont.*)

Author (s)	Number of countries studied	Inputs	Outputs	Main findings
		creation; 3) Innovation & entrepreneurship	performance expressed in terms of labor and business activities and their value added in innovative sectors and 2) Intellectual property measures they achieved in terms of successful know-how	*followers* (values above average efficiency); *moderate innovators* (range of different efficiencies); *catching up countries* (variety of efficiencies and the lowest of the average).
Pan (2007)	40	1) Total public education expenditure; 2) R&D expenditure; 3) FDI; 4) Goods and service imports; 5) Total R&D personnel employment	1) Patents granted to residents; 2) Patents granted in foreign offices	Improvement of NIS relative efficiency is linked to higher R&D resources and progress in the educational systems as well as in literacy.

Lee and Park (2005)	27	1) R&D expenditure and 2) number of researchers	1) Technology revenue; 2) Scientific and technical journal articles; and 3) triadic patents	A typology of countries related to relative efficiency by technological area. The first group efficient in production of patents (or inventors); a second group, efficient in technology revenue (or businessman); a third one, efficient in scientific and technical journal articles (or academician); and finally, a fourth group of inefficient countries in all the mentioned areas.
Nasierowski and Arcelus (2003)	45	1) Import of goods & commercial services; 2) GER&D; 3) Degree of private business involvement in R&D; 4) Employment in R&D; 5) Total educational expenditures	1) External patents by resident; 2) Patents by country's resident; 3) National productivity	The authors differentiate R&D contribution to national productivity and its ability to transform inputs into outputs. Also, they differentiate the country's role as a consumer and as generator of technological effort. The authors contrast two groups of countries. One group that overinvests in some aspect of technological effort to the detriment of its overall efficiency; its R&D effort is still at early stages of development. The other group consists of country leaders with signs of diminishing returns.

Source: Own elaboration based on authors cited.

efficient NIS, each taking values between zero and one. This methodology is based on a series of basic assumptions (see the assumptions of the DEA in Ramanathan [2009]), of which we will mention only two. First, the NIS, when compared to one another, operate uniformly: They receive the same inputs and produce the same outputs, although in different quantities. The concept of relative efficiency means that if an efficient NIS is capable of producing x units of output with y units of input, another NIS should also be capable of doing so if it operates efficiently. Second, the efficiency of each NIS is measured with the rate resulting from the sum of weighted outputs divided by the sum of weighted inputs. This rate is a number between zero and one. Points of efficiency provide guidelines and objectives for improving inefficient NIS.

We used the XLDEA 2.1 (2009) model, output-oriented with variable returns to scale.[7] In this section we describe the input and output variables, which we used to estimate the efficiency indices for each of the NIS objectives and their general index. In applying the model, the same input and output variables were used for both years in the study.

In a global system, a NIS efficient in creation could be one with the best relative performance and leadership in innovation; a NIS efficient in diffusion could be one in which firms are good at absorbing new technological knowledge and are relatively moderate innovators; and a NIS efficient in utilization could be recognized as a relative innovation follower. Although a NIS efficient in creation has the scientific and technological human skills and the infrastructure required to be an efficient technological knowledge disseminator and user, it could be specialized in creation. This is because countries that have built scientific and technological capabilities focused on creation have found such activities more profitable. It could be the case that these countries suffer relative backwardness in other main objectives. The same may happen with a NIS efficient in diffusion or in utilization, where the countries may lack the technological capabilities needed to be significant creators of innovation, for example. Thus, there seems to be a relative division of activities with an interaction of competition and cooperation among the NIS in the global system, with outstanding performance in creation seen in some NIS, and outstanding performance in diffusion and utilization in other NIS.

---

[7] For the theory of its two phases of application, see Ray (2004).

Creation Model. Creation is defined as a NIS capacity to generate new knowledge or improve previous knowledge (Whitley 2001). This model has as its inputs those variables associated with countries' efforts to build technological capabilities to obtain new scientific and technological knowledge. The first variable is linked with high human skills involved in research and development activities (number of R&D specialists per million inhabitants, World Data Bank on Science and Technology 2007 and 2014).[8] The second refers to the expenditures needed to make research and development possible, including researchers' earnings and the tangible and intangible capital invested as a percentage of gross domestic product (R&D expenditures as a percentage of GDP, according to the World Data Bank on Science and Technology 2007 and 2014). The third concerns foreign direct investment (FDI) and technology transfer (TT).[9] We included FDI because we consider it a key source of knowledge for firms needing access to advanced products and blueprints within each country. The indicators FDI and TT measure to what extent each variable is a key source of new technology (where 1= not at all and 7= to a great extent, World Economic Forum 2006 and 2014). "FDI encourages the transfer of technology and know-how between economies. It also provides an opportunity for the host economy to promote its products more widely in international markets. FDI, in addition to its positive effect on the development of international trade, is an important source of capital for a range of host and home economies." (OECD 2008: 17) (see Table 8.2).

For outputs, we used two variables. The first accounts for technological innovation with potential for exploitation at industrial and commercial scales as patents applied by residents in each country's intellectual property – IP – office (see WIPO) and also patent

---

[8] These are R&D spending figures reported by countries, although it is known that there are other efforts devoted to innovation, which are not classified as R&D. This is seen more in developing countries, but also in developed countries (Boyer and Didier 1998).

[9] "Direct investment is a category of cross-border investment made by a resident in one economy (the direct investor) with the objective of establishing a lasting interest in an enterprise (the direct investment enterprise) that is resident in an economy other than that of the direct investor. FDI provides a means for creating direct, stable and long-lasting links between economies. Under the right policy environment, it can serve as an important vehicle for local enterprise development, and it may also help improve the competitive position of both the recipient ('host') and the investing 'home' economy" (OECD 2008: 17).

Table 8.2 Variables for the National Innovation Systems REI – DEA models of creation, diffusion, utilization, and a general model

	Inputs	Outputs
Creation model	R&D Expenditure/GDP (%), 2007 and 2014. Researchers in R&D per million people, 2007 and 2012. Foreign Direct Investment and technology transfer, 2007 and 2014.	Scientific and technical journal articles per researcher in R&D, 2007 and 2013. Patent applications per residents per million people, 2007 and 2014. Triadic patents per million people, 2007 and 2014.
Diffusion model	Education index, 2007 and 2014. Researchers in R&D per million people 2007 and 2012. Patents applications of residents & non-residents per million pop., 2007 and 2014. Quality of overall infrastructure, 2008 and 2014. University-industry collaboration in R&D, 2008–2009. ICT goods imports (% total goods imports, 2007 and 2014.	Firm-level technology absorption, 2007 and 2014. Availability of latest technologies, 2008, 2014. Foreign direct investment and technology transfer, 2007 and 2014. Quality of scientific research institutions, 2007 and 2014.
Utilization model	Availability of latest technologies, 2008–2009 and 2014. Institutions' Efficiency Index 2007 and 2014. Quality of overall infrastructure, 2008 and 2014. Domestic market size index, 2007 and 2014. Fixed broadband subscriptions/100 pop, 2008 and 2014. Individuals using internet%, 2007 and 2014.	Quality of scientific research institutions, 2007 and 2014. GDP per capita, PPP, 2007 and 2014. Human Development Index, 2007 and 2012. Labor productivity, 2007 and 2014.
General model	Researchers in R&D per million people, 2007 and 2012. R&D/ GDP (%), 2007 and 2014.	Patent applications residents per million people, (2007 and 2014. Firm-level technology absorption, 2007 and 2014. Triadic patents per million pop., 2007 and 2014.

Source: Own proposal.

applications in the three main world offices (USPTO, EPO, and JPO), called triadic patents (OECD Patent Databases 2007 and 2011); both are normalized by dividing the number of patents per million inhabitants in each country. The second output variable shows the scientific or codified knowledge findings of each country as the number of scientific articles per million inhabitants in each country (Pan 2007; Cai 2011) (see Table 8.2).

Diffusion model. Diffusion is seen as a NIS capacity to spread innovation through transmission channels other than markets. For firms, such innovations are disseminated, even when the economic impact is not restricted to firms but spread throughout society (Whitley 2001). For this model, we have used as inputs indicators that express the level of education attained by each country's population (education index),[10] the high level education involved in R&D (R&D specialists per million inhabitants) and the inventive capabilities achieved by each country (resident patent applications). As to technological infrastructure, we included the quality of overall infrastructure and specifically that derived from the ICT technological paradigm (ICT goods imports as % of total goods imports). Finally, we added a variable that shows how two agents are connecting to generate new or incremental technological knowledge (university-industry collaboration in R&D). As outputs, we took into account variables that reveal, on one hand, how countries have acquired new technologies (availability of latest technologies, FDI, and technology transfer), and on the other hand, how the different agents have achieved certain development recognized as the knowledge-acquiring capacity of firms (firm-level technology absorption), the quality environment in those institutions focused on conducting scientific research (quality of scientific research institutions), and the impact of scientific production (citations in articles by one million inhabitants), which value the relevance of scientific production after it is disseminated (see Table 8.2).

Utilization model. The innovation process has utilization as its purpose and is the point of departure that drives creation and diffusion (Whitley 2001). In the utilization or usage model we used as inputs those variables showing, first, how institutions are efficient in regulating the acquisition of new technologies; second, the extent to which

---

[10]   The education level is calculated using Mean Years of Schooling and Expected Years of Schooling (Human Development Report Office 2013).

countries possess the quality of overall infrastructure needed to facilitate the use of new technologies; and third, the level of internet connectivity in the ICT paradigm (fixed broadband subscriptions/100 inhabitants and % individual internet users) " . . . not only for business purposes but also for access to knowledge" (Archibugi and Coco 2004: 14). Finally, we included as a variable the local market size index, to measure the population's ability to acquire innovations. As outputs of utilization, we have considered indicators accounting for human and institutional improvement once innovations are available to be used, as well as institutional efficiency and level (quality of scientific research institutions), population well-being either by increased income or access to better living conditions (per capita GDP; human development index), and the labor productivity achieved by each country (see Table 8.2).

General model. For the NIS general model, we included as inputs two variables, which summarize the effort countries make in NIS, R&D specialists per million inhabitants, and R&D spending as percentage of GDP. For output, we took into account three variables that show innovation outcomes and how firms have acquired technology knowledge absorption (see Table 8.2).

8.4.1 NIS Creation Model 2007 and 2014

We proceed briefly to look over the inputs and outputs variables selected for the NIS creation models for OECD and BRICS countries in 2007 and 2014. Accordingly, we show relative efficiency index (REI) results for NIS creation using DEA estimation. As to R&D efforts among the OECD and BRICS countries, the United States leads the world in spending on R&D by amount in US dollars (USD), followed by China (453.5 and 333.5 billion USD PPP, respectively). The United States and China are followed by Japan (160.2) and Germany (101.1) (UNESCO 2015). When this expenditure in R&D is divided by the GDP, we can identify how intensive R&D spending is, taking into account the size of each national economy. In 2007, the average R&D S/GDP of the thirty-nine countries in this study was 1.7 percent, with the United Kingdom at the median line, sixteen countries above and twenty-one below that line. In 2014, this average rose to 1.9 percent with similar distribution and some changes in the country ranking and with Iceland at the median line. The efforts made by South Korea (going from 3.0 percent in

2007 to 4.29 percent in 2014) and Israel (with more than 4 percent in 2007 and 2014) are noteworthy. The intensity of R&D is also remarkable in Japan, the Nordic countries, Switzerland, and the United States (with more than 3 percent in 2007 and 2014). On the other hand, Latin American countries showed lesser efforts to improve their R&D/GDP ratio: Chile and Mexico (slightly more than 0.3 percent, although Mexico increased its effort to 0.5 percent in 2014). Among emerging countries, some have made a quantitative leap, moving to or near 1 percent of R&D/GDP (Brazil, Turkey, Slovakia, India, and Greece). A special case is China, going from 1.38 percent in 2007 to 2.05 percent in 2014 (see Table 8A.1a).

The average number of R&D specialists per million inhabitants in the countries we studied was 3277.82 in 2007 and 3546.97 in 2012. Among the countries with above average percentage of researchers – from more than 5000 to 7000 per million inhabitants – are Japan, Israel, the Nordic countries (Finland, Denmark, Iceland, Norway, and Sweden), and Luxembourg. In South Korea, this indicator rose to 3.7 percent, reaching 5928 researchers/million inhabitants. India, Chile, Mexico, and South Africa have the smallest numbers of specialists in R&D activities per million inhabitants. In 2012, India reported 156.6, while Chile, Mexico, and South Africa reported more than three hundred (see Table 8A.1a).

Concerning FDI and technology transfer, we found that the average index for the countries we studied was 5.1 in 2007 and 4.8 in 2014 (World Economic Forum 2006 and 2014). In general, we observed that not a single country has reached outstanding results relying on FDI as a key source of new technology (estimated as 7 by WEF), though FDI is an important source of new technology for all countries. Ireland reported 6.4 in 2007 and 2014, the highest estimate index; followed by Slovakia (6 in 2007). Other countries with high FDI and TT indices were some Eastern European countries, such as the Czech Republic, Estonia, Slovakia, and Hungary in 2007, as well as Australia and Mexico (all with an FDI index between 5.5 to 5.9) (see Table 8A.1a).

In the creation model, we found that major technological innovations are concentrated in a few countries, although more countries are getting better results for arriving at new scientific findings. We found an important gap across the countries we studied as to patent applications by residents per million inhabitants. South Korea and Japan stand out with the largest numbers of patents applied for by residents in their own

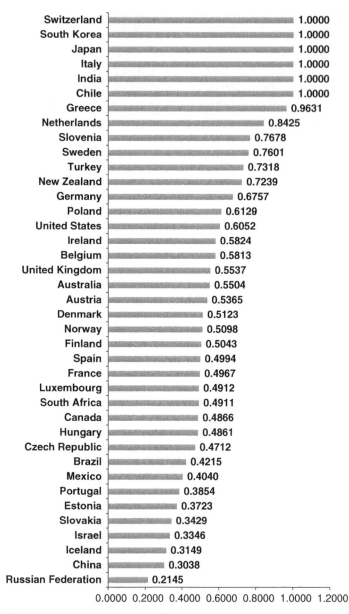

Figure 8.1a Creation relative efficiency index by OECD and BRICS countries, 2007

Source: Own elaboration based on the inputs and outputs data (see Table 8A.1a) and the creation relative efficiency DEA model.

countries; both had similar numbers in 2007 (2669.9 and 2620.8, respectively). South Korea's number of patent applications by residents increased to 3253.9 and Japan's fell to 2092 in 2014. Switzerland, Germany, the United States, the Nordic countries, and the Netherlands followed South Korea and Japan in 2007 with 500 to 1000 patent applications by residents per million inhabitants. Although the United States' leadership in innovation is widely recognized, the United States fell to fifth place in 2007 (800) and third place in 2014 (894.1) as to the number of patent applications by its population. China advanced rapidly from 116 patent applications per million inhabitants in 2007 to 587.2 patent applications per million inhabitants in 2014. The median of patent applications by residents per million inhabitants in all the countries we studied in 2007 was 399.4, with twelve countries above and twenty-seven below the median. The median of patent applications by residents per million inhabitants in those countries was 302.1 in 2014, with six countries above and twenty-eight below the median. India and Mexico were far from the median and showed the lowest relative endogenous capabilities for technological inventions per million inhabitants (see Table 8A.1a).

We found great differences in the index of triadic patents among the countries we studied. Trade activity and/or the presence of multinational corporations account for Japan and Switzerland having the most patent applications by residents per million inhabitants. Sweden, Germany, the Netherlands, Denmark, and South Korea follow Japan and Switzerland as having the most patent applications by residents per million inhabitants. Brazil, Chile, India, Mexico, and Turkey had marginal triadic patents per million inhabitants in 2007. India and Brazil have seen increases in the triadic patents index since then. India went from 0.17 in 2007 to 1.60 in 2014. Brazil went from 0.36 in 2007 to 3.35 in 2014. The Eastern European countries saw an increase in the triadic patents index as well between the years 2007 and 2014.

Switzerland led the way as to distribution and ranking of scientific and technological articles published by researchers in R&D with 0.639 articles per researcher in 2007. Chile led the way in 2013 with 0.8408 articles per researcher in R&D. It is noteworthy that, in 2007, Greece, Italy, Slovenia, and Turkey did not have high numbers of patent applications by residents per million inhabitants, but had high numbers of scientific articles published by researchers in R&D. Between 2007 and 2013, Chile, India, Australia, Luxembourg, Spain, and

South Africa had increased numbers of articles published by researchers in R&D. In 2007, the median for scientific articles by R&D researchers was 0.3792 with only ten countries above and twenty-three below the median. In 2013, the median for scientific articles by R&D researchers was 0.423, with only four countries above and twenty-nine countries below the median. In 2007 and 2013, the Russian Federation had the least number of scientific articles by R&D researchers (0.0603 in 2007 and 0.0797 in 2013) (see Table 8A.1a).

8.4.2 NIS Creation Relative Efficiency Index 2007 and 2014

Based on estimates of the relative efficiency index (REI) of NIS by the creation objective, in 2007, we identified six countries with an efficiency index of 1 (see Figure 8.1a). Among them are Japan, South Korea, and Switzerland, which showed higher investments in R&D activities and human capital, complemented by high scientific and technological absorption capabilities, high levels of technological innovation (patents), but not a higher volume of scientific production (articles by R&D researchers). The other three countries with relative efficiency in creation, Chile, India, and Italy, show a low level of patents and lesser efforts in innovation considered in the inputs of the REI creation model, but Chile and Italy, in particular, had the highest numbers of articles by R&D researchers, after Switzerland.

Among the most efficient countries (with REI index equal to 1) in NIS creation in 2007 are seven European countries that fell above the median (0.71) of all countries studied, including Greece, the Netherlands, Slovenia, Sweden, and Turkey, the Asian countries of India, Japan, and South Korea, the Latin American country of Chile, and New Zealand. Germany, Poland, and the United States fell below and near the median. Other European countries, such as Austria, Ireland, Belgium, the United Kingdom, the Nordic countries, and Australia showed a lower creation efficiency index. Among the countries with the lowest creation efficiency index are countries that have been recognized for their poor efforts in R&D and their limited creation products, such as the Russian Federation, China, Iceland, Slovakia, Estonia, and Portugal (see Figure 8.1a).

Estimates of REI in the NIS creation model in 2014 showed substantial changes. Chile, India, Italy, Japan, South Korea, and Switzerland were efficient in creation in 2007 and maintained a REI =1 in 2014.

China joined this efficient group of countries in 2014 when it substantially boosted its R&D efforts (R&D/GDP) and scientific production, and reported notable growth in number of patents. Luxembourg and South Africa were above the median in 2007, but fell under the median in 2014, although remaining close to it. Greece, the Netherlands, Slovenia, Sweden, Turkey, and New Zealand were no longer above the median in 2014, as they were in 2007, yet they each remained close to the median as well. Canada, the United States, Austria, the Nordic countries, and Spain showed improvement in NIS creation REI. Belgium, Ireland, France, Germany, Poland, and the United Kingdom saw their efficiency index fall slightly. The Czech Republic, Estonia, Hungary, Israel, Mexico, Slovakia, and especially the Russian Federation had the lowest efficiency indices in creation index (see Figure 8.1b). There are a number of countries that do not have large numbers of patents or scientific articles, but have increased efforts in some inputs with important results in their outputs, including some Eastern European countries, such as Slovenia. Other countries were relatively efficient in having more production even when their efforts, in per capita figures, were very low, such as China and India.

8.4.3 NIS Diffusion Model 2007 and 2014

As we previously explained, we took as inputs the human and institutional capabilities of countries and each country's physical infrastructure supporting the process of disseminating innovation. The countries in this study, with few exceptions, have medium to high levels of education. In 2007, the median education index was 0.78 (with a maximum value of 1), with Norway, Poland, and Australia having the highest education index of 0.91 and twenty-three other countries falling above the median. In 2007, China, India, and Turkey had the lowest education index (0.56, 0.43, and 0.56, respectively), and ten other countries fell below the median. In 2014, the median education index increased to 0.803 and the overall distribution of nations remained the same, but some countries improved their education levels, as was the case of South Korea (with an education index of 0.67 in 2007 and 0.86 in 2014), and in other cases, like in Mexico, education levels fell (from 0.75 in 2007 to 0.64 in 2014).

In 2007, the Western European countries of France, Switzerland, and Luxembourg, and also the United States, Canada, Japan, South

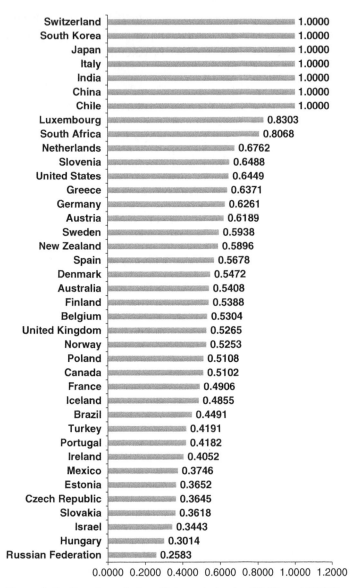

Figure 8.1b Creation relative efficiency index by OECD and BRICS countries, 2014

Source: Own elaboration based on the inputs and outputs data (see Table 8A.1a) and the creation relative efficiency DEA model.

Korea, and Australia had the highest quality of overall infrastructure with an index above the average of 4.93. In 2014, the distribution of countries as to overall quality of infrastructure remained almost the same as in 2007. The Netherlands, Switzerland, and Japan improved their overall quality of infrastructure, followed by Germany, the United Kingdom, and France. Brazil, Mexico, and South Africa had the lowest quality of overall infrastructure. Some BRICS and Eastern European countries improved their overall quality of infrastructure but remained below average.

In the case of ICT goods imports as % of total goods imports, only thirteen countries were above average (9.49 percent) in 2007, with China (24 percent) in the lead, followed by countries above 19 percent (Hungary and Ireland). The Netherlands, the Czech Republic, Mexico, South Korea, Slovakia, the United States, Finland, Japan, Australia, and Sweden had values ranging from the average of 9.49 percent up to 15 percent of ICT goods imports. By 2014, the median ICT goods/total goods imports was 8.31 percent and all countries had an overall lower ICT goods imports value. China maintained the highest number of ICT goods imports, followed by Mexico (see Table 8A.1b).

The variable university-industry collaboration in R&D by country shows that Australia, Japan, New Zealand, South Korea, the United States, and the Western European countries are more involved in this interinstitutional linkage, which favors the absorption of technological knowledge. The BRICS and Eastern European countries, Mexico, and Chile had less university-industry collaboration in R&D (see Table 8A.1b).

As to the products of diffusion, the countries we studied have an overall medium to high firm-level technology absorption, availability of latest technologies, and quality of scientific research. The median for firm-level technology absorption was 5.30. The Nordic countries, Japan, and the United States had the best firm-level technology absorption in 2007. In 2014, the United Kingdom led the rest of the countries we studied on firm-level technology absorption (6.5), followed in descending order by Iceland, the United States, Norway, and Japan. Firm-level technology absorption in Switzerland, Sweden, Luxembourg, and Israel was below that of the countries mentioned in the previous sentence. The Nordic countries and the United States had the best availability of latest technologies. In technology absorption and availability of latest technologies, some of the BRICS countries, Mexico, and Poland ranked behind the Nordic countries and the United States. Greece and Italy had higher levels of technology absorption and availability of latest technologies in 2014.

The median quality index of scientific research institutions in all the countries we studied was 4.84 during 2008–2009 and 5.03 in 2014, on a scale of 1 to 7. During those years, Switzerland was the leading country, followed by the United States, the United Kingdom, and Israel. China, Italy, and Slovakia increased the quality of their scientific research institutions in 2014. Greece, Mexico, Poland, and Turkey maintained the same low quality of scientific research institutions they had in 2007 (see Table 8A.1b).

Few countries had above average numbers of citations in articles by million inhabitants (the average being 3861.1 in 2007 and 6435.8 in 2014), which value the relevance of scientific production after diffusion. Yet, in 2007 and 2014 those countries saw a substantial increase of citations in articles. The Netherlands went from 53,844 citations in articles in 2007 to 93,138 in 2014. The United Kingdom went from 39,610.9 in 2007 to 61,832.9 in 2014. Ireland went from 16,458.3 in 2007 to 22,552.2 in 2014. Switzerland went from 7802 in 2007 to 20,057.5 in 2014. The United States went from 13,995 in 2007 to 16,726.5 in 2014. Germany went from 4804.1 in 2007 to 8313.2 in 2014 (see Table 8A.1b).

8.4.4 NIS Diffusion Relative Efficiency Index 2007 and 2014

The outcomes of the NIS *Diffusion relative efficiency index*, based on DEA estimates, show that, in 2007, nineteen of thirty-nine OECD and BRICS countries were relatively efficient. Among them were the United States, some European countries, Japan, Brazil, Chile, India, and Mexico. Other European and BRICS countries fell below the average of 98.46. Despite some countries' deficits in human and technological capabilities when compared to the countries with recognized leadership, either in the inputs or outputs selected, some achieved relative efficiency (see Figure 8.2a). In 2014, thirty-one of thirty-nine OECD and BRICS countries were relatively efficient in NIS diffusion, while the other six countries were below the median (0.994) (see Figure 8.2b). A probable interpretation is that countries with lower levels of education, specialists in R&D per million inhabitants, resident patent applications, quality of overall infrastructure, ICT goods imports as % of total goods

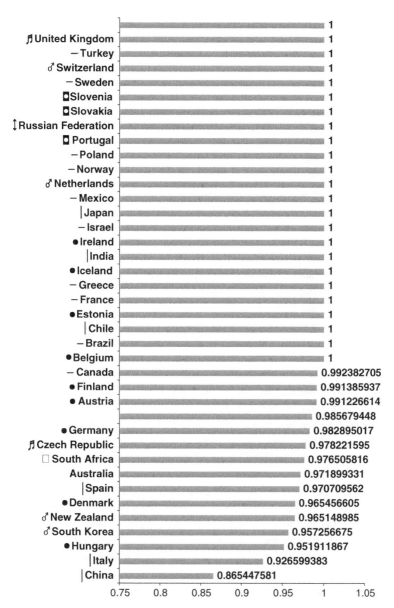

Figure 8.2a NIS diffusion relative efficiency index by OECD and BRICS countries, 2007

Source: Own elaboration based on the inputs and outputs data (see Table 8A.1b) and the diffusion relative efficiency DEA model.

Figure 8.2b NIS Diffusion relative efficiency index by OECD and BRICS countries, 2014

Source: Own elaboration based on the inputs and outputs data (see Table 8A.1b) and the diffusion relative efficiency DEA model.

imports, and university-industry collaboration in R&D have an efficient NIS diffusion. To the extent that such countries increase their efforts, they will improve the availability of latest technologies, FDI and technology transfer, firm-level technology absorption, quality of scientific research institutions, and the impact factor of scientific production efficiently, although with some relative changes.

8.4.5 NIS Utilization Model 2007 and 2014

For inputs into the objective of utilization, we identified two groups of countries with different levels of efforts to facilitate their populations' access to technological change (latest technologies in general and ICT technologies in particular, and overall infrastructure), by means of institutional efficiency and market size. The industrialized countries of Western Europe, North America, and Oceania showed the highest efforts to facilitate their populations' access to technological change. The BRICS countries, Mexico, Chile, and the Eastern European countries showed lower levels of efforts to facilitate their populations' access to technological change and fell below the overall average for the different inputs. Spain, Italy, Portugal, and Greece also showed lower levels of efforts to facilitate their populations' access to technological change and fell below average on some indicators (see Table 8A.1c).

In 2007 and 2014, the industrialized countries of Europe, North America, and Oceania had higher levels of institutional efficiency. In 2014, emerging and Eastern European countries, such as Slovakia, Italy, and Mexico, showed the lowest levels of institutional efficiency (3.3, 3.4, and 3.4, respectively; the median being 4.63); Finland and New Zealand showed the highest levels of institutional efficiency (6.08 and 6.09, respectively).

The average availability of the latest technologies in all the countries studied was relatively high (5.87 in 2007 and 5.69 in 2014, on a scale from 1 to 7). This may be due to the globalization process. To the extent that countries are involved in global production, their prospects for inflows of new technologies increase. BRICS countries showed backwardness in their availability of latest technologies. This became more evident when we considered the level of connectivity through the ICT paradigm in 2007. Examples of the extreme cases were India, with 0.4 fixed broadband subscriptions/100 population and with 3.95 percent of individuals using the internet, and South Africa, with 0.8 fixed broadband subscriptions/100 population and 8.07 percent individuals using the Internet. Mexico, Turkey, and Chile were also among the countries with lower connectivity. By 2014, almost all the countries we studied had made important improvements, especially in internet use. The leading countries have near 100 percent internet use among their populations. Countries where a quarter of the population had internet access in 2007 were close to 50 percent in 2014, such as China, Mexico, Turkey, and South Africa. Substantial catching up was achieved by Brazil, Greece, and the Russian Federation in 2014, increasing to more than 50 percent. India remained as the extreme case, going from 3.95 to 15.10 percent of individuals using the internet (see Table 8A.1c).

Developed and BRICS countries had above average local market size in 2007 and 2014. The United States and China had the largest local market size during both years. We noticed improvements in the human and institutional environment whenever countries gained access to innovation in products (notably access to ICT products), processes, or institutional changes. The quality of scientific research institutions was higher in the industrialized countries of Europe, North America, Israel, and Oceania, which have convergent levels of quality. The BRICS and Eastern European countries had below average local market sizes (the average was 4.8 in 2007 and 5.0 in 2014).

A large of number of countries showed a high human development index, evidencing concern for the general well-being of their populations. The BRICS countries had lower human development indices in 2007 and 2014. The human development index fell for every country in 2012, due to the world financial crisis of 2009. We found an enormous gap in per capita GDP across countries. In 2007, the mean per capita GDP for all the countries we studied was 34,412 US dollars (all figures in 2011 USD and PPP). In 2014, the per capita GDP reached a mean of 34,577 USD. Luxembourg had the highest per capita income in 2007 (96,711 USD), followed by Norway (65,781 USD) and the United States and Switzerland (with more than 50,000 USD). Ireland, the Netherlands, Denmark, Sweden, Austria, Iceland, Finland, Canada, Belgium, and Australia each had a per capita income between 40,000 and 50,000 USD. The United Kingdom, Italy, France, Japan, Spain, New Zealand, and Greece had a per capita income between 30,000 USD and 40,000 USD. India and China reported the lowest per capita incomes (3699 USD and 7225 USD, respectively). The other BRICS countries, Mexico, Chile, Turkey, Poland, and Hungary each had per capita incomes of less than 20,000 USD. The OECD and BRICS countries' per capita GDP had an average growth rate of 0.07 percent between 2007 and 2014, but the countries showed substantial differences in GDP growth rates. We note the significant GDP growth of some BRICS countries like China (8.3 percent), India (7.2 percent), and the Russian Federation (6.0 percent). Among industrialized countries, GDP growth was somewhat slower, as was the case in the United States (1.8 percent), Norway (3.31 percent), and Switzerland (3.3 percent).

Finally, the different levels of labor productivity achieved by each country also reflected their diversity in the use of new technologies. While the industrialized countries of Western Europe, North America, and Australia had above average levels of labor productivity (75,785 USD per worker in 2014), the BRICS and Eastern European countries fell below average in 2007 and 2014. The extreme cases are those with higher labor productivity, such as Luxembourg and Norway (128,663 USD and 125,650 USD per worker, respectively) and those with lower productivity, such India and China (13,091 USD and 22,318 USD per worker (see Table 8A.1c).

8.4.6 NIS Utilization Relative Efficiency Index 2007 and 2014

In 2007 and 2014, there were a large number of countries, including the industrialized countries of Eastern and Western Europe, North America, and some BRICS countries, with relative efficiency indices equal to one for the objective NIS utilization (see Figure 8.3a and Figure 8.3b). There were twenty-two relatively efficient countries in NIS utilization in 2007, but the remaining seventeen countries were close to becoming relatively efficient. In 2014, twenty-nine countries were relatively efficient and ten were close to efficient (see Figure 8.3b). Notwithstanding the important gaps across countries in the various inputs and outputs, we noted that even with deficient efforts to use new technologies and scarce derivative outputs that show improvement of human, economic, and institutional capabilities, some countries succeeded in achieving relative efficiency in NIS utilization.

8.4.7 NIS General Model 2007 and 2014

In the general model, countries' efforts to improve national innovation systems are mainly reflected in two input variables: specialists in R&D

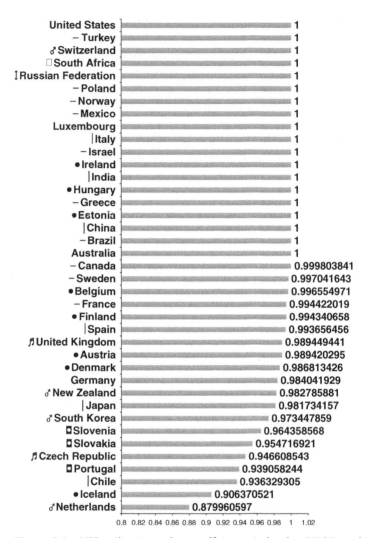

Figure 8.3a NIS utilization relative efficiency index by OECD and BRICS countries, 2007
Source: Own elaboration based on the inputs and outputs data (see Table 8A.1c) and the diffusion relative efficiency DEA model.

per million inhabitants and R&D spending as percentage of GDP. Both variables involve institutional efforts to facilitate the creation, diffusion, and utilization of new ideas and products. We included the two variables in the inputs of the NIS creation model. For output variables,

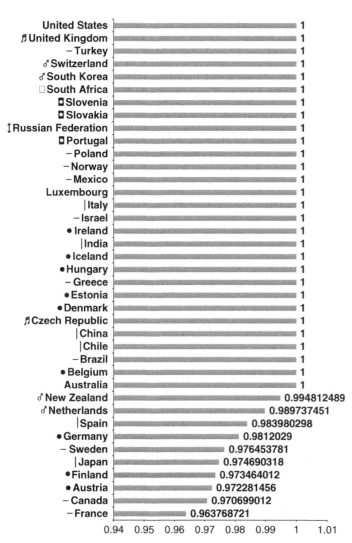

Figure 8.3b NIS utilization relative efficiency index by OECD and BRICS countries, 2014
Source: Own elaboration based on the inputs and outputs data (see Table 8A.1c) and the diffusion relative efficiency DEA model.

we used patent applications by residents per million inhabitants, triadic patents, and firm-level technology absorption. Patent applications by residents per million inhabitants and triadic patents show to what extent countries have maximized their innovation capabilities. We discussed firm-level technology absorption under our creation model section and triadic patent under our NIS diffusion model discussion.

8.4.8 NIS General Model Relative Efficiency Index 2007 and 2014

Our DEA estimates of the NIS relative efficiency index by objective allowed us to identify the strengths and weaknesses of national innovation systems in OECD and BRICS countries and, thus, to outline policies to improve each objective. One can expect that a NIS with a high stock of inputs would have the best possible outcomes and a high relative efficiency rating. Nevertheless, countries with comparatively fewer resources allocated to their innovation system and smaller comparative outcomes in absolute terms may achieve relative efficiency. We identified six countries as relatively efficient in the NIS general model in 2007: Switzerland, South Korea, Japan, India, Iceland, and Chile. The average efficiency index for all the NIS studied was relatively high at 0.903 (see Figure 8.4a).

The United Kingdom, Switzerland, South Korea, South Africa, New Zealand, Luxembourg, Japan, India, China, and Chile showed improved NIS general relative efficiency in 2014. The median relative efficiency in 2014 (0.897) was similar to that reported on the 2007 model (0.903) (see Figure 8.4b). The United States is a recognized leader in innovation, though some other industrialized and BRICS countries showed a high relative efficiency in the NIS general model. This may be explained by the fact that, although some countries are far behind the leaders in innovation, they have implemented measures to improve their relative efficiency and innovation systems; yet at the same time, they face important challenges to make effective gains and catch up in absolute terms.

8.4.9 Rates of Growth and Application of an Ordinary Least Square Model (OLS)

In this second stage of our study, we used a linear OLS model to relate the efficiency indices of the different objectives of the NIS with the

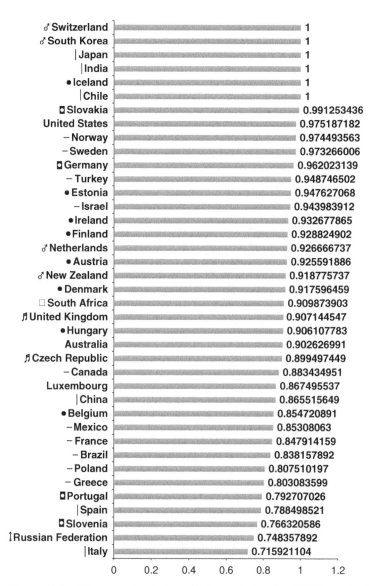

Figure 8.4a NIS general relative efficiency index by OECD and BRICS countries, 2007
Source: Own elaboration based on the inputs and outputs data (see Tables 8A.1a, 8A.1b and 8A.1c) and the general relative efficiency DEA model.

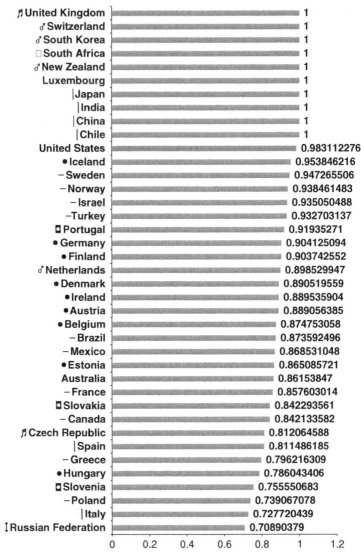

Figure 8.4b NIS general relative efficiency index by OECD and BRICS countries, 2014

Source: Own elaboration based on the inputs and outputs data (see Tables 8A.1a, 8A.1b and 8A.1c) and the general relative efficiency DEA model.

average long-term annual economic growth rates (2007–2014) of the countries we analyzed. The model is described here:

Model: $r_i = \alpha_0 + \alpha_1 I_{ci} + \alpha_2 I_{di} + \alpha_3 I_{ui} + \alpha_4 I_{gi} + \alpha_5 D_i + \alpha_6 I_{di} + \alpha_7 I_{ei} + u_i$

Where:

r_i = average economic growth rate during the period 2007–2014 of country i, where i = 1, …, 39
I_{ci} = relative efficiency index in creation of the NIS of country i;
I_{di} = relative efficiency index in diffusion of the NIS of country i;
I_{ui} = relative efficiency index in utilization of country i;
I_{gi} = relative efficiency index of the general model of country i;
D_i = *dummy* variable, with value 1 if country i has a high per capita GDP and 0 if it does not;
I_{di} = index of coefficient of dependency of country i;
I_{ei} = institutional efficiency index of country i;
α_j = parameters to be estimated by OLS, where j = 0, …,7;
u_i = errors in distribution N (0, 1).

Relative efficiency indices take values between 0 and 1. The values of the independent control variable coefficient of dependency is defined as the number of patent applications by foreign nationals divided by the number of patent applications by nationals (SEP-Conacyt 2000: 97) and the index of institutional efficiency is on a scale of 1 to 7. As shown in Table 8.3, the results of the OLS model of NIS efficiency indices in 2007 show two significant regression coefficients of the variables corresponding to the efficiency indices.[11] These were the coefficients corresponding to the diffusion and the general models indices. The values of the regression coefficients are elasticities; they point out the percentage increase in the dependent variable (growth rate) when the independent variable (efficiency index of the model) increases by 1 percent. For 2007, (1) the coefficient of the diffusion model index means that a one percent increase in the index would decrease the long run growth rate in 0.3 percent, (2) the coefficient of the general model index means that a one percent increase in that index would increase the long-run growth rate by 0.04 percent, and (3) the coefficient of institutions' efficiency index, a control variable, has a negative effect on the growth rate.

[11] The test for multicollinearity resulted in a vif equal to 1.61 in 2007 and 1.87 in 2014. This means a low correlation among the independent variables in both years.

Table 8.3 *OECD and BRICS countries: growth rate as function of relative efficiency indices and institutional variables by robust OLS, 2007 and 2014*

Variable	2007				2014			
	Coeff.		Robust Std. Err.	t	Coeff.		Robust Std. Err.	t
Creation model	-0.01		0.02	-0.57	0.00		0.01	0.33
Diffusion model	-0.30	**	0.17	-1.80	-0.45	**	0.25	-1.81
Utilization model	0.08		0.09	0.83	0.04		0.18	0.22
General model	0.17	*	0.05	3.52	0.14	***	0.06	2.56
Low GDP per capita	0.44		0.81	0.55	0.44		0.63	0.69
Dependency coefficient	0.09		0.07	1.28	0.18	***	0.08	2.30
Institutions Efficiency index	-1.00	***	0.47	-2.15	-0.75		0.50	-1.50
Constant	12.85		20.82	0.62	31.47		27.22	1.16
N	39				39			
R^2	0.505				0.488			

Own estimations
* Level of significance at 99%; ** Level of significance at 95%; *** Level of significance al 90%

For the year 2014, the results also show two significant regression coefficients for the efficiency index variables, for those of the general and diffusion models. Thus, (1) the coefficient for the diffusion model index variable indicates that a 1 percent increase in this index decreases the long-term growth rate by 0.45 percent; (2) the coefficient of the general model index shows that a 1 percent increase in the efficiency index of this model would increase the long-term growth rate by 0.14%; and (3) it is noteworthy that the coefficient of dependency has a positive impact on the long-term growth rate of the countries we analyzed.

We have two important results. The unexpected one is the negative relationship between the efficiency index of the diffusion model and the long-term rate of economic growth. In theory, any kind of allocative efficiency should result in a higher rate of economic growth; i.e. efficiency and economic growth seem to go hand-in-hand. In particular, one can expect that an increase in the diffusion of new ideas and technologies should result in higher economic growth. Our results, however, indicate that such is not always the case. We asked whether the relationship between efficiency and economic growth was the same for all countries independently of their GDP and rate of economic growth. The result we expected was a positive relationship between the efficiency index of the general model and the rate of economic growth. Looking for a reasonable explanation for our unexpected result, we divided the countries we analyzed into two groups: countries with an economic growth rate under the mean long-term economic growth rate of the thirty-nine countries we studied and countries with an economic growth rate above that mean long-term economic growth rate. Then, we applied an Ordered Probit model to the aforementioned variables.

8.5 NIS Efficiency Indices and Growth Rates: Application of an Ordered Probit Model

In order to conduct correlation analysis of efficiency indices with long-term economic growth rates, we applied an Ordered Probit model to data from 2007 and 2014. The regression equation is the same as that of the OLS model, but now the dependent variable, y_j, is redefined and takes two possible values (see Table 8.3).

y_j = High, if a country's economic growth rate is greater than the average economic growth rate of the thirty-nine countries we analyzed.

y_j = Low, if a country's economic growth rate is lower than the average economic growth rate of the thirty-nine countries we analyzed.

The econometric results of the general OProbit model do not allow for the interpretation of the regression coefficients and their sign. We estimated the marginal effects of independent variables on the dependent variable, as they are usually analyzed in applied econometric studies. In other words, in these models, the marginal values vary with the value of the independent variables. It is useful to calculate the marginal effects in order to interpret the results of the model (Green 2000: 812–817).

We grouped the countries' economic growth rates into two categories, one consisting of countries with high economic growth rates equal to or above the average (seventeen countries in 2007 and twenty countries in 2014). The other category we created consists of countries with below average economic growth rates (twenty-two countries in 2007 and nineteen countries in 2014). The results are shown in Table 8.4. As we have mentioned, the coefficients of a nonlinear model usually do not measure the marginal effects of independent variables on the dependent variable. Therefore, we proceed to commenting on the results of the marginal effects of the variables on the categories in which the dependent variable was divided.

In Table 8.4, the first row of results presents the probability of a country's economic growth rate falling into each of the categories in which the dependent variable was divided. In 2007, the probability of a country's economic growth rate being low was 51 percent and there was a 49 percent probability of a country's economic growth rate being high in 2014, these figures were 20 percent and 80 percent, respectively. The coefficient that measures a marginal effect (dy/dx) is read as the effect a marginal or unitary change of the independent variable (dx) has on the probability of a country's economic growth rate falling in a given category.

Table 8.4 shows the same econometric results for both categories of countries with low and high economic growth rates, although their coefficients have opposite signs. There are some differences in the results of the OLS and the OProbit models, and some of the efficiency indices seem to have a significant effect on the probability of a country's economic growth rate falling in any of the categories.[12] Thus, in the results

---

[12] We use STATA in the econometric analysis. This software provides the standard errors and z values for the null hypothesis that the regression coefficients of each of the independent variables are equal to zero. The interpretation of these values follows the traditional approach.

Table 8.4 *Marginal effects by Ordered Probit categories, 2007 and 2014*

Variable	2007			2014		
	dy/dx	Standard error	z	dy/dx	Standard error	z
Low rate probability	*0.5103*			*0.199*		
Creation model	-0.002	0.00494	-0.31	-0.010**	0.00476	-2.00
Diffusion model	0.015	0.02970	0.51	0.212*	0.08083	2.63
Utilization model	-0.087	0.05692	-1.52	-0.278*	0.09908	-2.80
General model	-0.017	0.01548	-1.12	-0.038**	0.01760	-2.15
Low GDP per capita	-0.483**	0.20073	-2.41	-0.774*	0.23976	-3.23
Dependency coefficient	-0.140*	0.04705	-2.97	-0.281*	0.07596	-3.69
Institutions Efficiency	0.140	0.21480	0.65	0.039	0.25527	0.15
High rate probability	*0.4897*			*0.801*		
Creation model	0.002	0.00494	0.31	0.010**	0.00476	2.00
Diffusion model	-0.015	0.02970	-0.51	-0.212*	0.08078	-2.63
Utilization model	0.087	0.05692	1.52	0.278*	0.09913	2.80
General model	0.017	0.01548	1.12	0.038**	0.01760	2.15
Low GDP per capita	0.483**	0.20073	2.41	0.774*	0.23976	3.23
Dependency coefficient	0.140*	0.04705	2.97	0.281*	0.07596	3.69
Institutions Efficiency	-0.140	0.21480	-0.65	-0.039	0.25527	-0.15

Own estimations

* Level of significance at 99%; ** Level of significance at 95%

for 2007 for the category of countries with low economic growth rates, the coefficients with marginal effects show: (1) that the efficiency index variables of all models did not have statistically significant coefficients. (2) The coefficients of the control variables indicate, first, that a low per capita GDP lowers a country's probability of having a low long-term economic growth rate by 0.48 percent; second, a 1 percent increase in a country's dependency rate lowers the country's probability of having a low long-term economic growth rate by 0.14 percent.

In 2007, in the category of countries with high economic growth rates, the regression coefficients showed the same effects, but with the opposite signs. Thus, (1) the efficiency index variables of all models did not have statistically significant coefficients and, (2) we found that a low per capita GDP increases a country's probability of having a high long-term economic growth rate by 0.48 percent, while a 1 percent increase in a country's dependency rate increases the country's probability of having a high long-term economic growth rate by 0.14 percent.

In 2014, in the category of countries with low economic growth rates, the coefficients of the marginal effects show: (1) that a 1 percent increase in the relative efficiency index of a country's creation model lowers the probability of that country having a low long-term economic growth rate by .01 percent; (2) that a one-percent increase in the relative efficiency index of a country's diffusion model increases that country's probability of having a low long-term economic growth rate by 0.21 percent; (3) that a 1 percent increase in the relative efficiency index of a country's utilization model lowers that country's probability of having a low long-term economic growth rate by 0.28 percent; (4) that a 1 percent increase in the relative efficiency index of a country's general model lowers that country's probability of having a low long-term economic growth rate by 0.04 percent; (5) the coefficients of the control variables indicate, first, that a low per capita GDP lowers a country's probability of having a low long-term economic growth rate by 0.77 percent, and second, that a 1 percent increase in a country's dependency coefficient lowers the country's probability of having a low long-term economic growth rate by 0.28 percent.

In 2014, in the category of countries with high economic growth rates, the regression coefficients show the same effects but with opposite signs. Thus, (1) a 1 percent increase in the relative efficiency index of a country's creation model would increase that country's probability of having a high long-term economic growth rate by 0.1 percent; (2) a

1 percent increase in the relative efficiency index of a country's diffusion model would lower that country's probability of having a high long-term economic growth rate by 0.21 percent; (3) a 1 percent increase in the relative efficiency index of a country's utilization model would increase a country's probability of having a high long-term economic growth rate by 0.28 percent; (4) a 1 percent increase in the relative efficiency index of a country's general model would increase that country's probability of having a high long-term economic growth rate by 0.04 percent; (5) the coefficients of the control variables indicate, first, that a high per capita GDP increases a country's probability of having a high long-term economic growth rate by 0.77 percent, and second, a 1 percent increase in a country's dependency coefficient increases the probability of the country having a high long-term economic growth rate by 0.28 percent. The opposite signs between the models' coefficients of relative efficiency indices, for example, of diffusion and utilization in 2014, show the presence of a trade-off or substitution between the two indices, moving along a line of equiprobability of being a country with a low or high long-term economic growth rate (see van Praag 2005: 215–216).

8.6 Conclusions

We found some differences and similarities in efforts among OECD and BRICS countries to develop, diffuse, and use new scientific and technological knowledge. Some countries have invested more in inputs that had yielded good outputs (results). But, the innovation leaders and main followers have not necessarily achieved higher relative efficiency in the main objectives of NIS: creation, diffusion, and utilization. In the creation relative efficiency indices, gaps among countries are evident. Few countries are leading the technological innovations, although more countries are getting good results at arriving at new scientific findings. Some emerging countries like Chile and India in 2007 and Chile, China, and India in 2014 reached the highest relative efficiency (an index of 1) in NIS creation, joining developed countries like Japan, South Korea, and Switzerland, but not the known leaders in building technological and innovation capabilities, such as Germany, the United States, and other European countries.

Developed countries have traditionally invested substantial resources in building human and institutional capabilities and the physical infrastructure supporting the process of disseminating innovation. These investments are the reason behind important gaps among the inputs and outputs of developed countries, the BRICS, and Eastern European countries of the OECD included in the DEA models we applied. However, our analysis showed a small gap in the NIS relative efficiency indices in diffusion and utilization among developed and less developed countries. This result might be explained by the globalization of the mechanisms of technology and knowledge diffusion. The gaps of the general relative efficiency indices between the NIS of the countries that we studied were a kind of synthesis of the relative efficiency indices of the partial objectives of such NIS.

Some NIS were relatively efficient in relation to some objectives but inefficient in relation to others. In spite of significant gaps in relative efficiency indices, we found that some emerging countries (India, China, and South Africa, for example) had relative efficiency in their NIS in some objectives, such as diffusion and utilization, similar to that of developed countries. Eastern European and BRICS countries must learn from the quantitative and qualitative private and public policies of developed countries, not only to accede to the scientific and technological frontier, but also to have economic growth and progress for the wellbeing of their population.

The econometric results we discussed in this study must be taken cautiously because they are dependent on the quality of the information used to estimate relative efficiency indices. However, we found some noteworthy trends. First, the efficiency index variable of the general model behaved independently of its three components or parts (relative efficiency index of models of creation, diffusion, and utilization), as was shown by our multicollinearity test among these variables. This fact reminds us of Aristotle's principle: The whole is more than the sum of its parts. Second, the efficiency indices of the diffusion model seemed to be negatively correlated with the rate of economic growth, especially in countries with high economic growth rates. More research on this result or topic is needed to support or reject this preliminary conclusion. Third, the regression coefficient of the efficiency index variable of the utilization model was consistently higher than the coefficients of the other efficiency index variables; this result suggests that improvements in this efficiency index would positively affect the long-term economic growth rate more than similar improvements in any other efficiency variable. This fact unquestionably underscores the need for further research on this topic.

ANNEX

Efficiency in DEA is expressed as the ratio of outputs to inputs. The most efficient DMUs have higher output/input ratios and are on the efficiency frontier. The efficiency index is equal to the unit along the entire efficiency frontier that surrounds the available data. DMUs, which are on the efficiency frontier, are the most efficient according to the available data, but the data does not offer insight as to the extent to which the most efficient DMUs can improve their performance. The performance of all other DMUs are evaluated in relation to the performance of the most efficient DMUs. Thus, we have obtained relative, not absolute, efficiencies (Ramanathan 2009; Productivity Tools 2009).

The main assumptions of a DEA model are weak and are fulfilled for any quasi-concave technology, such as: (1) the real input-output (x, y) combinations observed are feasible. (2) The set of output possibilities is convex. (3) DMUs may freely dispose of (eliminate without cost) their inputs and outputs. (4) If there are constant returns-to-scale and a feasible production plan (x, y), then for any k≥0, (kx, ky) is also feasible (Ray 2004). The model we used in this investigation was XLDEA 2.1 (Productivity Tools 2009), output oriented, in particular Phase one, which works with relative efficiency indices and efficient pair weights.

Phase 1. Maximization of the inverse efficiency index of DMUs in the population sample we analyzed.

$$\text{Max } \varphi$$
$$\text{s.a.: } x_0 - X\lambda \geq 0$$
$$-\varphi y_0 + Y\lambda \geq 0$$
$$\lambda \geq 0$$

Where:

(1) There are k inputs and m outputs
(2) x_0 and y_0 are vectors of inputs (k×1) and outputs (m×1) of the unit j, for j=1, 2, ..., n.
(3) X and Y are matrices (k×n) and (m×n) of inputs and outputs
(4) λ is the vector (n×1) of weights of efficient pairs
$\varphi^* \geq 1$; is the inverse efficiency index

Table 8A.1a *Inputs and outputs of NIS creation model*

	Inputs		Outputs									
	R&DE/GDP (%) 2007 (a)	R&DE/GDP (%) 2014 (a)	Researchers in R&D per million people, 2007 (a)	Researchers in R&D per million people, 2012 (a)	FDI and technology transfer, 2007 (Scale 1–7) (b)	FDI and technology transfer, 2014 (Scale 1–7) (c)	Scientific and technical journal articles per researcher in R&D (2007) (d)	Scientific and technical journal articles per researcher in R&D (2013) (d)	Patent applications residents per million people, 2007 (e)	Patent applications residents per million people, 2014 (e)	Triadic patents per million people, 2007 (f)	Triadic patents per million people, 2011 (f)
Australia	2.18	2.20	4231.78	4280.36	5.5	5.10	0.3899	0.4593	129.577	84.70	16.55	11.81
Austria	2.43	2.99	3815.74	4401.08	4.6	4.60	0.3100	0.3632	453.424	244.80	45.44	37.62
Belgium	1.84	2.46	3392.72	3878.19	5.1	5.00	0.3719	0.3549	219.901	79.15	40.51	36.33
Brazil	1.08	1.24	603.11	698.10	5.3	4.90	0.2595	0.3473	21.755	22.61	0.36	3.35
Canada	1.92	1.61	4588.22	4562.82	5.4	4.60	0.3373	0.3607	151.536	118.11	20.73	14.38
Chile	0.31	0.38	337.18	317.19	5.4	5.30	0.6125	0.8408	24.480	25.45	0.43	0.72
China	1.38	2.05	1078.63	977.70	4.4	4.50	0.1456	0.2724	115.987	587.23	0.52	12.89
Czech Republic	1.31	2.00	2698.60	2891.48	5.8	5.00	0.3462	0.3097	78.505	86.46	2.27	2.78
Denmark	2.51	3.08	5519.32	6805.83	4.9	4.80	0.2924	0.3148	561.369	244.21	57.72	39.65
Estonia	1.07	1.44	2745.06	3484.75	5.9	5.00	0.2707	0.3084	42.403	33.47	3.19	3.60
Finland	3.35	3.17	7373.24	7422.90	4.6	4.30	0.2321	0.2634	727.691	259.82	48.86	37.01
France	2.02	2.26	3580.19	3917.55	4.7	4.80	0.2862	0.2838	371.961	218.98	43.49	33.51
Germany	2.45	2.87	3597.24	4084.89	4.7	4.90	0.3002	0.3018	903.301	594.71	70.59	50.62
Greece	0.58	0.84	1887.83	2219.20	4.5	4.10	0.5158	0.4294	59.023	59.89	1.26	0.83
Hungary	0.96	1.37	1728.02	2302.80	5.5	5.10	0.3264	0.2536	78.099	55.36	5.86	3.55
Iceland	2.58	1.89	7230.49	7012.22	4.4	3.70	0.1630	0.2849	320.875	155.78	31.19	7.71
India	0.79	0.82	135.30	156.60	5.4	4.20	0.2720	0.4779	5.337	9.30	0.17	1.60
Ireland	1.23	1.52	2892.65	3354.53	6.4	6.40	0.4193	0.3969	287.562	56.98	20.74	12.32
Israel	4.41	4.11	9066.93	6602.34	5.4	5.40	0.1763	0.1924	233.356	136.93	48.74	38.49
Italy	1.13	1.29	1572.58	1747.94	4.4	3.70	0.5686	0.6355	230.763	141.49	12.48	10.28

Japan	3.46	3.58	5377.69	5157.52	4.8	4.70	0.1506	0.1613	2620.809	2091.99	138.73	107.78
Luxembourg	1.61	1.26	4635.72	5813.91	5.4	5.40	0.0972	0.4541	560.348	230.08	31.12	34.43
Mexico	0.37	0.54	335.25	386.43	5.5	5.10	0.2465	0.3041	5.560	9.94	0.17	0.11
Netherlands	1.70	1.97	3101.31	3506.93	5	5.00	0.4919	0.4124	551.478	136.02	65.02	49.28
New Zealand	1.16	1.17	3445.00	3692.86	5.2	5.10	0.3989	0.4067	446.435	362.77	13.45	9.29
Norway	1.56	1.71	5162.76	5507.56	4.9	4.70	0.3077	0.3612	259.722	215.31	22.27	15.44
Poland	0.56	0.94	1594.67	1678.67	4.6	4.60	0.3319	0.3730	64.857	103.68	0.66	1.44
Portugal	1.12	1.29	2670.52	4723.81	5.4	5.20	0.2609	0.3597	30.425	69.42	3.99	1.97
Russian Federation	1.12	1.19	3276.12	3125.30	4.1	3.80	0.0603	0.0797	193.574	167.38	0.54	7.90
Slovakia	0.45	0.89	2291.32	2832.16	6	5.10	0.2203	0.2998	47.666	38.94	0.67	1.99
Slovenia	1.42	2.39	3097.97	4255.19	4.3	3.90	0.4254	0.4084	221.071	229.27	5.70	3.65
South Africa	0.88	0.73	388.79	385.10	5.3	4.80	0.2963	0.4404	18.413	14.85	0.79	6.70
South Korea	3.00	4.29	4603.84	5928.28	4.5	4.60	0.1811	0.1826	2669.865	3253.87	40.68	43.32
Spain	1.23	1.23	2712.35	2799.90	5.3	4.70	0.3370	0.4475	100.709	63.54	5.70	3.94
Sweden	3.26	3.16	5004.96	5142.26	5.1	4.70	0.3603	0.2968	574.655	204.62	105.12	55.48
Switzerland	2.68	2.73	3457.99	3285.18	5.1	5.00	0.6389	0.5034	998.526	180.75	133.50	116.19
Turkey	0.72	1.01	714.49	987.00	5	5.10	0.4308	0.3405	28.094	62.77	0.13	0.32
United Kingdom	1.68	1.70	4131.53	4026.43	5.4	5.20	0.3495	0.3588	365.582	235.38	29.32	23.66
United States	2.63	2.77	3757.78	3978.73	5.1	4.90	0.3325	0.3108	800.074	894.12	46.16	36.66

Sources: (a) World Bank: World Development Indicators. Science and Technology, http://data.worldbank.org/indicator/SP.POP.SCIE.RD.P6

(b) World Economic Forum, The Global Competitiveness Report 2006–2007; Geneva, Switzerland, 2006, www3.weforum.org/docs/WEF_GlobalCompetitivenes sReport_2006–07.pdf

(c) Schwab, Klaus World Economic Forum, The Global Competitiveness Report 2014–2015; Geneva, Switzerland, 2014

(d) SCImago Journal & Country Rango, www.scimagojr.com/countryrank.php

(e) World Intellectual Property Organization, www.wipo.int/ipstats/en/statistics/country_profile/profile.jsp?code

(f) OECD Science, Technology and Patents. (Patents by technology), http://stats

Table 8A.1b *Inputs and outputs of NIS diffusion model*

	Education index, 2007 (1.00) (a)	Education index, 2013 (1.00) (a)	Researchers in R&D per million people, 2007 (b)	Researchers in R&D per million people, 2011 (b)	Patents applicati ons of residents & nonresid ents per million people, 2007 (c)	Patents applications of residents & nonresidents per million people, 2014 (c)	Quality of overall infrastru cture, 2008 (Scale 1–7) (d)	Quality of overall infrastruct ure, 2014 (Scale 1–7)(f)	University-industry collaborati on in R&D, 2008–2009 (Scale 1–7) (d)	University-industry collaboration in R&D, 2014 (Scale 1–7)(f)	ICT goods imports (% total imports, 2007 (g)	ICT imports (% total goods 2013 (g)
Country												
Australia	0.91	0.93	4231.779	4280.36	1279.56	1082.90	5.2	5.7	4.9	4.80	10.70	8.86
Austria	0.76	0.79	3815.744	4401.08	488.00	217.57	5.9	5.7	4.9	4.70	6.20	5.24
Belgium	0.80	0.81	3392.716	3878.19	235.13	262.60	5.6	5.5	5.3	5.60	3.79	2.75
Brazil	0.64	0.66	603.109	698.10	112.37	147.24	3.5	3.2	4.1	3.80	4.87	8.60
Canada	0.85	0.85	4588.222	4562.82	1216.74	997.00	5.9	5.4	5.2	4.90	8.30	7.30
Chile	0.72	0.75	337.183	317.19	231.19	174.81	4.9	4.6	3.9	4.20	7.50	7.64
China	0.56	0.61	1078.625	977.70	185.78	677.78	4.3	4.7	4.6	4.40	24.55	20.50
Czech Republic	0.85	0.87	2698.597	2891.48	97.09	108.04	4.3	4.1	4.4	4.00	14.74	13.69
Denmark	0.86	0.87	5519.315	6805.83	597.40	631.32	5.8	5.5	5.5	4.90	8.63	7.26
Estonia	0.85	0.86	2745.060	3484.75	56 54	65 34	4 7	4.4	4.1	4.40	6.67	10.72
Finland	0.81	0.82	7373.240	7422.90	767.58	682.71	5.9	5.4	5.6	6.00	12.36	5.77
France	0.80	0.82	3580.195	3917.55	410.48	423.40	6.5	6	3.9	4.60	7.17	6.25
Germany	0.87	0.88	3597.239	4084.89	1065.80	1136.28	5.5	6.1	5.2	5.30	8.86	7.20
Greece	0.79	0.80	1887.829	2219.20	60.82	69.45	4.3	4.8	3.2	3.10	5.85	3.95
Hungary	0.80	0.80	1728.017	2302.80	88.23	74.02	4	4.5	4.2	4.30	19.20	15.10
Iceland	0.84	0.85	7230.490	7012.22	494.41	320.79	5.9	5.3	4.8	4.60	5.73	4.79
India	0.43	0.47	135.300	156.60	29.85	33.08	3.5	4.1	3.8	3.90	7.38	5.80
Ireland	0.88	0.89	2892.646	3354.53	305.34	200.85	4.2	5.3	5	5.20	19.31	9.01
Israel	0.85	0.85	9066.935	6602.34	1157.24	790.10	4.4	4.9	4.6	5.50	8.48	8.76
Italy	0.78	0.79	1572.579	1747.94	245.47	217.83	4	5.4	3.4	3.70	5.42	4.64
Japan	0.79	0.81	5377.689	5157.52	3114.27	2571.00	5.8	6.2	4.7	5.00	11.46	10.89
Luxembourg	0.85	0.76	4635.721	5813.91	613.01	1214.58	6	5.7	4.7	4.90	6.08	3.79
Mexico	0.75	0.64	335.250	386.43	146.79	128.68	3.7	3.3	3.5	4.00	13.51	17.11
Netherlands	0.60	0.89	3101.312	3506.93	573.77	559.52	5.7	6.3	5.2	5.40	15.37	12.56
New Zealand	0.86	0.92	3445.004	3692.86	1850.86	1719.06	4.6	5.2	4.7	4.90	8.56	7.55
Norway	0.91	0.91	5162.762	5507.56	1411.19	405.79	5	5	4.9	5.00	7.77	6.91
Poland	0.91	0.82	1594.668	1678.67	74.23	118.57	2.9	4.3	3.3	3.50	7.73	8.62
Portugal	0.80	0.73	2670.524	4723.81	33.36	81.90	5.2	5.5	4.1	4.70	8.16	4.68
Russian Federation	0.68	0.78	3276.122	3125.30	276.92	283.11	3.6	4.8	3.3	3.60	8.60	6.80
Slovakia	0.77	0.80	2291.325	2832.16	67.33	48.13	3.9	4.3	3.3	3.40	13.02	14.23
Slovenia	0.80	0.86	3097.967	4255.19	228.51	60.02	4.8	4.8	4.2	4.00	3.97	3.28
South Africa	0.85	0.70	388.788	385.10	167.37	139.93	4.3	4.1	4.5	4.50	8.76	8.20
South Korea	0.67	0.86	4603.837	5928.28	3577.82	4199.59	5.6	5.8	4.6	4.60	13.26	10.44
Spain	0.75	0.79	2712.350	2799.90	106.57	100.32	5.4	5.9	3.7	3.80	7.38	4.54
Sweden	0.82	0.83	5004.962	5142.26	618.14	648.55	5.8	5.6	5.6	5.30	9.81	9.72
Switzerland	0.83	0.84	3457.994	3285.18	1043.76	1084.10	6.3	6.2	5.7	5.80	5.91	5.58
Turkey	0.56	0.65	714.486	987.00	31.13	70.96	3.9	4.4	3.4	3.70	5.03	4.57
United Kingdom	0.85	0.86	4131.534	4026.43	490.26	431.61	5.4	6	5.4	5.70	7.37	7.86
United States	0.88	0.89	3757.782	3978.73	1512.17	1811.88	5.9	5.9	5.9	5.80	12.80	12.96

Sources (a) United Nation Development Report, Human Development Report, International Human Development Indicators. Education Index, November, 2013. Calculated using Mean Years of Schooling and Expected Years of Schooling. http://hdr.undp.org/en/data

(b) World Bank: World Development Indicators. Science and Technology, http://data.world bank.org/indicator/SP.POP.SCIE.RD.P6

(c) World Intellectual Property Organization, www.wipo.int/ipstats/en/statistics/country_pro file/profile.jsp?code

(d) World Economic Forum, The Global Competitiveness Report 2008–2009, Geneva, Switzerland, www3.weforum.org/docs/WEF_GlobalCompetitivenessReport_2008–09.pdf

(f) Schwab, Klaus World Economic Forum, The Global Competitiveness Report 2014–2015; Geneva, Switzerland, 2014

(g) World Bank: World Development Indicators. The Information Society, http://wdi.world bank.org/table/5.12

(h) World Economic Forum, The Global Competitiveness Report 2006–2007; Geneva, Switzerland, 2006, www3.weforum.org/docs/WEF_GlobalCompetitivenessReport_2006–07.pdf

(i) SCImago Journal & Country Rango, www.scimagojr.com/countryrank.php

Outputs

ntry	Firm-level technology absorption, 2007 (d)	Firm-level technology absorption, 2014 (f)	Availability of latest technologies, 2008–2009 (d)	Availability of latest technologies 2014 (f)	FDI and technology transfer, 2007 (Scale 1–7) (h)	FDI and technology transfer, 2014 (f)	Quality of scientific research institutions, 2007 (h)	Quality of scientific research institution, 2014 (Scale 1–7) (f)	Citations received by articles by million people, 2007 (i)	Citations received by articles by million people, 2014 (i)
tralia	5.60	5.60	6.00	6.00	5.50	5.10	5.30	5.80	706.40	1166.44
tria	5.70	5.70	6.30	6.00	4.60	4.60	4.90	5.00	1175.10	2630.18
ium	5.20	5.60	6.20	6.30	5.10	5.00	5.60	6.10	390.50	379.02
zil	4.90	4.80	5.30	4.70	5.30	4.90	4.30	4.00	68.00	210.08
ada	5.50	5.40	6.30	6.20	5.40	4.60	5.50	5.50	1123.20	1209.09
e	5.20	5.20	5.80	5.70	5.40	5.30	4.00	4.00	75.90	209.15
na ch	5.10	4.70	4.30	4.30	4.40	4.50	3.70	4.30	52.40	142.42
ublic	5.40	5.00	5.30	5.20	5.80	5.00	4.60	4.50	403.10	823.32
mark	5.80	5.70	6.40	5.80	4.90	4.80	5.30	5.40	2886.60	3423.83
nia	5.60	5.40	5.90	5.80	5.90	5.00	4.70	5.00	80.30	452.06
and	6.00	5.80	6.60	6.60	4.60	4.30	5.70	5.70	373.80	906.08
ce	5.20	5.50	6.30	6.10	4.70	4.80	5.10	5.60	859.80	919.88
many	5.30	5.70	6.30	6.20	4.70	4.90	5.80	5.80	4804.10	8313.18
ce	4.40	4.50	4.90	5.00	4.50	4.10	3.70	3.70	1225.60	2427.28
gary	5.30	4.70	5.10	5.30	5.50	5.10	4.70	5.10	203.40	419.53
nd	6.50	6.20	6.80	6.40	4.40	3.70	4.60	4.80	32.70	146.65
a	5.80	4.20	5.50	4.10	5.40	4.20	5.30	4.00	12.20	48.33
nd	5.50	5.60	5.70	6.00	6.40	6.40	5.30	5.50	16458.30	22552.15
l	6.10	6.00	6.30	6.30	5.40	5.40	6.00	6.30	177.10	173.31
	4.20	4.20	4.90	5.00	4.40	3.70	3.40	4.50	529.60	1087.92
n emb	6.30	6.10	6.30	6.20	4.80	4.70	5.80	5.80	587.10	662.32
	5.20	6.00	6.10	6.20	5.40	5.40	3.90	5.00	10.50	26.95
co	4.50	4.60	4.60	4.90	5.50	5.10	3.90	3.90	12.10	28.22
erla										
	5.40	5.60	6.30	6.30	5.00	5.00	5.50	5.90	53844.30	93138.14
and	5.30	5.80	5.90	6.10	5.20	5.10	5.10	5.30	851.10	5801.16
way	5.90	6.10	6.60	6.50	4.90	4.70	5.10	5.20	139.70	137.53
d	4.40	4.20	4.50	4.50	4.60	4.60	3.80	3.90	307.70	777.97
ugal	4.70	5.60	5.90	6.30	5.40	5.20	4.30	5.40	27.00	98.34
ian rati										
	4.40	4.20	4.10	4.20	4.10	3.80	4.40	4.00	105.40	208.60
akia	5.30	4.80	5.40	5.20	6.00	5.10	3.60	3.90	283.80	580.51
nia	4.60	4.90	5.50	5.50	4.30	3.90	4.20	4.70	286.00	988.83
a	5.30	5.40	5.50	5.50	5.30	4.80	4.80	4.70	44.40	96.65
a	5.90	5.40	5.90	5.70	4.50	4.60	5.00	5.00	305.30	972.45
	4.70	4.90	5.50	5.60	5.30	4.70	4.00	4.50	343.30	503.29
en	6.10	6.00	6.70	6.40	5.10	4.70	5.60	5.50	355.30	573.11
zerl	6.10	6.00	6.60	6.40	5.10	5.00	6.30	6.40	7802.60	20057.52
	5.40	5.20	5.30	5.30	5.00	5.10	3.90	3.90	34.30	146.05
ey d do										
	5.50	6.50	6.20	5.70	5.40	5.20	6.00	6.30	39610.90	61832.92
d s	6.00	6.10	6.60	6.50	5.10	4.90	6.00	6.10	13995.60	16726.50

Table 8A.1c Inputs and outputs of NIS utilization model

	Availability of latest technologies, 2008–2009 (Scale 1–7). (a)	Availability of latest technologies, 2014 (Scale 1–7) (b)	Institutions' Efficiency Index, 2007 (Scale 1–7). (a)	Institutions' Efficiency Index, 2014 (Scale 1–7). (b)	Quality of overall infrastructure, 2008 (Scale 1–7). (b)	Quality of overall infrastructure, 2014 (Scale 1–7). (b)	Domestic market size index, 2007 (Scale 1–7). (a)	Domestic market size index, 2014 (Scale 1–7). (b)	Fixed broadband subscriptions /100 pop, 2008 ©	Fixed broadband subscriptions /100 pop, 2014. (c)	Individuals using internet, 2007 (%). (c)	Individuals using internet, 2014 (%). (c)
Australia	6.0	6.0	5.5	5.1	5.2	5.7	5.0	5.1	24.6	27.7	69.5	83.0
Austria	6.3	6.0	5.5	5.1	5.9	5.7	4.3	4.4	20.7	27.7	69.4	80.6
Belgium	6.2	6.3	4.9	5.1	5.6	5.5	4.5	4.4	27.7	36.0	64.4	82.2
Brazil	5.3	4.7	3.3	3.5	3.5	3.2	5.6	5.7	5.2	11.7	30.9	51.6
Canada	6.3	6.2	5.0	5.4	5.9	5.4	5.3	5.4	29.5	35.4	73.2	85.8
Chile	5.8	5.7	4.9	4.8	4.9	4.6	4.0	4.3	8.5	14.1	35.9	66.5
China	4.3	4.3	3.5	4.2	4.3	4.7	6.4	6.8	6.2	14.4	16.0	45.8
Czech Republic	5.3	5.2	3.8	3.8	4.3	4.1	4.2	4.1	16.9	27.9	51.9	74.1
Denmark	6.4	5.8	6.0	5.4	5.8	5.5	4.0	4.0	36.5	41.3	85.0	94.6
Estonia	5.9	5.8	4.7	5.0	4.7	4.9	2.8	2.7	22.5	28.9	66.2	80.0
Finland	6.6	6.6	6.1	6.1	5.9	5.4	4.0	4.0	30.4	32.3	80.8	91.5
France	6.3	6.1	4.9	4.7	6.5	6.0	5.7	5.6	28.5	40.2	66.1	81.9
Germany	6.3	6.2	5.6	5.2	5.5	6.1	5.8	5.8	27.2	35.8	75.2	84.0
Greece	4.9	5.0	4.4	3.6	4.3	4.8	4.5	4.2	13.6	28.4	35.9	59.9
Hungary	3.1	3.3	4.2	3.7	4.0	4.6	4.9	3.9	17.6	27.3	53.3	72.6
Iceland	6.8	6.4	6.0	5.1	5.9	5.3	4.0	2.1	34.3	35.9	90.6	96.5
India	5.5	4.1	4.6	3.8	3.5	4.1	2.2	6.2	0.4	1.2	4.0	15.1
Ireland	5.7	6.0	5.2	5.4	4.2	5.3	6.1	3.7	20.5	26.9	61.2	78.2
Israel	6.3	6.3	4.8	4.3	4.4	4.9	3.9	4.2	23.7	27.2	48.1	70.8
Italy	4.9	5.0	3.7	3.4	4.0	5.4	4.0	5.5	18.8	23.5	40.8	58.5
Japan	6.3	6.2	5.0	5.5	5.8	6.2	5.6	6.1	23.7	29.3	74.3	86.3
Luxembourg	6.1	6.2	5.7	5.7	6.0	5.7	6.1	2.6	29.4	34.8	78.9	93.8
Mexico	4.6	4.9	3.7	3.4	3.7	3.3	2.6	5.5	6.6	10.5	20.8	43.5
Netherlands	6.3	6.3	5.6	5.5	5.7	6.3	5.4	4.7	35.2	40.8	85.8	94.0
New Zealand	5.9	6.1	5.7	6.1	4.6	5.2	3.6	3.7	21.4	31.0	69.8	82.8
Norway	6.6	6.5	5.7	5.5	5.0	5.0	4.1	4.1	33.0	38.8	86.9	95.1
Poland	4.5	4.5	3.6	4.0	2.9	4.3	4.8	4.9	11.7	18.9	48.6	62.8
Portugal	5.9	6.3	4.8	4.4	5.2	5.5	4.2	4.1	15.5	25.7	42.1	62.1
Russian Federation	4.1	4.2	3.0	3.5	3.6	4.8	5.6	5.7	6.5	17.5	24.7	61.4
Slovakia	5.4	5.2	4.0	3.3	3.9	4.3	3.6	3.7	11.2	21.8	61.8	77.9
Slovenia	5.5	5.5	4.3	3.8	4.8	4.8	3.2	3.1	20.9	26.6	56.7	72.7
South Africa	5.5	5.5	4.5	4.5	4.3	4.1	4.6	4.8	0.8	3.2	8.1	48.9
South Korea	5.9	5.7	4.2	3.7	5.6	5.8	5.3	5.4	32.3	38.8	78.8	84.8
Spain	5.5	5.6	4.4	3.8	5.4	5.9	5.4	5.3	20.2	27.3	55.1	71.6
Sweden	6.7	6.4	5.5	5.4	5.8	5.6	4.3	4.4	31.4	34.1	82.0	94.8
Switzerland	6.6	6.4	5.7	5.6	6.3	6.2	4.3	4.3	33.4	42.5	77.2	86.7
Turkey	5.3	5.3	4.1	3.9	3.9	4.4	5.1	5.2	8.2	11.7	28.6	46.3
United Kingdom	6.2	5.7	5.4	5.4	5.4	6.0	5.7	5.7	28.2	37.4	75.1	89.8
United States	6.6	6.5	4.8	4.7	5.9	5.9	7.0	7.0	25.2	31.1	75.0	84.2

Sources: (a) World Economic Forum, The Global Competitiveness Report 2006–2007; Geneva, Switzerland, 2006;
(b) Schwab, Klaus World Economic Forum, The Global Competitiveness Report 2014–2015; Geneva, Switzerland, 2014;
(c) The World Bank. World Development Indicators. The Information Society, http://data.wor ldbank.org/indicator/IT.NET.BBND.P2
(d) United Nation Development Report, Human Development Report, International Human Development Indicators. Human Development Index, November, 2013. http://hdr.undp.org/en/ data
(e) TED Output Labor an Labor Productivity 1950–2015, May 2015, www.google.com.mx/url? url=https://www.conference-board.org/retrievefile.cfm%3Ffilename%3DTED–Output-Labor-and-Labor-Productivity-1950–2015.xlsx%26type%3Dsubsite&rct=j&q=&esrc=s&sa=U&ve d=0ahUKEwjusoK8vffPAhVJ7oMKHfEvBW4QFgglMAM&sig2=_Uv0639QtbtgXpBs5upDY Q&usg=AFQjCNH5tkxraWXKm9vSPeWeA6XbX5bLTA
(f)The World Bank. World Development Indicators. GDP per capita, http://databank.banco mundial.org/data/reports.aspx?source=2&series=NY.GDP.PCAP.PP.CD&country=

	Outputs							
	Quality of scientific research institutions, 2007 (1–7) (a)	Quality of scientific research institutions, 2014 (1–7) (b)	Human Development Index, 2007 (1.00) (d)	Human Development Index, 2012 (1.00) (d)	Labor productivity, 2007 (GDP per worker, USD constant prices 2014) (e)	Labor productivity, 2014 (GDP per worker USD constant prices 2014) (e)	GDP per capita, USD PPP, 2007 (constant prices 2011) (f)	GDP per capita, USD PPP, 2014 (constant prices 2011) (f)
lia	5.3	5.80	0.97	0.94	90300.59	95969.60	40617.01	43267.60
	4.9	5.00	0.955	0.90	94674.00	92004.71	43501.88	43871.72
n	5.6	6.10	0.953	0.90	105864.69	105626.50	41278.48	40777.78
	4.3	4.00	0.813	0.73	26914.59	29050.41	13150.01	15162.42
a	5.5	5.50	0.966	0.91	82653.42	86359.60	41647.39	42801.18
	4.0	4.00	0.878	0.82	50279.01	55180.49	18507.22	21923.39
	3.7	4.30	0.772	0.70	12771.75	22318.30	7224.91	12599.19
ic	4.6	4.50	0.903	0.87	60293.68	61605.15	28595.24	28674.81
rk	5.3	5.40	0.955	0.90	89681.36	90148.78	45609.29	43156.83
	4.7	5.00	0.883	0.85	56941.05	58829.39	26677.58	26593.51
d	5.7	5.70	0.959	0.89	92977.99	88717.16	42016.16	38577.21
	5.1	5.60	0.961	0.89	93364.52	95198.47	37638.99	37052.66
ny	5.8	5.80	0.947	0.92	87640.05	86978.91	40709.97	43552.29
	3.7	3.70	0.942	0.86	79879.58	72772.68	32669.20	24518.60
ry	4.7	5.10	0.964	0.83	58525.49	59009.95	23204.66	23723.25
	4.6	4.80	0.879	0.91	78984.70	80404.42	42585.49	41262.04
	5.3	4.00	0.969	0.55	8692.03	13091.18	3698.64	5391.69
	5.3	5.50	0.612	0.92	108224.99	118455.36	49974.90	48383.66
	6.0	6.30	0.965	0.90	67494.49	69387.37	28589.87	31521.32
	3.4	4.50	0.935	0.88	92364.18	87406.33	38105.69	33341.04
	5.8	5.80	0.951	0.91	71432.25	72973.58	35183.60	35587.17
bourg	3.9	5.00	0.96	0.88	143337.10	128662.66	96711.05	91368.11
	3.9	3.90	0.96	0.78	44137.19	42496.01	15859.47	16301.47
ands	5.5	5.90	0.854	0.92	91081.84	92032.87	46852.48	45662.07
d	5.1	5.30	0.95	0.92	67496.89	69040.68	33249.80	34262.73
y	5.1	5.20	0.971	0.96	128263.00	125649.85	65780.91	64161.49
	3.8	3.90	0.88	0.82	50854.50	60694.60	19360.83	23953.66
al	4.3	5.40	0.909	0.82	59774.12	62755.66	27731.95	26174.86
ion	4.4	4.00	0.817	0.79	45336.69	49949.31	22798.97	24873.89
a	3.6	3.90	0.88	0.84	61790.94	68657.27	23426.37	26469.90
a	4.2	4.70	0.929	0.89	65279.59	65691.05	29885.50	28156.30
frica	4.8	4.70	0.683	0.63	42306.00	43642.00	12066.65	12436.24
orea	5.0	5.00	0.937	0.91	61005.51	69482.50	28063.27	33639.61
	4.0	4.50	0.955	0.89	77444.26	86180.46	34825.21	31749.72
	5.6	5.50	0.963	0.92	93617.23	94596.71	44005.31	43976.29
land	6.3	6.40	0.96	0.91	96514.58	96085.95	54482.53	55270.98
	3.9	3.90	0.806	0.72	58428.88	58098.86	16546.18	18500.69
n	6.0	6.30	0.947	0.88	83679.37	83180.86	38227.53	38084.87
States	6.0	6.10	0.96	0.94	108611.54	117219.84	51011.43	51708.40

Table 8A.2 *National systems of innovation relative efficiency indexes across OECD and BRICS countries, 2007 and 2014*

Country	2007				2014			
	Creation	Diffusion	Utilization	General	Creation	Diffusion	Utilization	General
Australia	0.5504	0.9719	1.0000	0.9026	0.5408	1.0000	1.0000	0.8615
Austria	0.5365	0.9912	0.9894	0.9256	0.6189	0.9836	0.9685	0.8891
Belgium	0.5813	1.0000	0.9966	0.8547	0.5304	1.0000	1.0000	0.8748
Brazil	0.4215	1.0000	1.0000	0.8382	0.4491	1.0000	1.0000	0.8736
Canada	0.4866	0.9924	0.9998	0.8834	0.5102	0.9893	0.9707	0.8421
Chile	1.0000	1.0000	0.9363	1.0000	1.0000	1.0000	1.0000	1.0000
China	0.3038	0.8654	1.0000	0.8655	1.0000	0.9583	1.0000	1.0000
Czech Republic	0.4712	0.9782	0.9466	0.8995	0.3645	1.0000	1.0000	0.8121
Denmark	0.5123	0.9655	0.9868	0.9176	0.5472	0.9698	0.9988	0.8905
Estonia	0.3723	1.0000	1.0000	0.9476	0.3652	1.0000	1.0000	0.8651
Finland	0.5043	0.9914	0.9943	0.9288	0.5388	1.0000	0.9735	0.9037
France	0.4967	1.0000	0.9944	0.8479	0.4906	1.0000	0.9638	0.8576
Germany	0.6757	0.9829	0.9840	0.9620	0.6261	0.9759	0.9812	0.9041
Greece	0.9631	1.0000	1.0000	0.8031	0.6371	1.0000	1.0000	0.7962
Hungary	0.4861	0.9519	1.0000	0.9061	0.3014	1.0000	1.0000	0.7860
Iceland	0.3149	1.0000	0.9064	1.0000	0.4855	1.0000	1.0000	0.9538
India	1.0000	1.0000	1.0000	1.0000	1.0000	1.0000	1.0000	1.0000
Ireland	0.5824	1.0000	1.0000	0.9327	0.4052	1.0000	1.0000	0.8895
Israel	0.3346	1.0000	1.0000	0.9440	0.3443	1.0000	1.0000	0.9351

Italy	1.0000	0.9266	1.0000	0.7159	1.0000	1.0000	1.0000	0.7277
Japan	1.0000	1.0000	0.9817	1.0000	1.0000	1.0000	0.9747	1.0000
Luxembourg	0.4912	0.9857	1.0000	0.8675	0.8303	1.0000	1.0000	1.0000
Mexico	0.4040	1.0000	1.0000	0.8531	0.3746	1.0000	1.0000	0.8685
Netherlands	0.8425	1.0000	0.8800	0.9267	0.6762	1.0000	0.9897	0.8985
New Zealand	0.7239	0.9651	0.9828	0.9188	0.5896	1.0000	0.9948	1.0000
Norway	0.5098	1.0000	1.0000	0.9745	0.5253	1.0000	1.0000	0.9385
Poland	0.6129	1.0000	1.0000	0.8075	0.5108	0.9907	1.0000	0.7391
Portugal	0.3854	1.0000	0.9391	0.7927	0.4182	1.0000	1.0000	0.9194
Russian Federation	0.2145	1.0000	1.0000	0.7484	0.2583	0.9381	1.0000	0.7089
Slovakia	0.3429	1.0000	0.9547	0.9913	0.3618	1.0000	1.0000	0.8423
Slovenia	0.7678	1.0000	0.9644	0.7663	0.6488	1.0000	1.0000	0.7556
South Africa	0.4911	0.9765	1.0000	0.9099	0.8068	1.0000	1.0000	1.0000
South Korea	1.0000	0.9573	0.9734	1.0000	1.0000	0.9442	1.0000	1.0000
Spain	0.4994	0.9707	0.9937	0.7885	0.5678	1.0000	0.9840	0.8115
Sweden	0.7601	1.0000	0.9970	0.9733	0.5938	1.0000	0.9765	0.9473
Switzerland	1.0000	1.0000	1.0000	1.0000	1.0000	1.0000	1.0000	1.0000
Turkey	0.7318	1.0000	1.0000	0.9487	0.4191	1.0000	1.0000	0.9327
United Kingdom	0.5537	1.0000	0.9894	0.9071	0.5265	1.0000	1.0000	1.0000
United States	0.6052	1.0000	1.0000	0.9752	0.6449	1.0000	1.0000	0.9831

Source: Own estimations aplying Data Envelop Analysis (DEA).

References

Afzal, M. N. I. 2014. An empirical investigation of the National Innovation System (NIS) using Data Envelopment Analysis (DEA) and the TOBIT model. *International Review of Applied Economics* 28(4): 507–523. http://dx.doi.org/10.1080/02692171.2014.896880

Archibugi, D. and A. Coco. 2004. A New indicator of technological capabilities for developed and developing countries (ArCo). *World Development* 32(4): 629–654.

Balzat, M. 2002. The theoretical basis and the empirical treatment of National Innovation Systems. University of Augsburg, Institut für Volkswirtschaftslehre, Beitrag Nr. 232 December: 1–38. www.wiwi.uni-augsburg.de/vwl/institut/paper/232.pdf.

Balzat, M. and Hanusch, H. 2004. Recent trends in the research on National Innovation Systems. *Journal of Evolutionary Economics* 14: 197–210.

Barr, N. 2012. Higher education funding. *Oxford Review of Economic Policy* 20(2): 264–283.

Boyer, R. and Didier, M. 1998. *Innovation et Croissance*. Paris: Conseil d'Analyse économique, La documentation Française.

Cai, Y. 2011. Factors affecting the efficiency of the BRICS's National Innovation Systems: A comparative study based on DEA and panel data analysis. Economics. The Open-Access, Open-Assessment *E-Journal*, Discussion Paper No. 2011-52, December. www.economics-ejournal.or g/economics/discussionpapers/2011-52.

Cai, Y. and Hanley, A. 2012. Building BRICS: 2-Stage DEA analysis of R&D Efficiency, in: *Kiel Working Paper* No. 1788.

Charnes, A., Cooper, W. W., and Rhodes, E. 1978. Measuring the efficiency of decision making units. *European Journal of Operational Research* 2(6): 429–444.

Edquist, C. (ed.) 1997. *Systems of Innovation: Technologies, Institutions and Organizations*. London: Pinter Publishers/Cassell Academic.

Freeman, C. 1987. *Technology Policy and Economic Performance: Lessons from Japan*. London: Pinter Publishers.

Freeman, C. 1995. The national system of innovation in historical perspective. *Cambridge Journal of Economics* 19: 5–24.

Furman, J. L., Porter, M.E. and Stern, S. 2002. The determinants of national innovative capacity. *Research Policy* 31: 899–933.

Green, William H. (2000). *Econometric Analysis*, 4th edn. New Jersey: Prentice Hall.

Grupp, H. and Schubert, T. 2010. Review and new evidence on composite innovation indicators for evaluating national performance. *Research Policy* 39(1): 67–78.

Guan, J. and Chen, K. 2012. Modeling the relative efficiency of national innovation systems. *Research Policy* 41(1): 102–115. http://dx.do i:10.1016/j.respol.2011.07.001

Hollanders, H. and Celikel, F. 2007. Measuring innovation efficiency, *INNO-Metrics Thematic Paper*, December: 1–26. http://gent.uab.cat/diego_prior/si tes/gent.uab.cat.diego_prior/files/Reading_5_2_Innovation_efficiency.pdf.

Hu, J.-L., Yang, Ch.-H., and Chen, Ch.-P. 2014. R&D efficiency and the national innovation system: an international comparison using the distance function approach. *Bulletin of Economic Research* 66(1): 55–71. doi: 10.1111/j.1467-8586.2011.00417.x.

Kotsemir, Maxim. 2013. Measuring National Innovattion Systems efficiency – A review of DEA approach. *Basic Research Program Working papers* WP BRP 16/STI/2013, National Research University Higher School of Economics. https://papers.ssrn.com/sol3/papers.cfm?abstract_id=2304735.

Lee, H.-Y. and Park, Y.-T. 2005. An international comparison of R&D efficiency: DEA approach. *Asian Journal of Technology Innovation* 13(2): 207–222.

Lundvall, B. A. 1992. *National Systems of Innovation towards a Theory of Innovation and Interactive Learning*. London: Pinter Publishers.

Lundvall, B.-Å., Tomlinson, M. 2001. Learning by comparing: reflection on the use and abuse of benchmarking. In: Sweeney, G. (Ed.), *Innovation, Economic Progress and Quality of Life*. London: Edward Elgar.

Matei, M. and Aldea, A. 2012. Ranking national innovation systems according to their technical efficiency. *Procedia – Social and Behavioral Science* 62: 968–974.

Metcalfe, S. 1995. The economic foundations of technology policy: Equilibrium and evolutionary perspectives, in P. Stoneman (ed.), *Handbook of the Economics of Innovation and Technological Change*. Oxford/Cambridge, MA: Blackwell Publishers.

Nasierowski, W. and Arcelus, F. J. 2003. On the efficiency of National Innovation Systems. *Socio-Economic Planning Sciences an International Journal* 37(3): 215–234.

Nelson, R. R. (Ed.) 1993. *National Innovation Systems*. New York, NY: Oxford University Press.

Niosi, J. 2002. National systems of innovation are "x-efficient" (and x-effective). Why some are slow learners. *Research Policy* 31: 291–302.

Nooteboom, B. 2000. Learning by interaction: Absorptive capacity, cognitive distance and governance. *Journal of Management & Governance* 4(1): 69–92.

OECD. 2008. Benchmark Definition of Foreign Direct Investment. www.OE CD.org/daf/inv/investmentstatisticsandanalysis/40193734.pdf. Access June 10, 2016.

OECD. 1997. National Innovation Systems. Paris: OECD.

Pan, T.-W. 2007. Measuring the efficiency of national innovation system. *Journal of American Academy of Business, Cambridge* 11(2): 176–181.

Pan, T.-W., Hung, S.-W., and Lu, W.-M. 2010. DEA performance measurement of the national innovation system in Asia and Europe. *Asia-Pacific Journal of Operational Research* 27(3): 369–392.

Porter, M. E. and Stern, S. 2001. Innovation: Location matters. *MIT Sloan Management Review, Summer* 42(4): 28–36. www.clustermapping.us/sites/default/files/files/resource/Innovation%20-%20Location%20Matters.pdf.

Productivity Tools. 2009. *XLDEA 2.1*. Access January 1, 2016 in www.prod tools.com.

Ramanathan, Ram. 2009. *An Introduction to Data Envelopment Analysis*. New Delhi: Sage Publications.

Ray, Subhash C. 2004. *Data Envelopment Analysis. Theory and Techniques for Economics and Operations Research*. Cambridge: Cambridge University Press.

Romer, P. M. (1990). Endogenous technological change. *The Journal of Political Economy* 98(5): S71–S102.

Schumpeter, J.A. 1942. *Capitalism, Socialism, and Democracy*. NY: Harper.

Sep-Conacyt. 2000. Indicadores de Actividades Científicas y Tecnológicas 1990–1999, México.

Solow, R. 1957. Technical change and the aggregate production function. *The Review of Economics and Statistics* 39(3): 312–320.

United Nations, 2013. Human Development Report, The Rise of the South: Human Progress in a Diverse World. New York: United Nations.

Van Praag, Bernard M. S. 2005. The connection between old and new approaches of financial satisfaction, in Luigino Bruni and Pier Luigi Porta (eds.), *Economics and Happiness: Framing the analysis*. Oxford: Oxford University Press.

Weel B., Soete L. and Verspagen B. 2010. Systems of Innovation, CPB Discussion Paper. CPB Netherlands Bureau for Economic Policy Analysis.

Whitley, R. D. 2001. National Innovation Systems, in N. J. Smelser and P. B. Baltes (eds.), *International Encyclopedia of the Social & Behavioral Sciences*. Amsterdam: Elsevier Science: 10303–10309.

World Economic Forum. 2006. *The Global Competitiveness Report 2006–2007*. Geneva: Palgrave Macmillan.

Yuezhou, C. 2011. Factors Affecting the Efficiency of the BRICSs' National Innovation Systems: A Comparative Study based on DEA and Panel Data. Analysis, Economics, Discussion Paper No. 2011–52.

Zhang, J.-f. 2013. International comparison of national innovation system efficiency. *Tech Monitor*, April–June: 23–29. www.techmonitor.net/tm/images/d/da/13apr_jun_sf2.pdf.

9 | Differential Effects of Currency Undervaluation on Economic Growth in Mineral- vs Manufacturing-Exporting Countries

Revealing the Source of the Vicious Procyclicality in the Resource-cursed South[*]

SANIKA SULOCHANI RAMANAYAKE
AND KEUN LEE

9.1 Introduction

Manufacturing export-led growth has been regarded as the hallmark of the so-called Asian tigers, namely, South Korea, Singapore, Hong Kong, and Taiwan. Since the 1960s, resource-poor countries have outperformed resource-rich countries by a considerable margin (Auty 2001: 840). Fosu (1990)found that developing countries specializing in manufacturing achieved higher economic growth than those specializing in exporting primary goods (minerals). The World Bank (1993) report on the East Asian miracle de facto established manufacturing export-led growth as the standard growth prescription for developing countries. Razmi and Blecker (2008) stated that developing countries have significantly increased both their export orientation and the proportion of their exports in manufactured goods in the past two decades.

More recently, Setterfield (2010) argued that the export-led growth model is not a panacea for all developing nations, especially if they are driven by prolonged currency undervaluation, relative to competing developing countries. Some studies note the possibility of natural resource-based growth (Sachs and Warner 1999; Auty 2001; De Ferranti et al. 2002). De Ferranti et al. (2002) paid attention to the fact that several advanced economies, such as Canada, Australia,

---

[*] An earlier version of this paper was presented at the 2016 International Schumpeter Society Conference held in Montreal, Canada, on July 2016.

Sweden, and Finland, showed that relying on natural resources for growth can be a pathway to possible diversification and upgrade into other sectors at a later stage. Although this path of natural resource-based growth has been highlighted as a possibility for Latin American (LA) countries, others have warned that resource abundance may also hurt growth (Leite and Weidmann 1999; Gylfason 2002; Blum and Leamer 2004). Recently, many LA countries showed a decline in growth despite remaining rich in natural resources; many countries in Africa face the same phenomenon.

This chapter scrutinizes the effect of currency undervaluation or overvaluation in this growth-path debate. The development literature includes important debates regarding the effect of exchange rate undervaluation (depreciation) on growth. Some argue that undervaluation positively affects growth (especially in developing economies), but others contend that undervaluation negatively affects growth in the long run. Rodrik (2008; 2009) found that currency undervaluation stimulates economic growth and export expansion, particularly in developing countries.[1] Tradable sectors in developing countries tend to be smaller because they suffer from institutional weaknesses and market failures more than nontradable sectors (Rodrik 2009). By enhancing the sector's profitability in such a situation, undervaluation works as a second best policy that compensates for the negative effects of these distortions. High profitability promotes investment in tradable sectors, which subsequently expand and promote economic growth. Setterfield (2010) asserted that developing countries obtain significant growth benefits by maintaining low value of their currencies relative to competing developing countries. Yeyati and Sturzenegger (2007) claimed that undervalued currencies boost output and productivity growth. Korinek and Servén (2010) also asserted that currency undervaluation can raise growth through learning-by-doing externalities in tradable sectors.

Nevertheless, the undervaluation-growth argument is criticized, that is, undervaluation will hurt economic growth (Aguirre and Calderon

---

[1] Countries with per capita income below $2,500.

2005; Williamson 2012).[2] Eichengreen et al. (2012) argued that under-valuation is detrimental and slows down growth because an under-valued currency provides a disincentive to move up the technology ladder. Aguirre and Calderon (2005) explained that although small or moderate undervaluation enhances growth, large undervaluation hurts growth. Haddad and Pancaro (2010) claimed that undervalua-tion causes high and destabilizing liquidity growth and inflation, which lead to financial instability; undervaluation works only for low-income countries in the medium term. Pettinger (2011) specified that a falling currency value can be beneficial if the economy is uncompetitive and stuck in recession. Therefore, whether undervaluation is beneficial or harmful to growth remains debatable.

Given this background, this chapter delves deeply into the effects of undervaluation on growth. We identify one primary reason for this undervaluation debate within different industrial structures in different countries. Some countries exhibit manufacturing industry-based growth and others feature natural resource-based growth. If currency is more undervalued (for mineral exports) for countries highly depen-dent on natural resource exports, like many LA and African countries, then they earn lower income in terms of dollars. Natural resource exports are also insensitive to exchange rate valuation. Long-term currency undervaluation may not support economic growth.

We hypothesize that currency undervaluation differently affects the two groups of countries (mineral-exporting vs. manufacture-exporting countries). The empirical analysis of this currency valuation–growth linkage considers data from 1986 to 2012. Cross-sectional panel analysis is performed using five-year intervals. We tested two different samples, manufacturing-exporting countries versus mineral-exporting countries.[3] Apart from pooled OLS, panel fixed effect, and random effect estima-tions, we control for endogeneity using system GMM models. The estimation results suggest that currency overvaluation is good for mineral-exporting countries, whereas currency undervaluation may be

---

[2] Williamson (2012) demonstrated that undervalued currencies are likely to improve the current account surplus, stimulating capital flow out of the country instead of into it, thus impeding investment from entrepreneurs and, ultimately, economic growth.

[3] This study considers natural resource exports for mineral-exporting countries and excludes oil-exporting countries to avoid the sample bias problem (for additional details, see data and sources in Section 9.3).

good for manufacturing-exporting countries. This finding underscores the dilemma of resource-rich countries with the long-term goal of diversification into manufacturing. Given that manufacturing exports often requires currency undervaluation, this undervaluation sequentially undermines growth through its negative effect on dollar-based earnings from natural resource exports.

This paper is organized as follows. Section 9.2 discusses the literature and provides a theoretical background for empirical analysis in the following section. Section 9.3 discusses the data, regression models, and methodology. Section 9.4 presents and interprets the regression results. Finally, Section 9.5 summarizes the paper with concluding remarks.

9.2 Resource Abundance, Growth Performance, and Currency Valuation

Natural resources account for 20 percent of world trade and dominate the exports of many countries. Natural resource exports or mineral exports and growth are highlighted topics in economic history.[4] Many scholars argue that, on one hand, natural resource exports create a growth boom. On the other hand, natural resource abundance hurts growth. De Ferranti et al. (2002) cited the history of successful natural resource-abundant countries, such as Canada, Australia, Sweden, and Finland.[5] According to the standard economic theory, the wealth effects associated with natural resources should lead to increased investment and economic growth in the long run.

Some countries in the Global South (e.g. United Arab Emirates, Malaysia, and Botswana) have managed to harness the power of natural resources and maintain both strong investment and above-average growth rates. The economic history of Latin America also shows boom periods in natural resource exports leading to growth. In Bolivia, revenue from natural resource exports rose from 11 percent of GDP to 23 percent of GDP over a nine-year period, that is, between 1975

---

[4] Natural resource exports are defined as exports of agriculture, minerals, and fuels (Sachs and Warner 1997). Mineral exports are defined as only fuels and primary metals (Sachs and Warner 1999).

[5] Some argue that such success is due to locational proximity to a big market. Canada is close to the United States; Sweden and Finland to Europe; and Australia to New Zealand.

and 1984. In Ecuador, primary exports revenue rose by 19 percent of GDP in only two years (between 1972 and 1974). In Mexico, revenue from oil exports increased by 6 percent of GDP between 1978 and 1983 (Sachs and Warner 1999).

By contrast, another strand of literature argues that natural resource abundance is a curse for the economy, with Blum and Leamer (2004) asserting that natural resource abundance is a curse rather than a blessing. In addition, Gylfason (2001) stated that natural resource abundance may hurt growth by harming trade. Leite and Weidmann (1999) suggested that capital-intensive sectors involving natural resources are a major source of corruption. Paldam (1997) explained that natural resource abundance is, as a rule, accompanied by booms and busts. Sachs and Warner (1997) found in their analysis that economies with a high ratio of natural resource exports to GDP in 1970 tended to grow gradually during the subsequent twenty-year period.

Gylfason (2001) explained that natural resources bring risks; too many people become restricted to low-skill and intensive natural resource-based industries. He also found evidence that nations with abundant natural capital tend to have more corruption and less trade and foreign investment, education, and domestic investment than other nations. Leite and Weidmann (1999) discussed the direct and indirect effects of natural resources. The Dutch Disease is a direct effect, whereby large discoveries of natural gas has led to a recession in the Netherlands since the 1960s. Indirect effects include those on rent-seeking activities and institution building. Poelhekke and van der Ploeg (2009) also analyzed the direct effect of natural resource abundance on economic growth and its indirect effects through volatility of unanticipated output growth. They found that the direct effect can be positive, but can be swamped by the negative effect resulting from volatility.

Many countries with a high level of mineral-export share show a growth decline in the long run. Most mineral-exporting countries are struggling with declining economic and export growth, as is the case of many LA countries. Over the last few decades, the economy of Latin America has shown significant economic decline. Figure 9.1 shows the decreasing trend of GDP and export growth in LA and Caribbean countries in the long run. Export growth has been significantly declining since 1995, which is in contrast to the positive performance in other emerging countries.

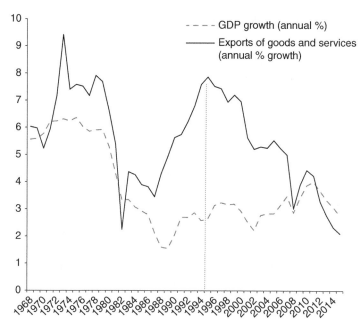

Figure 9.1 Economic performance of Latin American and Caribbean countries
Source: Data created by the authors using World Bank–World Development Indicators
(*Figures are in ten-year moving average)

Table 9.1 lists the twenty countries with the highest mineral-export contributions as a percentage of total merchandise exports in the selected years. Over time, many of the low-income countries have become increasingly reliant on export revenues from minerals as their main source of foreign exchange earnings. Many of these countries have low Human Development Index (HDI) scores, drawing attention to the potential for earnings from the mining sector to contribute to poverty reduction. In particular, in Chile, Ghana, and Brazil mining businesses contribute to poverty reduction and improve social development indicators more than nonmining ones (International Council on Mining and Metals or ICMM 2012). The ICMM suggests that the mining sector's contribution is important for sustaining development, especially in developing countries (ICMM 2012). According to the ICMM report in 2012, the nominal value of world mineral production was nearly four times higher than it was in 2002, which implied

Table 9.1 *Reliance on export of metallic minerals*

Rank by country (2010)	Mineral export contribution as % of total merchandise exports in 1996	Mineral export contribution as % of total merchandise exports in 2005	Mineral export contribution as % of total merchandise exports in 2010
1 Botswana	58.70%	86.50%	83.70%
2 Zambia	79.40%	64.00%	83.60%
3 Dem. Rep. of the Congo	72.40%	70.20%	78.30%
4 Mongolia	60.30%	70.10%	77.60%
5 Surinam	68.00%	64.30%	75.40%
6 French Polynesia	69.20%	55.30%	67.10%
7 Chile	47.70%	56.50%	65.90%
8 Guinea	77.10%	84.00%	65.20%
9 Peru	48.30%	57.90%	62.70%
10 Mauritania	36.10%	49.30%	60.40%
11 Northern Mariana Islands	3.30%	4.50%	58.90%
12 Mozambique	6.10%	66.90%	57.00%
13 Mali	8.50%	37.20%	54.80%
14 Sierra Leone	30.60%	58.20%	54.30%
15 Papua New Guinea	24.50%	39.20%	54.00%
16 Namibia	36.20%	41.20%	53.40%
17 Nauru	73.10%	25.20%	50.80%
18 Armenia	23.90%	39.80%	50.60%
19 Jamaica	49.70%	68.50%	49.60%
20 Cuba	15.10%	39.20%	47.70%

Source: Reproduced from ICMM (2012) (Mineral (non-fuel) exports in 2010 as % of total merchandise exports (UNCTAD data))

more earnings from the same amount of production. If this is the case, then currency overvaluation would also result in bigger earnings in terms of local currency and would thus be beneficial for economic growth.

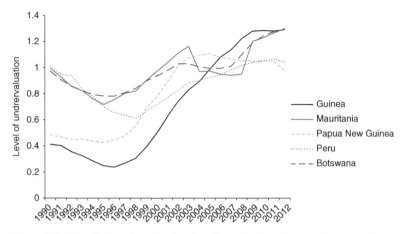

Figure 9.2 Trend of undervaluation in selected mineral-exporting countries
Source: Using exchange rate data from World Bank–World Development Indicators, undervaluation index is calculated by the authors, following Rodrik (2008).
Notes: (1) Figures are in a five-year moving average; data period is from 1986–2012.
(2) When undervaluation exceeds zero, the currency is undervalued and vice versa.

Given this contributing effect of natural resource exports, examining the effect of currency undervaluation or overvaluation on mineral exports is important. UNCTAD (2005) indicated that the real exchange rate reflects the underlying relative movement of prices at home and abroad. Generally, currency undervaluation, depreciation, or devaluation increases the competitiveness of exports and makes imports more expensive. Currency overvaluation or appreciation makes imports cheaper and exports more expensive.

In this regard, currencies in most mineral-exporting countries have been undervalued rather than overvalued. Figure 9.2 illustrates the situation in several countries (i.e. Botswana, Guinea, Mauritania, Papua New Guinea, and Peru) with shares of mineral exports over 40 percent of total exports, indicating the increasing trend of their currency undervaluation. Figure 9.3 depicts some cases that show long-term growth decline resulting from increasing the level of under-valuation in the long run. Given this background, examining whether currency undervaluation is truly responsible for the declining growth in these mineral-exporting countries is meaningful.

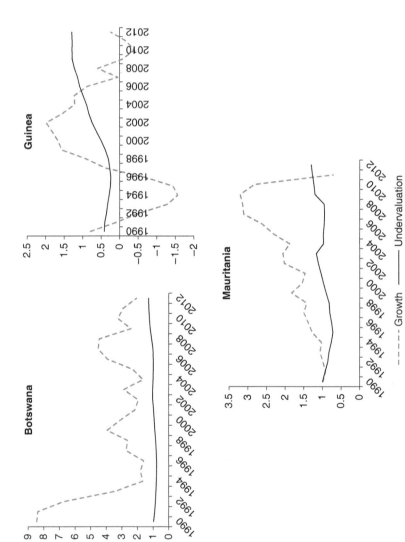

Figure 9.3 Increasing the level of undervaluation and growth decline in the long term

Source: Using exchange rate data form World Bank–World Development Indicators, undervaluation index is calculated by the authors following Rodrik (2008).

9.3 Data and Methodology

9.3.1 Dataset and Samples

This analysis consists of two different samples: manufacturing-exporting countries and natural resource-exporting countries. The natural resource-exporting sample consists of only mineral-exporting countries (excluding giant oil exporters). We limit the manufacturing-export sample to countries where manufacturing exports constitute at least 70 percent of their total exports (in at least one of the two years 1999 and 2001). This percentage corresponds to an average of 68 percent over 1999–2003, as reported by UNCTAD (2005). The eighteen countries that fit this criterion are Bangladesh, China, the Dominican Republic, Hong Kong, India, Jamaica, South Korea, Malaysia, Mauritius, Mexico, Pakistan, the Philippines, Singapore, Sri Lanka, Taiwan, Thailand, Tunisia, and Turkey. Nepal also meets this criterion but is excluded because of its land size. Taiwan is also excluded from our list because of lack of data. We include Vietnam in our list.[6] For the mineral-exporting country sample, we consider twenty-two countries: Armenia, Botswana, Brazil, Burkina Faso, Chile, Congo (Dem. Repub.), Cuba, French Polynesia, Guinea, Jamaica, Lao PDR, Mali, Mauritania, Mongolia, Montenegro, Mozambique, Namibia, Papua New Guinea, Peru, Surinam, Tanzania, and Zambia. To select this sample, we consider those countries with more than 40 percent share of mineral exports within total exports in 2010. We select the mineral-exporting countries based on ICMM (2012) country ranks.

Except for undervaluation index data, all the other variable data were taken from World Bank–World Development Indicators online database. We refer to the same estimation methodology that Rodrik (2008) used to calculate his undervaluation index; his sample comprises a maximum of 184 countries, and the data period is from 1950 to 2004. We calculate the undervaluation index from 1986–2012 for these countries. Rodrik's undervaluation index is the difference

---

[6] To select our manufacturing-exporting sample, we refer to existing literature (Blecker and Razmi 2008; Razmi and Blecker 2008; Setterfield 2010). We extended the sample data from 1986–2012. Razmi and Blecker's (2008) sample was from 1983–2001; Setterfield (2010) and Blecker and Razmi (2008) used data from 1984–2004.

Table 9.2 *Descriptive statistics*

Mineral export sample					
Variable	Obs.	Mean	Std. Dev.	Min	Max
Undervaluation	228	0.83	0.39	−0.60	1.64
GDP per capita growth	252	2.64	3.17	−10.48	13.17
Log initial GDP per capita	239	3.24	.64	2.07	4.58
Population growth	258	1.66	.97	−1.90	5.28
Human capital (school enrollment)	186	64.10	32.87	1.36	99.94
Gross capita formation (physical capital)	246	23.89	7.63	5.90	62.10
FDI (net inflow as % of GDP)	207	3.93	7.09	−21.95	48.58
Mineral exporter dummy	258	0.58	0.49	0	1
Manufacturing exporter dummy	258	0.42	0.49	1	0

between the actual real exchange rate and the Balassa–Samuelson adjusted rate with the following formula:

$$\ln UNDERVAL_{it} = \ln RER_{it} - \ln \widehat{RER}_{it},$$

where in $\widehat{RER}_{it}$ is the predicted value.[7] *UNDERVAL* is comparable across countries over time. When *UNDERVAL* exceeds zero, this condition indicates that the currency is undervalued and vice versa.

Table 9.2 presents the descriptive statistics of the variables. Detailed explanations for the definitions of the variables and data sources are presented in Table 9A.1 of the Appendix.

9.3.2 Methodology

This study uses cross-country panel data using a five-year average from 1986–2012.[8] To overcome observation problems, we combine both samples into one sample by including regressions in either of two

---

[7] ln RER_{it} is the predicted value from the equation
ln $RER_{it} = \alpha + \beta \ln RGDPCH_{it} + f_t + u_{it}$. See Rodrik (2008) for additional details. *RER* is the real exchange rate and *RGDPCH* is *RER* on per capita GDP.

[8] The periods considered are as follows: period 1 from 1986–1990, period 2 from 1991–1995, period 3 from 1996–2000, period 4 from 2001–2005, period 5 from 2006–2010, and period 6 from 2011–2012.

dummy variables, which correspond to mineral- or manufacturing-exporting countries. To ensure robustness of our results, estimations have been completed using pooled OLS, panel fixed effects, and random effects as well as system-generalized method-of-moments estimators (system GMM) to control for endogeneity issues.

We use the standard growth model specifications, consisting of typical control variables (X_{it}), a set of interest variables (Z_{it}), and other controls (O_{it}), as follows:

$$y_{it} = \text{Function}\ (X_{it},\ Z_{it},\ O_{it}) + e_{it},$$

where y_{it} is GDP per capita growth rate in country i in year t, and e_{it} is the error term. X_{it} variables include the (log) initial GDP per capita of a country i expressed in constant US dollars (*ln_intgdp*), population growth (*popgrowth*), human capital (*H_cap*) (school enrollment) measured by primary and secondary school enrollment, and gross capital formation (*P_cap*) as well as the variables of FDI net inflow as a percentage of GDP (FDI_{it}). Then, our variables (Z_{it}) of interest are undervaluation (Underval_{it}) as well as its interaction term with a mineral-exporting dummy or manufacturing-exporting dummy ($\text{Underval}^*\text{Mineral\_Dummy}_{it}$) or ($\text{Underval}^*\text{Manufact\_Dummy}_{it}$). Thus, we derive the following simple growth equation:

$$y_{it} = \alpha_1 + \beta_1\ ln\_intgdp_{it} + \beta_2 popgrowth_{it} + \beta_3 H\_cap_{it} + \beta_4 P\_cap_{it}$$
$$+ \beta_5 FDI_{it}$$

$$\beta_6(Underval_{it},\ Underval^*Mineral\_Dummy_{it},\ Mineral\_Dummy_{it})$$
$$+ e_{it}.$$

We begin with the pooled ordinary least square (POLS) estimation and move on to the panel estimation approach (Islam 1995) to control for omitted variable bias by estimating either fixed effect (FE) or random effect (RE) with the Hausman test. To further control possible endogeneity, a system GMM estimation developed by Arellano and Bover (1995) and Blundell and Bond (1998) is also applied. We use the following criteria to evaluate the system GMM estimation model specifications: the Hansen overidentification test and the test for second-order serial correlation (AR2) of the residuals in the first differenced equation. The AR2 test also provides additional verification of the specification of the model and the legitimacy of the instrumental variables in the difference equation. We attach the greatest reliability on the system GMM results for all estimation models.

9.4 Regression Results: Undervaluation to Economic Growth

The regression results of economic growth equation, with GDP per capita growth rate as the dependent variable, are shown in Table 9.3.

The coefficients of interaction term between undervaluation and either dummy of manufacturing- or mineral-exporting countries is significant, implying that the effect of undervaluation is significantly different between these two groups. The minus sign of this interaction term with a dummy of mineral-exporting countries suggests a possibly negative effect of undervaluation on economic growth, which is confirmed by reading the GMM estimation coefficient (–3.45) of the undervaluation variable in the equation with a dummy for manufacturing-exporting countries (model 1C in Table 9.3). The results are robust in all pooled OLS, random effect, and system GMM estimations. The results indicate that currency overvaluation may be good for economic growth in mineral-exporting countries.

By contrast, the coefficient of the interaction between undervaluation and manufacture-exporting countries is plus and significant, suggesting the possibility of positive effects on economic growth. However, the net effect of undervaluation for this group turns out to be insignificant, reading from the coefficient (0.11) of growth equation with a dummy for mineral-exporting countries (model 2C) in Table 9.3. This positive but insignificant effect is consistent with Lee and Ramanayake (2017), who found that undervaluation significantly affects growth in high-income countries but not in middle- or low-income countries. Their interpretation was that undervaluation only exerts significant effects in the presence of a strong manufacturing base at an adequate level of capabilities. Given the mixed nature of our manufacturing-exporting samples, that the overall effects are insignificant is expected. Managing exchange rates alone is not a solution for long-term growth in these countries; rather, they should develop technological capabilities (Lee and Mathews 2012).

Other control variables tend to show conventional effects. The variables of the initial GDP per capita and population growth show significant and negative effects on growth. Human capital is positive on growth but not that robust in the sense that only GMM results show

Table 9.3 *Undervaluation on economic growth in mineral- vs manufacturing-exporting countries*

Dep. variable: GDP per capita growth	Five-year average panel data					
	POLS	RE	GMM	POLS	RE	GMM
	(1A)	(1B)	(1C)	(2A)	(2B)	(2C)
Ln (initial GDP per capita)	−1.51**	−1.51**	−2.24***	−1.51**	−1.51**	−2.24***
	(−2.14)	(−2.14)	(−3.47)	(−2.14)	(−2.14)	(−3.47)
Population growth	−0.84***	−0.84***	−0.83***	−0.84***	−0.84***	−0.83***
	(−2.65)	(−2.65)	(−2.92)	(−2.65)	(−2.65)	(−2.92)
Human capital (school enrollment)	0.03	0.03	0.04**	0.03	0.03	0.04**
	(1.41)	(1.41)	(1.96)	(1.41)	(1.41)	(1.96)
Physical capital (gross capital formation)	0.24***	0.24***	0.24***	0.24***	0.24***	0.24***
	(6.30)	(6.30)	(4.58)	(6.30)	(6.30)	(4.58)
Undervaluation	−2.53**	−2.53**	−3.45**	0.19	0.19	0.11
	(−2.07)	(−2.07)	(−2.23)	(0.16)	(0.16)	(0.13)
Undervaluation* Mineral dummy				−2.73*	−2.73*	−3.56**
				(−1.66)	(−1.66)	(−2.16)
Undervaluation * Manufacturing dummy	2.72*	2.73*	3.56**			
	(1.66)	(1.66)	(2.16)			
Manufacturing exporter dummy	−1.72	−1.73	−2.05			
	(−1.12)	(−1.12)	(−1.28)			
Mineral exporter dummy				1.73	1.73	2.05
				(1.12)	(1.12)	(1.28)

Table 9.3 (*cont.*)

Five-year average panel data

Dep. variable: GDP per capita growth	POLS (1A)	RE (1B)	GMM (1C)	POLS (2A)	RE (2B)	GMM (2C)
FDI (% of GDP)	0.07	0.07	0.07*	0.07	0.07	0.07*
	(1.60)	(1.60)	(1.80)	(1.60)	(1.60)	(1.80)
Constant	2.65	2.65	4.73**	.92	.92	2.69
	(1.05)	(1.05)	(2.05)	(0.32)	(0.32)	(0.93)
R^2	0.39	0.39		0.39	0.39	
AR2			0.404			0.404
Sargan test			0.001			0.001
Number of Observations	130	130	130	130	130	130

Note: The dependent variable is GDP per capita growth. Five-year average panel data from 1986–2012 were used. Figures in brackets represent t and z ratios: *** Significant at 1%; ** significant at 5%; * significant at 10%

positive and significant coefficients. The coefficient of physical capital formation remains positive and significant on growth for these two groups. The coefficient of FDI is positive and significant on growth, but not that robust as only the GMM model results in a significant coefficient.

9.5 Summary and Concluding Remarks

Although manufacturing export-led growth has been regarded as the standard growth model for developing countries since the success of the so-called Asian tigers, resource-based economic growth has also received attention, as the strong mineral prices in the 2000s supported an economic boom in many mineral-exporting countries. This study explores the possibly differential effects of currency undervaluation or overvaluation in these two different growth paths, that is, manufacturing- versus mineral-exporting economies. The regression results in this study confirm a negative effect of undervaluation on growth in mineral-exporting groups and positive (no significant) effects of undervaluation in manufacturing-exporting groups. This finding is consistent with the fact that if currency is more undervalued in countries that highly depend on natural resource exports, then they earn less income in terms of dollars and natural resource exports are insensitive to exchange rates.

Apart from the logic of this finding and interpretation, it also underscores a policy dilemma of resource-rich countries aiming to eventually diversify into manufacturing. While they also need undervaluation to promote manufacturing exports, such a policy stance has immediate negative effects on economic growth through its negative effect on dollar-based earnings from natural resource exports. Also, as observed in several mineral-exporting countries, local currency has often tended to be undervalued rather than overvalued, indicating the difficulty of economic growth, such that undervaluation is not by choice, but often related to weak economic growth and associated recurrent balance-of-payment crises that necessitate depreciation. Thus, an important contrast between manufacturing- versus mineral-exporting countries is that depreciation often tends to exert countercyclical effects of recovering exports and growth in economies with a strong manufacturing base (or nonnegative effects on average), which is not the case in mineral-exporting economies. These mineral-exporting economies face the growth-impeding and procyclical effects of undervaluation during times of weak performance of the economy with a typical balance-of-payment crisis. This growth-impeding and procyclical effect of undervaluation underscores the difficulties facing economic growth in mineral-exporting economies and thus the dilemma of the so-called resource-based development model. The situation is close to being a vicious cycle, and the means to stop the cycle remain unclear.

Appendix

Table 9A.1 *Variable definitions and sources*

Variable	Definition
GDP per capita growth rate	Average annual growth for ten years of GDP per capita (Constant US$ 2000). *Source:* World Bank–World Development Indicators
Initial GDP per capita	(Constant US$ 2000), the period of 86–90 initial GDP per capita of 1986, 91–95, initial GDP per capita of 1991 and 96–00, initial GDP per capita of 1996, 2001–2005, initial GDP per capita of 2001, 2006–2010, initial GDP per capita of 2006, 2011–2012, initial GDP per capita of 2011. *Source:* World Bank–World Development Indicators
Human Capital (school enrollment)	Sum of School enrollment, primary (% gross) and school enrollment, Secondary education (% gross) divided by 2. *Source:* World Bank–World Development Indicators
Physical Capital (Gross capital formation)	Gross capital formation (% of GDP) *Source:* World Bank–World Development Indicators
FDI net inflow as % of GDP	FDI net inflow as % of GDP *Source:* World Bank–World Development Indicators

Table 9A.1 (*cont.*)

Variable	Definition
Undervaluation	The undervaluation data are the same data from Rodrik's undervaluation index (2008). In brief, undervaluation means the difference between the actual real exchange rate and the Balassa–Samuelson-adjusted rate. Rodrik (2008) defines undervaluation to be comparable across countries and over time. Whenever *Undervaluation* exceeds unity (zero), it indicates that the exchange rate is set such that goods produced at home are cheap in dollar terms: the currency is undervalued. When undervaluation is below unity (zero), the currency is overvalued (Rodrik 2008: 372) (For more details, see Rodrik 2008.)
Mineral export sample	Countries' share of mineral exports on total exports is higher than 40 percent in 2010; we only considered mineral exports (excluding oil exporters) (Armenia, Botswana, Brazil, Burkina Faso, Chile, Congo (Dem. Repub.), Cuba, French Polynesia, Guinea, Jamaica, Lao PDR, Mali, Mauritania, Mongolia, Montenegro, Mozambique, Namibia, Papua New Guinea, Peru, Surinam, Tanzania, and Zambia)
Manufacturing export sample	Over 70 percent of manufactured products in total exports (Bangladesh, China, the Dominican Republic, Hong Kong, India, Jamaica, South Korea, Malaysia, Mauritius, Mexico, Pakistan, the Philippines, Singapore, Sri Lanka, Taiwan, Thailand, Tunisia, and Turkey)

References

Aguirre, A. and Calderon, C. 2005. Real exchange rate misalignments and economic performance. *Documentos de Trabajo (Banco Central de Chile)* 315: 1–49.

Arellano, M. and Bover, O. 1995. Another look at instrumental variable estimation of error-component models. *Journal of Econometrics* 68: 29–51.

Auty, R. M. 2001. The political economy of resource-driven growth. *European Economic Review* 4(5): 839–946.

Blecker, R. A. and Razmi, A. 2008. The fallacy of composition and contractionary devaluations: The output impact of real exchange rate shocks in developing countries that export manufactures. *Cambridge Journal of Economics* 32(1): 83–109.

Blum, B. and Leamer, E. 2004. Can FTAA suspend the law of gravity and give Americas higher growth and better income distributions. *Integrating the Americas: FTAA and Beyond*: 539–572.

Blundell, R. and Bond, S. 1998. Initial conditions and moment restrictions in dynamic panel data models. *Journal of Econometrics* 87(1): 115–143.

De Ferranti, D., Perry, G. E., Lederman, D., and Maloney, W. E. 2002. *From Natural Resources to the Knowledge Economy: Trade and Job Quality*. Washington, DC: World Bank.

Eichengreen, B. Park, D. and Shin, K. 2012. When fast growing economies slow down: International evidence and implications for China. *Asian Economic Papers* 11: 42–87.

Fosu, A. K. 1990. Exports and economic growth: The African case. *World Development* 18(6): 831–835.

Gylfason, T. 2001. Natural resources, education, and economic development. *European Economic Review* 45(4): 847–859.

Gylfason, T. 2002. Natural resources and economic growth: What is the connection? in *Fostering Sustainable Growth in Ukraine*. Physica-Verlag, Heidelberg, 48–66.

Haddad, M. and Pancaro, C. 2010. *Can Real Exchange Rate Undervaluation Boost Exports and Growth in Developing Countries? Yes, But Not for Long*. Washington, DC: World Bank.

ICMM. 2012. In Brief The role of mining in national economies. *Mining's Contribution to Sustainable Development*. Available at www.icmm.com.

Islam, N. 1995. Growth empirics: A panel data approach. *Quarterly Journal of Economics* 110: 1127–1170.

Korinek, A. and Servén, L. 2010. Undervaluation through foreign reserve accumulation: Static losses, dynamic growth. *Policy Research Working Paper 5250*. Washington, DC: World Bank.

Lee, K. and Mathews, J. 2012. Firms in Korea and Taiwan, in *The Innovative Firms in the Emerging Market Economies*, edited by John Cantwell and Ed Amann. Oxford: Oxford Univ. Press, 223–245.

Lee, K. and Ramanayake, S.S. 2017. Adding-up problem and wage-productivity gap in exports of developing countries: A source of middle-income trap. *The European Journal of Development Research*: 1–20.

Leite C. and Weidmann, J. 1999. Does Mother Nature corrupt? Natural Resource resources, corruption, and economic growth. *Natural Resources, Corruption, and Economic Growth (June 1999). IMF Working Paper 99/85.*

Paldam, M. 1997. Dutch disease and rent seeking: The Greenland model. *European Journal of Political Economy* 13(1): 591–614.

Pettinger, T. 2011. What factors determine the price of gold?. *Economics Readers Quest*, www.economicshelp.org, Accessed February 12, 2012.

Poelhekke, S. and Van der Ploeg, F. 2009. Foreign direct investment and urban concentration: Unbundling spatial lags. *Journal of Regional Science* 49(4): 749–775.

Razmi, A. and Blecker, R. A. 2008. Developing country exports of manufactures: Moving up the ladder to escape the fallacy of composition? *Journal of Development Studies* 44(1): 21–48.

Rodrik, D. 2008. The real exchange rate and economic growth. *Brookings Papers on Economic Activity*: 365–412.

Rodrik, D. 2009. The real exchange rate and economic growth, in *Brookings Papers on Economic Activity*, Fall 2008, D. W. Elmendorf, N. G. Mankiw, and L. H. Summers (eds.). Washington, DC: Brookings Institution.

Sachs, J. D. and Warner, A. M. 1999. The big push, natural resource booms and growth. *Journal of Development Economics* 59(1): 43–76.

Sachs, J. D. and Warner, A. M. 1997. Sources of slow growth in African economies. *Journal of African economies* 6(3): 335–376.

Setterfield, M. (ed.). 2010. *Handbook of Alternative Theories of Economic Growth*. Cheltenham: Edward Elgar.

UNCTAD. 2005. Transnational corporations and the internationalization of R&D, in *World Investment Report*. New York, NY and Geneva: United Nations, 331.

Williamson, J. 2012. Some basic disagreements on development. *Panel at the High-Level Knowledge Forum for Rethinking Development Policy held by KDI and the World Bank in Seoul.*

World Bank. 1993. *The East Asian Miracle: Economic Growth and Public Policy.* NewYork, NY: Oxford University Press.

Yeyati, E. L. and Sturzenegger, F. 2007. Fear of Appreciation, in *Policy Research Working Paper 4387.* Washington, DC: World Bank.

PART III

Regional Innovation Systems and Policies

10 Innovation Policies and New Regional Growth Paths

A Place-Based System Failure Framework

MARKUS GRILLITSCH AND MICHAELA
TRIPPL

10.1 Introduction

Fundamental and enduring changes brought about by recurrent economic and financial crises, the digital revolution and ongoing globalisation processes of production and innovation activities are posing major challenges for regional and national economies to renew their industrial structures and develop innovations that break existing development trajectories. This calls for new innovation policy approaches that are well equipped to support transformation processes towards new industrial growth paths. This chapter aims to provide the conceptual underpinnings for such a reorientation of innovation policy. We take an innovation system (IS) perspective and develop a comprehensive place-based system failure framework for an innovation policy design that is suitable to promote structural change in different region-specific contexts.

Over the past ten years or so, the RIS concept has proven to be a powerful approach to inform policymakers and to legitimise their actions and interventions (Asheim et al. 2011; Coenen et al. 2017). A key point of departure in the innovation system policy literature is the notion of 'system failures'. Protagonists of the innovation system approach have convincingly argued that it is not only market failures (underinvestment in research due to the public good character of knowledge, spill overs and short time horizon applied by market actors in their investment decisions) that may lead to too low rates of innovation activities.

Structural failures (or deficiencies) at the system level, such as infrastructural, institutional, interaction (network) and capability failures

(Woolthuis et al. 2005) might also result in severe barriers suppressing innovation. The system failure concept has also been applied to the regional level, foregrounding the role of three main types of regional innovation system (RIS) deficiencies, that is, organisational thinness, negative lock-in and fragmentation (Tödtling and Trippl 2005). Recently, an attempt has been made to present an extended system failure concept by introducing a new focus on so-called transformational system failures, including directionality, demand articulation, policy coordination and reflexivity failures (Weber and Rohracher 2012).

These frameworks have offered many insights but they are only partially useful for identifying and conceptualising key barriers to the emergence and growth of new development paths. The older structural approaches mainly focus on existing innovation systems and innovation activities in established sectors and are thus rather limited in their explanatory power of what hinders (1) innovations that are required for new development paths and (2) the transformation of the whole IS. The more recent accounts of transformational system failures reflect the adoption of a more dynamic approach but they suffer from several shortcomings. Not only are the identified failures strongly overlapping but one can also critically ask if they are exhaustive. Furthermore, research on transformational system failures does hardly go beyond a mere identification of deficiencies, that is, it remains relatively vague in clarifying under what circumstances they make their appearance.

In this chapter we propose a place-based system failure framework that provides an advanced understanding of how regional context conditions shape and impede industrial renewal and diversification processes into new fields. Our framework rests on three pillars. First, we offer a nuanced view on barriers to regional structural change by distinguishing between failures to break with existing paths and failures to develop new industrial growth paths. Our framework acknowledges that such failures may emerge in all subsystems that form a RIS and relates them to actors, networks and institutions, which results in particular exploration/experimentation and exploitation dilemmas. Second, building on recent scholarly contributions on forms and directions of structural change (Isaksen et al. 2016) we differentiate between various types of new path development, namely

path upgrading, modernisation, branching, importation and new creation. Third, to capture varying regional characteristics we follow
Isaksen and Trippl (2016) and distinguish between thin, thick and
specialised, and thick and diversified RIS.

Our conceptual discussion reveals that each RIS type suffers from
particular combinations of region-specific failures and barriers to
structural change, which helps to assess which types of new development path are most likely to occur in peripheral, old industrial and core
regions. We argue that insights derived from such a place-based system
failure framework offer a sound basis for developing new policy
approaches to fashion regional structural change in various regional
contexts.

10.2 Regional Innovation Systems: Static or Dynamic?

A typical critique against the RIS approach flags its alleged static
perspective. Holding true, this critique would strongly undermine the
legitimacy of the RIS approach for understanding and analysing structural change in regions, and drawing adequate policy conclusions.
On the one hand, the critique is comprehensible given that numerous
empirical contributions to the RIS literature portray regional snap-
shots, ill-equipped to inform about structural change processes as
they unfold over time. On the other hand, we will show that the RIS
approach draws on concepts that are directed towards explaining
socio-economic change processes. In this section, these conceptual
underpinnings of the RIS approach are reviewed with the aim of preparing the ground for discussing how the RIS approach can be
extended to better conceptualise structural change processes.

The RIS approach emphasises the role of innovation as a key
driver for the competitiveness of firms and regions. It follows
thereby the evolutionary tradition emphasising what Schumpeter
(1943) called quality competition over ordinary (static price) competition. Quality competition refers to novel combinations of
knowledge and resources that create higher value through innovations (Asheim et al. 2016). The RIS approach recognises the variegated nature of innovation, encompassing product, process and
organisational innovations at the level of the firm as well as social
and institutional innovations at the level of the region or the industry (Morgan 2007).

Innovation explains industrial dynamics. Incremental innovations drive continuous upgrading processes and propel development along a technological trajectory. Incremental innovations, therefore, accompany path-dependent processes, which play an important role in the conceptual underpinnings of the RIS approach. Conversely, radical innovations are viewed as triggering structural change. Radical innovations devaluate existing knowledge bases, technologies and institutions. In a process of entrepreneurial discovery (Kirzner 1997) they lead to the reallocation of resources to more promising opportunities, contributing to the development of new knowledge, technologies and an adaptation of the institutional framework. In other words, incremental innovations reinforce development paths while radical innovations challenge them.

The RIS literature has dealt intensively with path-dependent processes, often associated with positive or negative lock-ins. On the positive side, lock-in processes describe an alignment of regional knowledge bases, collective resources, and the institutional framework. This alignment produces specialised suppliers, sophisticated demand, qualified labour, educational and research activities, and supporting services that are focused on a common theme or sector, thereby creating competitive advantage. The RIS approach emphasises the cumulative nature of localised learning processes embedded in an inert regional institutional context. The localised learning argument rests on the presumption that tacit knowledge plays a more important role in explaining competitive advantages than codified knowledge because the latter is more easily accessible globally (Maskell and Malmberg 1999). Furthermore, tacit knowledge is embedded in a social, cultural and institutional context, detached from which it quickly loses value (Gertler 2003). For these reasons, tacit knowledge is at best transferred or generated through interaction or practice (Polanyi 1958; Lam 2000) within a shared institutional context and through trust-based relationships. These 'untraded interdependencies' (Storper 1995) underpin learning and innovation dynamics and explain at the same time their cumulative and path-dependent nature.

A recent contribution to the RIS literature differentiates between cumulative and combinatorial knowledge dynamics (Strambach and Klement 2012). Cumulative knowledge dynamics refers to the continuous development of a knowledge base while combinatorial describes the process of bringing together different knowledge bases. Firms that combine knowledge bases either through holding them in-house or sourcing them externally are more likely to produce radical innovations (Tödtling and Grillitsch 2015; Grillitsch et al. 2017). Hence, the extent to which regions promote or hinder combinatorial knowledge dynamics can be expected to have an important effect on their adaptability and the potential of new path development.

The negative side of path-dependency and lock-in is the failure of regions to adapt when existing development trajectories are challenged by, for instance, radical innovations or new socio-economic trends. The RIS literature has addressed negative lock-ins in relation to the study of old industrial regions or regions facing structural challenges (Hassink 2005; Trippl and Otto 2009; Hassink 2010).

The conceptualisation of negative lock-in draws on Grabher's (1993) seminal contribution, in which he differentiates between cognitive, functional and political lock-in. Cognitive lock-in refers to a shared world view producing and reproducing similar interpretations of the environment. Homogeneous views limit the capacity to perceive environmental changes or draw adequate conclusions. Functional lock-in describes rigid, typically hierarchical inter-organisational relationships that limit the potential for individual players to reorient themselves and change strategy. Political lock-in captures efforts of established actors to protect vested interests and to resist change as well as formal and informal rules supporting the traditional sectors.

Hassink (2010) argues that economic-structural and political-institutional impact factors influence the renewal of clusters and regions. As regards the former, renewal is constrained by industrial mono-structure, and in particular if the leading industry is capital-intensive, has high-entry and exit barriers, exhibits above average company size, has an oligopolistic market structure and is highly influenced by trade unions. Political-institutional impact factors encompass the regional, national and supra-national level. Hassink (2010: 465) argues that 'it is of key importance when analysing regional lock-ins in old industrial areas to take the institutional context at all spatial levels, that is local, regional, national, and supra-national into account'.

Linking economic evolution with the institutional context, it has been argued that institutional variety contributes to the potential for radical innovations and new path development (Boschma 2015).

However, institutional variety alone is not sufficient, as it does not necessarily imply that actors from different institutional contexts interact and cooperate. Thus, also connectedness between different institutional contexts is required (Grillitsch and Asheim 2015). Institutional variety and connectedness together, for instance through individual mobility between variegated institutional contexts, double affiliations or positions, or networks are important explanatory factors for the potential of path-breaking innovations and entrepreneurial discoveries, as well as the coordination of interests and collective efforts in order to promote new development paths (Grillitsch 2015).

The RIS literature can be criticised for the frequent simplification of a static institutional framework, which applies in particular for empirical 'snap-shot analyses'. However, this does not per se obstruct a co-evolutionary perspective of RIS where institutional and economic changes are inherently linked. Sotarauta and Mustikkamaki (2015) show that institutional entrepreneurship is an important driver for institutional change and new path development. Grillitsch (2015) relates the adaptability of regional institutional contexts to structural characteristics such as institutional variety and connectedness as well as the position and power of actors within it.

Iammarino (2005) relates RIS to Dopfer et al.'s (2004) evolutionary micro-meso-macro framework implying that the interdependencies between the three levels (upward and downward causation) determine the paths of regions. The macro level encompasses institutions erected at the national and supra-national scale, while the meso level relates to the socio-institutional embededdness of regional innovation and knowledge linkages. Grillitsch and Rekers (2016: 167) argue that 'the shifts in behaviour of economic actors can be traced back to institutional changes at multiple scales. In other words, frequent opportunities for face-to-face interaction and the development of long-term trust-based relationships are not automatically available to firms that are located in close geographical proximity to competent partners. These localized assets are only assets when they are supported by the multi-scalar institutional environment in which organizations operate.'

Recent literature has reflected on the types of structural change in RIS (Trippl and Otto 2009; Tödtling and Trippl 2013): (i) incremental innovation-based adjustment processes of clusters towards new higher-value market niches, (ii) diversification of firms into established industries that are new to the region, (iii) the emergence of clusters in new industries based on knowledge-intensive activities. The importance of academic leadership and university spin-offs is highest for the third type of structural RIS change, leading to radical change. As the allocation of public funds to academic fields is to a large extent a political decision, often requiring long-term investments before economic results are realised, policy plays an important role in the emergence of research-based industries. Nevertheless, also more incremental forms of structural change depend on access to new knowledge and resources. Thus a reconfiguration of the knowledge infrastructure, institutional changes and policy support contribute to new path development in RIS (see, for instance, Morgan 2007; Tödtling and Trippl 2013).

Moreover, RIS 'with stronger social capabilities and a stronger knowledge base will tend to also be better equipped to exploit new technological opportunities, to adapt existing activities to emerging business environments, and to learn faster about how to build new regional advantages' (Iammarino 2005: 501). This can be reflected in different types of RIS. Isaksen and Trippl (2016) specify organisationally thick and diversified RIS (e.g. metropolitan areas), organisationally thick and specialised RIS (e.g. specialised clusters and old industrial regions) and thin RIS (typically peripheral areas). Accordingly, thick and diversified RIS offer the best pre-conditions for new path development, while thick and specialised RIS and, particularly, thin RIS provide a more constraining environment for the rise and further evolution of new growth paths.

10.3 Toward a New Understanding of Barriers to and Forms of Regional Structural Change

RIS consist of actors (individuals and organisations such as companies, cluster organisations, research institutes, educational bodies, knowledge transfer organisations, science parks and so on) that are connected through networks whereby the actors' behaviour and interactions are shaped by institutions, the cumulated knowledge base and technologies (Tödtling and Trippl 2005). From a RIS perspective, barriers to structural change can thus be related to actors, networks and institutions that result in – as will be explained in this section – various forms of knowledge exploration-exploitation dilemmas.

Table 10.1 *Barriers to breaking with existing paths and growing new paths*

	Barriers for breaking with existing paths	Barriers for growing new paths
Actors	Strong capabilities in existing paths	Weak capabilities in new paths
Networks	Strong connectedness and interdependencies in existing paths	Weak connectedness and interdependencies in new paths
Institutions	Strong institutional alignment for existing paths	Weak institutional alignment for new paths

Source: Author's own compilation

10.3.1 *Disentangling Barriers to Regional Structural Change*

Structural change results from a combination of breaking with existing structures (overcoming negative lock-ins) and growing new development paths (creating positive lock-ins) as illustrated in Table 10.1. These two essential processes of structural change face different types of barriers, which we address in this section.

A major barrier to breaking with existing paths relates to strong capabilities of RIS actors. Strong capabilities become a problem if changes in technologies or markets diminish the relevance and value of existing capabilities, inducing the classical cognitive lock-in (Grabher 1993). Similar worldviews and routines for perceiving, searching and interpreting new information lead to myopic behaviour, which is reinforced through localised learning within industry clusters (Maskell and Malmberg 2007). Typically, this is the case in mature industries, which are characterised by incremental innovations that often aim at cost-cutting or minor product adaptation (i.e. path extension). Strong capabilities have been built through investments into knowledge, organisational routines and infrastructure, which in the face of decline become sunk costs. Incumbents have strong vested interests to protect their past investments and profit opportunities.

In contrast, developing new growth paths is typically constrained by weak capabilities, which resonates closely with the organisational thinness argument (Isaksen 2001; Tödtling and Trippl 2005). Organisational thinness can be further differentiated in a quantitative and qualitative dimension (Grillitsch and Asheim 2015). The quantitative dimension refers to the existence or number of relevant RIS actors, while the qualitative dimension captures their level of capabilities. Weak capabilities also exist if the knowledge profiles of actors are incompatible, meaning that interactive learning is hindered due to a high cognitive distance (Boschma 2005).

As regards networks, relevant barriers for breaking with existing structures are strong connectedness and interdependencies in old paths. As industries mature, strong interdependencies between actors in the value chain emerge, creating functional lock-ins (Grabher 1993). These interdependencies might play out at the local scale in, for instance, industrial districts (Pyke et al. 1990; Asheim 2000). More often, however, they are realised in global production networks (Henderson et al. 2002; MacKinnon 2012) and are a powerful stabilising force for existing structures. These interdependencies are manifested in stable and thus relative rigid core-periphery network patterns, which develop due to preferential attachment to leading firms, the higher probability of weaker firms exiting the market and the tendency to collaborate with partners known from previous collaborations (Ter Wal and Boschma 2011).

While path-breaking struggles with strong connectedness and interdependencies, the opposite is true for growing new paths. Weak connectedness and interdependencies may exist at the regional and global level, hampering interactive learning and innovation related to the newly emerging fields. At the regional level, weak connectedness or fragmentation may exist between RIS sub-systems, for instance between universities and firms, as well as within the subsystems (Isaksen 2001; Tödtling and Trippl 2005). The latter is typically the case when a lack of social capital and highly competitive behaviour restricts interactive learning between firms. However, also a too strong regional focus hinders innovation (Fitjar and Rodríguez-Pose 2011). Innovative firms tend to combine regional knowledge sources with those on the national and international scale (Grillitsch and Trippl 2014; Tödtling and Grillitsch 2015).

Turning to institutions, it is interesting to note that the RIS literature has discussed negative institutional lock-ins at length as fundamental failure especially for old industrial regions (Isaksen 2001; Tödtling and

Trippl 2005; Hassink 2010). Institutions co-evolve with industries and technologies (Nelson 1994; Murmann 2003; Schamp 2010). Old industrial regions are characterised by a mono-industrial structure to which institutions are aligned. Regional actors that focus on the leading industry and protect vested interests, a national-political system where the regional actors can influence industrial policy and supra-national institutions that support the existing industry are key drivers of institutional lock-in (Hassink 2010). Geels (2004) argues that the alignment of institutions from different domains stabilises regimes, which is an argument that resonates well with the literature on institutional complementarities (Aoki 1994; Vitols 2001; Hall and Gingerich 2009). Hence, strong institutional alignment for existing paths is a significant barrier for structural change.

In contrast, growing new paths is constrained by weak institutional alignment and integration across institutional domains. Sotarauta and Mustikkamäki (2015) show that new path creation in an innovation system requires institutional entrepreneurship, i.e. deliberate action to make an institutional change (Garud et al. 2007; Battilana et al. 2009). A classic example is also the work of Zelizer (1978) showing that the diffusion of the life insurance policy was contingent to institutional change. Relating to this, diversity in the institutional framework reduces the risk of lock-in (Strambach 2010; Boschma 2015; Grillitsch 2015), while institutional integration captures the extent to which institutions promote or constrain interactions between different social groups and, consequently, learning between institutional domains (Grillitsch 2016).

10.3.2 Types of Regional Industrial Path Development

The distinction between existing paths and new paths outlined in the previous section serves as a point of departure for identifying basic types of failures preventing regional structural change to take place. As the development of new paths, however, can take on many shapes, partly contingent on the barriers developed earlier, this subsection introduces a fine-grained typology of path development.

Drawing on previous work (Martin and Sunley 2006; Tödtling and Trippl 2013), recent scholarly contributions have clarified and enriched the concept of path development by differentiating between five key forms (Isaksen et al. 2016), namely path extension,

Table 10.2 *Types and mechanisms of path development*

Forms of path development	Mechanisms
Path extension	Continuation of an existing industrial path based on incremental innovation in existing industries along well-established technological trajectories
Path upgrading	Major change of a regional industrial path related to enhancement of position within global production networks; moving up the value chain based on upgrading of skills and production capabilities
Path modernisation	Major change of an industrial path into a new direction based on new technologies or organisational innovations
Path branching	Development of a new industry based on competencies and knowledge of existing related industries (related variety)
Path importation	Setting up of an established industry that is new to the region (e.g. through foreign firms)
Path creation	Emergence and growth of entirely new industries based on radically new technologies and scientific discoveries or as outcome of search processes for new business models, user-driven innovation and social innovation

Source: Adapted from Isaksen et al. (2016).

modernisation, branching, importation and creation. We extend this typology by means of the notion of path upgrading (see Grillitsch et al. 2017) (Table 10.2).

Path extension occurs through incremental product and process innovations in existing sectors. It reflects continuity of regional industrial structures, path dependence and positive lock-in (see previous section). This may, however, lead to stagnation, decline and path exhaustion in the longer run due to weakly developed renewal capacities. Regional industries then suffer from negative lock-in. They become locked into innovation activities along well-established technological paths and practices, constraining their opportunities for experimentation and capacities to generate radical innovation.

Path upgrading describes transformation processes of a regional industrial path related to an improvement of its position within global production networks. This could occur through processes of value enhancement based on developing more advanced functions and more specialised skills, technological upgrading, and so on (Coe et al. 2004; MacKinnon 2012).

Path modernisation denotes fundamental intra-path changes, that is, transformation processes of established paths into a new direction. Such changes leading to a renewal and upgrading of existing paths may be based on the 'injection' of new technologies (e.g. the use of laser technology in the forest industry, Foray 2015) or organisational innovation (e.g. introduction of project organisation in creative industries, Grabher 2001).

Path branching represents a more radical form of regional structural change. Branching implies that new paths grow out of existing industries and capabilities (Boschma and Frenken 2011) often fuelled by related variety (Boschma 2015). A core mechanism of such processes is the diversification of incumbent firms into new fields and sectors based on the redeployment of existing assets and capabilities. Branching, however, can also take place through the establishment of new firms based on competencies in existing industries. Spin-offs from incumbents in related industries have been shown to play an important role for path branching (related diversification) processes (Klepper 2007).

Path importation means that established industries are transplanted to regions, in which they have not existed before. Arguably, they are new to the region but not new to the world. Importation of paths can occur through the settlement of foreign firms, arrival of qualified individuals and entrepreneurs with competences not available in the region or extra-regional networks (see, for instance, Trippl et al. 2017). Foreign direct investment is often seen to be a particularly important mechanism of path importation. It hinges on the condition that incoming firms perform high value-added functions in the region and establish linkages to regional actors to enhance their embeddedness in the regional economy.

Path creation in new industries represents the most radical form of regional structural change. It refers to the rise and growth of entirely new industries based on new technological and organisational knowledge assets. Creation of new paths may be the outcome of chance, contingent events, serendipity or historical accidents but more often than not new paths rest on pre-existing assets, resources or competencies in the region, such as an excellent scientific base (Tanner 2014) or the availability of highly skilled workers (Martin 2010). The rise of new high-tech and knowledge-intensive industries is nurtured by the formation of new companies and spin-offs (Frenken and Boschma 2007). Path creation in new industries requires a substantial transformation of the regional knowledge and support infrastructure and institutional change.

There are strong reasons to argue that regions differ substantially in their capacity to induce the forms of new path development outlined previously due to the prevalence of various types of barriers to structural change identified in Section 3.1. In a next step, we elaborate on this argument and discuss the policy implications following from it.

10.4 Regionalisation: RIS Types and Policy Approaches

Our point of departure is Isaksen and Trippl's (2016) distinction between three main RIS types, that is, organisationally thin RIS, organisationally thick and specialised RIS, and organisationally thick and diversified RIS. Thin RIS are often found in peripheral regions, while thick and specialised RIS are typical for old industrial areas. Finally, thick and diversified RIS tend to prevail in advanced core areas such as larger cities and metropolitan regions.

These RIS types suffer from particular combinations of barriers to breaking with existing and nurturing new paths, which helps to explain which forms and directions of structural change (that is, types of new path development) are likely to take place in each of the three region types considered in this chapter. This allows for a nuanced discussion of adequate policy strategies for peripheral, old industrial and core regions (see Table 10.3).

10.4.1 Thin RIS: Peripheral Regions

Peripheral regions are by definition characterised by a lack of a critical mass of strong actors in related or unrelated fields. On the one hand, it can be argued that for this reason barriers for breaking with existing paths are weaker compared to the other two regional types.

Table 10.3 *Place-based system failure framework for structural change in RIS*

Regional type	Barriers to structural change		Implication for new path development	
	Path breaking	Path development	Most promising types	Policy implication
Thin (Peripheral regions)	Possible monopolisation of networks and policies by key firms.	Pervasive failure due to weaknesses in whole innovation system.	Importation Upgrading	**Path breaking:** Broaden local and global networks Promote openness to external sources of knowledge **Path development:** Attract investments Strengthen capabilities of regional actors Promote inter-regional linkages
Thick and specialised (Old industrial regions)	Pervasive failure due to the existence of one dominant path	Partial failure due to strengths in exploitation but weakness in exploration	Modernisation Branching	**Path breaking:** Reduce public support for existing activities Break up tight-knit networks between incumbents and policy **Path development:** Increase variety in knowledge base Support linkages outside the dominant industry (global and local) Introduce new players

| Thick and diversified (Core regions) | Partial failure due to the existence of multiple paths at different stages of development | Partial failure due to strengths in exploration but weakness in exploitation | Modernisation
Branching
Path creation | **Path breaking (for 'old' paths in the region):**
Reduce public support for existing activities
Moving resources from old to new paths
Path development:
Increase regional connectedness between industries and sectors
Increase exploitation capabilities (in relation to the commercialisation of research-based knowledge)
Support institutional alignment and integration for newly emerging paths |

Source: own compilation

Simmie (2012: 770), for instance, argues that the introduction of wind power technologies in Denmark occurred in rural areas because 'the dominant urban, centralized and grid-connected electricity generation and supply system did not exist'. On the other hand, peripheral regions may be locked-in to global patterns of production and consumption. This is the case if transnational companies exploit basic, low-cost resources in the periphery, in particular cheap labour. MacKinnon (2012) argues that strong power asymmetries between the transnational firms and regional authorities, and a lack of local linkages with other firms imply a high degree of dependence and lock-in low-value-creating development paths.

Thus actor-related barriers for structural change in peripheral regions concern mainly weak capabilities of local actors in a broad sense. The competences of firms are essential for overcoming locational disadvantages (Grillitsch and Nilsson 2017). This directly relates to providing adequate educational and training facilities in the region. Peripheral regions typically lack universities and higher level education. Furthermore, the capacities of regional policy makers are essential to promote the growth of economic development paths, for instance through securing support and funding on the national level or encouraging regional embedding of key firms.

Due to the low number of relevant actors, innovation and production networks tend to be weakly developed in the periphery. However, a problem exists if one or a few strong regional actors monopolise the networks in an effort to protect vested interests. This could be the case, for instance, if one firm (or subsidiary) provides a large share of the jobs in the region, thus being a source for strong dependencies. A key question is then how to balance the power and position in the network, to allow other regional actors to be part in the network, and to open the network to complementary sources of knowledge and resources outside the region. Apart from this lock-in problem, actors in peripheral regions will – due to a lack of internal resources – always be in need of linking up to strong partners located elsewhere.

On the institutional side, peripheral regions may be characterised by a distinct regional culture. Westlund and Kobayashi (2013) argue that rural areas, due to a relatively homogeneous world view and strong bonding social capital, tend to be less inclined to engage in extra-regional networks. Too much region-mindedness has been identified as a hampering factor for innovation (Fitjar and Rodríguez-Pose 2011;

Malecki 2011), thereby constraining structural change processes. Peripheral regions have the advantage, in contrast, that institutions are not aligned to a specific type of economic activity (given a lack of specialisation in the regional economy), thus implying a relatively low degree of respective lock-in.

10.4.1.1 Policy Strategies

Due to the pervasive weaknesses of the innovation system in peripheral regions, viable policy strategies are limited to path importation and path upgrading. Typically, the available competencies in peripheral regions are too limited to create new paths even though exceptions may prove the rule (e.g. Simmie 2012). Furthermore, branching is not an option, as it requires a strong basis in at least one industry, which typically does not exist in peripheral regions.

Path-breaking policies play a role if existing players, such as one strong firm or subsidiary, monopolises regional networks and policies. Due to the dependency from the lead firm, this will most likely work in subtle ways. At the level of actors, the lead firm can be encouraged to engage more with other local actors while programmes to strengthen the capacities of the local actors will over time lead to an upgrading of the regional environment. As regards networks, policy makers may broaden their networks and engage new actors in regional decision making. On the institutional side, policies that encourage more openness towards the outside world can facilitate extra-regional knowledge linkages.

New path development policies shall focus on path upgrading and path importation. Path importation aims at attracting organisations including firms, universities, research institutes, educational facilities or public services, as well as individuals, to the region. Isaksen and Trippl (2017) show, for instance, how the arrival of several research institutes has led to the growth of the software industry in Mühlviertel, a peripheral Austrian region, or how two pioneering firms in the electronics sector stimulated a regional development path in Arendal-Grimstad, in Southern Norway. Such a policy should always include the commitment of upgrading the regional environment in an attempt to create positive self-reinforcing processes. This implies strengthening the competencies of organisations located in the region through (vocational) education and training as well as incentives to invest in innovation, creating support services and promoting networks within the region and with extra-regional sources of knowledge and resources.

10.4.2 Thick and Specialised RIS: Old Industrial Regions

Thick and specialised regions face major challenges to renew their economic structures and innovation systems. Barriers related to both breaking old paths and creating new ones tend to loom large and need to be overcome for structural change to occur. Breaking old industrial paths is pivotal and appears to be more in demand than in other regions due to the strong specialisation of these areas in a few, often traditional, industries and the prevalence of various forms of negative lock-ins (Hassink 2010). At the same time, assets for creating new paths are hardly available at the regional level as a result of the concentration of resources in well-established paths. Consequently, these regions have often been portrayed as 'centres of continuity', offering favourable conditions for path extension but not for new forms of path development (Isaksen and Trippl 2016). However, some of these regions may take advantage of a sufficiently large generic competence in their area of specialisation, which could provide the basis for path branching. Strengthening the research infrastructure to widen the exploration capacity of the region, building links to non-local sources of expertise and combining inflowing knowledge with the highly specialised competences residing within the region could essentially trigger such branching processes (Trippl et al. 2017). Diversification of oil and gas firms into offshore wind activities in Scotland (Dawley 2014) and Mid-Norway (Steen and Karlsen 2014) serve as a good example in this regard.

Actor-related barriers found in thick and specialised RIS are the outcome of long-standing, historically accumulated capabilities and experiences in traditional economic activities, which are difficult to abandon even if changes in markets and technological progress render existing competences obsolete. More often than not, actors' responses to changing environment conditions are characterised by cost-cutting measures or the adoption of incremental innovation strategies. Arguably, such responses and strategic orientations as well as the power of vested interest players are among important factors that explain why thick and specialised RIS face difficulties in breaking existing paths (Morgan 2013). At the same time, these regions tend to be short of capabilities that could provide the foundation for entirely new paths, that is, they lack the variety of capabilities and novel knowledge assets that often form the basis for new path creation (Isaksen and Trippl 2016).

Network-related barriers to structural change are well documented for thick and specialised regions. This RIS type often suffers from what Grabher (1993) has called 'the weakness of strong ties', that is, rigid, closed networks between well-established players, which underpin and further stabilise existing paths. Breaking existing paths will thus often precondition the dissolution of such network configurations, since they blind their members to seeing needs and opportunities for intra-path changes and new path development.

Finally, failures resulting from a strong alignment of institutions at various spatial scales to the dominant industries, lack of diversity in the institutional environment and low levels of institutional integration are salient features of thick and specialised RIS, reinforcing existing paths and bedevilling the rise of new ones.

To summarise, thick and specialised regions appear to be burdened with failures and rigidities found in the actor, network and institutional dimensions of their RIS. Their interplay provides a strong basis for expounding why path extension – and in some cases path branching – is often the dominant form of path development in these areas and why more radical forms of structural change are held down by too much exploitation and too little exploration.

10.4.2.1 Policy strategies

As elucidated previously, thick and specialised regions face the challenge of overcoming barriers to breaking existing paths and developing new ones. This calls for a policy approach that combines measures that help to destabilise and break with old paths and nurture the creation and growth of new ones. In other words: both path-breaking policies and new path development policies are required for structural change to take place.

Path-breaking policies range from withdrawal of public support for old industrial paths and technologies (removal of R&D and innovation funding, cutting subsidies, withdrawal of other institutional incentives, etc.), to breaking up close networks between government and private vested interest players, and so on. In essence, such policies are about weakening conditions that are favourable to the status quo.

New path development policies may cover a wide array of strategies and policy instruments, depending on the type of path development under consideration. Both path modernisation and path branching should rank high on the policy agenda. The former will entail support enabling firms to search for and create connections to providers of new technological and organisational knowledge and to strengthen their capacity to absorb new knowledge assets and combine them with their existing capabilities. Promotion of path branching might also be a suitable policy strategy to foster regional economic renewal and structural change in thick and specialised RIS. This calls for a proactive policy approach that supports the diversification of firms into new but related fields. Path branching will also benefit from policy actions geared towards a broadening of the specialised knowledge base, support of linkages outside the dominating path at the local and – even more importantly – at the non-local level and the introduction of new players in the RIS (e.g. establishment of research and educational bodies, nurturing local and attracting foreign firms that focus on new but related fields; see, for instance, Morgan's (2017) analysis of policy actions employed in the Basque country).

10.4.3 Thick and Diversified RIS: Core Regions

Thick and diversified regions often display multiple forms of regional industrial path development, that is, paths at later stages of their development co-exist and sometimes co-evolve with younger and emerging ones. Diversity in industrial structure (Boschma 2015) and the presence of a large number of different firms, knowledge and support organisations point to the availability of a large heterogeneity in competences and resources (Essletzbichler 2015) that can be used to initiate new paths. Beside favourable actor constellations, structural change in these areas is supported by diverse and geographically open networks and institutional heterogeneity, that is, the presence of both bonding and bridging social capital (Simmie 2003; Isaksen and Trippl 2016).

This should not imply, however, that challenges to new path development are absent in thick and diversified regions. Their nature, however, differs substantially from those observed in other RIS types. Barriers to grow new paths may be found in unbalanced exploration-exploitation capacities. These areas host actors with strong capabilities in experimentation and novelty generation (universities, young research-based firms, etc.). Actor-related barriers may mainly arise from comparatively poorly developed capabilities to exploit new knowledge for new path development. For instance, weak capacities of and little support for firms and universities to commercialise findings from the locally available excellent scientific base have hampered the rise of a new biotech path in Austria's capital city, Vienna (Trippl et al. 2017).

Focusing on the network dimension, weak connectedness and interdependencies may hinder new path development. At the regional level, fragmentation has been identified as a potential barrier to innovation and new industrial activities in thick and diversified regions (Tödtling and Trippl 2005). Fragmentation may stem from weak university-industry linkages, resulting in a poor commercialisation of new knowledge, which constrains new path creation based on scientific discoveries. Furthermore, cognitive and other barriers that prevent diverse firms and industries from connecting might be sources of fragmentation, impeding processes of path branching.

Barriers to path creation and path branching may also be related to the institutional dimension of diverse regions. Institutions tend to adapt slowly to emerging paths. Failures to align institutions to new industrial activities could lead to a loss of momentum in their development. Positive lock-in required for further path evolution of new industries may not take place.

One might also find barriers to breaking existing industrial paths, since diverse regions may also host traditional industries. In this case, too much exploitation and too little exploration – reflected in actors' capabilities, long-established networks and well-aligned institutional set-ups – may constrain structural change in parts of diverse innovation systems.

10.4.3.1 Policy Strategies

Diverse regions are regarded as centres of continuous change, offering favourable conditions for path creation and path branching. However, as discussed previously, there might be 'partial' failures that call for policy action.

Path-breaking policies might be on the policy agenda in order to avoid or escape from negative lock-in in traditional sectors. Withdrawal of support for traditional activities and other measures to break up old paths that bind resources that could be used for new development paths may thus be of vital importance.

New path development policies in thick and diversified regions should take into account the variegated nature of development paths in the region. In the case of mature industries, path-breaking policies can be complemented with activities to promote path modernisation. A good example is the food industry in Scania, a diversified region located in the South of Sweden. Injection of new scientific knowledge has led to the rise of functional food activities, i.e. substantial intra-path changes in a long-established industry (Zukauskaite and Moodysson 2016). Strengthening exploration capacity might be an essential policy goal in this regard. This should include a variety of measures. Fostering the creation of networks to sources of new science-based and other forms of knowledge, boosting the absorption capacities of traditional firms and provision of institutional incentives for path modernisation are important policy elements of exploration-enhancing strategies.

The main policy orientation, however, should be to support path branching and new path creation. This may best be achieved by enhancing the exploitation capacities and by targeting the sources that cause fragmentation. Active support for commercialisation of research-based knowledge and platform policies that bring together different (but related) firms and industries, allowing for an integration of dispersed knowledge and combination of resources should rank high on the policy agenda. Finally, adapting institutional structures to newly emerging paths to support them going beyond the early path creation or branching phase is of vital importance.

10.5 Conclusions

The regional innovation systems approach has been criticised for being rather static, while we argue that its theoretical and conceptual foundations capture dynamic processes such as innovation and learning. Hence, it provides a framework by which to analyse structural change of regional economies, contributing especially to understanding respective barriers in relation to region-specific conditions. The chapter shows conceptually why the regional context has far-reaching effects on the type of new path development that is most feasible and promising, leading to concrete policy recommendations for different types of regions.

A place-based system failure framework is proposed that combines three conceptual cornerstones. The first one differentiates between barriers that relate to rigidities of the current industrial, knowledge and institutional structures on the one hand and constraints that hinder the development of new growth paths on the other hand. The second conceptual cornerstone captures different forms of new path development, comprising path upgrading, modernisation, branching, importation and new path creation. The third cornerstone relates to regional characteristics. We differentiate between organisationally thin, organisationally thick and specialised and organisationally thick and diversified regions.

Our discussion shows that each region type is prone to a certain combination of barriers to structural change, which has profound implications for the most promising types of new path development and policy options. In organisationally thin regions (peripheral regions), a relatively low degree of negative lock-ins is expected, although a strong firm or subsidiary may monopolise regional networks and politics. However, new path creation is difficult due to the weaknesses in knowledge exploration and exploitation, and branching is unlikely because of the lack of specialisation in an industry. The most promising path development strategies, therefore, are to upgrade or import existing paths. This is best achieved by strengthening basic capabilities through attracting investments, enhancing capabilities of regional actors and promoting inter-regional linkages. In the case of one or a few actors monopolising regional networks and politics, path destabilisation policies that broaden local and global networks as well as promote openness to external sources of knowledge are recommended.

Organisationally thick and specialised regions suffer most from rigidities erected by the current industrial structure, knowledge assets and institutional configurations. Due to specialisation in one or a few industries, cognitive, functional and institutional lock-ins loom large. This is combined with barriers to new path development that relate to a lack of exploration capacities, in particular the capability to create novelty by combining knowledge from different domains. On the positive side, the accumulated knowledge and resources in the respective specialisation can be a basis for new path development. Accordingly, path modernisation and branching are the most promising development options. A combination of policies to destabilise the existing path and strengthen exploration capacities is recommended. Path destabilisation includes the reduction of public support for existing activities and the breaking up of tight-knit networks between incumbents and policy. Knowledge exploration can be strengthened by increasing variety in knowledge bases, supporting local and global linkages outside the dominant industry, and introducing new actors.

Organisationally thick and diversified regions are considered as core centres of new path development. Diversity in industrial and institutional structures, a large variety of knowledge assets and geographically open networks provide a fertile ground for path creation and path branching activities to occur. Nevertheless, 'partial' failures originating from unbalanced exploration-exploitation capacities may make their appearance, suppressing structural change. Too much exploration and experimentation may hamper positive lock-ins in newly emerging paths, while too much exploitation might prevent path modernisation taking place in more traditional industries. Consequently, diversified regions will benefit from a policy approach that enables mature paths to undergo major intra-path changes by building bridges to new knowledge sources and new paths to emerge and achieve positive-lock in by supporting exploitation activities in new fields. The latter targets path branching and new path creation and includes enhancing the regional connectedness between different industries, strengthening of the commercialisation of research-based knowledge and supporting institutional alignment and integration for new paths.

This chapter provides a conceptual discussion that contributes to a place-based system failure framework. It adds to traditional RIS failures by focussing on structural change and new path development, thus introducing a more dynamic perspective. Furthermore it advances the recent debate on transformative failure by linking it to the challenges different types of regions face. This chapter therefore translates the rather abstract thoughts on system transformation and structural change to place-specific conditions, which allows for a more concrete formulation of policy recommendations. Future research efforts will, however, need to empirically examine and test the proposed place-based system failure framework. In the real world, regions often deviate from the ideal types discussed in this chapter, which implies that the configuration of barriers and potentials for new path development may differ as well, and that consequently policy implications need to be adapted.

References

Aoki, M. 1994. The contingent governance of teams: Analysis of institutional complementarity. *International Economic Review* 35: 657–676.

Asheim, B., M. Grillitsch, and M. Trippl. 2016. Regional Innovation Systems: Past – presence – future, in *Handbook of the Geographies of Innovation*, D. Doloreux, R. Shearmur, and C. Carrincazeux (eds.), 46–62. Cheltenham: Edward Elgar.

Asheim, B. T. 2000. Industrial districts: The contributions of Marshall and beyond, in *The Oxford Handbook of Economic Geography*, G. L. Clark, M. P. Feldman, and M. S. Gertler (eds.), 413–431. Oxford; New York, NY: Oxford University Press.

Asheim, B. T., J. Moodysson, and F. Tödtling. 2011. Constructing regional advantage: Towards state-of-the-art regional innovation system policies in Europe? *European Planning Studies* 19: 1133–1139.

Battilana, J., B. Leca, and E. Boxenbaum. 2009. How actors change institutions: Towards a theory of institutional entrepreneurship. *The Academy of Management Annals* 3: 65–107.

Boschma, R. 2005. Proximity and innovation: A critical assessment. *Regional Studies* 39: 61–75.

Boschma, R. 2015. Towards an evolutionary perspective on regional resilience. *Regional Studies* 49: 733–751.

Boschma, R. and K. Frenken. 2011. Technological relatedness and regional branching, in *Beyond Territory. Dynamic geographies of knowledge creation, diffusion, and innovation*, H. Bathelt, M. Feldman, and D. Kogler (eds.), 64–81. London: Routledge.

Coe, N. M., M. Hess, H. W.-C. Yeung, P. Dicken, and J. Henderson. 2004. 'Globalizing' regional development: A global production networks perspective. *Transactions of the Institute of British Geographers* 29: 468–484.

Coenen, L., B. Asheim, M. M. Bugge, and S. J. Herstad. 2017. Advancing regional innovation systems: What does evolutionary economic geography bring to the policy table? *Environment and Planning C: Government and Policy* 35: 600–620.

Dawley, S. 2014. Creating new paths? Offshore wind, policy activism, and peripheral region development. *Economic Geography* 90: 91–112.

Dopfer, K.; J. Foster; and J. Potts. 2004. Micro-meso-macro. *Journal of Evolutionary Economics* 14: 263–279.

Essletzbichler, J. 2015. Relatedness, industrial branching and technological cohesion in US metropolitan areas. *Regional Studies* 49: 752–766.

Fitjar, R. D. and A. Rodríguez-Pose. 2011. When local interaction does not suffice: Sources of firm innovation in urban Norway. *Environment and Planning. A* 43: 1248–1267.

Foray, D. 2015. *Smart Specialization: Opportunities and Challenges for Regional Innovation Policies.* Abingdon: Routledge.

Frenken, K. and R. A. Boschma. 2007. A theoretical framework for evolutionary economic geography: Industrial dynamics and urban growth as a branching process. *Journal of Economic Geography* 7: 635–649.

Garud, R., C. Hardy, and S. Maguire. 2007. Institutional entrepreneurship as embedded agency: An introduction to the special issue. *Organization Studies* 28: 957–969.

Geels, F. W. 2004. From sectoral systems of innovation to socio-technical systems: Insights about dynamics and change from sociology and institutional theory. *Research Policy* 33: 897–920.

Gertler, M. S. 2003. Tacit knowledge and the economic geography of context, or the undefinable tacitness of being (there). *Journal of Economic Geography* 3: 75–99.

Grabher, G. 1993. The weakness of strong ties; the lock-in of regional development in the Ruhr area, in *The Embedded Firm: On the Socioeconomics of Industrial Networks*, G. Grabher (ed.), 255–277. London and New York, NY: Routledge.

Grabher, G. 2001. Locating economic action: Projects, networks, localities, institutions. *Environment and Planning A* 33: 1329–1331.

Grillitsch, M. 2015. Institutional layers, connectedness and change: Implications for economic evolution in regions. *European Planning Studies* 23: 2099–2124.

Grillitsch, M. 2016. Institutions, smart specialisation dynamics and policy. *Environment and Planning C: Government and Policy* 34: 22–37.

Grillitsch, M. and B. Asheim. 2015. Cluster Policy: Renewal through the integration of institutional variety. *Papers in Innovation Studies.*

Grillitsch, M., R. Martin, and M. Srholec. 2017. Knowledge base combinations and innovation performance in Swedish regions. *Economic Geography* 93: 458–479.

Grillitsch, M. and M. Nilsson. 2017. Firm performance in the periphery: On the relation between firm-internal knowledge and local knowledge spillovers. *Regional Studies* 51: 1219–1231.

Grillitsch, M. and J. V. Rekers. 2016. How does multi-scalar institutional change affect localized learning processes? A case study of the med-tech sector in Southern Sweden. *Environment and Planning A* 48: 154–171.

Grillitsch, M. and M. Trippl. 2014. Combining knowledge from different sources, channels and geographical scales. *European Planning Studies* 22: 2305–2325.

Grillitsch, M., B. Asheim, and M. Trippl. 2017. Unrelated knowledge combinations: Unexplored potential for new regional industrial path development. *Papers in Innovation Studies*.

Hall, P. A. and D. W. Gingerich. 2009. Varieties of capitalism and institutional complementarities in the political economy: An empirical analysis. *British Journal of Political Science* 39: 449–482.

Hassink, R. 2005. How to unlock regional economies from path dependency? From learning region to learning cluster. *European Planning Studies* 13: 521–535.

Hassink, R. 2010. Locked in decline? On the role of regional lock-ins in old industrial areas, in *The Handbook of Evolutionary Economic Geography*, R. Boschma and R. Martin (eds.), 450–468. Cheltenham: Edward Elgar.

Henderson, J., P. Dicken, M. Hess, N. Coe, and H. W.-C. Yeung. 2002. Global production networks and the analysis of economic development. *Review of International Political Economy* 9: 436–464.

Iammarino, S. 2005. An evolutionary integrated view of Regional Systems of Innovation: Concepts, measures and historical perspectives. *European Planning Studies* 13: 497–519.

Isaksen, A. 2001. Building regional innovation systems: Is endogenous industrial development possible in the global economy? *Canadian Journal of Regional Science* 14: 101–120.

Isaksen, A. and M. Trippl. 2017. Exogenously led and policy-supported new path development in peripheral regions: Analytical and synthetic routes. *Economic Geography* 93: 436–457.

Isaksen, A. and M. Trippl. 2016. Path development in different regional innovation systems, in *Innovation Drivers and Regional Innovation Strategies*, M. Parrilli, R. Fitjar, and A. Rodríguez-Pose (eds.), 66–84. New York, NY and London: Routledge.

Isaksen, A., F. Tödtling, and M. Trippl. 2016. Innovation policies for regional structural change: Combining actor-based and system-based strategies. In *56th ERSA Congress August 23–26*. Vienna, Austria.

Kirzner, I. M. 1997. Entrepreneurial discovery and the competitive market process: An Austrian approach. *Journal of Economic Literature* 35: 60–85.

Klepper, S. 2007. Disagreements, spinoffs, and the evolution of Detroit as the capital of the U.S. automobile industry. *Management Science* 53: 616–631.

Lam, A. 2000. Tacit knowledge, organizational learning and societal institutions: An integrated framework. *Organization Studies* 21: 487–513.

MacKinnon, D. 2012. Beyond strategic coupling: Reassessing the firm-region nexus in global production networks. *Journal of Economic Geography* 12: 227–245.

Malecki, E. J. 2011. Regional social capital: Why it matters. *Regional Studies* 46: 1023–1039.

Martin, R. 2010. Roepke lecture in economic geography – Rethinking regional path dependence: Beyond lock-in to evolution. *Economic Geography* 86: 1–27.

Martin, R. and P. Sunley. 2006. Path dependence and regional economic evolution. *Journal of Economic Geography* 6: 395–437.

Maskell, P. and A. Malmberg. 1999. Localised learning and industrial competitiveness. *Cambridge Journal of Economics* 23: 167–185.

Maskell, P. and A. Malmberg. 2007. Myopia, knowledge development and cluster evolution. *Journal of Economic Geography* 7: 603–618.

Morgan, K. 2007. The learning region: Institutions, innovation and regional renewal. *Regional Studies* 41: S147–S159.

Morgan, K. 2013. Path dependence and the state. In *Re-Framing Regional Development*, P. Cooke (ed.), 318–340. London and New York, NY: Routledge.

Morgan, K. 2017. Nurturing novelty: Regional innovation policy in the age of smart specialisation. *Environment and Planning C: Government and Policy* 35: 569–583.

Murmann, J. P. 2003. *Knowledge and Competitive Advantage: The Coevolution of Firms, Technology, and National Institutions*. Cambridge: Cambridge University Press.

Nelson, R. R. 1994. The co-evolution of technology, industrial structure, and supporting institutions. *Industrial and Corporate Change* 3: 47–63.

Polanyi, M. 1958. *Personal Knowledge : Towards a Post-Critical Philosophy*. London: Routledge & Kegan Paul.

Pyke, F., G. Becattini, and W. Sengenberger. 1990. *Industrial Districts and Inter-Firm Co-Operation in Italy*. Geneva: International Institute for Labour Studies.

Schamp, E. W. 2010. On the notion of co-evolution in economic geography, in *The Handbook of Evolutionary Economic Geography*, R. Boschma and R. Martin (eds.), 432–449. Cheltenham: Edward Elgar Publishing.

Schumpeter, J. 1943. *Capitalism, Socialism and Democracy*. New York, NY: Harper.

Simmie, J. 2003. Innovation and urban regions as national and international nodes for the transfer and sharing of knowledge. *Regional Studies* 37: 607–620.

Simmie, J. 2012. Path dependence and new technological path creation in the Danish wind power industry. *European Planning Studies* 20: 753–772.

Sotarauta, M. and N. Mustikkamäki. 2015. Institutional entrepreneurship, power, and knowledge in innovation systems: Institutionalization of regenerative medicine in Tampere, Finland. *Environment and Planning C: Government and Policy* 33: 342–357.

Steen, M. and A. Karlsen. 2014. Path creation in a single-industry town: The case of Verdal and Windcluster Mid-Norway. *Norsk Geografisk Tidsskrift – Norwegian Journal of Geography* 68: 133–143.

Storper, M. 1995. The resurgence of regional economies, ten years later: The region as a nexus of untraded interdependencies. *European Urban and Regional Studies* 2: 191–221.

Strambach, S. 2010. Path dependence and path plasticity: the co-evolution of institutions and innovation – the German customized business software industry, in *The Handbook of Evolutionary Economic Geography*, R. Boschma and R. Martin (eds.), 406–429. Cheltenham: Edward Elgar.

Strambach, S. and B. Klement. 2012. Cumulative and combinatorial micro-dynamics of knowledge: The role of space and place in knowledge integration. *European Planning Studies* 20: 1843–1866.

Tanner, A. N. 2014. Regional branching reconsidered: Emergence of the fuel cell industry in European regions. *Economic Geography* 90: 403–427.

Ter Wal, A. L. J. and R. Boschma. 2011. Co-evolution of firms, industries and networks in space. *Regional Studies* 45: 919–933.

Tödtling, F. and M. Grillitsch. 2015. Does combinatorial knowledge lead to a better innovation performance of firms? *European Planning Studies* 23: 1741–1758.

Tödtling, F. and M. Trippl. 2005. One size fits all? Towards a differentiated regional innovation policy approach. *Research Policy* 34: 1203–1219.

Tödtling, F. and M. Trippl. 2013. Transformation of regional innovation systems: From old legacies to new development paths. In *Reframing Regional Development*, P. Cooke (ed.), 297–317. London: Routledge.

Trippl, M., M. Grillitsch, and A. Isaksen. 2017. Exogenous sources of regional industrial change: Attraction and absorption of non-local knowledge for new path development. *Progress in Human Geography*. DOI:10.1177/0309132517700982.

Trippl, M. and A. Otto. 2009. How to turn the fate of old industrial areas: A comparison of cluster-based renewal processes in Styria and the Saarland. *Environment and Planning. A* **41**: 1217–1233.

Weber, K. M. and H. Rohracher. 2012. Legitimizing research, technology and innovation policies for transformative change: Combining insights from innovation systems and multi-level perspective in a comprehensive 'failures' framework. *Research Policy* 41: 1037–1047.

Westlund, H. and K. Kobayashi. 2013. Social capital and sustainable urban-rural relationships in the global knowledge society, in *Social Capital and Rural Development in the Knowledge Society*, H. Westlund and K. Kobayashi (eds.), 1–17. Cheltenham: Edward Elgar.

Vitols, S. 2001. Varieties of corporate governance: Comparing Germany and the UK, in *Varieties of Capitalism: The Institutional Foundations of Comparative Advantage*, P.A. Hall and D. Soskice (eds.), 337–360. Oxford; New York, NY: Oxford University Press.

Woolthuis, R. K., M. Lankhuizen, and V. Gilsing. 2005. A system failure framework for innovation policy design. *Technovation* 25: 609–619.

Zelizer, V. A. 1978. Human values and the market: The case of life insurance and death in 19th-century America. *American Journal of Sociology* 84: 591–610.

Zukauskaite, E. and J. Moodysson. 2016. Multiple paths of development: Knowledge bases and institutional characteristics of the Swedish food sector. *European Planning Studies* 24: 589–606.

11 | *Spinoffs and Clustering*

RUSSELL GOLMAN AND STEVEN KLEPPER

11.1 Introduction

Geographic clustering of people and organizations is a fact of modern economic life. At the aggregate level, around half the world's population is located in cities. At the industry level, Ellison and Glaeser (1997) and Duranton and Overman (2005) show that in the modal manufacturing industry in the United States and UK, respectively, plants are more clustered geographically than would be expected if they located randomly. These simple facts have been widely interpreted to reflect some sort of advantage of clustering. Wages and prices are higher in cities and in industry clusters such as Silicon Valley (Rosenthal and Strange 2004; Puga 2010). Consequently, businesses in clusters must enjoy some kind of advantages in order to be competitive.

These advantages appear to extend well beyond the natural advantages that some regions have for certain types of industries, such as the weather favoring the location of the movie industry in Hollywood (Ellison and Glaeser 1999). New Economic Geography models (Fujita et al. 1999) feature the role that costs of transporting goods play in inducing people and businesses to cluster in cities. Models of industry clustering commonly feature ideas proposed by Marshall (1890) about how clustering gives rise to agglomeration economies benefiting all firms located in clusters. These economies are related to the pooling of labor, the colocation of suppliers and producers, and localized spillovers of technological knowledge (Jaffe et al. 1993; Duranton and Puga 2004). Although it is difficult to test the mechanisms underlying clustering, numerous studies find evidence consistent with the advantages of clusters, such as firms in clusters performing better, entry being concentrated in clusters, and firms in different industries clustering to a greater degree the more they share similar types of labor, inputs, and knowledge (Audretsch and Feldman 2004; Rosenthal and Strange 2004; Ellison et al. 2010; Greenstone et al. 2010; Puga 2010).

In recent years, new evidence has emerged about how industry clusters evolve that calls out for explanation. Studies of the origins of firms in the automobile, tire, semiconductor, disk drive, and biotherapeutics industries, all of which were innovative in their time and evolved to be highly clustered, reveal a similar pattern. The regions where these industries ultimately clustered had one or at most a few related successful firms early on. What distinguished them from other regions that also had successful early producers was that, subsequently, they grew through entry of new firms that were mainly spinoffs descended from their early successful producers. (We define spinoffs as entrants founded by individuals who previously worked for incumbent firms in the same industry. We refer to the firm where the primary founder last worked as the spinoff's "parent.") In a number of instances, the early successful firms receded but the region nonetheless prospered, propelled forward by successive generations of spinoffs. Geographic modelers are increasingly recognizing the importance of entrepreneurship for clustering (Glaeser et al. 2010), but mainstream theories of clustering generally abstract from such forces and thus cannot readily address the accumulating evidence connecting clustering and spinoffs. Many studies of spinoffs in the last ten years have focused on innovative manufacturing industries, where clustering is also prominent (Feldman 1994; Audretsch and Feldman 2004), and the growing body of empirical evidence regarding spinoff formation and performance is now attracting increased attention in its own right (see Klepper 2009b).

The main purpose of this article is to organize the empirical evidence on spinoffs and clustering across industries and to develop a model to explain these stylized facts. Why do firms agglomerate especially in innovative industries? Why is so much of the entry driving the growth of agglomerative clusters coming in the form of spinoffs? And why are these spinoffs typically more successful, often becoming the industry leaders? We construct a simple theory of spinoffs that is related to firms growing over time through the discovery of new submarkets based on innovation. Spinoffs are assumed to locate close to their parents, as has been commonly found, in accordance with more general findings that new firms of all kinds tend to locate close to where their founders have previously worked and resided (Figueiredo et al. 2002; Romanelli and Feldman 2006; Stam 2007). We show that spinoffs (locating near their parents) naturally generate clustering.

Our model explains why the growth of an industry in a particularly concentrated region is typically marked by spinoffs, even if they only capture profits that would have gone to their parents. A simple insight powers the model. Innovation begets more innovation in a positive feedback cycle (Arthur 1990; Danneels 2002), creating more new profit opportunities for more successful firms. When this dynamic gets going, rapid innovation opens the door for spinoffs to enter, driving the entire region's growth. Innovative capabilities are not directly observable, but when we see clusters of spinoffs, we get a strong signal about their innovative potential.

We posit that a firm's innovations build on the expertise it already has. Evolving innovative capabilities reflect organizational learning (Mitchell 2000). Our model of new business opportunities growing out of existing ones is similar in spirit to recombinant growth (Weitzman 1998), endogenous technological change (Klette and Kortum 2004), combinatorial technological evolution (Arthur 2009), and creative development (Feinstein 2017). As in Klette and Kortum (2004), in particular, business units within a firm beget new business units. The new feature here is that newly created business units may be spun off into independent firms. As innovation makes spinoff entry possible, the implication is that spinoffs initially (upon entering the industry) produce products that are similar to their parents', and thus their performance correlates with their parents' performance. If an initial entrant in a region discovers a particularly rich vein of innovations, the spinoffs that descend there will be especially well-positioned for success.

Our model does not feature traditional agglomeration economies, but does include elements of such models as part of its structure. Indeed, in our model firms do not gain any advantages from being located in a booming cluster. We provide useful baseline estimates of the Ellison-Glaeser index of agglomeration in the absence of such localized externalities. Empirical measures of agglomeration could be compared against this baseline to assess the impact of localized (pecuniary or nonpecuniary) externalities over and above what can be attributed to a natural process of innovation and spinoff formation. The article is organized as follows. In Section 11.2 we relate the accumulating evidence about spinoffs and their role in industry clustering. Section 11.3 lays out our model. In Section 11.4 we show that the existence of spinoffs leads to clustering and offer an explanation why more innovative industries tend to be more highly clustered.

In Section 11.5 we show how spinoff entry contributes to the growth of a cluster in a particular region. In Section 11.6 we show that our model is consistent with the empirical regularities about spinoff formation and performance. In Section 11.7 we offer baseline estimates of levels of agglomeration that can be attributed solely to the process of innovation and spinoff formation. Section 11.8 discusses the absence of agglomeration economies – and the prospect of incorporating them – in our model. The appendix in the original publication contains proofs of all results as well as a glossary of symbols.

11.2 Industry Evidence

We consider the evolution of five US industries that are well known for clustering: automobiles around Detroit, tires around Akron (Ohio), semiconductors and disk drives around Silicon Valley, and biotherapeutics around San Francisco, Boston, and San Diego. Each of these industries was highly innovative and grew greatly over time, attracting many entrants. Various studies have attempted to piece together the organizational and geographic heritage of the entrants in each of the industries to understand the forces giving rise to clustering. The picture that emerges is most comprehensive for autos, semiconductors, and disk drives, reflecting the availability of data on the periodic market shares of the leading producers. For the tire industry, only the heritage of producers in Ohio was traced, and for the biotherapeutics industry the analysis largely focused on the San Diego cluster. Despite differences in coverage, the patterns in the five industries are remarkably similar. They can be summarized as eleven stylized facts (Table 11.1).

Fact #1 is inspired by the observation that the five industries chosen for their famous clusters have all experienced periods of rapid innovation. Indeed, this is no coincidence. Comparing across a host of industries, those that are more innovative – say, with greater total research and development expenditure as a percentage of sales – tend to be more concentrated geographically (Audretsch and Feldman 1996, 2004).

Fact #2 indicates that the clusters in each of these five industries typically had a flagship early entrant and then grew over time through entry. For example, Olds Motor Works was the first great firm in the Detroit area. It entered in 1901 and soon became the largest firm in the industry, attaining a peak market share of 26 percent in 1905. But Detroit was much more than Olds Motor Works. Over 100 firms

Table 11.1 *Patterns of cluster growth and spinoff entry*

1. More innovative industries have more often become highly clustered.
2. Clusters typically were characterized by an early successful firm and then grew subsequently through entry.
3. A greater percentage of entrants in the clusters than elsewhere were spinoffs.
4. Spinoffs accounted for a disproportionate share of the leaders in the clusters relative to their share of entrants overall.
5. Clusters prospered after spinoffs entered, even while in some cases the flagship firm that seeded the region subsequently declined.
6. Spinoffs performed better than other entrants.
7. Larger firms spawned spinoffs at a higher rate.
8. Spinoffs from larger firms were superior performers.
9. Spinoffs that entered at a larger size tended to perform better.
10. Spinoffs in clusters outperformed spinoffs elsewhere.
11. Spinoffs initially produced similar types of products as their parents.

entered in the Detroit area after Olds through 1924 (after which entry into the industry was negligible). By 1915, eleven of these firms were among the largest fifteen firms in the industry and the collective market share of the Detroit leaders was 83 percent (Klepper 2007, 2009a, 2010). Fairchild Semiconductor was the analog of Olds Motor Works in the semiconductor industry. It entered in 1957 and grew to be the second largest firm in the industry by 1966, when its market share peaked at 13 percent. Over 100 other firms entered the semiconductor industry in the Silicon Valley area from 1957 to 1986, and as of 1985, eight of the top sixteen firms with a collective market share of 42 percent were based in the Silicon Valley area (Klepper 2009a, 2010). BF Goodrich and IBM were the flagship firms in the Akron and Silicon Valley clusters in the tire and disk drives industries, respectively, both of which were spurred forward by entrants following the success of these two pioneers (Christensen 1993; McKendrick et al. 2000; Buenstorf and Klepper 2009). Hybritech appears to have played a similar role in the San Diego biotherapeutics cluster (Mitton 1990).

Facts #3 and 4 indicate that the entrants that fueled the growth of the clusters were disproportionately spinoffs of indigenous producers.[1]

---

[1] There are always some entrants that are challenging to classify, and the various studies document how these cases were handled.

The most extreme case was semiconductors. Every one of the leaders of the industry that were based in Silicon Valley was a spinoff of a Silicon Valley incumbent, which is not surprising given that nearly all the entrants in Silicon Valley were spinoffs of indigenous semiconductor firms. In contrast, most of the leaders of the industry based outside of Silicon Valley were experienced electronics producers and diversifiers from other industries, reflecting the much higher percentage of entrants outside Silicon Valley with these backgrounds (Klepper 2009a, 2010). Similarly, in autos and disk drives a much higher percentage of the entrants in Detroit and Silicon Valley than elsewhere were spinoffs,[2] and nearly all the later leaders in the two clusters were spinoffs of indigenous firms (Agarwal et al. 2004; Franco and Filson 2006; Klepper 2007, 2010). The percentage of entrants that were spinoffs in the biotherapeutics industry was also markedly higher in the San Diego, San Francisco, and Boston clusters than elsewhere (Romanelli and Feldman 2006), as was true as well for tire entrants originating around Akron versus the rest of Ohio (Buenstorf and Klepper 2009). These firms predominantly originated from incumbent firms located close by.

Fact #5 reflects that clusters prospered (i.e. grew faster than other regions) after spinoffs entered and became industry leaders, even though in the autos, semiconductors, and disk drive clusters the early flagship companies in these regions declined (Christensen 1993; Klepper 2009a). The semiconductor industry is particularly interesting because it allows for the construction of a counterfactual case involving an early flagship company in another region that did not give birth to so many spinoffs. The leading firm in the industry for many years was Texas Instruments (TI), which entered before Fairchild in 1952 in Dallas. TI and Fairchild were the pioneers of high performance silicon transistors and integrated circuits (ICs). Ultimately, Fairchild's management was overwhelmed by the wave of innovations it discovered, as discussed later. This tsunami sustained several spinoffs (and eventually sank the firm). TI had far fewer spinoffs than Fairchild (and did not decline like Fairchild) (Klepper 2009a). Of course, Silicon Valley and not Dallas became the center of the industry, suggesting that the flood

---

[2] Almost half of all spinoffs in the disk drive industry located in Silicon Valley (Kenney and von Burg 1999), whereas early pioneers in the industry were distributed across many other cities, including Tulsa, Minneapolis, and San Antonio, and were especially prominent in Los Angeles (Christensen 1993).

of spinoffs that emerged from Fairchild might actually have spurred the growth of the semiconductor cluster in Silicon Valley.

Fact #6 is that spinoffs were distinctive performers. In the automobile industry, spinoffs accounted for about half of firms classified as leaders of the industry between 1895 and 1966 despite making up only 20 percent of the 725 entrants (Klepper 2007). The performance of spinoffs is similar for semiconductor entrants (Klepper 2009a). The disk drive industry is an extreme case, with nearly all of the leading producers as of 1989 having descended from IBM over a period of about thirty years (Franco and Filson 2006). The available data for tires and biotherapeutics also seems consistent with this general pattern (Romanelli and Feldman 2006; Buenstorf and Klepper 2009).

Given the importance of spinoffs in all the industries, it is worthwhile stepping back for a moment to discuss the forces contributing to spinoffs. The studies of these industries discuss the circumstances behind many of the leading spinoffs. Many seem to have been founded due to some kind of disagreement in the parent firm about new technological ideas or management practices. It was not uncommon for leading firms to be managed by technologists with limited ability to assess the market potential of new ideas (Agarwal et al. 2004; Lécuyer 2006; Klepper 2007, 2009a). In other instances, individuals with limited industry experience gained control of leading firms; this occurred especially after the firms were acquired by firms in other industries (Klepper 2007, 2009a). These circumstances conspired at times to make firms unwilling to pursue ideas that turned out to have significant market potential. Sometimes others outside the firm could better evaluate the prospects of these ideas and would sponsor efforts by employees that worked on the ideas to form their own spinoff companies to pursue the ideas (Klepper 2007, 2009a). Fairchild illustrates these themes. It suffered three notable managerial mistakes. First, while managed by technologists with little management experience, it developed the first ICs but did not recognize their market potential (Moore and Davis 2004). Second, it was controlled by a defense contractor with little appreciation for the semiconductor industry's use of stock options as incentives. And third, it established R&D and manufacturing at separate locations and had difficulty mediating conflict between the divisions, making innovating difficult (Bassett 2002). Each of these disagreements caused top employees to leave and form spinoffs, including, famously, Intel (Lécuyer 2006). Fairchild was perhaps an extreme case, but other firms such as Olds Motor Works suffered similar conflicts that led to many spinoffs (Klepper 2007). Conflicts, even at well-established firms, are inevitable, and they appear to arise unpredictably.

Despite the ubiquity of disagreements in the origins of spinoffs, the existence of spinoffs does not indicate incompetence at the parent firm. Quite the contrary. As facts #7 and 8 indicate, the largest firms spawned spinoffs at the highest rate, and their spinoffs were superior performers. Fairchild was the exemplar. Among the seven leading semiconductor producers in Silicon Valley other than Fairchild as of 1985, five were spinoffs of Fairchild and the other two were founded by employees of other semiconductor firms that previously had worked at Fairchild (Klepper 2009a, 2010). Fairchild spawned so many spinoffs that its offspring were cleverly dubbed the Fairchildren.

IBM and its successful descendants had a similar effect on the disk drive industry.[3] Of forty spinoffs that entered the disk drive industry by 1993, twenty-eight had parents that ranked among the top ten leaders by market share at some point between 1976 and 1992, including nine out of the ten spinoffs that themselves made it onto this elite list (Franco and Filson 2006). These firms also survived longer than spinoffs with less distinguished parents.[4] As an example of this star-studded lineage, the very top firm in 1992, Conner, was a spinoff of Seagate (the top firm for much of the late 1980s), whose lineage traces through Shugart Associates, Memorex, and eventually back to IBM, all industry leaders at some point (Franco and Filson 2006).

In autos, all the leading spinoffs in the Detroit area either descended from Olds Motor Works or from three other early leaders, Cadillac, Ford, and Buick, that benefited from subcontracting from Olds (Klepper 2007). Similarly, tire spinoffs founded by individuals that had worked for the big three Akron firms – Goodrich, Goodyear, and Firestone – survived markedly longer than other spinoffs (Buenstorf and Klepper 2009). No information is reported about the performance of spinoffs in biotherapeutics, but similar to the other industries, the lead early producer in the San Diego cluster, Hybritech, was a fertile source of spinoffs with thirteen descendants over its first ten years (Mitton 1990).

---

[3] The spinoffs of a firm and all the spinoffs of its spinoffs are called the firm's descendants.

[4] Our calculations draw on data presented in Christensen's (1993) table 3 and figure 7, as well as Franco and Filson's (2006) table 1.

A few other stylized facts based on more limited data can also be established. Fact #9 is based on data on the entry sizes of spinoffs that were compiled for the automobile and tire industries (Klepper 2007, 2010; Buenstorf and Klepper 2009). In both industries, spinoffs that entered at larger sizes and had larger parents (at their time of entry) turned out to be superior performers. Fact #10, that spinoffs located in clusters performed better than spinoffs outside of these clusters, also relies on data on survival rates in the automobile and tire industries (Klepper 2007, 2010; Buenstorf and Klepper 2009), and accords with a study of Dutch publishing firms located inside and outside of Amsterdam (Heebels and Boschma 2011). Fact #11 is based on data that were compiled for the semiconductor and disk drive industries about the types of products that firms produced (Franco and Filson 2006; Klepper et al. 2011).[5] Not surprisingly, spinoffs initially produced products more like those produced by their parents than other firms in their industry.

These eleven facts reflect the key patterns about spinoffs and clustering that our model will address.

11.3 Innovation and Industrial Evolution

An industry is assumed to be composed of niches or submarkets that are discovered through innovation. Each submarket possesses certain characteristics or attributes, and we can identify a submarket by specifying its attributes. There is an uncountably infinite set S of possible attributes, and we represent a submarket as a finite subset $x \subset S$. That is, the set of attributes present in a submarket $\{s : s \in x\}$ fully characterizes that submarket, x. We let $|x|$ denote the number of attributes that describe and together define submarket x.[6] For simplicity, we assume that the existence of one submarket has no effect on the demand or costs in other submarkets.

New submarkets are discovered through innovation. A firm may innovate on any of its submarkets by incorporating a single new attribute. So, a firm with expertise in submarket x may discover a new submarket $x' = x \cup \{s\}$ for any $s \in S \backslash x$. This does not destroy the

---

[5] Data on the laser industry also support the overlap between the initial products of spinoffs and those of their parents (Klepper and Sleeper 2005).

[6] We might think of this as the complexity of the submarket.

preexisting submarket x. The firm simply may expand into the new submarket x' as well. We assume that a continuous probability distribution on S determines which attribute $\underline{s}$ is incorporated in the discovery of a new submarket.[7]

Our core idea is that the process of innovation is based on firms building on what they know. Because newly discovered attributes are combined with existing submarkets, a firm's innovative capabilities evolve as the firm gains experience in more submarkets. Firms thus expand into new submarkets that are related to submarkets with which they already have experience – related in the sense that they share one or more common attributes. This conforms to the insight that diversified firms generally develop products in related submarkets (Nelson and Winter 1982; Montgomery 1994). Let $X_{j,t}$ denote the set of submarkets that firm j has entered at time t and $N_{j,t}$ denote the number of these submarkets. We will explain later how a firm enters the industry and discovers its first submarket.

Innovations (by incumbents) are discovered according to a continuous-time Poisson branching process with mean intensity λ. The parameter λ captures the rate of incumbent innovation in the industry. For each submarket in which a firm already produces, the probability of the firm discovering a new submarket in the time interval dt is λdt. Then the expected number of new submarkets firm j discovers in time interval dt is $N_{j,t}\lambda dt$. Thus, more diversified firms tend to discover innovations more rapidly.

The demand in a new submarket depends on the attributes of that submarket as well as some degree of randomness. We represent the inverse demand function in submarket x as $p = \bar{p}(x) - mq$, where p is the price of the product, $q \geq 0$ is the total quantity demanded of the product (at any time), m is a parameter that sets the units for the quantity produced, and for any submarket x, the value of $\bar{p}(x)$ is a random draw on the price at which demand emerges. As described presently, the distribution of $\bar{p}(x)$ varies across submarkets (i.e. depends on the attributes they possess), but the random draws are independent (given these attributes). The unit cost of production in each submarket is k.

---

[7] Formally, we assume a non-atomic probability measure μ on S. That is, for any measurable set $\hat{S}$, the probability that the newly discovered attribute comes from this set is $Prob(\underline{s} \in \hat{S}) = \mu(\hat{S})$. The assumption that μ is non-atomic, along with the earlier assumption that S is uncountable, simply helps us avoid the case that the same exact submarket is discovered multiple times.

A firm monopolizes any submarket it discovers and so produces the monopoly output $q_m(x) = \frac{\bar{p}(x)-k}{2m}$ (as long as this is nonnegative) and charges the monopoly price $p_m(x) = \frac{\bar{p}(x)+k}{2m}$, which yields a revenue stream of $\frac{(\bar{p}(x))^2-k^2}{4m}$ and a profit stream of $\frac{(\bar{p}(x)-k)^2}{4m}$.[8]

Let $\underline{\eta}(x) = \max\left(\frac{\bar{p}(x)-k}{2m}, 0\right)$, so the firm's submarket output is $\underline{\eta}(x)$ and its profits are $m\left(\underline{\eta}(x)\right)^2$. If it turns out that $\underline{\eta}(x) = 0$, then the firm simply decides not to enter submarket x after all, and in the case of an arriving startup attempting to enter the industry, the firm would not be able to form. A firm's total output (or revenue / profit respectively) is simply the sum of the output (revenue / profit) it produces in each of its submarkets. So, letting $\pi_{j,t}$ denote the profit firm j earns at time t, we have

$$\pi_{j,t} = \sum_{x \in X_{j,t}} m\left(\underline{\eta}(x)\right)^2$$

The value of $\underline{\eta}(x)$ is determined by the value of $\bar{p}(x)$. We find it convenient to characterize the distribution of $\underline{\eta}(x)$ directly rather than through that of $\bar{p}(x)$. To do so, we introduce parameters z_s indicating the quality of any attribute s. In general, we assume that the distribution of $\underline{\eta}(x)$ is strictly increasing (in the sense of shifting its cumulative distribution function strictly downward at every point) in z_s for each $s \in x$, i.e. demand (and profit) is increasing with the quality of each attribute of the submarket. We let S_z denote the set of attributes having quality z. We assume some heterogeneity in quality, i.e. that $Prob(\underline{s} \in S_z) < 1$ for all z. The quality parameters are not directly observable, but realized profits in a submarket provide a signal of their values. We also do assume a nontrivial probability that any submarket x fails (i.e. generates no demand),

$$0 < Prob\left(\underline{\eta}(x)\right) < 1.$$

A specific example of a distribution that satisfies our assumptions for $\underline{\eta}(x)$ is the mixed geometric distribution,

---

[8] We could work out a similar profit function if the innovating firm were, say, a Stackelberg leader, but the monopolistic framework is simplest.

$$\text{Prob}\left(\underline{\eta}(x) = \eta\right) = \frac{1}{|x|} \sum_{s \in x} z_s^{\eta}(1 - z_s) \text{ for } \eta \in \{0, 1, 2, \dots\}.$$

With this functional form assumption, the probability that sub-market x is a success (i.e. generates positive demand) is simply the average of the quality parameters of its attributes, $\text{Prob}\left(\underline{\eta}(x) = \eta\right) = \frac{1}{|x|} \sum_{s \in x} z_s = \bar{z}_x$. For this distribution we find it reasonable to restrict $z_s \in (0, \frac{1}{2}]$ for all s as an acknowledgment that most innovations fail. We will make clear when we rely on this specific functional form.

The realizations of output $\underline{\eta}(x)$ in each submarket x are of course independent events. Yet, interestingly, related submarkets will appear to have correlated outputs (and profits) because they both depend on some of the same attributes. If $\underline{x}$ and $\underline{x}'$ refer to randomly chosen submarkets, then there will be positive correlation in their outputs $\underline{\eta}(\underline{x})$ and $\underline{\eta}(\underline{x}')$ whenever there is a possibility that these submarkets $\underline{x}$ and $\underline{x}'$ share common attributes.[9] Indeed, we have assumed that firms grow by discovering submarkets that share common attributes, so the profits in different submarkets discovered by the same firm will be positively correlated. The growth of a firm is path dependent because expansion into new submarkets depends on which submarkets it has already entered and because the profitability of these new submarkets correlates with the profitability of existing, related submarkets.

As discussed in Section 11.2, firms cannot always recognize the prospects of their innovations and sometimes fail to pursue promising submarkets. There are myriad reasons why this might occur, but our model does not require specification of the particular reason why an incumbent firm may be unable to enter a newly discovered submarket. We simply recognize that this may occur, and when it does, employees who contributed to the discovery of the innovation may then leave their old firm and form a spinoff (typically with financial support from another individual or company that can better evaluate the prospects of the innovation). Accordingly, we assume there is a probability $\alpha > 0$ that a firm will not pursue a newly discovered submarket x' (regardless

---

[9] Moreover, the more closely related the submarkets (holding fixed their complexity), as captured by the fraction of shared attributes, the greater the correlation (in their values of $\underline{\eta}$ and) in their profits.

of its attributes) and that employees at that firm break off on their own to pursue it. Then, if it turns out that $\eta(x') > 0$, they form a spinoff, which enters the submarket and hence the industry. The spinoff can continue to innovate on x', while the incumbent remains in the preexisting submarket x. Denote the number of spinoffs firm j spawns during the interval (t,t') as $\sigma_j(t,t')$.

Of course, new firms in the industry are sometimes formed by entrepreneurs with backgrounds outside of the industry. (Industry pioneers, for example, must by definition be outside entrants.) These outside startups, without expertise in any existing submarket, are assumed to enter an "entry-level" or single-attribute submarket with the attribute drawn from the aforementioned probability distribution on S. We let $\kappa(t)$ denote the mean arrival rate of outside startups at time t, with actual arrivals independent random events.

When a new firm enters the industry, it locates in one of R regions. We assume that the region in which an outside startup enters is random, with the probability of locating in any particular region r being equal to the share of economic activity in the region (across all industries), denoted as f_r. Spinoffs, however, locate in the same region as their parents. We will make use of the indicator variable $u_{j,r} = 1$ if firm j is located in region r and 0 otherwise. Aggregating by region simply involves summing over the firms in existence at time t, which we denote $\{1, ..., J_t\}$. So, $\varpi_{r,t} = \sum_j u_{j,r} \pi_{j,t}$ denotes the total profits in region r at time t, and $\varsigma_r(t,t') = \sum_j u_{j,r} \sigma_j(t,t'v)$ denotes the number of spinoffs forming in region r during the interval (t,t').[10] We denote the first entrant in region r as $\hat{j}_r$.

The fundamental insight underlying the process of spinoff formation is that spinoffs originate within incumbent firms from new ideas. Because spinoff formation is tied to innovation and innovations incorporate some already-known attributes into new submarkets, our model has built in the feature that spinoffs initially produce products that are similar to their parents', i.e. that are in related submarkets (Fact #11). Of course, after a spinoff enters the industry, it can then continue to

---

[10] The splitting probability α has no effect on regional profits (or output), but it does affect the number of firms in each region.

innovate on its own. While the spinoff's and parent's product lines will always share a common thread, they may gradually diverge.

We have accommodated Fact #11 directly, but the remaining facts in the list require explanation. In the following sections we work through the implications of the model and relate them to these stylized facts. We first tackle the occurrence of clusters, a notable phenomenon in and of itself.

11.4 Clustering

In this section we examine the phenomenon of clustering. We show that the formation of spinoffs implies that we can expect some clustering, and we then address Fact #1.

Ellison and Glaeser (1997) point out that some degree of geographic concentration in an industry is to be expected as a result of the lumpiness of plants, apart from any agglomerative forces that might contribute to clustering. Intuitively, if there are only a limited number of plants, then an industry's activity must be unevenly distributed in geographic space. For simplicity, we assume that all firms operate only one plant. Let $\theta_{j,t}$ denote the market share[11] of firm j at time t and let $\vartheta_{r,t} = \sum_j u_{j,r} \theta_{j,t}$ denote the market share of all firms located in region r at time t. Let $H_t = \sum_j \theta_{j,t}^2$ denote the industry Herfindahl index at time t. A standard measure of clustering at any point in time t is $L_t = \sum_r (\vartheta_{r,t} - f_r)^2$. Following Ellison and Glaeser, we can calculate the expected value of L_t, conditional on the firm-size distribution, in the case that (contrary to our assumption that spinoffs locate in the same region as their parent) all firms choose their locations independently with probability f_r of selecting region r.

Lemma 1 (Ellison and Glaeser (1997)) *If every firm were to independently locate in a region r according to the probability f_r, then*

$$E(L_t| J_t, \theta_{1,t}, ..., \theta_{J_t, t}) = \left(1 - \sum_r f_r^2\right) H_t.$$

Ellison and Glaeser thus propose an index of geographic concentration

---

[11] We could specify market share by output, revenue, or profit without affecting our results. We make use of the normalization $\sum_j \Theta_{j,t} = 1$.

$$\gamma_t = \frac{L_t - \left(1 - \sum_r f_f^2\right) H_t}{\left(1 - \sum_r f_f^2\right)(1 - H_t)}$$

that controls for the size distribution of firms. The index is normalized to have mean value $E(\gamma_t) = 0$ in the case that all firms choose their locations randomly (as if by throwing darts at a map) with no natural geographic advantages or industry-specific agglomerative forces. By Lemma, if there were no spinoffs, then there would be no clustering (beyond random fluctuation) in our model (i.e. we would have $E(\gamma_t) = 0$).

Using Ellison and Glaeser's index, we can establish that in our model, in which the only agglomerative force is the locational inertia of spinoffs, industries that have experienced spinoffs are expected to be clustered (see Corollary 1). Indeed, if we know the heritage of all firms in the industry, we can work out the expected value of the Ellison-Glaeser index. For any outside startup j^0, define $\beta(j^0)$ to be the set including the firm and all of its descendants (i.e. its spinoffs and spinoffs of its spinoffs, etc.). Let

$$\hat{\theta}_{j^0,t} = \sum_{j \in \beta j^0} \theta_{j,t}$$ denote the combined market share of these firms, and let

$$\hat{H}_t = \sum_{j^0} \hat{\theta}_{j^0,t}^2 \text{ (summing just over the outside startups)}.$$

Theorem 1

$$E(\gamma_t | J_t \theta_{1,t}, \dots, \beta(j^0)_{\{1,\dots,J_t\}}) = \frac{\hat{H}_t - H_t}{1 - H_t}$$

As a corollary of Theorem, we have:

Corollary 1

$$E(\gamma_t \mid \sum_r \varsigma_r(0, t)) > 0 \text{ if and only if } \sum_r \varsigma_r(0, t) > 0$$

Corollary 1 states that conditional on the existence of (one or more) spinoffs, an industry has a positive expected level of geographic concentration. Intuitively, if spinoffs locate in the same region as their parent, then firms will be more clustered in regions with successful initial entrants than would be expected randomly. We can think of it as a special case of firms being attracted to regions by the presence of others – specifically it is spinoffs being "attracted" to regions by the presence of their parents.

Spinoff formation requires two events: discovery of a successful submarket and splitting the resulting activity off from the parent firm. Only the first event – the innovation – contributes to the growth of industrial activity in those regions that initially get ahead. Yet Ellison and Glaeser's perspective is to take the firm size distribution as given and to correct for it when measuring the industry's concentration. From that perspective, in effect controlling for submarket discovery, the latter event – splitting activity off from the parent to form the spinoff – generates higher measured concentration only by distorting the correction for the finite sample of discrete-size firms. In our model, the profits generated by spinoffs could just as well have been generated by their parents if they had been able to follow through on their innovations, but the spinoff entry leads to the industry having more small firms and thus appearing to be more clustered because we over count the number of independent location choices. Still, as we explain in the next section, spinoff entry indicates fertile ground for innovation, which tends to lead to continued growth.

Now that we have established that clustering is a feature of our model, we can address the pattern that more innovative industries tend to become more clustered.

Theorem 2   *At any time t, $E(\gamma_t)$ is increasing in λ.*

In accordance with Fact #1, our model predicts that the expected level of geographic concentration in an industry is increasing in the pace of incumbent innovation. The intuition is that more innovative industries provide more opportunities for spinoffs to form, and it is (only) spinoffs that give rise to clustering. (Alternatively, as we decrease the rate of innovation and the number of outside startups gets large relative to the number of spinoffs, clustering eventually vanishes.) It is not surprising that industries like semiconductors and automobiles exhibit the most extreme clustering. They are famously innovative industries that underwent rapid expansion, and with so many new ideas being pursued – as well as not being pursued – by incumbent firms, they naturally had opportunities for spinoffs and hence ended up highly clustered.

11.5 The Growth of a Cluster

Having established in Section 11.4 that clustering will occur in our model, especially in innovative industries, we now shift our focus to the origins of a cluster in a particular region. Recall that Facts #2–5 tell a story of large business clusters prominently featuring spinoffs. Two main results in this section, Theorems 3 and 4, show what appears to be a virtuous cycle with spinoffs and regional growth. A region's market share is predictive of the birth of spinoffs, and spinoffs are predictive of a region's growth. These results directly address Facts #3 and #5, respectively. Underlying both phenomena, according to our model, is a process of innovation with inherent positive feedback. New innovations build on previous innovations, and they lead to spinoffs and to growth. This self-reinforcing dynamic can over time amplify an initial advantage in one particular region, an implication (Theorem) that conforms with Fact #2. We will defer discussion of Fact #4 to Section 11.6, after we have presented results about the correlates of successful spinoffs. We will come to see this fact as a natural consequence of a few other stylized facts in our list.

After recognizing that semiconductors and autos are natural candidates for clustering, we might still ask, why Silicon Valley or why Detroit? How does a particular region come to lead an industry? The key ingredient, according to our model, is innovation, and with innovation come spinoffs. Spinoffs should then be more common in highly active regions:

Theorem 3   *For any region r and times $t'' > t' \geq t$,*

$$cov\left(\varpi_{r,t}, \varsigma_r(t', t'')\right) > 0$$

Theorem states that there is a positive correlation between a region's share of the profits in the industry at a given time and the number of spinoffs subsequently spawned there. Intuitively, regions with greater market share are expected to generate more innovations and hence more spinoffs. On the other hand, for any particular region the rate of entry of outside startups is independent of the market share of the region. We thus have a very straightforward account of the stylized fact that a greater percentage of the entrants in clusters than elsewhere are spinoffs (Fact #3).

We have accounted for the pattern of spinoffs springing up in clusters, but, in addition, we observe spinoffs playing a dominant role in the growth of a cluster. In order to characterize a region's growth in our model, we introduce a bit of notation. Let $\Delta\varpi_{j,t,\Delta}t$ denote the (profit) growth of firm j during the interval $(t, t + \Delta t)$. Similarly, let $\Delta\varpi_{r,t,\Delta}t$ denote the growth of region r during the interval $(t, t + \Delta t)$.

It is straightforward to see that firms' ability to innovate on each of the submarkets they have already entered, as well as the correlation in profits between related submarkets, means that larger firms tend to grow more in absolute terms. Firm growth is approximately, but not precisely, in accordance with Gibrat's law, i.e. proportional to current size.[12] Similarly, by aggregation of all firms in a region, larger regions also tend to grow more in absolute terms. This means we often want to control for the current size of a region when examining the absolute growth of a region.

Even after controlling for the current size of a region, the number of spinoffs in the region should in our model correlate with the region's subsequent growth. We can establish this result formally in the case that there is no heterogeneity in the quality parameters (i.e. no uncertainty about the quality of each of the attributes discovered in the region). Let $X_{r,t} = \cup_{j:u_j,r=1} X_{j,t}$ denote the set of submarkets that firms in region r have entered at time t.

Theorem 4   *For any region r, time t and interval $\Delta t > 0$, and any quality z (that we shall assume characterizes all attributes discovered in the region) satisfying*

$$\text{Prob}(\underline{s} \in S_z) > 0,$$

$$\text{cov}(\varsigma_r(0, t), \Delta\varpi_{r,t,\Delta t} \,|\, \varpi_{r,t}, \cup X_{r,t} \subset S_z) > 0$$

In Theorem 4 we are conditioning on the quality of the attributes discovered by firms in the region, but not on the identity of these attributes, by restricting innovations to a subset of attributes with homogeneous quality. The theorem states that conditional on this homogeneous attribute quality and on a region's total profit, there is

---

[12] Firms pursue new submarkets in proportion to their current number of submarkets, but the profits generated in each submarket, while positively correlated within a firm or within a region, experience some reversion to the mean as well. This means that the relative growth rate of larger firms is less than that of smaller firms.

a positive correlation between the number of spinoffs that have formed in the region and the region's subsequent growth in profits. This conforms with Fact #5, which indicates that spinoffs stimulate the growth of highly clustered regions.

Intuitively, comparing two regions with the same total profits, the one with more past spinoffs can be expected to have discovered more new submarkets. Assuming no heterogeneity in the quality parameters allows us to fully attribute the success of the region with less spinoffs to a high (random) realization of demand as opposed to high quality of innovations discovered there in the past. The latter would bear on the future growth of the region (through the quality of the submarkets subsequently discovered there), which can now be ruled out. So, the region with more spinoffs would typically continue to be more innovative and to experience more subsequent growth.

The assumption of homogeneous quality simplifies our analysis, but is not a necessary condition. The higher realizations of demand in the region with fewer spinoffs signal higher quality parameters, but the relative lack of spinoffs itself signals the contrary. The net signal is equivocal. Moreover, newly discovered submarkets will gradually diverge from existing ones, so the quality of past innovations matters less over time. On the other hand, the greater pace of innovation in the region with more spinoffs continues to reinforce itself.

With this insight we can return to the exemplary Silicon Valley semiconductor cluster and address the question of what gives rise to such powerful growth. In particular, why did Silicon Valley grow faster than Dallas when both regions once had similar market shares and successful flagship firms? Theorem 4 suggests a particularly simple account: Silicon Valley had more spinoffs. Merely splitting off economic activity into separate corporate entities might not fundamentally cause explosive growth, but it might well indicate particularly fertile ground for innovation and hence for explosive growth.[13] Both Fairchild in Silicon Valley and Texas Instruments in Dallas discovered rich veins in which to innovate, openings into submarkets which would turn out to be immensely profitable. Yet perhaps the entry of so many

---

[13] Consistent with this account, regions with many small firms (alongside at least one big firm) are more innovative (i.e. produce more cited patents) and have a higher rate of spinoff formation than regions without so many small firms, even after controlling for the size of (i.e. the number of inventors in) each region (Agrawal et al. 2014).

spinoffs from Fairchild suggests that these firms had more innovative opportunities, that they were better positioned to discover the next great innovations that would drive the growth of Silicon Valley ahead of Dallas.

We have shown that in our model spinoffs accompany the growth of a cluster in a virtuous cycle. Discovery of new submarkets is at the heart of the spinoff process just as it also pumps up the growth of a region. To see how this process might get started, we apply Theorem 4 to the case of a region gaining its first firm in the industry. The size (profits) upon entry of the initial entrant in a region is predictive of the number of spinoffs subsequently spawned in that region. Letting t_j^0 be the time at which firm j formed (and $t_{j_r}^0$ specifically be the first time a firm formed in region r):

Theorem 5   *For any region r and times $t'' > t' > t_{j_r}^0$,*

$$\text{cov}\left(\pi_{j_r, t_{j_r}^0}, \varsigma_r(t', t'')\right) > 0.$$

Theorem 5 states that there is positive correlation between the profit upon entry of the initial firm in a region and the number of spinoffs subsequently spawned in the region. This means that regions with flagship firms (industry leading initial entrants) are expected to have more spinoff entrants. The profit of the initial entrant is a signal of the quality of the first attribute discovered in the region. This attribute will influence the quality of future submarkets discovered in the region, which in turn conditions whether potential spinoffs will actually form after an incumbent (potential parent) firm does not pursue a new submarket. Theorem 5 thus provides an account for the connection of flagship firms in a region and the subsequent number of spinoffs there (Fact #2).

11.6 Spinoff Entry and Performance

Sections 11.4 and 11.5 have shown how our model accounts for the remarkable connection between booming industry clusters and spinoffs. Still, it remains to show that our model accords with the observed patterns about spinoff formation and performance, as described by Facts #6–10, as well as Fact #4. We now derive results that illustrate these patterns as they arise in our model.

Some additional notation will help us present these results. Let $\underline{j}_t$ be a randomly selected firm drawn uniformly from among all firms in existence at time t, i.e. from $\{1, ..., J_t\}$. When we don't care about the particular time t at which the draw is made, we may neglect the subscript. Conditioning on the type of firm selected, we identify a randomly selected outside startup as $\underline{j}^0$ and a randomly selected spinoff firm as $\underline{j}^s$.

We begin with the pattern that spinoffs on average tend to be better performers (i.e. more profitable at every age) than other entrants. For this particular result, we adopt the specific functional form of the mixed geometric distribution for a submarket's output along with the restriction that most innovations fail. Our model then implies that spinoffs do better than outside startups.

Theorem 6   *Assume that for any submarket x, output $\eta(x)$ has a mixed geometric distribution, and restrict $z_s \in (0, \frac{1}{2}]$ for all s. At any age τ,*

$$E(\pi_{\underline{j}^s, \tau + t^0_{\underline{j}^s}}) > E(\pi_{\underline{j}^0, \tau + t^0_{\underline{j}^0}})$$

In accordance with Fact #6, our model predicts that spinoffs tend to be more profitable at any given age than outside startups at the same age. The intuition is that spinoffs are more likely to enter near a higher performing segment of submarkets. The fact that a firm is a spinoff instead of an outside startup carries information. The spinoff necessarily enters the industry in a submarket similar (in terms of shared attributes) to some other submarket that has already proven to be successful for its parent. Because these attributes are incorporated into the innovations the spinoff subsequently pursues, demand tends to be higher in the submarkets the spinoff enters than in randomly discovered submarkets stemming from an entry-level submarket. Consequently, the spinoff is expected to be more profitable than an outside startup.

Our model also predicts that firms with greater profits (or, similarly, greater market share) tend to spawn more spinoffs.

Theorem 7   *For times $t'' > t' \geq t$ and any firm j selected at time t,*

$$\text{cov}\left(\pi_{j,t}, \sigma_j(t', t'')\right) > 0$$

Theorem 7 states that there is a positive correlation between firm profits at a given time and the number of spinoffs that the firm subsequently spawns. This result is consistent with Fact #7. Intuitively, expanding into more submarkets adds to profits and also creates more opportunities for discovering innovations that occasionally lead to spinoffs. Additionally, finding high quality submarkets both increases current profits and also increases the likelihood that future innovations will be successful, thereby further enabling spinoff entry. As profits follow revenue and, more fundamentally, output, the same argument could be used to show a positive correlation between market share and subsequent spinoffs.

We can identify multiple factors that influence the quality of our spinoffs. Our model predicts that more successful spinoffs tend to have more successful parents. Additionally, spinoffs that are initially more successful tend to do better subsequently. Letting $\rho(j^s)$ denote the parent firm from which the spinoff j^s formed, we have:

Theorem 8   *For any spinoff j^s, profit upon entry correlates with its parent's profit:*

$$\text{cov}\left(\pi_{j^s,t_{j^s}^0}, \pi_{\rho(j^s),t_{j^s}^0}\right)$$

Moreover, both profit upon entry and parent's profit are predictive of a spinoff's subsequent profit growth.[14] *For any firm age τ, and over any time span $\Delta t > 0$, we have*

$$\text{cov}(\Delta\pi_{j^s,\tau+t_{j^s}^0,\Delta t}, \pi_{j^s,t_{j^s}^0} \mid \pi_{\rho(j^s),t_{j^s}^0}) > 0$$

and

$$\text{cov}(\Delta\pi_{j^s,\tau+t_{j^s}^0,\Delta t}, \pi_{\rho(j^s),t_{j^s}^0} \mid \pi_{j^s,t_{j^s}^0})$$

Theorem 8 indicates a positive correlation between a spinoff's profit upon entry and its parent firm's profit at that time, as well as between a spinoff's profit growth over time and both its profit upon entry and its parent's profit at that time, even after controlling for the other factor. The same correlations exist with revenues in place of profits. The correlation between a spinoff's performance and its parent's accords with Fact #8. The additional correlation with the spinoff's initial performance upon entry accords with Fact #9. Intuitively, because spinoffs enter the industry producing in submarkets that are

---

[14]   The positive correlation between profit growth and profit upon entry actually extends to all firms, not just to spinoffs.

related to their parents' (i.e. they initially enter a submarket that shares all but one of its attributes with one of the parent's submarkets), the demands in their submarkets are correlated, so we find that better-performing parent firms breed better-performing spinoffs. On top of this, starting with high initial profit is another good omen because it too signals that the firm may have found a rich vein in which to innovate, i.e. attributes that are retained in all their future innovations may have high quality, and thus demand in subsequently discovered submarkets is more likely to be strong. Moreover, even after controlling for the size (profits) of the parent, the size (profits) of the entire region should still be predictive of the profitability of a new spinoff. The same reasoning as in Theorem 8 applies here as well. The success of the entire region provides another informative signal about the quality of the attributes that (partially) characterize the submarkets that the spinoff will enter.

Theorem 9   *For any spinoff j^s in any region r (i.e., with $u_{j^s,r} = 1$) and any time $t' > t^0_{j^s}$,*

$$\lim_{t \nearrow t^0_{j^s}} \mathrm{cov}(\varpi_{r,t}, \pi_{j^s,t'} \,|\, \pi_{\rho(j^s),t^0_{j^s}}) > 0$$

Theorem 9 states that conditional on the parent's profit at the time it spawns a spinoff, there is still positive correlation between the total profit in the region at that time and the spinoff's profit subsequently. Looking to the extremely successful regions once again, we find that new spinoffs tend to be most successful in the leading (most highly clustered) region, as Fact #10 indicated.

Finally, we may return to Fact #4. The general pattern that spinoffs disproportionately became the industry leaders in the largest clusters follows naturally from two results already established: Spinoffs generally outperform other entrants (Theorem 6), and spinoffs in these regions in particular have the most success (Theorem 9). When combined with Fact #3, that the leading regions also have had more spinoffs, it is perhaps no surprise that in some of the industries that have been studied the top tier of leaders eventually consisted exclusively of spinoffs.

11.7 The Extent of Clustering

Sections 11.4–11.6 have established that our model of the process of innovation and spinoff formation yields a positive expected level of geographic concentration and accords with the eleven stylized facts described in Section 11.2. Still, for practical application, we would like to know how much geographic concentration can be attributed to the innovation and spinoff process so we can obtain better estimates of the role that traditional localized externalities play over and above it.

Theorem in Section 11.4 tells us precisely how much geographic concentration can be attributed to the innovation and spinoff process and even suggests a straightforward correction to the Ellison-Glaeser index that would measure the extent of geographic concentration over and above this level: simply pool the market shares of all firms with shared heritage in each region, as if these firms composed a single unit, when computing the Herfindahl index, i.e. replace H_t with $\hat{H}_t$. Application of this result requires us to trace the industry's entire heritage. In practice, tracking the organizational heritage of all the firms in an industry takes a lot of hard work and has only been done for a few select industries. Until researchers collect this empirical data, we find it useful to make some numerical estimates of the degree of clustering that arises in our model solely from the innovation and spinoff process, in the absence of localized externalities.

Each panel of Figure 11.1 shows the Ellison-Glaeser index of geographic concentration over time from 100 simulated runs of the model[15] with reasonable parameter values.[16] Each simulation was run until there were 1000 submarkets. The time required to reach this many submarkets varies between runs, but in all cases the long-run behavior of the index becomes clear by this point. The Ellison-Glaeser index appears to converge asymptotically to a level that is path dependent. Remarkably, it does not decay toward 0 nor explode toward 1. Two opposing forces are in balance. Over time the pace of spinoff entry picks up, and that causes clustering. However, the effect can be seen as distorting the correction for the finite sample of firms, and the number of firms grows large over time, so this correction would fade if it were not for the spinoff and innovation dynamics. If the largest family of firms were to occupy merely an infinitesimal share of the industry as the

[15] Our simulation takes the regions to be the fifty states plus the District of Columbia ($R=51$) and takes the share of total economic activity in each region f_r to be the share of manufacturing employment there, using December 2013 BLS data from www.bls.gov.

[16] The particular specification assumes a constant arrival rate of outside startups, $\kappa(t)=1$, a mixed geometric distribution for the output $\eta(x)$ in submarket x, and a uniform distribution over $[0, \frac{1}{2}]$ for the quality of a randomly discovered attribute z_S.

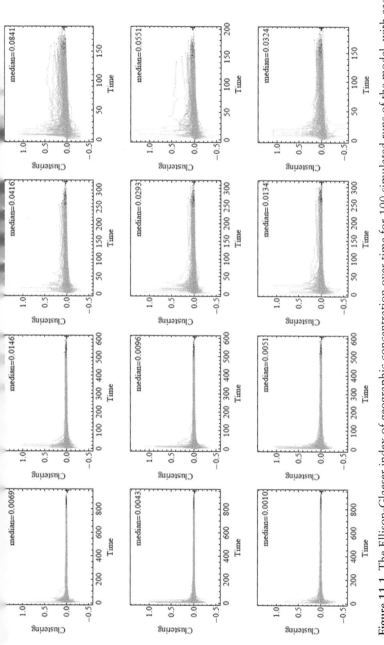

Figure 11.1 The Ellison-Glaeser index of geographic concentration over time for 100 simulated runs of the model, with each run terminating upon reaching 1000 submarkets. The innovation rate λ varies across the columns, taking on values 0.01, 0.02, 0.05, and 0.1 from left to right. The splitting probability α varies across the rows, taking on values 0.05, 0.1, and 0.2 from bottom to top.

383

number of families grew large, then the correction would fade entirely and the index would decay toward 0. However, the positive feedback in the innovation process implies that larger families of firms grow more quickly and do not ever become inconsequential.[17] The population of firms does not inevitably spread out evenly across locations.[18] Thus, clustering can persist.

For each specification of the innovation rate λ (the column) and the splitting probability α (the row), the median asymptotic value of the Ellison-Glaeser index (estimated when reaching 1000 submarkets) is noted in Figure 11.1. As Theorem 2 claims, the index is increasing in λ. We also see that the index is increasing in α, consistent with the intuition that more spinoff formation makes an industry appear more highly clustered. If the pace of innovation is too slow ($\lambda=.01$) and splitting from one's parent firm is relatively unlikely ($\alpha=.05$), then clustering practically vanishes. At the other extreme, with rapid innovation ($\lambda=.1$) and a relatively high probability of splitting from one's parent firm ($\alpha=.2$), then the index is atypically large (median value 0.084 and topping out near 0.4 in the largest of the 100 simulated runs). For comparison, Ellison and Glaeser (1997) report the median value of their index across 459 US manufacturing industries as 0.026, along with mean value 0.051, and they identify only four industries with an index greater than 0.4. We do not have much basis for a precise specification of realistic parameter values (which may well vary across industries) in our model, but we might use $\lambda=.02$ and $\alpha=.1$ to make a point estimate of 0.010 as the typical level of the Ellison-Glaeser index with our model. This estimate suggests that the dynamics of innovation and spinoffs might account for a large part, but not all, of the observed geographic concentration of manufacturing industries.

Figure 11.2 shows scatter plots of the Ellison-Glaeser index and the percentage of firms that are spinoffs at the termination of each run, upon reaching 1000 submarkets. A straightforward consequence of spinoff formation requiring both innovation and splitting off of this

[17] Bottazzi and Secchi (2006) and Luttmer (2007) present models of firm growth in which new technologies or business opportunities grow out of existing ones, and this positive feedback causes the firm size distribution to have a fat tail. A similar mechanism in our model is the reason why the largest family of firms retains a nonnegligible market share.

[18] The population of families of firms does spread out proportionally across locations in the long run, but the largest families continue to account for a disproportionate share of the industry.

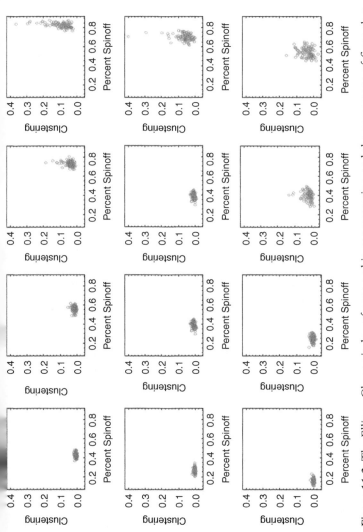

Figure 11.2 The Ellison-Glaeser index of geographic concentration and the percentage of firms that are spinoffs, recorded upon reaching 1000 submarkets, across all 100 simulated runs of the model. The innovation rate λ varies across the columns, taking on values 0.01, 0.02, 0.05, and 0.1 from left to right. The splitting probability α varies across the rows, taking on values 0.05, 0.1, and 0.2 from bottom to top.

activity is that the percentage of spinoffs (just like the Ellison-Glaeser index) is increasing in the innovation rate λ (moving to the right across the columns) and in the splitting probability α (moving up the rows). Additionally, there is some degree of correlation between the percentage of spinoffs and the Ellison-Glaeser index within each scatter plot, but the variation within a plot is less pronounced than the variation between plots. This cross-sectional view shows that more spinoffs lead to greater clustering. The precise value of the percentage of spinoffs, however, depends on our arbitrary termination point. If the process were to run forever, the population of firms would come to be completely dominated by spinoffs. This clearly unrealistic implication of our model is a result of the absence here of any shakeout process, which surely does operate in the real world.[19]

Recall that the Ellison-Glaeser index is designed to control for the lumpiness of firms so that if each firm's location were independent of its size, the index would not depend on the Herfindahl. A distinguishing feature of our model is that firms in the same region are correlated in size (because of the possibility of shared heritage), so the Ellison-Glaeser index does correlate with the Herfindahl index.

11.8 Discussion and Conclusion

The empirical pattern of clusters in various innovative industries growing principally through spinoff entry – and, moreover, of these spinoffs coming to dominate their industries – is striking and calls out for explanation. Traditional economic theory is mostly silent on the origins of a firm. In passing, standard theory might at best suggest that entry is more likely to take place in clusters because of the advantages of clustering. Perhaps entrants founded by individuals leaving incumbent firms in the industry somehow have a unique ability to exploit these advantages. In essence, conventional wisdom attributes observed patterns of clustering to firms' incentives. We take a different perspective and suggest that opportunity matters as much as incentives.[20]

---

[19] Allowing submarkets to perish with an exogenous hazard rate would let us address patterns of firm exit and perhaps capture industry shakeouts as well, as in Klepper and Thompson (2006). Spinoffs' longer survival could possibly account for the higher survival rate in clusters (cf. Dumais et al. 2002).

[20] These perspectives really are complements, not substitutes. Incentives and opportunity both, no doubt, shape firm behavior. So, too, rational allocation of

Innovation creates the opportunity for spinoff firms to form and for an industry cluster to grow (Schumpeter 1934, 1942). We develop a theory based on an underlying process of innovation with positive feedback to account for the close connection between spinoffs and clustering. Our theory explains empirical regularities about the clustering of innovative industries, the growth of a cluster in a particular region where spinoffs have proliferated, and the entry and performance of these spinoffs.

Clusters emerge in our model even in the absence of agglomeration economies. Obviously, the presence of other firms in the same industry can affect the economic climate in a particular region. Our model, however, cautions against jumping from the observation of pervasive industry clustering to the conclusion that powerful agglomeration economies are universal. We noted in Section 11.1 that firms in clusters perform better, that entry is concentrated in these regions, and that firms in related industries tend to locate near each other as well. Each of these patterns could be driven exclusively by spinoffs, which happen to spring up where there is already activity in the industry and which then outperform other firms. (To explain the third pattern, we could allow innovations to occasionally cross the boundaries between industries.) Indeed, in many cases the superior performance of firms in clusters does not extend beyond spinoffs. In the US automobile industry (Klepper 2007), the tire industry (Buenstorf and Klepper 2009, 2010), the Dutch book publishing industry (Heebels and Boschma 2011), the fashion design industry (Wenting 2008), and the British automobile industry (Boschma and Wenting 2007) spinoffs in the respective industry clusters tend to be superior performers, but other new entrants inside industry clusters have comparable performance to other entrants elsewhere.[21] A survey across industries shows strong evidence that clusters promote entry, but little evidence that they enhance firm growth or survival (Frenken et al. 2015).[22]

capital (i.e. responsiveness to incentives) and discovery of innovation (i.e. exploitation of opportunity) are both necessary ingredients for economic growth. We merely suggest that the latter constraint is sometimes binding.

[21] A conspicuous absence of positive externalities in clusters has also been noted in the metal-working (Appold 1995), footwear (Sorenson and Audia 2000), knitwear (Staber 2001), biotechnology (Stuart and Sorenson 2003), and machine tool (Buenstorf and Guenther 2011) industries.

[22] These null findings are consistent with the observation that the development of economic institutions in a region tends to lag firm growth rather than to precipitate it (Feldman 2001).

The evidence (e.g. higher spinoff rates inside clusters [even after controlling for firm characteristics]) and our model are consistent with a view of knowledge spillovers, traditionally thought to benefit an entire cluster, as a Marshallian externality that is specific to entrepreneurship.[23] These spillovers primarily support the formation of spinoffs, which have access to the technical knowledge developed by their parents. Tacit knowledge facilitates innovation, and such knowledge is difficult to acquire without being inside an organization that possesses it. Knowledge can be transferred both through founders and employees that entrants hire from incumbent firms (Breschi and Lissoni 2009; Cheyre et al. 2015). A desire to hire employees from their parents, to tap into their specialized knowledge base, may well be an important motive for spinoffs to locate close to their parents (Carias and Klepper 2010), which is of course the critical ingredient for clustering in our model.[24]

The phenomenon of spinoffs locating near their parents can occur on top of more broadly based agglomeration economies or natural advantages that favor a particular region. Such complementary forces surely do contribute to the agglomeration of at least a few notable industries (e.g. the movie industry in Hollywood, finance in New York City, steel in Pittsburgh, and wine in northern California) and our calculations of the extent of geographic concentration showing up in our model in Section 11.7 reveal that the model has room for them. It would be straightforward to accommodate agglomeration economies and natural regional advantages in our model by conditioning $\eta(x)$ (i.e. the firm's output in a given submarket and, in turn, the firm's profit in that submarket) on the location of the firm as well as the level of industry activity in the region.[25] This would generate even more concentrated regional clusters and a stronger correlation between the market share of a region and the success of a new firm there. This correlation would then extend beyond spinoffs to all firms entering the region, but would

---

[23] There could also be a demonstration effect encouraging entrepreneurship (Nanda and Sørensen 2010).

[24] The notion that spinoffs might in their formative stages need to recruit labor from their parents helps us understand why congestion costs in clusters might persist and not drive spinoffs away. (See Stam 2007 for a careful treatment of relocation costs.)

[25] Conditioning a firm's output on its location would be equivalent to assuming that all submarkets include an attribute characterizing their locations. It would be as if all firms in each region were related.

still be stronger for spinoffs than for other entrants. Additionally, this extension of the model would not interfere with, and actually would strengthen some of, the other patterns we have described.

Our model of the dynamics of spinoff formation and clustering fits naturally into a framework for evolutionary economic geography that conceives of innovation as a branching process that generates industrial and urban growth (Boschma and Frenken 2006; Frenken and Boschma 2007; Buendia 2013). Economic development is a complex system. Our model formalizes the intuition that clusters form endogenously, driven by entrepreneurs building their own firms (Feldman et al. 2005). Firms grow over time, discovering new submarkets through innovation. Occasionally, spinoffs form to pursue these opportunities. We suggest that in some cases clusters arise as an artifact of the spinoff process, rather than as the basis for it. Nevertheless, business clusters are still indicative of rapid technological change and industrial growth.

References

Agarwal, R., Echambadi, R., Franco, A., and Sarkar, M. 2004. Knowledge transfer through inheritance: Spinout generation, development, and survival. *Academy of Management Journal* 47: 501–522.

Agrawal, A., Cockburn, I., Galasso, A., and Oettl, A. 2014. Why are some regions more innovative than others? The role of small firms in the presence of large labs. *Journal of Urban Economics* 81: 149–165.

Appold, S. 1995. Agglomeration, interorganizational networks, and competitive performance in the U.S. metalworking sector. *Economic Geography* 71: 27–54.

Arthur, W. B. 1990. Positive feedbacks in the economy. *Scientific American* 262: 92–99.

Arthur, W. B. 2009. *The Nature of Technology: What It Is and How It Evolves*. New York, NY: Free Press.

Audretsch, D. and Feldman, M. 1996. R&D spillovers and the geography of innovation and production. *American Economic Review* 86: 253–273.

Audretsch, D. and Feldman, M. 2004. Knowledge spillovers and the geography of innovation, in *Handbook of Regional and Urban Economics* 4, J. V. Henderson and J. F. Thisse (eds.). Amsterdam: Elsevier.

Bassett, R. *To the Digital Age*. 2002. Baltimore, MD: Johns Hopkins University Press.

Boschma, R. and Frenken, K. 2006. Why is economic geography not an evolutionary science? Towards an evolutionary economic geography. *Journal of Economic Geography* 6: 273–302.

Boschma, R. and Wenting, R. 2007. The spatial evolution of the British automobile industry: Does location matter? *Industrial and Corporate Change* 16: 213–238.

Bottazzi, G. and Secchi, A. 2006. Explaining the distribution of firm growth rates. *The RAND Journal of Economics* 37: 235–256.

Breschi, S. and Lissoni, F. 2009. Mobility of skilled workers and co-invention networks: An anatomy of localized knowledge flows. *Journal of Economic Geography* 9: 439–468.

Buendia, F. 2013. Increasing returns economics and generalized polya processes. *Complexity* 19: 21–37.

Buenstorf, G. and Guenther, C. 2011. No place like home? Relocation, capabilities, and firm survival in the German machine tool industry after World War II. *Industrial and Corporate Change* 20: 1–28.

Buenstorf, G. and Klepper, S. 2009. Heritage and agglomeration: The Akron tire cluster revisited. *Economic Journal* 119: 705–733.

Buenstorf, G. and Klepper, S. 2010. Why does entry cluster geographically? Evidence from the U.S. tire industry. *Journal of Urban Economics* 68: 103–114.

Carias, C. and Klepper, S. 2010. Entrepreneurship, the initial labor force, and the location of new firms. Working Paper.

Cheyre, C., Klepper, S., and Veloso, F. 2015. Spinoffs and the mobility of US merchant semiconductor inventors. *Management Science* 61: 487–506.

Christensen, C. 1993. The rigid disk drive industry: A history of commercial and technological turbulence. *Business History Review* 67: 531–588.

Danneels, E. 2002. The dynamics of product innovation and firm competences. *Strategic Management Journal* 23: 1095–1121.

Dumais, G., Ellison, G., and Glaeser, E. 2002. Geographic concentration as a dynamic process. *Review of Economics and Statistics* 84: 193–204.

Duranton, G. and Puga, D. 2004. Micro-foundations of urban agglomeration economies, in *Handbook of Regional and Urban Economics* 4, J. V. Henderson and J. F. Thisse (eds.). Amsterdam: Elsevier.

Duranton, G. and Overman, H. 2005. Testing for localization using micro-geographic data. *Review of Economic Studies* 72: 1077–1116.

Ellison, G. and Glaeser, E. 1997. Geographic concentration in U.S. manufacturing industries: A dartboard approach. *Journal of Political Economy* 105: 889–927.

Ellison, G. and Glaeser, E. 1999. The geographic concentration of industry: Does natural advantage explain agglomeration? *American Economic Review* 89: 311–316.

Ellison, G., Glaeser, E., and Kerr, W. 2010. What causes industry agglomeration? Evidence from coagglomeration patterns. *American Economic Review* 100: 1195–1213.

Feinstein, J. 2017. The creative development of fields: Learning, creativity, paths, implications. *Journal of the Knowledge Economy* 8: 23–62.

Feldman, M. 1994. *The Geography of Innovation*. Boston, MA: Kluwer Academic Publishers.

Feldman, M. 2001. The entrepreneurial event revisited: Firm formation in a regional context. *Industrial and Corporate Change* 10: 861–891.

Feldman, M., Francis, J., and Bercovitz, J. 2005. Creating a cluster while building a firm: Entrepreneurs and the formation of industrial clusters. *Regional Studies* 39: 129–141.

Figueiredo, O., Guimaraes, P., and Woodward, D. 2002. Home-field advantage: Location decisions of Portuguese entrepreneurs. *Journal of Urban Economics* 52: 341–361.

Franco, A. and Filson, D. 2006. Spin-outs: Knowledge diffusion through employee mobility. *RAND Journal of Economics* 37: 841–860.

Frenken, K. and Boschma, R. 2007. A theoretical framework for evolutionary economic geography: Industrial dynamics and urban growth as a branching process. *Journal of Economic Geography* 7: 635–649.

Frenken, K., Cefis, E., and Stam, E. 2015. Industrial dynamics and clusters: A survey. *Regional Studies* 49: 10–27.

Fujita, M., Krugman, P., and Venables, A. 1999. *The Spatial Economy: Cities, Regions, and International Trade*. Cambridge, MA: Massachusetts Institute of Technology Press.

Glaeser, E., Rosenthal, S., and Strange, W. 2010. Urban economics and entrepreneurship. *Journal of Urban Economics* 67: 1–14.

Greenstone, M., Hornbeck, R., and Moretti, E. 2010. Identifying agglomeration spillovers: Evidence from winners and losers of large plant openings. *Journal of Political Economy* 118: 536–598.

Heebels, B. and Boschma, R. 2011. Performing in Dutch book publishing 1880–2008. The importance of entrepreneurial experience and the Amsterdam Cluster. *Journal of Economic Geography* 11: 1007–1029.

Jaffe, A., Trajtenberg, M., and Henderson, R. 1993. Geographic localization of knowledge spillovers as evidenced by patent citations. *The Quarterly Journal of Economics* 108: 577–598.

Kenney, M. and von Burg, U. 1999. Technology, entrepreneurship and path dependence: Industrial clustering in Silicon Valley and Route 128. *Industrial and Corporate Change* 8: 67–103.

Klepper, S. 2007. Disagreements, spinoffs, and the evolution of Detroit as the capital of the U.S. automobile industry. *Management Science* 53: 616–631.

Klepper, S. 2009a. Silicon Valley – A chip off the old Detroit bloc, in *Entrepreneurship, Growth, and Public Policy*, Z. Acs, D. Audretsch and R. Strom (eds.). Cambridge: Cambridge University Press.

Klepper, S. 2009b. Spinoffs: A review and synthesis. *European Management Review* 6: 159–171.

Klepper, S. 2010. The origin and growth of industry clusters: The making of Silicon Valley and Detroit. *Journal of Urban Economics* 67: 15–32.

Klepper, S., Kowalski, J., and Veloso, F. 2011. *Technological Spillovers and the Agglomeration of the Semiconductor Industry in Silicon Valley*. Mimeo.

Klepper, S. and Sleeper, S. 2005. Entry by spinoffs. *Management Science* 51: 1291–1306.

Klepper, S. and Thompson, P. 2006. Submarkets and the evolution of market structure. *The RAND Journal of Economics* 37: 861–886.

Klette, T. J. and Kortum, S. 2004. Innovating firms and aggregate innovation. *Journal of Political Economy* 112: 986–1018.

Lécuyer, C. 2006. *Making Silicon Valley*. Cambridge, MA: Massachusetts Institute of Technology Press.

Luttmer, E. 2007. Selection, growth, and the size distribution of firms. *Quarterly Journal of Economics* 122: 1103–1144.

Marshall, A. 1890. *Principles of Economics*. London: Macmillan.

McKendrick, D., Doner, R., and Haggard, S. 2000. *From Silicon Valley to Singapore*. Stanford, CA: Stanford University Press.

Mitchell, M. 2000. The scope and organization of production: Firm dynamics over the learning curve. *RAND Journal of Economics* 31: 180–205.

Mitton, D. 1990. Bring on the clones: A longitudinal study of the proliferation, development, and growth of the biotech industry in San Diego, in *Frontiers of Entrepreneurship*, N. Churchill, W. Bygrave, J. Hornday, D. Muzyka, K. Vesper, and W. Wetzel Jr. (eds.). Babson Park, MA: Babson College.

Montgomery, C. 1994. Corporate diversification. *Journal of Economic Perspectives* 8: 163–178.

Moore, G. and Davis, K. 2004. Learning the Silicon Valley way, in *Building High-Tech Clusters: Silicon Valley and beyond*, T. Bresnahan and A. Gambardella (eds.). Cambridge: Cambridge University Press.

Nanda, R. and Sørensen, J. 2010. Workplace peers and entrepreneurship. *Management Science* 56: 1116–1126.

Nelson, R. and Winter, S. 1982. *An Evolutionary Theory of Economic Change*. Cambridge, MA: Harvard University Press.

Puga, D. 2010. The magnitude and causes of agglomeration economies. *Journal of Regional Science* 50: 203–219.

Romanelli, E. and Feldman, M. 2006. The anatomy of cluster development: The case of U.S. biotherapeutics, 1976–2003. *Cluster Genesis* 27: 87–113.

Rosenthal, S. and Strange, W. 2004. Evidence on the nature and sources of agglomeration economies, in *Handbook of Regional and Urban Economics* 4, J. V. Henderson and J. F. Thisse (eds.). Amsterdam: Elsevier.

Schumpeter, J. 1934. *Theory of Economic Development*. Cambridge, MA: Harvard University Press.

Schumpeter, J. 1942. *Capitalism, Socialism, and Democracy*. New York, NY: Harper & Row.

Sorenson, O. and Audia, P. 2000. The social structure of entrepreneurial activity: Geographic concentration of footwear production in the United States, 1940–1989. *American Journal of Sociology* 106: 424–462.

Staber, U. 2001. Spatial proximity and firm survival in a declining industrial district: The case of knitwear firms in Baden-Württemberg. *Regional Studies* 35: 329–341.

Stam, E. 2007. Why butterflies don't leave: Locational behavior of entrepreneurial firms. *Economic Geography* 83: 27–50.

Stuart, T. and Sorenson, O. 2003. The geography of opportunity: Spatial heterogeneity in founding rates and the performance of biotechnology firms. *Research Policy* 32: 229–253.

Weitzman, M. 1998. Recombinant growth. *Quarterly Journal of Economics* 113: 331–360.

Wenting, R. 2008. Spinoff dynamics and the spatial formation of the fashion design industry, 1858–2005. *Journal of Economic Geography* 8: 593–614.

12 Examining the Technological Innovation Systems of Smart Cities

The Case of Japan and Implications for Public Policy and Institutional Design

MASARU YARIME AND MARTIN KARLSSON

12.1 Introduction

Smart cities are considered as a key area where innovation plays a critical role in making system transformation toward sustainability. Smart cites are based on advanced systems of hardware and software for mutual exchanges of energy and information between supply and demand sides for efficient, flexible, and resilient services, incorporating the behavior of different actors including generators, distributors, technology developers, and consumers through an intelligent network. Improvement in the efficiency of energy consumption will reduce emissions coming from energy generation, particularly those from coal power plants. Flexibility in balancing energy supply and demand through smart meters and affiliated technologies will facilitate the introduction of renewable energy sources such as solar and wind, substituting pollution-laden fossil fuels. Electrification of urban infrastructure will also support the deployment of electric vehicles, which do not emit pollutants, unlike the conventional vehicles driven by internal combustion engines.

As a diverse mixture of hardware as well as software are involved in a complex way, however, a variety of approaches to implementing the concept of smart cities would be possible in practice. Therefore, innovation systems of smart cities exhibit a significant degree of diversity in knowledge, actors, and institutions, depending on the economic, social, and environmental conditions. In-depth examination of the

394

processes of creating innovation on smart cities is expected to generate useful lessons for implementing system transformation. Policy and strategic implications of the experiences of the industrialized countries will be particularly important for many countries in the developing world, where urbanization is proceeding rapidly in many major cities, producing many energy and environmental challenges. They require effective integration of various types of science and technological knowledge through close collaboration with relevant stakeholders in academia, industry, and the public sector.

In this paper, we examine the innovation system of smart cities in Japan and its implications for system transformation toward sustainability. This research is aimed at understanding the processes of implementing innovation on smart cities in the economic and social contexts of the country. Detailed analysis is conducted on what knowledge and technologies are focused on, what actors are involved at which stages of innovation, what factors influence the behavior of the actors, and what effects and impacts are made by policy interventions. Projects on smart cities are analyzed in terms of the actors involved, the technological areas emphasized, and the processes in which the actors collaborate with each other. Information was collected through various sources, such as project reports, academic articles, corporate reports, trade journals, and web sites, and interviews were conducted with relevant stakeholder, including academia, firms, industry association, and government organizations. Network analysis is conducted to identify key stakeholders involved in innovation on smart cities and to analyze the relationships between them, illustrating how important organizations are located and interacted in the communities on smart cities. The functions in the innovation system of smart cities are also examined to understand the process of developing and introducing smart cities. Based on the analysis of the experience of Japan, implications are discussed for policy measures and approaches for making system transformation toward sustainability.

12.2 Innovation Systems of Smart Cities

Smart cities are widely seen as a future trajectory of technological change in the energy system. In smart cities a key role is played by smart grids, which would be understood as an electricity network that can intelligently integrate the actions of all users connected to it, including both generators and consumers, in order to efficiently deliver sustainable, economic, and secure electricity supplies (European Technology Platform for Electricity Networks for the Future 2016). Bundling various types of equipment and practices, smart grids constitute an aggregate system to improve electricity generation, distribution, and consumption by introducing new functionalities. Based on smart grids, smart cites have been evolving into sophisticated systems of hardware and software assembling, and processing an increasing amount of information on multifaceted dimensions of cities, providing diverse types of products and services.

The concept of smart cities, therefore, would reflect different dimensions of complex technological assemblages, and as such there are significant differences in the nuance and emphasis of the concept, depending upon the specific contexts and conditions. In Europe a focus is given on creating an infrastructure that can use information collected and distributed among all connected users, to ensure that the various objectives of the electricity grid are achieved in a more intelligent way (Clastres 2011). In the United States there is a specific emphasis on security, involving key features such as self-healing and resilience against physical and cyber threats. Because the functionalities discussed as part of the smart city are many, there is also a breadth of benefits envisioned for society when a smart city is implemented. Potential benefits include higher overall energy efficiency, lower cost of operating the electricity grid, lower environmental impact, higher resilience of the energy system, and more empowerment to end-users in the energy system. Given the desirability of these benefits for societies facing climate change and increasing energy prices, and the high hurdles such a complex systemic technology area face, it is important that governments facilitate the introduction of smart cities. This study takes a systemic approach to examining the experience in Japan to extract valuable lessons and implications for governments and entrepreneurs seeking to promote smart cities.

This study takes a holistic approach to examining the processes of innovation on smart cities. Given the relatively short period of time in which smart cities have evolved, there have not been many studies with macroscopic views of innovation on smart cities, particularly those studies conducted from policy perspectives (Lin, Yang, and Shyua 2013). One of the major analytical approaches to studying innovation processes is the approach of innovation systems. It has been built upon the notion that it is not only activities by firms and researchers that determine the character of technological change but also broader societal and institutional structures. The idea of the system of innovation was originally developed to examine the functioning of national systems of innovation, particularly how the key actors in the system could actively promote innovation through interactions and networking in the national context (Freeman 1988; Lundvall 1988; Nelson 1993).

For understanding the characteristics of innovation in a particular sector, it would be useful to identify a sectoral innovation system. A sectoral innovation system is understood to consist of three main dimensions: namely, knowledge, actors, and institutions (Malerba 2002, 2004). The knowledge dimension deals with the specificities of knowledge and technological domains that are relevant to the innovation. The actors involved in the innovation system show heterogeneity, networks, and interactions among them. Institutions include formal ones such as policies, regulations, and standards as well as informal ones like norms, customs, and established practices. Within a sectoral systems framework, innovation is considered to be a process that involves systematic interactions among a wide variety of actors for the generation and exchange of knowledge relevant to innovation and its commercialization, influenced by institutional conditions (Malerba and Adams 2014).

From this perspective, innovation can be understood as a coevolutionary process of knowledge/technological and institutional developments (Nelson 1994, 1995). Knowledge at the base of innovative activities changes over time and affects the boundaries and structure of the sectoral innovation system. Actors and networks are highly affected by the characteristics of and changes in the knowledge base. And changes in the knowledge base or in demand affect the characteristics of the actors, the organization of research and development (R&D) and of the innovative process, the type of networks, and the structure of the market and the relevant institutions. These variables in turn lead to further modifications in the technology, the knowledge base, and demand. In the emergence of the knowledge-based economies, a focus has been placed on the role of the main actors in the innovation system, namely, universities, firms, and the government, and their relationships and interactions within the innovation system. The experience of recent decades, however, has shown that other influences, such as activities by end users and discourses in society, can also have an important role in driving innovation.

To investigate broad societal structures and processes, the approach of technological innovation systems would be effective in capturing the activities directed toward development, diffusion, and use of a particular technology (Bergek, Jacobsson, Carlsson, Lindmark, and Rickne 2008). A technological innovation system is defined as networks of agents interacting in a specific technology area under a particular institutional infrastructure to generate, diffuse, and utilize technology (Carlsson and Stankiewicz 1991). It is stressed that it is the analysis of the functions that should receive the most attention, as the aim of a technological innovation system is to fulfil its functions, rather than to achieve a structure (Bergek, Carlsson, Jacobsson, Lindmark, and Rickne 2008). The functions identified include knowledge development and diffusion, guidance of the search, resource mobilization, entrepreneurial experimentation, market formation, legitimation, and development of positive externalities. In efforts to find ways to accelerate and enhance innovation processes, the approach of technological innovation systems has mostly been applied to the study of green innovation, which is aimed at addressing societal values of environment protection and sustainability. Examples include wind turbines (Kamp, Smits, and Andriesse 2004), renewable energy systems (Jacobsson and Bergek 2004), and renewable vehicle fuels (Suurs 2009).

The innovation system of smart cities would involve complex interactions of advanced technologies for efficient, flexible, and resilient energy supply and applications and the behavior of the actors, including generators, distributors, technology developers, and end users. To capture a broad understanding of the processes of introducing and implementing innovation on smart cities in Japan, we analyze the knowledge and technological domains concerning smart cities, the key actors and stakeholders including academia, firms, industry associations, and government organizations, and the institutional conditions and environments in which these stakeholders interact and examine the drivers or obstacles in innovation by paying attention to the functions of the innovation system of smart cities.

12.3 The Case of Japan

The Japanese government's interest in smart cities grew out of the government's promotion of renewable energy sources, an area in which Japan was an early champion. In the first decade of the millennium, the New Energy Development Organisation (NEDO), a governmental agency under the Ministry of Economy, Trade and Industry (METI), promoted domestic projects aiming at developing grid-connecting technologies for renewable energy projects. Projects supported included clustered photovoltaic (PV) generation, mega solar generation, wind power stabilizing and power quality management, and micro grids. Although these projects were not necessarily carried out under the label of smart cities, they touched upon some of the functionalities now associated with the concept. In 2010, smart city innovation efforts started when METI launched four large-scale smart city demonstration projects in different areas of Japan. These were called "Next-Generation Energy and Social Systems Demonstration Areas," later known as "Smart Communities." The projects are all based on an important role of local authorities and one coordinating corporation per project, which receives support from METI and coordinates with other partners, and focus on creating practical examples of different smart energy technologies (Uetake 2013). Other innovative efforts on smart cities in Japan have been mainly conducted by potential vendors of smart grid technologies, often in collaboration with other enterprises such as real estate developers.

12.3.1 Knowledge and Technological Domains

Knowledge is a major driving force of development and transformation in economic systems, and learning and knowledge by individuals and organizations are at the base of innovation. Therefore, to understand the characteristics of the innovation system of smart cities, it is important to analyze what kinds of knowledge and technologies are involved. Bibliometric analysis was conducted on the academic articles concerning smart cities in Japan. The result is visualized as a semantic network, where more commonly occurring words are represented with larger nodes, and a connecting edge between two words in close positions means a high level of their co-occurrence (Vlieger and Leydesdorff 2010).

Figure 12.1 shows the knowledge and technological domains in the innovation systems of smart cities in Japan. The most important knowledge domains were found to be energy system and power system. The smart grid concept, although not at the core of the network,

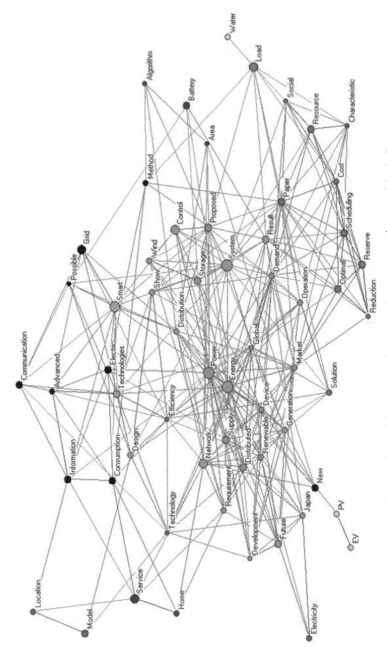

Figure 12.1 Knowledge and technological domains in the innovation systems of smart cities in Japan

occupies a relatively central role. Other core knowledge and technological domains include renewable energy, distributed energy and energy storage, distributed generation, the creation of new service markets, EV charging infrastructure, and energy storage and security. There are some close relationships, for example, among home, service, and consumption, probably related to smart home functionalities. Concepts such as social, cost, load, reduction, reserve, and optimal form a separate cluster, probably showing an interest in economic and management dimensions of smart cities. There is also a region linking domains like communication, information, and smart grid. It can be said that knowledge and technological domains related to application sides are relatively well-represented.

12.3.2 Actors and Their Network

Many government organizations are involved in the Japanese innovation systems of smart cities. Among them, METI is the most prominent actor, having a broad portfolio of relevant policy areas. Traditionally characterized by a strong relationship with the business sector, METI's main mission has been to support the development of the Japanese industry. Situated under METI, the New Energy and Industrial Technology Development Organization (NEDO) is Japan's largest public R&D funding and management organization. As one of the responses from the government to the oil crisis of the 1970s, NEDO was formed in 1980 to promote the development and diffusion of new energy technologies in Japan. Prior to the year 2000, NEDO-supported research on electricity grids focused on extending grid connection to single producers of renewable energy. In the first decade of the new millennium, NEDO shifted its focus to inclusion of large-scale, multiple renewable energy producers. Since 2010, a broader focus has been made on the concept of "smart communities," with more attention to consumer-domain technologies (Morozumi 2010).

METI and NEDO conduct their efforts for innovation on smart cities in close collaboration with the business sector. Local governments, especially the cities that were allocated financial resources through the Japan Smart Cities project and the Future Environment City project, are very active in smart grid activities. Several cities have partnered with private companies or universities; for example, Fujisawa is partnering with one of the largest electronic companies in Japan,

Panasonic, and Toshima ward in Tokyo has collaborated with the Tokyo Institute of Technology (Hirai 2013).

The most important actors in Japanese efforts on smart cities are large firms with strong corporate networks and technological knowledge, such as Hitachi, Toshiba, and Mitsubishi. The size of these companies and their networks with other firms provide them with access to expertise in various aspects of smart grid technologies (Office of Energy and Environmental Industries 2012). Because of their large portfolios of business activities, these companies tend to take a broader definition of smart cities, with many products and services available for residential end-users of electricity. Companies and consultancies in the information and communication technology sector are also active, mostly in the development and provision of software components and services. Residential developers and department stores are also important stakeholders, as they aim to provide customers with additional services and the potential for cost reduction through installing smart energy technologies.

While regional monopolistic utilities have traditionally dominated most of Japan's electricity system, they are currently operating in a very uncertain and economically difficult situation since the Fukushima nuclear accident and the liberalization of energy markets. TEPCO, the largest of the utilities in Japan and one of the largest utilities in the world, previously did not show much enthusiasm for the concept of the smart grid. Prior to the Fukushima accident, it was argued that the Japanese energy system was based on world-class technology and thus smart grids would not be necessary (Dasher 2012). In the post-Fukushima era, the financial standing of the utilities would make it difficult for them to make much investment.

Japan Smart Community Alliance (JSCA) was formed in April 2010 by METI and NEDO, which hosts the secretariat, following the recommendation of a roadmap produced internally that international standardization efforts were needed. By February 2013, 408 companies had joined the organization, with Toshiba serving as the president (Japan Smart Community Alliance 2013).

The Energy Conservation and Homecare Network (ECHONET) Consortium is a network of private companies in the area of smart housing. Active since 1997, the consortium has developed communication standards for smart appliances, which are open and universal, to promote the emergence of home networks connected to these smart appliances (ECHONET Consortium 2013a). As of January 2013, the consortium has eight core members representing some of the largest electronics producers in Japan, including Panasonic, Sharp, and Toshiba, as well as Japan's largest utility company, TEPCO (ECHONET Consortium 2013b). After its establishment, ECHONET experienced a steady decline of activities in the early 2000s, as consumer interest in smart appliances remained quite low, and a proliferation of communication protocols meant high cost and uncertainty for vendors. In 2011, the consortium released an enhanced and WiFi-based standard, ECHONET-lite, which was swiftly endorsed for the home energy management system (HEMS) by the Japanese government, with financial support provided to HEMS adopting the standard. This led to a sharp spike in interest and membership in the ECHONET consortium (Mochizuki 2013).

In some areas, local associations have been established for private companies and research institutes involved in smart city or smart house developments. One example is the Yokohama Smart Community Association, which was created following the beginning of the Yokohama Smart City project. It is an association of local small and medium enterprises (SMEs) working in collaboration with smart city initiatives and acting as suppliers for some of the companies involved (Uetake 2013).

The network structure of the actors in the field of smart cities was analyzed by collecting data on projects and consortia related to smart cities through trade journals, research reports, web sites, and interviews with relevant stakeholders. As a result, a database was constructed with twenty-two projects and two consortia. Network analysis was conducted to identify key stakeholders in the Japanese system of innovation of smart cities and to analyze the relationships between them. In the network, when multiple organizations join the same joint project, they are connected with one another.

Figure 12.2 illustrates the entire structure of the Japanese network of the actors involved in smart city projects. Figure 12.3 shows the central area of the network.

Table 12.1 lists key actors in the network involved in the innovation systems of smart cities in Japan. They are listed in the order of the most connected organizations according to the measurement of betweenness centrality, which illustrates how important the location of an organization is for the other organizations connected with each other in the

Figure 12.2 Actor network of the innovation systems of smart cities in Japan

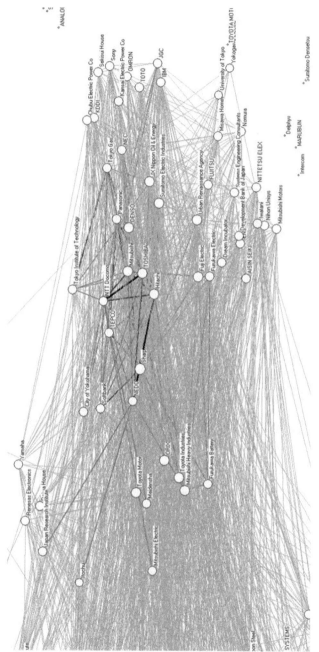

Figure 12.3 Central area of the actor network of the innovation systems of smart cities in Japan

405

Table 12.1 *Key actors in the innovation systems of smart cities in Japan*

Organization	Sector	Betweenness centrality	Degree centrality
Hitachi	Electronics company	5212.7	74
Toshiba	Electronics company	3735.6	64
Mitsubishi Corporation	Trading company	2908.3	67
NEDO	Governmental funding agency	2735.7	28
Sharp	Consumer electronics company	1603.5	91
Denso	Automotive component supplier	1567.2	55
Fuji Electric	Infrastructure provider	1516.7	53
JX Nippon Oil & Energy	Petroleum company	1481.1	55
Panasonic	Electronics company	1276.7	35
Furukawa Electric	Infrastructure provider	1187.1	47
University of Tokyo	University	1154.3	13
Sumitomo Electric Industries	Infrastructure provider	1123.1	55
Urban Renaissance Agency	Real estate agency	960.8	47
TOTO	White ware company	917.4	30
IBM	Software provider	917.4	30
Omron	Electronic component supplier	770.8	24
Kansai Electric Power Co	Electric utility	770.8	24
Iwatani	Gas equipment provider	658.8	29
Nittetsu Elex	Infrastructure provider	658.8	29
Tokyo Gas	Gas utility	609.8	31

network. The table also shows the degree of centrality, which measures the number of connections to the organization.

As can be seen from Figure 12.2, Figure 12.3, and Table 12.1, the key actors identified from the network analysis are mainly large conglomerates with broad portfolios, covering both electronics and infrastructure areas. They are also members of both JSCA and ECHONET and are participating in several demonstration projects. The top two, Hitachi and Toshiba, are of particular importance, and the government-funding agency NEDO also plays a prominent role in the network. The large electricity utilities, on the other hand, are not centrally connected in the network, and their presence is relatively invisible.

12.3.3 Functional Analysis of the Innovation System of Smart Cities

Knowledge creation and diffusion would be considered as one of the most important functions of a technological innovation system. It encompasses the creation of different kinds of knowledge concerning scientific, technological, market, and institutional dimensions. In Japan, the relevant stakeholders rated the knowledge creation and diffusion process as positive, overall. The smart city projects are regarded as especially important collaborative platforms in which novel technological functionalities could be tried out. While the tightly knit groups involved in the smart city projects are producing valuable knowledge, the sharing of that knowledge is still limited. Within the smart house and appliances sector, knowledge creation has proceeded further, and diffusion platforms have been seen as better developed, especially since the Fukushima accident, after which the government started to promote standardization and to provide financial support to consumers for purchasing home energy management systems (HEMS).

The function of guidance of the search refers to the way in which society creates incentives for a certain type of technology to emerge from a technological innovation system. If this function is performing well, there is a clear common understanding of the expectation and probabilities of technology development and diffusion, shared by industry actors, the government, and consumers. This is particularly important as it addresses the often-overlooked phase of interactions among different groups of interest and power within innovation processes (Smith, Stirling, and Berkhout 2005). While a vaguer vision could be helpful to mobilize a broad coalition, if the interpretative flexibility is too great, the innovation system will not be pulling in the same direction and therefore will not be effective as a system. In Japan the process of the guidance of the search has been performing relatively well, as there is a shared understanding about the basic concept and acceptance of the smart grid, although the emphasis varies to a certain extent between different stakeholders. NEDO has been regarded as the most important actor in facilitating consensus building. As the public sector manages the financial resources for many of the demonstration projects on smart cities, it has a significant amount of capacity to influence the focus and direction of the development of technologies relevant to smart cities.

Innovation requires various kinds of capital and assets for further development. Financial and human capitals are the most important among these, and the availability of these resources is crucial in enabling innovation. The financial resources provided by METI and NEDO to relevant projects have functioned as important stimuli for innovation, especially through funding the smart city projects. Since the Fukushima accident, in particular, many of the electricity utilities have relatively limited financial capabilities to initiate and implement new technological development. This has directly affected their engagements on smart city initiatives that already existed. The activities of the electricity utilities that are still ongoing are mostly funded by government grants, which illustrate the significant role played by resource mobilization for keeping the momentum on innovation.

Entrepreneurial experimentation refers to experiments carried out by the actors who intend to utilize smart energy technologies to implement something novel for achieving their aims. Their activities would be indispensable for a process to be innovative. From a societal perspective, the experimentation of entrepreneurs would make uncertainty about the development and use of technology lower, as they create hard evidence for the likelihood of success or failure of certain types of technology. In Japan this function has been performing relatively poorly. While established manufacturing firms are making efforts to tap into new markets, the traditional monopolistic structure of the electricity market and the uncertainty about future policies and regulations have discouraged ambitious activities of entrepreneurship. Moreover, the membership in the smart city projects has remained relatively closed, with new entrants very limited, and the area of smart cities tends to be regarded as a field giving advantage to the established industrial giants. The smart house and appliance sector sees more involvement and engagement by smaller firms, in addition to the large electronic companies.

For the benefits of innovation to become widespread, a market for technologies needs to be created and well established. As an emerging technological innovation system often has only a very small and weak market, particularly at an initial stage, a strong expectation of market formation in the future with ample possibilities and opportunities for profit making will accelerate the process of innovation. The creation of a market for technologies related to smart cities in Japan is at this moment considered to face many problems and challenges. While a very limited market exists, it is still at a very early stage, and the uncertainties surrounding the current environment and future development of the electricity market would make potential investors wary. In the smart home and appliances sector, the market has developed further and some demand has already been emerging. Residential developers have played a key role in popularizing various applications for smart homes and appliances. The residential developers, however, while actively engaged with the concept of smart homes and appliances, only cater to the upper-income groups, with HEMS remaining relatively expensive. The high prevalence and popularity of residential photovoltaics in Japan has also been an important driver for the smart house market.

Creation of legitimacy refers to the process in which technologies become socially accepted and institutionally incorporated into the legal system. When this function is not fulfilled, search guidance and market formation would not be effective ultimately, and regulatory barriers can create obstacles to innovation. In the case of Japan the creation of legitimacy has not been a serious problem for facilitating innovation on smart cities. Although knowledge about smart cities is not necessarily shared widely in the general public, energy security and efficiency have basically been understood as areas to be supported since the oil crises in the 1970s. Hence the planned outages by the electricity utilities following the Fukushima accident received strong criticisms, as regions of less economic importance had to endure more blackouts. Accordingly, smart energy technologies that are considered to contribute to reducing energy consumption are socially accepted, without much resistance due to concerns about privacy or health effects. In the smart house and smart appliance sector, the situation has been less problematic, as consumers generally appreciate smart appliances for the benefits provided by these technologies.

Empirical studies have shown that the existence of complementary innovation systems is important for a technological innovation system to be successful (Bergek, Jacobsson, Carlsson, Lindmark, and Rickne 2008). For example, the success of civilian nuclear power technology benefited greatly from the advances in nuclear weapon technology, even though they basically belong to two distinctive innovation systems. Similarly, the development of positive externalities has also been observed in the evolution of technologies on smart cities. A crucial area of coevolutionary development is the fast-developing field of smart home and appliances. The appliance manufacturers who also have interests in the grid equipment market have been the most active stakeholders in the technological innovation systems of smart cities. The electric vehicle has also been an innovation area of critical importance. While being at a too early stage to contribute significantly, the development and diffusion of electric vehicles will benefit considerably from smart city innovation. Renewable energy development has also been an adjacent innovation area. The influence of renewable energy is still relatively small, however, as the electricity utilities currently allow only limited amounts of electricity to be connected to the grids, because of concern about the grid capacities to absorb the fluctuation and interruption of the electricity produced by renewable energy sources, particularly solar power.

12.4 Implications for Public Policy and Institutional Design

Based on the analysis of the Japanese innovation system of smart cities, we consider lessons and implications for public policy and institutional design for facilitating system transformation in the future. As an important background for developing smart cities, large-scale induction of renewable energy requires us to maintain high quality of electricity in terms of voltage and frequency. After the Fukushima accident, it has also become critical to save energy and cut back its consumption during peak periods. As new technologies concerning energy supply and distribution are emerging, their safety and reliability need to be tested and verified. Smart cities are expected to improve energy efficiency and facilitate energy resilience by utilizing advanced technologies, including ICTs and storage batteries, with cogeneration and renewable energy through distributed energy systems.

Given these backgrounds, there are several objectives identified for promoting smart cities in Japan. First, it is of critical importance to strengthen the resilience of energy supply against disruptions and disasters such as earthquakes and typhoons through distributed energy systems. At the same time, we need to reduce environmental burdens, including carbon dioxide emissions, by increasing renewable energy sources and efficient energy usage. Efficient and resilient energy systems require effective utilization of energy management systems (EMSs), including demand-response systems to manage the balance between energy supply and demand efficiently through consumers' participation in cutting energy consumption during peak periods. It would also be possible to reduce the capacities of thermal power generation prepared for peak energy consumption by establishing efficient electricity systems from a mid- to long-term perspective.

While smart cities have initially been understood as a system based on mutual exchange of energy and information between supply and demand sides, as expansion and integration of smart cities progress, there are various aspects in which diversity and complexity are influencing further development of smart cities. Smart cities consist of various types of hardware as well as software for efficient and resilient energy supply and applications, involving a large amount of different kinds of data. Actors and stakeholders are also diverse in the entire supply chain, including energy generators, distributors, technology developers, system operators, local communities, and consumers. This implies that various kinds of interests and concerns exist, such as energy efficiency, economic costs, environmental impacts, resilience to external shocks and disasters, accessibility and inclusiveness to end users, privacy, and cyber security.

Reflecting the diversity and complexity of smart cities, it would be possible to interpret the concept of smart cities and to create and implement innovation in various ways, depending on the local conditions and contexts. Semantic analysis of discourse on smart cities suggests that Japan has basically focused on improving sophistication of application technologies for extensive use of home appliances and electric vehicles, whereas the United States has paid attention to creating and maintaining security through improvement in resilience against physical as well as virtual threats. Network analysis of the key actors involved in smart city projects in Japan shows a relatively concentrated structure dominated by a small number of large actors, mainly government organizations and electricity and electronic companies. In contrast, the US network reveals a distributed structure with many actors, such as utilities and smart meter manufacturers, including SMEs and start-ups.

There are several policy approaches and instruments that are considered to have influenced the development of smart cities in Japan. They include liberalization of energy markets for new entrants; the feed-in-tariff (FIT) program for promoting renewable energy; technological road-mapping to social system demonstration; localization of demonstration projects adjusted to economic environments, major actors, and technological orientation; platforms for strategic partnerships among stakeholders including academia, industry, government, and local communities; and standard setting for smart meters and equipment.

The Japanese government has recently started to introduce a series of policy measures to accelerate the liberalization of energy markets. One is the Amended Electricity Business Act enacted in November 2013. This legislation established the Organization for Cross-regional Coordination of Transmission Operators (OCCTO) in 2015 to promote wide-area electrical grid operation. And the liberalization of the retail sale of electricity was initiated in April 2016. Furthermore, separation of power generation and power transmission is expected to take place in 2018–2020. Another policy measure is the Strategic Energy Plan introduced in April 2014. This plan has accelerated the introduction of renewable energy sources. For example, it is expected that the energy produced by photovoltaics will be increased to 53 GW and by wind to 10 GW by 2030. A strong emphasis has been placed on R&D and demonstration of transmission and distribution equipment. It is also specified that regional or interregional grids for renewables will be established.

The policy instrument of the feed-in-tariff (FIT) was very important for promoting the adoption of renewable energy sources. The shutdown of nuclear power plants following the Fukushima accident in March 2011 has effectively accelerated the expansion of renewable energy as a strategy to make up for lost power generation and to reduce Japan's dependence on imported oil and natural gas. The government announced, in June 2011, a target of putting PV systems on 10 million roofs by 2030. The FIT program was introduced in 2012 to encourage the installation of renewable energy, particularly solar PV. Revised FIT for PV is expected to account for more than 80 percent of newly installed capacity in the coming decade. On the other hand, while more than 80 GW of solar power capacity has been approved, by the end of 2014, only 23 GW had been installed. Consequently, installations of PV have been slowed, as utilities have denied additional grid access to new solar farms. The current grid infrastructure has not been set up for large-scale adoption of renewables such as solar and wind power, with further deployment disrupting the operations of the grid.

The gradual shift from technological road mapping to social system demonstration was also important in facilitating systemic approaches to innovation on smart cities. Iterative processes of revising the technological roadmap on PV were conducted by the funding agency NEDO. NEDO PV 2030 roadmap was initially published in 2004. Then NEDO PV Challenges replaced the roadmap in 2009 with a revised one, NEDO PV 2030+ and again in 2014. In this process the main focus was placed on technological development. Then the support provided by NEDO shifted gradually from technological development to social system demonstration. Prior to 2000, the funding agency mainly supported the development of specific technologies for introducing renewable energy to the electricity grid. In the period from 2000 to 2010 support was provided for the development and demonstration of multiple, large-scale technologies coordinated for introducing renewable energy to the grid. And since then, demonstration of smart cities incorporating social needs has been encouraged with financial assistance.

Demonstration of smart cities in various parts of the country has been critical for testing promising technologies and raising awareness among the general public. Smart city projects were implemented in Yokohama, Toyota, Keihanna, and Kitakyushu in the period from 2011 to 2014. They were mainly aimed at verifying emerging advanced technologies concerning smart cities, including cogeneration, renewable energy, energy storage, electric vehicles, and energy management systems (EMSs). At the same time, these projects were also targeted at establishing robust business models with active participation of relevant stakeholders, including local communities and residents as well as technology providers in the private sector.

What was important in implementing these demonstration projects was that they were locally adjusted, considering the specificities of the economic and social conditions and contexts. In Yokohama, which is a major metropolitan city close to Tokyo, the aim was to facilitate large-scale introduction of renewable energy and electric vehicles, with participation of 4,000 households equipped with HEMS, ten large-scale building, and multiple storage batteries. In Toyota local production of energy for local consumption was the target, involving sixty-seven households equipped with solar panels, household fuel cells, storage batteries, and advanced transportation systems including electric vehicles and plug-in hybrid vehicles. Keihanna Science City intended to test the visualization of energy for control and management in a housing complex of 700 households, as well as HEMS and the feasibility of consulting business on energy saving. In Kitakyushu, which has a designated energy supply area, optimization of various sources of energy was explored, with power supplied by large steel and metal companies and a dynamic pricing system introduced for 180 households.

These demonstration projects had a significant effect of accelerating technological integration, reliability, and learning through trial and error. For establishing smart cities, various types of new promising technologies need to be verified, adopted, and integrated, including facilities for renewable energy, energy storage batteries, and energy management systems. As it is usually difficult to show the economic advantages of emerging technologies over conventional energy systems, their deployment for smart communities would be a disadvantage under normal conditions. Through these demonstration projects, large-scale adoption and intensive learning became possible, inducing the prices of component technologies and the cost of operating energy systems to decline.

Standard-setting for component technologies, particularly smart meters, also played an important role in facilitating the introduction of smart cities. Proprietary standards among competing providers have initially slowed down the market's take-off. The Open Automated Demand Response (OpenADR) 2.0 technology standard was adopted, following feasibility, interoperability, and connectivity testing in the summer of 2013. With an application-programming interface (API), the efficient development of applications was also promoted, including HEMS and building energy management system (BEMS). The adoption of HEMS had a significant impact on driving Japan's smart household appliance industry, as LED lights, smart thermostats, plug-in electric vehicles, rooftop solar, demand-flexible water heaters, battery energy storage, and other appliances are now integrated with the IT network. HEMS Alliance has been formed by leading companies to create a multi-vendor device environment. On the other hand, new standards have recently started to emerge in other sectors, particularly in fields related to what is called the Internet of Things (IoT), in which virtually everything will be connected for information exchange and communication so that many activities that used to be conducted separately can now be coordinated with each other efficiently. Various standards, such as ZigBee and Bluetooth Low Energy, are currently under rapid development, leading to an urgent need to consider cooperation and coordination among the major players.

12.5 Conclusion

Based on the analysis of the development of smart cities in Japan, we can identify several challenges in implementing system transformation. We need to have a clear vision of what kinds of smart cities we would like to establish and then match the visions with feasible plans for implementation. Strong leadership for projects and transparency in the process of decision-making and implementation are also important. Under the existence of a significant degree of symmetry of knowledge and expertise between large technology companies on the one side and local government and communities on the other side, we also need to consider how it would be possible to secure serious and active participation of end users. Robust business models are currently missing, which has an effect of discouraging private companies to take over the demonstration projects that have been mainly financed by the public sector. It is also critical to nurture human resources with skills and capacities necessary to understand and integrate technical and societal dimensions of smart cities. As smart cities consist of various types of hardware and software, coordination among different standards is also indispensable for facilitating the development and adoption of technologies for them. Policy measures and instruments need to be well coordinated on the institutional landscape at the macro level and specific technologies at the micro level. This was particularly important for the creation and liberalization of energy markets in encouraging new entrants and entrepreneurship and consequent competition. Iterated processes of road mapping of technological development to social system demonstration evolved through up-to-date and diverse inputs from relevant stakeholders. Standard setting needs to be carefully managed to facilitate connectivity among the existing technologies while paying close attention to emerging technologies in related fields.

References

Bergek, B. Carlsson, S. Jacobsson, S. Lindmark, and A. Rickne. 2008. Analyzing the functional dynamics of technological innovation systems: A scheme of analysis. *Research Policy* 37: 407–429.

Bergek, Anna, Staffan Jacobsson, Bo Carlsson, Sven Lindmark, and Annika Rickne. 2008. Analyzing the functional dynamics of technological innovation systems: A scheme of analysis. *Research Policy* 37: 407–429.

Carlsson, B. and R. Stankiewicz. 1991. On the nature, function, and composition of technological systems. *Journal of Evolutionary Economics* 1: 93–118.

Clastres, Cédric. 2011. Smart grids: Another step towards competition, energy security and climate change objectives. *Energy Policy* 39(9): 5399–5408.

Dasher, Richard B. 2012. The outlook for smart grids, in *Fresh Currents – Japan's Flow from a Nuclear Past to a Renewable Future.* Kyoto: Kyoto Journal, Heian-kyo Media.

ECHONET Consortium. 2013a). Application Areas. Retrieved on February 12, 2013. ECHONET Consortium. www.echonet.gr.jp/english/echo/application.htm.

ECHONET Consortium. 2013b). List of Members. Retrieved on February 12, 2013. ECHONET Consortium. www.echonet.gr.jp/english/membership/kigyo.htm.

European Technology Platform for Electricity Networks for the Future. 2016. The SmartGrid European Technology Platform. European Technology Platform for Electricity Networks for the Future. www.smartgrids.eu/ETPSmartGrids. Accessed on February 1, 2016.

Freeman, Christopher. 1988. Japan: A new national innovation system?, in *Technical Change and Economic Theory.* London: Pinter Publishers.

Hirai, Toshihiro (2013). Personal interview, Tokyo Institute of Technology, Tokyo, February 18.

Jacobsson, Staffan and Anna Bergek. 2004. Transforming the energy sector: The evolution of technological systems in renewable energy technology. *Industrial and Corporate Change* 13(5): 815–849.

Japan Smart Community Alliance. 2013. Membership (as of February 8, 2013). Retrieved February 13, 2013. Japan Smart Community Alliance: www.smart-japan.org/memberslist/tabid/189/Default.aspx.

Kamp, Linda, Ruud Smits, and Cornelis Andriesse. 2004. Notions on learning applied to wind turbine development in the Netherlands and Denmark. *Energy Policy* 32: 1625–1637.

Lin, Chen-Chun, Chia-Han Yang, and Joseph Z. Shyua. 2013. A comparison of innovation policy in the smart grid industry across the pacific: China and the USA. *Energy Policy* 57: 119–132.

Lundvall, Bengt-Ake. 1988. Innovation as an interactive process: From user-producer interaction to the national system of innovation, in Dosi, Giovanni, Christopher Freeman, Richard Nelson, Gerald Silverberg, and Luc Soete (eds.), *Technical Change and Economic Theory*. London: Pinter.

Malerba, Franco. 2002. Sectoral systems of innovation and production. *Research Policy* 31(2): 247–264.

Malerba, Franco, ed. 2004. *Sectoral Systems of Innovation: Concepts, Issues and Analyses of Six Major Sectors in Europe*. Cambridge: Cambridge University Press.

Malerba, Franco and Pamela Adams. 2014. Sectoral systems of innovation, in Dodgson, Mark, David M. Gann, and Nelson Phillips (eds.), *Oxford Handbook of Innovation Management*. Oxford: Oxford University Press.

Mochizuki, Shoji (2013). Personal interview, ECHONET Consortium, Tokyo, October 17.

Morozumi, Satoshi. 2010. NEDO's Grid Connection Related Research Activities. *Expert Group on New and Renewable Energy Technologies*.

Nelson, Richard, ed. 1993. *National Innovation Systems: A Comparative Analysis*. New York, NY: Oxford University Press.

Nelson, Richard R. 1994. The co-evolution of technology, industrial structure, and supporting institutions. *Industrial and Corporate Change* 3(1): 47–63.

Nelson, Richard R. 1995. Co-evolution of industry structure, technology and supporting institutions, and the making of comparative advantage. *International Journal of the Economics of Business* 2(2): 171–184.

Office of Energy and Environmental Industries. 2012. Japan's Electricity Market and Opportunities for U.S. Renewable Energy and Smart Grid Exporters. Market Intelligence Brief, Manufacturing and Services, International Trade Administration, Department of Commerce, United States.

Smith, Adrian, Andy Stirling, and Frans Berkhout. 2005. The governance of sustainable socio-technical transitions. *Research Policy* 34: 1491–1510.

Suurs, Roald. 2009. *Motors of Sustainable Innovation: Towards a Theory on the Dynamics of Technological Innovation Systems*. Utrecht: University of Utrecht.

Uetake, Kaori. 2013. Smart City Project, Yokohama City, March 19.

Vlieger, Esther and Loet Leydesdorff. 2010. *How to Analyze Frames Using Semantic Maps of a Collection of Messages?: Pajek Manual. leydesdorff .net*, Amsterdam: Amsterdam School of Communications Research (ASCoR), University of Amsterdam.

13 | Agglomeration of Invention in the Bay Area

Not Just ICT

CHRIS FORMAN, AVI GOLDFARB, AND
SHANE GREENSTEIN[*]

Does invention agglomerate, and if so, where does it agglomerate? In this chapter we examine changes in patterns of agglomeration in invention over time, using data on patent applications from all granted US patents.

There are plenty of reasons to expect invention to agglomerate. Carlino and Kerr's (2015) recent handbook chapter summarizes many such results, emphasizing the role of input sharing, labor market matching, and knowledge spillovers, among others. Knowledge spillovers received an especially large fraction of attention in their chapter, and in the literature overall (e.g. Jaffe, Trajtenberg, and Henderson 1993; Audretsch and Feldman 1996; Moretti 2012; Kerr and Kominers 2015).

Simple economics might forecast that most invention agglomerates in the same area as the primary using industry (Carlino and Kerr 2015). For example, patents related to automotive technology are clustered in Detroit (Hannigan, Cano-Kollmann, and Mudambi 2015). Or causality could be reversed: The location of a break-through invention can lead to industry agglomeration and localized follow-on invention (Duranton 2007). We label this "colocation" between invention and industry production.

However, other forces push away from colocation. Invention itself is an economic activity and it shares inputs, such as specialized labor institutions, particular intellectual property contracts, and

* Max Koven and Yasin Ozcan provided excellent research assistance.
We thank Maryann Feldman and seminar participants at the University of Toronto, Stanford University, and the 2016 American Economic Association meetings for helpful comments. Avi Goldfarb thanks SSHRC for research support.

information spillovers from one type of invention to another. If such forces are strong, they could lead to agglomeration of many types of invention in one place. We call this "coagglomeration of invention." For many industries, the key inventions could be in a location distinct from the place where production for the downstream industries resides.

Using patent data to measure invention, there are two approaches to investigate colocation and coagglomeration of invention. One is to map the agglomeration of downstream industries and invention and measure the geographic correlation. We take another approach. We look for evidence of coagglomeration of invention – namely, invention from distinct areas appearing in the same location, irrespective of downstream industry.

We find evidence consistent with the hypothesis of coagglomeration. We demonstrate a strong trend toward the clustering of patenting in the San Francisco Bay Area from 4 percent of US patents in 1976 to 16 percent of US patents in 2008, a time period when the fraction of the US population in the Bay Area did not increase substantially relative to the US population as a whole.[1] While this increase in Bay Area patenting is partly driven by the increasing fraction of patents in information and communication technologies (ICTs), ICTs cannot fully explain the trend. The San Francisco Bay Area has seen a substantial increase in its share of patents, even for patents that seem quite distant from ICTs, rising from 3.9 percent of such patents in 1976 to 6.9 percent in 2008.[2]

Our results are consistent with coagglomeration of invention in the Bay Area. While others have documented a tendency toward agglomeration of patenting by industry, we believe we are the first to

---

[1] According to the US Census, the Bay Area grew from 2.54 per cent of the US population in 1980 (5.74 million residents) to 2.65 per cent of the US population in 2010 (8.15 million residents).

[2] One unusual aspect of patenting in the San Francisco Bay Area is that invention is not centered in the city but in Silicon Valley. Therefore, while we refer to other cities by the city names, we refer to the "Bay Area" rather than "San Francisco" to describe the San Francisco Consolidated Metropolitan Statistical Area. We use the 2013 definition, which includes the following twelve counties and their FIPS codes: Alameda (06001), Contra Costa (06013), San Francisco (06075), San Mateo (06081), Marin (06041), Santa Clara (06085), San Benito (06069), San Joaquin (06077), Sonoma (06097), Solano (05095), Santa Cruz (06087), and Napa (06055).

document a general tendency toward agglomeration in patenting across industries and patent classes. Further, our study is unique in its documentation of agglomeration in one particular region, the Bay Area.

Coagglomeration in production and invention has been documented in other settings and other industries. For example, Rosenberg (1963) analyzes sewing machines, bicycles, and automobiles located in northern Ohio and southeastern Michigan and their sharing of common inventions in machine tools, and shows how growing downstream industries induced additional improvements in those innovations over time. Glaeser (2005) discusses coagglomeration of production across many industries in New York City, starting in the nineteenth century. A number of recent researchers have explored the causes and consequences of coagglomeration, including Ellison, Glaeser, and Kerr (2010), Helsley and Strange (2014), and Delgado, Porter, and Stern (2014).

At this point, our results do not provide a definitive cause for this broad increase in coagglomeration in invention. A variety of mechanisms are possible including regulation, financing, shared labor markets across invention types, and knowledge spillovers across invention types.

Of course, we are not the first to document the agglomeration of economic activity in ICT in the Bay Area. Garcia-Vicente, Garcia-Swartz, and Campbell-Kelly (2014) show that such agglomeration began to arise in the 1980s and 1990s. Our results are consistent with this timing. A variety of authors have explored the reasons behind the agglomeration of the ICT industry in the Bay Area and its dynamics in generating new firms and new ideas (e.g. Saxenian 1994; Franco and Mitchell 2008; Chen et al 2010; Marx, Singh and Fleming 2015; Kerr and Kominers 2015). Our contribution relates to the finding of the increasing role of the Bay Area in patenting overall.

13.1 Data and Empirical Strategy

We use patents granted by the US Patent and Trademark Office (USPTO) as our measure of invention. Because of the delay between patent application and grant date, we date patents using the year of application. We have data on patents granted between 1976 and 2012, and our analysis data set includes patents with application dates between 1976 and 2008. We cut off the last four years of the data because of lags between year granted and year filed. Generally, we start to see a decline in patenting in 2008, suggesting right truncation may be an issue for the last few years of our data. The trends we identify appear long before 2008.

Patents have been shown to provide a useful measure of a firm's intangible stock of knowledge (Hall, Jaffe, and Trajtenberg 2005). Their limitations are well known. Not all patents meet the USPTO criteria for patentability (Jaffe and Trajtenberg 2002), and not all inventors seek to patent. Further, the propensity to patent has changed over time during our sample (e.g. Hall and Ziedonis 2001); this was particularly the case for patents related to software, which grew rapidly toward the end of our sample period due to changes that strengthened their legal rights (e.g. Graham and Mowery 2003; Hall and MacGarvie 2010). We are comfortable with using patents in this context because our primary focus is on changes in the geographic distribution of patenting within broad technology areas over time. While the propensity to patent has changed across patent classes over time, we rely on the assumption that it has not changed significantly across geographic locations.

We map inventors to counties and MSAs using the zip code of the location of the inventor. We used consolidated MSAs (CMSAs) where those were present. This will be particularly important for our analysis of the Bay Area.

For the analysis that follows, we do not weight by citations. For multi-author patents, we divide by the number of authors. For example, if a patent has one author in the Bay Area and two authors in Boston, it would count as one third of a patent in the Bay Area and two thirds of a patent in Boston. Our results are generally robust, and often stronger, using three-year and five-year citation-weighted measures. For example, using either three- or five-year citation weights, the Bay Area surpasses New York City as the location with the most patents three years earlier than with the unweighted measure.

Our analysis requires us to identify patents that represent inventions related to ICT, or inventions that draw upon the stock of knowledge related to ICT. As is well known, identifying such inventions through the patent data is difficult (see, e.g. Graham and Mowery 2003; Bessen and Hunt 2007; Hall and MacGarvie 2010). As a result, we use different definitions based on the primary class of the patent and explore the robustness of our results to alternatives.

We present our results at the year level, as aggregated means over the thirty-three years from 1976 to 2008 inclusive. In particular, our results are presented as graphs of time trends of the fraction of patents each year that meet some criteria such as location in the Bay Area. This is therefore a descriptive exercise that tests whether the results are consistent with increasing coagglomeration of invention in the San Francisco Bay Area over time.

13.2 Results

13.2.1 Patenting across Locations

Given the overall rise in the propensity to patent, all major urban areas had an increase in the number of patents. We explore the fraction of all US patents by area, thereby controlling for the overall trend.

Figure 13.1 shows the increasing importance of the Bay Area as a fraction of US patenting. It compares the top ten areas in the United States, defined by the total number of patents between 1976 and 2008. In 1976, the New York City area was the dominant center for patenting, with just under 15 percent of all patents. Generally, patenting was highly correlated with population. The Bay Area rose steadily as a fraction of patenting in the 1970s and 1980s, and then the trend increased in the 1990s before settling down at the earlier rate of increase in the 2000s. In 1995, the Bay Area surpassed New York City as the US location with the largest number of patents.

Figure 13.2 combines locations into four groups: the Bay Area, New York City, the eighteen other cities in the top 20, and all other locations. Generally, while New York and locations outside the top 20 are falling as a proportion of patenting, the Bay Area is rising quickly, and the other eighteen cities in the top 20 are rising slightly (42.6 percent in 1976 to 46.1 percent at the peak level in 2004).

13.2.2 Patenting across Types of Patents

The Bay Area has had a cluster of ICT firms for many years. Therefore, one reason the Bay Area is becoming an increasingly large fraction of

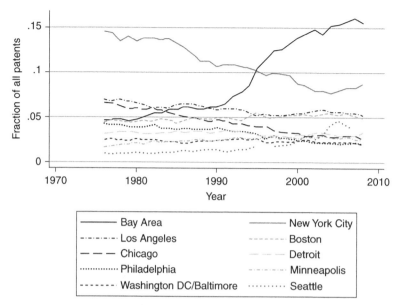

Figure 13.1 Fraction of patents in top 10 cities

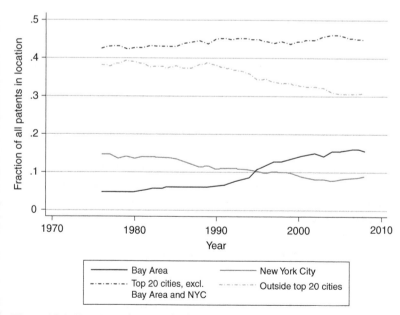

Figure 13.2 Fraction of patents by location type

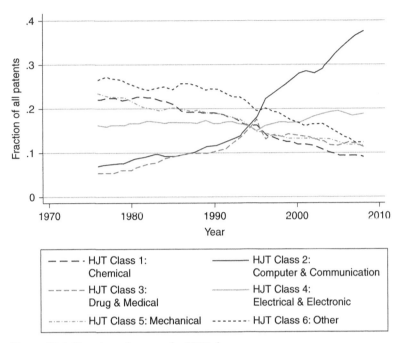

Figure 13.3 Fraction of patents by HJT class

patenting is the increase in ICT patents as a fraction of total patenting. Figure 13.3 displays this increase using the Hall, Jaffe, and Trajtenberg (HJT) definitions of patent classes. Computers and Communication (Class 2) went from under 10 percent of patents to over 30 percent of patents between 1980 and 2005. Some of this growth may reflect changes in the propensity to patent software and other ICT inventions (e.g. Graham and Mowery 2003; Hall and Ziedonis 2001) that have been encouraged by sympathetic treatment in the courts and the PTO. Drugs and Medical (Class 3) tracked the increase in Computers and Communication until the mid-1990s but then settled back to around 13 percent of patents.

We offer the first evidence supporting the coagglomeration hypothesis with Figure 13.4, which shows the fraction of patents that are in the Bay Area by broad class. The increase is sharpest in Computers and Communication and in Electrical and Electronic (Class 4). It is also noticeable in Chemicals (Class 1), Drugs and Medical, and Mechanical (Class 5). In Other (Class 6) the increase is smaller, rising from

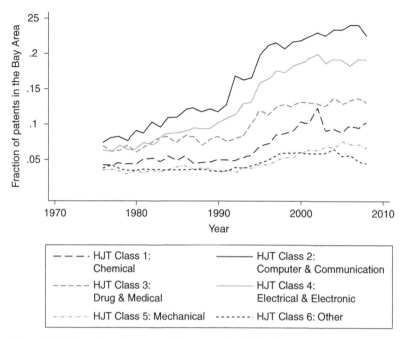

Figure 13.4 Fraction of patents in bay area by HJT class

3.8 percent in 1976 to a peak of 6.3 percent in 2004 before falling back to 4.4 percent in 2008. Thus, for five of six broad patent classes, we see a noticeable rise in the proportion of patents coming from the Bay Area.

One possibility is that many of the patents in the Chemicals, Drugs and Medical, and Mechanical classes are ICT-based. Software has increasingly been used as an input into a wider array of inventions in other patent categories (Arora, Branstetter, and Drev 2013; Branstetter, Drev, and Kwon 2015). Figure 13.5 shows our preferred measures of ICT and non-ICT patents to account for this possibility, and examines the trend over time. We define ICT patents as all patents in Computers and Communication (HJT Class 2) or Electrical and Electronic patents (HJT Class 4) plus software patents as defined by Graham and Mowery (2003). The general results are robust to dropping HJT Class 4 or software patents, or to including a broader definition of software patents that includes patents identified through a keyword search as in Bessen and Hunt (2007) and software patents identified in Graham and Vishnubhakat (2013).

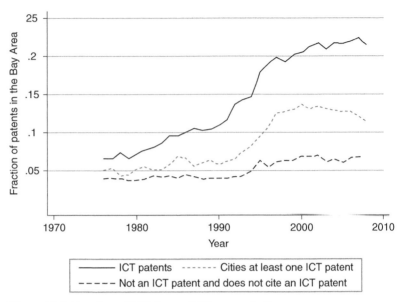

Figure 13.5 Fraction of ICT & non-ICT patents in Bay area

The solid line at the top of the graph shows the increasing proportion of ICT patents that are in the Bay Area. The dotted line identifies all patents that cite ICT patents but are not explicitly categorized as ICT using the definition in this chapter. Instead, they are connected through citation and therefore build on ICT invention. There is a clear trend toward an increasing proportion of these patents in the Bay Area, providing another explanation for the rise of Bay Area patents.

Together, the above suggest the following: ICT is an increasingly large fraction of patents; the Bay Area is an increasingly large (and even dominant) fraction of ICT patents; and the Bay Area is an increasingly large fraction of patents that cite ICT patents. Given prior results on agglomeration of the ICT industry in the Bay Area, perhaps none of these results are surprising, though we believe that the results on geography of patents that cite ICT are not previously documented. These all could result from agglomeration of software invention near the location of the firms producing electronics, computing, and communications.

The evidence for coagglomeration of invention appears in the dashed line in Figure 13.5: The Bay Area is an increasing fraction of non-ICT US patents, rising from 3.9 percent to 6.9 percent from 1976 to 2008.

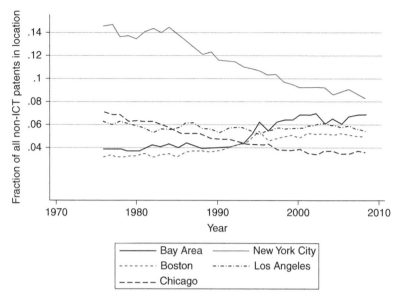

Figure 13.6 Fraction of non-ICT patents by city

While these figures are more modest than the increase in ICT patents, they still suggest an increasingly important role for the Bay Area, relative to all other areas, in US non-ICT patenting. Figure 13.6 compares the Bay Area to the four other top patenting cities in the United States. The Bay Area was second behind New York for most of the period from 1997 to 2008.

Overall, we interpret these results to suggest that we cannot reject coagglomeration of invention. The increase in patenting in the Bay Area is not entirely attributable to the increasing fraction of ICT patents in overall patenting.

13.3 Conclusions

We have documented an increase of the fraction of US patenting of all kinds that occurs in the Bay Area that is disproportionate to population growth and occurs within a variety of patent classes. This partly results from the agglomeration of invention near the production of firms who use the invention, and who themselves agglomerate in one area. We also think it offers evidence of coagglomeration, the clustering of invention from many distinct types of invention into one geographic area.

While we do not know the cause of the rise in coagglomeration of many patent types in the Bay Area, our results suggest that any possible explanation must be broad-based. In particular, any explanation must account for growth in the fraction of ICT and non-ICT patents in the Bay Area.

References

Arora, Ashish, Lee G. Branstetter, and Matej Drev. 2013. Going soft: How The rise of software-based innovation led to the decline of Japan's IT industry and the resurgence of Silicon Valley. *Review of Economics and Statistics* 95(3): 757–775.

Audretsch, David and Maryann Feldman. 1996. R&D spillovers and the geography of innovation and production. *American Economic Review* 86: 630–640.

Bessen, James and Robert Hunt. 2007. An empirical look at software patents. *Journal of Economics and Management Strategy* 16(1): 157–189.

Branstetter, Lee, Matej Drev, and Manho Kwon. 2015. Get with the Program: Software-Driven Innovation in Traditional Manufacturing. Working paper.

Carlino, Gerald and William Kerr. 2015. Agglomeration and Innovation. In Gilles Duranton, Vernon Henderson, and William Strange (eds.), *Handbook of Regional and Urban Economics Volume 5*. 349–404.

Chen, Henry, Paul Gompers, Anna Kovner, and Josh Lerner. 2010. Buy local? The geography of venture capital. *Journal of Urban Economics* 67(1): 90–102.

Delgado, Mercedes, Michael Porter, and Scott Stern. 2014. Clusters, convergence, and economic performance. *Research Policy* 43(10): 1785–1799.

Duranton, G. 2007. Urban evolutions: the fast, the slow, and the still. *American Economic Review* 97: 197–221.

Ellison, Glenn, Edward L. Glaeser, and William R. Kerr. 2010. What causes industry agglomeration? Evidence from coagglomeration patterns. *American Economic Review* 100(3): 1195–1213.

Franco, April and Matthew Mitchell. 2008. Covenants not to compete: labor mobility and industry dynamics. *Journal of Economics and Management Strategy* 17(3): 581–606.

Garcia-Vicente, Florencia, Daniel Garcia-Swartz, and Martin Campbell-Kelly. 2014. The Hydra of Lerna: Economic-Geography Perspectives on America's Early Computer Clusters. Working paper, Warwick University.

Glaeser, Edward. 2005. Urban colossus: Why is New York America's largest city? *FRBNY Economic Policy Review* December: 7–24.

Graham, Stuart and David Mowery. 2003. Intellectual property protection in the U.S. software industry, in Wesley Cohen and Stephen Merrill (eds.) *Patents in the Knowledge Economy.* Washington, DC: National Research Council, 219–258.

Graham, Stuart and Saurabh Vishnubhakat. 2013. Of smart phone wars and software patents. *Journal of Economic Perspectives* 27(1): 67–86.

Hall, Bronwyn, Adam Jaffe, and Manuel Trajtenberg. 2005. Market value and patent citations. *RAND Journal of Economics* 36(1): 16–38.

Hall, Bronwyn and Megan MacGarvie. 2010. The private value of software patents. *Research Policy* 39(7): 994–1009.

Hall, B. H. and R. Ziedonis. 2001. The patent paradox revisited: An empirical study of patenting in the US semiconductor industry, 1979–1995. *RAND Journal of Economics* 32: 101–128.

Hannigan, Thomas J., Marcelo Cano-Kollmann, and Ram Mudambi. 2015. Thriving innovation amidst manufacturing decline: The Detroit auto cluster and the resilience of local knowledge production. *Industrial and Corporate Change* 24(6): 1–22.

Helsley, Robert W. and William C. Strange. 2014. Coagglomeration, Clusters, and the Scale and Composition of Cities. *Journal of Political Economy.* 122(5),1064–1093.

Jaffe, A., M. Trajtenberg, and R. Henderson. 1993. Geographic localization of knowledge spillovers as evidenced by patent citations. *Quarterly Journal of Economics* 108(3): 577–598.

Jaffe, Adam and Manuel Trajtenberg. 2002. *Patents, Citations, and Innovations: A Window on the Knowledge Economy.* Cambridge, MA: MIT Press.

Kerr, William and Scott Kominers. 2015. Agglomerative forces and cluster shapes. *Review of Economics and Statistics*, forthcoming.

Marx, M. J. Singh and L. Fleming. 2015. Regional disadvantage? Employee non-compete agreements and brain drain. *Research Policy* 44(2): 394–404.

Moretti, E. 2012. *The New Geography of Jobs.* New York: Houghton Mifflin Harcourt.

Rosenberg, Nathan. 1963. Technology change in the machine tool industry, 1840–1910. *The Journal of Economic History* 23(4): 414–443.

Saxenian, A. 1994. *Regional Advantage: Culture and Competition in Silicon Valley and Route 128.* Cambridge, MA: Harvard University Press.

PART IV

Innovation Management and its Links with Policy

14 Knowledge-Intensive Entrepreneurship and Future Research Directions

FRANCO MALERBA AND MAUREEN MCKELVEY

14.1 Introduction

Entrepreneurship as a more general field of research has exploded in recent decades. Many different scientific disciplines have contributed to the understanding of entrepreneurship. The definitions, approaches, and results are so diverse that the concept of entrepreneurship may well have become a "catch-all" term (Davidson et al. 2001; OECD 2008). Despite this broad scope, the entrepreneurship literature has contributed a range of interesting theoretical and empirical results, which focus attention upon specific dimensions of how and why founders, teams, and firms act upon the process of entrepreneurship as well as more broadly within the economy and society. Numerous articles and handbooks have endeavored to define the field of entrepreneurship as a research field as well as to define the phenomena and the appropriate lines of enquiry for future research (Shane 2000; Shane & Venktaraman 2000; Carlsson et al. 2013; Landström et al. 2012; Venktaraman et al. 2012). Instead of tackling the broad field of entrepreneurship in general, this chapter focuses upon a more specific phenomenon within entrepreneurship, namely knowledge-intensive entrepreneurship (KIE),[*] which is highly relevant to economics and management theories inspired by Schumpeter.

We focus upon the concept of knowledge-intensive entrepreneurship (KIE) and discuss future research trajectories, which can enrich related

[*] We thank Yannis Caloghirou, Slavo Radosevic, and Nicholas Vonortas for continuous interactions and feedbacks and for several comments on previous versions of the paper. For useful comments and suggestions, we also thank the participants of the KEINS and AEGIS projects; the workshop held in Gothenburg 2015 on "Evolutionary approaches informing research on entrepreneurship and regional development"; the Montreal Schumpeter Society Conference (ISS 2016); the SPRU 50th anniversary Conference in Sussex in 2016; and the European Association for Evolutionary Political Economy (EAEPE) in Manchester in 2016.

fields inspired by Schumpeter such as entrepreneurship, innovation systems, and evolutionary economics. Our approach follows in the tradition of a Schumpeterian approach, in the sense that entrepreneurship is driven by innovation and the activities of entrepreneurs, who are responding to opportunities in markets and technology (Schumpeter 1934, 1942 and 1949; Malerba 2004). Moreover, entrepreneurial activities introduce uncertainty and disequilibrium into the economy, which in turn promote economic development. More specifically, this chapter focuses upon the particular case where advanced knowledge and innovation are the basis of competitive advantage for entrepreneurs. We propose that KIE firms, which introduce disequilibrium and rely upon advanced knowledge, can be identified across all types of manufacturing and service sectors, and they do so by taking advantage of diverse innovative opportunities.

Hence, the purpose of this chapter is to expand the discussion of how to conceptualize the existence, and importance, of knowledge-intensive entrepreneurship in order to propose directions for future research. More specifically, the definition and stylized process model of KIE that we have presented in other research (Malerba and McKelvey 2011; Malerba and McKelvey 2015; Malerba and McKelvey forthcoming 2017) highlight questions related to how and why the process of entrepreneurship helps translate knowledge into economic value, through innovations commercialized in firms and their network connections with actors in the innovation systems. More specifically, this chapter focuses upon the special case where advanced knowledge and innovation are the basis of competitive advantage for entrepreneurs.[1]

This is a rich area, and there are many ways to discuss future research. We will do so in terms of taking stock of existing concepts, in order to align indicators/measurements and interesting topics. Section 14.2 provides a definition, briefly linked to relevant literature. Section 14.3 presents results from a large-scale microdata survey, while Sections 14.4 and 14.5 focus on operationalization and future research agendas, respectively. Given that KIE represents a new phenomenon not previously studied theoretically and empirically except in selected literature, these sections address research about KIE in general and KIE ventures in particular.

---

[1] More detailed analysis of the phenomenon can be found in the four books (Malerba 2010; McKelvey and Lassen 2013a; McKelvey and Lassen 2013b; Malerba et al. 2015). These books were supported by the European projects KEINS and AEGIS, see references.

The conclusion provides many areas for future research. One point has to do with the particular role of knowledge and institutions that stimulate the transformation of knowledge and ideas into innovations. Another large topic is to further develop analyses of innovation, entrepreneurship, and performance in different varieties of knowledge-intensive entrepreneurship. For example, science-based industries and creative industries are thought to differ on many points, so there is a need to compare and contrast them. Moreover, research should contextualize the role of sectoral systems of innovation relative to theories of industrial evolution and industrial dynamics.

Thus, much is left to be done in future research and in debates with policy makers. The conceptualization of KIE is also important, because public policy makers and related innovation policy literature argue that phenomena similar to what we call KIE are important due to the increasingly important role of advanced knowledge and innovation for economic growth and societal development.

14.2 Conceptualization of Knowledge-Intensive Entrepreneurship More Generally and KIE Ventures More Specifically

Our approach starts from a Schumpeterian analysis of how innovation and entrepreneurship drive economic development. By drawing explicitly upon Schumpeter, evolutionary economics, and innovation systems, Malerba and McKelvey (2017) propose the following definition: Knowledge-intensive entrepreneurial ventures are new learning organizations that use and transform existing knowledge and generate new knowledge in order to innovate within innovation systems. This more theoretical concept also requires a definition, which can be operationalized in empirical work, as used and discussed in Section 14.4. Hence, an early definition useful for operationalization by Malerba and McKelvey (2011 and 2015) proposes that a KIE venture has the following four characteristics, namely (i) is an entrepreneurial venture formalized as a new firm; (ii) is innovative; (iii) has a significant knowledge intensity; and (iv) can exploit innovative opportunities across many sectors.

The concept of KIE entrepreneurship and of KIE ventures tries to unite different levels of analysis – there are the founders and teams who act as entrepreneurs; there is usually a project that accesses resources;

there may be a firm that is consolidated as a formal organization; and there is a broad phenomenon affecting society and the economy called entrepreneurship.

Entrepreneurs take risks, under conditions of uncertainty, by introducing innovations and they aim to capture temporary returns to their innovations. Based upon a substantial review, Bull and Willard (1993) conclude that most definitions of entrepreneurship are related to the Schumpeterian view in the sense that "an entrepreneur creates value by carrying out new combinations causing discontinuity." They propose it is possible to make predictions about the conditions under which a person may become an entrepreneur, specifically by considering: (1) Task-related motivation, (2) Expertise, (3) Expectation of personal gain, and (4) A supportive environment (Bull and Willard 1993). Hence, the specific person of an entrepreneur has certain characteristics, and a related discussion analyzes business organizations as having entrepreneurial orientation. Ardichvili et al. (2003) argue that the individual entrepreneur is more or less able to identify these market opportunities and develop a venture, based upon: (a) entrepreneurial alertness, (b) information asymmetries and prior (individual) knowledge, (c) social networks, (d) personality traits, and (e) the type of opportunity. Hence, the main structural explanation for entrepreneurial opportunities can be seen in the "market," especially in relation of how market imperfections enable arbitrage profits. However, given that these market imperfections could theoretically be visible to all entrepreneurs, much of the literature stressing this type of opportunity tends to try to find explanations at the level of characteristics and traits of the individual entrepreneur. This has also lead to a central discussion in entrepreneurship research about the origin of opportunities (Shane and Venkataraman 2002; Eckhardt and Shane 2003; Vaghely and Julien 2010).

There are also the wider effects of the process of entrepreneurship. Schumpeter (1942: 82) stated that "The fundamental impulse that sets and keeps the capitalist engine in motion comes from the new consumers' goods, the new methods of production or transportation, the new markets, the new forms of industrial organization that capitalist enterprise creates." In accordance with a large literature, we mean that the broader concept of entrepreneurship can be primarily analyzed as a function of the economic system, which promotes growth, and this means that entrepreneurs will play a particularly important function in introducing disequilibrium into the economic system (Andersen 2009; Metcalfe and Foster 2012).

More specifically, we have introduced the knowledge-intensive entrepreneurship concept, because of the need to better conceptualize the linkages between innovation, entrepreneurship, and performance in these processes. Hence, from our perspective, knowledge is at the vase of entrepreneurship and helps reduce uncertainty during these processes but it may also introduce new uncertainty in a restless capitalist perspective (Metcalfe 1998). Another way to consider this is that knowledge is embedded in new elements – such as a technology, a product, an organization, or a market – which keep introducing new dynamics into the economy (Holmèn et al. 2007).

Our discussion of the generation, use, and diffusion of different types of knowledge is also related to how that knowledge is changed into value for the firm. Schumpeter had a classical distinction between invention, which is closer to the idea, and innovation, which requires some return on the market.

Similarly within entrepreneurship literature, another recent line of research tries to move from the previous focus upon the individual and the start-up company to understand the broader systemic process of entrepreneurship (Acs et al. 2009; Malerba 2010; Carlsson et al. 2013). Entrepreneurs, in fact, interact with, and benefit from, the various components of the national, regional, and sectoral systems (Nelson 2019; Lundvall 1993; Cooke et al. 1997; Malerba 2002). In the KIE process, as well as in analyzing a specific KIE venture, we would like to stress the inherent uncertainty involved in the creation and translation of knowledge into products and services, or what is known as identifying innovative opportunities and creating value. Based on our previous work, we focus upon network relationships between the KIE venture and the surrounding innovation systems.

In summary, we follow the Schumpeterian theoretical tradition that entrepreneurship is driven by innovation and the activities of entrepreneurs, who are responding to opportunities in markets and technology. Moreover, entrepreneurial activities introduce uncertainty and disequilibrium into the economy, which in turn promote economic development. The phenomenon of knowledge-intensive entrepreneurship involves these broader processes. The entrepreneur, team, and ventures are involved in entrepreneurship in the broad sense of systemic, problem-solving processes; embedded in innovation systems;

affected by their institutional context; and take advantage of diverse innovative opportunities. While we recognize the impact of founders, teams, and projects, we are interested here in the actual process of how entrepreneurs and teams move to starting and managing a company.

14.3 What We Know about KIE Ventures in Europe

This section builds upon the existing empirical evidence about knowledge-intensive entrepreneurial ventures in Europe, in order to illustrate how the theoretical propositions are backed up by survey data and case studies. The first subsection introduces a survey of KIE ventures in Europe; the second subsection introduces the analysis of eighty-six case studies of KIE ventures in Europe; and the final subsection presents descriptive data and illustrations related to the characteristics of these KIE ventures.

14.3.1 A Survey of KIE Ventures in Europe

Both sets of evidence reported here were integral parts of the European Union project known as AEGIS,[2] which followed upon the European Union project KEINS.

In AEGIS, a major survey of KIE ventures was carried out in 2010. The survey was intended to sample KIE ventures across a range of sectors and countries within Europe. See Caloghirou et al. 2011, 2015 for more details and empirical overview. The sectors included were sampled from high-tech manufacturing, medium- to high-tech manufacturing, low-tech manufacturing, medium to low manufacturing, and knowledge-intensive business services (KIBS). The countries included were Croatia, Czech Republic, Denmark, France, Germany, Greece, Italy, Portugal, Sweden, and the United Kingdom.

Survey questions from other surveys that have been validated previously – e.g. GEM, CIS, Yale survey, etc. – have been used as well as additional new questions, which are designed to be interesting from a theoretical perspective. The survey questions were developed collaboratively within the AEGIS project, with questions being developed by the researchers in the AEGIS scientific committee (from Bocconi University, NTUA Athens, IMIT / University of Gothenburg, and UCL)

---

[2] See also Aegis Research Project 2013.

and the development of the survey questions was presented and discussed several times with the full AEGIS consortium.

The sample of potential companies was pulled primarily from the population of firms found in the Amadeus database. The survey also included a series of control questions, to ensure they met the previously described definition of KIE ventures. Amadeus database also gives financial and other data per company. Four thousand and four companies were sampled, through telephone survey in the main language of each country.

The main purpose of this survey of KIE ventures has been to investigate whether KIE ventures indeed exist across different sectors, as well as to identify a series of variables and relationships deemed important theoretically. These primarily focus around firm-level variables, set in relation to impacts from the wider innovation system.

Key dimensions of the survey included the following six points:

- The founder/team and origins of the company.
- Knowledge characteristics of the firm.
- The knowledge lifecycle of the company, set in relation to innovation system factors.
- Business, market, and institutional conditions.
- Innovation.
- Aspects of firm-specific strategy and performance.

These six points were divided into approximately forty questions in the survey. These dimensions are further explained in Section 14.3, in connection with a description of the results.

14.3.2 An Analysis of Eighty-Six Case Studies of KIE Ventures in Europe

A series of eighty-six case studies were performed of KIE ventures in Europe – see Ljungberg et al. (2012), McKelvey and Lassen (2013b), and McKelvey et al. (2015). The various case studies were analyzed in accordance with the three phases of a KIE venture proposed in McKelvey and Lassen (2013a), namely the phase of accessing resources and ideas; managing and developing the venture; and evaluating performance and output.

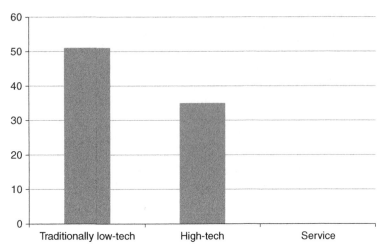

Figure 14.1 Distribution in terms of high-tech manufacturing, low-tech manufacturing, and services

In total, eighty-six case studies of KIE ventures at the firm level have been conducted and analyzed. The majority of cases concern firms within industries that traditionally are characterized as low-tech, as shown in Figure 14.1.

The case studies were, however, concentrated in certain industries as seen in Figure 14.2. Both high-tech (IT) and low-tech (Machine tools) were studied in detail.

Moreover, the case studies were performed in different European countries, as seen in Figure 14.3.

These eighty-six case studies of KIE ventures address several of the conceptual issues that have related KIE ventures to innovation systems, growth, and performance as identified in this chapter. Many of the case studies focus upon strategy, business models, mobilization of resources, and other internal processes of venture creation, as related to a temporal, sectoral, and geographical relationship to the innovation system. The AEGIS case studies are primarily theory-driven, based upon an explicit research design to address very specific questions/puzzles that are not answered through qualitative data. Case studies may primarily focus upon qualitative data but may also combine qualitative and quantitative data in multiple case study design. A few case studies are chosen upon a sampling strategy, which implies that the projects have first identified (often surveyed or otherwise gather

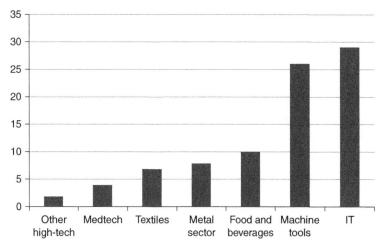

Figure 14.2 Distribution by sector

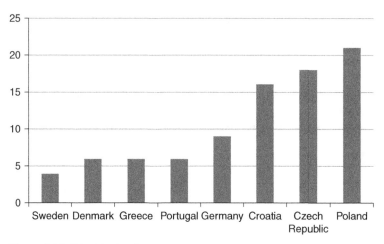

Figure 14.3 Distribution by country

quantitative data) a total population and then selected relevant case studies. Others were chosen for illustrative purposes.

14.3.3 Evidence from Both Survey and Analysis of Eighty-six Case Studies

This section uses evidence from both the survey and analysis of the eighty-six case studies, in order to provide descriptive statistics and insights into these KIE ventures in Europe. The categories follow the ones described previously for the survey.

14.3.3.1 The Founder/Team and Origins of the Company

The issue of founder/team and origins of the venture referred especially to the founder or founding team, as well as the early phase of moving from a project to a venture. Hence, examples of variables analyzed include characteristics of the founders of the company; determinants of why they decided to start up the company; the type of formation the company had, such as university spin-off or corporate spin-off; the type and amount of funding obtained; and the opportunities and obstacles that the company faced in the early phase.

From the survey, the data show that the origins of the firms were individual founders or small teams. Eight-six percent of the firms had three or fewer founders, and of the total, 37 percent had one founder. Eighty-two percent of founders were male, and 18 percent female, which were more likely to be founders of low-tech firms.

From the case studies, many of those studied are also small and remain small, but a few have many employees. Thus a skewed distribution (which also exists in the survey data) is present.

As seen in Figure 14.4, four categories of KIE ventures are identified as studied in the case studies: Corporate entrepreneurship, Academic spin- offs, Corporate spin-offs, and Independent start-ups. Note that

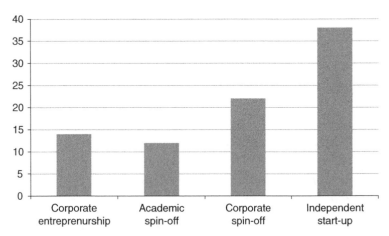

Figure 14.4 Distribution by origin of company

this categorization of the cases is based on conceptual idea of the sources of knowledge to the KIE venture, i.e. the sources of the ideas, knowledge, and opportunities leading to the foundation of the venture.

Most of the ones selected for study (thirty-eight) can be classified as independent start-ups, e.g. without support from their parent organization, and include serial entrepreneurs, experienced employees of existing firms, etc. Fourteen cases concern corporate entrepreneurship within existing firms, which later led to company formation. Twelve cases concern academic spin-offs, which are firms founded by researchers employed at universities or research institutes, but in a few cases also by recent graduates who established the firm based on ideas and knowledge gained during their academic studies. Corporate spin-offs are, similarly, firms founded based on knowledge and opportunities identified by existing firms.

14.3.3.2 Knowledge Characteristics of the Firm

These characteristics were focused upon the constituting knowledge assets and skills. This included variables about the founders of the company in terms of their experience, skills, and training as well as educational attainment of the employees. In the survey, questions were asked not only about scientific and technical training but also other types such as design. In the case studies, a key issue was to identify the types of knowledge produced and used by the firm, through both internal absorptive capacities and through knowledge networks.

Of the founders, approximately 43 percent had a degree, of which 29 percent had a postgraduate degree and only 6 percent had a PhD. About 41 percent of founders had previously been employed in the same industry, and another 19 percent had been employed in a different industry. The founders had an average of professional (corporate) experience of 12.2 years. In terms of forming the company, four variables that represent knowledge useful to act upon opportunities were listed as very/extremely important to firms, namely work experience in the current activity field (83 percent); market knowledge (73 percent); technical/engineering knowledge in the field (68 percent); and networks built during previous career (63 percent). Many founders had prior industry experience.

In the case studies, the characteristics of the founder – including previous education and experience – have an important effect not only on the initial start-up phase but also in the later management and development of the KIE venture. There are many illustrations that help us understand why the founders often have extensive prior experience of the industry of their start-ups, which is commonly also accompanied with related technical knowledge.

Here is an illustration from a KIE venture operating within the food industry:[3]

The entrepreneurs had professional competences in different fields such as business management, baking, logistic and finance, but they all had basic knowledge of the food processing industry. With the common knowledge as solid foundation, they could contribute with the expert knowledge in the respective fields to build up the new business. All three entrepreneurs had knowledge of the industry from former work experience and the major investor, who is also the chairman of the board, also had many years of experience in convenience food market.

This example illustrates how three founders have combined their complementary prior knowledge, and that they all have industrial and market experience in this industry.

14.3.3.3 The Knowledge Lifecycle of the Company, Set in Relation to Innovation System Factors

These are variables that can affect the formation, growth, and performance of the KIE venture. For network relationships, questions focused on issues such as the role of customers, the sources of knowledge such as universities, public research organizations, suppliers, and so on; the links and networking; and the types of alliances established.

The survey has a series of questions related to how important different sources of information were for exploring new opportunities. The most important sources were clients or customers (86%), followed by in-house knowledge (knowhow, R&D laboratories, and similar (53%) and suppliers (51%). KIE ventures in all three areas – high-tech sector, low-tech sector, and KIBS – reported other SMEs as their most important customer. Similarly, networks were important in being able to contact customers and suppliers (76 percent), recruit skilled labor (52 percent), select suppliers (51 percent), and develop new products and

---

[3] The quotes have been extracted from the analysis of 86 case studies in the AEGIS project and made anonymous. Please see McKelvey et a.l 2015 for an analysis of all the case studies.

services (47 percent). Alliances were particularly important in relation to subcontracting and strategic alliances.

Similarly in the eighty-six case studies, customers play a key role in linking the KIE venture to the innovation system, and in helping to define possible market opportunities. For an illustration, "Since CMDK1 is a custom-made product manufacturer, it is important to cooperate closely with the customers. To satisfy customers' specific needs, the company has to involve customers in the development phase." This quote indicates that companies are involved in innovation processes.

Here is an illustration, of why having specific knowledge built upon networks and commercial experience can help the KIE venture to pursue market opportunities:

Mr L has been an experienced entrepreneur for 36 years. He has already founded fourteen companies in different sectors like IT, electronics or leasing services but had no business experience in the textile industry so far. Mr L has no formal education. He broke up the secondary education and a professional education as a mechanics, worked as a vendor and purchaser without any formal commercial apprenticeship. He picked up his commercial know-how on the job. In the age of 22 he founded his first company. Before the establishment of CTGE1 Mr L sold a former company in the electronics sector to a leading company for metal fittings and took a timeout from business. Mr L is considered as creative and as a professional in marketing and sales. He widened the business strategy for consumer products which is supposed to lead to the main volume of sales in a few years by licensing to big manufacturers. Moreover, he organised the investors for commercialising the new fibres from his social network. The motivation of Mr L can be described as intrinsic. At this time he was 51 years old and had earned enough money by his entrepreneurial activities to retire. He was fascinated by the platform technology and its numerous fields of application and felt challenged by this risky situation that no one else of the sector felt encouraged to join this venture.

This longer quote illustrates many aspects of the entrepreneurial process, but in particular we would like to highlight how cumulative experience matters for commercialization of a new technology.

14.3.3.4 Business, Market, and Institutional Conditions
There are many interesting variables related to examining the institutional and market environment that surrounds KIE and that can be a source of growth as well as obstacles to firm-level outcomes such as commercialization, innovation, and growth. Financing is one important aspect as well.

446Franco Malerba and Maureen McKelvey

The survey questions captured respondents' self-reported perceptions of their business environment, as well as how these conditions either promoted opportunities or acted as barriers to the firm. Similar aspects can be captured through semi-structured interviews in case studies.

In the survey, a key aspect of the business environment was the focus upon competition over quality (61 percent) but also competition over price/low cost (52 percent). Innovation was considered important, especially introducing new products and services (49 percent). Firms considered it important to be able to offer products and goods to specific needs of different market niches (82 percent), but also the capacity to offer premium price (62 percent) and at low cost (42 percent). Key institutional barriers reported were high tax rates (57 percent), regulatory requirements (44 percent), and labor market regulation (39 percent). For financing at the time of starting up the company, the majority relied upon informal sources including own financial resources (80 percent) and family members (43 percent). For more formal financing, this included banks (52 percent), venture capital (45 percent), previous employer (44 percent), and national/local authority or EU (34 percent).

In the case studies, the struggle was often reported between producing unique goods at a higher price, while at the same time also providing goods or services wanted by the market at a reasonable price. Finding this balance can be illustrated, with consideration of why KIE ventures stress the relationships with customers.

The firm's most important relationships are those with its customers. These relationships and its internal resources are the most important resources in product development. Relationships with suppliers and research institutes play a minor role as well. The knowledge gained as a result of these relationships relates most importantly to finding new customers; other important areas include information about the competition and tax and legal advice. To some extent the relationships are also useful for product development (note that this form of profit from relationships is of secondary importance), operations management and finding new distribution channel.

Moreover, in terms of financing for the case studies, the majority of these firms only relied upon the informal financing of family or own financing, although several had received EU grants as well. An example of public policy as financing for a KIE venture in the food industry in Germany follows.

The company made use of a funding program called EXIST-SEED for academic start-ups in 2006/07 kick starting formal establishment as a legal entity and building up production facilities. This program is the standard tool of the technology transfer office of the University of Kassel. It has a competitive selection process of the applicants which guarantees a certain quality of the funded ideas. According to the founders the grant was vital for the firm and they do not know if they would have pursued establishment of the firm without it.

Public policy may thus play a key role in start-up for a few companies and was a trigger for later development.

14.3.3.5 Innovation

Innovation is an important topic. In the economics of science and technology, a key idea is to differentiate ideas and inventions from the innovation, where value should be created. A series of survey questions were asked regarding whether the company had engaged in innovation during the past five years, the type of innovation, and the relative degree of novelty of that innovation. Similar taxonomies were used in the case studies.

For the survey results, in total, 64 percent of the firms had introduced at least one product innovation. Each firm could introduce one or more innovation. In terms of degree of novelty, the majority of innovations were new to firm (64 percent of firms reported), while 55 percent reported that they had introduced an innovation new to the market and 22 percent had an innovation new to the world. In terms of process and organizational innovations, the most common ones introduced were IT knowledge management systems (50 percent), followed by supporting process activities (49 percent), methods of manufacturing (43 percent), logistics/supply chain (35 percent), and changes in management organization (31 percent).

In the case studies, a variety of different innovations were studied, ranging from one based upon technologies to services in IT and medical devices sectors, to manufacturing products. Sometimes, introducing a product innovation had the follow-on effect of introducing an organizational change. This was the case of a venture related to a corporate spin-out firm, illustrated here:

[The firm] decided to form a separate business area for the non-dental products. It was called Cranio-Facial Reconstruction and Audiology

("CFRA")/ . . . / In 1997, the top management decided that [the firm] should become "a dentistry company" with two complementary businesses, viz., implants and prosthetics. The Chief Financial Officer therefore got the assignment to find a new environment for the CFRA business area. As preparation for sale a business plan for a conceivable new company was made.

Hence, in this case study, the source of the resources and ideas for the KIE venture was an established firm. The established firm was active in the medical technology industry, but felt it had identified a business opportunity that was deemed to lie outside the scope of the current business of the firm and hence helped the KIE venture to start-up.

14.3.3.6 Aspects of Firm-Specific Strategy and Performance

These aspects include a variety of different ones such as strategy, the sensing, and seizing of opportunities and the business models and performance. These aspects thus address many key areas about how the firm is managed and developed over time, as well as variables useful for evaluating performance and output.

In the survey, reports about the key aspects of strategy included confidentiality agreements (55 percent), lead-time advantage over competitors (54 percent), complexity of design (46 percent), trademarks (41 percent), and secrecy (40 percent). Only 17 percent reported patents as a method of intellectual property methods that they used. Innovative opportunities were primarily identified in relation to market and customers, as indicated in previous paragraphs. In terms of performance, the average trend for 2007–2009 was an increase in sales, a stable level of employment, and a stable level of exports.

In the case studies, similar types of intellectual property strategies as those mentioned earlier can be illustrated: only nineteen of eighty-six firms in the case studies have and actively use patents. Many of these firms have grown in terms of employees, albeit modestly. The evaluation of performance is more mixed, with wide fluctuations at the firm level and distribution at the sample level over better or worse performing KIE ventures.

Many of these types of entrepreneurs find ideas or inventions without a market and are forced to create a new market, such as for medical devices. This is illustrated here as a link between globalization, network, experience, and financing: "While the networking with local users has become crucial for Promimic's development, the relationship to the research environment from which Promimic was once spun off has lost much of its initial importance. The responsibility for developing the technology has been taken over by the company and it is no longer dependent on Chalmers for its competence development." This illustration indicates that market opportunities had to be developed, and at that time, the earlier network relationships for research were less important.

14.5 Promoting Research on KIE

Given that KIE represents a new phenomenon not previously studied theoretically and empirically, we have written this section, in order to go through some issues related to research design and operationalization. The purpose of this appendix is thus to help promote research about KIE in general and KIE ventures in particular. The KIE venture, or the firm level, is used as the definitional level here, because of the strength of microdata to analyze both processes of firms and aggregate processes such as industrial dynamics. The research envisioned is related to our specific interest in the firm's relationship to the innovation system, and to the patterns of accessing resources and ideas, development, performance, and growth patterns of interest here.

14.5.1 Alignment in Research Design

Thus, we wish to promote solid research design, which can address new trajectories for research, such as those specified in the concluding section. By solid research design, we mean alignment between elements of research, namely the conceptual framework, nuanced definitions, clever operationalization, and interesting questions. The reason for doing so is that without solid research design, it is difficult to develop research on a new phenomenon.

Let us go back to the basics of research to explain further why this appendix focuses upon issues related to how to measure and analyze KIE ventures.

Figure 14.5 visualizes that in order to address interesting research questions, the quality of the resulting research depends to a large extent

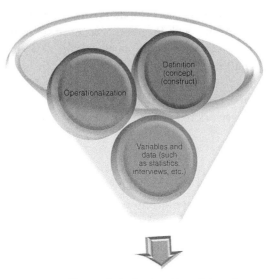

Research design to address interesting
research question in the conceptual
framework

Figure 14.5 Visualization of how the research design includes definitions, operationalization, variables, and data

upon the design. Issues have to be solved related to reliability (e.g. it is consistent over different settings) as well as validity (e.g. it measures the construct or concept under study). One way of thinking about validity is to consider alignment. The Merriam-Webster dictionary gives an example of alignment as "the state or condition of agreeing with or matching something else." By alignment, we mean that all elements of the research design are aligned (talk about the same thing), as illustrated in Figure 14.5.

Key elements visualized in Figure 14.5 include the following:

Model (conceptual framework): Models or conceptual frameworks are ways to organize ideas and relationships, or organizing devices for phenomena under study.

This chapter refers to a broader conceptual framework for identifying vital elements of the phenomenon of entrepreneurship, which has different varieties presented in different research (Malerba and

McKelvey 2011, 2015, and 2017). The model was not reproduced here.

Definition (concept; construct): Definitions are key to defining the phenomenon under study, and in our case that of knowledge-intensive entrepreneurship. There are often concepts or constructs within the definition, which can be thought of as explanatory elements not directly observable. These are usually derived from theoretical explanations or are linked together to form an explanation.

Based on our previous work, the definition of a KIE venture includes the following four characteristics, namely it (i) is an entrepreneurial venture formalized as a new firm; (ii) is innovative; (iii) has a significant knowledge intensity; and (iv) can exploit innovative opportunities across many sectors.

Operationalization: operationalization refers to the process of defining the measurement of specific concepts and variables included in the definition and/or model. Many elements of a definition, including concepts and constructs, are often not directly measureable. Operationalization leads us to identify variables and data and to examine, discuss, and measure the phenomena of interest. Variables and data are used in quantitative studies as well as qualitative studies.

Let us think about these issues by considering the example of how to measure high quality science. In quantitative data, an indicator of high quality science could be number of total publications, number of publications in journals with an average in the top 5 percent of journals in that field, or number of citations. In qualitative data, interview guides and software coding are often available in order to help gather, organize, and understand the results. In this example, the indicator of high quality science could include having an expert read the papers and evaluate relative quality or else conducting interviews to discuss the university environment and how it affected the impact, quantity, and results of the scientific endeavor.

Understanding the phenomena requires research, which may add knowledge about a series of related knowledge relevant to the phenomenon, as visualized in Figure 14.6.[4]

---

[4] This visualization was inspired by a similar model in McKelvey and Lassen (2013a).

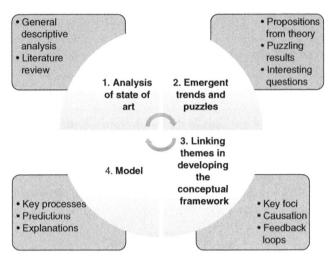

Figure 14.6 Research as a process

In summary then, alignment is needed in developing the research design, and in order to turn ideas into a framework of understanding that is useful to answer the research questions.

14.5.2 Operationalizing Key Elements in the Definition of Knowledge-Intensive Entrepreneurship

Based upon our previous work, we have proposed that empirical work on a KIE venture has the following four characteristics, namely it (i) is an entrepreneurial venture formalized as a new firm; (ii) is innovative; (iii) has a significant knowledge intensity; and (iv) can exploit innovative opportunities across many sectors. This definition was also used to organize the European Union project AEGIS, and particularly the large-scale survey reported in this chapter.

We feel that later work may not have the opportunity to do a survey and may therefore benefit from a discussion of the choices that can be made to define these four characteristics, with a specific focus upon how to operationalize them.

14.5.2.1 Characteristic of Being an Entrepreneurial Venture Formalized as a New Firm

This criterion focuses our attention upon the creation of an organization, formalized as a firm, which has a profit motive. Given the profit motive, other types of entrepreneurship such as necessity and lifestyle entrepreneurship are excluded. Official statistics are available in most countries. They can identify a firm, as well as add dates and sometimes also the persons involved in starting the firm, such as the founder and board members. Different countries tend to have somewhat different laws, as well as a multitude of types of firms, so specific knowledge of organizational forms of firms is needed.

Moreover, the construct "the KIE venture" focuses upon the actual company. Naturally, events matter that happened before the start-up of the firm, as extensively documented in the entrepreneurship literature. Hence, this focus does not mean that the founder (or founder team) is not important. Extensive literature now exists that suggests that characteristics and traits of the founder and founder team matter for the latter development of the firm (see, for example, the discussion in Klepper 2015). Key attributes of the founder appear to be industrial experience and education. In this way, these studies may tackle a number of very specific issues of interest to literature in both entrepreneurship and innovation, such as how founder education affects opportunity recognition.

One issue requiring a thoughtful choice relates to the concept of "new," defined in relation to a time frame. Following previous literature and policy, a new venture has been defined in the previous AEGIS project as eight years or less. Eight years is used in our quantitative studies of KIE ventures, because those studies are focused on newly formed companies – their strategies, opportunities, and challenges. In contrast, the case studies tend to run for longer, including both early and late phases. Case studies are not restricted to the company per se, given our interest in a long process. Case studies generally include the period when the entrepreneurial founder and team may be active before the firm is formed, such as how they gather resources, experience, and ideas, as well as a longer term perspective on how and why the firm has developed over time to evaluate performance.

Classifications can also be used to nuance the definition of an entrepreneurial venture in order to do comparisons. Examples of classifications in the literature that can be developed include whether or not the KIE venture is a spin-off from a large company or university; the founder's background in terms of education and experience; the origins of the initial ideas that were later commercialized; the availability of resources; the role of public policy both in supporting the production of relevant knowledge and providing financing; the role of demand in forming the innovative opportunities; or the availability of financing, including both formal and informal types.

In summary, an entrepreneurial venture formalized as a new firm includes two main ways of developing indicators to capture these criteria. For quantitative studies, the indicators used focus upon official statistics to identify a population or sample of firms that are formalized according to law, and are also less than eight years old. For qualitative studies, the indicators used often identify one or more KIE ventures of interest, and then also follow a much longer process of starting, managing, and creating output over time.

14.5.2.2 Characteristic of Being Innovative

One rationale for focusing upon KIE ventures is the proposition that they are highly important for economic development and societal well-being, because they are innovative. Innovation is another criteria within the definition that can be measured in very different ways. The literature streams in science policy evaluation and in the economics of science and technology have proposed many types and measures of innovations that should be used.

There has been significant work by national statistics offices to use surveys to define many different types of innovations, and then allocate the degree of innovations to the degree of innovativeness of an organization. The types of innovations as well as types of research have been used for many years in official statistics, many of which were based upon the OECD manuals. The so-called Community Innovation Survey (CIS) asks firms to report whether they have engaged in a number of different types of innovations – such as product, service, and organizational innovations – in a period of time as well the percentage of sales based upon new goods and services. Questions of whether the innovation is new to the firm, new to the industry, new to the country, or new to the world are often also used as indicators of the degree of novelty. Examples of taxonomies include disruptive innovations for industries, radical vs incremental, modular vs architectural technologies, and service vs manufacturing (goods) innovations. These questions from national statistics offices were generally created in dialogue with researchers, and also used in surveys sent out by other researchers.

Innovation, and relative degree of innovativeness, are thus theoretical constructs that one can measure and discuss in different ways. If one wishes to capture the phenomenon across a population (or sample), then one must have an indicator that is considered valid and reliable over many observations. Two common indicators are patents and scientific publications. Patents are often used as an indicator in the study of innovations. This measure is well-established and often used because patents cover all sectors and technologies. However, there are debates among scholars about whether patents mostly measure technology or whether they are useful to measure innovations, e.g. the economic value of the resulting invention. Moreover, it is well-known that many small firms do not patent, and that patents are less applicable to creative industries and service industries. Hence, patents may be more useful for capturing advanced technologies in some sectors than in others. Patents are more accepted as a measure of invention than of innovation.

Many of the narrower concepts such as gazelles assume that the firm grows at a specific rate. We have not included performance within the definition, because that is an empirical question about whether or not these types of firms perform better or worse than a matched sample. Innovation as discussed earlier can be considered a type of performance. More usual measures for financial performance include sales, turnover, market share, exports, and number of employees.

In summary, the definition of innovation is based upon the conceptualization of innovation being a novelty of potential economic value. Innovation is distinguished from performance, but the relationship between the two is very interesting to study empirically. For quantitative studies, national statistical offices have used standardized questions and also developed new ones, which can be reproduced in surveys managed by a researcher. For qualitative studies, the definition of innovation needs to be carefully considered, but a more complex process is generally reported concerning how individuals, teams, ventures, and firms interact with the surrounding innovation system.

14.5.2.3 Characteristic of Having Significant Knowledge Intensity

This characteristic has a wide range of possible ways in which it can be used to operationalize this construct. Theoretically, knowledge intensity is thought to matter because the firm can deliver services and create goods that translate knowledge into organization knowledge and profits, usually by competing on unique or similar abilities.

We suggest there is a strong need to go beyond two measures – academic entrepreneurship and microdata of firms in high-tech sectors – which are often used in the literature as a shortcut to identify certain types of KIE. For academic entrepreneurship, there is often a focus upon spin-offs from universities, or the engagement of university researchers and more recently of students. The assumption is that university knowledge is the key motor to generate innovation (if coupled with market and application knowledge). A second measure often used is that of microdata of firms in high-tech sectors, e.g. with a high percentage of sales invested in research and development (R&D). This indicator assumes that all of these new firms that enter a high-technology sector have to be innovative and/ or that they are knowledge intensive. These two assumptions are quite strong and influence the interpretation of results. Our proposed definition proposes the need to recognize the contributions of these two streams of literature and include them in our definition, but also to go beyond them to understand the wide variety of ways in which knowledge and a high level of knowledge intensity occurs across the economy.

One way to do so is to focus upon the existence and use of *highly skilled human capital*, irrespective of the sector. Human capital can be measured in terms of the education of the entrepreneur or teams, and the experience, education, and skills of the employees. In this way, also new firms active in the so called traditional sectors may be considered KIE.

Another way to do so is to consider access to knowledge, both internally through absorptive capacities and externally through mechanisms such as sources of knowledge and what are known today as open innovation and entrepreneurial ecosystems.

14.5.2.4 Characteristic of Exploiting Innovative Opportunities across Many Sectors

This criteria is used both to design studies that go across many different types of sectors and types of innovations. This leads to a straightforward recommendation to study KIE ventures in many different types of sectors, including services, cultural and creative industries, manufacturing, and so forth. These sectors have quite different technological and market opportunities that need to be taken into account for a better understanding of the process of KIE.

Moreover, this characteristic captures the core concept within entrepreneurship from a Schumpeterian perspective, namely opportunities. The underlying conceptual view is thus that innovative opportunities are created and exploited by the KIE venture, in combination with relationships to innovation systems.

For quantitative studies, one problem with linking the KIE venture to the innovation system generally has to do with the lack of sectoral, regional, and country level quantitative indicators that are valid and reliable. These indicators are not easily available, nor does a comprehensive one exists. Often, the alternative is to focus upon either an industry and/ or a country, and then use a portfolio of company indicators, which are often available via large databases, often commercial ones.

For both quantitative and qualitative studies, interest in the link between the entrepreneur, the venture, and the innovation system often revolves around the sources and importance of knowledge sources, as well as processes that promote entrepreneurship in the innovation system. Examples of aspects that are linked to the recognition and exploitation of innovative opportunities include knowledge from users; knowledge from suppliers; knowledge from competitors; type of cooperation; and role of university. These aspects can all be inquired upon within surveys (self-reported) or else studied in depth in case studies. Many qualitative studies also rely upon quantitative data, in order to analyze specific theoretical constructs.

14.6 Issues for Future Research

Let us conclude by proposing new directions and questions for future research. Hypotheses could be generated for each, and some discussion is devoted to available data and research methods. This analysis is based upon our proposed definitions, as well as a very selective review of key points from literature, and leads us to propose interesting areas for future research, given the limitations of the current state-of-the-art.

First, large investments in knowledge generation (R&D) do not lead automatically to economic growth. This implies that providing incentives for R&D – such as tax subsidies – is not enough. Instead, there are institutional and organizational issues to be considered. In particular, the sum of the barriers related to converting research into commercialized knowledge (called by some authors knowledge filter) and the existence of a transformative mechanism such as entrepreneurship determines the effectiveness of the conversion of knowledge into economic activity. Future research should address the transformative mechanisms for knowledge into growth, as well as additional institutional and organization issues that affect these processes.

Second, knowledge-intensive entrepreneurship can definitely be found within science-based industries, advanced technologies, or R&D-intensive manufacturing (high-tech) industries. Science-based industries by definition use very advanced knowledge and technologies. For example, one can associate this concept with nanotech or autonomous self-driving or alternative-fuel green vehicles. R&D intensity remains an important determinant of technological opportunities, even if the process of translation to value is not automatic. Future research issues should focus upon the speed and direction of science-based industries – like nanotechnology and life sciences – in terms of commercialization, asking questions such as why and how do science-based industries differ? Aspects related to the linkages between KIE ventures and national and regional innovation systems should be studied, in particular in relation to the role of different markets, clusters, and agglomerations in stimulating or hindering the phenomena. Related to this is how different types of knowledge are, or are not, embedded in organizational learning as well as the individual entrepreneur or team. Finally, an important issue is how demand and markets exist in not only helping to create opportunities but also shaping the trajectory of the firm, and of industries facing creative destruction by knowledge-intensive entrepreneurship.

Third, knowledge intensive entrepreneurship is not restricted to science-based industries, advanced technologies, or R&D-intensive manufacturing (high-tech) industries. Instead, due to the broad diffusion of innovative opportunities, knowledge entrepreneurship is relevant in other manufacturing sectors – such as non–R&D-intensive manufacturing (low tech) and traditional industries – as well as in service sectors and the creative and cultural industries. The particular features of knowledge and of later innovations may differ and have specific features, as compared to high-tech manufacturing sectors. In other sectors, the knowledge may be constituted in new forms, such as design knowledge, organizational knowledge, and so forth, and innovations may be coproduced with suppliers or with customers. Future research has many issues to address here, given the need to better understand both knowledge and innovation in these sectoral contexts, as well as how they create opportunities for these entrepreneurs.

Fourth, the broader industrial dynamics of knowledge-intensive entrepreneurship is highly sector specific. Its features and impact depend on the knowledge base of a sector, the main public and private actors embedded in the sector, and the associated institutions. Hence, future research should concentrate on the specific interplay between science, technological advancement, industrial dynamics, and economic growth, and the relationship with human resources and the entrepreneur within sectoral innovation systems.

Fifth, there are market and institutional aspects – which constitute innovation systems – that influence the production, use, and diffusion of advanced knowledge, as well as the appropriation of the returns to innovations. For example, the knowledge filter will vary over time and depend very much on a wide variety of socioeconomic factors, including the institutional set-up, cultural factors, and the prevailing intellectual climate. Moreover, market and institutional factors give rise to different sets of opportunities for innovation and knowledge-intensive entrepreneurship. Future research should focus upon how the sectoral context interacts with market and institutional contexts of particular industries and countries or regions.

Sixth, knowledge-intensive entrepreneurship appears to play out in different ways in different regions. Regional contexts that are rich in knowledge appear to generate more entrepreneurial opportunities, and also allow the KIE entrepreneur to access more and more specialized resources. Hence, a host of factors in regional innovation systems, such as institutions, laws, traditions, and culture, shape the amount of region-specific entrepreneurship capital (i.e. the willingness of individuals to serve as conduits of technology transit to commercialization). Regions characterized by a high propensity for entrepreneurship would be expected to exhibit high levels of economic growth, ceteris paribus. Given the advance of this line of research in general, future research could test several of these propositions.

Seventh, in terms of analyzing entrepreneurship and how well it functions in society, we argue that one needs to take into account not only the level of entrepreneurship but also its quality, type, potential, and sustainability. This implies that policy makers should not only try to promote small-business ownership or starting a company in general but should have a more nuanced view of which types of entrepreneurship are more likely to impact the economy. Economic contexts with a greater extent of certain types of entrepreneurship exhibit higher growth rates. This holds at the country, sectoral, and spatial levels. Hence, future research could examine whether and how entrepreneurship promotes economic growth by penetrating the knowledge filter and serving as a conduit of knowledge spillovers.

Eighth, market demand – both private as well as public – plays a key role in affecting knowledge-intensive entrepreneurship, as well as its impact on overall innovation and economic growth. Demand is at the heart of the notion that knowledge has to be translated into commercial value – in the sense that someone needs to purchase or pay for the idea, invention, or innovation. Future research should focus upon the relative importance of demand as compared to advanced knowledge, and especially how the KIE venture combines both within business model innovations.

Ninth, this type of entrepreneurship is based upon a broad range of not only innovative technology but also advanced knowledge in the KIE venture, which seems to take many different forms than R&D knowledge. An interesting observation is that there are spillover effects, both in terms of knowledge spillovers but also in terms of imitation effects and of economic indirect spillovers, whereby the KIE venture will challenge established firms. Future research should examine the extent to which both the direct and indirect effects of entrepreneurship are important stimuli for overall economic growth, or whether creative destruction becomes destructive destruction.

Tenth, the entrepreneurs must create KIE ventures that have to deliver. Dynamic organizational capabilities lie behind continuous growth at firm level and represent the core of a dynamic market-driven economy. Entrepreneurs act on opportunities given their resources, capabilities, and strategies. Entrepreneurial dynamics are generated when market and institutional factors are aligned with firm-specific capabilities and when they mutually reinforce each other. Hence, one might assume that successful knowledge-intensive entrepreneurship implies not just effective entry but also continuous growth and profitability. Future research should consider the extent to which KIE ventures indeed develop dynamic organizational capabilities, which translates into growth, and/or whether the individual entrepreneurs move between KIE ventures, which, in themselves, arise and disappear quickly.

In summary, these ten points represent our selective review from the literature, but which also generate a number of important and interesting topics for future research.

References

Acs, Z. J., Braunerhjelm, P., Audretsch, D., and Carlsson, B. 2009. The knowledge spillover theory of entrepreneurship. *Small Business Economics* January. 32(1): 15–30.

AEGIS Research Project 2013 (Advancing Knowledge-Intensive Entrepreneurship and Innovation for Economic Growth and Social Well-being in Europe), Grant Agreement number 225134) European Commission, DG Research, Brussels.

Andersen, E. S. 2009. *Schumpeter's Evolutionary Economics: A Theoretical, Historical and Statistical Analysis of the Engine of Capitalism.* London: Anthem Press.

Ardichvili, A., Cardozo, R., and Ray, S. 2003. A theory of entrepreneurial opportunity identification and development. *Journal of Business Venturing* 18: 105–123.

Bull, I. and Willard, G. 1993. Towards a theory of entrepreneurship. *Journal of Business Venturing* 8(3): 183–195.

Caloghirou, Y., Protogerou, A., and Tskanikas, A. (2015) Knowledge Intensive Entrepreneurship: Exploring a taxonomy based on the AEGIS survey, in Malerba, F., Caloghirou, Y., McKelvey, M., and Radosevic, S. (eds.), *Dynamics of Knowledge-Intensive Entrepreneurship: Business Strategy and Public Policy.* London: Routledge.

Caloghirou, Y., Protogerou, A., and Tsakanikas, A. 2011. Final report summarizing survey methods and results. *AEGIS – 7th Framework Programme for Research and Technological Development,* Deliverable 7.1.5.

Carlsson, B., Braunerhjelm, P., McKelvey, M., Olofsson, C., Persson, L., and Ylinenpää, H. 2013. The Evolving Domain of Entrepreneurship Research. *Small Business Economics* 41: 913–930.

Cooke, P., Gomez Uranga, M., and Etzebarria, G. 1997. Regional innovation systems: Institutional and organisational dimensions. *Research Policy* 26 (4–5): 475–491.

Davidson, P. Low, M. and Wright M. 2001. Low and MacMillan ten years on: Achievements and future directions for entrepreneurship research. *Entrepreneurship Theory and Practice* 25(4):5–15.

Eckhardt, J. and Shane, S. 2003. Opportunities and entrepreneurship. *Journal of Management* 29 (3): 333–349.

Holmén, M., Magnusson, M., and McKelvey, M. 2007. What are innovative opportunities? *Industry and Innovation* 14(1): 27–45.

KEINS Research Project (Knowledge base entrepreneurship: Institutions, networks and systems, EU project n.CT2-CT-2004–506022) supported by European DG Research.

Klepper S. 2015. *Experimental Capitalism: The Nanoeconomics of American High-Tech Industries.* Princeton University Press.

Landström, H., Harirchi, G., and Åström, F. 2012. Entrepreneurship: Exploring the knowledge base. *Research Policy* 41(7): 1154–1181.

Ljungberg, D., McKelvey, M., and Lassen, A. H. 2012. Final report on case studies: Emerging trends, lessons and methodological issues. The AEGIS case study analysis. *AEGIS – 7th Framework Programme for Research and Technological Development*, Deliverable D7.2.3.

Lundvall, B. A. 1992. *National Systems of Innovation.* London: Pinter Publishers.

Malerba, F. 2002. Sectoral systems of innovation and production. *Research Policy* 31(2): 247–264.

Malerba, F. (ed.). 2004. *Sectoral Systems of Innovation.* Cambridge: Cambridge University Press.

Malerba, F. 2010. Knowledge-intensive entrepreneurship and innovation systems in Europe, in Malerba, F. (ed.), *Knowledge-Intensive Entrepreneurship and Innovation Systems: Evidence from Europe.* Abington; New York, NY: Routledge.

Malerba, F., Caloghirou, Y., McKelvey, M., and Radosevic, S. (eds.). 2015. *Dynamics of Knowledge-Intensive Entrepreneurship: Business Strategy and Public Policy.* London: Routledge.

Malerba, F. and McKelvey, M. 2011. Conceptualizing knowledge-intensive entrepreneurship: Concepts and models. *AEGIS – 7th Framework Programme for Research and Technological Development*, Deliverable 1.1.1.

Malerba, F. and McKelvey, M. 2015. Knowledge intensive entrepreneurship: Conceptual framework, in Malerba, F., Caloghirou, Y., McKelvey, M., and Radosevic, S. (eds.), *Dynamics of Knowledge-Intensive Entrepreneurship: Business Strategy and Public Policy.* Routledge.

Malerba, F. and McKelvey, M. 2018. Knowledge-intensive innovative entrepreneurship: Integrating Schumpeter, evolutionary economics and innovation systems. *Small Business Economics.*

McKelvey, M. and Lassen, A. H. 2013a. *Managing Knowledge Intensive Entrepreneurship*. Cheltenham: Edward Elgar Publishers.

McKelvey, M. and Lassen A. H. 2013b. *How Entrepreneurs Do What They Do: Case Studies of Knowledge Intensive Entrepreneurship*. Cheltenham: Edward Elgar Publishers.

McKelvey, M., Ljungberg, D. and Lassen, A. H., 2015. Structuring the process of knowledge intense entrepreneurship: A meta-analysis of 86 case studies of ventures. In Malerba et al 2015. *Dynamics of Knowledge Intensive Entrepreneurship*. London: Routledge.

Metcalfe, J. S. 1998. *Evolutionary Economics and Creative Destruction*. London: Routledge.

Metcalfe, J. S. and Foster, J. 2012 Economic emergence: An evolutionary economics perspective. *Journal of Economic Behaviour & Organization* 82(2–3): 420–432.

Nelson, R. 1993. *National Innovation Systems*. Oxford UK: Oxford University Press.

OECD (2008) Fostering entrepreneurship for innovation, OECD Science, Technology and Industry Working Papers 2008/5, OECD Publishing.

Shane, S. 2000. Prior knowledge and the discovery of entrepreneurial opportunities. *Organization Science* 11(4): 448–469.

Shane, S. and Venkataraman, S. 2002. The promise of entrepreneurship as a field of research. *Academy of Management Review* 25: 217–226.

Schumpeter, J. 1934. The theory of Economic Development.

Schumpeter, J. 1942. Capitalism, Socialism and Democracy.

Schumpeter, J. 1949. Economic theory and entrepreneurial History, in *Change and the Entrepreneur. Postulates and Patterns for Entrepreneurial History*. Cambridge, MA: Harvard University Press.

Vaghely, I. P. and Julien, P.-A. 2010. Are opportunities recognized or constructed? An information perspective on entrepreneurial opportunity identification. *Journal of Business Venturing* 25(1): 73–86.

15 | The Three Great Issues Confronting Europe – Economic, Environmental and Political

JAN FAGERBERG, STAFFAN LAESTADIUS
AND BEN R. MARTIN

15.1 Introduction

Europe today is confronted by fundamental changes in its external environment as well as internally, giving rise to several daunting policy challenges. First, there is *the economic challenge* manifest in slow growth or even stagnation in many countries, which, although also present in other parts of the world, is particularly severe in Europe. Second, there is *the challenge posed by the climate crisis*, the solution of which requires nothing less than a fundamental transformation from carbon-based growth to a new, sustainable economy. Without this, future generations will be in dire straits. The third challenge concerns *the governance and policy crisis now facing Europe* and the difficulties this poses for policy making and implementation. It might be argued that the recent rapid growth of immigration to Europe represents a *fourth* challenge. Although we do not deny the institutional challenges now confronting many European countries, our contention is that addressing the three main challenges analysed below will be essential in our long-term capacity to absorb new citizens.[1] This chapter argues that a completely new policy stance is required, one that simultaneously addresses the challenges created by economic stagnation, climate change, and problems of governance.

---

[1] In addition, it should be noted that Europe absorbs just a fraction of the growing global migration total (GMDAC 2016).

464

15.2 The Economic Challenge for Europe

Over the longer term, European economic integration has delivered very substantial benefits to Europe's citizens. For example, during the first two or three decades of integration efforts in (Western) Europe, the economy grew very fast, and the gap in productivity and income vis-à-vis the world's technologically and economically leading country, the United States, was considerably reduced (Abramovitz 1994). The European Union has also been notably successful in supporting transitions from authoritarian regimes to democracy in large parts of Europe, first from the mid-1970s onwards when the fascist dictatorships in Southern Europe were swept away, and later – and on a much larger scale – in the 1990s onwards following the disintegration of the former Soviet Union. The gradual integration of the countries in Eastern Europe, followed by substantial inflows of investment from the rest of Europe, led to very rapid growth in the new member countries and markedly reduced differences in productivity and income across Europe as a whole (Fagerberg and Verspagen 2015).

Around the turn of the millennium, several European initiatives were taken to sustain the positive dynamics of the previous decades in the expectation that this would lead to a further narrowing of the gap in GDP per capita between the United States and Europe. For example, at the EU summits in Lisbon and Barcelona in 2000 and 2002, member states agreed on the goal of making Europe "the most competitive and dynamic knowledge-based economy in the world capable of sustainable economic growth with more and better jobs and greater social cohesion" by increasing R&D investments (as a share of GDP) to a level superior to that of the United States by the end of the decade.[2] Moreover, a common European currency, the Euro, was introduced in 2002 as part of the strategy to further deepen European integration and spur economic growth.

To what extent did European policy makers succeed in their aims? Figure 15.1 traces the development of GDP per capita from the mid-1990s onwards for three groups of European countries and the EU as a whole relative to that of the United States. As the figure shows, there is little evidence of Europe catching up with the United States during this period. In fact, in 2015 GDP per capita in the European Union

---

[2] See www.consilium.europa.eu/en/uedocs/cms_data/docs/pressdata/en/ec/00100-r1.en0.htm (accessed 7 October 2016).

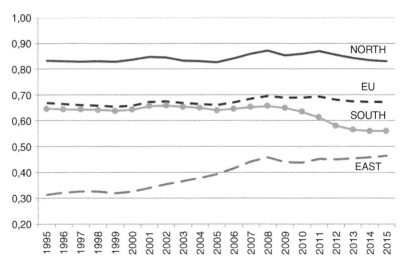

Figure 15.1 Europe: GDP per capita relative to the US, constant US$ (PPP), 1995–2015

Note: Authors' calculations on GDP per capita, in constant US$ (PPP-adjusted) at 2011 price levels, based on data from the World Bank (http://data .worldbank.org/indicator/NY.GDP.PCAP.PP.KD), accessed 1 October 2016. EU includes all member countries, NORTH consists of Denmark, Sweden, Finland, Germany, Netherlands and Austria; SOUTH comprises Greece, Italy, Portugal and Spain; while EAST includes the eleven previously socialist countries in the East of Europe (that became members after the collapse of the Soviet Union).

was two-thirds of the US level, exactly the same as twenty years earlier. Among the European countries, only the new members from Eastern Europe managed to substantially reduce the productivity gap with respect to the United States, rising from 32 per cent to 46 per cent of the US level between 2000 and 2008, after which the catch-up of Eastern Europe came to an abrupt halt. In Southern Europe the average GDP per capita relative to that of the United States was roughly constant and equal to the EU average until the outbreak of the financial crisis. However, between 2008 and 2015 it dropped from 66 per cent to 56 per cent of the US level, a 15 per cent decline compared to the pre-crisis level. Thus, rather than the convergence in GDP per capita that characterized Europe during the previous decade, the years after 2007–2008 have witnessed a process of

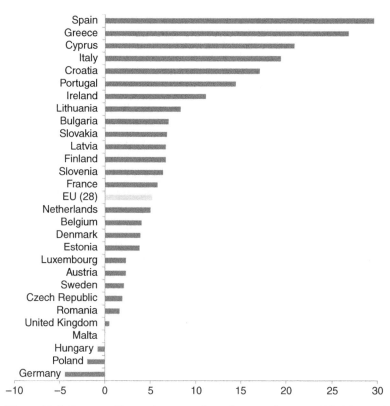

Figure 15.2 Europe: Change in rates of youth unemployment (20–24 years), per cent, 2007–2015
Note: Authors' calculations based on data from Eurostat (http://appsso .eurostat.ec.europa.eu/ (yth_empl_090)), accessed 1 October 2016.

divergence, with several countries, particularly in the southern part of the continent, falling further behind economically.

Should we be concerned about these developments? Yes – and to see why, consider Figure 15.2, which shows the change in unemployment rates for young adults aged 20–24 in Europe since the crisis struck. Apart from a few countries (and especially Germany), youth unemployment has been on the increase everywhere. The situation is especially severe in Southern Europe (where the level of youth unemployment has more than doubled compared to the situation before the financial crisis) and in parts of Eastern Europe. If this situation is not reversed, large numbers of young people in Europe risk being permanently marginalized, the social, economic and political consequences of which are likely to be highly detrimental to Europe's future. Why is Europe's performance so disappointing? The economic changes that have taken place in Europe during the last two or three decades have occurred within an international context characterized by globalization. The gradual inclusion of China in the global capitalist economy, adding hundreds of millions of lower-paid manufacturing workers to the global labour pool, provided a substantial boost to this process, and similar although less spectacular developments have taken place in other developing nations. This process also poses a challenge, however, because it tends to undermine the competitive position of established industries throughout the developed world, especially in low skill, labour-intensive manufacturing sectors. The evidence (e.g. Fagerberg and Verspagen 2015; Landesmann 2015) suggests that the effects of globalization on the growth performance of different parts of Europe have been very uneven. While the advanced economies in the North of Europe have to a certain extent managed to adapt to the changing competitive conditions by selling advanced products to customers in emerging markets (and substantially increasing their exports as a percentage of GDP), countries in the Southern part of the continent (and some in the East) have generally failed to do so. Hence, they have become 'losers' in the globalization process.

However, European integration and EU policies have also had an impact. The introduction of the Euro in 2002 meant that the economies of the Eurozone became more interdependent. A natural consequence of this might well have been a greater degree of coordination of economic policies among the participating countries, but instead the Eurozone countries continued to shape their economic policies based largely on domestic considerations, effectively disregarding the consequences for other countries and for the wider Eurozone. For example, Germany, following the costly re-unification with former East Germany, decided to restrain growth in wages and domestic demand in order to boost the competitiveness of its industry and to run a trade surplus with the rest of the world. However, this policy implied that other, less competitive, members of the Eurozone, with far less scope for growing through increasing exports, would have to practice austerity as well if increased trade deficits were to be avoided. Initially, several countries in the South shied away from austerity, leading to rising deficits and foreign indebtedness (Fagerberg and Verspagen

2015; Landesmann 2015), a situation which clearly was not sustainable. However, eventually the financial crisis brought governments in different parts of Europe together under the umbrella of austerity, leading to slow growth, rising unemployment (especially in the South) and increasing divergence in the Union as whole.

15.3 Europe Facing the Climate Challenge

There is near-consensus among climate analysts that the globe is currently heading towards a 3–6°C warmer Earth than a century ago, and that this global warming is primarily caused by greenhouse gas (GHG) emissions from human activities (IPCC 2012, 2013a,b, 2014; World Bank 2012, 2013). In order to confine temperature rises to 2°C, global GHG emissions have to be reduced substantially by 2050, and almost completely eliminated by the end of the century (IPCC 2014). These demanding goals are equivalent to reductions by approximately 3–4 per cent annually for the rest of this century (e.g. Smil 2010). More recent analyses deliver a still tougher message: the additions to the accumulated stock of GHGs in the atmosphere must decrease faster. To have a real impact on climate change – i.e. to offer a reasonable chance of keeping the temperature increase below 2°C (not to say 1.5°C) – global GHG-emissions (including non-energy-related emissions) must *decline* by some 5–6 per cent annually from present levels over the decades ahead, leaving much less of the reduction to the second half of the century (IEA 2015b; Reilly et al. 2015; Hansen et al. 2016a, b). However, global CO_2 emissions are still *increasing* at a global level and have done so every year since 2009 (BP 2016b). In addition, it would seem only reasonable that the developed part of the world, which has benefitted most from previous emissions, should shoulder the largest burden of the reductions ahead.

European politicians pride themselves on having already substantially reduced greenhouse-gas emissions and hence for being on broadly the right track (European Council 2014). But is this correct? To explore this, Figure 15.3 traces the development of European GHG emissions from 1990 onwards for three country groups: Eastern Europe, Germany (including the former GDR) and the rest of Europe.

What the figure shows is that, for Europe as a whole, there was a reduction in emissions in the early 1990s, but this can be almost entirely explained by the rapid changes that took place (including the

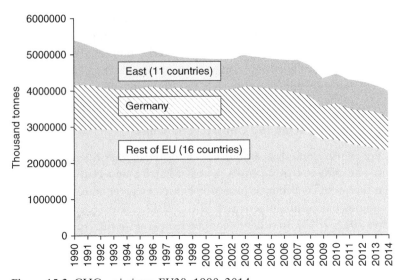

Figure 15.3 GHG emissions, EU28, 1990–2014
Note: Authors' calculations based on data from Eurostat (http://appsso
.eurostat.ec.europa.eu/ [env_air_gge], accessed 1 October 2016.

closure of inefficient plants) in the previously socialist countries in the
East. For the rest of Europe, emissions were essentially stable until the
outbreak of the financial crisis. This raises the question of whether
the more recent decline in GHG emissions represents a shift towards
a new, more sustainable path, or whether it is mainly a consequence of
the financial crisis, and hence is likely to be reversed should the economy recover.

To investigate this, Figure 15.4 includes data on GHG emissions and
growth of GDP for the European Union as a whole between 1995 and
2014. It reveals that the GHG intensity (i.e. GHG emissions per unit of
output) has declined steadily, as it has in the United States (Nordhaus
2013). But until shortly before the financial crisis, this decline was not
enough to reduce Europe's overall emissions. Moreover, as the figure
shows, had growth continued at the same pace as before the crisis,
emissions would probably have stayed roughly constant. Thus, the
recent decline in emissions does not reflect a change towards a more
sustainable path for the European economy, but is mainly a reflection
of continuing economic stagnation. And, according to recent BP statistics, the European CO_2 emissions turned upwards again in 2015,

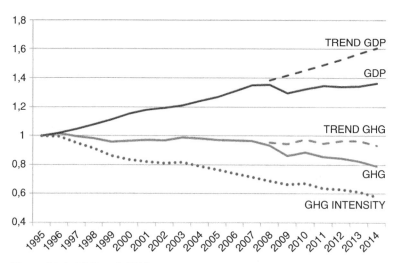

Figure 15.4 GDP and GHG emissions, EU28, 1995–2014
Note: Authors' calculations based on data from Eurostat (http://appsso
.eurostat.ec.europa.eu/ [nama_10_gdp] and [env_air_gge], accessed
1 October 2016). Trend-GDP is a continuation of the 1995–2007 trend for
GDP, while Trend-GHG is what the emissions would have been in that case
(with actual GHG intensity).

suggesting that the growth effect now more than outweighs increased
carbon efficiency (BP 2016b). In fact, European consumption of oil and
natural gas in 2015 *increased* by 1.5 per cent and 4.6 per cent, respectively, which – from an emissions perspective – more than offset the
decline in coal consumption of 1.8 per cent (BP 2016a).

This raises serious questions about Europe's ability to cope with the
challenges discussed in this chapter. A revival of the economy, which is
required to reduce unemployment and increase welfare, appears to be
in direct conflict with the need to combat climate change. Or to put it
differently, to realize both objectives, the European economy has to
shift to a completely new trajectory when it comes to the emission of
greenhouse gases. For example, to allow for 'classic' economic growth
of 1.5 per cent per year for Europe as a whole, the annual decline in the
GHG intensity needs to be around 6–7 per cent per year during the
decades ahead. This is a truly formidable challenge and will require
a fundamental transformation of the content of European economic
activities.

In October 2014, EU leaders met to consider European policies on climate change and agreed to reduce GHG emissions by 40 per cent (compared to the 1990 level) by 2030 (European Council 2014). This also became the intended nationally determined contributions (INDCs) from Europe to the Paris negotiations in late 2015. If one takes into account that half of this reduction had been achieved already as explained earlier, this agreement implies an annual 1.8 per cent reduction only in emissions between 2014 and 2030, less than half the annual reduction needed to reach the long-term target that both the European Council and the European Parliament agreed to five years earlier. This is also closer to a third of what would be a reasonable European contribution to keep world temperature increase below 2°C (Rogelj et al. 2016; Hansen et al. 2016a, b). Hence, current EU leaders would seem to have ducked their responsibility, tacitly opting to leave most of the required efforts to future generations, by which time the task, according to IPCC analyses, will have become much harder (and the costs far greater).

15.4 Is Europe Doomed to a Stalemate in Transformation and Growth Policy?

The climate challenge and the economic challenge that Europe is facing are intimately interrelated.[3] Without growth, greenhouse gas emissions may continue to decline, although almost certainly not at the pace necessary for their elimination in the latter half of the twenty-first century. But employment would undoubtedly continue to suffer, too. A return to the type of growth that prevailed before the financial crisis, on the other hand, might be good for employment – in the short run at least – but certainly not for the climate, as emissions would continue at unsustainably high levels. Is there a way out of this dilemma?

As a start, it may be noted that economic growth does not necessarily mean doing more of the same. It can also mean getting more out of a given level of resources by doing things in a smarter way than before or developing other, and sustainable, resources – that is, by innovation.

---

[3] The interrelated nature of these challenges, obvious at it may seem, has apparently not yet penetrated EU policy thinking to any great extent. For example, in the conclusions from the European Council meeting of October 2014 (European Council 2014), climate change and stagnation are both highlighted, but there is no mention of their interrelated nature.

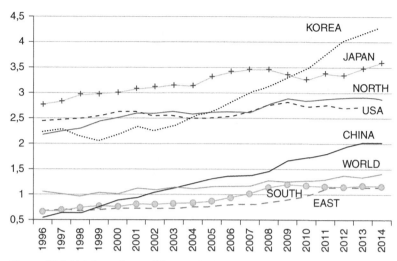

Figure 15.5 R&D as share of GDP, 1996–2014

Note: Authors' calculations based on data from data from UNESCO (http://data.uis.unesco.org/), accessed 1 October 2016. "WORLD" is the average value for the sixty-four countries for which reasonably comprehensive data exist. NORTH, EAST and SOUTH are groups of European countries (for definitions see note to Figure 15.1).

There are important and sceptical voices with regard to the potential of future innovation, not the least Gordon (2012, 2016). But are there really reasons to believe that humankind is less capable now of coming up with smart solutions than, say, fifty or hundred years ago? We believe the answer to this question is a clear 'No'. Smart solutions, or innovations, typically mean combining different sources of information, knowledge and other resources in a novel way, for which education is a great advantage (if not a must). Never have levels of education been as high as they are today. The same holds for our knowledge on how to mobilize the global resources to be used for new and better ways of doing things as evidenced, for example by the rapidly increasing share of R&D expenditure in GDP globally (Figure 15.5).

Northern Europe, in particular, joins a club of high R&D performers together with the United States, Japan and, not least, Korea, which have doubled their investment in R&D as a percentage of GDP over the last two decades. Similarly rapid growth has occurred in China, which clearly aspires to join the countries on the R&D frontier. In fact, albeit

Jan Fagerberg, Staffan Laestadius and Ben R. Martin

starting at a very low level two decades ago, China's share of R&D in GDP is currently around 50 per cent above the world average. It is disturbing, therefore, that Southern and Eastern Europe continue to lag well behind the world average, and that the difference has been increasing in recent years. Hence, these countries appear to be falling behind not only economically but also with respect to science, technology and innovation. This provides further evidence of the European divergence noted earlier.

The main message in Gordon's (2016) *magnum opus* is the declining productivity effects of what he terms *great inventions*. According to Gordon, these great inventions – largely related to more efficient production and intensified use of energy – served as the main drivers for the period of high growth in total factor productivity (TFP) between 1920 and 1970. He also notes that there was also a shorter and less impressive period of TFP increases around the turn of the millennium (1994–2004) which, following Gordon, can be largely explained by the penetration of ICT in the economy. However, according to Gordon, the large scale TFP increases obtained from these great inventions cannot be sustained.[4] What follows subsequently, in his view, is much smaller (incremental) improvements.

In addition, and partly related, he identifies various countervailing factors – what he calls 'headwinds' – contributing to slower growth in income (or GDP per capita). He points specifically to demography (and an aging population), reduced scope for increasing the qualifications of the labour force (through investments in education), globalization, increasing inequality (which he identifies as arguably the most important 'headwind'), and the large public and private debts that need to be reduced. The joint effect of these 'headwinds' may well be to restrict future growth of GDP per capita in the United States to almost zero (Gordon 2016).

However, what (perhaps) holds for the United States does not necessarily hold for the world as a whole. For example, countries at a lower level of development can gain a lot by exploiting technologies already in place in more technologically advanced nations (Abramovitz 1994). As pointed out above, GDP per capita in Europe is just two-thirds of that in the United States, so there should still be plenty of scope for

---

[4] This may be looked upon as an analogue to the Ricardian theory on the declining marginal productivity of land.

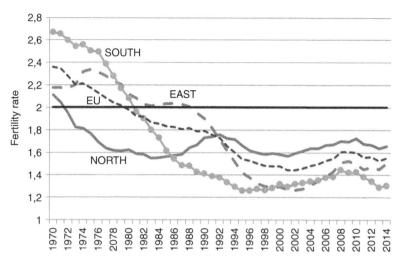

Figure 15.6 Europe: Fertility rates (live births per woman), 1970–2014
Note: Authors' calculations based on data from Eurostat (http://appsso
.eurostat.ec.europa.eu/[demo_frate]), accessed 1 October 2016. NORTH,
EAST and SOUTH are groups of European countries (for definitions see note
to Figure 15.1).

catching up and hence for faster growth than in the United States,
especially in the poorer EU member states in Eastern Europe.

The issue of declining and aging populations, emphasized by
Gordon, clearly represents a challenge for Europe.[5] In fact, fertility
rates have declined all over Europe for several decades (Figure 15.6)
and presently only a handful of European countries have fertility rates
sufficient to ensure a constant population. This challenge is especially
evident in Southern Europe as well as in some Eastern European
countries (with Poland being the most prominent case).

It is interesting to observe that fertility rates in Europe actually
increased during the period of inclusive growth, characterized by
rapid catch-up by poorer member countries, which preceded the financial crisis. However, in the years after the crisis struck, fertility rates
declined markedly, particularly in Southern Europe, which received the
biggest hit from the crisis and from the German-inspired austerity

---

[5] But not necessarily for the world as a whole; for example, an aging population is
clearly not a problem in Africa, home to some of the fastest-growing countries in
recent years.

drive. Thus, as with several other challenges, the demographic challenge facing Europe is something policy can influence, notably by breaking with austerity but also through other changes in the policy stance, for example by creating favourable conditions for families with children, and allowing for more integration of young, entrepreneurial job-seekers from countries outside the EU, of which there appears to be an abundant supply. Hence, the growing anti-immigration sentiments in several European countries are both backward-looking and counterproductive.

Furthermore, while education levels are high in large parts of Europe, particularly in the North, average education levels in the South of Europe continue to lag substantially behind. Investing in education there, including the education of the current adult population who will continue to dominate the labour force for some time to come, may prove to be an essential element in a long-term policy for reviving the depressed economies in this part of Europe.[6] Finally, while the distribution of income generally is much more equitable in Europe than in the United States (Piketty 2014), a factor which (according to recent research) should be good for growth (Cingano 2014), Southern Europe (together with the UK) represents something of an exception in this regard (Figure 15.7). Therefore, policy aimed at reviving these economies may need to pay particular attention to the distributional aspects of economic development, unlike the current austerity policies.

Let us return, therefore, to Gordon's hypothesis of the declining productivity effects of what he calls great inventions. It may be argued that the cognitive foundation – or paradigm – behind much of the scientific and innovative activities of humankind has been related to 'mastering nature' rather than 'adapting' to it. However, while there may be a declining productivity advance along the old fossil-based technological trajectory, we are perhaps just at the beginning of learning how to transform the economy towards sustainability within our planetary boundaries (cf. Steffen et al. 2015) – in other words, at the start of a new technological trajectory.

Not least is this shift in trajectory related to energy use. Gordon (2016: ch. 16) frequently discusses the important role played by the

---

[6] Similarly, average education levels are still low in most developing countries, so continuing investments in education there should be expected to bring large payoffs.

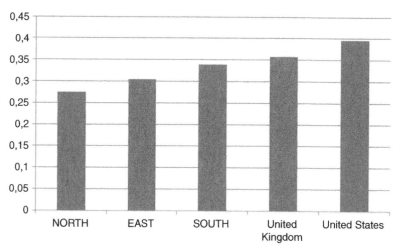

Figure 15.7 Inequality (gini-coefficient), total population, 2013
Note: Authors' calculations based on data from OECD Income Distribution Database (IDD), http://www.oecd.org/social/income-distribution-database .htm, accessed 1 October 2016. The coefficient is for disposable income (post taxes and transfers). NORTH, EAST and SOUTH are groups of European countries (for definitions see note to Figure 15.1).

growing input of energy – fossil fuels as well as (fossil-based) electricity – as an explanation of the rapid increase of TFP during the period from 1920 to 1970. This great acceleration of fossil dependence is, however, not fundamentally connected to climate change in Gordon's analysis.[7] Nevertheless, it adds to the headwinds. To maintain existing TFP levels for the future – and even more so if we are to *increase* productivity – all this energy input has to be substituted in one way or another by sustainable or renewable solutions. This will require major innovations.

In theory, at least, this can be done – for the United States as well as for the rest of the world. Although the inflow of solar energy to the Earth every hour is many times as large as mankind uses in a whole year (Sandén 2008), there will be a strong need to economize with energy in the transformation towards a sustainable trajectory (Moriarty and Honnery 2016). In the language of the International Energy Agency this will include innovations throughout society to *avoid*, as well as to

---

[7] For an in-depth analysis of the 'Great Acceleration', see McNeill and Engelke (2016).

improve and *substitute*, energy-related activities (IEA 2014). The implication of the IEA 'avoid' concept is that significant fossil-based systems (and routines) have to be abandoned or radically transformed. In essence, this is an example of what Schumpeter labelled *creative destruction*.

In summary, we do not think that the continuing economic stagnation in Europe can be explained mainly in terms of there being less scope for innovation, or indeed in terms of 'headwinds' of the type emphasized by Gordon. It also has to do with developing the necessary policies to confront the governance challenge and shift Europe to a path for transforming our economies towards sustainability, the topic to which we now turn.

15.5 The Governance Challenge Facing Europe

In this section, we examine the governance challenge faced by Europe with regard to developing the necessary policies for economic recovery and transformation and confronting issues related to climate change and sustainability.

A first issue has to do with the increasingly global nature of the problems confronting governments, requiring internationally coordinated, multilateral efforts that are hard to bring about, as evidenced by the failure, at least until the Paris climate conference in December 2015, to come up with a comprehensive international agreement on how to deal with climate change. Nevertheless, as pointed out by Laestadius (2015) and Schmitz and Lema (2015), there may be other possibilities for international cooperation affecting climate change, such as alliances of like-minded countries (with Europe taking the lead) pioneering new solutions and encouraging others to follow.

Second, not only are the problems to be confronted today large-scale, but they are also more likely to cross-cut organizational boundaries, particularly within governments (Bauer et al. 2012) and to interact in an increasingly complex manner. Energy policy, for instance, must give careful consideration to a range of issues, including security, for example (Geels 2015). Therefore, effective policies for transforming the economy towards sustainability may require the development of new forms of governance, characterized by a holistic perspective and by close coordination between different parts of government.

A third issue relates to the increasing involvement of non-government actors, not least in Europe (Biermann 2007; Biermann and Pattberg 2008; Biermann and Gupta 2011; Bauer et al. 2012). However, while making governance more complex, the involvement of non-governmental actors may also introduce a much needed new dynamics in policy-making, as evidenced, for example, by the German *Energiewende* (see Box 15.1, and also Lauber and Jacobsson 2015).

Fourth, there is a heightened sensitivity to risk and uncertainty (Biermann 2007). The fundamentally uncertain nature of technological advance means that policies for transformation should place the emphasis on pursuing a broad portfolio of different energy technologies and on not getting locked into a specific path of development that at one point may appear more cost-effective or promising. The German *Energiewende* (see Box 15.1) is an excellent example of how this can be achieved.

BOX 15.1: Germany's Transition to Sustainable Electricity Production – the *Energiewende*

One of the most remarkable achievements of any European country when it comes to transforming its economy in a sustainable direction is provided by Germany. In just over fifteen years, from 1998 to 2015, the share of renewables in German electricity consumption increased from less than five to over 30 per cent (Figure 15.8). The German *Energiewende* – literally energy transition – had its origins in the environmental and anti-nuclear movements of the 1970s and 1980s (in particular, the Green Party). Renewable energy was seen as critical for phasing out nuclear generators, and the first national scheme requiring utilities to purchase renewable power from private sources at a fixed rate (the so-called 'feed-in tariff') was adopted by parliament in 1990. The coalition between Social Democrats and Greens that came to power in 1998 continued and expanded these policies. The feed-in tariff was set at different levels for different technologies (e.g. solar, bio, on-shore wind, off-shore wind, etc.) depending on how far these had come with respect to becoming commercially viable. It is thus an example of a policy supporting technological development on a broad front, allowing different technologies time to deliver on their promise, and thus avoiding premature lock-in to a specific technology.

BOX 15.1: (cont.)

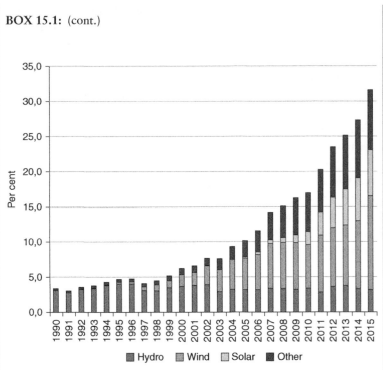

Figure 15.8 Renewables as a share of total German electricity consumption, 1990–2015
Note: Authors' calculations based on data from Bundesminister für Wirtschaft und Energie, (http://www.bmwi.de/DE/Themen/Energie/Energiedaten-und-analysen/Energiedaten/gesamtausgabe), accessed 1 October 2016.

The process acquired substantial momentum after the turn of the millennium, and growth has been especially rapid in recent years. A substantial German capital-goods industry also developed and costs declined as envisaged. However, as a result of its success, the policy has also become more controversial. For example, it has come under fire from electricity utilities (with huge sunk costs in coal-based plants) and politicians from coal-producing regions. The policy's support for a broad range of renewables, rather than concentrating on the currently most cost-effective (and hence most mature) technologies, has also been repeatedly criticized for being too costly. The entry of China into certain segments of renewable energy technology, which to a certain extent has come at the expense of jobs in Europe, has also weakened the popularity of the policy in some circles.

Source: Lauber and Jacobsson (2015).

A fifth factor adding to the governance challenges facing the EU is the growing number and diversity of member states. Now that there are twenty-eight member states, EU countries have become quite different in terms of economic, industrial and institutional characteristics, and policies based on the philosophy of 'one size fits all' appear less appropriate than ever.

Lastly, and again a factor specific to the governance challenge faced by the EU, is the fact that the scale of resources at the disposal of the EU is in most cases very limited compared with those allocated by national governments (Begg 2015). Hence, the ability to influence and coordinate national governments becomes essential.

The declining trust in (and diminishing popular support for) European institutions (Begg 2015) indicates that the failure of EU politicians in dealing effectively with the challenges that Europe faces is now coming back to haunt the entire European project. This clearly underscores the need for a new policy stance (Mowery et al. 2010). As pointed out previously, simply pumping up demand would quickly come into conflict with climate concerns and hence not be sustainable. Therefore, a policy aiming at a new form of green growth in Europe in order to increase employment and welfare must simultaneously speed up the transformation to a sustainable economy. The challenge with this transformation is briefly analysed in Box 15.2.

The best way to achieve this, we argue, is to target innovation, the diffusion of new technology and, not the least, transformative investments in areas such as energy supply and distribution, increased energy efficiency, public transport, infrastructure for cars driven by electricity and fuel cells, and so on. Many of these investments, in the energy sector for example, would be necessary anyway (ECF 2013), but undertaking them sooner rather than later (and using reduced GHG emissions as a yardstick in the selection process) may accelerate the transformation while at the same time reviving growth. As pointed out earlier, such a policy stance has to take into account the fact that the economies of Europe are very different, so there is no point in just mimicking the same policy, whether patterned on the German experience or that of some other country, everywhere.

While such transformative investments are needed in all member countries, it is natural to place the emphasis on those countries that

BOX 15.2: The Transformation Challenge

The conditions for transformation can – inspired by Pasinetti (1981) – be formulated in macro-economic terms using a three-sector model:

*	*green* sector	sustainable
*	*blue* sector	sustainability enabling
*	*black* sector	climate-impacting sector

The *green* sector consists of non–CO_2-generating activities (non–CO_2-emitting goods, services and investments in human and cultural capital). Bio-based products from sustainable forestry and agriculture also belong to this category.

The *blue* sector consists of activities that in themselves may be polluting but which, in their use, will contribute to a reduction of CO_2 emissions. On the consumption side this includes energy-saving and long-lasting artefacts (e.g. heat pumps). Among blue investments we may identify railway tracks as well as wind-power systems and investments in energy efficiency.

To the *black* sector we allocate all activities involving consumption of – and investment in – products, systems and services that generate CO_2 emissions.

The policy challenge from a macroeconomic point of view is not to unconditionally 'pump up demand' in general to increase employment but, with help from the *blue* sector, to rapidly transform demand away from the *black* sector towards the *green*. It is not enough to reduce the relative size of the *black* sector; it must be reduced in absolute terms, eventually to a negligible level.

This transformation of activities may generate 'green growth' if the green and blue sectors expand more than the decline of the black. Whether there is a creation of net employment depends on the labour absorption capacity of the growing green and blue activities relative to the declining black.

This requires, in contrast to the standard response from economists, highly selective policies all over the economy at the expense of general macro-economic policies. This includes strongly differentiated and higher VAT rates, purchase taxes and fees on black products and activities, probably compensated by lower general taxes, e.g. on labour. A world where transformation is the main task requires a rapid shift from general to selective macro-economic policies.

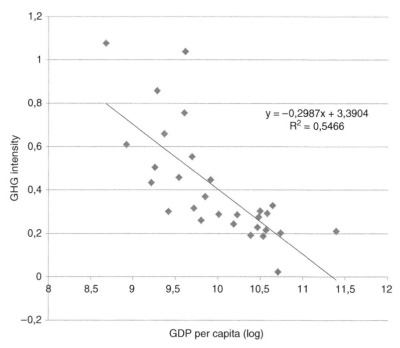

Figure 15.9 GHG intensity and GDP per capita, EU28, 2014
Note: Authors' calculations based on data from Eurostat (http://appsso
.eurostat.ec.europa.eu/ [naida_10_gdp]; [env_air_gge], and http://ec.europa.e
u/eurostat/web/population-demography-migration-projections/population-
data/main-tables/ [tps00001]), accessed 1 October 2016.

have further to go with respect to achieving sustainability. As
Figure 15.9 shows, the countries most in need of transforming their
economies in the direction of sustainability are poorer member states
(which are also, in general, the ones most adversely affected by the
current stagnation). Thus, a programme for transformative investment
based on these principles would not only be good for climate change
and economic growth generally, but also deliver growth where it is
most needed, thereby contributing to improved social cohesion in the
Union as a whole.

In recent years, the governing bodies of the EU, in particular the
European Commission and the European Central Bank, have started to
devote more attention to the need to get Europe out of the present
slump by increasing investments (European Commission 2014) and

adopting a more expansionary monetary policy. However, although these initiatives are surely welcome, they will do little to stimulate the much-needed European transformation towards sustainable growth unless most – say 90 per cent – of the funds made available are allocated to investments in the green and blue sectors.[8]

The crucial question for policy, therefore, must be how to get the European economy out of its present depressed state and simultaneously mobilize the European population in a collective innovation journey in the direction of a sustainable economy and society. Innovation is not, as sometimes presented, primarily about creating new ideas that may (or may not) have profound effects sometime in the distant future. Rather it is about trying out promising new solutions and ways of doing things, learning from the experience, and on this basis improving the technologies in question. Therefore, a good innovation policy is one that also promotes diffusion, use, learning and continuous improvement.

To achieve this transformation, creating demand for innovative and sustainable solutions may be essential. In fact, as the Norwegian example of supporting the demand for electric cars shows (Figenbaum and Kolbenstvedt 2013; Fagerberg, Laestadius and Martin 2016), demand-oriented policies can lead to surprisingly large changes in a relatively short time. This matters because, in order to minimize the adverse consequence of climate change, the transformation process has to occur rather rapidly.

Although, as this paper has shown, there are large differences among European countries in relation to the crisis, they have one thing in common: their transport sectors have similarities in their heavy dependence – on average 83 per cent of inland passenger transport (2014) – on fossil-fuelled personal cars and life styles strongly related to that. This creates an option for the formulation of a common European policy for a rapid decarbonization of the transport sector. This arguably offers a low hanging fruit compared with the more complex challenge of transforming the lignite-based European energy sectors.[9]

---

[8] For example, in a presentation of the EU investment plan, Vice-President Jyrki Katainen did not once mention climate change or sustainability (see Vice-President Jyrki Katainen explains the EU investment plan, http://ec.europa.eu/p riorities/jobs-growth investment/plan/index_en.htm accessed 9 October 2016).

[9] A recent illustration on how such a policy can be implemented is given from a Nordic perspective in the policy study *Nordic Transport Ways* (Global Utmaning 2015).

15.7 Conclusions

Europe (like many parts of the world but perhaps even more so) is confronted by an intimidating triple challenge comprising economic stagnation, climate change and a governance crisis. This paper demonstrates how these three challenges are closely inter-related. In particular, a return to economic growth cannot come at the expense of greater risk of irreversible climate change. Instead, what is required is a fundamental transformation of the economy to a new 'green' trajectory based on rapidly diminishing emission of greenhouse gases.

Boosting Europe's economy and its transition to a sustainable 'green' economy through transformative investments should be seen as a core element of European policy for innovation and growth (Mazzucato and Perez 2015). Innovation is not primarily about scientific breakthroughs, although these are often very important, but more about continuous experimentation, learning, gradual improvements, cost reductions and increased performance of technologies that are, in most cases, already on the table (Mathews 2014). Policy makers can exert great influence on innovative activities by emphasizing the most pressing challenges or problems that need to be addressed. This type of innovation policy, which provides a sense of direction to the collective innovation journey and rallies potential contributors behind it, would be relevant for a wide range of activities essential for the transition to a sustainable economy, such as energy production, distribution and use, and also transport and construction. In order to be effective, such a policy must link to and coordinate different policy arenas (energy, transport, regional development, research, innovation, etc.). Thus, sustainable growth requires more than technological innovation; new – innovative – forms of governance and institutions are also required. This aspect should not be neglected. Many (perhaps even most) of the technologies needed for the decarbonization process are available already – or almost available. And many of them have recently experienced significant cost reductions. But the prevailing low prices of de facto subsidized fossil-based solutions still make actors reluctant to invest in sustainable systems, solutions and life styles.

The dominant policy approach to dealing with climate change in Europe up to now has tended to focus on getting 'the prices right', with the Emissions Trading Scheme (ETS) as the central instrument. Yet this has proved far from successful.[10] The reason is not that there is something inherently wrong with getting 'the prices right' but rather than getting political support for the necessary adjustments in prices (through increasing taxes or cutting quotas or in other ways) has proved very difficult. This is well illustrated by the difficulties in closing down existing European coal-powered energy systems. One way to overcome this stalemate is to agree on taxation paths for the coming decade. Such paths have to be delivered with credibility by the political system and allow actors to adapt. This may also be a means to get success with the necessary taxation of international bunker fuels.[11]

Moreover, timing is crucial here. Arguably, acquiring the necessary momentum in the transformation process is critically dependent on mobilizing broad segments of society through advocating and experimenting with new solutions. It is very notable that successful transformation policies, such as the German *Energiewende* and the Norwegian programme for electric cars, were not created through top-down initiatives by political leaders, but by pressure from below from green movements and environmental activists, which gradually received increasing support for these policies as they acquired momentum.

These programmes are examples of what economists often call 'second best' policies, reserving the term 'first best' for 'getting the prices right'. Yet it is fallacious (even from an economic theory point of view) to criticize these policies on the argument that they are more expensive than 'first best' policies when it is quite obviously illusory to assume that the latter will deliver the goods in time. Moreover, if combatting climate change requires a considerable amount of innovation, as almost everybody seems to agree, then it is not only the costs of particular policies here and now that matter but also the effects on innovation. In this respect, a policy such as *Energiewende* is an inspiring example because it creates opportunities for experimenting, learning and innovating with a broad range of energy technologies, instead of becoming locked in to what observers at a certain point might see as

[10]   The ETS (see Begg 2015) has completely failed in terms of creating a price-level for GHG emissions that would stimulate a transition towards increased sustainability. As argued by Laestadius (2015), CO_2 prices will have to increase to around €40/ton or more in order to contribute to this transformation, yet during 2012–2017 they only sporadically exceeded €8.00/ton.

[11] CO_2 emissions from international bunkers have grown 79 per cent between 1990 and 2014, much faster than overall growth of energy-related CO_2 emissions (IEA 2016).

the most 'cost-effective' approach. Arguably, incorrect assessments of this kind can have considerable costs.

As pointed out earlier, other parts of the world are also facing varying forms of the triple challenge. Given the global character of the problem, and the many actors involved at different levels all round the world who may have a say in what happens, the ability to influence actors in other countries becomes of central importance. One key way to achieve this, and one for which Europe seems eminently well placed, would be to lead by example, providing solutions for how the climate challenge can be effectively dealt with. Taking the lead may, of course, incur significant costs. Nevertheless, doing nothing will undoubtedly have a major detrimental impact in the years ahead in many areas of life. By taking the lead in addressing the triple challenge, Europe may not only attract followers, thereby ensuring that climate change is kept within manageable bounds; it may also lead to considerable benefits in the longer term in the form of strengthened industrial competitiveness, enhanced exports and new jobs.[12] Moreover, addressing the triple challenge may provide Europe and its citizens with a new sense of purpose, revitalizing the EU, 'the European project' and Europe's role in the world over the decades to come.

Acknowledgements

An earlier version of this chapter was presented at the 16th International Schumpeter Society in Montreal, Canada, 6–8 July 2016. The chapter draws heavily on the book edited by the authors (Fagerberg et al. 2015), and on an earlier article summarizing the message from the volume (Fagerberg et al. 2016). The authors are grateful to the contributors to the 2015 book, and to various reviewers, for their helpful comments.

References

Abramovitz, M. 1994. Catch-up and convergence in the post-war growth boom and after, in W. J. Baumol, R. R. Nelson and E. N. Wolf (eds.), *Convergence of Productivity – Cross-National Studies and Historical Evidence*. Oxford: Oxford University Press, 86–125.

---

[12] Mathews (2014) argues that China's leadership is well aware of this possibility, and that China is already on the path to becoming the global leader in green technologies.

Bauer, A., J. Feichtinger, and R. Steurer. 2012. The governance of climate change adaptation in 10 OECD countries: Challenges and approaches. *Journal of Environmental Policy & Planning* 14: 279–304.

Begg, I. 2015. EU policy and governance: Part of the problem or part of the solution? in J. Fagerberg, S. Laestadius, and B. R. Martin, 204–228.

Biermann, F. 2007. Earth system governance as a crosscutting theme of global change research. *Global Environmental Change* 17: 326–337.

Biermann, F. and A. Gupta. 2011. Accountability and legitimacy in earth system governance: A research framework. *Ecological Economics* 70: 1856–1864.

Biermann, F. and P. Pattberg 2008. Global environmental governance: Taking stock, moving forward. *Annual Review of Environmental Resources* 33: 277–294.

BP. 2016a. *BP Statistical Review of World Energy, June 2016* (downloaded from www.bp.com/en/global/corporate/energy-economics/statistical-review-of-world-energy.html on 10 October 2016).

BP. 2016b. *BP Statistical Review of World Energy, June 2016, Carbon Dioxide Emissions* (downloaded from www.bp.com/en/global/corporate/energy-economics/statistical-review-of-world-energy.html on 10 October 2016).

Cingano, F. 2014. Trends in income inequality and its impact on economic growth, OECD *Social, Employment and Migration* Working Papers, No. 163, Paris: OECD Publishing (downloaded from www.oecd.org/els/soc/trends-in-income-inequality-and-its-impact-on-economic-growth-SEM-WP163.pdf on 10 October2016).

ECF. 2013. *From Roadmaps to Reality – A Framework for Power Sector Decarbonisation in Europe.* Brussels: European Climate Foundation.

European Commission. 2014. An investment plan for Europe, Brussels: European Commission (downloaded from http://ec.europa.eu/priorities/jobs-growth-investment/plan/index_en.htm on 10 October 2016).

European Council. 2014. Conclusions from the European Council 23 and 24 October 2014, EUCO 169/14, Brussels: European Council. (downloaded from http://register.consilium.europa.eu/doc/srv?l=EN&f=ST%20169%202014%20INIT on 10 October 2016).

Fagerberg, J., S. Laestadius, and B. R. Martin. 2015. *The Triple Challenge for Europe: Economic Development, Climate Change and Governance.* Oxford: Oxford University Press.

Fagerberg, J., S. Laestadius, and B. R. Martin (eds.). 2016. The triple challenge for Europe: The economy, climate change, and governance. *Challenge* 59: 178–204.

Fagerberg, J. and B. Verspagen. 2015. One Europe or several? Causes and consequences of the European stagnation, in Fagerberg, J., S. Laestadius, and B. R. Martin, B. R. 33–59.

Figenbaum, E., and M. Kolbenstvedt. 2013. Electromobility in Norway – experiences and opportunities with Electric Vehicles, Report 1281/2013, The Institute of Transport Economics (downloaded from www.toi.no/pub likasjoner/elektromobilitet-i-norge-erfaringer-og-muligheter-med-elkjoretoy -article32103-8.html on 10 October 2016).

Geels, F. W. 2015. The arduous transition to low-carbon energy: A multi-level analysis of renewable electricity niches and resilient regimes, in Fagerberg, J., S. Laestadius, and B. R. Martin, B. R. 91–118.

Global Utmaning. 2015. Nordic Transport Ways (a report from the independent Swedish think tank Global Utmaning) (downloaded from www.globalutmaning.se/rapporter/ on 10 October 2016).

GMDAC. 2016. IOM Global Migration Data Analysis Centre (downloaded from http://iomgmdac.org on 10 October 2016).

Gordon, R. 2012. Is US Economic growth over? Faltering innovation confronts the six headwinds, NBER Working Paper 18315. Cambridge, MA: NBER.

Gordon, R. 2016. *The Rise and Fall of American Growth – the U.S. Standard of Living Since the Civil War*. Princeton, NJ and Oxford: Princeton University Press.

Hansen, J. et al. 2016a. Ice melt, sea level rise and superstorms: Evidence from paleoclimatic data, climate modeling, and modern observations that 2°C global warming could be dangerous. *Atmospheric Chemistry and Physics* 16: 3761–3812.

Hansen, J. et al. 2016b. Young people's burden: Requirement of negative CO_2 emissions (discussion paper publ. 161004 by *Earth System Dynamics*, an open access journal of the European Geosciences Union, (downloaded from www.earth-syst-dynam-discuss.net/esd-2016–42/ on 10 October 2016).

IEA. 2014. *Energy Technology Perspectives – Harnessing Electricity's Potential*. Paris: OECD, International Energy Agency.

IEA. 2015b. *Energy and Climate Change – World Energy Outlook Special Report*. Paris: OECD/IEA.

IEA. 2016. *Key CO_2 Emissions Trends, Excerpt from: CO_2 Emissions from Fuel Combustion*. Paris: OECD/IEA.

IPCC. 2012. *Managing the Risks of Extreme Events and Disasters to Advance Climate Change Adaption*. Cambridge: Cambridge University Press.

IPCC. 2013a. *Climate Change 2013 – Mitigation of Climate Change*. Cambridge: Cambridge University Press.

IPCC. 2013b. *Climate Change 2013 – The Physical Science Basis.* Cambridge: Cambridge University Press.

IPCC. 2014. *Climate Change 2014 – Mitigation of Climate Change* (WGIII contribution to AR5) (downloaded from www.ipcc.ch/pdf/assessment-report/ar5/wg3/ipcc_wg3_ar5_frontmatter.pdf on 10 October 2016).

Laestadius, S. 2015. Transition paths: Assessing conditions and alternatives, in Fagerberg, J., S. Laestadius, and B. R. Martin, 143–169.

Landesmann, M. A. 2015. The new North-South divide in Europe – Can the European convergence model be resuscitated? in Fagerberg, J., S. Laestadius, and B. R. Martin, 60–87.

Lauber, V. and S. Jacobsson. 2015. Lessons from Germany's Energiewende, in Fagerberg, J., S. Laestadius, and B. R. Martin, 173–203.

Mathews, J. 2014. *Greening of Capitalism: How Asia Is Driving the Next Great Transformation.* Stanford, CA: Stanford University Press.

Mazzucato, M. and C. Perez. 2015. Innovation as growth policy: The challenge for Europe, in Fagerberg, J., S. Laestadius and B. R. Martin, 229–264.

McNeill, J. R. and P. Engelke. 2016. *The Great Acceleration – An Environmental History of the Anthropocene since 1945.* Cambridge, MA: Harvard University Press.

Moriarty, P. and D. Honnery. 2016. Can renewable energy power the future? *Energy Policy* 93: 3–7.

Mowery, D.C., R. R. Nelson and B. R. Martin. 2010. Technology policy and global warming: Why new policy models are needed (or why putting new wine in old bottles won't work), *Research Policy*, 39: 1011–1023.

Nordhaus, W. 2013. *The Climate Casino – Risk, Uncertainty and Economics for a Warming World.* New Haven, CT and London: Yale University Press.

Pasinetti, L. 1981. *Structural Change and Economic Growth: A Theoretical Essay on the Dynamics of the Wealth of Nations.* Cambridge: Cambridge University Press.

Piketty, T. 2014. *Capital in the Twenty-First Century.* Cambridge, MA: The Belknap Press.

Rogelj, J. et al. 2016. Paris agreement climate proposals need a boss to keep warming well below 2°C. *Nature* 534: 631–639.

Schmitz, H. and R. Lema. 2015. The global green economy: Competition or cooperation between Europe and China? in J. Fagerberg, S. Laestadius, and B. R. Martin, 119–142.

Reilly, J. et al. 2015. *Energy and Climate Outlook – Perspectives from 2015*, MT Joint Program on the Science and Policy of Global Change, Cambridge, MA: Massachusetts Institute of Technology.

Sandén, B. 2008. Solar solution: the next industrial revolution. *Materials Today* 11(2): 22–24.

Smil, V. 2010. *Energy Transitions – History, Requirements Prospects*. Santa Barbara, CA: Praeger.

Steffen, W. et al. 2015. Planetary boundaries: Guiding human development on a changing planet. *Science* 347(6223): paper 1259855.

World Bank. 2012. *Turn Down the Heat – Why a 4°C Warmer World Must be Avoided*. Washington, DC: World Bank.

World Bank. 2013. *Turn Down the Heat – Climate Extremes, Regional Impact, and the Case for Resilience*. Washington, DC: World Bank.

Index